CRE**A**TIVE
HOMEOWNER®

THE
BIG BOOK
OF HOME PLANS

CREATIVE HOMEOWNER®, Upper Saddle River, New Jersey

COPYRIGHT © 2005

CRE▲TIVE
HOMEOWNER®

A Division of Federal Marketing Corp.
Upper Saddle River, NJ

VP/Business Development: Brian H. Toolan
VP/Editorial Director: Timothy O. Bakke
Production Manager: Rose Sullivan

Home Plans Publishing Consultant: James D. McNair III
Editorial Assistants: Nicole Porto, Evan Lambert,
   Lauren Manoy

Design and Layout: Arrowhead Direct (David Kroha,
   Cindy DiPierdomenico, Judith Kroha)

Cover Design: David Geer

Current Printing (last digit)
10 9 8 7 6 5 4 3 2 1

The Big Book of Home Plans
Library of Congress Control Number: 2004116480
ISBN: 1-58011-249-8

CREATIVE HOMEOWNER®
A Division of Federal Marketing Corp.
24 Park Way
Upper Saddle River, NJ 07458
www.creativehomeowner.com

Printed In China

Note: The homes as shown in the photographs and renderings in this book may differ from the actual blueprints. When studying the house of your choice, please check the floor plans carefully.

PHOTO CREDITS

Front cover: *center* plan 131032, page 146; *bottom row* (from left to right) plan 121094, page 31; plan 111004, page 82; plan 111004, page 82; plan 121081, page 301

back cover: *top* plan 181151, page 30; center plan 121088, page 69; *bottom row* (from left to right) plan 131028, page 8; plan 161036, page 286; plan 111004, page 84

page 1: plan 131030, page 360

page 3: *top* plan 131032, page 146; *bottom* plan 151020, page 258

page 5: courtesy of Western Wood Products

page 6: *top* Freeze Frame Studio/CH; *bottom* courtesy of Trus Joist MacMillan

page 7: Timothy O. Bakke/CH

pages 110–117: Gary David Gold/CH

page 196: *left* courtesy of Johnson Hardware; *top right and center* courtesy of Kohler; *bottom right* courtesy of American Standard

page 197: courtesy of Velux America

page 198: both courtesy of Kohler

page 199: George Ross/CH

page 200: *left* courtesy of Kohler; right courtesy of York Wallcoverings

page 201: *top left* courtesy of Robern Inc.; *top right* courtesy of Ondine Shower Systems; *bottom* courtesy of Jacuzzi

page 280: courtesy of Motif Designs

page 281: John Parsekian/CH

pages 282–283: *top left* George Ross/CH; center courtesy of York Wallcoverings

page 356: *top* courtesy of Trex Decks; *bottom* courtesy of the Hickson Corp.

page 357: courtesy of Arch Wood Protection

page 358: both courtesy of the California Redwood Association

page 359: courtesy of Trex Decks

Contents

Getting Started

Maybe you can't wait to bang the first nail. Or you may be just as happy leaving town until the windows are cleaned. The extent of your involvement with the construction phase is up to you. Your time, interests, and abilities can help you decide how to get the project from lines on paper to reality. But building a house requires more than putting pieces together. Whoever is in charge of the process must competently manage people as well as supplies, materials, and construction. He or she will have to

- Make a project schedule to plan the orderly progress of the work. This can be a bar chart that shows the time period of activity by each trade.
- Establish a budget for each category of work, such as foundation, framing, and finish carpentry.
- Arrange for a source of construction financing.
- Get a building permit and post it conspicuously at the construction site.
- Line up supply sources and order materials.
- Find subcontractors and negotiate their contracts.
- Coordinate the work so that it progresses smoothly with the fewest conflicts.
- Notify inspectors at the appropriate milestones.
- Make payments to suppliers and subcontractors.

You as the Builder

You'll have to take care of every logistical detail yourself if you decide to act as your own builder or general contractor. But along with the responsibilities of managing the project, you gain the flexibility to do as much of your own work as you want and subcontract out the rest. Before taking this path, however, be sure you have the time and capabilities. Do you also have the

time and ability to schedule the work, hire and coordinate subs, order materials, and keep ahead of the accounting required to manage the project successfully? If you do, you stand to save the amount that a general contractor would charge to take on these responsibilities, normally 15 to 30 percent of the construction cost. If you take this responsibility on but mismanage the project, the potential savings will erode and may even cost you more than if you had hired a builder in the first place. A subcontractor might charge extra for hav-

Acting as the builder, above, requires the ability to hire and manage subcontractors.

Building a home, opposite, includes the need to schedule building inspections, at the appropriate milestones.

ing to return to the site to complete work that was originally scheduled for an earlier date. Or perhaps because you didn't order the windows at the beginning, you now have to pay for a recent cost increase. (If you had hired a builder in the first place he or she would absorb the increase.)

Hiring a Builder to Handle Construction

A builder or general contractor will manage every aspect of the construction process. Your role after signing the construction contract will be to make regular progress payments and ensure that the work for which you are paying has been completed. You will also consult with the builder and agree to any changes that may have to be made along the way.

Leads for finding builders might come from friends or neighbors who have had contractors build, remodel, or add to their homes. Real-estate agents and bankers may have some names handy but are more likely familiar with the builder's ability to complete projects on time and budget than the quality of the work itself.

The next step is to narrow your list of candidates to three or four who you think can do a quality job and work harmoniously with you. Phone each builder to see whether he or she is interested in being considered for your project. If so, invite the builder to an interview at your home. The meeting will serve two purposes. You'll be able to ask the candidate about his or her experience, and you'll be able to see whether or not your personalities are compatible. Go over the plans with the builder to make certain that he or she understands the scope of the project. Ask if they have constructed similar houses. Get references, and check the builder's standing with the Better Business Bureau. Develop a short list of builders, say three, and ask them to submit bids for the project.

Contracts

Lump-Sum Contracts

A lump-sum, or fixed-fee, contract lets you know from the beginning just what the project will cost, barring any changes made because of your requests or unforeseen conditions. This form works well for projects that promise few surprises and are well defined from the outset by a complete set of contract documents. You can enter into a fixed-price contract by negotiating with a single builder on your short list or by obtaining bids from three or four builders. If you go the latter route, give each bidder a set of documents and allow at least two weeks for them to submit their bids. When you get the bids, decide who you want and call the others to thank them for their efforts. You don't have to accept the lowest bid, but it probably makes sense to do so since you have already honed the list to builders you trust. Inform this builder of your intentions to finalize a contract.

Cost-Plus-Fee Contracts

Under a cost-plus-fee contract, you agree to pay the builder for the costs of labor and materials, as verified by receipts, plus a fee that represents the builder's overhead and profit. This arrangement is sometimes referred to as "time and materials." The fee can range between 15 and 30 percent of the incurred costs. Because you ultimately pick up the tab—whatever the costs—the contractor is never at risk, as he is with a lump-sum contract. You won't know the final total cost of a cost-plus-fee contract until the project is built and paid for. If you can live with that uncertainty, there are offsetting advantages. First, this form allows you to accommodate unknown conditions much more easily than does a lump-sum contract. And rather than being tied down by the project documents, you will be free to make changes at any point along the way. This can be a trap, though. Watching the project take shape will spark the desire to add something or do something differently. Each change costs more, and the accumulation can easily exceed your budget. Because of the uncertainty of the final tab and the built-in advantage to the contractor, you should think twice before entering into this form of contract.

Contract Content

The conditions of your agreement should be spelled out thoroughly in writing and signed by both parties, whatever contractual arrangement you make with your builder. Your contract should include provisions for the following:

- The names and addresses of the owner and builder.
- A description of the work to be included ("As described in the plans and specifications dated . . .").
- The date that the work will be completed if time is of the essence.
- The contract price for lump-sum contracts and the builder's allowed profit and overhead costs for changes.
- The builder's fee for cost-plus-fee contracts and the method of accounting and requesting payment.
- The criteria for progress payments (monthly, by project milestones) and the conditions of final payment.
- A list of each drawing and specification section that is to be included as part of the contract.
- Requirements for guarantees. (One year is the standard period for which contractors guarantee the entire project, but you may require specific guarantees on

When submitting bids, all of the builders should base their estimates on the same specifications. Once the work begins, communicate with your builder to keep the work proceeding smoothly.

Inspect your newly built home, if possible, before the builder closes it up and finishes it.

certain parts of the project, such as a 20-year guarantee on the roofing.)

- Provisions for insurance.
- A description of how changes in the work orders will be handled.

The builder may have a standard contract that you can tailor to the specifics of your project. These contain complete specific conditions with blanks that you can fill in to fit your project and a set of "general conditions" that cover a host of issues from insurance to termination provisions. It's always a good idea to have an attorney review the draft of your completed contract before signing it.

Working with Your Builder

The construction phase officially begins when you have a signed copy of the contract and copies of any insurance required from the builder. It's not unheard of for a builder to request an initial payment of 10 to 20 percent of the total cost to cover mobilization costs, those costs associated with obtaining permits and getting set up to begin the actual construction. If you agree to this, keep a careful eye on the progress of the work to ensure that the total paid out at any one time doesn't get too far out of sync with the actual work completed.

What about changes? From here on, it's up to you and your builder to proceed in good faith and to keep the channels of communication open. Even so, changes of one sort or another beset every project, and they usually add to its cost.

Light at the End of the Tunnel.

The builder's request for a final inspection marks the end of the construction phase—almost. At the final inspection meeting, you and the builder will inspect the work, noting any defects or incomplete items on a "punch list." When the builder tidies up the punch list items, you should reinspect. Sometimes, builders go on to another job and take forever to clean up the last few details, so only after all items on the list have been completed satisfactorily should you release the final payment, which often accounts for the builder's profit.

Some Final Words

Having a positive attitude is important when undertaking a project as large as building a home. A positive attitude can help you ride out the rigors and stress of the construction process.

Stay Flexible. Expect problems, because they certainly will occur. Weather can upset the schedule you have established for subcontractors. A supplier may get behind on deliveries, which also affects the schedule. An unexpected pipe may surprise you during excavation. Just as certain, every problem that comes along has a solution if you are open to it.

Be Patient. The extra days it may take to resolve a construction problem will be forgotten once the project is completed.

Express Yourself. If what you see isn't exactly what you thought you were getting, don't be afraid to look into changing it. Or you may spot an unforeseen opportunity for an improvement. Changes usually cost more money, though, so don't make frivolous decisions.

Finally, watching your home go up is exciting, so stay upbeat. Get away from your project from time to time. Dine out. Take time to relax. A positive attitude will make for smoother relations with your builder. An optimistic outlook will yield better-quality work if you are doing your own construction. And though the project might seem endless while it is under way, keep in mind that all the planning and construction will fade to a faint memory at some time in the future, and you will be getting a lifetime of pleasure from a home that is just right for you.

Plan #131028

Dimensions: 69'2" W x 50'2" D
Levels: 2
Square Footage: 2,696
Main Level Sq. Ft.: 1,960
Upper Level Sq. Ft.: 736
Bedrooms: 4
Bathrooms: 3
Foundation: Crawl space, slab,
or basement
Materials List Available: Yes
Price Category: G

Imagine owning a home with Victorian styling and a dramatic, contemporary interior design.

Features:

• Foyer: Enter from the curved covered porch into this foyer with its 17-ft. ceiling.

• Great Room: A vaulted ceiling sets the tone for this large room, where friends and family are sure to congregate.

• Dining Room: A 14-ft. ceiling here accentuates the rounded shape of this room.

• Kitchen: From the angled corner sink to the angled island with a snack bar, this room has character. A pantry adds convenience.

• Master Suite: A 13-ft. tray ceiling exudes elegance, and the bath features a spa tub and designer shower.

• Upper Level: The balcony hall leads to a turreted recreation room, two bedrooms, and a full bath.

Main Level Floor Plan

Upper Level Floor Plan

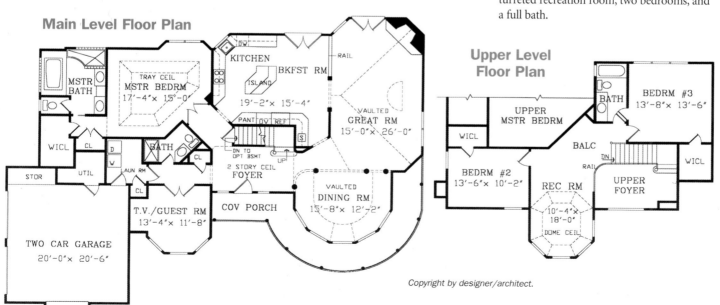

Copyright by designer/architect.

Rear View

Entry

Dining Room

Kitchen View to Great Room   Great Room

Plan #101005

Dimensions: 63' W x 57'2" D
Levels: 1
Square Footage: 1,992
Bedrooms: 3
Bathrooms: 2½
Foundation: Slab, crawl space, basement
Materials List Available: Yes
Price Category: D

Images provided by designer/architect.

Rear View

This midsized ranch is accented with Palladian windows and inviting front porch.

Features:

- Ceiling Height: 9 ft. unless otherwise noted.

- Special Ceilings: Tray or vaulted ceilings adorn the living room, family room, dining room, and master suite.

- Kitchen: This bright and airy kitchen is designed to be a pleasure in which to work. It shares a big bay window with the contiguous breakfast room.

- Breakfast Room: The light streaming in from the bay window makes this the perfect place to linger with coffee and the Sunday paper.

- Master Suite: This exceptional suite has a sitting area and direct access to the deck, as well as a sitting area, full-featured bath, and spacious walk-in closet.

- Secondary Bedrooms: The other bedrooms each measure about 13 ft. x 11 ft. They have walk-in closets and share a "Jack-and-Jill" bath.

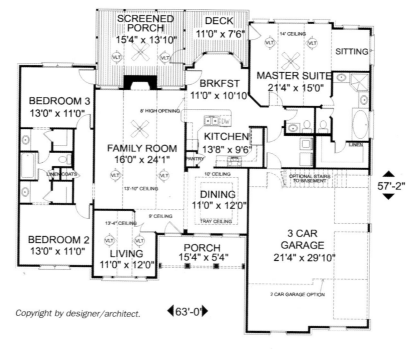

Copyright by designer/architect.

Plan #121091

Dimensions: 56' W x 50' D
Levels: 2
Square Footage: 2,689
Main Level Sq. Ft.: 1,415
Upper Level Sq. Ft.: 1,214
Bedrooms: 4
Bathrooms: 2½
Foundation: Basement
Materials List Available: Yes
Price Category: F

Images provided by designer/architect.

You'll love the unusual details that make this home as elegant as it is comfortable.

Features:

- **Entry:** This two-story entry is filled with natural light that streams in through the sidelights and transom window.

- **Den:** To the right of the entry, French doors open to this room, with its 11-ft. high, spider-beamed ceiling. A triple-wide,

transom-topped window brightens this room during the daytime.

- **Family Room:** A fireplace and built-in entertainment center add comfort to this room, and the cased opening to the kitchen area makes it convenient.

- **Kitchen:** With an adjoining breakfast area, this kitchen is another natural gathering spot

Main Level Floor Plan

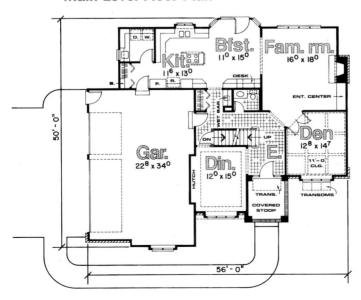

Upper Level Floor Plan

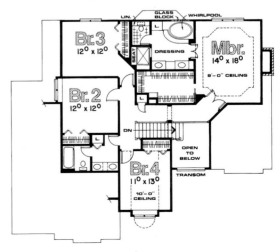

Copyright by designer/architect.

Plan #131006

Dimensions: 61' W x 53'6" D
Levels: 1
Square Footage: 2,193
Bedrooms: 3
Bathrooms: 2
Foundation: Basement, crawl space, or slab
Materials List Available: Yes
Price Category: E

Images provided by designer/architect.

This compact home is perfect for a small lot, but even so, has all the features of a much larger home, thanks to its space-saving interior design that lets one area flow into the next.

Features:

- Great Room: This wonderful room is sure to be the heart of your home. Visually, it flows from the foyer and dining room to the rear of the house, giving you enough space to create a private nook or two in it or treat it as a single, large room.

- Dining Room: Emphasize the formality of this room by decorating with subdued colors and sumptuous fabrics.

- Kitchen: Designed for efficiency, this kitchen features ample counter space and cabinets in a layout guaranteed to please you.

- Master Suite: You'll love the amenities in this private master suite, with its lovely bedroom and a bath filled with contemporary fixtures.

Rear View

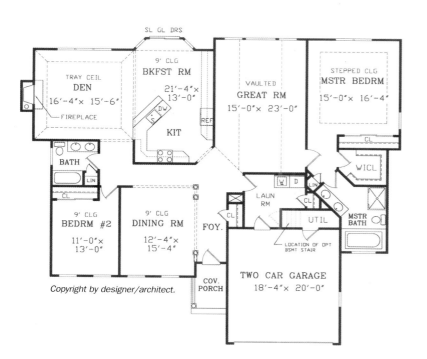

TRAY CEIL
DEN
16'-4"x 15'-6"

FIREPLACE

SL GL DRS

9' CLG
BKFST RM
21'-4"x
13'-0"

DW

KIT

REF

VAULTED
GREAT RM
15'-0"x 23'-0"

STEPPED CLG
MSTR BEDRM
15'-0"x 16'-4"

CL

WICL

BATH

LIN

CL

9' CLG
BEDRM #2
11'-0"x
13'-0"

9' CLG
DINING RM
12'-4"x
15'-4"

FOY.

W D

CL

LAUN
RM

LIN

CL

UTIL

MSTR
BATH

LOCATION OF OPT
BSMT STAIR

COV.
PORCH

TWO CAR GARAGE
18'-4"x 20'-0"

Copyright by designer/architect.

Alternate Floor Plan

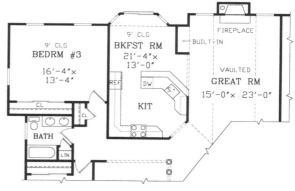

9' CLG
BEDRM #3
16'-4"x
13'-4"

9' CLG
BKFST RM
21'-4"x
13'-0"

FIREPLACE

BUILT-IN

REF

DW

VAULTED
GREAT RM
15'-0"x 23'-0"

CL

BATH

LIN

CL

KIT

Foyer /Dining Room

Kitchen

Great Room

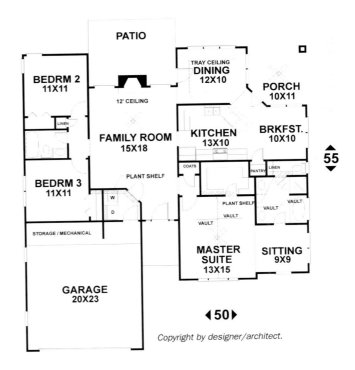

Images provided by
designer/architect.

Copyright by designer/architect.

Plan #101002

Dimensions: 46' W x 42' D
Levels: 1
Square Footage: 1,296
Bedrooms: 3
Bathrooms: 2
Foundation: Crawl space, slab,
basement
Materials List Available: No
Price Category: B

SMARTtip

Preparing Walls for Paint

Poor surface preparation is the number-one cause of
paint failure. Preparing surfaces properly—including
removing loose paint and thoroughly sanding—may
be tedious, but it's important for a good-looking and
long-lasting finish.

Plan #101003

Dimensions: 50' W x 54'10" D
Levels: 1
Square Footage: 1,593
Bedrooms: 3
Bathrooms: 2
Foundation: Slab, crawl space,
basement
Materials List Available: Yes
Price Category: C

Images
provided by
designer/
architect.

Copyright by designer/architect.

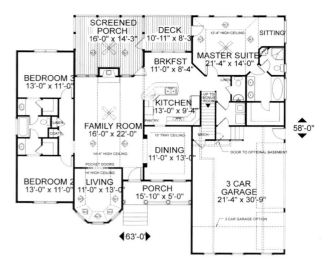

Plan #101006

Dimensions: 63' W x 58' D
Levels: 1
Square Footage: 1,982
Bedrooms: 3
Bathrooms: 2½
Foundation: Slab, crawl space, or basement
Materials List Available: Yes
Price Category: D

SMARTtip

Art in Pools

The tiled walls and floor of a pool make great canvases for art, so incorporate a serious or whimsical design. Also, make the stairs wide and shallow to form a wading area for kids.

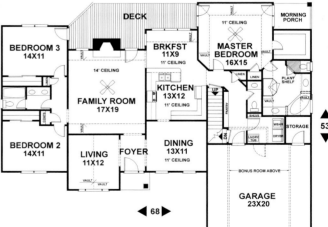

Plan #101008

Dimensions: 68' W x 53' D
Levels: 1
Square Footage: 2,088
Bedrooms: 3
Bathrooms: 2½
Foundation: Slab, crawl space, or basement
Materials List Available: Yes
Price Category: D

SMARTtip

Accentuating Your Bathroom with Details

No matter how big or small the room, details will pull the style together. Some of the best details that you can include are the smallest—drawer pulls from an antique store or shells in a glass jar or just left on the countertop. Add period flavor with crown molding, or dress up contemporary fixtures with polished stone fittings.

Plan #121093

Dimensions: 62' W x 60'8" D
Levels: 2
Square Footage: 2,603
Main Level Sq. Ft.: 1,800
Upper Level Sq. Ft.: 803
Bedrooms: 4
Bathrooms: 3½
Foundation: Basement
Materials List Available: Yes
Price Category: F

Images provided by designer/architect.

If you love family life but also treasure your privacy, you'll appreciate the layout of this home.

Features:

• Entry: This two-story, open area features plant shelves to display a group of lovely specimens.

• Dining Room: Open to the entry, this room features 12-ft. ceilings and corner hutches.

• Den: French doors lead to this quiet room, with its bowed window and spider-beamed ceiling.

• Gathering Room: A three-sided fireplace, shared with both the kitchen and the breakfast area, is the highlight of this room.

• Master Suite: Secluded for privacy, this suite also has a private covered deck where you can sit and recharge at any time of day. A walk-in closet is practical, and a whirlpool tub is pure comfort.

Main Level Floor Plan

Upper Level Floor Plan

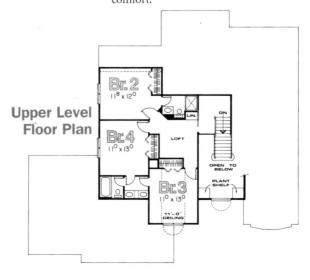

Copyright by designer/architect.

Plan #121078

Dimensions: 50' W x 48' D
Levels: 2
Square Footage: 2,248
Main Level Sq. Ft.: 1,568
Upper Level Sq. Ft.: 680
Bedrooms: 4
Bathrooms: 2½
Foundation: Slab
Materials List Available: Yes
Price Category: E

Images provided by designer/architect.

This design is wonderful for any family but has features that make it ideal for one with teens.

Features:

- Family Room: A vaulted ceiling gives a touch of elegance here and a corner fireplace makes it comfortable, especially when the weather's cool.

- Living Room: Both this room and the dining room have a formal feeling, but don't let that stop you from making them a family gathering spot.

- Kitchen: A built-in desk, butler's pantry, and a walk-in pantry make this kitchen easy to organize. The breakfast nook shares an angled eating bar with the family room.

- Master Suite: A walk-in closet and corner whirlpool tub and shower make this suite feel luxurious.

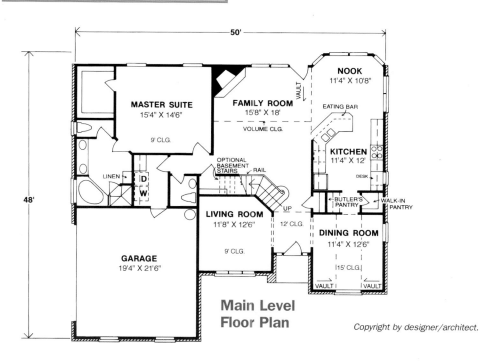

Main Level Floor Plan

Copyright by designer/architect.

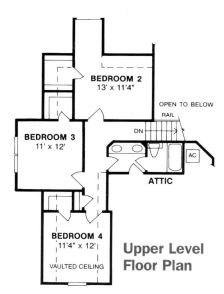

Upper Level Floor Plan

Plan #321001

Dimensions: 83' W x 42' D

Levels: 1

Square Footage: 1,721

Bedrooms: 3

Bathrooms: 2

Foundation: Basement, crawl space, or slab

Materials List Available: Yes

Price Category: C

You'll love the atrium that creates a warm, naturally lit space inside this gracious home, as well as the roof dormers that give it wonderful curb appeal from the outside.

Features:

- Great Room: Bathed in light from the atrium window wall, this room, with its vaulted ceiling, will be the hub of your family life.

- Dining Room: This room also has a vaulted ceiling and is lit by the atrium, but you can draw drapes at night to create a cozy, warm feeling.

- Kitchen: Designed for functionality, this step-saving kitchen is easy to organize and makes cooking a pleasure.

- Breakfast Room: For convenience, this room is located between the kitchen and the rear covered porch.

- Master Suite: Retire with pleasure to this lovely retreat, with its luxurious bath.

Rear View

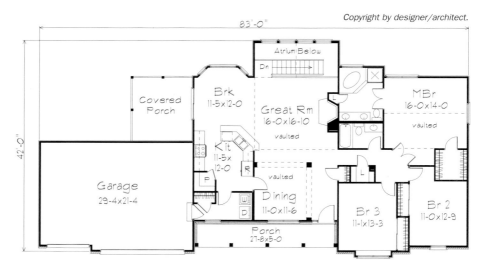

Plan #221024

Dimensions: 43' W x 40' D
Levels: 2
Square Footage: 1,732
Main Level Sq. Ft.: 1,289
Upper Level Sq. Ft.: 544
Bedrooms: 3
Bathrooms: 2½
Foundation: Basement
Materials List Available: No
Price Category: C

Images provided by designer/architect.

If your family loves contemporary split-level designs and large rooms with an open feeling, this is the home of their dreams.

Features:

- **Living Room:** A vaulted ceiling adds dimension to this large room, which is open to the dining room.

- **Dining Room:** Vaulted ceilings here and in the adjacent kitchen add to the spacious feeling. Sliding glass doors that open to the backyard make a practical pathway for the children.

- **Family Room:** This huge room features a fireplace for cozy comfort on chilly nights.

- **Master Suite:** A tray ceiling, walk-in closet, and private bath make this upstairs suite a joy.

- **Bonus Room:** Finish this 18-ft. x 29-ft.-9-in. space on the lower level as a home office or game room.

- **Bedrooms:** Both bedrooms have good closet space and share a full bath off the hallway.

Basement Level Floor Plan

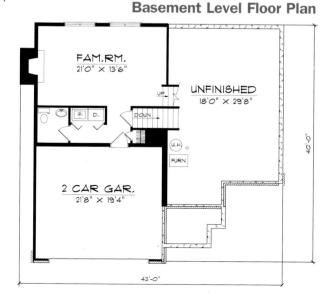

Copyright by designer/architect.

Main Level Floor Plan

Plan #121079

Dimensions: 50' W x 60' D
Levels: 2
Square Footage: 2,688
Main Level Sq. Ft.: 1,650
Upper Level Sq. Ft.: 1,038
Bedrooms: 4
Bathrooms: 3½
Foundation: Slab
Materials List Available: Yes
Price Category: F

Images provided by designer/architect.

You'll love this open design if you're looking for a home that gives a spacious feeling while also providing private areas.

Features:

- **Entry:** The cased openings and corner columns here give an attractive view into the dining room.

- **Living Room:** Another cased opening defines the entry to this living room but lets traffic flow into it.

- **Kitchen:** This well-designed kitchen is built around a center island that gives you extra work space. A snack bar makes an easy, open transition between the sunny dining nook and the kitchen.

- **Master Suite:** An 11-ft. ceiling sets the tone for this private space. With a walk-in closet and adjoining full bath, it will delight you.

Main Level Floor Plan

NOOK 12'4" X 11'8"

EATING BAR

KITCHEN ISLAND 13" X 12'

PANTRY

UP

LIVING ROOM 16' X 19'6" 9' CLG.

OPTIONAL BASEMENT STAIRS

MASTER SUITE 16'2" X 13'6" 11' CLG.

AC

9' CLG.

DINING ROOM 10'8" X 15'

OPTIONAL STUDY

FOYER 9' CLG.

3 CAR GARAGE 20'4" X 28'6"

PORCH

50'

60'

D   W

Upper Level Floor Plan

WINDOW SEAT

SLOPE   SLOPE

PLAY ROOM 16' X 16'

AC

ATTIC

DN

BEDROOM 4 12'6" X 11'4"

BEDROOM 2 11'6" X 13'6"

LIN

BEDROOM 3 10'8" X 15'

SLOPE

Copyright by designer/architect.

Plan #121080

Dimensions: 56' W x 49' D

Levels: 2

Square Footage: 2,384

Main Level Sq. Ft.: 1,616

Upper Level Sq. Ft.: 768

Bedrooms: 4

Bathrooms: 2½

Foundation: Slab

Materials List Available: Yes

Price Category: E

Images provided by designer/architect.

This design is ideal if you want a generously sized home now and room to expand later.

Features:

- Living Room: Your eyes will be drawn towards the ceiling as soon as you enter this lovely room. The ceiling is vaulted, giving a sense of grandeur, and a graceful balcony from the second floor adds extra interest to this room.

- Kitchen: Designed with lots of counter space to make your work convenient, this kitchen also shares an eating bar with the breakfast nook.

- Breakfast Nook: Eat here or go out to the adjoining private porch where you can enjoy your meal in the morning sunshine.

- Master Suite: The bayed area in the bedroom makes a picturesque sitting area. French doors in the bedroom open to a private bath that's fitted with a whirlpool tub, separate shower, two vanities, and a walk-in closet.

Main Level Floor Plan

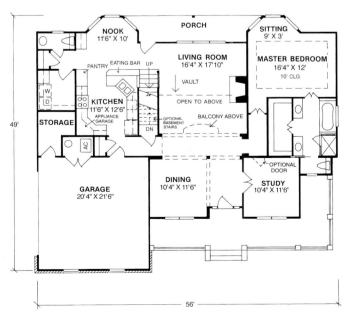

Upper Level Floor Plan

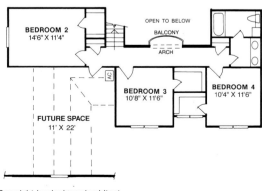

Copyright by designer/architect.

Plan #121090

Dimensions: 60' W x 58' D

Levels: 2

Square Footage: 2,645

Main Level Sq. Ft.: 1,972

Upper Level Sq. Ft.: 673

Bedrooms: 4

Bathrooms: 2½

Foundation: Basement

Materials List Available: Yes

Price Category: F

Images provided by designer/architect.

You'll be amazed at the amenities that have been designed into this lovely home.

Features:

- Den: French doors just off the entry lead to this lovely room, with its bowed window and spider-beamed ceiling.

- Great Room: A trio of graceful arched windows highlights the volume ceiling in this room. You might want to curl up to read next to the see-through fireplace into the hearth room.

- Kitchen: Enjoy the good design in this room.

- Hearth Room: The shared fireplace with the great room makes this a cozy spot in cool weather.

- Master Suite: French doors lead to this well-lit area, with its roomy walk-in closet, sunlit whirlpool tub, separate shower, and two vanities.

Main Level Floor Plan

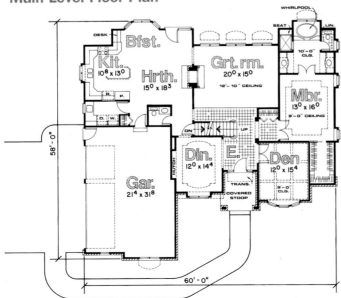

Upper Level Floor Plan

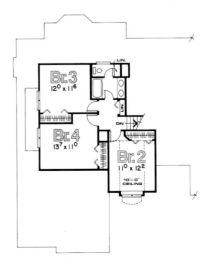

Copyright by designer/architect.

Plan #121064

Dimensions: 44' W x 40' D
Levels: 2
Square Footage: 1,846
Main Level Sq. Ft.: 919
Upper Level Sq. Ft.: 927
Bedrooms: 4
Bathrooms: 2½
Foundation: Basement
Materials List Available: Yes
Price Category: D

Images provided by designer/architect.

You'll love the features and design in this compact but amenity-filled home.

Features:

- Entry: A balcony overlooks this two-story entry, where a plant shelf tops the coat closet.
- Great Room: A trio of tall windows points up the large dimensions of this room, which is sure to be the hub of your home. Arrange the

furniture to create a cozy space around the fireplace, or leave it open to the room.

- Kitchen: You'll love to work in this well-designed kitchen area.
- Master Suite: On the second floor, this master suite features a tiered ceiling and two walk-in closets. In the bath, you'll find a double vanity, whirlpool tub, and separate shower.

Main Level Floor Plan

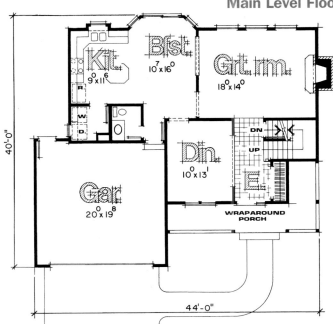

Upper Level Floor Plan

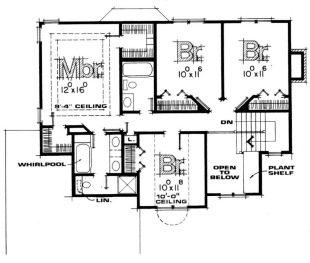

Copyright by designer/architect.

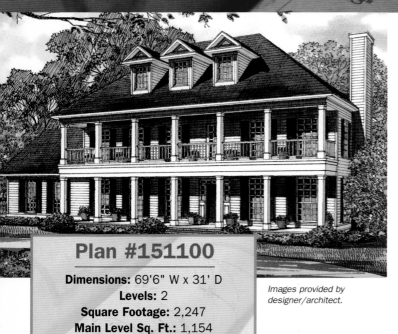

Plan #151100

Dimensions: 69'6" W x 31' D

Levels: 2

Square Footage: 2,247

Main Level Sq. Ft.: 1,154

Upper Level Sq. Ft.: 1,093

Bedrooms: 3

Bathrooms: 2½

Foundation: Crawl space, slab, or basement

Materials List Available: Yes

Price Category: E

Images provided by designer/architect.

Main Level Floor Plan

Upper Level Floor Plan

Copyright by designer/architect.

Plan #151118

Dimensions: 54'2" W x 73'6" D

Levels: 2

Square Footage: 2,784

Main Level Sq. Ft.: 1,895

Upper Level Sq. Ft.: 889

Bedrooms: 4

Bathrooms: 2½

Foundation: Crawl space, slab, or basement

Materials List Available: Yes

Price Category: F

Images provided by designer/architect.

Upper Level Floor Plan

Main Level Floor Plan

Copyright by designer/architect.

Plan #281007

Dimensions: 37' W x 31' D

Levels: 2

Square Footage: 1,206

Main Level Sq. Ft.: 670

Upper Level Sq. Ft.: 536

Bedrooms: 3

Bathrooms: 1 full, 2 half

Foundation: Full basement

Materials List Available: Yes

Price Category: B

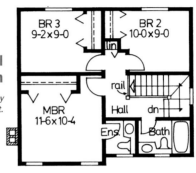

Images provided by designer/architect.

Main Level Floor Plan

DR 11-6x9-0
Nook
KITCHEN 12-2 x 9-0
dw
F R
up
rail
dn
GARAGE 13-6 x 20-6
LIVINGROOM 11-6 x17-8
BRM
Foyer
Lav
Porch

Upper Level Floor Plan

Copyright by designer/architect.

BR 3 9-2x9-0
BR 2 10-0x9-0
lin
rail
dn
MBR 11-6 x 10-4
Ens
Hall
Bath

Plan #291011

Dimensions: 68'6" W x 33' D

Levels: 2

Square Footage: 1,898

Main Level Sq. Ft.: 1,182

Upper Level Sq. Ft.: 716

Bedrooms: 4

Bathrooms: 2½

Foundation: Basement

Materials List Available: No

Price Category: D

Main Level Floor Plan

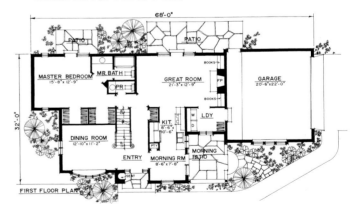

68'-0"

PATIO
PATIO
BOOKS
MASTER BEDROOM 15'-8" x 12'-9"
MR. BATH
GREAT ROOM 21'-3" x 12'-9"
FP
GARAGE 20'-6" x 22'-0"
PR
BOOKS
32'-0"
KIT. 10'-6"
W
LDY
D
DINING ROOM 12'-10" x 11'-2"
PT
MORNING PATIO
ENTRY
MORNING RM 8'-6" x 7'-2"
SEAT
FIRST FLOOR PLAN

Copyright by designer/architect.

Images provided by designer/architect.

Upper Level Floor Plan

BATH #2
BEDROOM #4 11'-6" x 10'-2"
BEDROOM #2 13'-4" x 14'-4"
DN
BEDROOM #3 11'-0" x 14'-11"

Plan #161021

Dimensions: 48' W x 38' D
Levels: 2
Square Footage: 1,897
Main Level Sq. Ft.: 1,036
Upper Level Sq. Ft.: 861
Bedrooms: 3
Bathrooms: 2½
Foundation: Basement
Materials List Available: No
Price Category: D

If you're looking for a home where you can create a loving family-life, you'll love this one.

Features:

- **Foyer:** The view from the foyer through the great room and its rear windows to the back yard gives a spacious feeling to this home.
- **Great Room:** French doors topped by arched windows add quiet elegance to this room.
- **Dining Room:** A furniture alcove in this formal room adds convenience.
- **Kitchen:** Enjoy the extra storage space the pantry provides in this well-designed area.
- **Laundry Room:** This large room makes even the most complicated laundry jobs a snap.

- **Stairs:** The split stairs feature a wood rail that leads to a window seat at the top with a balcony that overlooks the great room.

Images provided by designer/architect.

Rear Elevation

Main Level Floor Plan

Upper Level Floor Plan

Copyright by designer/architect.

Plan #151089

Dimensions: 84' W x 55'6" D
Levels: 1
Square Footage: 1,921
Bedrooms: 3
Bathrooms: 3
Foundation: Crawl space, slab, or basement
Materials List Available: Yes
Price Category: D

If your family loves to combine indoor and outdoor living, this home's fabulous porches and deck space make it perfect.

Features:

- **Porches:** A huge wraparound front porch, sizable rear porch, and deck that joins them give you space for entertaining or simply lounging.

- **Living Room:** A fireplace and built-in media center could be the focal points in this large room.

- **Hearth Room:** Open to both the living room and kitchen, this hearth room also features a fireplace.

- **Kitchen:** This step-saving kitchen includes ample storage and work space, as well as an angled bar it shares with the hearth room. Atrium doors lead to the rear porch.

- **Bonus Upper Level:** A large game room and a full bath make this area a favorite with the children.

Images provided by designer/architect.

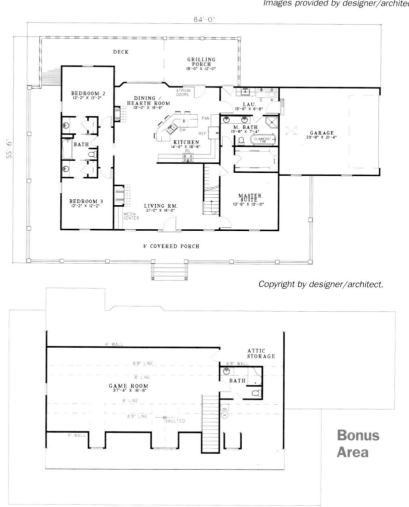

Copyright by designer/architect.

Bonus Area

Plan #121066

Dimensions: 46' W x 41'5" D

Levels: 2

Square Footage: 2,078

Main Level Sq. Ft.: 1,113

Upper Level Sq. Ft.: 965

Bedrooms: 4

Bathrooms: 2½

Foundation: Basement

Materials List Available: Yes

Price Category: D

Images provided by designer/architect.

This lovely home has an unusual dignity, perhaps because its rooms are so well-proportioned and thoughtfully laid out.

Features:

- Family Room: This room is sunken, giving it an unusually cozy, comfortable feeling. Its abundance of windows let natural light stream in during the day, and the fireplace warms it when the weather's chilly.

- Dining Room: This dining room links to the parlor beyond through a cased opening.

- Parlor: A tall, angled ceiling highlights a large, arched window that's the focal point of this room.

- Breakfast Area: A wooden rail visually links this bayed breakfast area to the family room.

- Master Suite: A roomy walk-in closet adds a practical touch to this luxurious suite. The bath features a skylight, whirlpool tub, and separate shower.

Main Level Floor Plan

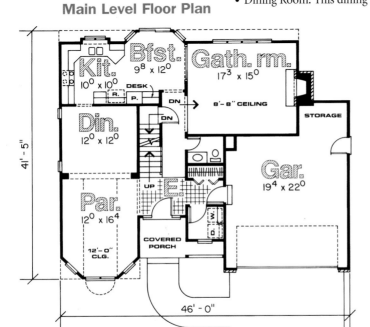

Upper Level Floor Plan

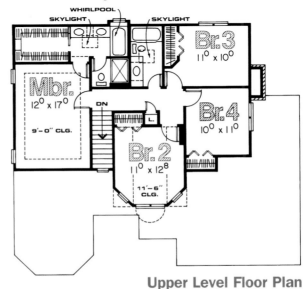

Copyright by designer/architect.

Plan #211070

Dimensions: 46' W x 68' D
Levels: 2
Square Footage: 1,700
Main Level Sq. Ft.: 1,160
Upper Level Sq. Ft.: 540
Bedrooms: 3
Bathrooms: 2½
Foundation: Crawl space, optional slab, or basement
Materials List Available: Yes
Price Category: C

Images provided by designer/architect.

You'll be charmed by the three roof dormers and the full-width covered porch on this traditional home.

Features:

- Living Room: With 9-ft. ceilings throughout the living room, dining room, and kitchen merge to maximize usable space and create a spacious, airy feeling in this home. You'll find a fireplace here and three pairs of French doors.

- Dining Room: Walk through this room to the rear covered porch beyond that connects the house to the garage.

- Kitchen: Designed for convenience, this kitchen features a wet bar that is centrally located so that it can easily serve both the living and dining rooms.

- Master Suite: A sloped ceiling with a skylight and French doors leading to the front porch make this area luxurious. The bath includes a raised marble tub, dual-sink vanity, and walk-in closet.

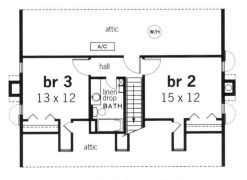

Main Level Floor Plan

Upper Level Floor Plan

Copyright by designer/architect.

Plan #211003

Dimensions: 62' W x 64'8" D
Levels: 1
Square Footage: 1,865
Bedrooms: 3
Bathrooms: 2
Foundation: Slab
Materials List Available: Yes
Price Category: D

SMARTtip

Fire Extinguishers

The word PASS is an easy way to remember the proper way to use a fire extinguisher.

Pull the pin at the top of the extinguisher that keeps the handle from being accidentally pressed.

Aim the nozzle of the extinguisher toward the base of the fire.

Squeeze the handle to discharge the extinguisher. Stand approximately 8 feet away from the fire.

Sweep the nozzle back and forth at the base of the fire. After the fire appears to be out, watch it carefully because it may reignite!

The traditional style of this home is blended with all the amenities required for today's lifestyle.

Features:

- Ceiling Height: 8 ft. unless otherwise noted.
- Front Porch: Guests will feel welcome arriving at the front door under this sheltering front porch.
- Dining Room: This large room will accommodate dinner parties of all sizes, from large formal gatherings to more intimate family get-togethers.
- Living Room: Guests and family alike will feel right at home in this inviting room. Sunlight streaming through the skylights in the 12-ft. ceiling, combined with the handsome fireplace, makes the space both airy and warm.

- Back Patio: When warm weather comes around, step out the sliding glass doors in the living room to enjoy entertaining or just relaxing on this patio.
- Kitchen: A cathedral ceiling soars over this efficient modern kitchen. It includes an eating area that is perfect for informal family meals.

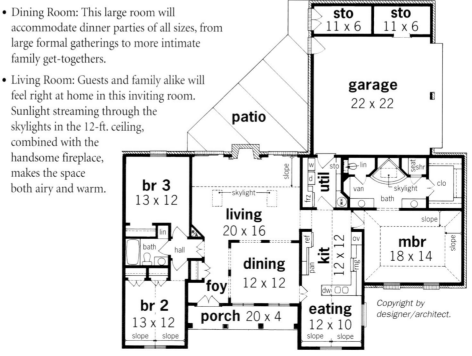

Copyright by designer/architect.

Plan #121094

Dimensions: 40'8" W x 46' D

Levels: 2

Square Footage: 1,768

Main Level Sq. Ft.: 905

Upper Level Sq. Ft.: 863

Bedrooms: 3

Bathrooms: 2½

Foundation: Basement

Materials List Available: Yes

Price Category: C

Images provided by designer/architect.

You'll love this design if you're looking for a home to complement a site with a lovely rear view.

Features:

- **Great Room:** A trio of lovely windows looks out to the front entry of this home. The French doors in this room open to the breakfast area for everyone's convenience.

- **Kitchen:** Designed to suit a gourmet cook, this kitchen includes a roomy pantry and an island with a snack bar.

- **Breakfast Area:** The boxed window here is perfect for houseplants or a collection of culinary herbs. A door leads to the rear porch, where you'll love to dine in good weather.

- **Master Suite:** On the upper level, the bedroom features a cathedral ceiling, two walk-in closets, and a window seat. The bath also has a cathedral ceiling and includes dual lavatories, a large dressing area, and a sunlit whirlpool tub.

Main Level Floor Plan

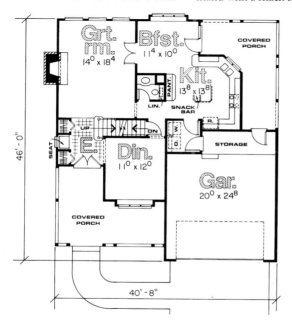

Upper Level Floor Plan

Copyright by designer/architect.

Plan #121042

Dimensions: 48' W x 49' D
Levels: 2
Square Footage: 2,354
Main Level Sq. Ft.: 1,207
Upper Level Sq. Ft.: 1,147
Bedrooms: 4
Bathrooms: 3½
Foundation: Basement
Materials List Available: Yes
Price Category: E

Images provided by designer/architect.

Careful attention to traffic flow in this open layout result in a convenient and comfortable home.

Features:

- Ceiling Height: 8 ft. unless otherwise noted.
- Family Room: This sunny room is perfectly suited for family activities.
- Breakfast Area: You'll want to linger over breakfast in this sunlight-filled bayed area that flows into the family room.
- Kitchen: The breakfast area flows into this kitchen, which features a pantry and center island that doubles as a snack bar.
- Dining Room. Corner columns lend elegance to this room, making it perfect for formal entertaining as well as family gatherings.
- Computer Loft: This loft, designed to accommodate the family computer, overlooks the two-story entry.
- Master Suite: This comfortable retreat offers a walk-in closet, whirlpool, and separate shower.

Main Level Floor Plan

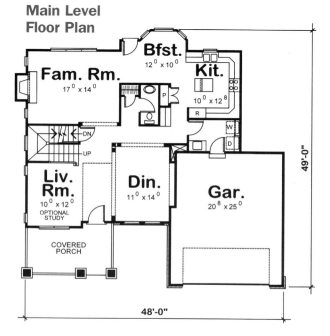

Upper Level Floor Plan

Copyright by designer/architect.

Plan #121027

Dimensions: 46' W x 48' D
Levels: 2
Square Footage: 1,660
Main Level Sq. Ft.: 1,265
Upper Level Sq. Ft.: 395
Bedrooms: 3
Bathrooms: 2½
Foundation: Basement
Materials List Available: Yes
Price Category: C

Images provided by designer/architect.

This elegant home is designed for architectural interest and gracious living.

Features:

- Ceiling Height: 8 ft. unless otherwise noted.

- Great Room: Family and guests will be drawn to this inviting, sun-filled room with its 13-ft. ceiling and raised-hearth fireplace.

- Formal Dining Room: An angled ceiling lends architectural interest to this elegant room. Alternately, this room can be used as a parlor.

- Master Bedroom: Corner windows are designed to ease window placement.

- Master Bath: The master bedroom is served by a private bath. The sunlit whirlpool bath invites you to take time to luxuriate and rejuvenate. There's a double vanity, separate shower, and a walk-in closet.

- Garage: This two bay garage offers plenty of space for storage in addition to parking.

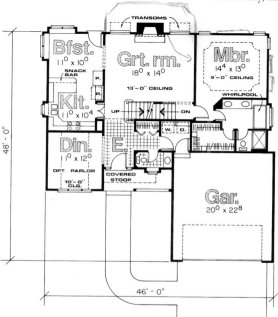

Main Level Floor Plan

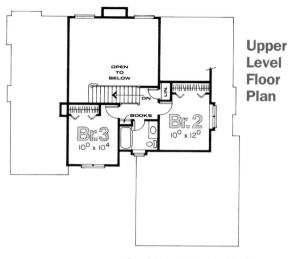

Upper Level Floor Plan

Copyright by designer/architect.

Images provided by designer/architect.

Plan #111001

Dimensions: 66'8" W x 76'11" D

Levels: 1

Square Footage: 2,832

Bedrooms: 4

Bathrooms: 2½

Foundation: Slab

Materials List Available: No

Price Category: F

Copyright by designer/architect.

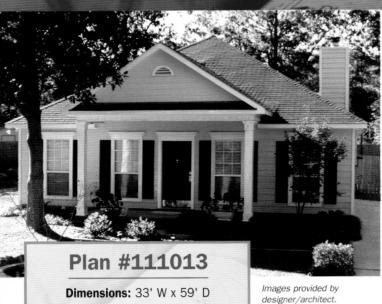

Copyright by designer/architect.

Images provided by designer/architect.

Plan #111013

Dimensions: 33' W x 59' D

Levels: 1

Square Footage: 1,606

Bedrooms: 3

Bathrooms: 2

Foundation: Slab

Materials List Available: No

Price Category: C

Plan #111008

Dimensions: 43' W x 69' D

Levels: 2

Square Footage: 2,011

Main Level Sq. Ft.: 1,331

Upper Level Sq. Ft.: 680

Bedrooms: 3

Bathrooms: 2½

Foundation: Slab

Materials List Available: No

Price Category: D

Images provided by designer/architect.

Main Level Floor Plan

Upper Level Floor Plan

Copyright by designer/architect.

Extra Storage 19'4"x 3'4"

Two-Car Carport 20'0"x 24'0"

Patio 20'0"x 8'0"

Great Room 22'8"x 14'0"

Utility

Master Bath

WIC

Breakfast 10'0"x 10'0"

Kitchen 11'4"x 10'10"

Master Bedroom 13'6"x 13'0"

Porch 11'0"x 5'0"

Dining Room 11'4"x 12'0"

Open to Below

Bedroom 11'4"x 15'0"

Bedroom 10'4"x 10'6"

Study 11'10"x 9'2"

Plan #111023

Dimensions: 46'11" W x 73'5" D

Levels: 2

Square Footage: 2,356

Main Level Sq. Ft.: 1,516

Upper Level Sq. Ft.: 840

Bedrooms: 4

Bathrooms: 2½

Foundation: Slab

Materials List Available: No

Price Category: E

Images provided by designer/architect.

Main Level Floor Plan

Two Car Garage 22'x 23'6"

Porch

Breakfast

Master Bedroom 15'x 15'4"

Living 18'x 17'6"

Dining 13'6"x 12'

Porch

Upper Level Floor Plan

Copyright by designer/architect.

Bedroom 14'x 11'

Bedroom 15'5"x 12'

Bedroom 14'x 11'6"

Open To Below

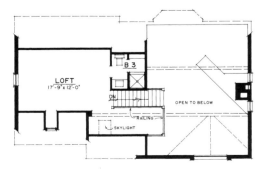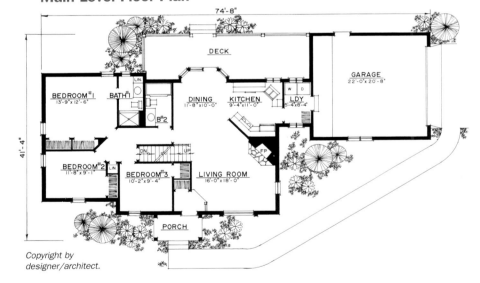

Plan #291009

Dimensions: 74'8" W x 41'4" D

Levels: 2

Square Footage: 1,655

Main Level Sq. Ft.: 1,277

Upper Level Sq. Ft.: 378

Bedrooms: 3

Bathrooms: 2

Foundation: Basement

Materials List Available: No

Price Category: C

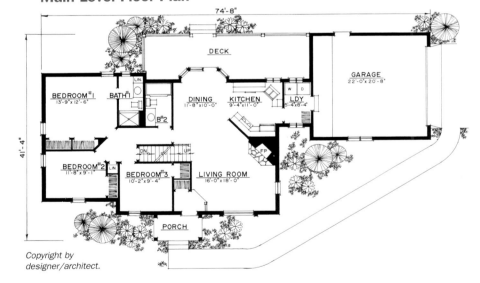

Main Level Floor Plan

Copyright by designer/architect.

Upper Level Floor Plan

Images provided by designer/architect.

If your family loves a northern European look, they'll appreciate the curved eaves and arched window that give this lovely home its character.

Features:

- **Entryway:** The front door welcomes both friends and family into a lovely open design on the first floor of this home.

- **Living Room:** The enormous arched window floods this room with natural light in the daytime. At night, draw drapes across it to create a warm, intimate feeling.

- **Dining Room:** Windows are the highlight of this room, too, but here, the angled bay window area opens to the rear deck.

- **Kitchen:** The family cook will be delighted with this well-planned kitchen, which is a snap to organize.

- **Master Suite:** Located on the first floor, this suite includes a private bath for total convenience.

Plan #151117

Dimensions: 66' W x 55' D
Levels: 1
Square Footage: 1,957
Bedrooms: 3
Bathrooms: 3
Foundation: Crawl space, slab, or basement
Materials List Available: Yes
Price Category: D

You'll love this home if you have a family-centered lifestyle and enjoy an active social life.

Features:

Foyer: A 10-ft. ceiling sets the tone for this home.

- Great Room: A 10-ft. boxed ceiling and fireplace are the highlights of this room, which also has a door leading to the rear covered porch.

- Dining Room: Columns mark the entry from the foyer to this lovely formal dining room.

- Study: Add the French doors from the foyer to transform bedroom 3, with its vaulted ceiling, into a quiet study.

- Kitchen: This large kitchen includes a pantry and shares an eating bar with the adjoining, bayed breakfast room.

- Master Suite: You'll love the access to the rear porch, as well as the bath with every amenity, in this suite.

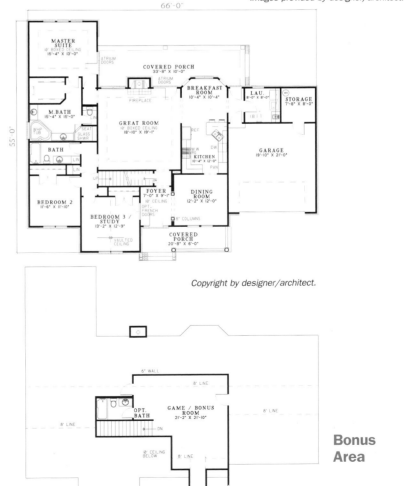

Bonus Area

Plan #121032

Dimensions: 54'8" W x 45'4" D
Levels: 2
Square Footage: 2,339
Main Level Sq. Ft.: 1,665
Upper Level Sq. Ft.: 674
Bedrooms: 4
Bathrooms: 2½
Foundation: Basement
Materials List Available: Yes
Price Category: E

Images provided by designer/architect.

This home is designed for gracious living and is distinguished by many architectural details.

Features:

• Ceiling Height: 8 ft. unless otherwise noted.

• Foyer: This is truly a grand foyer with a dramatic ceiling that soars to 18 ft.

• Great Room: The foyer's 18-ft. ceiling extends into the great room where an open staircase adds architectural windows. Warm yourself by the fireplace that is framed by windows.

• Kitchen: An island is the centerpiece of this handsome and efficient kitchen that features a breakfast area for informal family meals. The room also includes a handy desk.

• Private Wing: The master suite and study are in a private wing of the house.

• Room to Expand: In addition to the three bedrooms, the second level has an unfinished storage space that can become another bedroom or office.

Main Level Floor Plan

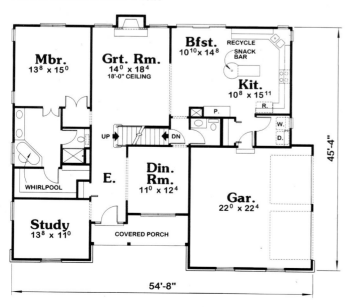

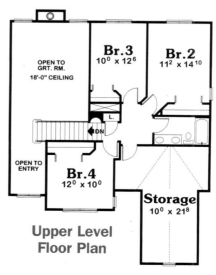

**Upper Level
Floor Plan**

Copyright by designer/architect.

Plan #121001

Dimensions: 56' W x 58' D
Levels: 1
Square Footage: 1,911
Bedrooms: 3
Bathrooms: 2
Foundation: Basement
Materials List Available: Yes
Price Category: D

Images provided by designer/architect.

Detailed, soaring ceilings and top-notch amenities set this distinctive home apart.

Features:

- Ceiling Height: 8 ft. except as noted.

- Great Room: A soaring ceiling and six tall transom-topped windows make this a light and airy spot for entertaining.

- Formal Dining Room: The entry enjoys a pleasing view of this dining room's detailed 12-ft. ceiling and picture window.

- Great Room: At the back of the home, a see-through fireplace in this great room is joined by a built-in entertainment center.

- Hearth Room: This bayed room shares the see-through fireplace with the great room.

- Master Suite: Enjoy the stars and the sun in the private bath's whirlpool and separate shower. The bath features the same decorative ceiling as the dining room.

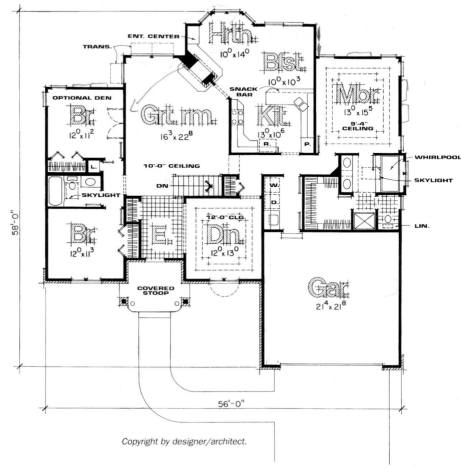

Copyright by designer/architect.

Main Level Floor Plan

Images provided by designer/architect.

Plan #101024

Dimensions: 53' W x 57' D

Levels: 2

Square Footage: 3,135

Main Level Sq. Ft.: 1,600

Upper Level Sq. Ft.: 1,535

Bedrooms: 5

Bathrooms: 4

Foundation: Basement

Materials List Available: No

Price Category: G

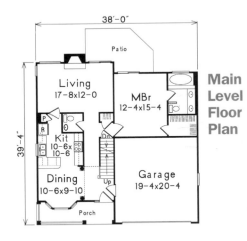

Upper Level Floor Plan

Copyright by designer/architect.

Plan #321075

Dimensions: 38' W x 39'4" D

Levels: 2

Square Footage: 1,524

Main Level Sq. Ft.: 951

Upper Level Sq. Ft.: 573

Bedrooms: 3

Bathrooms: 2½

Foundation: Basement

Materials List Available: Yes

Price Category: C

Images provided by designer/architect.

Main Level Floor Plan

Upper Level Floor Plan

Copyright by designer/architect.

Main Level Floor Plan

Plan #181137

Dimensions: 68' W x 34' D

Levels: 2

Square Footage: 2,353

Main Level Sq. Ft.: 1,281

Upper Level Sq. Ft.: 1,072

Bedrooms: 3

Bathrooms: 2½

Foundation: Full basement

Materials List Available: Yes

Price Category: E

Images provided by designer/architect.

Upper Level Floor Plan

Copyright by designer/architect.

Plan #251014

Dimensions: 53'8" W x 61' D

Levels: 2

Square Footage: 2,210

Main Level Sq. Ft.: 1,670

Upper Level Sq. Ft.: 540

Bedrooms: 3

Bathrooms: 2½

Foundation: Crawl space, basement

Materials List Available: Yes

Price Category: E

Images provided by designer/architect.

Main Level Floor Plan

Upper Level Floor Plan

Copyright by designer/architect.

Plan #121002

Dimensions: 42' W x 54' D
Levels: 1
Square Footage: 1,347
Bedrooms: 3
Bathrooms: 2
Foundation: Basement
Materials List Available: Yes
Price Category: B

This home's convenient single level and luxury amenities are a recipe for gracious living.

Features:

- Ceiling Height: 8 ft. except as noted.

- Great Room: The entry enjoys a long view into this great room where a pair of transom-topped windows flanks the fireplace and a 10-ft. ceiling visually expands the space.

- Snack Bar: This special feature adjoins the great room, making it a real plus for informal entertaining, as well as the perfect spot for family get-togethers.

- Kitchen: An island is the centerpiece of this well-designed convenient kitchen that features an island, a door to the backyard, a pantry, and convenient access to the laundry room.

- Master Suite: Located at the back of the home for extra privacy, the master suite feels like its own world. It features a tiered ceiling and sunlit corner whirlpool.

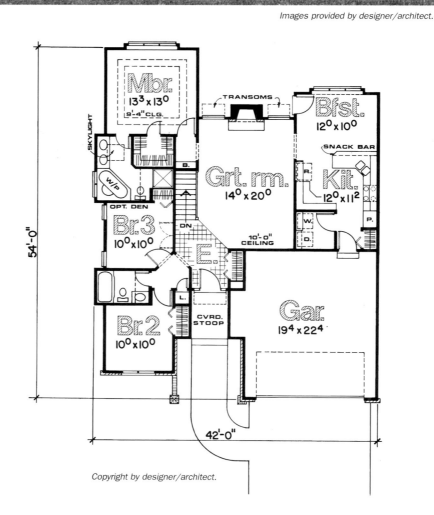

Copyright by designer/architect.

Plan #121005

Dimensions: 48' W x 52' D
Levels: 1
Square Footage: 1,496
Bedrooms: 3
Bathrooms: 2
Foundation: Basement
Materials List Available: Yes
Price Category: B

Images provided by designer/architect.

A beautiful starter or retirement home with all the amenities you'd expect in a much bigger house.

Features:

- Ceiling Height: 8 ft.

- Great Room: A cathedral ceiling visually expands the great room making it the perfect place for family gatherings or formal entertaining.

- Formal Dining Room: This elegant room is ideal for entertaining dinner guests. It conveniently shares a wet bar and service counter with a bayed breakfast area next door.

- Breakfast Area: In addition to the service area shared with the dining room, this cozy area features a snack bar, pantry, and desk that's perfect for household paperwork.

- Master Suite: The master bedroom features special ceiling details. It's joined by a private bath with a whirlpool, shower, and spacious walk-in closet.

- Garage: The two-bay garage offers plenty of storage space.

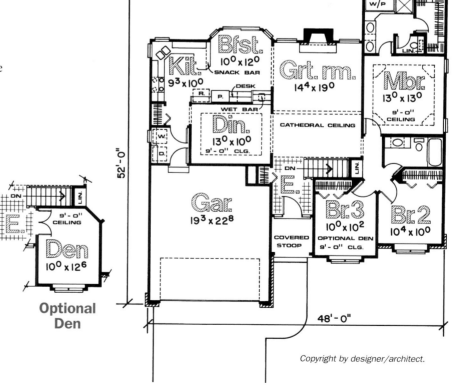

Optional Den

Copyright by designer/architect.

Main Level Floor Plan

Garage
29 x 24-4

Family
17-6 x 14

Nook

Patio

Util.

Kit.

Living
14-6 x 12

Dining
10 x 12

Entry

UP

Cov'd. Porch

Images provided by designer/architect.

Plan #231013

Dimensions: 71'6" W x 40' D
Levels: 2
Square Footage: 2,780
Main Level Sq. Ft.: 1,200
Upper Level Sq. Ft.: 1,580
Bedrooms: 4
Bathrooms: 3½
Foundation: Crawl space
Materials List Available: No
Price Category: F

Playroom
13 x 19

DESK

Br #4
10 x 10

M. Br
15 x 14

DESK

LINEN

Br #3
11 x 10

DN.

BALCONY

Br #2
11 x 12

Upper Level Floor Plan

Copyright by designer/architect.

Nook

Patio

Kit.

Dining
10 x 12-6

Family
15 x 14-2

DN.

PANT

Garage
21-4 x 35-4

Living
12 x 15-8

DN.

UP

Util.

Foyer

Porch

Main Level Floor Plan

Plan #231015

Dimensions: 63' W x 42' D
Levels: 2
Square Footage: 2,360
Main Level Sq. Ft.: 1,054
Upper Level Sq. Ft.: 1,306
Bedrooms: 4
Bathrooms: 2½
Foundation: Crawl space
Materials List Available: No
Price Category: E

Images provided by designer/architect.

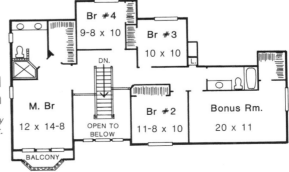

Br #4
9-8 x 10

Br #3
10 x 10

DN.

Upper Level Floor Plan

Copyright by designer/architect.

M. Br
12 x 14-8

OPEN TO BELOW

Br #2
11-8 x 10

Bonus Rm.
20 x 11

BALCONY

Main Level Floor Plan

Gathering
18x17

Nook
9-6x9

Kitchen

Dining
11x12

Garage
27-8x23-4

Utility

Pantry

Den
12-6x12

Covered Porch

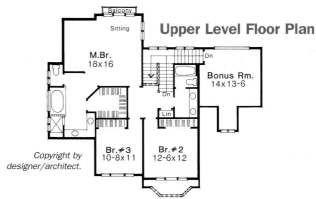

Upper Level Floor Plan

Balcony

Sitting

M.Br.
18x16

Bonus Rm.
14x13-6

Lin

Br.#3
10-8x11

Br.#2
12-6x12

Plan #231025

Dimensions: 66' W x 46' D

Levels: 2

Square Footage: 2,501

Main Level Sq. Ft.: 1,170

Upper Level Sq. Ft.: 1,331

Bedrooms: 3

Bathrooms: 2½

Foundation: Crawl space

Materials List Available: No

Price Category: E

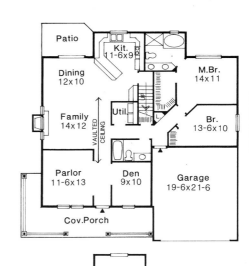

Patio

Kit.
11-6x9

Dining
12x10

M.Br.
14x11

Family
14x12

VAULTED CEILING

Util

Br.
13-6x10

Parlor
11-6x13

Den
9x10

Garage
19-6x21-6

Cov.Porch

Main Level Floor Plan

Upper Level Floor Plan

OPEN TO BELOW

DN

Br.
11x12-4

Loft

Plan #231035

Dimensions: 50' W x 50' D

Levels: 2

Square Footage: 1,954

Main Level Sq. Ft.: 1,508

Upper Level Sq. Ft.: 446

Bedrooms: 3

Bathrooms: 3

Foundation: Crawl space, slab

Materials List Available: No

Price Category: D

Plan #281011

Dimensions: 50' W x 54' D

Levels: 1

Square Footage: 1,314

Bedrooms: 3

Bathrooms: 2

Foundation: Basement

Materials List Available: Yes

Price Category: B

Images provided by designer/architect.

This attractive ranch home takes advantage of views at both the front and rear.

Features:

- Ceiling Height: 8 ft.
- Porch: This large, inviting porch welcomes your guests and provides shade for the big living-room window on hot summer days.
- Living Room: This large main living area has plenty of room for entertaining and family activities.
- Dining Room: This room can accommodate large dinner parties. It's located near the living room and the kitchen for convenient entertaining.
- Deck: Family and friends will enjoy stepping out on this large covered sun deck that is accessible from the living room, dining room, and kitchen.
- Master Suite: You'll enjoy retiring at the end of the day to this luxurious master suite, which features its own walk-in closet and bathroom.

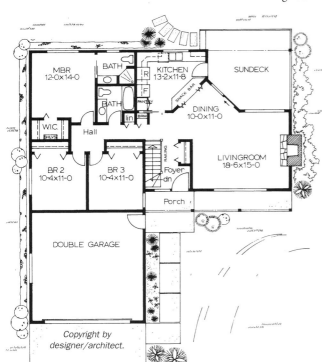

Copyright by designer/architect.

Rear Elevation

SMARTtip

Rag-Rolling Off

Paint Tip: Work with a partner. One person can roll on the glaze while the other lifts it off with the rag in a rhythmic pattern of even, steady strokes.

Plan #221004

Dimensions: 67'8" W x 43' D

Levels: 1

Square Footage: 1,763

Bedrooms: 3

Bathrooms: 2

Foundation: Basement

Materials List Available: No

Price Category: C

Images provided by designer/architect.

You'll love the spacious feeling provided by the open design of this traditional ranch.

Features:

- Ceiling Height: 8 ft.

- Dining Room: This formal room is perfect for entertaining groups both large and small, and the open design makes it easy to serve.

- Living Room: The vaulted ceiling here and in the dining room adds to the elegance of these rooms. Use window treatments that emphasize these ceilings for a truly sumptuous look.

- Kitchen: Designed for practicality and efficiency, this kitchen will thrill all the cooks in the family. An attached dining nook makes a natural gathering place for friends and family.

- Master Suite: The private bath in this suite features a double vanity and whirlpool tub. You'll find a walk-in closet in the bedroom.

- Garage: You'll love the extra storage space in this two-car garage.

Rear Elevation

Copyright by designer/architect.

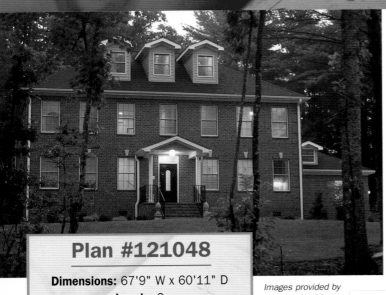

Main Level Floor Plan

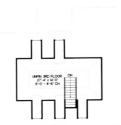

Images provided by designer/architect.

Copyright by designer/architect.

Plan #121048

Dimensions: 67'9" W x 60'11" D
Levels: 2
Square Footage: 2,975
Main Level Sq. Ft.: 1,548
Upper Level Sq. Ft.: 1,427
Bedrooms: 4
Bathrooms: 3½
Foundation: Slab
Materials List Available: Yes
Price Category: F

Upper Level Floor Plan

Bonus Area

Plan #121095

Dimensions: 65'4" W x 48'8" D
Levels: 2
Square Footage: 2,282
Main Level Sq. Ft.: 1,597
Upper Level Sq. Ft.: 685
Bedrooms: 4
Bathrooms: 2½
Foundation: Basement
Materials List Available: Yes
Price Category: E

Main Level Floor Plan

Images provided by designer/architect.

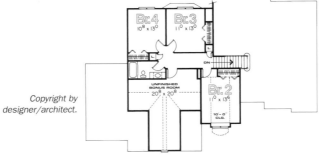

Copyright by designer/architect.

Upper Level Floor Plan

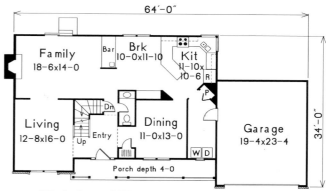

Main Level Floor Plan

Upper Level Floor Plan

Copyright by designer/architect.

Plan #321066

Dimensions: 64' W x 34' D

Levels: 2

Square Footage: 2,286

Main Level Sq. Ft.: 1,283

Upper Level Sq. Ft.: 1,003

Bedrooms: 4

Bathrooms: 2½

Foundation: Basement, crawl space, or slab

Materials List Available: No

Price Category: E

Images provided by designer/architect.

Copyright by designer/architect.

Rear Elevation

Plan #161007

Dimensions: 66'4" W x 43'10" D

Levels: 1

Square Footage: 1,611

Bedrooms: 3

Bathrooms: 2

Foundation: Basement

Materials List Available: Yes

Price Category: C

Images provided by designer/ architect.

Plan #131026

Dimensions: 55'10" W x 41' D
Levels: 2
Square Footage: 2,796
Main Level Sq. Ft.: 1,481
Upper level Sq. Ft.: 1,315
Bedrooms: 4
Bathrooms: 2½
Foundation: Basement, crawl space, or slab
Materials List Available: Yes
Price Category: G

Images provided by designer/architect.

Handsome half rounds add to curb appeal.

Features:

- Ceiling Height: 8 ft.

- Library: This room features a10-ft. ceiling with a bright bay window.

- Great Room: A 10-ft. ceiling adds to the spacious feeling of this room, while the corner fireplace gives it an intimate feeling. Sliding glass doors at the rear of the room open to the backyard.

- Dining Room: This formal room adjoins the great room, allowing guests and family to flow between the rooms, and it opens to the backyard through sliding glass doors.

- Breakfast Room: Turrets add a Victorian feeling to this room, which is just off the kitchen and overlooks the front porch.

- Master Suite: Privacy is assured in this suite, which is separated from the main part of the house. A compartmented bath and large walk-in closet add convenience to its beauty.

Master Bathroom

Family Room

Rear
Elevation

Upper Level Floor Plan

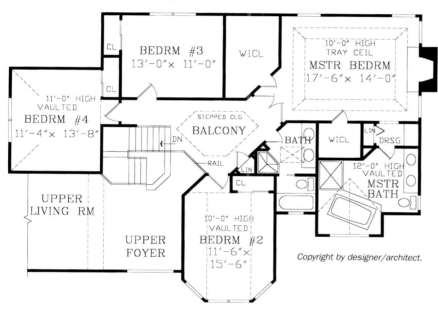

CL
BEDRM #3
13'-0" x 11'-0"

WICL

10'-0" HIGH
TRAY CEIL
MSTR BEDRM
17'-6" x 14'-0"

CL

11'-0" HIGH
VAULTED
BEDRM #4
11'-4" x 13'-8"

STEPPED CLG
BALCONY

DN

RAIL

BATH

WICL

LIN

DRSG

LIN

12'-0" HIGH
VAULTED
MSTR
BATH

CL

UPPER
LIVING RM

UPPER
FOYER

10'-0" HIGH
VAULTED
BEDRM #2
11'-6" x
15'-6"

Copyright by designer/architect.

Main Level Floor Plan

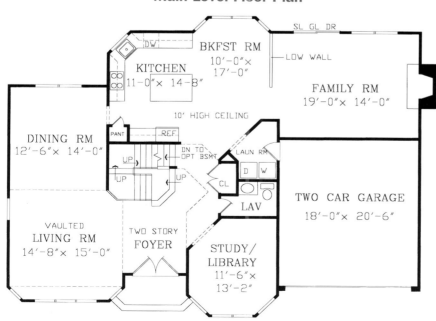

DW

BKFST RM
10'-0" x
17'-0"

SL GL DR

LOW WALL

KITCHEN
11'-0" x 14'-8"

FAMILY RM
19'-0" x 14'-0"

10' HIGH CEILING

DINING RM
12'-6" x 14'-0"

PANT

REF

DN TO
OPT BSMT

LAUN RM

UP

UP

UP

D W

CL

LAV

TWO CAR GARAGE
18'-0" x 20'-6"

VAULTED
LIVING RM
14'-8" x 15'-0"

TWO STORY
FOYER

STUDY/
LIBRARY
11'-6" x
13'-2"

Paint Basics

Most interior paints are either alkyd-resin (oil-based) products or latex (water-based) varieties. Oil and water don't mix, and generally neither do the paints based on them. For multi-layered effects, stick to one type or the other.

Alkyd paints are somewhat lustrous, translucent, and hard-wearing. But alkyds, and the solvents needed for cleaning up, are toxic and combustible, requiring good work-site ventilation and special disposal methods. Professional decorative painters often prefer slower-drying alkyds, which allow more time to achieve complex special effects. Alkyd paints are better suited to techniques such as combing and ragging, where glaze is brushed on in sections and then manipulated.

Latex paints, which now approach alkyd's durability and textural range, are nontoxic and quick-drying, and they clean up easily with soap and water. Most nonprofessionals find latex paint easier to deal with and capable of creating many popular decorative finishes. In general, latex paints are best suited to effects that are dabbed on over the base coat, as in sponging or stenciling. The short drying time can be an advantage, because mistakes can be painted over and redone.

Latex paint is usually the best choice for covering an entire wall, too, because the job can be completed from start to finish in just a few hours.

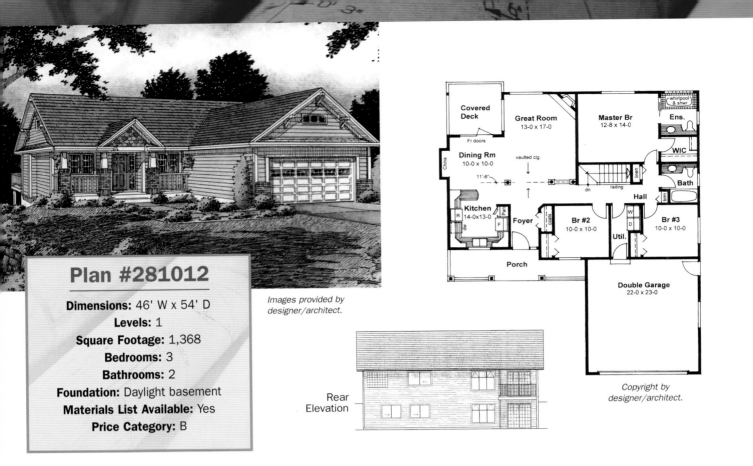

Plan #281012

Dimensions: 46' W x 54' D

Levels: 1

Square Footage: 1,368

Bedrooms: 3

Bathrooms: 2

Foundation: Daylight basement

Materials List Available: Yes

Price Category: B

Images provided by designer/architect.

Rear Elevation

Copyright by designer/architect.

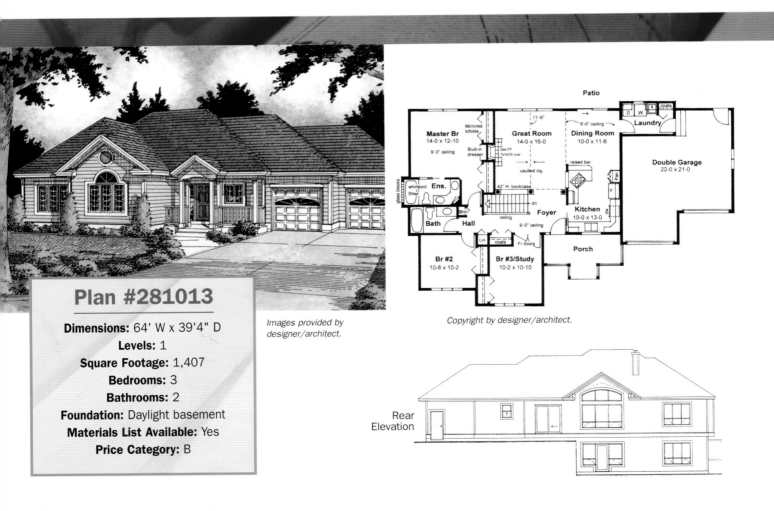

Plan #281013

Dimensions: 64' W x 39'4" D

Levels: 1

Square Footage: 1,407

Bedrooms: 3

Bathrooms: 2

Foundation: Daylight basement

Materials List Available: Yes

Price Category: B

Images provided by designer/architect.

Copyright by designer/architect.

Rear Elevation

Main Level Floor Plan

Plan #241009

Dimensions: 62'9" W x 38'6" D

Levels: 2

Square Footage: 1,974

Main Level Sq. Ft.: 1,480

Upper Level Sq. Ft.: 494

Bedrooms: 3

Bathrooms: 2½

Foundation: Slab

Materials List Available: No

Price Category: D

Images provided by designer/architect.

Upper Level Floor Plan

Copyright by designer/architect.

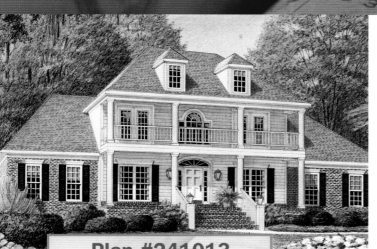

Main Level Floor Plan

Plan #241013

Dimensions: 68' W x 46' D

Levels: 2

Square Footage: 2,779

Main Level Sq. Ft.: 1,918

Upper Level Sq. Ft.: 861

Bedrooms: 4

Bathrooms: 3½

Foundation: Slab

Materials List Available: No

Price Category: F

Images provided by designer/architect.

Upper Level Floor Plan

Copyright by designer/architect.

Plan #121034

Dimensions: 92'8" W x 59'4" D

Levels: 1

Square Footage: 2,223

Bedrooms: 2

Bathrooms: 2

Foundation: Basement

Materials List Available: Yes

Price Category: E

Images provided by designer/architect.

This home features a flowing, open floor plan coupled with an abundance of amenities.

Features:

- Ceiling Height: 8 ft. unless otherwise noted.

- Foyer: This elegant entry features a curved staircase and a view of the formal dining room.

- Formal Dining Room: Magnificent arched openings lead from the foyer into this dining room. The boxed ceiling adds to the architectural interest.

- Great Room: A wall of windows, a see-through fireplace, and built-in entertainment center make this the perfect gathering place.

- Covered Deck: The view of this deck, through the wall of windows in the great room, will lure guests out to this large deck.

- Hearth Room: This room shares a panoramic view with the eating area.

- Kitchen: This kitchen features a corner pantry, a built-in desk, and a curved island.

Main Level Floor Plan

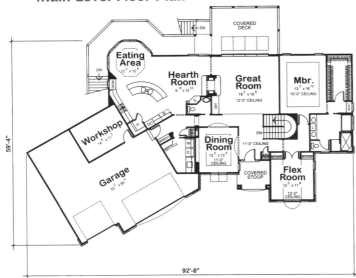

Optional Basement Level Floor Plan

Copyright by designer/architect.

Plan #121013

Dimensions: 40' W x 55'8" D
Levels: 1
Square Footage: 1,375
Bedrooms: 1
Bathrooms: 2
Foundation: Basement
Materials List Available: Yes
Price Category: B

Images provided by designer/architect.

This convenient open plan is well-suited to retirement or as a starter home.

Features:

- Ceiling Height: 8 ft., unless otherwise noted.
- Den: To the left of the entry, French doors lead to a den that can convert to a second bedroom.
- Kitchen: A center island doubles as a snack bar while the breakfast area includes a pantry and a desk for compiling shopping lists and menus.

- Open Plan: The sense of spaciousness is enhanced by the large open area that includes the family room, kitchen, and breakfast area.
- Family Room: A handsome fireplace invites family and friends to gather in this area.
- Porch: Step through the breakfast area to enjoy the fresh air on this secluded porch.
- Master Bedroom: This distinctive bedroom features a boxed ceiling. It's served by a private bath with a walk-in closet.

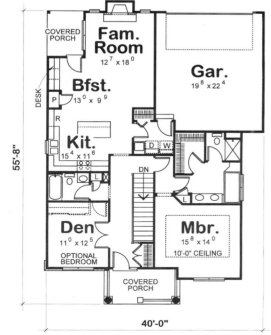

Copyright by designer/architect.

SMARTtip

Paint Color Choices for Your Home

Earth tones are easy to decorate with because they are neutral colors. Use neutral or muted tones, such as light grays, browns, or greens with either lighter or darker shades for accenting.

Use bright colors sparingly, to catch the eye. Painting the front door a bright color creates a cheerful entryway.

Investigate home shows, magazines, and houses in your area for color ideas. Paint suppliers can also give you valuable tips on appropriate color schemes.

Colors that look just right on a color card may need to be toned down for painting large areas. If in doubt, buy a quart of paint and test it.

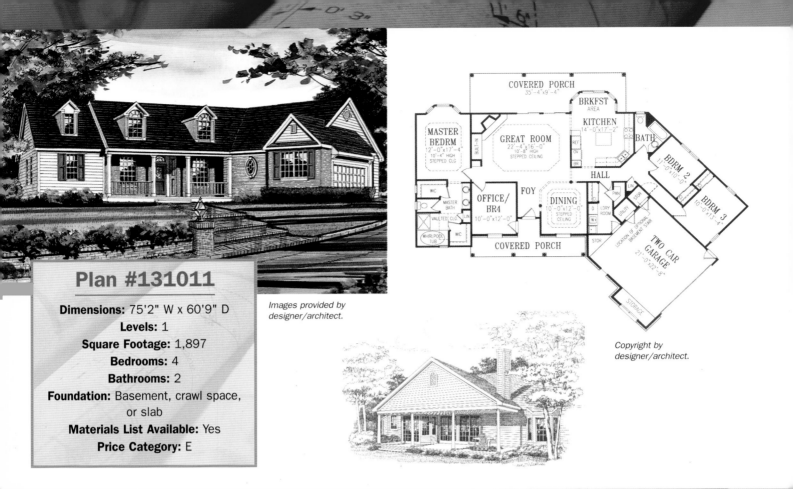

Plan #131011

Dimensions: 75'2" W x 60'9" D

Levels: 1

Square Footage: 1,897

Bedrooms: 4

Bathrooms: 2

Foundation: Basement, crawl space, or slab

Materials List Available: Yes

Price Category: E

Images provided by designer/architect.

Copyright by designer/architect.

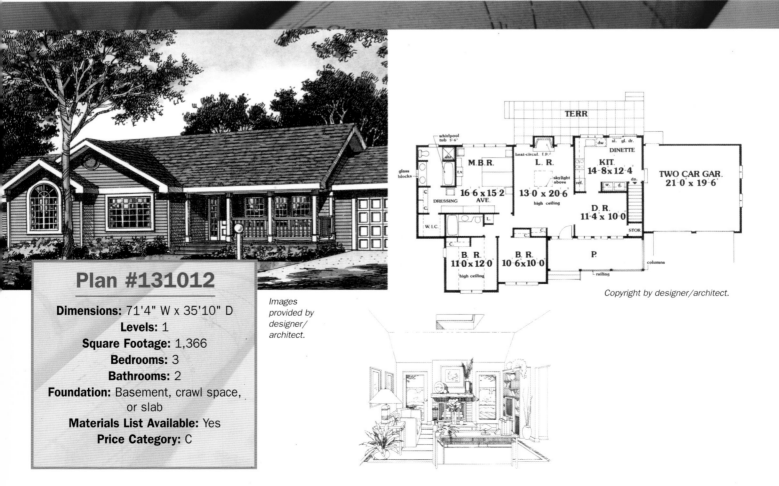

Plan #131012

Dimensions: 71'4" W x 35'10" D

Levels: 1

Square Footage: 1,366

Bedrooms: 3

Bathrooms: 2

Foundation: Basement, crawl space, or slab

Materials List Available: Yes

Price Category: C

Images provided by designer/ architect.

Copyright by designer/architect.

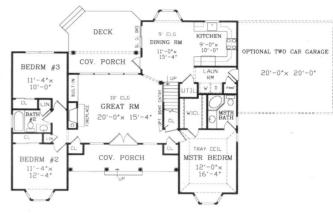

Copyright by designer/architect.

Images provided by designer/architect.

Plan #131014

Dimensions: 48' W x 43'4" D
Levels: 1
Square Footage: 1,380
Bedrooms: 3
Bathrooms: 2
Foundation: Basement, crawl space, or slab
Materials List Available: Yes
Price Category: C

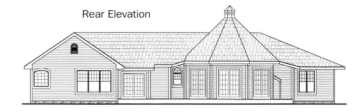

Rear Elevation

FUTURE EXPANSION
20'-0" x 15'-4"

Bonus Room

Rear Elevation

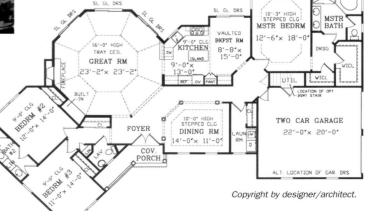

Plan #131019

Dimensions: 83'6" W x 53'4" D
Levels: 1
Square Footage: 2,243
Bedrooms: 3
Bathrooms: 2½
Foundation: Basement, crawl space, or slab
Materials List Available: Yes
Price Category: F

Images provided by designer/architect.

Copyright by designer/architect.

Plan #121028

Dimensions: 54'8" W x 42' D

Levels: 2

Square Footage: 2,644

Main Level Sq. Ft.: 1,366

Upper Level Sq. Ft.: 1,278

Bedrooms: 4

Bathrooms: 2½

Foundation: Basement

Materials List Available: Yes

Price Category: F

Images provided by designer/architect.

This home is filled with special touches and amenities that add up to gracious living.

Features:

• Ceiling Height: 8 ft.

• Formal Living Room: This large, inviting room is the perfect place to entertain guests.

• Family Room: This cozy, comfortable room is accessed through elegant French doors in the living room. It is sure to be the favorite family gathering place with its bay window, see-through fireplace, and bay window.

• Breakfast Area: This area is large enough for the whole family to enjoy a casual meal as they are warmed by the other side of the see-through fireplace. The area features a bay window and built-in bookcase.

• Master Bedroom: Upstairs, enjoy the gracious and practical master bedroom with its boxed ceiling and two walk-in closets.

• Master Bath: Luxuriate in the whirlpool bath as you gaze through the skylight framed by ceiling accents.

Main Level Floor Plan

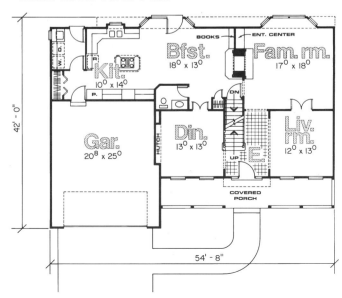

Upper Level Floor Plan

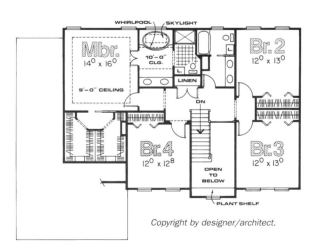

Copyright by designer/architect.

Plan #121030

Dimensions: 58' W x 44'4" D

Levels: 2

Square Footage: 2,613

Main Level Sq. Ft.: 1,333

Upper Level Sq. Ft.: 1,280

Bedrooms: 4

Bathrooms: 2½

Foundation: Basement

Materials List Available: Yes

Price Category: F

Images provided by designer/architect.

This home is packed with all the amenities you need for a gracious and comfortable lifestyle.

Features:

- Ceiling Height: 8 ft. unless otherwise noted.

- Foyer: The elegant entry opens into the living room and formal dining room.

- Adaptable Space: An area linking the formal living room and the family room would make a great area for the family computer. Alternately, it can become a wet bar with window seat.

- Breakfast Area: The family will enjoy informal meals in this sun-bathed area.

- Snack Bar: Perfect for a quick bite, this angled area joins the kitchen to the breakfast area.

- Master Suite: Two walk-in closets make this suite convenient as well as luxurious. The bayed whirlpool tub under a cathedral ceiling invites you to unwind and relax.

- Bonus Room: The second level includes a large room that could become an extra bedroom, a guest room, or a home office.

Main Level Floor Plan

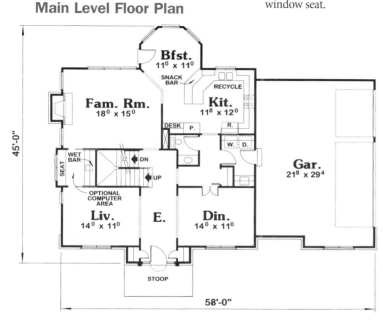

Upper Level Floor Plan

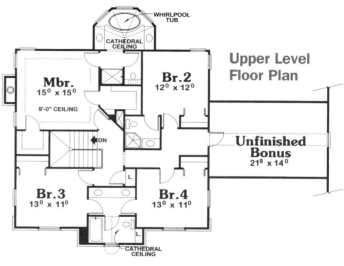

Copyright by designer/architect.

Plan #161039

Dimensions: 61' W x 41'8" D
Levels: 2
Square Footage: 2,320
Main Level Sq. Ft.: 1,595
Upper Level Sq. Ft.: 725
Bedrooms: 4
Bathrooms: 2½
Foundation: Basement
Materials List Available: Yes
Price Category: E

A touch of old-world charm combines with the comfort and convenience of modern amenities to create a delightful home.

Images provided by designer/architect.

Features:

- **Great Room:** This great room is the focal point of this lovely home. The wonderful room has a two-story ceiling, fireplace, and French doors to the rear yard. Split stairs lead to a second floor balcony.

- **Dining Room:** Adjacent to the foyer, this formal dining room has a boxed window, furniture alcove, and butler's pantry.

- **Kitchen:** This kitchen is a wonderful food-preparation area, consisting of a walk-in pantry, oven cabinet, and center island.

- **Master Suite:** This master bedroom has a sloped ceiling and relaxing garden bath that showcases a whirlpool tub, shower, double-bowl vanity, and large walk-in closet.

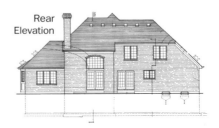

Rear Elevation

Main Level Floor Plan

Upper Level Floor Plan

Copyright by designer/architect.

Plan #321002

Dimensions: 72' W x 28' D
Levels: 1
Square Footage: 1,400
Bedrooms: 3
Bathrooms: 2
Foundation: Basement, crawl space
Materials List Available: Yes
Price Category: B

Images provided by designer/architect.

If you're looking for a well-designed compact home with contemporary amenities, this could be the home of your dreams.

Features:

- **Porch:** Just the right size for some rockers and a swing, this porch could become your outdoor living area when the weather is fine.

- **Living Room:** A vaulted ceiling adds to the spacious feeling in this room, where friends and family are sure to gather.

- **Kitchen:** This space-saving design, in combination with the ample counter and cabinet space, makes cooking a pleasure.

- **Utility Room:** This large room is fitted with cabinets for extra storage space. You'll find storage space in the large garage, too.

- **Master Bedroom:** This room is somewhat secluded for privacy, making it an ideal place for some quiet time at the end of the day.

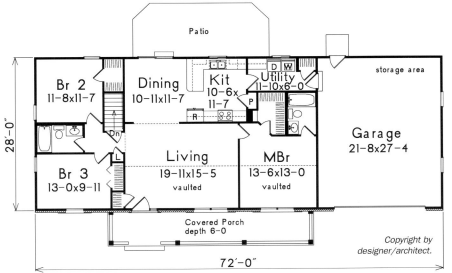

Copyright by designer/architect.

SMARTtip

Fabric Draping Ability

Test a fabric's draping ability by looking at a large piece in a fabric store. Gather at least two to three yards of material, holding one end in your hand. Check how it drapes. Does it fall into folds easily? Also look at the pattern when it is gathered. Does the design become lost in the folds? Ask a salesclerk or a friend to hold the fabric, and look at it from a few feet away.

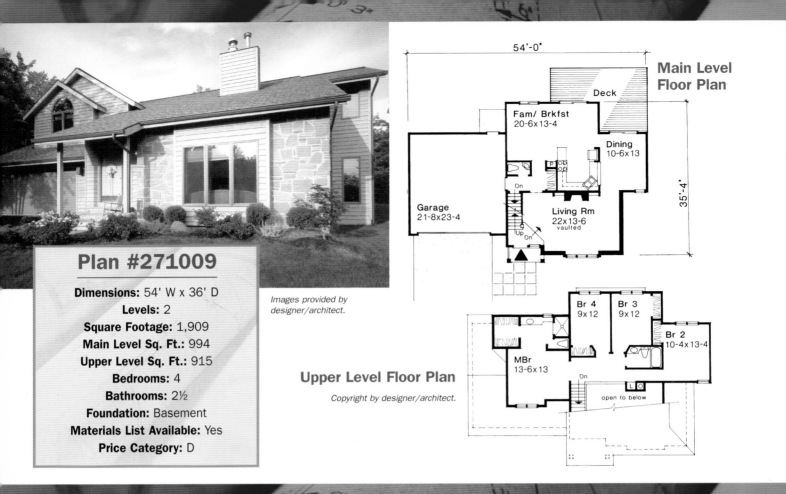

Plan #271009

Dimensions: 54' W x 36' D
Levels: 2
Square Footage: 1,909
Main Level Sq. Ft.: 994
Upper Level Sq. Ft.: 915
Bedrooms: 4
Bathrooms: 2½
Foundation: Basement
Materials List Available: Yes
Price Category: D

Images provided by designer/architect.

Main Level Floor Plan

54'-0"

Deck

Fam/ Brkfst
20-6x13-4

Dining
10-6x13

Garage
21-8x23-4

Living Rm
22x13-6 vaulted

35'-4"

Upper Level Floor Plan

Copyright by designer/architect.

Br 4
9x12

Br 3
9x12

Br 2
10-4x13-4

MBr
13-6x13

open to below

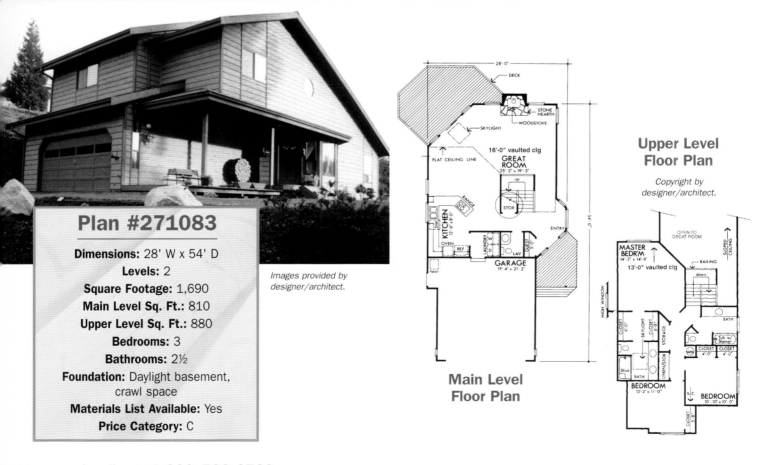

Plan #271083

Dimensions: 28' W x 54' D
Levels: 2
Square Footage: 1,690
Main Level Sq. Ft.: 810
Upper Level Sq. Ft.: 880
Bedrooms: 3
Bathrooms: 2½
Foundation: Daylight basement, crawl space
Materials List Available: Yes
Price Category: C

Images provided by designer/architect.

Upper Level Floor Plan

Copyright by designer/architect.

28'-0"

DECK

STONE HEARTH
WOODSTOVE

SKYLIGHT

FLAT CEILING LINE

16'-0" vaulted clg
GREAT ROOM
25'-2" x 19'-3"

up

STOR

KITCHEN
12'-6" x 8'-0"

RANGE

OVEN

REF

LAUNDRY

GUEST

LAV

ENTRY

GARAGE
19'-4" x 21'-2"

heat

OPEN TO GREAT ROOM

MASTER BEDR'M
14'-2" x 14'-6"
13'-0" vaulted clg

RAILING

SLOPED CEILING

down

BATH

CLOSET
6'-0"

SKYLIGHT

CLOSET
6'-0"

STORAGE

LINEN/STOR

CLOSET
4'-0"

CLOSET
4'-0"

Tub w/ Shower

BATH

Shwr

BEDROOM
12'-2" x 11'-0"

BEDROOM
10'-10" x 10'-0"

Main Level Floor Plan

Main Level Floor Plan

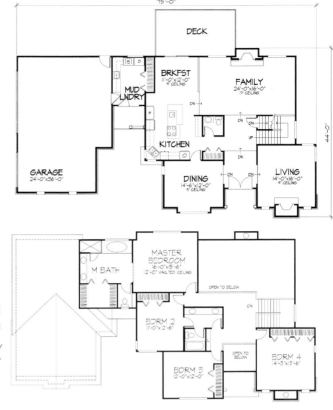

Images provided by designer/architect.

Upper Level Floor Plan

Copyright by designer/architect.

Plan #271024

Dimensions: 75' W x 44' D

Levels: 2

Square Footage: 3,107

Main Level Sq. Ft.: 1,639

Upper Level Sq. Ft.: 1,468

Bedrooms: 4

Bathrooms: 2½

Foundation: Basement

Materials List Available: Yes

Price Category: G

Images provided by designer/architect.

Main Level Floor Plan

Upper Level Floor Plan

Copyright by designer/architect.

Plan #271036

Dimensions: 44' W x 50' D

Levels: 2

Square Footage: 1,602

Main Level Sq. Ft.: 1,112

Upper Level Sq. Ft.: 490

Bedrooms: 3

Bathrooms: 2½

Foundation: Basement

Materials List Available: No

Price Category: C

Plan #121033

Dimensions: 50'4" W x 47'4" D
Levels: 2
Square Footage: 1,987
Main Level Sq. Ft.: 929
Upper Level Sq. Ft.: 1,058
Bedrooms: 4
Bathrooms: 2½
Foundation: Basement
Materials List Available: Yes
Price Category: D

Images provided by designer/architect.

This spacious and practical home is designed with the growing family in mind.

Features:

- Ceiling Height: 8 ft.

- Great Room: This inviting room features a see-through fireplace that is sure to make it the central gathering place of the home.

- Flex Room: French doors flanking the see-through fireplace lead from the great room into this room that can be used as a dining room, music room or study.

- Breakfast Area: Also accessible through the great room French doors, this breakfast area is the perfect spot for informal family meals.

- Garage: In addition to parking for two cars, this garage offers plenty of storage space. At the garage entrance, you'll find a powder room and a recycling area.

- Room to Grow: In addition to four bedrooms and a laundry room, the second level has 163 ft. of unfinished space for future expansion.

Main Level Floor Plan

Upper Level Floor Plan

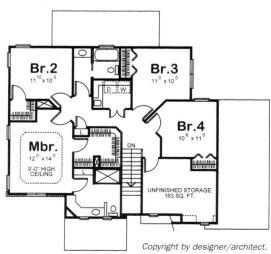

Copyright by designer/architect.

Plan #121070

Dimensions: 50' W x 58' D

Levels: 2

Square Footage: 2,139

Main Level Sq. Ft.: 1,506

Upper Level Sq. Ft.: 633

Bedrooms: 4

Bathrooms: 2½

Foundation: Basement

Materials List Available: Yes

Price Category: D

You'll love this design if you're looking for a bright, airy home where you can easily entertain.

Features:

- Entry: A volume ceiling sets the tone for this home when you first walk in.

- Great Room: With a volume ceiling extending from the entry, this great room has an open feeling. Transom-topped windows contribute

natural light during the day.

- Dining Room: Because it is joined to the great room through a cased opening, this dining room can serve as an extension of the great room.

- Kitchen: An island with a snack bar, desk, and pantry make this kitchen a treat, and a door from the breakfast area leads to a private covered patio where dining will be a pleasure.

Main Level Floor Plan

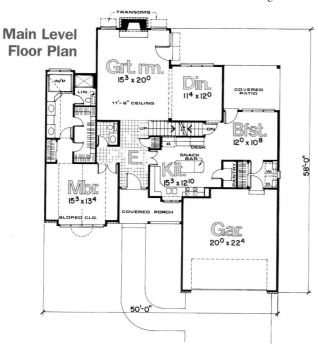

Upper Level Floor Plan

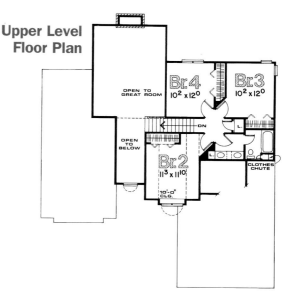

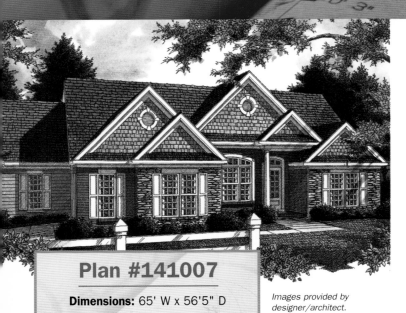

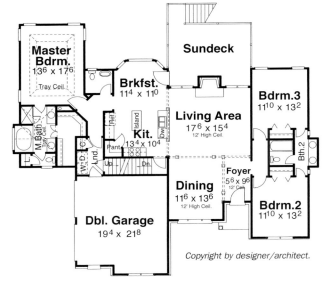

Images provided by designer/architect.

Copyright by designer/architect.

Plan #141007

Dimensions: 65' W x 56'5" D
Levels: 1
Square Footage: 1,854
Bedrooms: 3
Bathrooms: 2½
Foundation: Basement
Materials List Available: No
Price Category: D

Images provided by designer/architect.

Copyright by designer/architect.

Plan #141011

Dimensions: 54' W x 60'6" D
Levels: 1
Square Footage: 1,869
Bedrooms: 3
Bathrooms: 2
Foundation: Basement, crawl space, or slab
Materials List Available: Yes
Price Category: D

Storage
21-6x6-0

Brick Patio

Garage
21-6x21-3

M.Bath
16-1x13-0
9' ceiling

Porch
25-3x10-0
10' ceiling

Sitting
9-0x8-0
9' ceiling

Master
Bedroom
16-1x15-0
9' ceiling

Bath
2

Laun.
7-3x6-6
Shelves

Bath

Greatroom
17-0x18-3
10' ceiling

Kitchen
14-10x12-10

9'

Bedroom 2
11-3x11-6
9' ceiling

Bedroom 3
11-6x12-3
9' ceiling

Foyer

Dining
12-9x11-0
10' ceiling

Breakfast
10-0x9-6
9' ceiling

Pantry

Porch
36-2x6-8
Arched Barrel
Ceiling

Copyright by designer/architect.

Rear View

Images provided by designer/architect.

Plan #311001

Dimensions: 65'11" W x 67'9" D

Levels: 1

Square Footage: 2,085

Bedrooms: 3

Bathrooms: 2½

Foundation: Slab, crawl space, or basement

Materials List Available: No

Price Category: D

Future
11-2x12-5
8' ceiling line

Step Down

Future
10-9x12-5
8' ceiling line

Step Down

Future
35-0x19-6
8' ceiling line

Optional Bonus Area

Copyright by designer/architect.

Master
Bedroom
14-0x17-6

Porch
32-2x8-0

Breakfast
11-8x10-6

Bath
9-0x15-3

Bedroom
11-10x11-6

Greatroom
17-6x17-6

Kitchen
11-8x14-11

Laundry
11-6x7-6

Storage
11-6x7-10

shelving   linen   shelving

Bath

Bedroom
11-10x11-6

Foyer

Dining
13-0x11-6

1/2
Bath

Garage
23-4x21-8

Porch
36-4x8-0

Plan #311004

Dimensions: 68'2" W x 57'4" D

Levels: 1

Square Footage: 2,046

Bedrooms: 3

Bathrooms: 2½

Foundation: Slab, crawl space, or basement

Materials List Available: Yes

Price Category: D

Images provided by designer/architect.

Rear View

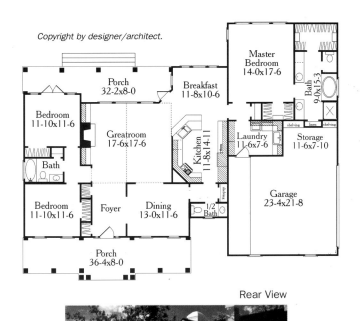

Plan #121041

Dimensions: 49' W x 46'4" D

Levels: 2

Square Footage: 2,705

Main Level Sq. Ft.: 1,369

Upper Level Sq. Ft.: 1,336

Bedrooms: 4

Bathrooms: 3

Foundation: Basement

Materials List Available: Yes

Price Category: F

Images provided by designer/architect.

This is a traditional family home with plenty of space and plenty of amenities.

Features:

- Ceiling Height: 8 ft.

- Family Room: Everyone will gravitate to the family room with its two-sided fireplace joined by an entertainment center.

- Hearth Room: This cozy room on the other side of the fireplace is the perfect spot for reading or quiet conversation.

- Kitchen: This open kitchen will inspire you to new culinary creations. Its center island is flanked by columns and doubles as a snack bar.

- Computer Loft: This upper level loft is the ideal spot for a computer.

- Walk-in Closets: The master suite offers two walk-in closets, and you'll find walk-ins in all the other bedrooms as well.

- Garage: With two bays this garage provides plenty of space for storage as well as cars.

Main Level Floor Plan

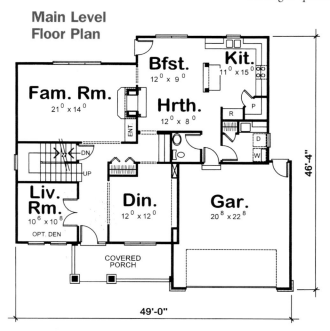

Upper Level Floor Plan

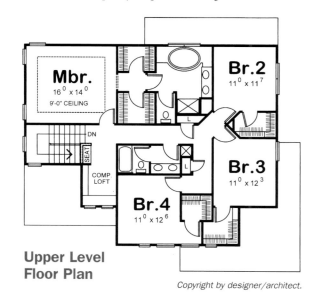

Copyright by designer/architect.

Plan #121088

Dimensions: 56' W x 48' D

Levels: 2

Square Footage: 2,340

Main Level Sq. Ft.: 1,701

Upper Level Sq. Ft.: 639

Bedrooms: 4

Bathrooms: 2½

Foundation: Basement

Materials List Available: Yes

Price Category: E

Images provided by designer/architect.

You'll love this cheerful home, with its many large windows that let in natural light and cozy spaces that encourage family gatherings.

Features:

• **Entry:** Use the built-in curio cabinet here to display your best collector's pieces.

• **Den:** French doors from the entry lead to this room, with its built-in bookcase and triple-wide, transom-topped window.

• **Great Room:** The 14-ft. ceiling in this room accentuates the floor-to-ceiling windows that frame the raised-hearth fireplace.

• **Kitchen:** Both the layout and the work space make this room a delight for any cook.

• **Master Suite:** The bedroom has a tray ceiling for built-in elegance. A skylight helps to light the master bath, and an oval whirlpool tub, separate shower, and double vanity provide a luxurious touch.

Main Level Floor Plan

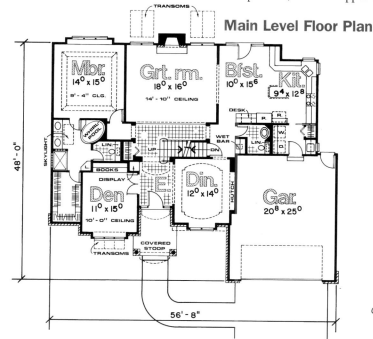

Upper Level Floor Plan

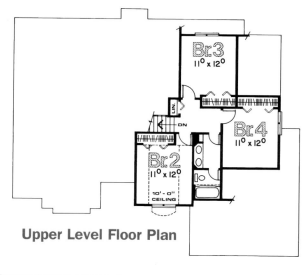

Copyright by designer/architect.

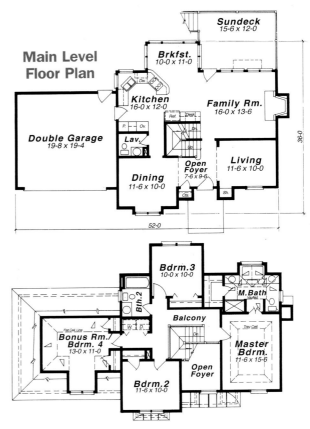

Main Level Floor Plan

Sundeck 15-6 x 12-0

Brkfst. 10-0 x 11-0

Kitchen 16-0 x 12-0

Family Rm. 16-0 x 13-6

Double Garage 19-8 x 19-4

Lav.

Open Foyer 7-6 x 9-6

Living 11-6 x 10-0

Dining 11-6 x 10-0

36-0

52-0

Images provided by designer/architect.

Upper Level Floor Plan

Bdrm.3 10-0 x 10-0

M.Bath

Bth.2

Balcony

Bonus Rm./ Bdrm. 4 13-0 x 11-0

Open Foyer

Master Bdrm. 11-6 x 15-6

Bdrm.2 11-6 x 10-0

Copyright by designer/architect.

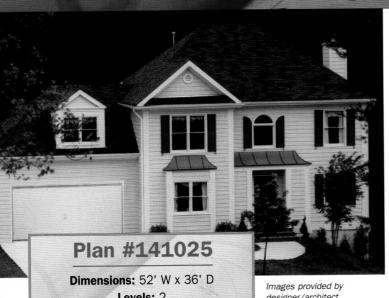

Plan #141025

Dimensions: 52' W x 36' D

Levels: 2

Square Footage: 1,721

Main Level Sq. Ft.: 902

Upper Level Sq. Ft.: 819

Bedrooms: 4

Bathrooms: 2½

Foundation: Basement

Materials List Available: Yes

Price Category: C

Plan #141027

Dimensions: 46' W x 38' D

Levels: 2

Square Footage: 2,088

Main Level Sq. Ft.: 1,048

Upper Level Sq. Ft.: 1,040

Bedrooms: 3

Bathrooms: 2½

Foundation: Basement

Materials List Available: Yes

Price Category: D

Images provided by designer/ architect.

Main Level Floor Plan

© 1996 Jannnis Vann & Associates, Inc.

Sundeck 21-0 x 12-0

Brkfst. 12-10 x 13-8

Kitchen 12-6 x 13-4

Living Area 20-0 x 13-4

Dining 13-0 x 14-8

Open Foyer

Double Garage 19-8 x 21-4

38-4

Porch

46-0

Upper Level Floor Plan

M.Bath

Bdrm.3 13-0 x 10-10

Master Bdrm. 13-0 x 18-6

Open To Foyer

Bth.2

Bdrm.2 13-0 x 10-0

Copyright by designer/architect.

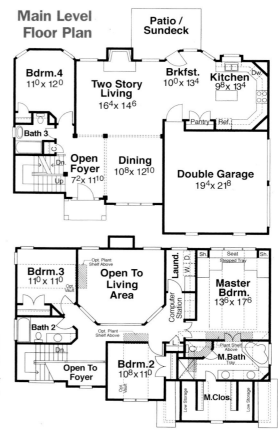

Main Level Floor Plan

Patio / Sundeck

Bdrm. 4
11^0 x 12^0

Two Story Living
16^4 x 14^6

Brkfst.
10^0 x 13^4

Kitchen
9^8 x 13^4

Bath 3

Open Foyer
7^2 x 11^0

Dining
10^8 x 12^{10}

Pantry Ref.

Double Garage
19^4 x 21^8

Bdrm. 3
11^0 x 11^0

Opt. Plant Shelf Above

Open To Living Area

Laund. W./D.

Sh. Seat Stepped Tray Sh.

Master Bdrm.
13^6 x 17^6

Computer Station

Bath 2

Opt. Plant Shelf Above

Plant Shelf Above

M. Bath Tray

Upper Level Floor Plan

Open To Foyer

Bdrm. 2
10^8 x 11^0

Low Storage M. Clos. Low Storage

Copyright by designer/architect.

Plan #141028

Dimensions: 48' W x 36'4" D

Levels: 2

Square Footage: 2,215

Main Level Sq. Ft.: 1,075

Upper Level Sq. Ft.: 1,140

Bedrooms: 4

Bathrooms: 3

Foundation: Basement

Materials List Available: Yes

Price Category: E

Images provided by designer/architect.

Main Level Floor Plan

Sundeck
12-0 x 11-0

Lnd. Lav.

Brkfst.
10-4 x 11-0

Living Area
16-10 x 15-6

Master Bdrm.
13-6 x 15-6

Command Center

Kit.
12-4 x 9-4

Dining
10-6 x 12-6

Open Foyer

M. Bath

Double Garage
21-4 x 20-8

© 1999, Jannis Vann & Associates, Inc.

55-0

Upper Level Floor Plan

Open To Living Area

Unfinished Storage
13-6 x 10-0

Computer Station

Bdrm. 4
12-4 x 11-4

Bdrm. 2
10-0 x 12-6

Open To Foyer

Bth. 2

Bdrm. 3
14-8 x 11-8

Copyright by designer/architect.

Plan #141029

Dimensions: 55' W x 42' D

Levels: 2

Square Footage: 2,289

Main Level Sq. Ft.: 1,382

Upper Level Sq. Ft.: 907

Bedrooms: 4

Bathrooms: 2½

Foundation: Basement

Materials List Available: Yes

Price Category: E

Images provided by designer/architect.

Plan #121043

Dimensions: 47' W x 42'8" D
Levels: 2
Square Footage: 2,363
Main Level Sq. Ft.: 1,048
Upper Level Sq. Ft.: 1,315
Bedrooms: 4
Bathrooms: 2½
Foundation: Basement
Materials List Available: Yes
Price Category: E

Images provided by designer/architect.

An open, flowing floor plan makes this the perfect home for today's busy lifestyle.

Features:

- Ceiling Height: 8 ft.

- Great Room: Cased opening define this airy and open room that is sure to be a favorite gathering place for social gatherings of all kinds.

- Dining Room: Accessible from the great room through a cased opening, this distinctive dining room features display niches that flank a double-wide window.

- Kitchen: The convenience of this kitchen is enhanced by a snack bar, pantry, and a planning desk. It includes a breakfast area that's perfect for quick impromptu meals.

- Computer Left: The second floor landing hosts this loft, which is specifically designed to house the family computer.

- Master Suite: This private retreat includes a window seat, optional bar, his and her walk-in closets, and a sunlit corner whirlpool.

Main Level Floor Plan

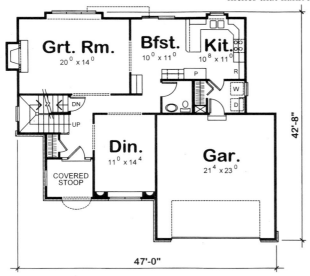

Upper Level Floor Plan

Copyright by designer/architect.

Plan #121075

Dimensions: 57'4" W x 30' D

Levels: 2

Square Footage: 2,345

Main Level Sq. Ft.: 1,000

Upper Level Sq. Ft.: 1,345

Bedrooms: 4

Bathrooms: 3½

Foundation: Basement

Materials List Available: Yes

Price Category: E

Images provided by designer/architect.

Imagine owning a home with a Colonial-styled exterior and a practical, amenity-filled interior with both formal and informal areas.

Features:

- **Family Room:** This room will be the heart of your home. A bay window lets you create a special nook for reading or quiet conversation, and a fireplace begs for a circle of comfortable chairs or soft cushions around it.

- **Living Room:** Connected to the family room by a set of French doors, you can use this room for formal entertaining or informal family fun.

- **Kitchen:** This kitchen has been designed for efficient work patterns. However, the snack bar that links it to the breakfast area beyond also invites company while the cook is working.

- **Master Suite:** Located on the second level, this suite features an entertainment center, a separate sitting area, built-in dressers, two walk-in closets, and a whirlpool tub.

Main Level Floor Plan

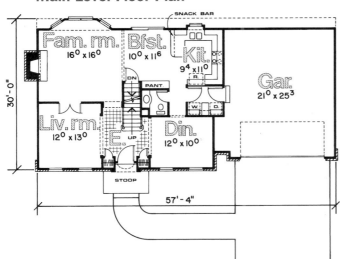

Upper Level Floor Plan

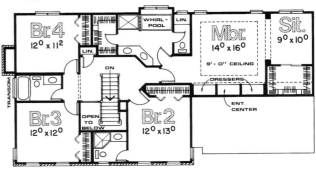

Copyright by designer/architect.

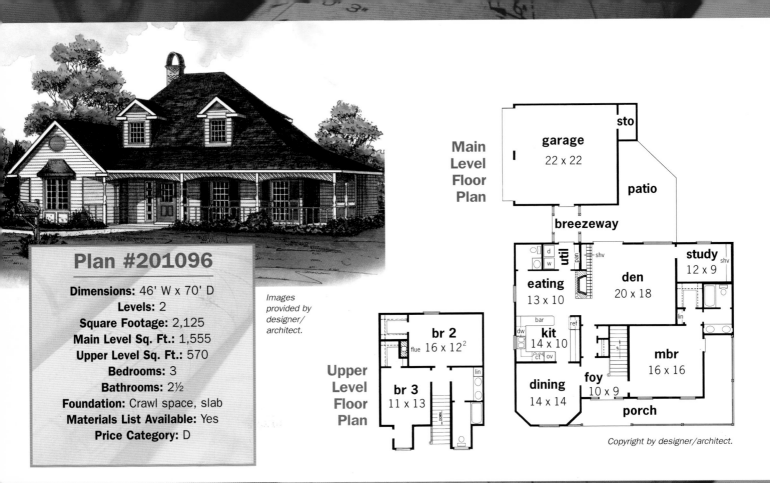

Plan #201096

Dimensions: 46' W x 70' D
Levels: 2
Square Footage: 2,125
Main Level Sq. Ft.: 1,555
Upper Level Sq. Ft.: 570
Bedrooms: 3
Bathrooms: 2½
Foundation: Crawl space, slab
Materials List Available: Yes
Price Category: D

Images provided by designer/architect.

Main Level Floor Plan

sto
garage 22 x 22
patio
breezeway
util
shv
study 12 x 9
eating 13 x 10
den 20 x 18
bar
kit 14 x 10
ref
mbr 16 x 16
dining 14 x 14
foy 10 x 9
porch

Upper Level Floor Plan

br 2 16 x 12²
flue
br 3 11 x 13
lin

Copyright by designer/architect.

Plan #301006

Dimensions: 60' W x 32' D
Levels: 2
Square Footage: 2,162
Main Level Sq. Ft.: 1,098
Upper Level Sq. Ft.: 1,064
Bedrooms: 3
Bathrooms: 2½
Foundation: Crawl space, slab
Materials List Available: Yes
Price Category: D

Images provided by designer/architect.

Main Level Floor Plan

WOOD DECK
BREAKFAST 9-8 x 9-8
KITCHEN 12-0 x 13-6
LAUNDRY
GARAGE 22-0 x 22-0
GREAT ROOM 13-6 x 27-4
DINING 13-6 x 13-6
FOYER
PORCH
60-0

Copyright by designer/architect.

Optional Third Level

BATH
ATTIC STORAGE
SLOPE CLG
BEDROOM 4 11-0 x 12-0
HALL
BEDROOM 5 11-0 x 12-0
SLOPE CLG
ATTIC STORAGE

Upper Level Floor Plan

GARDEN TUB
BATH
WALK-IN CLOSET
BEDROOM 2 13-6 x 12-0
WALK-IN CLOSET
BATH
HALL
CLOSET
M. BEDROOM 13-6 x 16-0
TELEPHONE NICHE
BEDROOM 3 13-6 x 12-0
READING NOOK

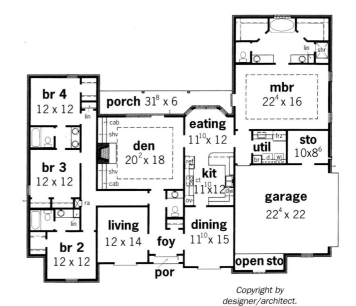

Plan #201069

Dimensions: 70'10" W x 64'10" D

Levels: 1

Square Footage: 2,735

Bedrooms: 4

Bathrooms: 3½

Foundation: Crawl space, slab

Materials List Available: Yes

Price Category: F

Images provided by designer/architect.

Copyright by designer/architect.

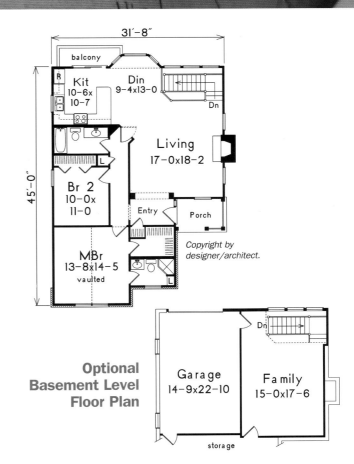

Plan #321039

Dimensions: 31'8" W x 45' D

Levels: 1

Square Footage: 1,231

Bedrooms: 2

Bathrooms: 2

Foundation: Basement

Materials List Available: Yes

Price Category: B

Images provided by designer/architect.

Copyright by designer/architect.

Optional Basement Level Floor Plan

Plan #241010

Dimensions: 56' W x 44'5" D
Levels: 2
Square Footage: 2,044
Main Level Sq. Ft.: 1,203
Upper Level Sq. Ft.: 841
Bedrooms: 3
Bathrooms: 2½
Foundation: Slab
Materials List Available: No
Price Category: D

You will be immediately drawn by the warmth and charm of this award-winning Victorian design, which features an inviting front porch with corner gazebo.

Features:

- **Great Room:** Friends and family will gravitate to this comfortable great room and its cozy fireplace, well suited for holiday entertaining.
- **Kitchen:** This wonderful kitchen, which features a large pantry and cooktop island with eating bar, will become a natural gathering place for conversation and informal dining.
- **Master Suite:** Separated for privacy, this first-floor master suite features his and her walk-in closets, separate vanities, a deluxe corner tub, and a walk-in shower.
- **Additional Rooms:** Two secondary bedrooms and a large playroom—perfect for a growing family—are located on the second floor.

Main Level Floor Plan

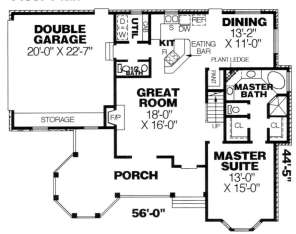

Upper Level Floor Plan

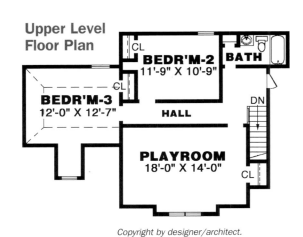

Plan #241008

Dimensions: 65' W x 56'8" D

Levels: 1

Square Footage: 2,526

Bedrooms: 4

Bathrooms: 3

Foundation: Slab

Materials List Available: No

Price Category: E

Images provided by designer/architect.

A covered back porch—with access from the master suite and the breakfast area—makes this traditional home ideal for siting near a golf course or with a backyard pool.

Features:

- **Great Room:** From the foyer, guests enter this spacious and comfortable great room, which features a handsome fireplace.

- **Kitchen:** This kitchen—the hub of this family-oriented home—is a joy in which to work, thanks to abundant counter space, a pantry, a convenient eating bar, and an adjoining breakfast area and sunroom.

- **Master Suite:** Enjoy the quiet comfort of this coffered-ceiling master suite, which features dual vanities and separate walk-in closets.

- **Additional Bedrooms:** Two secondary bedrooms, which share a full bath, are located at the opposite end of the house from the master suite. Bedroom 4—in front of the house—can be converted into a study.

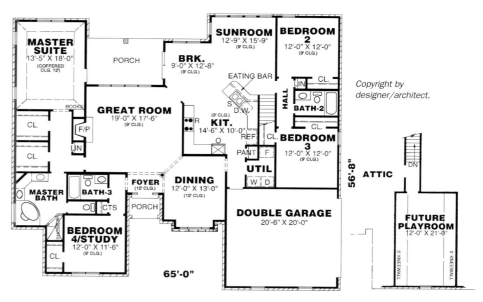

Copyright by designer/architect.

SMARTtip

Traditional-Style Kitchen Cabinetry

You can modify stock kitchen cabinetry to enjoy fine furniture-quality details. Prefabricated trims may be purchased at local lumber mills and home centers. For example, crown molding, applied to the top of stock cabinetry and stained or painted to match the door style, may be all you need. Likewise, you can replace hardware with reproduction polished-brass door and drawer knobs or pulls for a finishing touch.

Plan #161019

Dimensions: 54'6" D x 41'10" W
Levels: 2
Square Footage: 2,428
Main Level Sq. Ft.: 1,309
Upper Level Sq. Ft.: 1,119
Bedrooms: 4
Bathrooms: 2½
Foundation: Basement
Materials List Available: No
Price Category: E

Images provided by designer/architect.

Elegant and designed for comfortable family living, this home is full of amenities.

Features:

- Foyer: The elegant staircase and arched opening to the living room are visible from this foyer, and a balcony on the upper level lets you look into it.

- Family Room: Let the family relax and play here so that you can save the formal living room for entertaining and quiet activities.

- Kitchen: The central location of this kitchen makes it the heart of this home. It's visually open to the family room and breakfast area and naturally lit by a bank of rear windows.

- Master Suite: Relax in this quiet area, or enjoy the luxury of the master bath, with its whirlpool tub, separate shower, and dual vanities.

- Upper Level: 3 bedrooms and a bath with a skylight and double-bowl vanity make this area comfortable for guests or family.

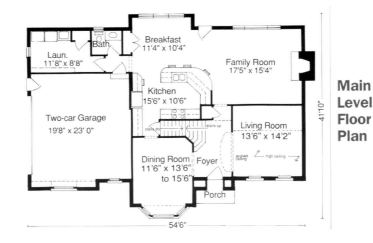

Main Level Floor Plan

Upper Level Floor Plan

Copyright by designer/architect.

Plan #121068

Dimensions: 54' W x 49'10" D

Levels: 2

Square Footage: 2,391

Main Level Sq. Ft.: 1,697

Upper Level Sq. Ft.: 694

Bedrooms: 4

Bathrooms: 2½

Foundation: Basement

Materials List Available: Yes

Price Category: E

Images provided by designer/architect.

This home allows you a great deal of latitude in the way you choose to finish it, so you can truly make it "your own."

Features:

• Living Room: Located just off the entryway, this living room is easy to convert to a stylish den. Add French doors for privacy, and relish the style that the 12-ft. angled ceiling and picturesque arched window provide.

• Great Room: The highlight of this room is the two-sided fireplace that easily adds as much design interest as warmth to this area. The three transom-topped windows here fill the room with light.

• Kitchen: A center island, walk-in pantry, and built-in desk combine to create this wonderful kitchen, and the attached gazebo breakfast area adds the finishing touch.

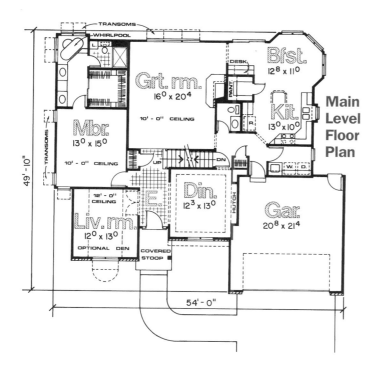

Main Level Floor Plan

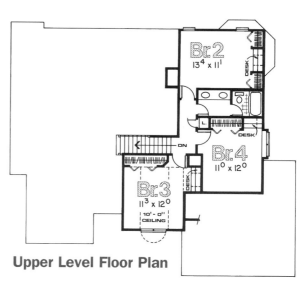

Upper Level Floor Plan

Copyright by designer/architect.

Plan #131022

Dimensions: 54'8" W x 43' D

Levels: 2

Square Footage: 2,092

Main Level Sq. Ft.: 1,152

Upper Level Sq. Ft.: 940

Bedrooms: 3

Bathrooms: 2½

Foundation: Basement, crawl space, or slab

Materials List Available: Yes

Price Category: E

Images provided by designer/architect.

You'll love the way this charming home reminds you of an old-fashioned farmhouse.

Features:

• Ceiling Height: 8 ft.

• Living Room: This large living room can be used as guest quarters when the need arises.

• Dining Room: This bayed, informal room is large enough for all your dining and entertaining needs. It could also double as an office or den.

• Garage: An expandable loft over the garage offers an ideal playroom or fourth bedroom.

Rear Elevation

Main Level Floor Plan

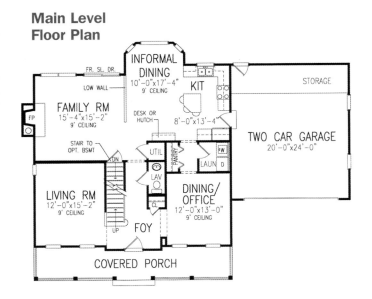

Upper Level Floor Plan

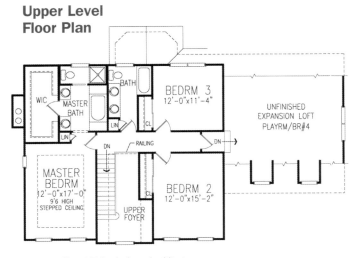

Copyright by designer/architect.

Plan #121071

Dimensions: 72'8" W x 51'4" D
Levels: 2
Square Footage: 2,957
Main Level Sq. Ft.: 2,063
Upper Level Sq. Ft.: 894
Bedrooms: 4
Bathrooms: 4½
Foundation: Basement
Materials List Available: Yes
Price Category: F

Images provided by designer/architect.

You'll appreciate the mix of open public areas and private quarters that the layout of this home guarantees.

Features:

• Entry: From this entry, the formal living and dining rooms, as well as the great room, are all visible.

• Great Room: A soaring cathedral ceiling sets an elegant tone for this room, and the fireplace that's flanked with lovely transom-topped windows adds to it.

• Den: French doors from the great room lead to this den, where you'll find a generous bay window, a wet bar, and a decorative ceiling.

• Master Suite: On the main floor to give it needed privacy, this master suite will make you feel at home the first time you walk into it. The private bath has an angled ceiling and a whirlpool tub.

Main Level Floor Plan

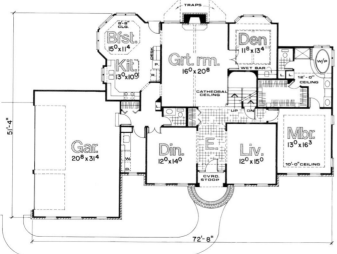

Upper Level Floor Plan

Copyright by designer/architect.

Plan #111014

Dimensions: 78' W x 47' D
Levels: 1
Square Footage: 1,865
Bedrooms: 4
Bathrooms: 2
Foundation: Crawl space
Materials List Available: No
Price Category: D

Images provided by designer/architect.

Copyright by designer/architect.

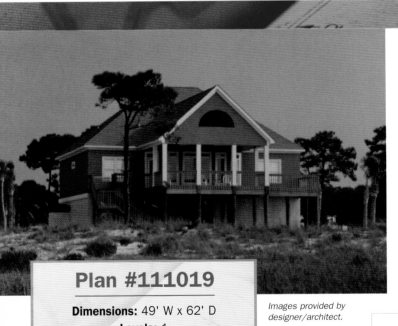

Plan #111019

Dimensions: 49' W x 62' D
Levels: 1
Square Footage: 1,936
Bedrooms: 4
Bathrooms: 2
Foundation: Pier
Materials List Available: No
Price Category: D

Images provided by designer/architect.

Optional Gameroom

Copyright by designer/architect.

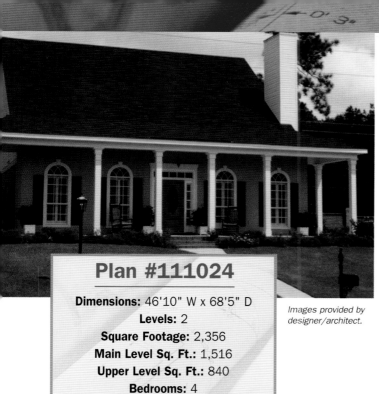

Plan #111024

Dimensions: 46'10" W x 68'5" D

Levels: 2

Square Footage: 2,356

Main Level Sq. Ft.: 1,516

Upper Level Sq. Ft.: 840

Bedrooms: 4

Bathrooms: 2½

Foundation: Slab

Materials List Available: No

Price Category: E

Images provided by designer/architect.

Main Level Floor Plan

Two Car Garage 22'x 23'6"

Porch

Utility

Master Bath

Breakfast 11'x 12'8"

WIC

Master Bedroom 15'x 15'4"

Kitchen 12'5"x 12'8"

Dining 13'6"x 12

Living 18'x 17'6"

Porch

Upper Level Floor Plan

Copyright by designer/architect.

Bath

WIC

Bedroom 14'x 11'

Bedroom 15'5"x 12'

Balcony

Bedroom 14'x 11'6"

Open To Below

Plan #111025

Dimensions: 45'10" W x 48'5" D

Levels: 2

Square Footage: 2,428

Main Level Sq. Ft.: 1,533

Upper Level Sq. Ft.: 895

Bedrooms: 4

Bathrooms: 2½

Foundation: Basement

Materials List Available: No

Price Category: E

Images provided by designer/architect.

Main Level Floor Plan

Utility

Porch 24'x 8'

Breakfast 9'2"x 9'11"

Living 18'8"x 15'

Kitchen 11'6"x 12'

Dining 12'8"x 11'6"

Foyer 8'8"x 6'6"

Master Bedroom 14'10"x 13'

Porch 35'10"x 5'

Optional Basement Level Floor Plan

Two-Car Garage 26'5"x 24'10"

Upper Level Floor Plan

Bedroom 13'7"x 11'9"

Open to Below

Bedroom 15'x 11'11"

Bedroom 11'11"x 11'4"

Copyright by designer/architect.

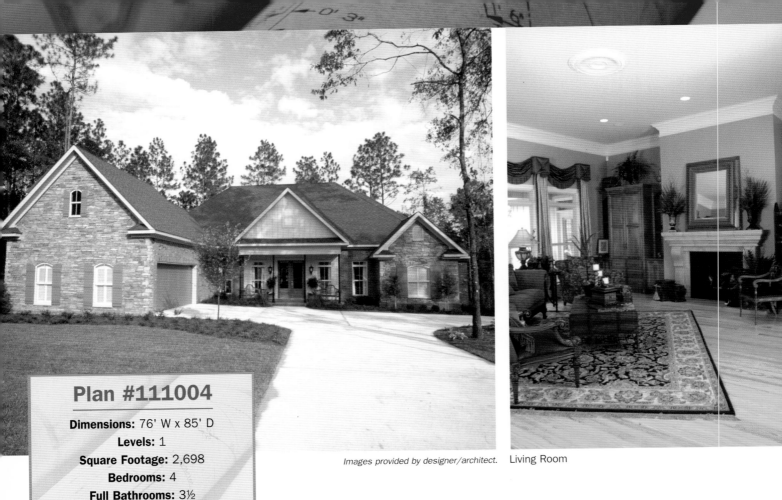

Images provided by designer/architect.   Living Room

Plan #111004

Dimensions: 76' W x 85' D

Levels: 1

Square Footage: 2,698

Bedrooms: 4

Full Bathrooms: 3½

Foundation: Slab

Materials List Available: No

Price Category: F

If you've been looking for a home that includes a special master suite, this one could be the answer to your dreams.

Features:

- **Living Room:** Make a sitting area around the fireplace here so that the whole family can enjoy the warmth on chilly days and winter evenings. A door from this room leads to the rear covered porch, making this room the heart of your home.

- **Kitchen:** An island with a cooktop makes cooking a pleasure in this well-designed kitchen, and the breakfast bar invites visitors at all times of day.

- **Utility Room:** A sink and a built-in ironing board make this room totally practical.

- **Master Suite:** A private fireplace in the corner sets a romantic tone for this bedroom, and the door to the covered porch allows you to sit outside on warm summer nights. The bath has two vanities, a divided walk-in closet, a standing shower, and a deluxe corner bathtub.

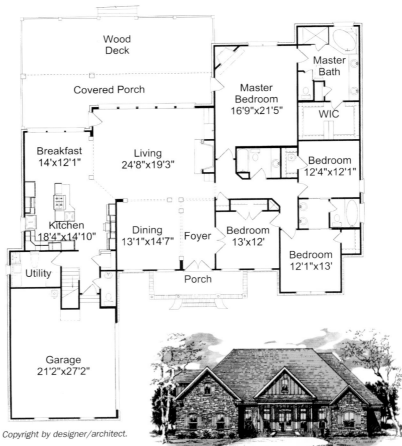

Copyright by designer/architect.

Kitchen

Dining Room

Master Bath

Master Bath

SMARTtip

How to Quit Smoking — Lighting Your Fireplace

Before attempting to light a wood fire, make certain that the damper is open all the way. This allows a good draft (flow of air up the chimney) to prevent smoke from blowing back into the room. To ensure a good draft—particularly if your home is well insulated—open a window a bit when lighting a fire.

The opposite of draft is downdraft, which occurs when cold air flows down the chimney and into the room. If the fireplace is properly designed and maintained, the smoke shelf will prevent backpuffing from downdraft most of the time by redirecting cold air currents back up the chimney. The open damper also helps prevent backpuffing.

Also, build a fire slowly to let the chimney liner heat up, which will create a good draft and minimize the chances of downdraft.

Don't wait until fall to inspect the chimney. Do this job, or call a chimney sweep, when the weather is mild. Because some repairs take a while to make, it's best to have them done when the fireplace is not normally in use. If you do the inspection yourself, wear old clothes, eye goggles, and a mask.

Plan #121084

Dimensions: 40' W x 42' D
Levels: 2
Square Footage: 1,728
Main Level Sq. Ft.: 845
Upper Level Sq. Ft.: 883
Bedrooms: 4
Bathrooms: 2½
Foundation: Basement
Materials List Available: Yes
Price Category: C

Images provided by designer/architect.

If you're looking for a home where the whole family will be comfortable, you'll love this design.

Features:

- **Great Room:** The heart of the home, this great room has a fireplace with a raised hearth, a sloped ceiling, and transom-topped windows.

- **Dining Room:** A cased opening lets you flow from the great room into this formal dining room. A built-in display hutch is the highlight here.

- **Kitchen:** What could be nicer than this wraparound kitchen with peninsula snack bar? The sunny, attached breakfast area has a pantry and built-in desk.

- **Master Suite:** A double vanity, whirlpool tub, shower, and walk-in closet exude luxury in this upper-floor master suite.

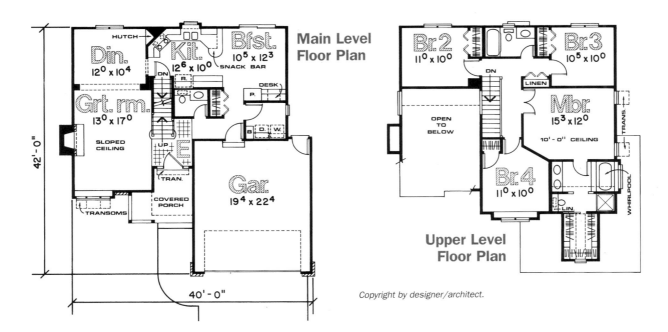

Plan #121085

Dimensions: 42' W x 54' D
Levels: 2
Square Footage: 1,948
Main Level Sq. Ft.: 1,517
Upper Level Sq. Ft.: 431
Bedrooms: 4
Bathrooms: 3
Foundation: Basement
Materials List Available: Yes
Price Category: D

Images provided by designer/architect.

You'll love the spacious feeling in this home, with its generous rooms and excellent design.

Features:

- **Great Room:** This room is lofty and open, thanks in part to the transom-topped windows that flank the fireplace. However, you can furnish to create a cozy nook for reading or a private spot to watch TV or enjoy some quiet music.

- **Kitchen:** Wrapping counters add an unusual touch to this kitchen, and a pantry gives extra storage area. A snack bar links the kitchen with a separate breakfast area.

- **Master Suite:** A tiered ceiling adds elegance to this area, and a walk-in closet adds practicality. The private bath features a sunlit whirlpool tub, separate shower, and double vanity.

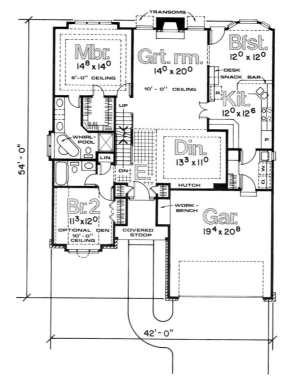

Main Level Floor Plan

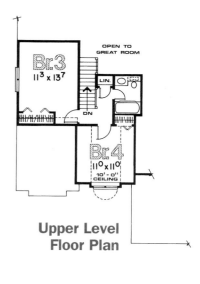

Upper Level Floor Plan

Copyright by designer/architect.

- **Upper-Level Bedrooms:** The upper-level placement is just right for these bedrooms, which share an amenity-filled full bathroom.

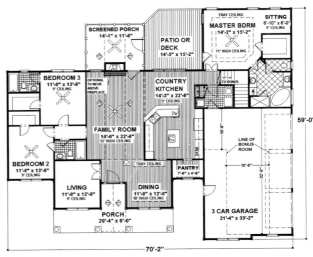

Images provided by designer/architect.

Copyright by designer/architect.

Plan #101009

Dimensions: 70'2" W x 59' D

Levels: 1

Square Footage: 2,097

Bedrooms: 3

Bathrooms: 3

Foundation: Slab

Materials List Available: No

Price Category: D

Images provided by designer/ architect.

Copyright by designer/architect.

Plan #101013

Dimensions: 72' W x 66' D

Levels: 1

Square Footage: 2,564

Bedrooms: 3

Bathrooms: 2½

Foundation: Slab, crawl space, basement

Materials List Available: No

Price Category: E

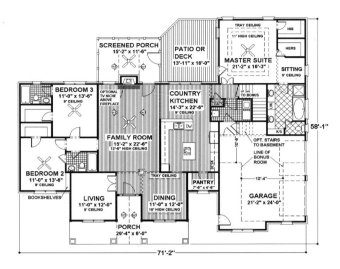

Images provided by designer/architect.

Copyright by designer/architect.

Plan #101011

Dimensions: 71'2" W x 58'1" D
Levels: 1
Square Footage: 2,184
Bedrooms: 3
Bathrooms: 3
Foundation: Slab, crawl space, basement
Materials List Available: No
Price Category: D

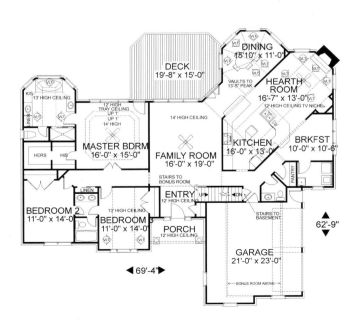

Images provided by designer/architect.

Copyright by designer/architect.

Plan #101012

Dimensions: 69'4" W x 62'9" D
Levels: 1
Square Footage: 2,288
Bedrooms: 3
Bathrooms: 2½
Foundation: Slab, crawl space, basement
Materials List Available: No
Price Category: E

Plan #121086

Dimensions: 55'4" W x 37'8" D

Levels: 2

Square Footage: 1,998

Main Level Sq. Ft.: 1,093

Upper Level Sq. Ft.: 905

Bedrooms: 3

Bathrooms: 2½

Foundation: Basement

Materials List Available: Yes

Price Category: D

You'll love the open design of this comfortable home if sunny, bright rooms make you happy.

Features:

- Entry: Walk into this two-story entry, and you're sure to admire the open staircase and balcony from the upper level.
- Dining Room: To the left of the entry, you'll see this dining room, with its special ceiling detail and built-in display cabinet.
- Living Room: Located immediately to the right, this living room features a charming bay window.
- Family Room: French doors from the living room open into this sunny space, where a handsome fireplace takes center stage.
- Kitchen: Combined with the breakfast area, this kitchen features an island cooktop, a large pantry, and a built-in desk.

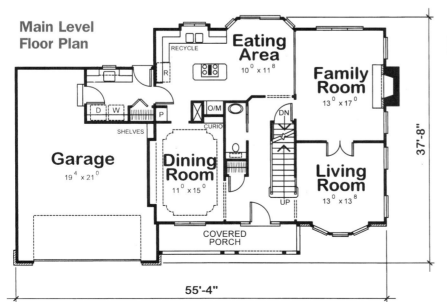

Main Level Floor Plan

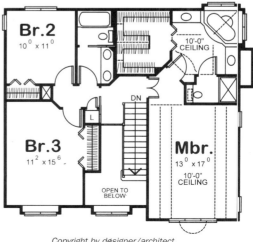

Upper Level Floor Plan

Plan #121087

Dimensions: 50' W x 40' D
Levels: 2
Square Footage: 2,103
Main Level Sq. Ft.: 1,082
Upper Level Sq. Ft.: 1,021
Bedrooms: 4
Bathrooms: 2½
Foundation: Basement
Materials List Available: Yes
Price Category: D

Images provided by designer/architect.

You'll love the comfort and the unusual design details you'll find in this home.

Features:

- **Entry:** A T-shaped staircase frames this two-story entry, giving both visual interest and convenience.

- **Family Room:** Bookcases frame the lovely fireplace here, so you won't be amiss by decorating to create a special reading nook.

- **Breakfast Area:** Pass through the cased

opening between the family room and this breakfast area, for convenience.

- **Kitchen:** Combined with the breakfast area, this kitchen features an island, pantry, and desk.

- **Master Suite:** On the upper floor, this suite has a walk-in closet and a bath with sunlit whirlpool tub, separate shower, and double vanity. A window seat makes the bedroom especially cozy, no matter what the outside weather.

Main Level Floor Plan

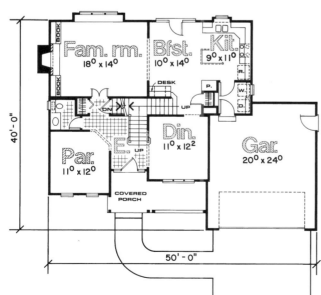

Upper Level Floor Plan

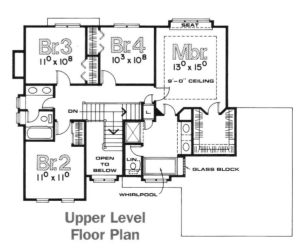

Copyright by designer/architect.

Plan #121056

Dimensions: 48' W x 50' D

Levels: 1

Square Footage: 1,479

Bedrooms: 2

Bathrooms: 2

Foundation: Basement

Materials List Available: Yes

Price Category: B

Images provided by designer/architect.

Copyright by designer/architect.

Optional Third Bedroom Floor Plan

Plan #151083

Dimensions: 63'4" W x 58'6" D

Levels: 1

Square Footage: 2,034

Bedrooms: 4

Bathrooms: 2

Foundation: Crawl space, slab (basement option for fee)

Materials List Available: Yes

Price Category: D

Images provided by designer/architect.

Copyright by designer/architect.

Optional Upper Level Floor Plan

Plan #121039

Dimensions: 49' W x 40' D
Levels: 2
Square Footage: 2,200
Main Level Sq. Ft.: 1,130
Upper Level Sq. Ft.: 1,070
Bedrooms: 4
Bathrooms: 2½
Foundation: Basement
Materials List Available: Yes
Price Category: E

Images provided by designer/architect.

This handsome family home beautifully blends architectural grace with modern amenities.

Features:

- Ceiling Height: 8 ft.
- Cased Openings: Joining the formal living to the dining rooms and the family room to the bedroom, these openings create efficient traffic patterns while providing architectural beauty and continuity from room to room.
- Kitchen: The family will want to gather around the center island in this bright and airy kitchen. A pantry and planning desk add to the kitchen's efficiency.
- Hall Bookcase: Hallways provide a lot of wall space that often go unused. Not in this house, where bookcases in the upstairs hall provide plenty of bedtime reading.
- Master Suite: Luxuriate at the end of a busy day in this master suite that includes a walk-in closet, a whirlpool, a shower, and a double vanity.

Main Level Floor Plan

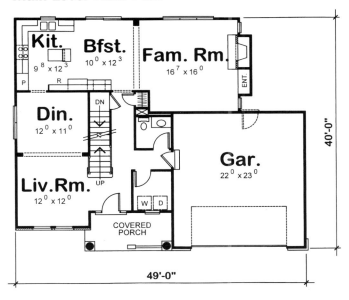

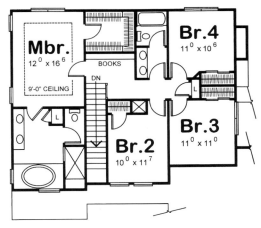

Copyright by designer/architect.

Upper Level Floor Plan

Plan #271050

Dimensions: 40' W x 40' D
Levels: 2
Square Footage: 1,188
Main Level Sq. Ft.: 936
Upper Level Sq. Ft.: 252
Bedrooms: 3
Bathrooms: 2
Foundation: Daylight basement
Materials List Available: Yes
Price Category: B

This open and attractive design features multilevel construction and efficient use of living space.

Features:

- **Living Room:** A fireplace and a dramatic 15-ft. vaulted ceiling make family and friends gravitate to this area.

- **Kitchen/Dining:** A U-shaped counter with a snack bar facilitates meals and entertaining. A stacked washer/dryer unit makes weekend chores a breeze.

- **Secondary Bedrooms:** Five steps up, two sizable bedrooms with vaulted ceilings share

a nice hall bath. One of the bedrooms could serve as a den and features sliding glass doors to a deck.

- **Master Suite:** On a level of its own, this private space includes a personal bathroom and a romantic deck for stargazing.

- **Basement/Garage:** The home's lower level offers plenty of space for expansion or storage, plus a tandem, tuck-under garage.

Main Level Floor Plan

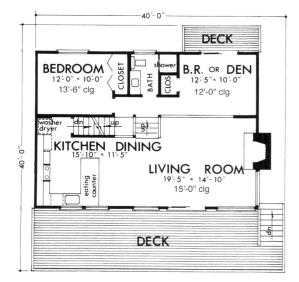

Basement Level Floor Plan

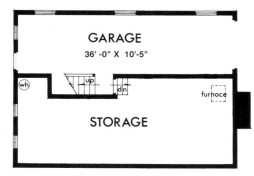

Upper Level Floor Plan

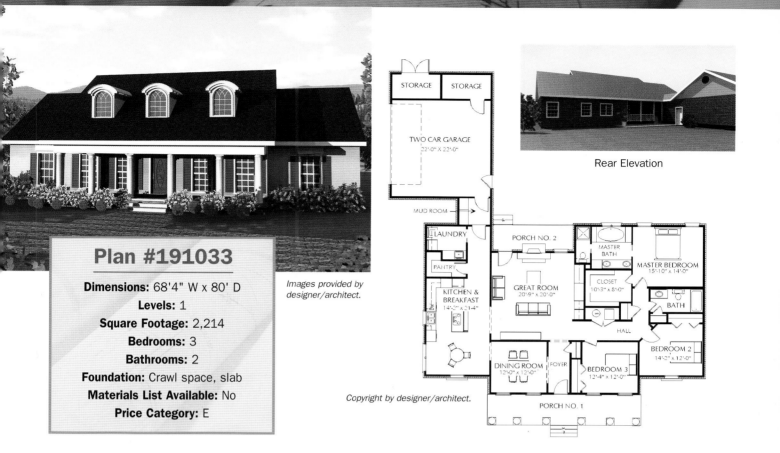

Plan #191033

Dimensions: 68'4" W x 80' D

Levels: 1

Square Footage: 2,214

Bedrooms: 3

Bathrooms: 2

Foundation: Crawl space, slab

Materials List Available: No

Price Category: E

Images provided by designer/architect.

Rear Elevation

Copyright by designer/architect.

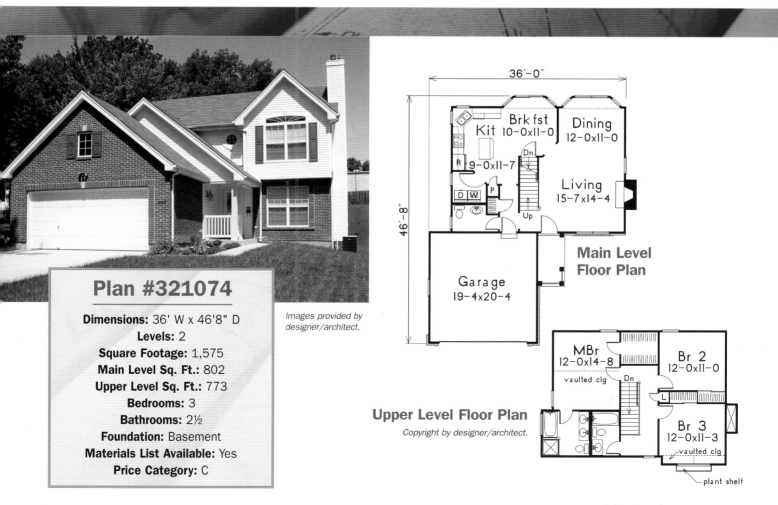

Plan #321074

Dimensions: 36' W x 46'8" D

Levels: 2

Square Footage: 1,575

Main Level Sq. Ft.: 802

Upper Level Sq. Ft.: 773

Bedrooms: 3

Bathrooms: 2½

Foundation: Basement

Materials List Available: Yes

Price Category: C

Images provided by designer/architect.

Main Level Floor Plan

Upper Level Floor Plan

Copyright by designer/architect.

Plan #161017

Dimensions: 61' W x 37'6" D
Levels: 2
Square Footage: 2,653
Main Level Sq. Ft.: 1,365
Upper Level Sq. Ft.: 1,288
Bedrooms: 4
Bathrooms: 2½
Foundation: Basement
Materials List Available: No
Price Category: F

Images provided by designer/architect.

If a traditional look makes you feel comfortable, you'll love this spacious, family-friendly home.

Features:

- Family Room: Accessorize with cozy cushions to make the most of this sunken room. Windows flank the fireplace, adding warm, natural light. Doors leading to the rear deck make this room a family "headquarters."

- Living and Dining Rooms: These formal rooms open to each other, so you'll love hosting gatherings in this home.

- Kitchen: A handy pantry fits well with the traditional feeling of this home, and an island adds contemporary convenience.

- Master Suite: Relax in the whirlpool tub in your bath and enjoy the storage space in the two walk-in closets in the bedroom.

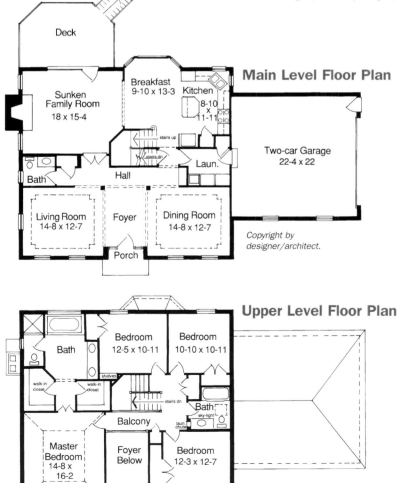

Main Level Floor Plan

Copyright by designer/architect.

Upper Level Floor Plan

Plan #271010

Dimensions: 47' W x 43' D
Levels: 2
Square Footage: 1,724
Main Level Sq. Ft.: 922
Upper Level Sq. Ft.: 802
Bedrooms: 3
Bathrooms: 2½
Foundation: Basement
Materials List Available: Yes
Price Category: C

Images provided by designer/architect.

This traditional home features a wide assortment of windows that flood the interior with light and accentuate the open, airy atmosphere.

Features:

- **Entry:** A beautiful Palladian window enlivens this two-story-high space.

- **Great Room:** A second Palladian window brightens this primary gathering area, which is topped by a vaulted ceiling.

- **Dining Room:** Sliding glass doors connect this formal area to a large backyard deck.

- **Kitchen:** Centrally located, this kitchen includes a boxed-out window over the sink, providing a nice area for plants.

- **Family/Breakfast Area:** Smartly joined, this open space hosts a snack bar and a wet bar, in addition to a warming fireplace.

- **Master Suite:** Located on the upper floor, the master bedroom boasts corner windows, a large walk-in closet, and a split bath with a dual-sink vanity.

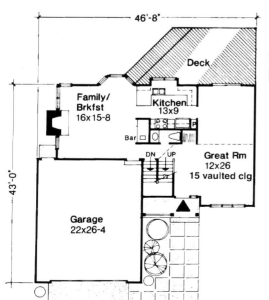

Main Level Floor Plan

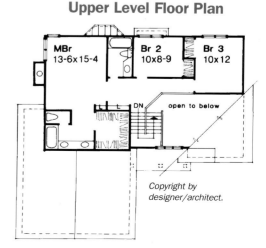

Upper Level Floor Plan

Copyright by designer/architect.

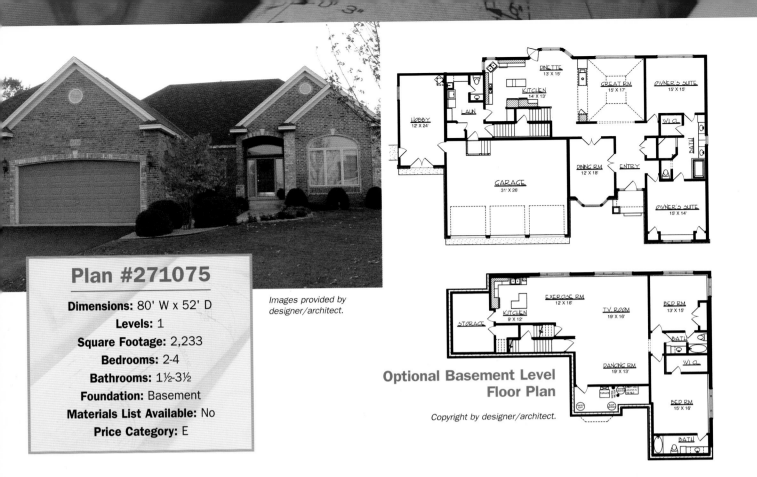

Plan #271075

Dimensions: 80' W x 52' D
Levels: 1
Square Footage: 2,233
Bedrooms: 2-4
Bathrooms: 1½-3½
Foundation: Basement
Materials List Available: No
Price Category: E

Images provided by designer/architect.

Optional Basement Level Floor Plan

Copyright by designer/architect.

Plan #271076

Dimensions: 69' W x 57' D
Levels: 1
Square Footage: 2,188
Bedrooms: 2-4
Bathrooms: 1½-2½
Foundation: Daylight basement
Materials List Available: No
Price Category: D

Images provided by designer/architect.

Optional Basement Level Floor Plan

Copyright by designer/architect.

Main Level Floor Plan

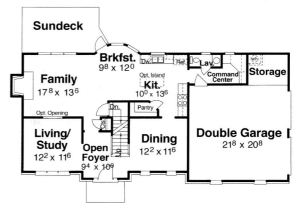

Sundeck

Brkfst.
9^8 x 12^0

Family
17^8 x 13^6

Opt. Island

Kit.
10^0 x 13^6

Dw.

Ref.

Lav.

Command Center

Storage

W/H

Opt. Opening

Dn.

Pantry

Living/Study
12^2 x 11^6

Open Foyer
9^4 x 10^0

Up

Dining
12^2 x 11^6

Double Garage
21^8 x 20^8

Images provided by designer/architect.

Opt. Opening

Opt. Sink

Bdrm.2
12^2 x 12^4

Ks.

Bth.2

Lnd.

W.D.

Sh.

Storage

Computer Station

Sh.

Master Bdrm.
18^{10} x 13^2

Tray Ceil.

Upper Level Floor Plan

Copyright by designer/architect.

Dn.

Balcony

Bdrm.3
12^2 x 12^4

Open Foyer

Bdrm.4/Study
12^2 x 11^6

Opt. Opening To Sitting

Ks.

M.Bath

Plan #141031

Dimensions: 58'4" W x 30' D

Levels: 2

Square Footage: 2,367

Main Level Sq. Ft.: 1,025

Upper Level Sq. Ft.: 1,342

Bedrooms: 4

Bathrooms: 2½

Foundation: Basement

Materials List Available: No

Price Category: E

Main Level Floor Plan

Patio / Deck

Storage

Computer Station

P

Dw.

Brkfst.
8^8 x 11^2

Two Story Family Rm.
17^4 x 13^6

Lav.

Kit.
10^0 x 13^6

Ref.

C.

Up

Dn.

Double Garage
21^4 x 21^6

Dining
12^0 x 12^6

Foyer
5^8 x 15^{10}

Living
11^4 x 12^{10}

Images provided by designer/architect.

M.Bath
Tray Ceil.

Bdrm.2
11^0 x 11^6

Opt. Vault W/ Plant Shelf

Bth.2

Two Story Family Rm.

Balcony

Dn.

Master Bdrm.
15^4 x 14^6
Tray Ceil.

Opt. Vault W/ Plant Shelf

Bdrm.3
11^8 x 10^6

Opt. Vault W/ Plant Shelf

W.D.

Laund.

Open To Foyer

Bdrm.4
11^4 x 11^0

Upper Level Floor Plan

Copyright by designer/architect.

Opt. Closet

Sitting
10^0 x 7^0

Plan #141032

Dimensions: 52' W x 44' D

Levels: 2

Square Footage: 2,476

Main Level Sq. Ft.: 1,160

Upper Level Sq. Ft.: 1,316

Bedrooms: 4

Bathrooms: 2½

Foundation: Basement

Materials List Available: Yes

Price Category: E

Plan #191003

Dimensions: 56' W x 42' D
Levels: 1
Square Footage: 1,785
Bedrooms: 3
Bathrooms: 3
Foundation: Crawl space, slab, or basement
Materials List Available: No
Price Category: C

Images provided by designer/architect.

Enjoy the amenities you'll find in this gracious home, with its traditional Southern appearance.

Features:

- **Great Room:** This expansive room is so versatile that everyone will gather here. A built-in entertainment area with desk makes a great lounging spot, and the French doors topped by transoms open onto the lovely rear porch.

- **Dining Room:** An arched entry to this room helps to create the open feeling in this home.

- **Kitchen:** Another arched entryway leads to this fabulous kitchen, which has been designed with the cook's comfort in mind. It features a downdraft range, many cabinets, a snack bar, and a sunny breakfast area, where the family is sure to gather.

- **Laundry:** A sink, shower, toilet area, and cabinets galore give total convenience in this room.

- **Master Suite:** Enjoy the walk-in closet and bath with toilet room, whirlpool tub, and shower.

Copyright by designer/architect.

56'-0" Width

Plan #191009

Dimensions: 62' W x 76' D
Levels: 1
Square Footage: 2,172
Bedrooms: 4
Bathrooms: 2
Foundation: Crawl space, slab
Materials List Available: No
Price Category: D

Images provided by designer/architect.

This charming home is equally attractive in a rural or a settled area, thanks to its classic lines.

Features:

- **Porches:** Covered front and back porches emphasize the comfort you'll find in this home.

- **Great Room:** A tray ceiling gives elegance to this spacious room, where everyone is sure to gather. A fireplace makes a nice focal point, and French doors open onto the rear covered porch.

- **Dining Room:** Arched openings give distinction to this room, where it's easy to serve meals for the family or host a large group.

- **Kitchen:** You'll love the cooktop island, walk-in pantry, wall oven, snack bar, and view out of the windows in the adjoining breakfast area.

- **Master Suite:** The large bedroom here gives you space to spread out and relax, and the bath includes a corner whirlpool tub, shower, and dual sinks. An 8-ft. x 10-ft. walk-in closet is off the bath.

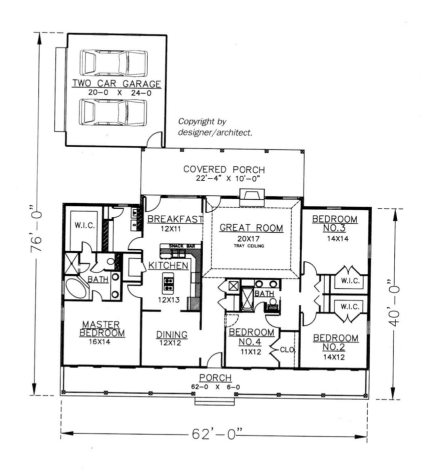

Copyright by designer/architect.

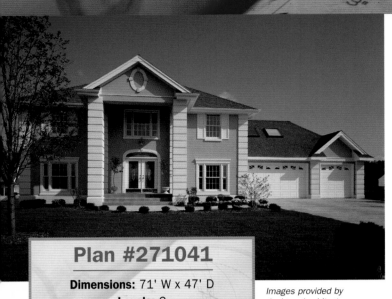

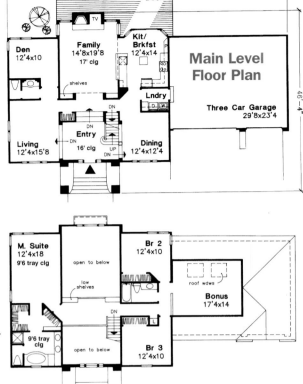

Main Level Floor Plan

Deck

Den
12'4x10

Family
14'8x19'8
17' clg

Kit/Brkfst
12'4x14

71'-0"

Main Level
Floor Plan

Three Car Garage
29'8x23'4

46'-4"

shelves

Lndry

Living
12'4x15'8

Entry
16' clg

DN
UP
DN

Dining
12'4x12'4

Images provided by designer/architect.

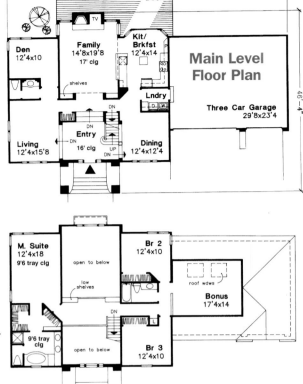

M. Suite
12'4x18
9'6 tray clg

open to below

low shelves

Br 2
12'4x10

roof wdws

Bonus
17'4x14

Upper Level Floor Plan

9'6 tray clg

open to below

DN

Br 3
12'4x10

Copyright by designer/architect.

Plan #271041

Dimensions: 71' W x 47' D
Levels: 2
Square Footage: 2,416
Main Level Sq. Ft.: 1,416
Upper Level Sq. Ft.: 1,000
Bedrooms: 4
Bathrooms: 2½
Foundation: Basement
Materials List Available: No
Price Category: E

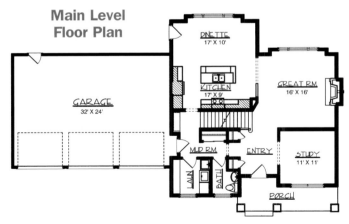

Main Level Floor Plan

DINETTE
17' X 10'

KITCHEN
17' X 9'

GREAT RM
16' X 16'

GARAGE
32' X 24'

MUD RM

ENTRY

STUDY
11' X 11'

LAUN

BATH

PORCH

Images provided by designer/architect.

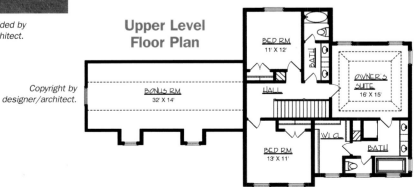

Upper Level Floor Plan

BED RM
11' X 12'

BATH

OWNER'S SUITE
16' X 15'

BONUS RM
32' X 14'

HALL

W.I.C.

BED RM
13' X 11'

BATH

Copyright by designer/architect.

Plan #271057

Dimensions: 66' W x 41' D
Levels: 2
Square Footage: 2,195
Main Level Sq. Ft.: 1,095
Upper Level Sq. Ft.: 1,100
Bedrooms: 3
Bathrooms: 2½
Foundation: Daylight basement
Materials List Available: No
Price Category: D

**Main Level
Floor Plan**

*'Images provided by
designer/architect.*

Plan #271055

Dimensions: 68' W x 53' D

Levels: 2

Square Footage: 3,159

Main Level Sq. Ft.: 1,819

Upper Level Sq. Ft.: 1,340

Bedrooms: 4

Bathrooms: 2½

Foundation: Daylight basement

Materials List Available: No

Price Category: G

Upper Level Floor Plan

Copyright by designer/architect.

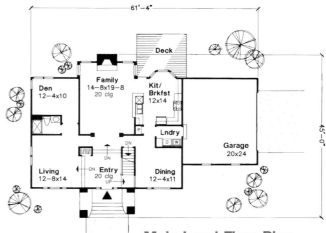

Main Level Floor Plan

*Images provided by
designer/architect.*

Plan #271088

Dimensions: 62' W x 45' D

Levels: 2

Square Footage: 2,493

Main Level Sq. Ft.: 1,346

Upper Level Sq. Ft.: 1,147

Bedrooms: 3

Bathrooms: 3

Foundation: Basement

Materials List Available: Yes

Price Category: C

**Upper Level
Floor Plan**

*Copyright by
designer/architect.*

Plan #221015

Dimensions: 69'8" W x 46' D

Levels: 1

Square Footage: 1,926

Bedrooms: 3

Bathrooms: 2½

Foundation: Basement (Walk-out basement option for fee)

Materials List Available: No

Price Category: D

You'll love the open plan in this lovely ranch and admire its many features, which are usually reserved for much larger homes.

Features:

- Ceiling Height: 8 ft.

- Great Room: A vaulted ceiling and tall windows surrounding the centrally located fireplace give distinction to this handsome room.

- Dining Room: Positioned just off the entry, this formal room makes a lovely spot for quiet dinner parties.

- Dining Nook: This nook sits between the kitchen and the great room. Central doors in the bayed area open to the backyard.

- Kitchen: An island will invite visitors while you cook in this well-planned kitchen, with its corner pantry and ample counter space.

- Master Suite: A tray ceiling, bay window, walk-in closet, and bath with whirlpool tub, dual-sink vanity, and standing shower pamper you here.

Images provided by designer/architect.

Rear Elevation

Copyright by designer/architect.

Plan #271012

Dimensions: 48' W x 29'10" D
Levels: 2
Square Footage: 1,359
Main Level Sq. Ft.: 668
Upper Level Sq. Ft.: 691
Bedrooms: 3
Bathrooms: 2½
Foundation: Basement
Materials List Available: Yes
Price Category: B

Images provided by designer/architect.

This traditional home blends an updated exterior with a thoroughly modern interior.

Features:

- Living Room: This sunny, vaulted gathering room offers a handsome fireplace and open access to the adjoining dining room.

- Dining Room: Equally suited to intimate family gatherings and larger dinner parties, this space includes access to a spacious backyard deck.

- Kitchen/Breakfast Nook: Smartly joined, these two rooms are just perfect for speedy weekday mornings and lazy weekend breakfasts.

- Master Suite: A skylighted staircase leads to this upper-floor masterpiece, which includes a private bath, a walk-in closet, and bright, boxed-out window arrangement.

- Secondary Bedrooms: One of these is actually a loft/bedroom conversion, which makes it suitable for expansion space as your family grows.

Main Level Floor Plan

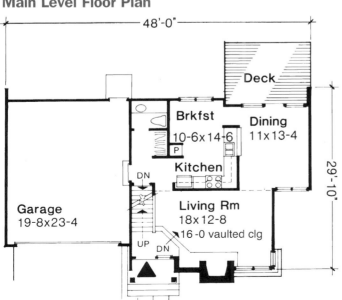

Upper Level Floor Plan

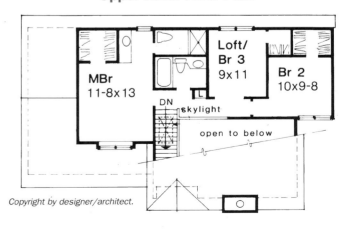

Copyright by designer/architect.

**Main Level
Floor Plan**

**Upper Level
Floor Plan**

*Images provided by
designer/architect.*

Copyright by designer/architect.

Plan #251010

Dimensions: 53' W x 52' D

Levels: 2

Square Footage: 1,854

Main Level Sq. Ft.: 1,317

Upper Level Sq. Ft.: 537

Bedrooms: 3

Bathrooms: 2½

Foundation: Basement

Materials List Available: Yes

Price Category: D

**Upper Level
Floor Plan**

**Main Level
Floor Plan**

*Images provided by
designer/architect.*

Copyright by designer/architect.

Plan #251011

Dimensions: 49' W x 47' D

Levels: 2

Square Footage: 2,008

Main Level Sq. Ft.: 1,318

Upper Level Sq. Ft.: 690

Bedrooms: 4

Bathrooms: 2½

Foundation: Basement

Materials List Available: Yes

Price Category: D

Plan #251012

Dimensions: 57'9" W x 62'10" D
Levels: 2
Square Footage: 2,009
Main Level Sq. Ft.: 1,520
Upper Level Sq. Ft.: 489
Bedrooms: 3
Bathrooms: 2½
Foundation: Basement
Materials List Available: Yes
Price Category: D

Images provided by designer/architect.

Main Level Floor Plan

Upper Level Floor Plan

Copyright by designer/architect.

Plan #251013

Dimensions: 58' W x 44' D
Levels: 2
Square Footage: 2,073
Main Level Sq. Ft.: 1,441
Upper Level Sq. Ft.: 632
Bedrooms: 4
Bathrooms: 2½
Foundation: Basement
Materials List Available: Yes
Price Category: D

Images provided by designer/architect.

Main Level Floor Plan

Upper Level Floor Plan

Copyright by designer/architect.

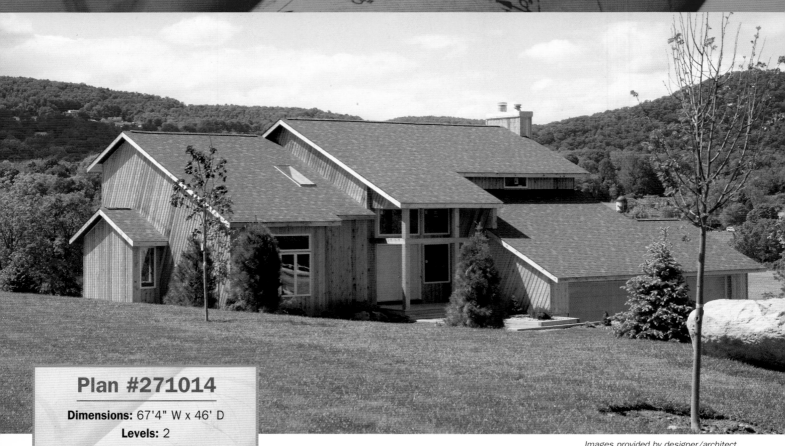

Plan #271014

Dimensions: 67'4" W x 46' D
Levels: 2
Square Footage: 2,444
Main Level Sq. Ft.: 1,364
Upper Level Sq. Ft.: 1,080
Bedrooms: 4
Bathrooms: 3
Foundation: Basement
Materials List Available: Yes
Price Category: E

This traditional home is poised to capture every ray of sun.

Features:

• Living Room: This generous space boasts its own transom-topped windows and a two-story, vaulted ceiling.

• Kitchen: Stretching between the formal dining room and the sunny breakfast room, this kitchen enjoys wide windows of its own. Nearby deck access is another plus.

• Family Room: Sunlight floods this space, too, which is warmed by a homey fireplace and served by a wet bar, tucked carefully out of the way.

• Master Suite: Sprawling across one end of the upper floor, this master suite welcomes the sunlight, too, through six windows. Its private bath hosts a dual-sink vanity, a tub, and a separate shower.

• Den: Neighboring the master suite, this den could expand that suite or serve as a fourth bedroom. All the bedrooms overlook the backyard.

Main Level Floor Plan

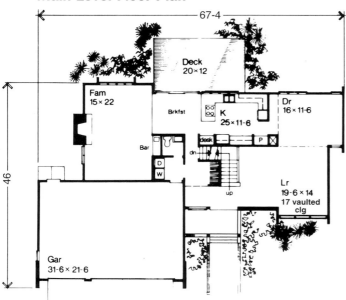

Upper Level Floor Plan

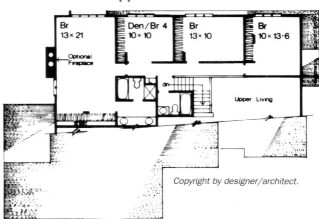

Plan #271017

Dimensions: 50' W x 37'2" D
Levels: 2
Square Footage: 1,835
Main Level Sq. Ft.: 928
Upper Level Sq. Ft.: 907
Bedrooms: 3
Bathrooms: 2½
Foundation: Basement
Materials List Available: Yes
Price Category: D

Images provided by designer/architect.

This inviting and popular home combines interesting window arrangements and brick accents for a winning facade.

Features:

• Entry: A high ceiling expands this welcome center, for a dramatic effect.

• Living Room: A handsome fireplace is the highlight here. A dramatic vaulted ceiling is shared with the adjacent formal dining room. Imagine entertaining your extended family in this space during the holidays.

• Country Kitchen: An efficient layout keeps the family chef happy and productive in this room. The home's second fireplace warms family members while they enjoy casual meals or simply relax. A bay window is a nice touch.

• Master Suite: This suite's bedroom area is certainly generous, and the master bath features a private toilet and a walk-in closet, as well as a separate tub and shower.

Main Level Floor Plan

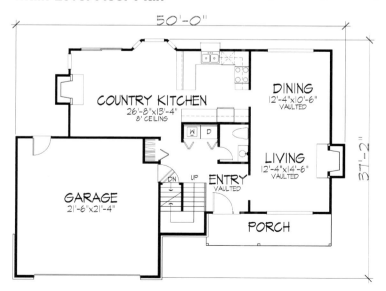

Upper Level Floor Plan

Copyright by designer/architect.

Trimwork Basics

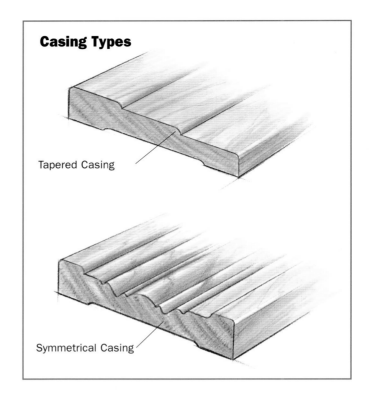
There are two basic types of window casings: tapered and symmetrical. Tapered casing is thinner on the edge closest to the window or door and thicker on the outside edge. Stock Colonial and clamshell casings are tapered casings. When you form corners with tapered casings, you must miter the joints.

Symmetrical casing is the same thickness on both edges and has a uniform pattern across its face. This type of casing rests on top of a plinth block or window stool and joins corner blocks or headers with square-cut butt joints. These casings often look more decorative than stock Colonial-style casings, and they are easier for most do-it-yourselfers to install because you don't have to miter symmetrical casings.

Casing Reveals

The edge of a doorjamb is flush with the surface of the adjoining wall, and there is usually a narrow gap between the jamb and the nearby drywall. Casing has to bridge that gap. Typically, the door side of the casing covers most but not all of the jamb, leaving a narrow edge called a reveal. This helps to add definition to the molding and avoids an unsightly seam where the edge of one board lines up directly over another. When you're working on a new jamb, you have to establish the reveal and stick with it to maintain a uniform appearance. If you're replacing existing trim, you may need to clean up the edge of an old jamb with a sharp scraper and a sander even if you duplicate the old reveal. Although there are several varieties of casing treatments, they all share this detail—a slight setback of at least ⅛ inch from the edge of the jamb. If you install plinths or corner blocks, which are slightly wider than the casing, you may need to experiment with their exact placement to maintain the reveal.

A typical reveal between a doorjamb and casing creates a handsome transition at cased openings.

Door casings can be built up with molding, including an outer strip of backband molding, showing multiple reveals.

Three-Piece Victorian-Style Casing

Although three-piece built-up casing looks large compared with most stock Colonial casing, its scale actually is about halfway between the scale of modern molding and the overwhelming trimwork of the Victorian era. Finished with a clear sealer, it may be a little heavy in modest-size rooms with standard 8-foot ceilings. Finished with paint that complements the wall color, it will add decoration and detail to any room.

The easiest approach is to prepare built-up lengths of this casing on a workbench in three basic steps: sanding, routing, and assembling.

Sanding. Clamp the 1x2 and 1x4 boards to a workbench one at a time, and sand them with a random-orbit sander loaded with 120-grit sandpaper. Sand just the face side of the 1x4s. Sand both sides and the good edge of the 1x2s, but don't tip the sander and round the edge too much. You should ease the edge slightly with a few quick strokes of fine sandpaper.

Detail A

1 x 2 Top Cap
Base Cap Molding
1 x 4
Routed Edge

Detail B

Base Cap Molding
1 x 2 Top Cap
1 x 4
Horn
Stool
Apron

Victorian-Style Mitered Casing

Head Casing
A
Window Casing
B
Leg Casing

Routing. Mill a ¾-inch ogee detail onto the bottom edge of the 1x4. You can do this yourself with a router or a router mounted in a specialized worktable, or look around for a small woodworking shop that will perform this work on a shaper with an automatic feed. Working on your own, clamp the stock securely to the bench, and make at least two passes: one to remove about two-thirds of the depth, and a final pass at full depth. Of course, you can rout another shape if you don't happen to have the right-sized ogee bit.

Remember that there is no one correct combination of moldings, as long as you pay attention to basic design principles. You may like the idea of a complex shape built up from different components. Or you may prefer a simpler approach, such as installing a wide casing trimmed on its outside edges with a backband.

Assembly. Start by attaching the 1x2 top cap to the edge of the 1x4. Clamp the 1x4 to the top of the bench with the milled edge down and away from you. (Even two 2x4s spiked together and laid across sawhorses can serve as a bench for this job.) Spread glue along the edge of the 1x4, and nail the top cap to it. Keep the back edges flush. Work from one end to the other, adjusting the free end to keep the surfaces flush.

Release the clamps, and flip the casing over to apply the base cap molding. Apply glue to the back of a length of molding, set it in place, and nail it off, continually pushing it into place as you work from one end to the other.

Installing the Casing

Mark a ⅛-inch reveal line along the edges of all three sides of the window or door frame. Then square off the bottom of the leg casings, and stand one leg casing in place. Make a mark on its inside edge at the point where the inside edge of the leg casing intersects the reveal line on the head casing. Repeat the same process for the other leg casing before mitering at the mark. Then tack the components into place.

Cut and fit the head casing next. If the profiles line up, you can pull the casings off the wall and install them permanently using glue and nails. Use carpenter's glue between the casing and the jamb and in the miters, and dots of panel adhesive between the casing and the wall. When mitering large casings, clamp the casing firmly so that it won't move during the cut. It's difficult to get perfect miter joints with large casings, so you may have to fill some gaps with caulk.

The horns of a window stool typically extend beyond the casing.

Symmetrical Arts &
Crafts–Style Casing

A hybrid approach to trimming openings resembles the Arts and Crafts style in some respects but blends with a simplified version of the Neoclassical approach. The leg casings are not fluted, of course, because Arts and Crafts detailing calls for a flat profile and a sometimes almost rugged-looking use of lumber. The idea of this style is to avoid fussy details and use wood more in its natural state with simple joints. In some cases, Arts and Crafts leg casings may be stock boards, with the same-dimension material laid across the top of the opening and overhanging the legs on each side by approximately an inch or so.

You can use the facsimile shown below with or without simple plinth blocks at the base of the leg casings, and make other alterations to suit the style of your house. For example, if you want to stay closer to pure Arts and Crafts style, you may want to dispense with elaborate cornice molding with end returns at the top of the assembly and use something more basic, such as strips of backband molding.

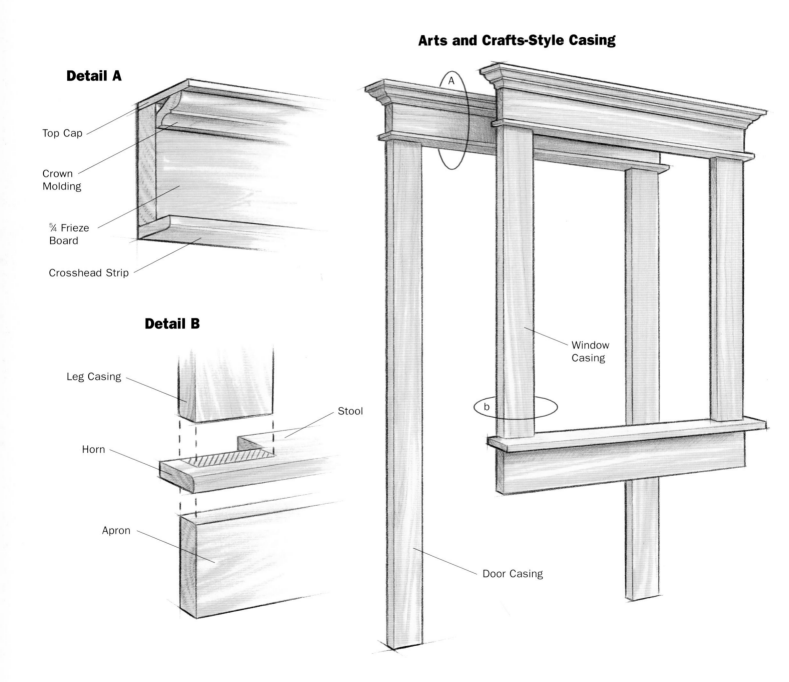

Detail A

Top Cap

Crown Molding

⁵⁄₄ Frieze Board

Crosshead Strip

Detail B

Leg Casing

Horn

Apron

Stool

Arts and Crafts-Style Casing

A

Window Casing

b

Door Casing

Building Decorative Crossheads

A crosshead strip is simply a narrow piece of wood that runs horizontally across the top of the opening. It adds depth to the molding treatment and allows you to use basic butt joints on the leg casings.

Depending on the scale of the casings and other moldings you're using, you could select a piece of lattice to use for the crosshead or one-by lumber or even ¾ material. The larger size used below may look better if you're planning a fairly elaborate cap treatment above the opening. (See the illustration at left.)

Basic Installation

Start by measuring the distance between the outside edges of the leg casings, and cut the ¾ x 6 frieze board to this measurement. Cut a length of 1½-inch-wide bullnose stop molding ¾ inch longer (for a ⅜-inch reveal) as the crosshead strip. Next, cut a strip of crown molding 6 inches longer. Center the length of crown molding on the top edge of the board, with 3 inches hanging off each end. Mark the ends of the crown on its bottom edge. These marks represent the short points of the compound miter cuts that form the outside corners at each end of the crosshead cap. This detail allows the crown molding to return to the wall on both ends of the frieze board.

Making these outside corners is identical to turning outside corners with crown molding on a ceiling. When making the small return pieces, cut the miter onto a piece of molding at least 12 inches long. Remember that to work safely you should never hold small pieces of wood against the fence of a power miter saw.

When you have cut the returns, predrill them to avoid splitting; then glue and nail the molding to the face of the board first, and attach the returns. Now you can make the top cap. If you're using lattice, a typical reveal is ⅜ inch. Measure the distance between the outside edges of the returns, and add ¾ inch. Cut the lattice; then center and fasten it over the crown moldings.

You can build the complete decorative crosshead assembly, above, on a bench. Clamp it in place on the jamb reveal line, right, as you fasten it to the studs.

"Arts and Crafts detailing calls for a flat profile and a sometimes almost rugged-looking use of lumber"

Neoclassical Fluted Casing

Many people can picture flutes as a feature of great stone columns on public buildings. But this design motif, which looks like a series of shallow troughs in the material's surface, is widely used in wood.

You're likely to find that stock fluted casings are too small and special-order casings are too expensive. So you may want to make your own or have a local woodworking shop make them for you.

With this design variation, the troughs become increasingly shallow and finally disappear, leaving several inches of unfluted wood just before the casing joins the top blocks and bottom plinths. This feature takes a lot of planning and some nifty router work. Professional woodworkers have an easier time than amateurs creating boards where the fluted pattern gradually diminishes to nothing near the ends. Do-it-yourselfers will find it much easier to run the flutes through to the ends of the boards.

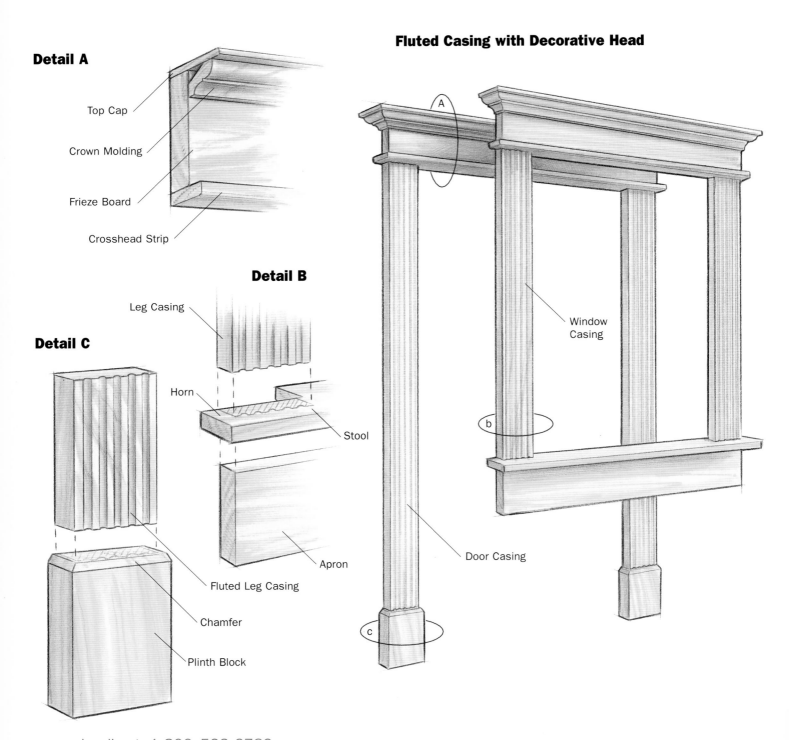

Detail A

Top Cap

Crown Molding

Frieze Board

Crosshead Strip

Detail B

Leg Casing

Detail C

Horn

Stool

Apron

Fluted Leg Casing

Chamfer

Plinth Block

Fluted Casing with Decorative Head

Window Casing

Door Casing

Alternative Window Trim

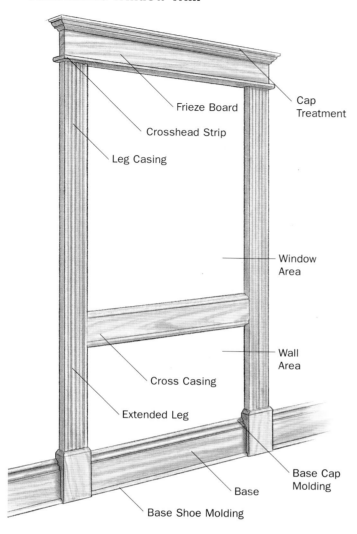

- Frieze Board
- Crosshead Strip
- Leg Casing
- Cap Treatment
- Window Area
- Wall Area
- Cross Casing
- Extended Leg
- Base Cap Molding
- Base
- Base Shoe Molding

Installation

Using a combination square, establish reveal lines along all three sides of the jamb, and install the plinth blocks flush with the inside edges of the leg jambs. This approach calls for some additional planning because you need to accommodate the plinth blocks in your base-trim treatment.

Next, square off the bottoms of the leg casings. Position one of the leg casings on top of one of the plinth blocks, and mark the spot where the reveal line on the head jamb hits the casing. Then square-cut each leg casing to length and install it. Measure from the top outside edge of one leg casing to the top outside edge of the other leg casing, and use this measurement (plus an allowance for a small overhang on each side) to build a decorative crosshead over the opening.

On windows, you have a couple of options. You can stop the leg casings at a window stool or run them down to plinth blocks on the floor. This second approach takes more wood and more time. But it can make short windows, and the room in general, look more expansive. If you run leg casings down to plinth blocks on the floor, you'll need to trim the bottom of the window along the reveal mark on the lower jamb with a piece of cross casing.

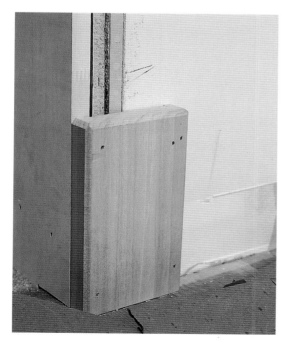

A plinth block at the edge of a passageway is chamfered on the side and top edges to provide a transition between the block and the fluted casing above it.

Plan #131007

Dimensions: 59'10" W x 47'8" D
Levels: 1
Square Footage: 1,595
Bedrooms: 3
Bathrooms: 2
Foundation: Crawl space, slab, basement, or walkout
Materials List Available: Yes
Price Category: D

Imagine living in this home, with its traditional country comfort and individual brand of charm.

Features:

- Exterior elements: The mixture of a front porch with a cameo front door, decorative posts, bay windows, and dormers will delight you.

- Great Room: A tray ceiling gives distinction to this large room, and a wet bar eases entertaining.

- Screened Porch: At dusk and dawn, this porch is sure to be your favorite outdoor spot.

- Kitchen: Eat any meal in this large kitchen for a touch of homey charm.

- Dining Room: Perfect for hosting a formal dinner, this bayed dining room can increase your enjoyment of simple family meals.

- Master Bedroom: For the sake of privacy, this room is somewhat secluded. Decorate to emphasize the elegant tray ceiling.

Images provided by designer/architect.

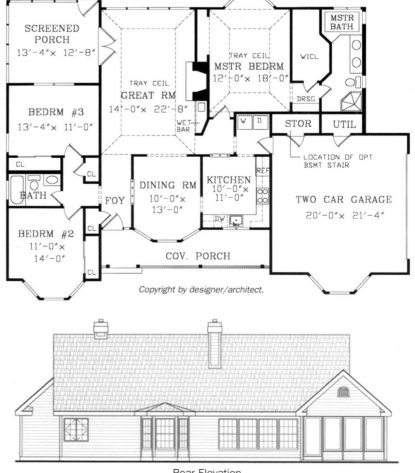

Copyright by designer/architect.

Rear Elevation

Alternate Front View

Foyer / Dining Room

Great Room

Add the Extras

Simple or plain, it's the little conveniences and miscellaneous touches that push the dining experience to perfection. Here are some extra things to think about.

- You can never have too many serving trays when you entertain outside. For carrying food or drinks from the kitchen or the grill, trays are indispensable.

- A serving cart on wheels makes a perfect movable outdoor bar and provides an additional serving surface. Look for one at yard sales or buy one new.

- Chances are you won't have a sideboard, but a few small tables to hold excess items are great substitutes for one. They're also easier to position in the different places where you need them.

- For cooler weather or even a summer's evening with a bit of nip in the air, nothing beats an outdoor fireplace for comfort. You could build one into the house, but various types of stand-alone units are sold in home centers. To add a Southwest ambiance, consider a chiminea, a clay fireplace. Try burning some piñon pine, and you'll feel as if you're in Santa Fe. Be sure to follow manufacturers' instructions when using these fireplaces. You might also have to store them during the winter.

- Pots of fragrant plants—lavender, scented geraniums, flowering tobacco, or jasmine—provide a sensual aroma. Flowers such as roses climbing up an arbor or trellis are beautiful, evoke a romantic feeling, and lend a delicate scent to the atmosphere as well.

Nothing adds romance and intrigue to an evening soiree as candlelight does. Include just a few candles for an intimate dinner. Use more for a larger gathering, placing one or more on each table. Scatter luminaries around the yard. As the beautiful evening dusk begins, light candles, a few at a time, so your eyes can adjust to the dimming light. Not only do the candles illuminate the night in a magical way but they can also keep bugs at bay.

Plan #271020

Dimensions: 68' W x 37' D
Levels: 2
Square Footage: 2,198
Main Level Sq. Ft.: 1,288
Upper Level Sq. Ft.: 910
Bedrooms: 3
Bathrooms: 2½
Foundation: Basement
Materials List Available: Yes
Price Category: D

Images provided by designer/architect.

This traditional home attracts attention with a striking columned entry and inviting front porch.

Features:

- Living Room: This sunken formal gathering area has a vaulted ceiling, a corner fireplace, and eye-catching windows with transoms.

- Dining Room: A china hutch services this quiet dining room. A nearby powder room is handy for last-minute hand-washing.

- Kitchen: Well planned and stylish, this kitchen offers a snack bar and a built-in desk. A pantry and laundry facilities are just steps away, as is the bayed breakfast nook, which may be closed off from the foyer with French doors.

- Family Room: This sunken space boasts a second fireplace next to built-in bookshelves. Sliding glass doors open to a backyard patio.

- Master Suite: On the upper floor, this getaway spot boasts a vaulted ceiling and private bar.

Main Level Floor Plan

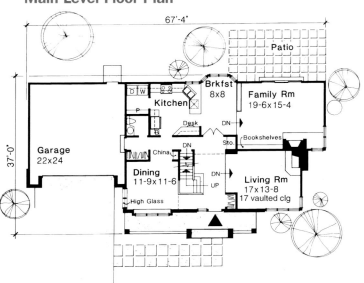

Upper Level Floor Plan

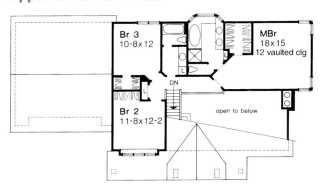

Copyright by designer/architect.

Plan #271021

Dimensions: 39' W x 58' D
Levels: 2
Square Footage: 1,551
Main Level Sq. Ft.: 1,099
Upper Level Sq. Ft.: 452
Bedrooms: 3
Bathrooms: 2½
Foundation: Basement
Materials List Available: Yes
Price Category: C

Images provided by designer/architect.

The exterior of this cozy country-style home boasts a charming combination of woodwork and stone that lends an air of England to the facade.

Features:

• Living Room: An arched entryway leads into the living room, with its vaulted ceiling, tall windows, and fireplace.

• Dining Room: This space also features a vaulted ceiling, plus a view of the patio.

• Master Suite: Find a vaulted ceiling here, too, as well as a walk-in closet, and private bath.

Living Room

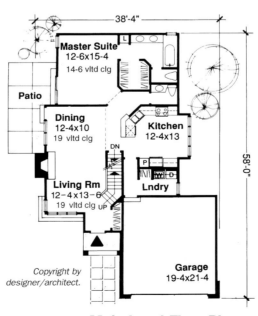

Main Level Floor Plan

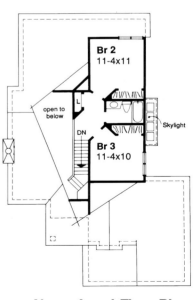

Upper Level Floor Plan

Main Level Floor Plan

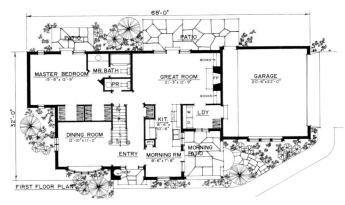

Copyright by designer/architect.

Plan #291010

Dimensions: 68'6" W x 33' D

Levels: 2

Square Footage: 1,776

Main Level Sq. Ft.: 1,182

Upper Level Sq. Ft.: 594

Bedrooms: 3

Bathrooms: 2½

Foundation: Basement

Materials List Available: No

Price Category: C

Images provided by designer/architect.

Upper Level Floor Plan

Copyright by designer/architect.

Main Level Floor Plan

Plan #291012

Dimensions: 68'6" W x 33' D

Levels: 2

Square Footage: 1,898

Main Level Sq. Ft.: 1,182

Upper Level Sq. Ft.: 716

Bedrooms: 4

Bathrooms: 2½

Foundation: Basement

Materials List Available: No

Price Category: D

Images provided by designer/architect.

Upper Level Floor Plan

Copyright by designer/architect.

Images provided by designer/architect.

Rear Elevation

Plan #221012

Dimensions: 71' W x 51' D

Levels: 1

Square Footage: 1,802

Bedrooms: 3

Bathrooms: 2½

Foundation: Basement

Materials List Available: No

Price Category: D

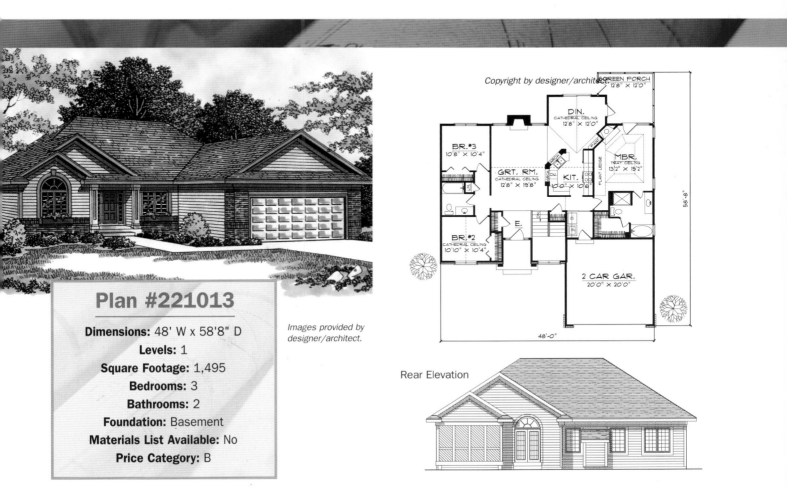

Copyright by designer/architect.

Images provided by designer/architect.

Rear Elevation

Plan #221013

Dimensions: 48' W x 58'8" D

Levels: 1

Square Footage: 1,495

Bedrooms: 3

Bathrooms: 2

Foundation: Basement

Materials List Available: No

Price Category: B

Images provided by designer/architect.

Plan #131020

Dimensions: 67'2" W x 48'10" D

Levels: 1

Square Footage: 1,735

Bedrooms: 3

Bathrooms: 2

Foundation: Basement, crawl space, or slab

Materials List Available: Yes

Price Category: D

Copyright by designer/architect.

Kitchen   Foyer/Dining Room

Plan #131045

Dimensions: 81'4" W x 68'3" D

Levels: 1

Square Footage: 2,347

Bedrooms: 4

Bathrooms: 2½

Foundation: Basement, crawl space, or slab

Materials List Available: Yes

Price Category: F

Images provided by designer/architect.

Bonus Area

Copyright by designer/architect.

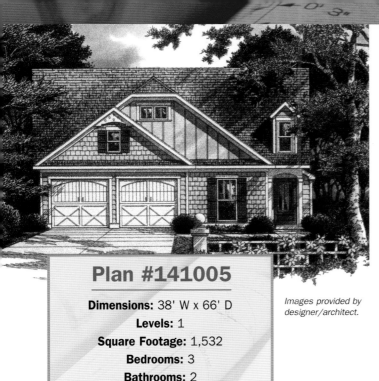

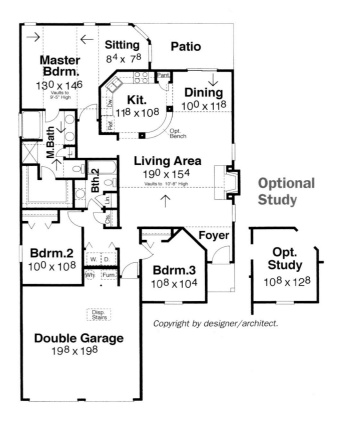

Plan #141005

Dimensions: 38' W x 66' D

Levels: 1

Square Footage: 1,532

Bedrooms: 3

Bathrooms: 2

Foundation: Slab, basement

Materials List Available: No

Price Category: C

Images provided by designer/architect.

Copyright by designer/architect.

Plan #141006

Dimensions: 64' W x 52' D

Levels: 1

Square Footage: 1,787

Bedrooms: 3

Bathrooms: 2½

Foundation: Basement

Materials List Available: No

Price Category: C

Images provided by designer/architect.

Copyright by designer/architect.

SMARTtip

Arts and Crafts Style in Your Kitchen

The heart of this style lies in its earthy connection. The more you can bring nature into it, the more authentic it will appear. An easy way to do this is with plants. Open the space up to nature with glass doors that provide a view to a green garden.

Plan #271026

Dimensions: 48' W x 50' D
Levels: 2
Square Footage: 2,170
Main Level Sq. Ft.: 1,169
Upper Level Sq. Ft.: 1,001
Bedrooms: 3
Bathrooms: 2½
Foundation: Basement
Materials List Available: Yes
Price Category: D

Images provided by designer/architect.

This fresh design presents a friendly facade to neighbors and passersby. Inside, you'll find a floor plan that is up to date.

Features:

• Entry: In this area, a two-story-high ceiling welcomes visitors in a dramatic fashion.

• Great Room: Triple windows in front and back brighten this expansive gathering space, which is both sunken and vaulted. Formal meals could be hosted at the rear of this room.

• Kitchen: With lots of counter space, this entertaining hub is efficient and well planned. A bayed dinette nearby looks out over a sizable deck and the backyard vistas beyond.

• Family Room: The highlight here is the striking fireplace, which will be the focal point of any casual occasion.

• Master Suite: A vaulted ceiling adds a special touch to the sleeping area. The private bath showcases a separate tub and shower, dual sinks, and two walk-in closets.

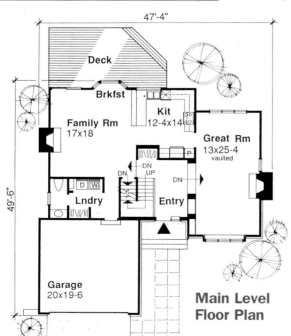

Main Level Floor Plan

Upper Level Floor Plan

Copyright by designer/architect.

Plan #271027

Dimensions: 61' W x 44' D
Levels: 2
Square Footage: 2,463
Main Level Sq. Ft.: 1,380
Upper Level Sq. Ft.: 1,083
Bedrooms: 4
Bathrooms: 2½
Foundation: Basement
Materials List Available: Yes
Price Category: E

This post-modern design uses half-round transom windows and a barrel-vaulted porch to lend elegance to its facade.

Features:

- **Living Room:** A vaulted ceiling and a striking fireplace enhance this formal gathering space.

- **Dining Room:** Introduced from the living room by square columns, this formal dining room is just steps from the kitchen.

- **Kitchen:** Thoroughly modern in its design, this walk-through kitchen includes an island cooktop and a large pantry. Nearby, a sunny, bayed breakfast area offers sliding-glass-door access to an angled backyard deck.

- **Family Room:** Columns provide an elegant preface to this fun gathering spot, which sports a vaulted ceiling and easy access to the deck.

- **Master suite:** A vaulted ceiling crowns this luxurious space, which includes a private bath and bright windows.

Main Level Floor Plan

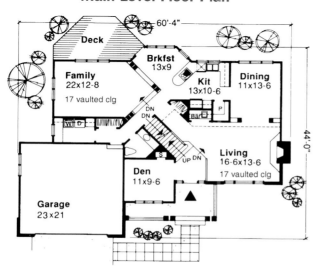

Upper Level Floor Plan

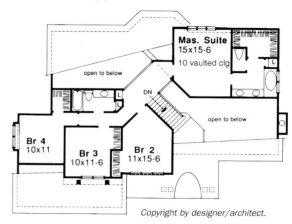

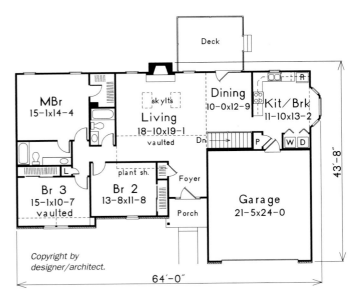

Copyright by
designer/architect.

64'-0"

43'-8"

Plan #321014

Dimensions: 64' W x 43'8" D

Levels: 1

Square Footage: 1,676

Bedrooms: 3

Bathrooms: 2

Foundation: Basement

Materials List Available: Yes

Price Category: C

Images provided by designer/architect.

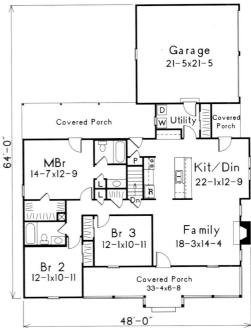

64'-0"

48'-0"

Plan #321015

Dimensions: 48' W x 64' D

Levels: 1

Square Footage: 1,501

Bedrooms: 3

Bathrooms: 2

Foundation: Basement

Materials List Available: Yes

Price Category: C

Images provided by designer/architect.

Copyright by designer/architect.

Plan #321017

Dimensions: 77' W x 36'8" D

Levels: 1

Square Footage: 2,531

Bedrooms: 1-4

Bathrooms: 1-2½

Foundation: Daylight basement

Materials List Available: Yes

Price Category: E

Rear View

Images provided by designer/architect.

Optional Basement Level Floor Plan

Copyright by designer/architect.

Plan #321018

Dimensions: 88'4" W x 48'4" D

Levels: 1

Square Footage: 2,523

Bedrooms: 3

Bathrooms: 2

Foundation: Basement

Materials List Available: Yes

Price Category: E

Images provided by designer/architect.

Copyright by designer/architect.

SMARTtip

Tiebacks

You don't have to limit yourself to tiebacks made from matching or contrasting fabric. Achieve creative custom looks by making tiebacks from unexpected items. Some materials to consider are old cotton bandannas or silk scarves, strings of beads, lengths of leather, or old belts and chains.

Plan #271030

Dimensions: 55'8" W x 45' D
Levels: 2
Square Footage: 1,926
Main Level Sq. Ft.: 1,490
Upper Level Sq. Ft.: 436
Bedrooms: 3
Bathrooms: 2½
Foundation: Basement
Materials List Available: Yes
Price Category: D

Images provided by designer/architect.

This traditional home's main-floor master suite is hard to resist, with its inviting window seat and delightful bath.

Features:

• Master Suite: Just off from the entry foyer, this luxurious oasis is entered through double doors, and offers an airy vaulted ceiling, plus a private bath that includes a separate tub and shower, dual-sink vanity, and walk-in closet.

• Great Room: This space does it all in style, with a breathtaking wall of windows and a charming fireplace.

• Kitchen: A cooktop island makes dinnertime tasks a breeze. You'll also love the roomy pantry. The adjoining breakfast room, with its deck access and built-in desk, is sure to be a popular hangout for the teens.

• Secondary Bedrooms: Two additional bedrooms reside on the upper floor and allow the younger family members a measure of desired—and necessary—privacy.

Main Level Floor Plan

Upper Level Floor Plan

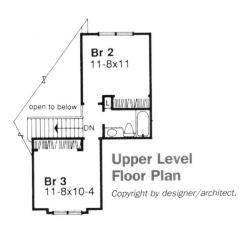

Copyright by designer/architect.

Plan #271046

Dimensions: 50' W x 43' D
Levels: 2
Square Footage: 2,445
Main Level Sq. Ft.: 1,237
Upper Level Sq. Ft.: 1,208
Bedrooms: 3
Bathrooms: 2½
Foundation: Basement
Materials List Available: Yes
Price Category: E

Images provided by designer/architect.

Charming window seats, built-in shelves, and dazzling windows grace this two-story home.

Features:

- **Living Room:** The sidelighted entry introduces this formal charmer, which is brightened by large windows. A tray ceiling rises overhead.

- **Dining Room:** Low half-walls separate the living room from this formal dining room. Large windows here give nice outdoor views.

- **Kitchen/Breakfast:** A work island enhances this open kitchen, which is bordered by a bayed breakfast nook. A door from the nook opens onto a comfortable backyard deck.

- **Family Room:** Here, a wonderful fireplace and large windows make for a enviable destination point.

- **Master Suite:** On the upper floor, the master bedroom pampers you with a cozy deck. The private bath includes a separate tub and shower, plus an ample walk-in closet.

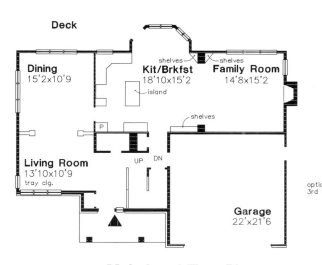

Main Level Floor Plan

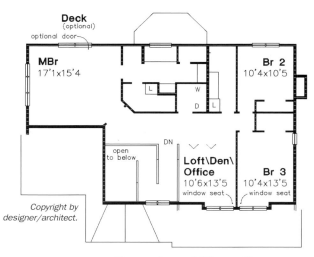

Upper Level Floor Plan

Plan #271001

Dimensions: 52'8".W x 35'4" D

Levels: 1

Square Footage: 1,400

Bedrooms: 3

Bathrooms: 2

Foundation: Basement

Materials List Available: Yes

Price Category: B

Deck

Images provided by designer/architect.

Master Br
15-4x11

Great
Room
16-8x19

Dining

Kitchen/
Brkfst
13-8x12-8

Bar

dn

Garage
19-4x19-4

35'-4"

Den/Br 3
11-4x12-4

Br 2
11x10

52'-8"

Copyright by designer/architect.

This contemporary design builds on the basics, creating a comfortable home that offers possibilities for entertaining or quiet downtime.

Features:

- Great room: The heart of the home, this massive gathering room features a handsome fireplace and a handy wet bar, and flows into the dining space. Sliding glass doors between the two spaces lead to a deck.

- Kitchen/Breakfast: This combination space uses available space efficiently and comfortably.

- Master Suite: The inviting master bedroom includes a private bath.

SMARTtip

Candid Camera for Your Landscaping

To see your home and yard as others see them, take some camera shots. Seeing your house and landscaping on film will create an opportunity for objectivity. Problems will become more obvious, and you will then be better able to prioritize your home improvements, as well as your landscaping plan.

Plan #271048

Dimensions: 60' W x 32'6" D
Levels: 2
Square Footage: 2,143
Main Level Sq. Ft.: 1,200
Upper Level Sq. Ft.: 943
Bedrooms: 4
Bathrooms: 3
Foundation: Basement, crawl space
Materials List Available: No
Price Category: D

Images provided by designer/architect.

With a nod to historical architecture, this authentic Cape Cod home boasts a traditional exterior with an updated floor plan.

Features:

- **Living Room:** This spacious area is warmed by an optional fireplace and merges with the dining room.

- **Kitchen:** Efficient and sunny, this walk-through kitchen handles almost any task with aplomb.

- **Family Room:** The home's second optional fireplace can be found here, along with a smart log-storage bin that can be loaded from the garage. Sliding-glass-door access to a backyard patio is a bonus.

- **Guest Bedroom:** Private access to a bath and plenty of room to relax make this bedroom a winner.

- **Master Suite:** Amenities abound in the master bedroom, including two closets, a separated dressing spot, and a dormer as a sitting area.

Main Level Floor Plan

Copyright by designer/architect.

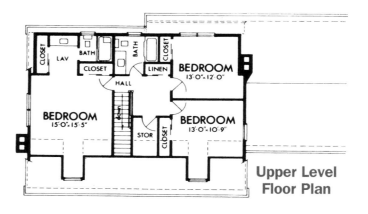

Upper Level Floor Plan

Plan #161046

Dimensions: 58'6" W x 49' D
Levels: 2
Square Footage: 2,338
Main Level Sq. Ft.: 1,633
Upper Level Sq. Ft.: 705
Bedrooms: 4
Bathrooms: 2½
Foundation: Basement
Materials List Available: Yes
Price Category: E

The brick-and-stone exterior and covered porch draw your eyes to this exciting two-story home.

Images provided by designer/architect.

Features:

- **Great Room:** Multiple windows light up this delightful great room, which is warmed by an inviting fireplace. You will appreciate the easy access to the kitchen and enjoy the indoor-outdoor effect created by triple French doors to the breakfast room.

- **Kitchen:** A convenient angled island with seating provides a view of the great room from this kitchen. Enjoy easy access to the formal dining room for special occasions.

- **Master Suite:** This master suite, with deluxe bath and large walk-in closet, completes the first floor.

- **Additional Bedrooms:** Angled stairs from the foyer lead to a second-floor balcony with built-ins, a bonus space above the garage, and two bedrooms, each with walk-in closets.

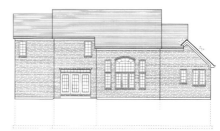

Rear Elevation

Main Level Floor Plan

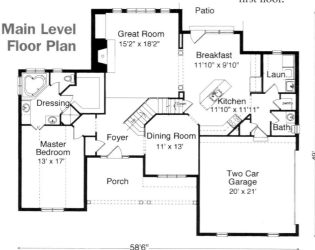

Patio

Great Room 15'2" x 18'2"

Breakfast 11'10" x 9'10"

Laun.

Dressing

Kitchen 11'10" x 11'11"

pantry

Master Bedroom 13' x 17'

Foyer

Dining Room 11' x 13'

Bath

Porch

Two Car Garage 20' x 21'

49'

58'6"

Upper Level Floor Plan

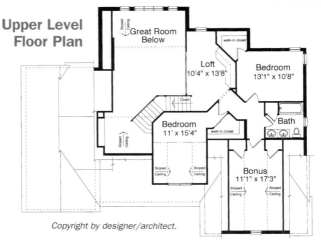

Great Room Below

walk-in closet

Loft 10'4" x 13'8"

Bedroom 13'1" x 10'8"

Bedroom 11' x 15'4"

walk-in closet

Bath

Bonus 11'1" x 17'3"

Copyright by designer/architect.

Plan #141004

Dimensions: 48' W x 29' D

Levels: 1

Square Footage: 1,514

Bedrooms: 3

Bathrooms: 2

Foundation: Slab, basement

Materials List Available: No

Price Category: C

Images provided by designer/architect.

Designed for the narrow lot, this cottage-style home features Craftsman-style exterior columns.

Features:

- Ceiling Height: 8 ft. unless otherwise noted.

- Entry: There's no defined foyer, so you enter immediately into the living area, with its vaulted ceiling that flattens over the dining area at a soaring 14 ft.

- Living/Dining Areas: The see-through fireplace flanked by bookcases is a main focal point of the home. It serves as the divider between the living room and dining room.

- Kitchen: This kitchen shares the vaulted ceiling with the dining room and living room. A plant shelf over the cabinets facing the dining room defines the space without obstructing the view of the fireplace.

- Master Suite: This private retreat has its own entrance away from the other bedrooms and boasts a cathedral ceiling over both bedroom and bath.

Copyright by designer/architect.

Images provided by designer/architect.

Plan #271045

Dimensions: 56' W x 47' D
Levels: 2
Square Footage: 2,409
Main Level Sq. Ft.: 1,463
Upper Level Sq. Ft.: 946
Bedrooms: 4
Bathrooms: 2½
Foundation: Basement
Materials List Available: No
Price Category: E

This traditional home is so attractive, guests will walk right up to visit!

Features:

- **Living Room:** They'll be drawn first to this comfortable room, which boasts a vaulted ceiling and an eye-catching bump-out.

- **Dining Room:** From the living room, columned half walls define and introduce this formal dining room, which flaunts an elegant tray ceiling.

- **Kitchen:** This gourmet island-equipped kitchen offers a handy pantry. The attached breakfast bay hosts a useful menu desk and easy access to an inviting backyard deck.

- **Family Room:** A fireplace warms this expansive family room, which also opens onto the deck.

- **Master Suite:** Upstairs, the master bedroom boasts a vaulted ceiling and two walk-in closets. The private bath shows off a garden tub and a dual-sink vanity with a makeup area.

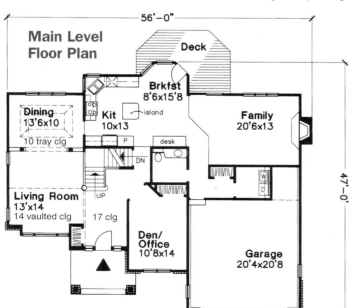

Copyright by designer/architect.

Plan #271062

Dimensions: 54' W x 45' D
Levels: 2
Square Footage: 2,356
Main Level Sq. Ft.: 1,222
Upper Level Sq. Ft.: 1,134
Bedrooms: 4
Bathrooms: 2½
Foundation: Daylight basement
Materials List Available: No
Price Category: E

Images provided by designer/architect.

The covered front porch of this traditional home includes enough space for a pair of rocking chairs.

Features:

- Living Room: To the right of the entry, this large living room is enhanced by a focal-point bay window and is the perfect spot for conversations with guests.

- Dining Room: This bright, formal dining room is situated near the kitchen, making meal service a breeze.

- Kitchen: A U-shaped counter defines this open kitchen, which flows nicely into the adjacent dinette and a versatile sunroom beyond.

- Family Room: Casual gatherings are destined for this huge family room. A crackling fireplace sets a warm and friendly mood.

- Master Suite: Upstairs, this spacious master bedroom sits next to a walk-in closet and a private bath, where a whirlpool tub is complemented by a separate shower.

Main Level Floor Plan

54'0"

SUN ROOM 10'0" x 8'0"
MUD
KITCHEN 11'0" x 12'8"
DINETTE 10'0" x 12'8"
FAMILY ROOM 15'0" x 17'0"
DINING 12'0" x 11'6"
ENTRY
GARAGE 22'4" x 24'4"
COVERED PORCH
LIVING 12'0" x 14'0"
45'0"
DN
UP

Upper Level Floor Plan

MASTER SUITE 14'8" x 17'0"
BDRM 4 12'0" x 13'0"
W.I.C.
BDRM 3 11'6" x 11'0"
BDRM 2 12'4" x 14'0"
DN

Copyright by designer/architect.

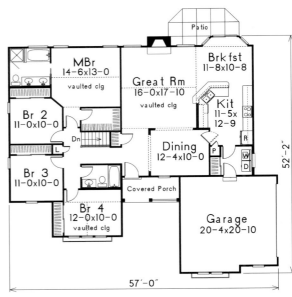

Images provided by designer/architect.

Copyright by designer/architect.

Plan #321008

Dimensions: 57' W x 52'2" D

Levels: 1

Square Footage: 1,761

Bedrooms: 4

Bathrooms: 2

Foundation: Basement

Materials List Available: Yes

Price Category: C

SMARTtip

Hanging Wallpaper

Use liner paper to smooth out a damaged wall and to provide uniform support for expensive paper.

Copyright by designer/architect.

Images provided by designer/architect.

Plan #221014

Dimensions: 72' W x 44'8" D

Levels: 1

Square Footage: 1,906

Bedrooms: 3

Bathrooms: 2½

Foundation: Basement

Materials List Available: No

Price Category: D

Rear Elevation

Images provided by designer/architect.

Copyright by designer/architect.

Plan #151037

Dimensions: 50' W x 56' D

Levels: 1

Square Footage: 1,538

Bedrooms: 3

Bathrooms: 2

Foundation: Crawl space, slab, or basement

Materials List Available: Yes

Price Category: C

Plan #151050

Dimensions: 69'2" W x 74'10" D

Levels: 1

Square Footage: 2,096

Bedrooms: 3

Bathrooms: 2½

Foundation: Crawl space, slab, or basement

Materials List Available: Yes

Price Category: D

Images provided by designer/architect.

Copyright by designer/architect.

Plan #271064

Dimensions: 76' W x 54' D

Levels: 2

Square Footage: 2,864

Main Level Sq. Ft.: 1,610

Upper Level Sq. Ft.: 1,254

Bedrooms: 4

Bathrooms: 2½

Foundation: Daylight basement

Materials List Available: No

Price Category: E

Images provided by designer/architect.

Tall windows and a colonnaded porch lend a touch of style to this traditional home.

Features:

- **Family Room:** A bay window enhances this sizable family room, which shares a see-through fireplace with a cozy hearth room.

- **Kitchen:** This room's island presents a unique serving bar that facilitates meals and entertaining. The versatile dinette incorporates sliding glass doors for easy access to a nice backyard deck.

- **Dining Room:** This formal space is the perfect locale for holiday feasts and special meals.

- **Study:** Double doors introduce this quiet study, which could easily serve as a guest-room or a home office.

- **Master Suite:** This fabulous area boasts a tray ceiling and a bay window in the sleeping chamber. The deluxe private bath offers a whirlpool tub, separate shower, dual-sink vanity, and walk-in closet.

Main Level Floor Plan

Copyright by designer/architect.

Upper Level Floor Plan

Plan #271072

Dimensions: 76' W x 38' D
Levels: 2
Square Footage: 3,081
Main Level Sq. Ft.: 1,358
Upper Level Sq. Ft.: 1,723
Bedrooms: 3
Bathrooms: 2½
Foundation: Basement, crawl space
Materials List Available: No
Price Category: G

This updated farmhouse design features a wraparound porch for savoring warm afternoons.

Features:

- Living Room: Striking columns invite visitors into this relaxing space. Double doors provide direct access to the casual family room beyond.

- Family Room: A focal-point fireplace warms this friendly space, while windows overlook impressive backyard vistas.

- Kitchen: An island cooktop and a menu desk simplify meal preparation here. A versatile dinette offers outdoor access through sliding glass doors.

- Dining Room: Neatly situated near the kitchen, this room will host important meals with style.

Images provided by designer/architect.

- Master Suite: Double doors and a tray ceiling make a good first impression. Two walk-in closets organize lots of clothes. A spa tub anchors the private bath.

- Bonus Room: A unique phone booth is found in this versatile room, which could serve as a playroom or an art studio.

Main Level Floor Plan

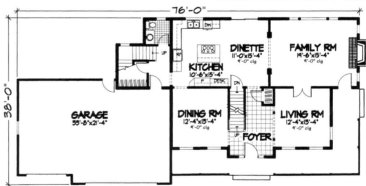

Upper Level Floor Plan

Copyright by designer/architect.

Plan #271077

Dimensions: 70' W x 53' D

Levels: 1

Square Footage: 1,786

Bedrooms: 1-4

Bathrooms: 1½-2½

Foundation: Daylight basement

Materials List Available: No

Price Category: C

Images provided by designer/architect.

Optional Basement Level Floor Plan

Copyright by designer/architect.

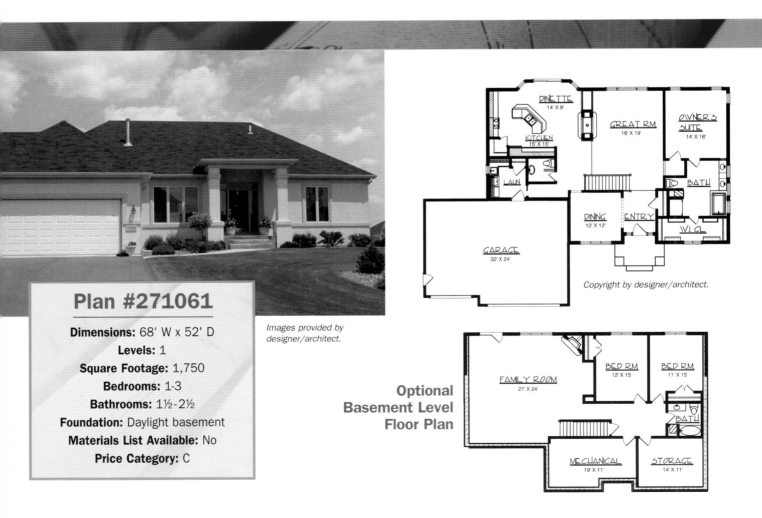

Plan #271061

Dimensions: 68' W x 52' D

Levels: 1

Square Footage: 1,750

Bedrooms: 1-3

Bathrooms: 1½-2½

Foundation: Daylight basement

Materials List Available: No

Price Category: C

Images provided by designer/architect.

Copyright by designer/architect.

Optional Basement Level Floor Plan

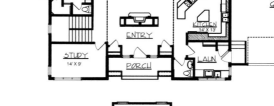

Plan #271078

Dimensions: 83' W x 52' D

Levels: 1

Square Footage: 1,855

Bedrooms: 1-2

Bathrooms: 1½-2½

Foundation: Daylight basement

Materials List Available: No

Price Category: D

Images provided by designer/architect.

Optional Basement Level Floor Plan

Copyright by designer/architect.

Plan #271060

Dimensions: 72' W x 52' D

Levels: 1

Square Footage: 1,726

Bedrooms: 2-4

Bathrooms: 2½-3½

Foundation: Daylight basement

Materials List Available: No

Price Category: C

Images provided by designer/architect.

Copyright by designer/architect.

Optional Basement Level Floor Plan

Plan #311003

Dimensions: 70'10" W x 65'4" D

Levels: 2

Square Footage: 2,428

Main Level Sq. Ft.: 2,348

Upper Level Sq. Ft.: 80

Bedrooms: 3

Bathrooms: 2½

Foundation: Slab, crawl space, or basement

Materials List Available: Y

Price Category: E

Images provided by designer/architect.

If you admire the gracious colonnaded porch, curved brick steps, and stunning front windows, you'll fall in love with the interior of this home.

Features:

• Great Room: Enjoy the vaulted ceiling, balcony from the upper level, and fireplace with flanking windows that let you look out to the patio.

• Dining Room: Columns define this formal room, which is adjacent to the breakfast room.

• Kitchen: A bayed sink area and extensive curved bar provide visual interest in this well-designed kitchen, which every cook will love.

• Breakfast Room: Huge windows let the sun shine into this room, which is open to the kitchen.

• Master Suite: The sitting area is open to the rear porch for a special touch in this gorgeous suite. Two walk-in closets and a vaulted ceiling and double vanity in the bath will make you feel completely pampered.

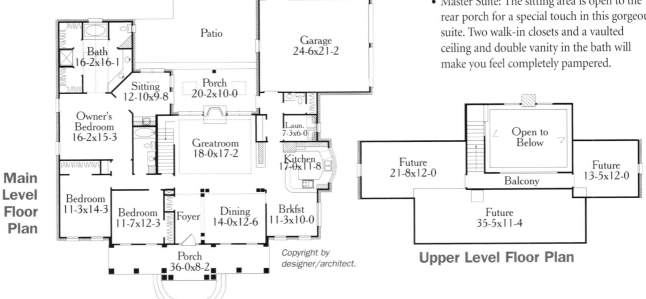

Main Level Floor Plan

Bath 16-2x16-1

Patio

Garage 24-6x21-2

Sitting 12-10x9-8

Porch 20-2x10-0

Owner's Bedroom 16-2x15-3

Laun. 7-3x6-0

Greatroom 18-0x17-2

Kitchen 17-0x11-8

Bedroom 11-3x14-3

Bedroom 11-7x12-3

Foyer

Dining 14-0x12-6

Brkfst 11-3x10-0

Porch 36-0x8-2

Copyright by designer/architect.

Upper Level Floor Plan

Future 21-8x12-0

Open to Below

Future 13-5x12-0

Balcony

Future 35-5x11-4

Plan #311005

Dimensions: 87' W x 57'3" D
Levels: 1
Square Footage: 2,497
Bedrooms: 3
Bathrooms: 3½
Foundation: Slab, crawl space, or basement
Materials List Available: Yes
Price Category: E

Images provided by designer/architect.

You'll love this home, which mixes practical features with a gracious appearance.

Features:

- Great Room: A handsome fireplace and flanking windows that give a view of the back patio are the highlights of this gracious room.

- Kitchen: A curved bar defines the perimeter of this well-planned kitchen.

- Breakfast Room: Open to both the great room and the kitchen, this sunny spot leads to the rear porch, which in turn, leads to the patio beyond.

- Master Suite: Vaulted ceilings, a huge walk-in closet, and deluxe bath create luxury here.

- Bonus Room: Finish this 966-sq.-ft. area as a huge game room, or divide it into a game room, study, and sewing or craft room.

- Additional Bedrooms: Each bedroom has a private bath and good closet space.

Main Level Floor Plan

Copyright by designer/architect.

Bonus Area Floor Plan

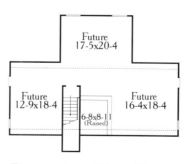

SMARTtip
Front Porch

A front porch proclaims you to the outside world, so furnish it in a way that expresses what you want the world to know about you. Use the walls of your porch to hang interesting items such as sundials or old shutters. Set a mirror into an old window to reflect a portion of the garden.

Plan #131032

Dimensions: 69'2" W x 46' D
Levels: 2
Square Footage: 2,455
Main Level Sq. Ft.: 1,499
Upper Level Sq. Ft.: 956
Bedrooms: 4
Bathrooms: 3
Foundation: Crawl space, slab, or basement
Materials List Available: Yes
Price Category: F

Images provided by designer/architect.

If you love Victorian styling, you'll be charmed by the ornate, rounded front porch and the two-story bay that distinguish this home.

Features:

• Living Room: You'll love the 13-ft. ceiling in this room, as well as the panoramic view it gives of the front porch and yard.

• Kitchen: Sunlight streams into this room, where an angled island with a cooktop eases both prepping and cooking.

• Breakfast Room: This room shares an eating bar with the kitchen, making it easy for the family to congregate while the family chef is cooking.

• Guest Room: Use this lovely room on the first level as a home office or study if you wish.

• Master Suite: The dramatic bayed sitting area with a high ceiling has an octagonal shape that you'll adore, and the amenities in the private bath will soothe you at the end of a busy day.

Rear View

Upper Level Floor Plan

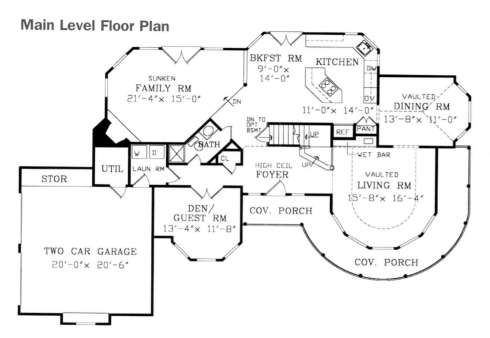

MSTR BATH

WICL

LIN

BEDRM #3
11'-0" x 11'-4"

BATH

LIN

BEDRM #2
10'-0" x 13'-6"

CL

CL

BALC.

DN

MSTR BEDRM
20'-8" x 14'-6"

UPPER FOYER

PLANT LEDGE

TRAY CLG
SITTING AREA
10'-4" x 8'-0"

Copyright by designer/architect.

Main Level Floor Plan

BKFST RM
9'-0" x 14'-0"

KITCHEN

DW

OV

SUNKEN
FAMILY RM
21'-4" x 15'-0"

DN

VAULTED
DINING RM
13'-8" x 11'-0"

11'-0" x 14'-0"

DN TO
OPT
BSMT

UP

REF

PANT

W D

BATH

CL

UP

WET BAR

VAULTED
LIVING RM
15'-8" x 16'-4"

UTIL

LAUN RM

HIGH CEIL
FOYER

STOR

DEN/
GUEST RM
13'-4" x 11'-8"

COV. PORCH

TWO CAR GARAGE
20'-0" x 20'-6"

COV. PORCH

Dining Room

Living Room

Kitchen

Breakfast

Foyer

Plan #271065

Dimensions: 63'10" W x 34' D

Levels: 2

Square Footage: 2,508

Main Level Sq. Ft.: 1,368

Upper Level Sq. Ft.: 1,140

Bedrooms: 4

Bathrooms: 2½

Foundation: Basement, crawl space

Materials List Available: No

Price Category: E

This flawlessly rendered Colonial-style home blends a historically accurate facade with a modern floor plan.

Features:

- **Living Room:** To one side of the entry foyer, this quiet and secluded living room is the perfect spot for an afternoon of conversation.

- **Dining Room:** Formal and sophisticated, this space is bright and cheery, and easily hosts special dinners.

- **Kitchen:** With a central island and a handy menu desk, this room flows smoothly into the adjacent dinette. Sliding glass doors give way to a breezy and inviting backyard porch.

- **Family Room:** A fancy bay window and a crackling fireplace make this the spot to which guests and family alike will gravitate.

- **Master Suite:** Upstairs, the master suite features a sizable walk-in closet, a whirlpool tub, a separate shower, and a dual-sink vanity.

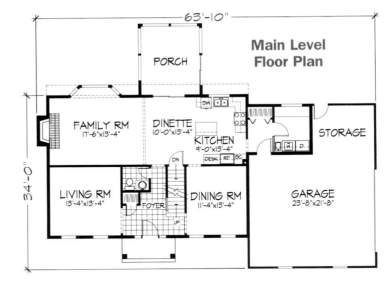

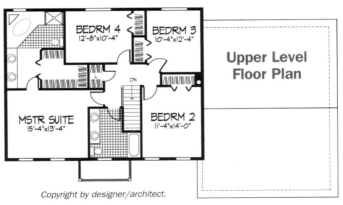

Copyright by designer/architect.

Plan #271054

Dimensions: 63' W x 49' D
Levels: 2
Square Footage: 2,654
Main Level Sq. Ft.: 1,384
Upper Level Sq. Ft.: 1,270
Bedrooms: 4
Bathrooms: 2½
Foundation: Daylight basement
Materials List Available: No
Price Category: F

Images provided by designer/architect.

This updated farmhouse attracts comments from passersby with its shuttered windows and welcoming wraparound porch.

Features:

- **Great Room:** This popular gathering spot includes a fireplace flanked by a media center and abundant shelves, and a wall of windows.

- **Dining Room:** This formal dining room is closed off with a pocket door for peace and quiet during meals. The bayed window facing the front is a nice touch.

- **Kitchen:** This thoroughly modern kitchen boasts an island with two sinks, a good-sized pantry, and a bayed dinette with sliding doors to the backyard.

- **Sun Porch:** Accessed via double doors from the dinette, this warm getaway spot flaunts a wood floor, ample angled windows, and a French door to the backyard.

- **Owner's Suite:** This master bedroom has a gorgeous tray ceiling in the sleeping chamber, plus a private bath with a corner whirlpool tub, a separate shower, and an endless walk-in closet.

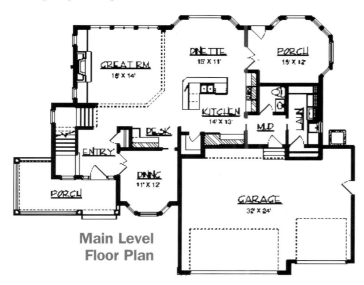

Main Level Floor Plan

Upper Level Floor Plan

Copyright by designer/architect.

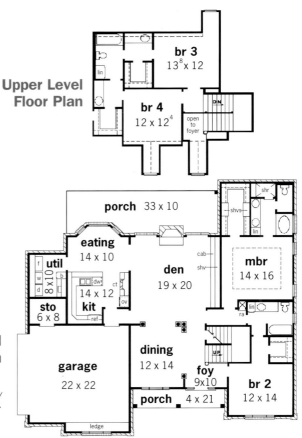

Upper Level Floor Plan

br 3
13⁸ x 12

br 4
12 x 12⁴

open to foyer

Main Level Floor Plan

porch 33 x 10

eating
14 x 10

util
8 x 10

den
19 x 20

mbr
14 x 16

kit
14 x 12

sto
6 x 8

garage
22 x 22

dining
12 x 14

foy
9x10

br 2
12 x 14

porch 4 x 21

ledge

Images provided by designer/architect.

Copyright by designer/architect.

Plan #201103

Dimensions: 57'10" W x 56'10" D
Levels: 2
Square Footage: 2,490
Main Level Sq. Ft.: 1,911
Upper Level Sq. Ft.: 579
Bedrooms: 4
Bathrooms: 3
Foundation: Crawl space, slab
Materials List Available: Yes
Price Category: E

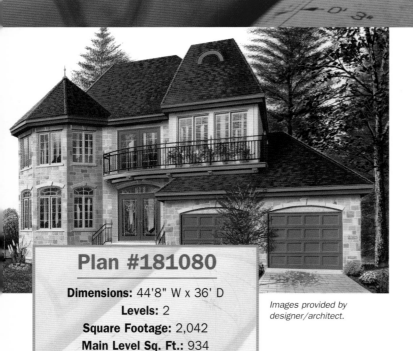

Main Level Floor Plan

36'-0"
10,8 m

14'-0" X 9'-4"
4,20 X 2,80

18'-6" X 11'-8"
5,60 X 3,50

12'-4" X 22'-8"
3,70 X 6,80

19'-8" X 22'-0"
5,90 X 6,80

44'-8"
13,4 m

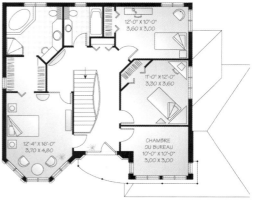

Upper Level Floor Plan

12'-0" X 10'-0"
3,60 X 3,00

11'-0" X 12'-0"
3,30 X 3,60

12'-4" X 16'-0"
3,70 X 4,80

CHAMBRE OU BUREAU
10'-0" X 10'-0"
3,00 X 3,00

Images provided by designer/architect.

Copyright by designer/architect.

Plan #181080

Dimensions: 44'8" W x 36' D
Levels: 2
Square Footage: 2,042
Main Level Sq. Ft.: 934
Upper Level Sq. Ft.: 1,108
Bedrooms: 3
Bathrooms: 2½
Foundation: Full basement
Materials List Available: Yes
Price Category: D

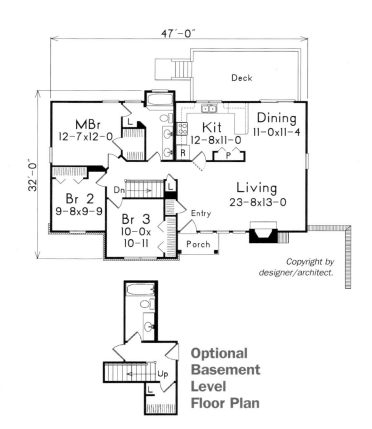

Plan #321024

Dimensions: 47' W x 32' D

Levels: 1

Square Footage: 1,403

Bedrooms: 3

Bathrooms: 1-2

Foundation: Daylight basement

Materials List Available: Yes

Price Category: B

Images provided by designer/architect.

Optional Basement Level Floor Plan

Copyright by designer/architect.

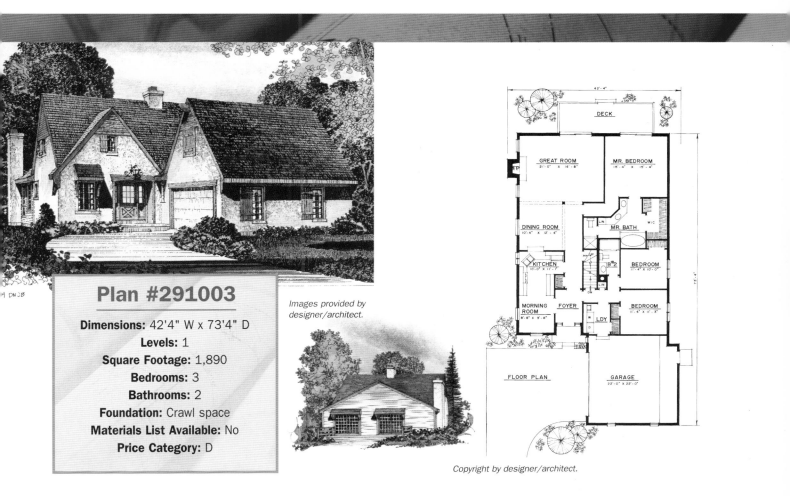

Plan #291003

Dimensions: 42'4" W x 73'4" D

Levels: 1

Square Footage: 1,890

Bedrooms: 3

Bathrooms: 2

Foundation: Crawl space

Materials List Available: No

Price Category: D

Images provided by designer/architect.

Copyright by designer/architect.

Plan #271069

Dimensions: 63'5" W x 51'8" D
Levels: 2
Square Footage: 2,376
Main Level Sq. Ft.: 1,248
Upper Level Sq. Ft.: 1,128
Bedrooms: 4
Bathrooms: 2½
Foundation: Basement, crawl space
Materials List Available: No
Price Category: E

This home's Federal-style facade has a simple elegance that is still popular among today's homeowners.

Features:

- Living Room: This formal space is perfect for serious conversation or thoughtful reflection. Optional double doors would open directly into the family room beyond.

- Dining Room: You won't find a more elegant room than this for hosting holiday feasts.

- Kitchen: This room has everything the cook could hope for—a central island, a handy pantry, and a menu desk. Sliding glass doors in the dinette let you step outside for some fresh air with your cup of coffee.

- Family Room: Here's the spot to spend a cold winter evening. Have hot chocolate in front of a crackling fire!

- Master Suite: With an optional vaulted ceiling, the sleeping chamber is bright and spacious. The private bath showcases a splashy whirlpool tub.

Main Level Floor Plan

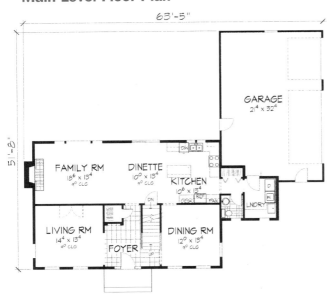

Upper Level Floor Plan

Plan #271080

Dimensions: 71' W x 83' D

Levels: 1

Square Footage: 2,581

Bedrooms: 3

Bathrooms: 3

Foundation: Basement

Materials List Available: Yes

Price Category: E

Images provided by designer/architect.

An open floor plan and beautiful adornments promise comfortable living within this appealing one-story home.

Features:

• **Living Room:** Beyond the sidelighted entry, this spacious living room is bordered on two sides by striking arched openings.

• **Kitchen:** This island kitchen flows into a bayed eating nook, which shares a two-sided fireplace with the living room.

• **Master Suite:** A bright sitting room is a nice feature in this luxurious suite, which is secluded to the rear of the home. The private bath boasts a corner tub, a separate shower, two vanities, and a walk-in closet.

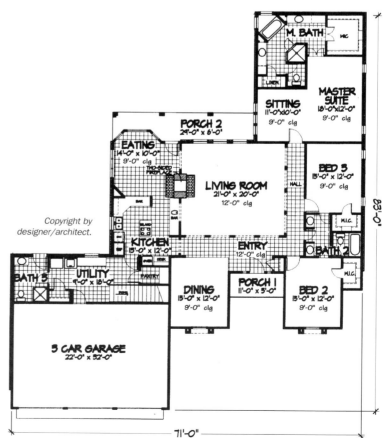

Copyright by designer/architect.

Plan #321077

Dimensions: 55' W x 49'4" D
Levels: 2
Square Footage: 3,169
Main Level Sq. Ft.: 1,679
Upper Level Sq. Ft.: 1,490
Bedrooms: 4
Bathrooms: 2½
Foundation: Basement
Materials List Available: Yes
Price Category: G

Images provided by designer/architect.

You'll love the spacious interior of this gorgeous home, which is built for comfortable family living but includes amenities for gracious entertaining.

Features:

- Entry: This large entry gives a view of the handcrafted staircase to the upper floor.
- Living Room: Angled French doors open into this generously sized room with a vaulted ceiling.
- Family Room: You'll love to entertain in this huge room with a masonry fireplace, built-in entertainment area, gorgeous bay window, and well-fitted wet bar.
- Breakfast Room: A door in the bayed area opens to the outdoor patio for dining convenience.
- Kitchen: The center island provides work space and a snack bar, and the walk-in pantry is a delight.
- Master Suite: Enjoy the vaulted ceiling, two walk-in closets, and luxurious bath in this suite.

Main Level Floor Plan

Upper Level Floor Plan

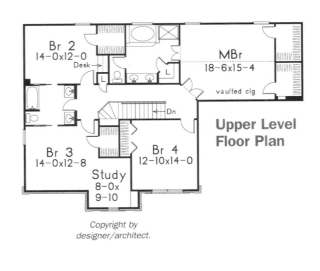

Copyright by designer/architect.

Plan #161010

Dimensions: 50'8" W x 54'2" D
Levels: 1
Square Footage: 1,544
Bedrooms: 3
Bathrooms: 2
Foundation: Basement
Materials List Available: Yes
Price Category: C

Images provided by designer/architect.

Right Side Elevation

Left Side Elevation

Rear Elevation

This one-story home's many distinctive and elegant features—including arched openings and sloped ceilings—will surprise and excite you at every turn.

Features:

- Great Room: Decorative columns frame the entrance from the foyer to this great room and are repeated at the opening to the formal dining area.

- Kitchen: Designed for quick meals or to accommodate an oversized crowd, this kitchen features a curved countertop with seating that functions as a delightful bar.

- Master Bedroom: This master bedroom is split to afford you more privacy and features a compartmented bath that forms a separate vanity area.

- Additional Bedrooms: Take advantage of the double doors off the foyer to allow one bedroom to function as a library.

Covered Porch 16' x 10'

Master Bedroom 12' x 14'

Great Room 16'4" x 18'

Dining 14'2" x 11'8"

Kitchen 14'2" x 8'10"

Bath

Laun.

Two-Car Garage 20' x 20'

Foyer

Library/ Bedroom 10'9" x 11'

Hall

Bath

Bedroom 10' x 11'6"

Porch

Copyright by designer/architect.

Plan #271081

Dimensions: 86' W x 54' D
Levels: 1
Square Footage: 2,539
Bedrooms: 4
Bathrooms: 2
Foundation: Slab
Materials List Available: No
Price Category: E

This traditional home is sure to impress your guests and even your neighbors.

Features:

• **Living Room:** This quiet space off the foyer is perfect for pleasant conversation.

• **Family Room:** A perfect gathering spot, this room is nicely enhanced by a fireplace.

• **Kitchen:** This room easily serves the bayed morning room and the formal dining room.

• **Master Suite:** The master bedroom overlooks a side patio, and boasts a private bath with a skylight and a whirlpool tub.

• **Library:** This cozy room is perfect for curling up with a good novel. It would also make a great extra bedroom.

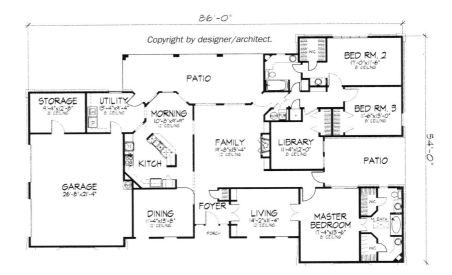

SMARTtip

Determining Curtain Length

Follow length guidelines for foolproof results, but remember that they're not rules. Go ahead and play with curtain and drapery lengths. Instead of shortening long panels at the hem, for instance, take up excess material by blousing them over tiebacks for a pleasing effect.

Plan #151172

Dimensions: 76'10" W x 53'4" D

Levels: 1½

Square Footage: 2,373

Upper Sq. Ft. (Bonus): 776

Bedrooms: 4

Bathrooms: 3

Foundation: Crawl space, slab (basement or daylight basement option for fee)

Materials List Available: Yes

Price Category: E

Main Level Floor Plan

Images provided by designer/architect.

Upper Level Floor Plan

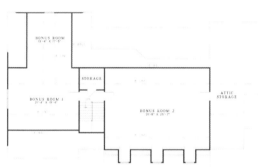

Copyright by designer/architect.

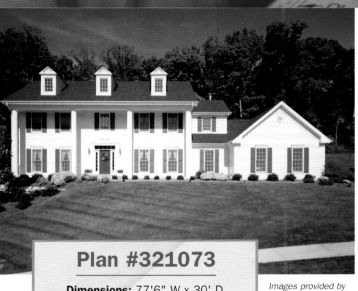

Plan #321073

Dimensions: 77'6" W x 30' D

Levels: 2

Square Footage: 3,216

Main Level Sq. Ft.: 1,834

Upper Level Sq. Ft.: 1,382

Bedrooms: 4

Bathrooms: 4½

Foundation: Basement

Materials List Available: Yes

Price Category: G

Main Level Floor Plan

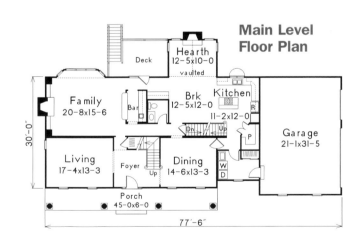

Images provided by designer/architect.

Copyright by designer/architect.

Upper Level Floor Plan

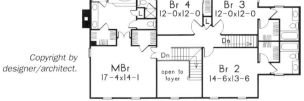

Main Level Floor Plan

61'-0"

49'-4"

Deck

Great Rm
22-1x18-2
vaulted

Brk
10-8x15-1
vaulted

Kit
9-10x12-2

skylts

Bar

Dn

MBr
17-0x16-0

Up Entry

Dining
12-3x12-5

Garage
20-8x20-1

Porch depth 4-0

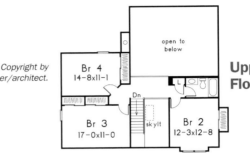

open to below

Br 4
14-8x11-1

Upper Level Floor Plan

Dn

Br 3
17-0x11-0

skylt

Br 2
12-3x12-8

Images provided by designer/architect.

Copyright by designer/architect.

Plan #321072

Dimensions: 61' W x 49'4" D
Levels: 2
Square Footage: 2,618
Main Level Sq. Ft.: 1,804
Upper Level Sq. Ft.: 814
Bedrooms: 4
Bathrooms: 2½
Foundation: Basement
Materials List Available: Yes
Price Category: F

Copyright by designer/architect.

MBR.
13'x14'6"

LIV.
VAULTED CEILING
14'x18'

DIN.
13'6"x11'

KIT.
13'6"x12'

PAN.

BR. #2
11'x11'6"

BR. #3
10'-1 1/8" CEILING
12'x10'6"

E.
VAULTED CEILING

2 CAR GAR.
20'x22'

46'-0"

52'-0"

Plan #221002

Dimensions: 52' W x 46' D
Levels: 1
Square Footage: 1,508
Bedrooms: 3
Bathrooms: 2
Foundation: Basement
Materials List Available: No
Price Category: C

Images provided by designer/architect.

Rear Elevation

Plan #221003

Dimensions: 69' W x 51'4" D

Levels: 1

Square Footage: 1,802

Bedrooms: 3

Bathrooms: 2

Foundation: Basement

Materials List Available: No

Price Category: D

Images provided by designer/architect.

Copyright by designer/architect.

Rear Elevation

Plan #221007

Dimensions: 48' W x 56'4" D

Levels: 1

Square Footage: 1,472

Bedrooms: 3

Bathrooms: 2

Foundation: Basement

Materials List Available: No

Price Category: B

Images provided by designer/architect.

Copyright by designer/architect.

Plan #271082

Dimensions: 71' W x 62' D
Levels: 1
Square Footage: 2,074
Bedrooms: 4
Bathrooms: 2
Foundation: Crawl space or slab
Materials List Available: No
Price Category: D

Magnificent pillars and a huge transom window add stature to the impressive entry of this traditional home.

Features:

• Living Room: A corner fireplace warms this spacious room, which shares a 12-ft. ceiling with the dining room and the kitchen.

• Backyard: A French door provides direct access to a covered porch, which in turn flows into a wide deck and a sunny patio.

• Master Suite: A cathedral ceiling enhances the master bedroom, which offers a large walk-in closet. The private bath is certainly luxurious, with its whirlpool tub and two vanities

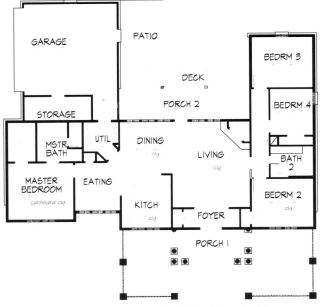

Copyright by designer/architect.

SMARTtip

Making a Cornice

Any new cornice or cornice shelf includes mounting hardware and directions for its installation. But you'll probably need to purchase mounting brackets to install older or homemade cornices. If you're not comfortable with the idea of working on a ladder, especially while handling the cornice and various tools, call a pro. A professional installer will charge a flat rate for coming to your house plus an additional fee for each treatment. Prices vary, but your location, the size of the treatment (measured by the foot), and the difficulty of the job will determine its price.

Plan #271047

Dimensions: 68' W x 47' D

Levels: 2

Square Footage: 2,729

Main Level Sq. Ft.: 1,778

Upper Level Sq. Ft.: 951

Bedrooms: 4

Bathrooms: 2½

Foundation: Basement

Materials List Available: No

Price Category: F

Constructed of materials chosen with your health in mind, this two-story home promises to pamper your body and soul.

Features:

- Great Room: Not only does this room host a media nook and a two-story ceiling, it also includes a sealed gas fireplace for zero emissions.

- Kitchen: Here, cultured-marble countertops replace traditional pressed-wood and laminate.

- Master Suite: Here's a lovely retreat. A tray ceiling, cavernous walk-in closet, and private bath are just the beginning.

- Air Safety: A radon-detection system and exhaust fan in the garage help to eliminate airborne irritants. Tile floors replace carpet in much of the home, too.

Images provided by designer/architect.

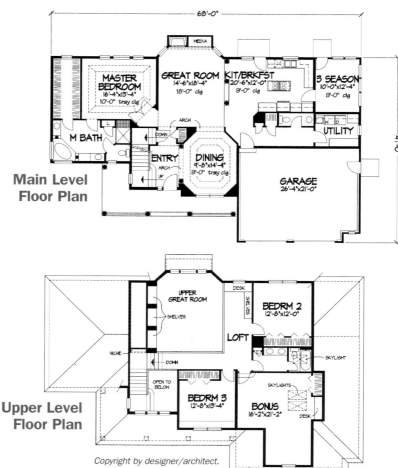

Main Level Floor Plan

Upper Level Floor Plan

Copyright by designer/architect.

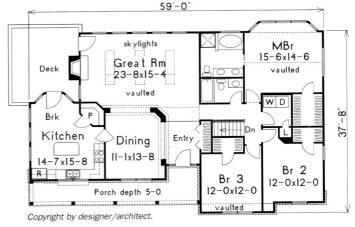

Copyright by designer/architect.

Plan #321010

Dimensions: 59' W x 37'8" D
Levels: 1
Square Footage: 1,787
Bedrooms: 3
Bathrooms: 2
Foundation: Basement
Materials List Available: Yes
Price Category: C

Images provided by designer/architect.

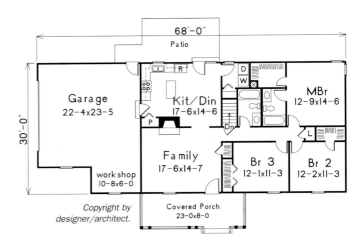

Copyright by designer/architect.

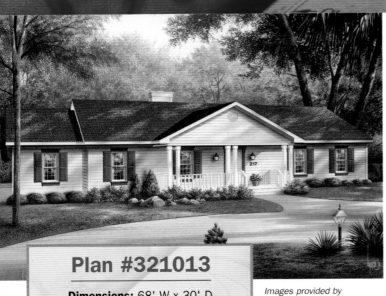

Plan #321013

Dimensions: 68' W x 30' D
Levels: 1
Square Footage: 1,360
Bedrooms: 3
Bathrooms: 2
Foundation: Basement
Materials List Available: Yes
Price Category: B

Images provided by designer/architect.

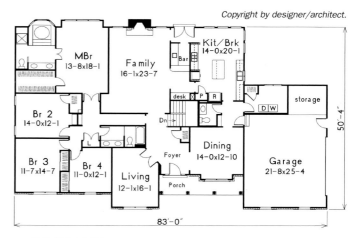

Copyright by designer/architect.

Plan #321011

Dimensions: 83' W x 50'4" D
Levels: 1
Square Footage: 2,874
Bedrooms: 4
Bathrooms: 2½
Foundation: Basement
Materials List Available: Yes
Price Category: F

Images provided by designer/architect.

SMARTtip

Drilling for Kitchen Plumbing

Drill holes for plumbing and waste lines before installing the cabinets. It is easier to work when the cabinets are out in the middle of the floor, and there is no danger of knocking them out of alignment when creating the holes if they are not screwed to the wall studs or one another yet.

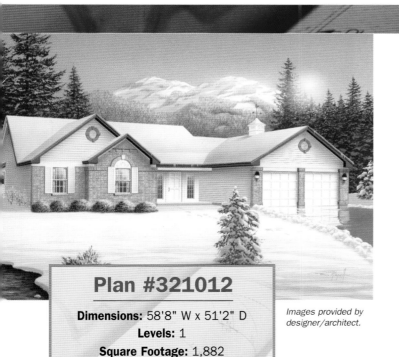

Plan #321012

Dimensions: 58'8" W x 51'2" D
Levels: 1
Square Footage: 1,882
Bedrooms: 3
Bathrooms: 2
Foundation: Basement
Materials List Available: Yes
Price Category: D

Images provided by designer/architect.

Copyright by designer/architect.

Plan #151009

Dimensions: 44' W x 86'2" D
Levels: 1
Square Footage: 1,601
Bedrooms: 3
Bathrooms: 2
Foundation: Crawl, slab
Materials List Available: Yes
Price Category: C

This can be the perfect home for a site with views you can enjoy in all seasons and at all times.

Features:

- Porches: Enjoy the front porch with its 10-ft. ceiling and the more private back porch where you can set up a grill or just get away from it all.

- Foyer: With a 10-ft. ceiling, this foyer opens to the great room for a warm welcome.

- Great Room: Your family will love the media center and the easy access to the rear porch.

- Kitchen: This well-designed kitchen is open to the dining room and the breakfast nook, which also opens to the rear porch.

- Master Suite: The bedroom has a 10-ft. boxed ceiling and a door to the rear. The bath includes a corner whirlpool tub with glass block windows.

- Bedrooms: Bedroom 2 has a vaulted ceiling, while bedroom 3 features a built-in desk.

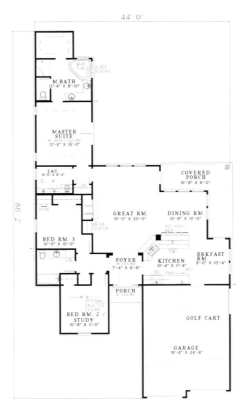

Copyright by designer/architect.

SMARTtip

Fertilizing Your Grass

Fertilizers contain nutrients balanced for different kinds of growth. The ratio of nutrients is indicated on the package by three numbers (for example, 10-10-10). The first specifies nitrogen content; the second, phosphorus; and the third, potash.

Nitrogen helps grass blades to grow and improves the quality and thickness of the turf. Fertilizers contain up to 30 percent nitrogen.

Phosphorus helps grass to develop a healthy root system. It also speeds up the maturation process of the plant.

Potash helps grass stay healthy by providing amino acids and proteins to the plants.

Plan #131003

Dimensions: 60' W x 39'10" D
Levels: 1
Square Footage: 1,466
Bedrooms: 3
Bathrooms: 2
Foundation: Basement, crawl space, or slab
Materials List Available: Yes
Price Category: B

Victorian styling adds elegance to this compact and easy-to-maintain ranch design.

Features:

- Ceiling Height: 8 ft.

- Foyer: Bridging between the front door and the great room, this foyer is a surprise feature.

- Great Room: A 10-ft. ceiling adds to the spacious feeling of this room, while the corner fireplace gives it an intimate feeling. Sliding glass doors at the rear of the room open to the backyard.

- Dining Room: This formal room adjoins the great room, allowing guests and family to flow between the rooms.

- Breakfast Room: Turrets add a Victorian feeling to this room that's just off the kitchen and overlooks the front porch.

- Master Suite: Privacy is assured in this suite, which is separated from the main part of the house. A compartmented bath and large walk-in closet add convenience to its beauty.

Images provided by designer/architect.

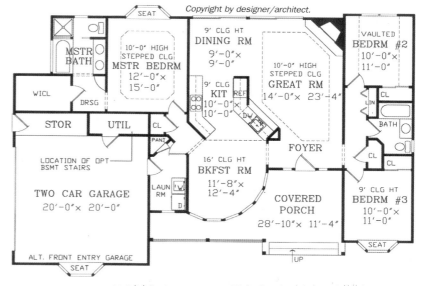

Copyright by designer/architect.

Breakfast Room

Plan #321071

Dimensions: 66' W x 40' D
Levels: 2
Square Footage: 2,411
Main Level Sq. Ft.: 1,293
Upper Level Sq. Ft.: 1,118
Bedrooms: 3
Bathrooms: 2½
Foundation: Basement, crawl space, or slab
Materials List Available: Yes
Price Category: E

The classic exterior of this spacious home is well complemented by the clean lines and elegant features of the interior design.

Features:

- Foyer: Situated between the living and dining rooms, the two-story foyer has a vaulted ceiling.

- Family Room: A wet bar and fireplace flanked by built-in shelves make this an ideal gathering spot.

- Breakfast Room: Enjoy the sunshine in this well-placed room, or step outside to the adjacent deck.

- Kitchen: Designed for a cook, the kitchen is marked by generous counters and cabinets. A large pantry and laundry room are adjacent to it.

- Study: Convert this room to a bedroom, media room, or craft and sewing area if you wish.

- Master Suite: The walk-in closet, oversized tub, separate shower, and double vanity make this private area luxurious.

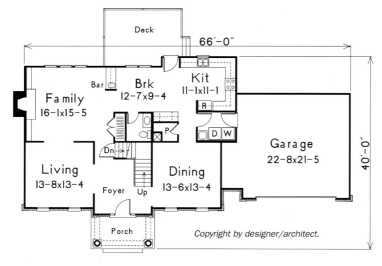

Copyright by designer/architect.

Main Level Floor Plan

Upper Level Floor Plan

Plan #101022

Dimensions: 66'2" W x 62' D

Levels: 1

Square Footage: 1,992

Bedrooms: 3

Bathrooms: 3

Foundation: Basement, crawl space, or slab

Materials List Available: Yes

Price Category: D

Images provided by designer/architect.

The exterior of this lovely home is traditional, but the unusually shaped rooms and amenities are contemporary.

Features:

- Foyer: The two-story foyer is open to the family room, but columns divide it from the dining room.

- Family Room: A gas fireplace and TV niche, flanked by doors to the covered porch, sit at the rear of this seven-sided, spacious room.

- Breakfast Room: Set off from the family room by columns, this area shares a snack bar with the kitchen and has windows looking over the porch.

- Bedroom 3: Use this room for a living room if you wish, and transform the guest room to a media room or a family bedroom.

- Master Suite: The bedroom features a tray ceiling, has his and her dressing areas, and opens to the porch. The bath has a large corner tub, a separate shower, linen closet, and two vanities.

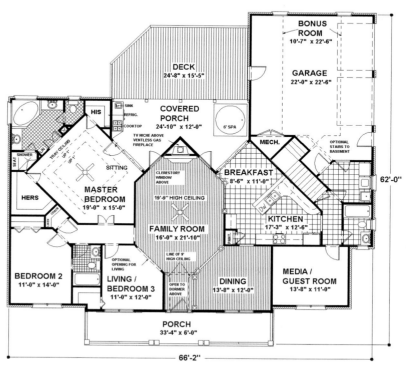

Copyright by designer/architect.

Plan #161015

Dimensions: 55'4" W x 40'4" D
Levels: 2
Square Footage: 1,768
Main Level Sq. Ft.: 960
Upper Level Sq. Ft.: 808
Bedrooms: 3
Bathrooms: 2½
Foundation: Basement
Materials List Available: No
Price Category: C

Images provided by designer/architect.

One look at this dramatic exterior—a 12-ft. high entry with a transom and sidelights, multiple gables, and an impressive box window—you'll fall in love with this home.

Features:

- **Foyer:** This 2-story area announces the grace of this home to everyone who enters it.

- **Great Room:** A natural gathering spot, this room is sunken to set it off from the rest of the house. The 12-ft. ceiling adds a spacious feeling, and the access to the rear porch makes it ideal for friends and family.

- **Kitchen:** The kids will enjoy the snack bar and you'll love the adjoining breakfast room with its access to the rear porch.

- **Master Suite:** A whirlpool in the master bath and walk-in closets in the bedroom spell luxury.

- **Laundry Area:** Two large closets are so handy that you'll wonder how you ever did without them.

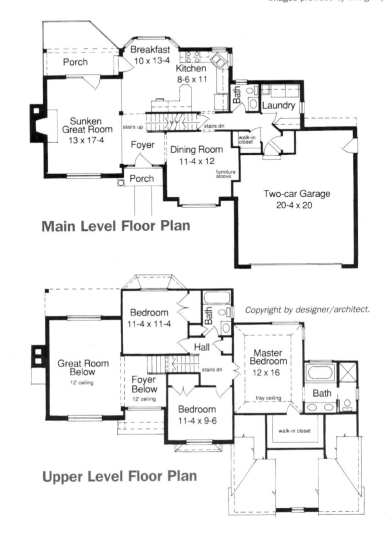

Main Level Floor Plan

Copyright by designer/architect.

Upper Level Floor Plan

Plan #161018

Dimensions: 74'4" W x 69'11" D
Levels: 2
Square Footage: 2,816
+ 325 Sq. Ft. bonus room
Main Level Sq. Ft.: 2,231
Upper Level Sq. Ft.: 624
Bedrooms: 3
Bathrooms: 3 full, 2 half
Foundation: Basement
Materials List Available: No
Price Category: F

Images provided by designer/architect.

If you love classic European designs, look closely at this home with its multiple gables and countless conveniences and luxuries.

Features:

- **Foyer:** Open to the great room, the 2-story foyer offers a view all the way to the rear windows.

- **Great Room:** A fireplace makes this room cozy in any kind of weather.

- **Kitchen:** This large room features an island with a sink, and an angled wall with French doors to the back yard.

- **Dining Room:** The furniture alcove and raised ceiling make this room both formal and practical.

- **Master Suite:** You'll love the quiet in the bedroom and the luxuries—a whirlpool tub, separate shower, and double vanities—in the bath.

- **Basement:** The door from the basement to the side yard adds convenience to outdoor work.

Rear View

Main Level Floor Plan

Porch

Patio

Breakfast
13' x 10'5"

Laun.

Bath

Hall

Kitchen
17' x 13'2"

Great Room
19'4" x 17'9"

Master Bedroom
13'8" x 17'9"

Garage
21'10" x 32'4"

Dining Room
13' x 12'9"

Foyer

Hall

Bath

Porch

Bath

Dressing

69'-11"

74'-4"

2192 Sq. Ft.

Upper Level Floor Plan

Bedroom
13' x 13'11"

Bath

Bonus Room
16'8" x 15

Balcony

Great Room
Below

Bedroom
13' x 13'4"

949 Sq. Ft.

Copyright by designer/architect.

Foyer/Dining Room

Plan #271028

Dimensions: 48' W x 39'6" D

Levels: 2

Square Footage: 2,335

Main Level Sq. Ft.: 1,168

Upper Level Sq. Ft.: 1,167

Bedrooms: 4

Bathrooms: 2½

Foundation: Daylight basement

Materials List Available: Yes

Price Category: E

Images provided by designer/architect.

Main Level Floor Plan

Upper Level Floor Plan

Copyright by designer/architect.

Plan #271097

Dimensions: 60' W x 42' D

Levels: 2

Square Footage: 1,645

Main Level Sq. Ft.: 1,136

Upper Level Sq. Ft.: 509

Bedrooms: 3

Bathrooms: 2

Foundation: Basement

Materials List Available: No

Price Category: C

Images provided by designer/architect.

Main Level Floor Plan

Upper Level Floor Plan

Copyright by designer/architect.

Main Level Floor Plan

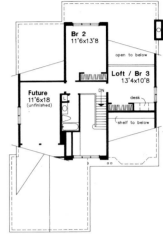

Upper Level Floor Plan

Copyright by designer/architect.

Plan #271040

Dimensions: 44' W x 66'8" D

Levels: 2

Square Footage: 2,272

Main Level Sq. Ft.: 1,750

Upper Level Sq. Ft.: 522

Bedrooms: 3

Bathrooms: 2½

Foundation: Basement

Materials List Available: Yes

Price Category: E

Images provided by designer/architect.

Plan #271058

Dimensions: 68' W x 53' D

Levels: 2

Square Footage: 2,924

Main Level Sq. Ft.: 1,579

Upper Level Sq. Ft.: 1,345

Bedrooms: 3

Bathrooms: 2½

Foundation: Daylight basement

Materials List Available: No

Price Category: F

Images provided by designer/architect.

Main Level Floor Plan

Upper Level Floor Plan

Copyright by designer/architect.

Plan #271073

Dimensions: 69' W x 56' D

Levels: 1

Square Footage: 1,920

Bedrooms: 3

Bathrooms: 2

Foundation: Daylight basement

Materials List Available: No

Price Category: B

Images provided by designer/architect.

A great floor plan and plenty of space make this home perfect for people who welcome family members back home to visit.

Features:

- Great Room: This vaulted space shares a see-through fireplace with a cozy hearth room.

- Kitchen: An angled island and a step-in pantry are the highlights of this room.

- Study: Double doors introduce this versatile space, which shows off a nice bay window.

- Master Suite: Double doors lead to the bedroom. The private bath hosts a whirlpool tub and a separate shower.

- Basement: This level contains more bedrooms and family spaces for visiting relatives.

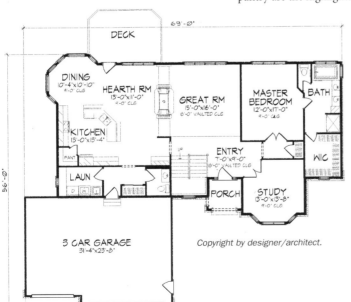

Copyright by designer/architect.

Basement Level Floor Plan

Plan #161022

Dimensions: 52'10" W x 38'2" D
Levels: 2
Square Footage: 1,898
Main Level Sq. Ft.: 1,065
Upper Level Sq. Ft.: 833
Bedrooms: 3
Bathrooms: 2½
Foundation: Basement
Materials List Available: No
Price Category: D

A covered porch and boxed window add to the charm of the stone exterior of this home.

Features:

- **Great Room:** This sunken room can be warmed by a fireplace on winter days and chilly evenings, and lit by natural light flowing through the bank of windows on the rear wall.

- **Kitchen:** You'll love the companionship that the snack bar in the kitchen naturally encourages. A large pantry in this area gives you ample storage space and helps to keep you organized.

- **Breakfast Room:** Quiet elegance marks this room with its sloped ceiling and arched windows that look out into the rear yard.

- **Master Suite:** Enjoy the vaulted ceiling and bath with a whirlpool tub.

- **Extra Spaces:** A loft on the second floor and a bonus room allow endless possibilities in this comfortable home.

Rear Elevation

Main Level Floor Plan

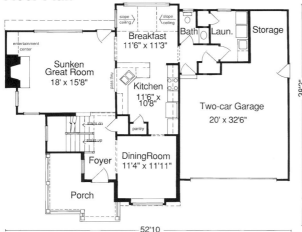

Upper Level Floor Plan

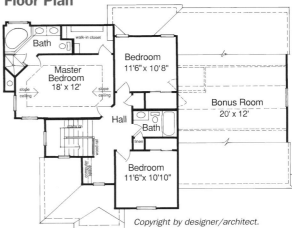

Plan #221008

Dimensions: 60'4" W x 46' D

Levels: 1

Square Footage: 1,540

Bedrooms: 3

Bathrooms: 2

Foundation: Basement

Materials List Available: Yes

Price Category: C

Images provided by designer/architect.

Copyright by designer/architect.

Rear Elevation

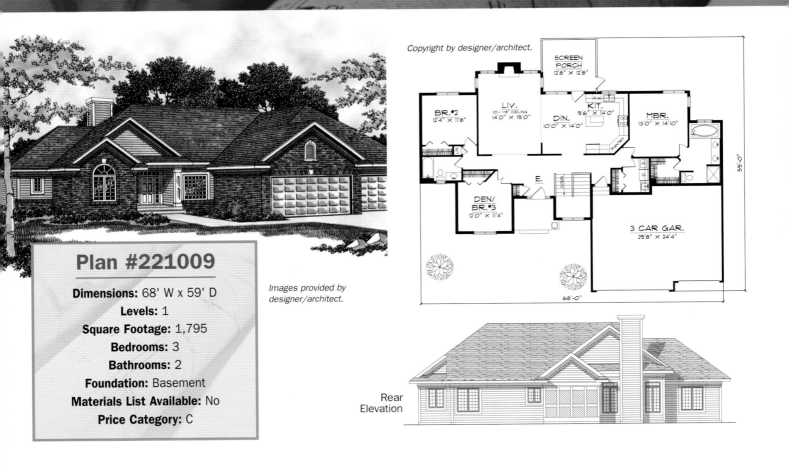

Plan #221009

Dimensions: 68' W x 59' D

Levels: 1

Square Footage: 1,795

Bedrooms: 3

Bathrooms: 2

Foundation: Basement

Materials List Available: No

Price Category: C

Images provided by designer/architect.

Copyright by designer/architect.

Rear Elevation

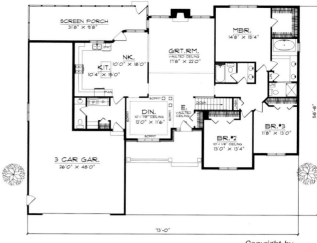

Plan #221010

Dimensions: 73' W x 58'8" D

Levels: 1

Square Footage: 2,196

Bedrooms: 3

Bathrooms: 2½

Foundation: Basement

Materials List Available: Yes

Price Category: D

Images provided by designer/architect.

Copyright by designer/architect.

Rear Elevation

Plan #221011

Dimensions: 59' W x 58' D

Levels: 1

Square Footage: 1,756

Bedrooms: 3

Bathrooms: 2

Foundation: Basement

Materials List Available: No

Price Category: C

Images provided by designer/architect.

Copyright by designer/architect.

Rear Elevation

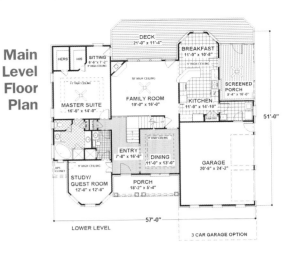

Main Level Floor Plan

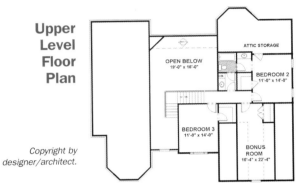

Upper Level Floor Plan

Images provided by designer/architect.

Copyright by designer/architect.

Plan #101017

Dimensions: 57' W x 51' D

Levels: 2

Square Footage: 2,253

Main Level Sq. Ft.: 1,719

Upper Level Sq. Ft.: 247

Bedrooms: 4

Bathrooms: 2½

Foundation: Basement

Materials List Available: No

Price Category: E

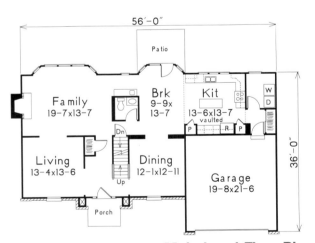

Main Level Floor Plan

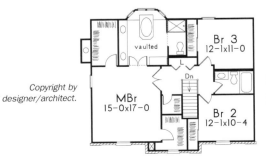

Upper Level Floor Plan

Images provided by designer/architect.

Copyright by designer/architect.

Plan #321069

Dimensions: 56' W x 36' D

Levels: 2

Square Footage: 2,401

Main Level Sq. Ft.: 1,355

Upper Level Sq. Ft.: 1,046

Bedrooms: 3

Bathrooms: 2½

Foundation: Basement, crawl space, or slab

Materials List Available: Yes

Price Category: E

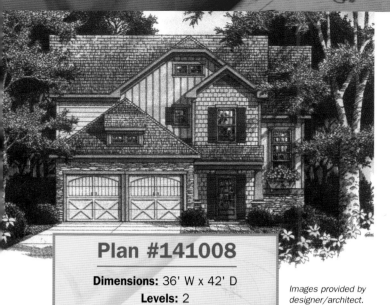

Plan #141008

Dimensions: 36' W x 42' D

Levels: 2

Square Footage: 1,577

Main Level Sq. Ft.: 737

Upper Level Sq. Ft.: 840

Bedrooms: 3

Bathrooms: 2½

Foundation: Slab, basement

Materials List Available: No

Price Category: C

Images provided by designer/architect.

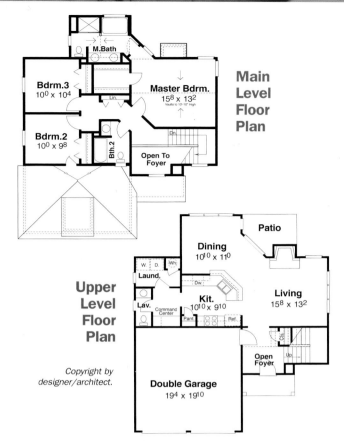

Main Level Floor Plan

Upper Level Floor Plan

Copyright by designer/architect.

Plan #321067

Dimensions: 70' W x 40' D

Levels: 2

Square Footage: 2,505

Main Level Sq. Ft.: 1,436

Upper Level Sq. Ft.: 1,069

Bedrooms: 3

Bathrooms: 2½

Foundation: Basement, crawl space

Materials List Available: Yes

Price Category: E

Images provided by designer/architect.

Main Level Floor Plan

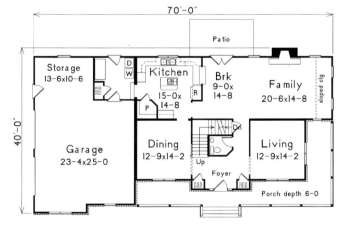

Upper Level Floor Plan

Copyright by designer/architect.

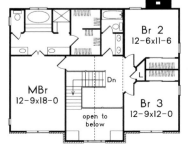

Plan #131005

Dimensions: 70' W x 37'4" D
Levels: 1
Square Footage: 1,595
Bedrooms: 3
Bathrooms: 2
Foundation: Basement, crawl space, or slab
Materials List Available: Yes
Price Category: D

SMARTtip

Create a Courtyard

Create a private walled-garden retreat with fences covered by climbing vines. Add height with trellises, and divide spaces with clipped boxwood hedges. Include an (almost) instant patio by digging away an area of sod and then covering it with a layer of sand and landscaping mesh to discourage weeds. Then cover it with pea gravel, and add a garden bench, statuary, and perhaps an antique or two. The result? European ambiance for even the most nondescript suburban yard.

Images provided by designer/architect.

With the finest features of an open design in the main living areas, this home gives privacy where you need it. Best of all, it's wheelchair accessible.

Features:

- **Foyer:** A high ceiling gives this area real presence and serves to blend it seamlessly with the great room and the dining room.

- **Great Room:** The open design allows you to use this room as an extension of the dining room or, if you wish, furnish it to create a private reading nook or visually separate media center.

- **Breakfast Room:** Both this room and the adjacent well-appointed kitchen flow into the rest of the living area. However, access to the rear porch, where you can sit out and enjoy the weather while you eat, distinguishes this room.

- **Master Suite:** Located in the same wing as the other bedrooms, this suite has a separate entrance and features a vaulted ceiling, three closets, and a compartmented bath.

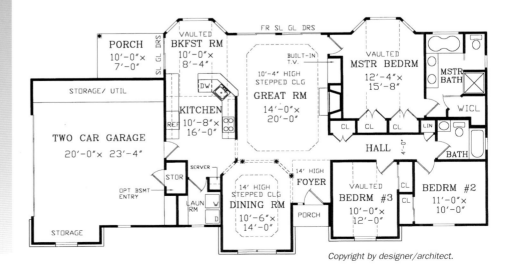

Copyright by designer/architect.

Foyer

Dining Room

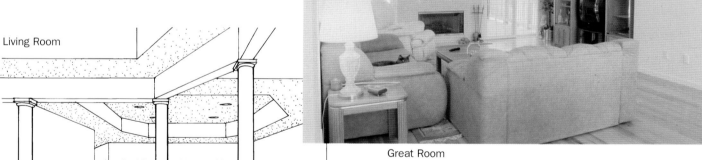

Great Room

Living Room

SMARTtip
Natural Trellis

Create a natural rustic trellis that might even, if growing conditions are right, produce its own pretty blooms. Cut and place saplings in the ground as uprights. Then weave old grapevines with smaller saplings for the lattice.

Plan #321006

Dimensions: 76' W x 45' D
Levels: 1, optional lower
Square Footage: 1,977
**Optional Basement Level
Sq. Ft.:** 1,416
Bedrooms: 4
Bathrooms: 2½
Foundation: Basement
Materials List Available: Yes
Price Category: D

Images provided by designer/architect.

Optional Basement Level Floor Plan

Copyright by designer/architect.

Plan #321007

Dimensions: 76' W x 55'2" D
Levels: 1
Square Footage: 2,695
Bedrooms: 3
Bathrooms: 2½
Foundation: Basement
Materials List Available: Yes
Price Category: F

Images provided by designer/architect.

Copyright by designer/architect.

SMARTtip

Decorative Poles

Drapery poles are supported by the brackets fastened to the window frame or wall. The brackets that are provided with the poles generally coordinate and blend in with the pole finish. Brackets can be simple but also decorative. If you opt for a spectacular, attention-grabbing bracket, consider choosing less showy finials for the ends of the pole.

Plan #101023

Dimensions: 52' W x 42' D

Levels: 1

Square Footage: 1,197

Bedrooms: 3

Bathrooms: 2

Foundation: Crawl space, or slab

Materials List Available: No

Price Category: B

Images provided by designer/architect.

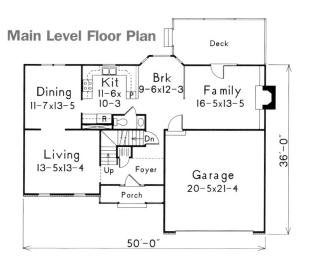

Copyright by designer/architect.

OPTIONAL BAY

MASTER BEDROOM 14 x 12

FAMILY ROOM 14 x 16

DINING

VAULT

PLANT SHELF

KIT.

D W

VAULT

BEDROOM 12 x 11

BEDROOM 12 x 11

GARAGE 19 x 20

42

52

Plan #321068

Dimensions: 50' W x 36' D

Levels: 2

Square Footage: 2,058

Main Level Sq. Ft.: 1,098

Upper Level Sq. Ft.: 960

Bedrooms: 3

Bathrooms: 2½

Foundation: Basement, crawl space, or slab

Materials List Available: Yes

Price Category: D

Images provided by designer/architect.

Main Level Floor Plan

Deck

Dining 11-7x13-5

Kit 11-6x 10-3

Brk 9-6x12-3

Family 16-5x13-5

R

Dn

Living 13-5x13-4

Up

Foyer

Garage 20-5x21-4

Porch

36'-0"

50'-0"

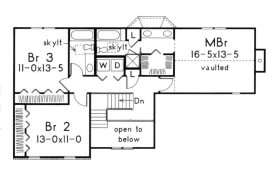

Upper Level Floor Plan

Copyright by designer/architect.

skylt

Br 3 11-0x13-5

skylt

W D

L

L

MBr 16-5x13-5 vaulted

Dn

Br 2 13-0x11-0

open to below

Plan #101004

Dimensions: 55'8" W x 56'6" D

Levels: 1

Square Footage: 1,787

Bedrooms: 3

Bathrooms: 2

Foundation: Slab, crawl space, basement

Materials List Available: No

Price Category: C

This carefully designed ranch provides the feel and features of a much larger home.

Features:

- Ceiling Height: 9 ft. unless otherwise noted.

- Foyer: Guests will step up onto the inviting front porch and into this foyer, with its impressive 11-ft. ceiling.

- Dining Room: Open to the entry and to its left is this elegant dining room, perfect for entertaining or informal family gatherings.

- Family Room: This family gathering place features an 11-ft. ceiling to enhance its sense of spaciousness.

- Kitchen: This intelligently designed kitchen has an open plan. A breakfast bar and a serving bar are features that add to its convenience.

- Master Suite: This suite is loaded with amenities, including a double-step tray ceiling, direct access to the screened porch, a sitting room, deluxe bath, and his and her walk-in closets.

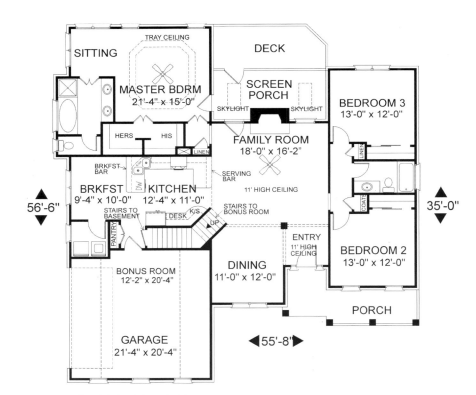

Copyright by designer/architect.

Images provided by designer/architect.

Plan #101016

Dimensions: 31'2" W x 42' D
Levels: 2
Square Footage: 1,985
Main Level Sq. Ft.: 1,009
Upper Level Sq. Ft.: 976
Bedrooms: 3
Bathrooms: 2½
Foundation: Slab, crawl space, or basement
Materials List Available: No
Price Category: D

This delightful Victorian-style home has a compact footprint that is perfect for narrow lots.

Features:

• Ceiling Height: 9 ft. unless otherwise noted.

• Family Room: From the entry you'll step into this inviting family room. Family and friends alike will be drawn to the room's warming fireplace. A set of French doors leads out to a porch.

• Dining Room: Pass through another set of French doors from the family room into this elegant dining room.

• Deck: Yet another set of French doors from the living room lead to this enormous deck.

• Kitchen: Food preparation will be a pleasure, thanks to the 3-ft. x 5-ft. island that you'll find in this bright and airy open kitchen.

• Breakfast Area: This bayed breakfast area has a fourth set of French doors that leads to the deck.

• Master Suite: This master bedroom has a 9-ft.-6-in. tray ceiling and a 7-ft. x 11-ft. walk-in closet.

Main Level Floor Plan

DECK
30'-6" x 11'-7"

BRKFST

KITCHEN
15'-0" x 17'-0"

DINING
14'-8" x 12'-8"

UP

ENTRY
7'-11" x 15'-6"

FAMILY
18'-8" x 16'-0"

COATS

PORCH
30'-6" x 7'-7"

42'-0"

◄ 31'-2" ►

Upper Level Floor Plan

TRAY CEILING

MASTER BDRM
16'-4" x 15'-0"

D W

DN

BEDROOM 2
12'-0" x 12'-8"

BEDROOM 3
12'-8" x 12'-0"

WINDOW SEAT

Copyright by designer/architect.

Plan #161024

Dimensions: 54'4" W x 26'8" D
Levels: 2
Square Footage: 1,698
Main Level Sq. Ft.: 868
Upper Level Sq. Ft.: 830
Bonus Space Sq. Ft.: 269
Bedrooms: 3
Bathrooms: 2½
Foundation: Basement
Materials List Available: No
Price Category: C

The covered porch, dormers, and center gable that grace the exterior let you know how comfortable your family will be in this home.

Features:

- **Great Room:** Walk from windows overlooking the front porch to a door into the rear yard in this spacious room, which runs the width of the house.

- **Dining Room:** Adjacent to the great room, the dining area gives your family space to spread out and makes it easy to entertain a large group.

- **Kitchen:** Designed for efficiency, the kitchen area includes a large pantry.

- **Master Suite:** Tucked away on the second floor, the master suite features a walk-in closet in the bedroom and a luxurious attached bathroom.

- **Bonus Room:** Finish the 269-sq.-ft. area over the 2-bay garage as a guest room, study, or getaway for the kids.

Images provided by designer/architect.

Main Level Floor Plan

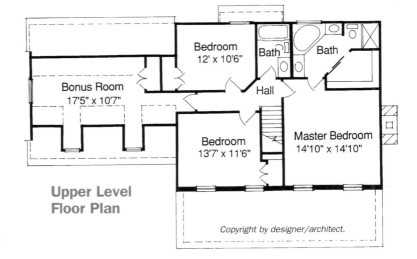

Upper Level Floor Plan

Copyright by designer/architect.

Plan #161025

Dimensions: 63'4" W x 48' D
Levels: 2
Square Footage: 2,738
Main Level Sq. Ft.: 1,915
Upper Level Sq. Ft.: 823
Bedrooms: 4
Bathrooms: 3½
Foundation: Basement
Materials List Available: No
Price Category: F

Images provided by designer/architect.

One look at the octagonal tower, boxed window, and wood-and-stone trim, and you'll know how much your family will love this home.

Features:

- **Foyer:** View the high windows across the rear wall, a fireplace, and open stairs as you come in.
- **Great Room:** Gather in this two-story-high area.
- **Hearth Room:** Open to the breakfast room, it's close to both the kitchen and dining room.
- **Kitchen:** A snack bar and an island make the kitchen ideal for family living.
- **Master Suite:** You'll love the 9-ft. ceiling in the bedroom and 11-ft. ceiling in the sitting area. The bath has a whirlpool tub, double-bowl vanity, and walk-in closet.
- **Upper Level:** A balcony leads to a bedroom with a private bath and 2 other rooms with private access to a shared bath.

Main Level Floor Plan

Upper Level Floor Plan

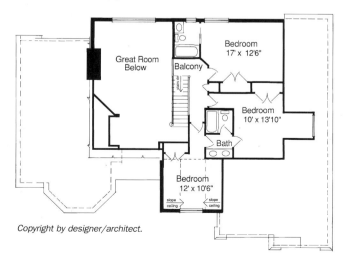

Copyright by designer/architect.

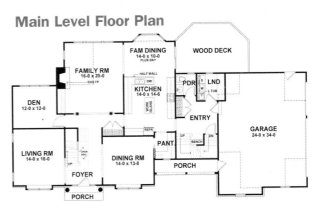

Main Level Floor Plan

WOOD DECK

FAM DINING
14-0 x 10-0
PLUS BAY

HALF WALL

FAMILY RM
16-0 x 20-0
GAS FP

DEN
12-0 x 12-0

KITCHEN
14-0 x 14-6
WORK ISLAND

PDR

LND
L TUB

ENTRY

GARAGE
24-0 x 34-0

REFR

UP

DN

PANT

BENCH

LIVING RM
14-0 x 16-0

DINING RM
14-0 x 13-8

OPEN ABV

FOYER

PORCH

PORCH

Images provided by designer/architect.

Upper Level Floor Plan

Copyright by designer/architect.

ROOF

M BEDRM
14-6 x 20-0

WPOOL TUB

M BATH

SHWR

BEDRM 2
14-0 x 12-0

BATH 2

HALL

BALC

RAILING

BONUS RM
AREA: 571 SQ FT

BEDRM 3
14-0 x 12-4

BALC

BUILT INS SEAT

LINEN

SHWR

BEDRM 4
14-0 x 13-0

BATH 3

ROOF

ROOF

Rear Elevation

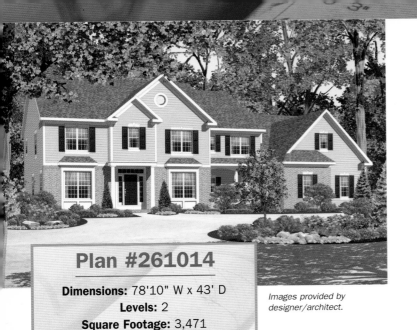

Plan #261014

Dimensions: 78'10" W x 43' D

Levels: 2

Square Footage: 3,471

Main Level Sq. Ft.: 1,873

Upper Level Sq. Ft.: 1,598

Bedrooms: 4

Bathrooms: 3½

Foundation: Basement

Materials List Available: No

Price Category: G

Plan #261013

Dimensions: 81'8" W x 34' D

Levels: 2

Square Footage: 3,193

Main Level Sq. Ft.: 1,735

Upper Level Sq. Ft.: 1,458

Bedrooms: 4

Bathrooms: 3½

Foundation: Basement

Materials List Available: No

Price Category: G

Main Level Floor Plan

WOOD DECK

SCREENED PORCH
12-0 x 12-0

Copyright by designer/architect.

KITCHEN
12-0 x 15-10

DW

DEN
13-0 x 12-0

DINETTE
11-4 x 15-10

OPT BUILT INS

FAMILY RM
21-6 x 16-0

GAS FP

REFR

GARAGE
24-0 x 34-0

ENTRY

BENCH

DN

PANTRY

DN

LANDING

DINING RM
14-0 x 16-2

FOYER
OPEN ABV

LIVING RM
14-0 x 16-0

L TUB

PDR

LND

PORCH

UP

PORCH

Images provided by designer/architect.

Rear Elevation

Upper Level Floor Plan

ROOF

ROOF

SHOWER

WPOOL TUB

BED RM 4
12-8 x 12-0

M BATH

MASTER BED RM
17-8 x 13-8

SHWR

BATH 3

HALL

LANDING

CLOS

BATH 2

SHWR

DN

BED RM 3
14-0 x 12-2

BALCONY

RAILING

BED RM 2
14-0 x 12-8

ROOF

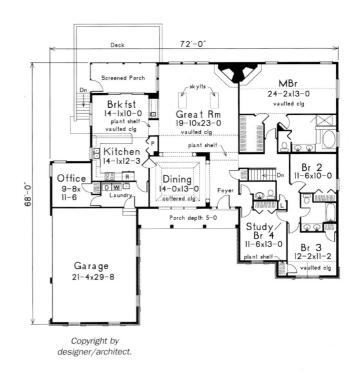

Plan #321027

Dimensions: 72' W x 68' D

Levels: 1

Square Footage: 2,758

Bedrooms: 4

Bathrooms: 2½

Foundation: Basement

Materials List Available: Yes

Price Category: F

Images provided by designer/architect.

Copyright by designer/architect.

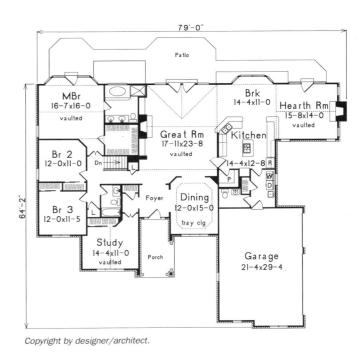

Plan #321028

Dimensions: 79' W x 64'2" D

Levels: 1

Square Footage: 2,723

Bedrooms: 3

Bathrooms: 2½

Foundation: Basement

Materials List Available: Yes

Price Category: F

Images provided by designer/architect.

Copyright by designer/architect.

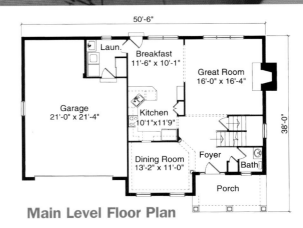

Main Level Floor Plan

Plan #161043

Dimensions: 50'6" W x 38' D
Levels: 2
Square Footage: 1,856
Main Level Sq. Ft.: 980
Upper Level Sq. Ft.: 876
Bedrooms: 3
Bathrooms: 2½
Foundation: Basement
Materials List Available: Yes
Price Category: D

Images provided by designer/architect.

Rear Elevation

Upper Level Floor Plan

Copyright by designer/architect.

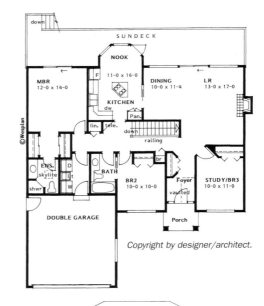

Copyright by designer/architect.

Plan #281009

Dimensions: 46' W x 52' D
Levels: 1
Square Footage: 1,423
Bedrooms: 3
Bathrooms: 2
Foundation: Walk-out basement
Materials List Available: Yes
Price Category: B

Images provided by designer/architect.

Rear Elevation

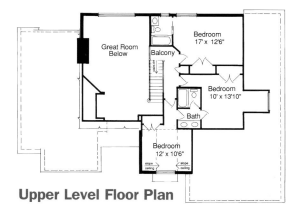

Upper Level Floor Plan

Plan #161041

Dimensions: 63'4" W x 48' D
Levels: 2
Square Footage: 2,738
Main Level Sq. Ft.: 1,915
Upper Level Sq. Ft.: 823
Bedrooms: 4
Bathrooms: 3½
Foundation: Basement
Materials List Available: Yes
Price Category: F

Images provided by designer/architect.

Rear Elevation

Main Level Floor Plan

Copyright by designer/architect.

Plan #321070

Dimensions: 65' W x 37' D
Levels: 2
Square Footage: 2,521
Main Level Sq. Ft.: 1,375
Upper Level Sq. Ft.: 1,146
Bedrooms: 4
Bathrooms: 2½
Foundation: Basement
Materials List Available: Yes
Price Category: E

Images provided by designer/architect.

Main Level Floor Plan

Upper Level Floor Plan

Copyright by designer/architect.

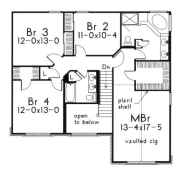

Plan #321078

Dimensions: 71' W x 54'7" D
Levels: 2
Square Footage: 3,368
Main Level Sq. Ft.: 2,150
Upper Level Sq. Ft.: 1,218
Bedrooms: 4
Full Bathrooms: 3
Half Bathrooms: 2
Foundation: Basement
Materials List Available: Yes
Price Category: G

Inside this traditional exterior lies a home filled
with contemporary amenities and design features
that are sure to charm the whole family.

Features:

- Great Room: Relax in this sunken room with a
  cathedral ceiling, wooden beams, skylights, and
  a masonry fireplace.

- Breakfast Room: Octagon-shaped with a domed
  ceiling, this room leads to the outdoor patio.

- Library: Situated for privacy and quiet, this
  room opens from the master bedroom and
  the foyer.

- Kitchen: The central island here adds to the
  ample work and storage space.

- Dining Room: Just off the foyer, this room is
  ideal for formal dinners and quiet times.

- Master Suite: Enjoy the large bedroom and bath
  with a luxurious corner tub, separate shower,
  two vanities, walk-in closet, and dressing area.

Images provided by designer/architect.

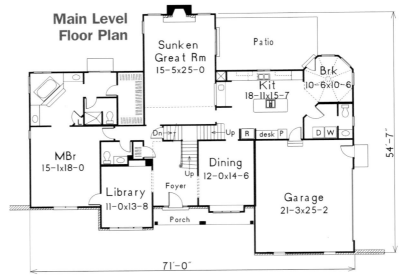

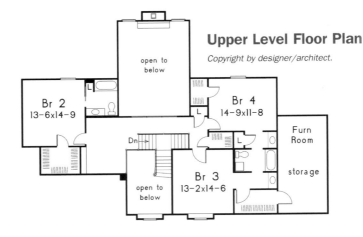

Upper Level Floor Plan

Copyright by designer/architect.

Plan #141010

Dimensions: 43'4" W x 37' D
Levels: 2
Square Footage: 1,765
Main Level Sq. Ft.: 1,210
Upper Level Sq. Ft.: 555
Bedrooms: 3
Bathrooms: 3
Foundation: Basement
Materials List Available: No
Price Category: C

Images provided by designer/architect.

A Palladian window in a stone gable adds a new twist to a classical cottage design.

Features:

- Ceiling Height: 8 ft. unless otherwise noted.

- Living Area: Dormers open into this handsome living area, which is designed to accommodate gatherings of any size.

- Master Suite: This beautiful master bedroom opens off the foyer. It features a modified cathedral ceiling that makes the front Palladian window a focal point inside as well as out. The master bath offers a dramatic cathedral ceiling over the tub and vanity.

- Balcony: U-shaped stairs lead to this elegant balcony, which overlooks the foyer while providing access to two additional bedrooms.

- Garage: This garage is tucked under the house to improve the appearance from the street. It offers two bays for plenty of parking and storage space.

Main Level Floor Plan

Sundeck 15-4 x 12-0
Brkfst. 12-0 x 7-4
Kit. 12-0 x 8-0
Dining 12-0 x 11-10
Living 21-4 x 13-6
M.Bath
Master Bdrm. 15-4 x 13-6
43-4
37-0

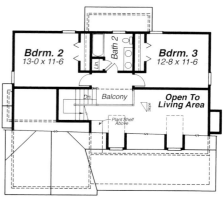

Upper Level Floor Plan

Bdrm. 2 13-0 x 11-6
Bath 2
Bdrm. 3 12-8 x 11-6
Balcony
Open To Living Area

Copyright by designer/architect.

Basement Floor Plan

Storage 14-4 x 11-0
Double Garage 18-2 x 24-8
Future Fin. 13-8 x 13-0

SMARTtip

Stone Tables

Marble- and stone-topped tables with plants are perfect for use in light-filled rooms. Warmed by the sun during the day, the tabletops catch leaf droppings and can stand up to the splatters of watering cans and plant sprayers.

Plan #351011

Dimensions: 73'8" W x 53'2" D

Levels: 1

Square Footage: 2,251

Bedrooms: 3

Bathrooms: 2½

Foundation: Basement, crawl space, or slab

Materials List Available: Yes

Price Category: E

Images provided by designer/architect.

Bonus Room

Copyright by designer/architect.

Plan #211089

Dimensions: 56' W x 61' D

Levels: 2

Square Footage: 1,956

Main Level Sq. Ft.: 1,320

Upper Level Sq. Ft.: 636

Bedrooms: 3 or 4

Bathrooms: 4

Foundation: Slab, crawl space

Materials List Available: Yes

Price Category: D

Images provided by designer/architect.

Copyright by designer/architect.

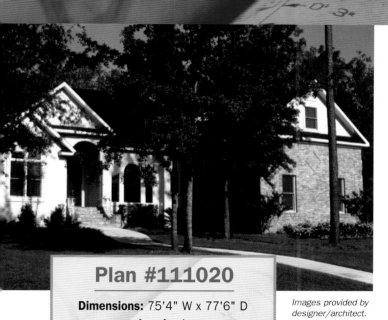

Copyright by
designer/architect.

*Images provided by
designer/architect.*

Plan #111020

Dimensions: 75'4" W x 77'6" D

Levels: 1

Square Footage: 2,987

Bedrooms: 4

Bathrooms: 3

Foundation: Slab

Materials List Available: No

Price Category: F

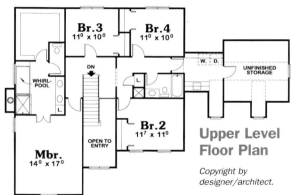

Bonus Area

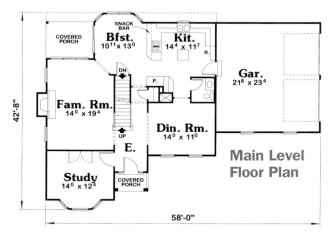

**Main Level
Floor Plan**

**Upper Level
Floor Plan**

Copyright by
designer/architect.

Plan #121097

Dimensions: 58' W x 42'8" D

Levels: 2

Square Footage: 2,417

Main Level Sq. Ft.: 1,162

Upper Level Sq. Ft.: 1,255

Bedrooms: 4

Bathrooms: 2½

Foundation: Basement

Materials List Available: Yes

Price Category: E

*Images
provided by
designer/
architect.*

Plan #161034

Dimensions: 56' W x 53' D
Levels: 2
Square Footage: 2,156
Main Level Sq. Ft.: 1,605
Upper Level Sq. Ft.: 551
Bedrooms: 3
Bathrooms: 2½
Foundation: Basement
Materials List Available: No
Price Category: D

Images provided by designer/architect.

Multiple gables, a covered porch, and circle-topped windows combine to enhance the attractiveness of this exciting home.

Features:

- Great Room: A raised foyer introduces this open combined great room and dining room. Enjoy the efficiency of a dual-sided fireplace that warms both the great room and kitchen.

- Kitchen: The kitchen, designed for easy traffic patterns, offers an abundance of counter space and features a cooktop island.

- Master Suite: This first-floor master suite, separated for privacy, includes twin vanities and a walk-in closet. A deluxe corner bath and walk-in shower complete its luxurious detail.

- Additional Rooms: Two additional bedrooms lead to the second-floor balcony, which overlooks the great room. You can use the optional bonus room as a den or office.

Copyright by designer/architect.

Main Level Floor Plan

Upper Level Floor Plan

Plan #221001

Dimensions: 87' W x 60' D
Levels: 1
Square Footage: 2,600
Bedrooms: 2
Bathrooms: 2½
Foundation: Basement
Materials List Available: No
Price Category: F

Images provided by designer/architect.

Copyright by designer/architect.

You'll love this traditional ranch for its unusual spaciousness and many comfortable amenities.

Features:

- **Great Room:** As you enter the home, you'll have a clear view all the way to the backyard through the many windows in this huge room. Built-ins here provide a practical touch, and the fireplace makes this room cozy when the weather's cool.

- **Kitchen:** This large kitchen has been thoughtfully designed to make cooking a pleasure. It flows into a lovely dining nook, so it's also a great place to entertain.

- **Master Suite:** Relaxing will come naturally in this lovely suite, with its two walk-in closets, private sitting area, and large, sumptuous bathroom that features a Jacuzzi tub.

- **Additional Bedrooms:** Located on the opposite side of the house from the master

Rear Elevation

suite, these bedrooms are both convenient to a full bath. You can use one room as a den if you wish.

Kitchen

Ideas for Master Baths

A master bath is a must-have on any new homebuyer's list of desired features. In fact, some new homes have two of them. One is located on the main level, and another one is upstairs or in another wing of the house. Homeowners know that although today they may prefer the privacy of a master suite that is located away from the main living areas, there may come a time when the accessibility of a centrally located bedroom and bathroom is a necessity. In the meantime, this room is often part of a second master suite that is reserved for visiting friends and family.

What are you looking for? According to a recent survey conducted by the National Association of the Remodeling Industry (NARI), most people want quality personal time today—the kind of serious convenience, comfort, and luxury that a new high-style master bath can provide. A bathroom equipped with personal spa amenities and outfitted in glamorous fixtures and materials offers the level of pampering that people had to leave home to find—until now.

Bathtub styles are numerous today. Here are just a few: cast iron in a wood surround, right top; a whirlpool drop-in, right middle; and a claw-foot reproduction, right bottom.

A trend in master bathroom design is to compartmentalize the space, below, designating separate private or semiprivate areas for bathing, toileting, grooming, and dressing.

Luxurious Personal Haven

Master bathrooms in general have been getting grander in scale and in scope for more than a decade. For some people, a sumptuous bathroom may be a status symbol, but the reality is that contemporary life is hectic, and people are working longer hours, leaving home earlier, and returning later than they used to a generation ago. "Me time" is getting harder to find. For this person, an at-home getaway is the answer.

Top of the Line

At the highest end of the market, everything is designed for the convenience of two people. You don't have to wait your turn when there's both an oversized tub and a separate and spacious walk-in shower at your disposal. Cancel the day spa, because both your bathtub and shower can be outfitted with strategically placed water or air jets designed to relax you or invigorate you, head to toe, with a therapeutic message.

Steam and More. Experts have been touting the health benefits of steam for years, and now many upscale homeowners request a steam-equipped shower or personal sauna to complete their at-home spa. Other luxurious master-bath amenities almost always include a separate toilet compartment (sometimes referred to as a "private toileting room"). Some homeowners also request a bidet.

In addition to two sinks and either a large double-sized vanity or two separate vanities, custom-designed dressing areas that are integrated into the suite (sometimes as the link from bedroom to bathroom) are expanding the concept of the walk-in closet. More than a place to store clothes, a dressing area is practically a room unto itself, except that it has no door. Dressing areas might feature custom cabinetry for clothes and linen storage, an exercise area, media equipment, or even laundry facilities.

Various types of fixtures and bulbs may be part of a high-end custom-designed lighting plan. In addition to general overall lighting and task lighting for applying

Abundant glass and light add drama to a master bathroom. Elevating the tub within a bay of windows makes it the focal point of the room and takes advantage of the view.

makeup, shaving, and hairstyling, upscale bathrooms often feature decorative accent lighting underneath soffits, within coves, and even inside the tub.

High-End Surfacing. Luxurious stone (mostly granite, slate, limestone, or marble in slab or tile form) is the preferred material, although ceramic tile is classic, especially custom or hand-painted versions. Exquisite glass tiles are also desirable because of their wonderful reflective quality. Stone and tile may be appealing to the eye, but they are also cold to the touch, so designers are specifying warming devices such heat lamps over the tub and shower areas, radiant heating systems (under the floor), and toe-kick heaters (under the

vanity) to keep bathers comfortable. Heated towel bars are also becoming a standard amenity in master bathrooms.

If people have fewer hours to relax, they want more from their relaxing experience. One way to do this is by incorporating elements of nature into the environment. Therefore, whenever it is possible, a deluxe master bath is also connected to an outdoor area. This may be small private garden, a deck with an outdoor spa or hot tub, or a pool area. Health-conscious homeowners may also want to make the master bath accessible to a swim spa that is used as part of a daily exercise routine. At the least, glass doors, large windows, skylights, or roof windows will enhance a bath's connection to the outdoors.

Marvelous at Midrange

Want a master bathroom that is as pleasing to your mind and body as it is to your pocketbook? Depending on the size of the room, you may be able fit a separate tub and shower into your layout. Locate a walk-in shower adjacent to the tub, for example. This conserves space and saves money because you don't have to pay to install long lines of plumbing. Using a glass enclosure around the shower compensates for the tight squeeze, keeping the room light and airy.

Another space- and money-saving option is a standard-size whirlpool. But if you prefer a shower and rarely if ever take a bath, eliminate the tub, especially if there is one in another bathroom in the house. Install a larger shower, one with a roomy seat for two, built-in storage nooks, and perhaps a spa feature, such as massage jets or a rainbar. However, you could gain a foot or two if you gave up a closet in an adjacent hallway or another room. Or talk to the builder about bumping out an outside wall a few feet over the foundation.

Also, sometimes it's possible to position a tub, sink, shower, or even a toilet at an

angle. This conserves space and, if planned properly, doesn't require long and expensive lines of plumbing.

Creating Privacy. If you can't accommodate a separate enclosure for the toilet, you may be able to install a partial partition with a half wall. Glass-block or sandblasted-glass walls offer some privacy without closing off the light, as well. If you can

sacrifice the potential storage, you might forego a linen closet if it will be adjacent to a plumbing line.

In a master bathroom with limited space, a double-bowl vanity is a more practical choice than a pair of pedestal sinks because you will need the storage the cabinet will provide. If you like the look of pedestal sinks so much that you're willing to sacrifice storage, try to space them far enough apart so that you can install a slim cabinet between the two. A shelf and a recessed medicine cabinet (deep enough to store an extra roll of toilet paper or a hair dryer) for each sink should compensate for some of the lost storage. When you select the pedestal sinks, look for a style that has a generous deck surrounding the bowl so that there is a landing spot for cosmetics, brushes, and the like when you're grooming. Make sure there's good task lighting in near the sink, even if you've provided adequate general lighting.

Light. Don't overlook natural light in your plans. If privacy demands that you keep windows to a minimum, consider supplementing a single or small window with a skylight or a roof window. The view by day could be magnificent treetops and by night a dramatic skyscape.

In a European-inspired design, left, classical styling extends even to the bidet and toilet. Coordinated hardware and the floor and wall treatments pull the look together.

Building a new Victorian? You can find old, restorable fixtures at a selvage company, or you can buy new ones, left, that are faithful reproductions.

Beadboard paneling, opposite, evokes cottage style. Other elements, such as a gooseneck faucet and cross-handle valves, are new but designed to look vintage.

"In a master bathroom with limited space, a double-bowl vanity is a more practical choice than a pair of pedestal sinks because you will need the storage the cabinet will provide."

Decorate the bathroom with the same commitment to style as you would any other room in the house. Surround a tub with elegant woodwork, above. A trompe l'oeil mural is a creative wall accent over the built-in storage bench.

Customize your bathing experience with features that suit your lifestyle. A shower tower, left, can immerse you in a waterfall or provide a relaxing or invigorating full-body massage.

Big Ideas, Small Budget

A handsome, practical master bath doesn't have to be the size of the Taj Mahal, nor does it require a marble countertop and tub surround. There are attractive and hard-working materials, such as standard ceramic tile and high-quality plastic-laminate products, that will serve you well. Stick to standard fixtures and fittings, avoiding special effects, fancy finishes, and special-order colors if you have limited funds. Another way to keep costs down: eliminate all spa amenities. However, the price range of whirlpool tubs is wide, and there are models available for the budget-minded, as well.

Again, depending upon your bathing habits, you could simply install a shower. A shower without a threshold that is separated from the rest of the room by a glass enclosure saves space and looks great. You might investigate the flow options of many affordable showerheads, also. You don't have to settle for the old standard, which came with a single boring setting. But it is interesting that consumer testing conducted recently by one major manufacturer revealed that most people use only one or two shower settings anyway.

Storage becomes a challenge in a small space, so a modest-size vanity with a single sink is a good idea. Storage nooks built between the wall studs can provide point-of-use storage for bottles and small toiletries in the bath or shower and near the sink. Shelving is another option, and is handy for storing extra towels and grooming supplies. As a bonus, good-looking bath linens can add a nice color accent to the room, especially if the permanent fixtures are a neutral color.

Sometimes thinking outside the box can expand the function of a small master bath in a unique way. If you want but can't fit two sinks, consider using a large trough-style or farmhouse-style sink and installing two separate taps or faucets.

Bathroom Lighting

Good lighting puts illumination where you need it. A superb lighting scheme also enhances the mood of the room.

There are several types of artificial light and various sources. In all but the smallest bathrooms, ceiling-mounted lights are nec-

Reflective materials, such as a glass sink and countertop and mirrored surfaces, above, look glamorous in a bathroom.

An electronic touch pad, above right, lets you preprogram different settings for water temperature and frequency of intervals between pulses from the water jets.

A deluxe prefabricated shower system, right, comes with an array of built-in features that include numerous pulsating jets, adjustable and handheld showerheads, a TV, and a sound system.

essary for sufficient general, also called "ambient," illumination.

Recessed fixtures are a good choice by the shower or tub, in the toilet compartment, and in the dressing room. The number of required recessed fixtures varies by the size of the room.

Task lighting is necessary for grooming. To look good in the mirror, task lighting should come at you from both sides, radiating from the middle of your face (60 to 66 inches from the floor for most adults.) Avoid lighting the vanity area from above, which will cause shadows.

Accent lighting isn't necessary in a bathroom, but it can add a decorative touch. Small strip lights mounted under a raised tub or lights recessed into a soffit above a vanity are good examples.

Plan #161026

Dimensions: 67'6" W x 63'6" D
Levels: 1
Square Footage: 2,041
Bedrooms: 3
Bathrooms: 2
Foundation: Basement
Materials List Available: No
Price Category: D

You'll love the special features of this home, which has been designed for efficiency and comfort.

Images provided by designer/architect.

Features:

- Foyer: This raised foyer offers a view through the great room and beyond it to the covered deck.

- Great Room: Elegant windows allow versatility — decorate casually or more formally.

- Kitchen: You'll find ample counter space and cabinets in this spacious room, which adjoins the dining room and opens onto the rear yard.

- Library: Curl up on the window seat that wraps around the tower in this quiet spot.

- Laundry Room: A tub makes this large room practical for crafts as well as laundry.

- Master Suite: A vaulted ceiling gives grace to the sitting area, and the garden bath with a walk-in closet and whirlpool tub adds luxury.

Rear Elevation

Main Level Floor Plan

Basement Level Floor Plan

Copyright by designer/architect.

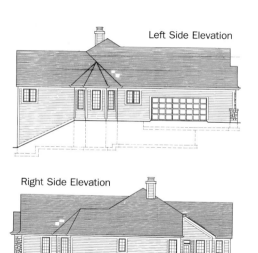

Left Side Elevation

Right Side Elevation

Front View

Living Room

Plan #321079

Dimensions: 69'8" W x 46' D

Levels: 2

Square Footage: 2,624

Main Level Sq. Ft.: 1,774

Upper Level Sq. Ft.: 850

Bedrooms: 4

Bathrooms: 2½

Foundation: Basement

Materials List Available: Yes

Price Category: F

The dramatic exterior design allows natural light to flow into the spacious living area of this home.

Features:

- Entry: This two-story area opens into the dining room through a classic colonnade.

- Dining Room: A large bay window, stately columns, and doorway to the kitchen make this room both beautiful and convenient.

- Great Room: Enjoy light from the fireplace or the three Palladian windows in the 18-ft. ceiling.

- Kitchen: The step-saving design features a walk-in pantry as well as good counter space.

- Breakfast Room: You'll love the light that flows through the windows flanking the back door.

- Master Suite: The vaulted ceiling and bayed areas in both the bed and bath add elegance. You'll love the two walk-in closets and bath with a sunken tub, two vanities, and separate shower.

Images provided by designer/architect.

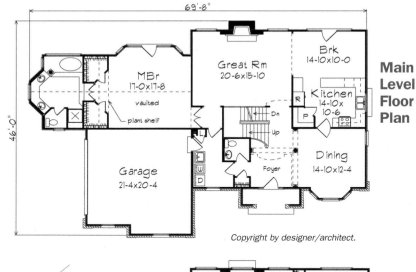

Main Level Floor Plan

Copyright by designer/architect.

Great Room

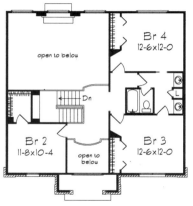

Upper Level Floor Plan

Images provided by designer/architect.

Plan #151014

Dimensions: 70'2" W x 51'4" D

Levels: 2

Square Footage: 2,698

Main Level Sq. Ft.: 1,813

Upper Level Sq. Ft.: 885

Bedrooms: 5

Bathrooms: 3

Foundation: Crawl space, slab, optional basement for fee

Price Category: D

A comfortable front porch welcomes you into this home that features a balcony over the great room, a study, and a kitchen designed for gourmet cooks.

Features:

- Ceiling Height: 9 ft.

- Front Porch: Stately 12-in.-wide pillars form the entryway.

- Foyer: Open to upper story.

- Great Room: A fireplace, vaulted 9-ft. ceiling, and balcony from the second floor add character to this lovely room.

- Dining Room: Open to the kitchen for convenience.

- Kitchen: A large walk-in pantry, well-designed work areas, and eat-in bar make this room a treasure.

- Breakfast Room: Enjoy this spot that opens to both the kitchen and a large covered porch at the rear of the house.

- Study: This quiet room has French doors leading to the yard.

- Master Suite: This spacious area has cozy window seats as well as his and her walk-in closets. The master bathroom is fitted with a whirlpool tub, a glass shower, and his and her sinks.

Upper Level Floor Plan

Main Level Floor Plan

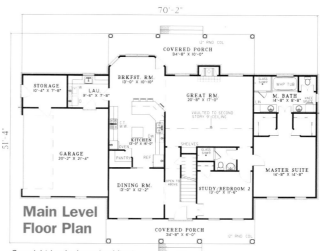

Copyright by designer/architect.

Plan #191010

Dimensions: 62' W x 40' D

Levels: 1

Square Footage: 2,189

Bedrooms: 3

Bathrooms: 2½

Foundation: Crawl space, slab

Materials List Available: No

Price Category: D

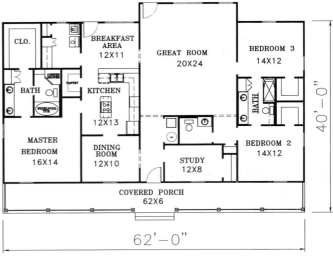

Images provided by designer/architect.

Copyright by designer/architect.

Plan #271039

Dimensions: 45'4" W x 46' D

Levels: 2

Square Footage: 1,565

Main Level Sq. Ft.: 1,105

Upper Level Sq. Ft.: 460

Bedrooms: 3

Bathrooms: 2½

Foundation: Basement

Materials List Available: Yes

Price Category: C

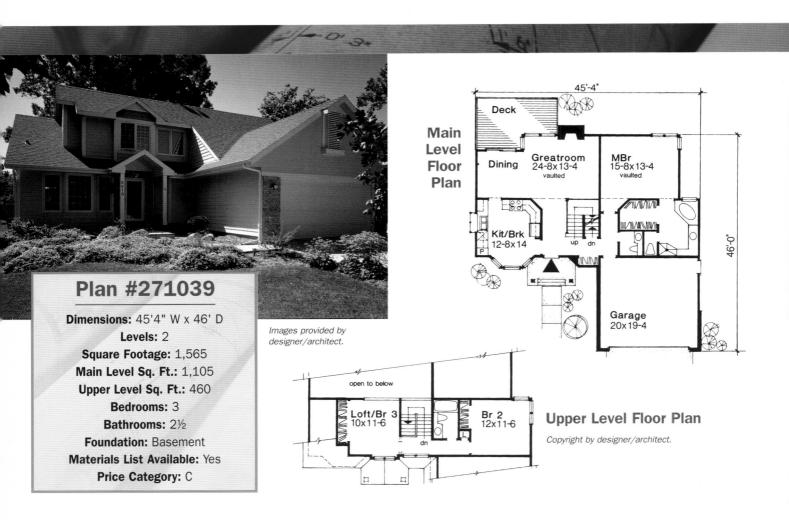

Images provided by designer/architect.

Copyright by designer/architect.

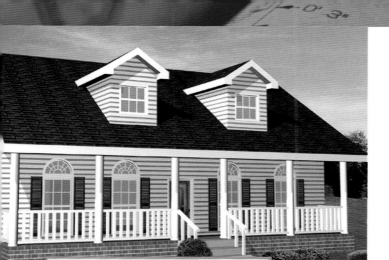

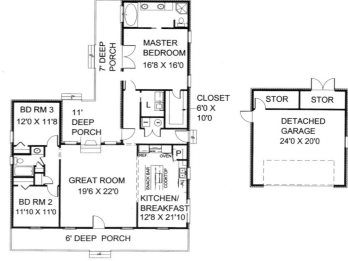

Plan #191002

Dimensions: 44' W x 65' D
Levels: 1
Square Footage: 1,716
Bedrooms: 3
Bathrooms: 2
Foundation: Crawl space, slab
Materials List Available: No
Price Category: C

Images provided by designer/architect.

MASTER BEDROOM 16'8 X 16'0
7' DEEP PORCH
CLOSET 6'0 X 10'0
BD RM 3 12'0 X 11'8
11' DEEP PORCH
REF
OVEN
P
SNACK BAR
COOKTOP
GREAT ROOM 19'6 X 22'0
KITCHEN/ BREAKFAST 12'8 X 21'10
BD RM 2 11'10 X 11'0
6' DEEP PORCH
STOR
STOR
DETACHED GARAGE 24'0 X 20'0

44'-0" WIDE X 65'-0" DEPTH - WITHOUT GARAGE

Copyright by designer/architect.

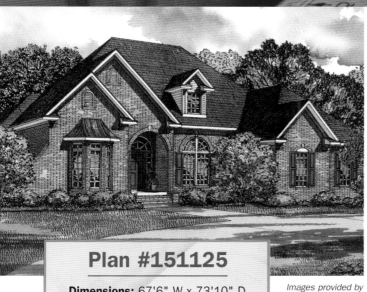

Plan #151125

Dimensions: 67'6" W x 73'10" D
Levels: 1
Square Footage: 2,606
Bedrooms: 3
Bathrooms: 2½
Foundation: Crawl space, slab, or basement
Materials List Available: Yes
Price Category: F

Images provided by designer/architect.

Copyright by designer/architect.

67'-6"
M. BATH
BEDROOM 3
GRILLING PORCH
HEARTH ROOM
BEDROOM 1
MASTER SUITE
GREAT RM.
BRKFST RM.
KITCHEN
PATIO
FOYER
DINING RM.
LAU.
STORAGE
STUDY / BEDROOM 4
ENTRY
GARAGE
73'-10"

PROPOSED BONUS ROOM
WINDOW SEAT
WINDOW SEAT

Optional Bonus Area Floor Plan

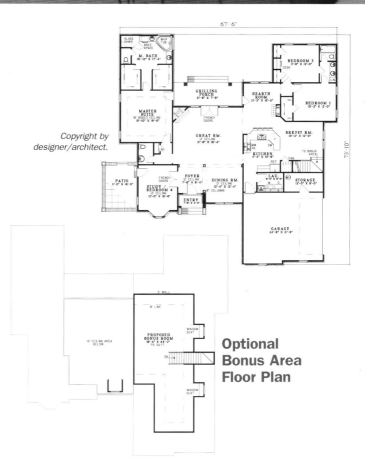

Plan #271002

Dimensions: 44'8" W x 50'8" D

Levels: 1

Square Footage: 1,252

Bedrooms: 3

Bathrooms: 2

Foundation: Basement

Materials List Available: Yes

Price Category: B

Images provided by designer/architect.

This traditional home combines a modest square footage with stylish extras.

Features:

- Living Room: Spacious and inviting, this gathering spot is brightened by a Palladian window arrangement, warmed by a fireplace, and topped by a vaulted ceiling.

- Dining Room: The vaulted ceiling also crowns this room, which shares the living room's fireplace. Sliding doors lead to a backyard deck.

- Kitchen: Smart design ensures a place for everything.

- Master Suite: The master bedroom boasts a vaulted ceiling, cheery windows, and a private bath.

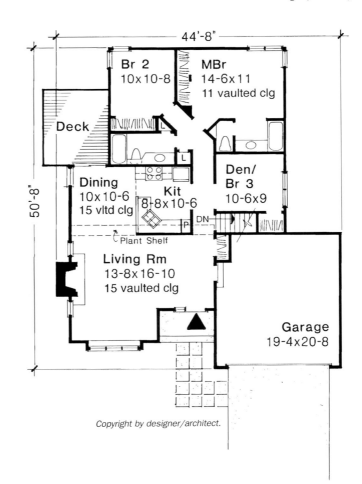

Copyright by designer/architect.

Plan #151005

Dimensions: 58' W x 54'10" D
Levels: 1
Square Footage: 1,940
Bedrooms: 4
Bathrooms: 2
Foundation: Basement, crawl space, or slab
Materials List Available: Yes
Price Category: D

Images provided by designer/architect.

A covered front porch with stately 10-in. round columns and a classically-styled foyer invite family and guests into this well-designed, traditional 4-bedroom home.

Features:

- **Great Room:** The 9-ft. boxed-ceiling, radiant fireplace, and built-in shelving add up to create a cozy and practical room where friends and family will love to gather.

- **Dining Room:** Open access from this dining room to the kitchen, and from there to the breakfast room, makes this room an ideal place for entertaining.

- **Master Suite:** This luxuriously appointed suite, with a 9-ft. pan ceiling in the bedroom, is located just of the breakfast room. The spectacular bath is fitted with a whirlpool tub, separate shower, and double vanities.

- **Bedrooms 2 and 3:** Large walk-in closets make these rooms easy to organize and keep tidy.

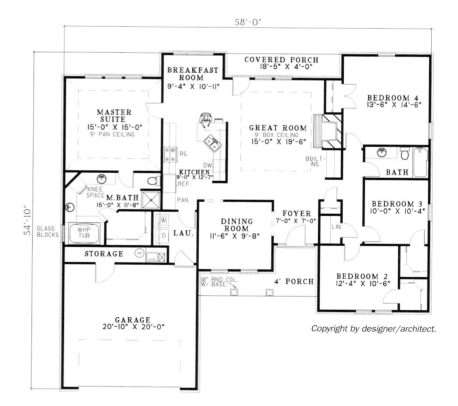

Copyright by designer/architect.

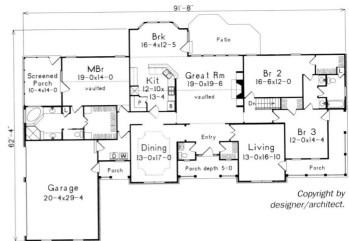

Copyright by designer/architect.

Images provided by designer/architect.

Plan #321004

Dimensions: 91'8" W x 62'4" D
Levels: 1
Square Footage: 2,808
Bedrooms: 3
Bathrooms: 2½
Foundation: Basement
Materials List Available: Yes
Price Category: F

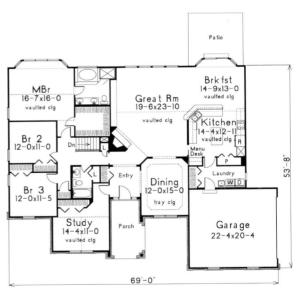

Copyright by designer/architect.

Images provided by designer/architect.

Plan #321005

Dimensions: 69' W x 53'8" D
Levels: 1
Square Footage: 2,483
Bedrooms: 4
Bathrooms: 2
Foundation: Basement
Materials List Available: Yes
Price Category: E

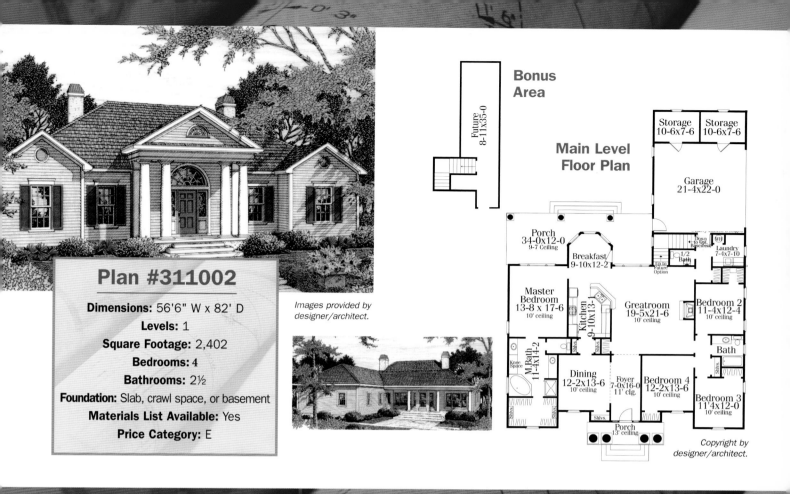

Plan #311002

Dimensions: 56'6" W x 82' D

Levels: 1

Square Footage: 2,402

Bedrooms: 4

Bathrooms: 2½

Foundation: Slab, crawl space, or basement

Materials List Available: Yes

Price Category: E

Images provided by designer/architect.

Bonus Area

Future 8-11x35-0

Main Level Floor Plan

Storage 10-6x7-6

Storage 10-6x7-6

Garage 21-4x22-0

Porch 34-0x12-0 9-7 Ceiling

Breakfast 9-10x12-2

Down to Opt. Basement

1/2 Bath

WH

Laundry 7-4x7-10

Up to Future Option

Master Bedroom 13-8 x 17-6 10' ceiling

Kitchen 9-10x13-1

Greatroom 19-5x21-6 10' ceiling

Bedroom 2 11-4x12-4 10' ceiling

M.Bath 11-4x14-2

Knee Space

Dining 12-2x13-6 10' ceiling

Foyer 7-0x16-0 11' clg.

Bedroom 4 12-2x13-6 10' ceiling

Bath

Bedroom 3 11'4x12-0 10' ceiling

Shlvs.

Porch -13' ceiling

Copyright by designer/architect.

Plan #321003

Dimensions: 67'4" W x 48' D

Levels: 1

Square Footage: 1,791

Bedrooms: 4

Bathrooms: 2

Foundation: Basement

Materials List Available: Yes

Price Category: C

Images provided by designer/architect.

Copyright by designer/architect.

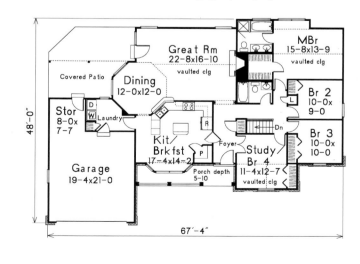

Great Rm 22-8x16-10 vaulted clg

MBr 15-8x13-9 vaulted clg

Covered Patio

Dining 12-0x12-0

Br 2 10-0x 9-0

Stor 8-0x 7-7

D W Laundry

Kit/ Brkfst 17-4x14-2

Foyer

Dn

Study Br 4 11-4x12-7 vaulted clg

Br 3 10-0x 10-0

Garage 19-4x21-0

Porch depth 5-10

48'-0"

67'-4"

Plan #241005

Dimensions: 53' W x 55'9" D
Levels: 1
Square Footage: 1,670
Bedrooms: 3
Bathrooms: 2
Foundation: Slab
Materials List Available: No
Price Category: C

This charming starter home, in split-bedroom format, combines big-house features in a compact design.

Features:

- **Great Room:** With easy access to the formal dining room, kitchen, and breakfast area, this great room features a cozy fireplace.

- **Kitchen:** This big kitchen, with easy access to a walk-in pantry, features an island for added work space and a lovely plant shelf that separates it from the great room.

- **Master Suite:** Separated for privacy, this master suite offers a roomy bath with whirlpool tub, dual vanities, a separate shower, and a large walk-in closet.

- **Additional Rooms:** Additional rooms include a laundry/utility room—with space for a washer, dryer, and freezer—a large area above the garage, well-suited for a media or game room, and two secondary bedrooms.

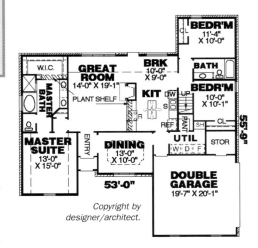

Copyright by designer/architect.

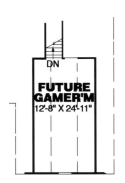

SMARTtip

Window Scarf

The best way to wrap a window scarf around a pole is as follows:

- Lay out the material on a large, clean surface. Gather the fabric at the top of each jabot, and use elastic to hold it together.

- Swing one jabot into place over the pole and, starting from there, wind the swag portion as many times as you need around the pole until you reach the elastic at the second jabot, which should have landed at the opposite pole end.

- Readjust wraps along the pole. Generally, wrapped swags just touch or slightly overlap.

- For a dramatic effect, stuff the wrapped swags with tissue paper or thin foam, depending on the translucence and weight of fabric.

- Release elastics at tops of jabots.

Images provided by designer/architect.

Plan #141015

Dimensions: 46' W x 36'8" D
Levels: 2
Square Footage: 2,350
Main Level Sq. Ft.: 1,155
Upper Level Sq. Ft.: 1,195
Bedrooms: 4
Bathrooms: 2½
Foundation: Basement
Materials List Available: Yes
Price Category: E

This home offers classic Victorian details combined with modern amenities.

Features:

- Ceiling Height: 9 ft. unless otherwise noted.
- Porch: Enjoy summer breezes on this large wraparound porch, with its classic turret corner.
- Family Room: This room has a fireplace and two sets of French doors. One set of doors leads to the porch; the other leads to a rear sun deck.
- Living Room: This large room at the front of the house is designed for formal entertaining.
- Kitchen: This convenient kitchen features an island and a writing desk.
- Master Bedroom: Enjoy the cozy sitting area in the turret corner. The bedroom offers access to a second story balcony.
- Laundry: The second-floor laundry means you won't have to haul clothing up and down stairs.

Main Level Floor Plan

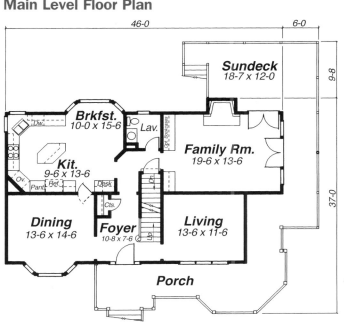

Upper Level Floor Plan

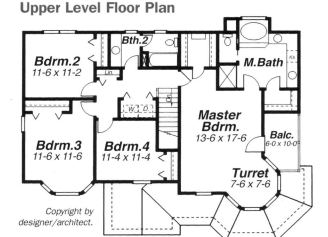

Copyright by designer/architect.

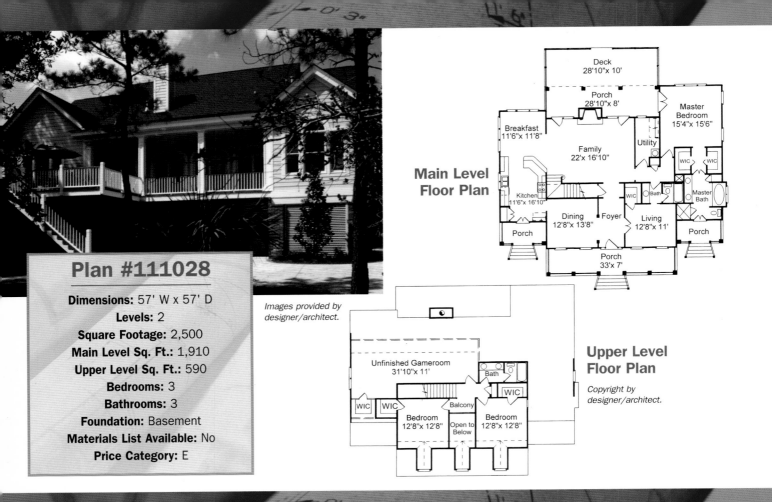

Plan #111028

Dimensions: 57' W x 57' D

Levels: 2

Square Footage: 2,500

Main Level Sq. Ft.: 1,910

Upper Level Sq. Ft.: 590

Bedrooms: 3

Bathrooms: 3

Foundation: Basement

Materials List Available: No

Price Category: E

Images provided by designer/architect.

Main Level Floor Plan

Deck 28'10"x 10'
Porch 28'10"x 8'
Breakfast 11'6"x 11'8"
Family 22'x 16'10"
Master Bedroom 15'4"x 15'6"
Utility
WIC WIC
Kitchen 11'6"x 16'10"
Bath
Master Bath
Dining 12'8"x 13'8"
Foyer
Living 12'8"x 11'
WIC
Porch
Porch
Porch 33'x 7'

Upper Level Floor Plan

Copyright by designer/architect.

Unfinished Gameroom 31'10"x 11'
Bath
WIC
WIC WIC
Balcony
Bedroom 12'8"x 12'8"
Open to Below
Bedroom 12'8"x 12'8"

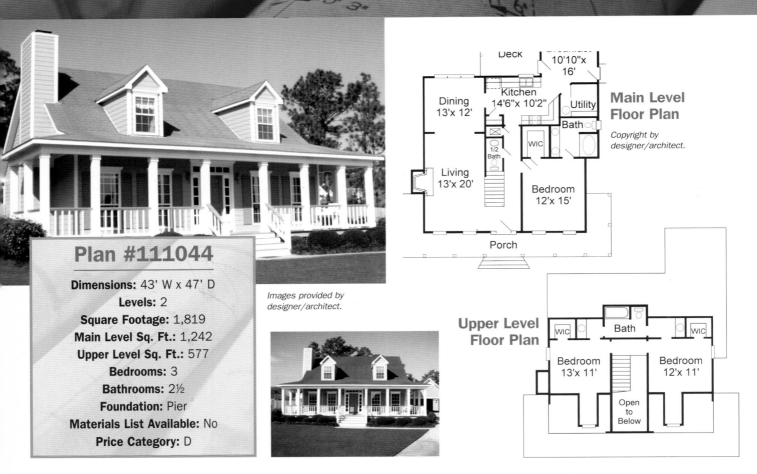

Plan #111044

Dimensions: 43' W x 47' D

Levels: 2

Square Footage: 1,819

Main Level Sq. Ft.: 1,242

Upper Level Sq. Ft.: 577

Bedrooms: 3

Bathrooms: 2½

Foundation: Pier

Materials List Available: No

Price Category: D

Images provided by designer/architect.

Main Level Floor Plan

Copyright by designer/architect.

Deck
10'10"x 16'
Kitchen 14'6"x 10'2"
Dining 13'x 12'
Utility
Bath
Living 13'x 20'
1/2 Bath
WIC
Bedroom 12'x 15'
Porch

Upper Level Floor Plan

WIC
Bath
WIC
Bedroom 13'x 11'
Bedroom 12'x 11'
Open to Below

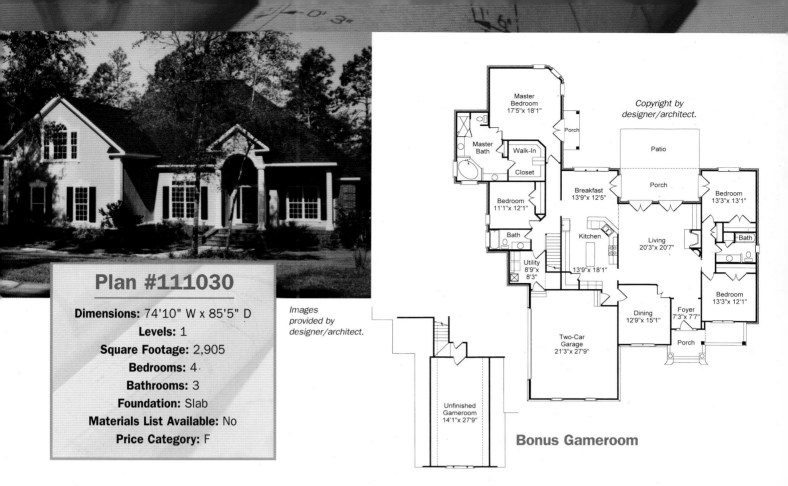

Plan #111030

Dimensions: 74'10" W x 85'5" D

Levels: 1

Square Footage: 2,905

Bedrooms: 4

Bathrooms: 3

Foundation: Slab

Materials List Available: No

Price Category: F

Images provided by designer/architect.

Bonus Gameroom

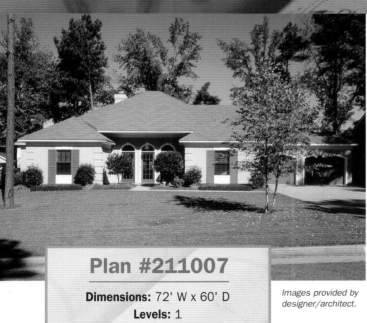

Plan #211007

Dimensions: 72' W x 60' D

Levels: 1

Square Footage: 2,252

Bedrooms: 4

Bathrooms: 2

Foundation: Slab

Materials List Available: Yes

Price Category: E

Images provided by designer/architect.

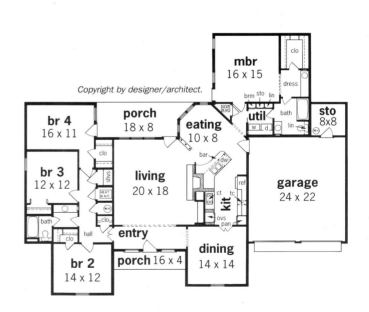

Plan #131050

Dimensions: 72'8" W x 47' D
Levels: 2
Square Footage: 2,874
Main Level Sq. Ft.: 2,146
Upper Level Sq. Ft.: 728
Bedrooms: 4
Bathrooms: 3
Foundation: Crawl space, slab, or basement
Materials List Available: Yes
Price Category: G

Images provided by designer/architect.

A gazebo and long covered porch at the entry let you know that this is a spectacular design.

Features:

- **Foyer:** This vaulted foyer divides the formal living room and dining room, setting the stage for guests to feel welcome in your home.

- **Great Room:** This large room is defined by several columns; a corner fireplace and vaulted ceiling add to its drama.

- **Kitchen:** An island work space

separates this area from the bayed breakfast nook.

- **Master Suite:** You'll have privacy in this main-floor suite, which features two walk-in closets and a compartmented bath with a dual-sink vanity.

- **Upper Level:** The two large bedrooms share a bath and a dramatic balcony.

- **Bonus Room:** Walk down a few steps into this large bonus room over the 3-car garage.

Main Level Floor Plan

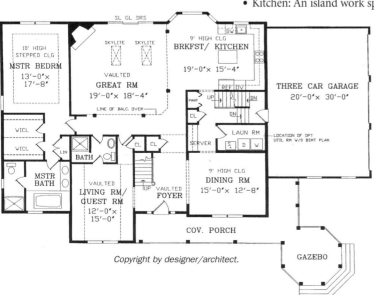

Copyright by designer/architect.

Upper Level Floor Plan

Rear Elevation

Plan #131036

Dimensions: 72' W x 69'10" D
Levels: 1
Square Footage: 2,585
Bedrooms: 4
Bathrooms: 3
Foundation: Crawl space, slab, or basement
Materials List Available: Yes
Price Category: F

Images provided by designer/architect.

This sprawling brick home features living spaces for everyone in the family and makes a lovely setting for any sort of entertaining.

Features:

- **Foyer:** Pass through this foyer, which leads into either the living room or dining room.
- **Living Room:** An elegant 11-ft. stepped ceiling here and in the dining room helps to create the formality their lines suggest.
- **Great Room:** This room, with its 10-ft.-7-in.-high stepped ceiling, fireplace, and many built-ins, leads to the rear covered porch.
- **Kitchen:** This kitchen features an island, a pantry closet, and a wraparound snack bar that serves the breakfast room and gives a panoramic view of the great room.
- **Master Suite:** Enjoy a bayed sitting area, walk-in closet, and private bath with garden tub.
- **Office:** A private entrance and access to a full bath give versatility to this room.

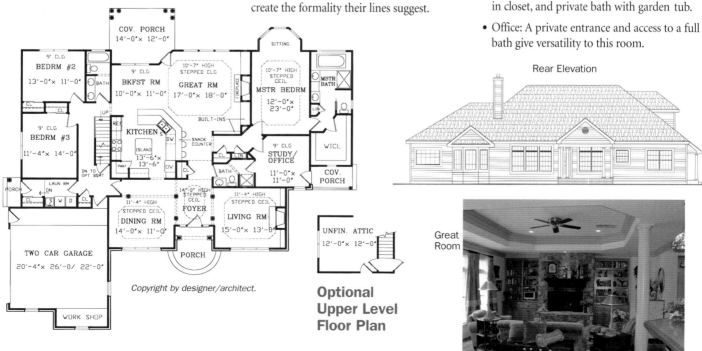

Copyright by designer/architect.

Optional Upper Level Floor Plan

Rear Elevation

Great Room

Plan #201027

Dimensions: 58'10" W x 46'10" D
Levels: 1
Square Footage: 1,494
Bedrooms: 3
Bathrooms: 2
Foundation: Crawl space, slab
Materials List Available: Yes
Price Category: B

Images provided by designer/architect.

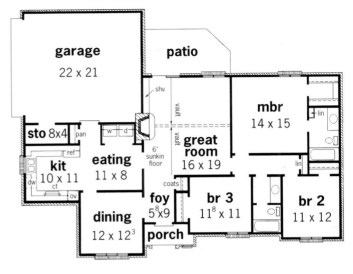

Copyright by designer/architect.

Plan #201028

Dimensions: 66'4" W x 38'10" D
Levels: 1
Square Footage: 1,484
Bedrooms: 3
Bathrooms: 2
Foundation: Crawl space, slab
Materials List Available: Yes
Price Category: B

Images provided by designer/architect.

Copyright by designer/architect.

SMARTtip

Creating a Comfortable Bedroom

Whites, neutrals, or pale colors—blues, greens, or pinks—create a restful ambiance in the bedroom, making sleeping easier. Cheery colors, such as yellow, work for those who like rising with the sun (or those who need help waking up). All-over wallpaper patterns, particularly large-scale ones, can make a bedroom feel too enclosed, so use bold patterns sparingly.

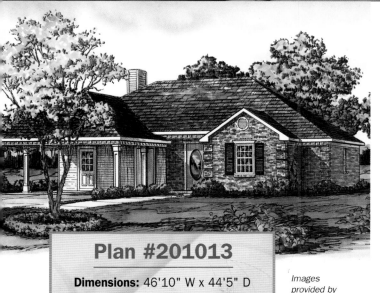

Plan #201013

Dimensions: 46'10" W x 44'5" D
Levels: 1
Square Footage: 1,211
Bedrooms: 3
Bathrooms: 2
Foundation: Crawl space, slab
Materials List Available: Yes
Price Category: B

Images provided by designer/architect.

46'-10"

PORCH 16'-0"x4'-0"

DINING 11'-0"x11'-0"

CLO

MASTER BEDROOM 13'-6"x12'-0"

BATH-2

GREAT ROOM 15'-0"x15'-0"

FLAT HEARTH

HVAC

REF. RANGE

KITCHEN 8'-6"x12'-0"

DBL. SINK w/DISPOSAL

DW

SHELVES

10'-6" CEILING

BATH-1

BEDROOM-2 10'-0"x10'-6"

44'-5"

DRY WASH

STORAGE 8'-6"x4'-0"

CLO

FOYER

HALL

CLO

PORCH

LINE OF PORCH

BEDROOM-3 11'-0"x11'-0"

GARAGE 20'-0"x21'-0"

Copyright by designer/architect.

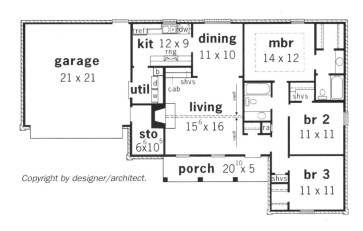

Plan #201015

Dimensions: 63'10" W x 38'10" D
Levels: 1
Square Footage: 1,271
Bedrooms: 3
Bathrooms: 2
Foundation: Crawl space, slab
Materials List Available: Yes
Price Category: B

Images provided by designer/architect.

SMARTtip

Basic Triangle-Kitchens

Draw up your kitchen plan in this order: sink, range, refrigerator. Once you have the basic triangle located, add the other appliances, such as wall ovens and a dishwasher, and then the cabinets, counters, and eating areas.

ref

dw

kit 12 x 9

rng

dining 11 x 10

mbr 14 x 12

garage 21 x 21

util

b

d

w

shvs

cab

living 15'6" x 16

shvs

br 2 11 x 11

sto 6'x10'5"

vault

vault

porch 20'10" x 5

shvs

br 3 11 x 11

Copyright by designer/architect.

Plan #131023

Dimensions: 78'8" W x 36'2" D
Levels: 2
Square Footage: 2,460
Main Level Sq. Ft.: 1,377
Upper Level Sq. Ft.: 1,083
Bedrooms: 4
Bathrooms: 2½
Foundation: Basement, crawl space, or slab
Materials List Available: Yes
Price Category: F

Images provided by designer/architect.

Rear Elevation

You'll love the modern floor plan inside this traditional two-story home, with its attractive facade.

Features:

- Ceiling Height: 8 ft.

- Living Room: The windows on three sides of this room make it bright and sunny. Choose the optional fireplace for cozy winter days and the wet bar for elegant entertaining.

- Family Room: Overlooking the rear deck, this spacious family room features a fireplace and a skylight.

- Dining Room: The convenient placement of this large room lets guests flow into it from the living room and allows easy to access from the kitchen.

- Kitchen: The island cooktop and built-in desk make this space both modern and practical.

Main Level Floor Plan

Copyright by designer/architect.

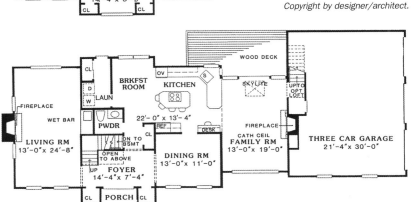

Upper Level Floor Plan

Plan #321076

Dimensions: 54' W x 57'4" D

Levels: 2

Square Footage: 3,138

Main Level Sq. Ft.: 1,958

Upper Level Sq. Ft.: 1,180

Bedrooms: 4

Bathrooms: 3½

Foundation: Basement

Materials List Available: Yes

Price Category: G

Images provided by designer/architect.

This elegant home is spacious enough for an active family and lovely enough for entertaining.

Features:

- Family Room: Host a crowd in this enormous room, or enjoy a cozy chat beside the fireplace.

- Breakfast Room: Open to the family room, this breakfast room leads to the outdoor patio.

- Study: Situated for privacy and quiet, this study has large windows and handsome double doors.

- Dining Room: This large, private room is equally suitable for formal parties and family dinners.

- Master Suite: The vaulted ceiling and bay window make the bedroom elegant, while the two walk-in closets, linen closet, double vanity, tub, and separate shower make the suite luxurious.

- Loft: Use this spacious area as a playroom when the children are small and a media area later on.

Main Level Floor Plan

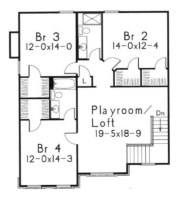

Upper Level Floor Plan

Copyright by designer/architect.

Plan #201031

Dimensions: 60'10" W x 41'5" D
Levels: 1
Square Footage: 1,531
Bedrooms: 3
Bathrooms: 2
Foundation: Crawl space, slab
Materials List Available: Yes
Price Category: C

Images provided by designer/architect.

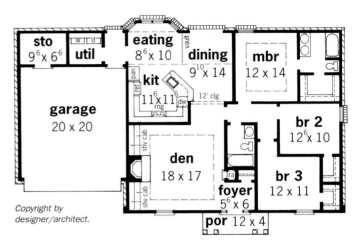

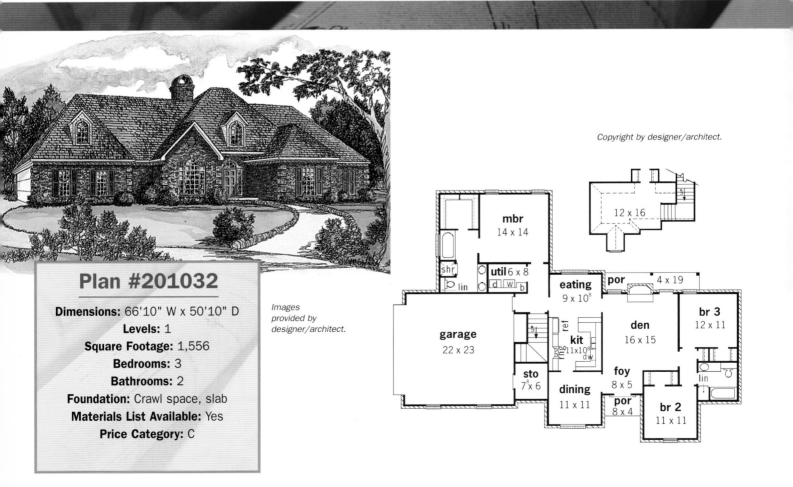

Plan #201032

Dimensions: 66'10" W x 50'10" D
Levels: 1
Square Footage: 1,556
Bedrooms: 3
Bathrooms: 2
Foundation: Crawl space, slab
Materials List Available: Yes
Price Category: C

Images provided by designer/architect.

Plan #241002

Dimensions: 65' W x 59'8" D

Levels: 1

Square Footage: 2,154

Bedrooms: 4

Bathrooms: 2½

Foundation: Slab

Materials List Available: No

Price Category: D

Images provided by designer/architect.

Copyright by designer/architect.

Plan #241006

Dimensions: 51' W x 53' D

Levels: 1

Square Footage: 1,744

Bedrooms: 3

Bathrooms: 2

Foundation: Slab

Materials List Available: No

Price Category: C

Images provided by designer/architect.

Copyright by designer/architect.

Plan #161061

Dimensions: 90' W x 69'10" D
Levels: 2
Square Footage: 3,816
Main Level Sq. Ft.: 2,725
Upper Level Sq. Ft.: 1,091
Bedrooms: 4
Bathrooms: 3½
Foundation: Basement, walkout basement
Materials List Available: Yes
Price Category: H

Images provided by designer/architect.

Luxurious amenities make living in this spacious home a true pleasure for the whole family.

Features:

• **Great Room:** A fireplace, flanking built-in shelves, a balcony above, and three lovely windows create a luxurious room that's always comfortable.

• **Hearth Room:** Another fireplace with surrounding built-ins and double doors to the outside deck (with its own fireplace) highlight this room.

• **Kitchen:** A butler's pantry, laundry room, and mudroom with a window seat and two walk-in closets complement this large kitchen.

• **Library:** Situated for privacy and quiet, this spacious room with a large window area may be reached from the master bedroom as well as the foyer.

• **Master Suite:** A sloped ceiling and windows on three walls create a lovely bedroom, and the huge walk-in closet, dressing room, and luxurious bath add up to total comfort.

Main Level Floor Plan

Upper Level Floor Plan

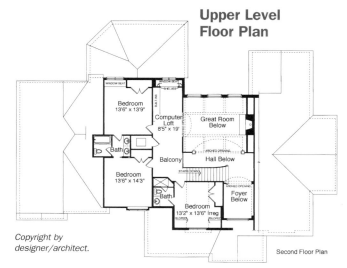

Copyright by designer/architect.

Rear Elevation

Right Side Elevation

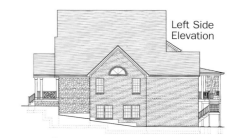

Left Side Elevation

Great Room

Hearth Room

Kitchen

Dining Room

Library

Plan #281001

Dimensions: 54' W x 47' D
Levels: 2
Square Footage: 2,423
Main Level Sq. Ft.: 1,388
Second Level Sq. Ft.: 1,035
Bedrooms: 3
Bathrooms: 2½
Foundation: Basement
Materials List Available: Yes
Price Category: E

This stately manor appears larger than it is and is filled with amenities for comfortable living.

Features:

- Ceiling Height: 8 ft. unless otherwise noted.
- Foyer: The grand entrance porch leads into this spacious two-story foyer, with an open staircase and architecturally interesting angles.

- Balcony: This second story has a balcony that overlooks the foyer.
- Living Room: This delightful living room seems even more spacious, thanks to its sloped vaulted ceiling.
- Dining Room: This elegant dining room shares the living room's sloped vaulted ceiling.
- Kitchen: This beautiful kitchen will be a real pleasure in which to cook. You'll love lingering over morning coffee in the breakfast nook, which is located on the sunny full-bayed wall.
- Family Room: Relax in this roomy family room, with its 9-ft. ceiling.

Images provided by designer/architect.

Main Level Floor Plan

Upper Level Floor Plan

Copyright by designer/architect.

Plan #271099

Dimensions: 71' W x 74'2" D
Levels: 2
Square Footage: 2,949
Main Level Sq. Ft.: 2,000
Upper Level Sq. Ft.: 949
Bedrooms: 3
Bathrooms: 2½
Foundation: Crawl space
Materials List Available: No
Price Category: F

Gracious symmetry highlights the lovely facade of this traditional two-story home.

Features:

- Foyer: With a high ceiling and a curved staircase, this foyer gives a warm welcome to arriving guests.

- Family Room: At the center of the home, this room will host gatherings of all kinds. A fireplace adds just the right touch.

- Kitchen: An expansive island with a cooktop anchors this space, which easily serves the adjoining nook and the nearby dining room.

- Master Suite: A cozy sitting room with a fireplace is certainly the highlight here. The private bath is also amazing, with its whirlpool tub, separate shower, dual vanities, and walk-in closet.

- Bonus Room: This generous space above the garage could serve as an art studio or as a place for your teenagers to play their electric guitars.

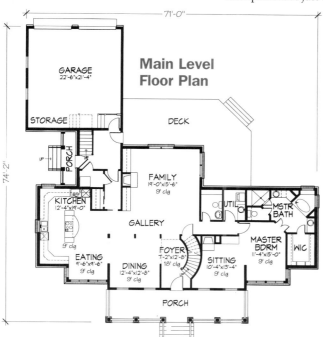

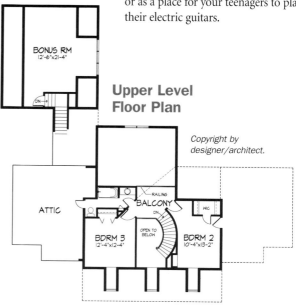

Copyright by designer/architect.

Plan #321020

Dimensions: 58' W x 47'6" D
Levels: 1
Square Footage: 1,882
Bedrooms: 4
Bathrooms: 2
Foundation: Basement
Materials List Available: Yes
Price Category: D

Images provided by designer/architect.

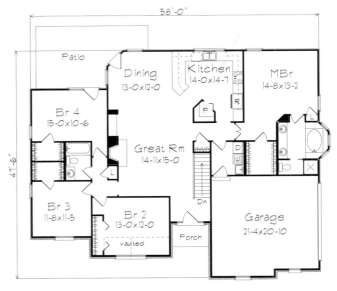

Copyright by designer/architect.

Plan #321021

Dimensions: 80' W x 42' D
Levels: 1
Square Footage: 1,708
Bedrooms: 3
Bathrooms: 2
Foundation: Basement
Materials List Available: Yes
Price Category: C

Images provided by designer/architect.

SMARTtip

Planning a Safe Children's Room

Keep safety in mind when planning a child's room. Make sure that there are covers on electrical outlets, guard rails on high windows, sturdy screens in front of radiators, and gates blocking any steps. Other suggestions include safety hinges for chests and nonskid backing for rugs.

Copyright by designer/architect.

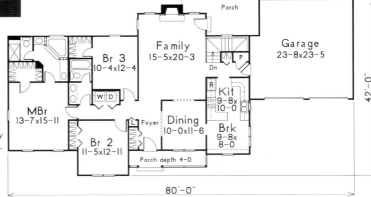

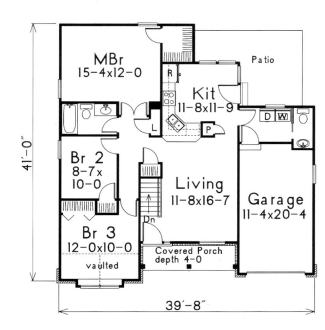

Plan #321022

Dimensions: 44' W x 27' D

Levels: 1

Square Footage: 1,140

Bedrooms: 3

Bathrooms: 2

Foundation: Basement

Materials List Available: Yes

Price Category: B

Images provided by designer/architect.

SMARTtip

Basement Moldings

Keep moldings simple in a basement with lower ceilings. Elaborate moldings around the ceiling or floor can shorten the height of the room.

Plan #321023

Dimensions: 39'8" W x 41' D

Levels: 1

Square Footage: 1,092

Bedrooms: 3

Bathrooms: 1½

Foundation: Basement

Materials List Available: Yes

Price Category: B

Images provided by designer/architect.

Copyright by designer/architect.

Plan #161038

Dimensions: 58'6" W x 49' D
Levels: 2
Square Footage: 2,209
Main Level Sq. Ft.: 1,542
Upper Level Sq. Ft.: 667
Bedrooms: 3
Bathrooms: 2½
Foundation: Basement
Materials List Available: No
Price Category: E

Brick trim, sidelights, and a transom window at the entry are a few of the many features that convey the elegance and style of this exciting home.

Images provided by designer/architect.

Features:

- Great Room: This great room is truly the centerpiece of this elegant home. The ceiling at the rear wall is 14 ft. and slopes forward to a second floor study loft that overlooks the magnificent fireplace and entertainment alcove. The high ceiling continues through the foyer, showcasing a deluxe staircase.

- Kitchen: This modern kitchen is designed for efficient work patterns and serves both the formal dining room and breakfast area.

- Master Suite: The highlight of this master suite is a wonderful whirlpool tub. Also

included are two matching vanities and a large walk-in closet.

- Bonus Room: A bonus room above the garage completes this exciting home.

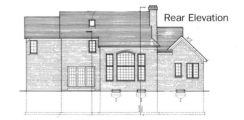

Rear Elevation

Main Level Floor Plan

Great Room 15'6" x 18'1"
Breakfast 11'7" x 12'0"
Laun.
Bath
walk-in closet
Hall
Kitchen 11'9" x 11'
Bath
Master Bedroom 13' x 13'11"
Foyer
Dining Room 11' x 13'
Porch
Two-car Garage 20' x 21'

Copyright by designer/architect.

58'6"
49'

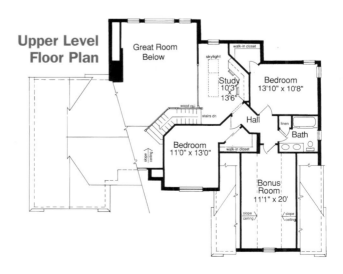

Upper Level Floor Plan

Great Room Below
skylight
walk-in closet
Study 10'3" x 13'6"
Bedroom 13'10" x 10'8"
Hall
linen
Bath
Bedroom 11'0" x 13'0"
walk-in closet
Bonus Room 11'1" x 20'
slope ceiling

Plan #131044

Dimensions: 57'6" W x 42'4" D
Levels: 1
Square Footage: 1,994
Bedrooms: 4
Bathrooms: 2
Foundation: Basement, crawl space, or slab
Materials List Available: Yes
Price Category: E

Images provided by designer/architect.

Under a covered porch, Victorian-detailed bay windows grace each side of the brick-faced facade at the center of this ranch-style home, giving it a formal air.

Features:

- **Ceiling Height:** 10-ft. ceilings grace the central living area and the master bedroom of this home.

- **Entry:** Round top windows make this area and the flanking rooms bright and cheery.

- **Great Room:** A fireplace and built-ins that are visible from anywhere in this large room make it a natural gathering place for friends and family.

- **Optional Office:** Use the room just off the central hall as a home office, fourth bedroom, or study.

- **Master Suite:** You'll love the bay window, tray ceiling, two walk-in closets, and private bath.

- **Bonus Space:** Finish this large area in the attic for extra living space, or use it for storage.

Rear Elevation

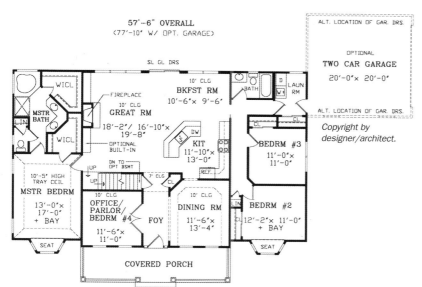

Copyright by designer/architect.

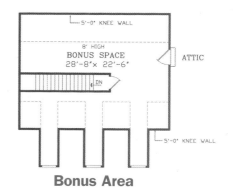

Bonus Area

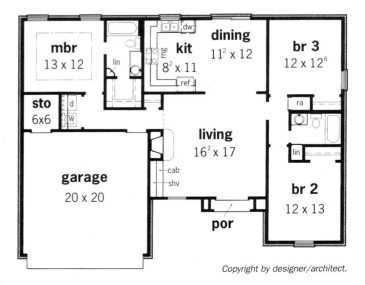

Copyright by designer/architect.

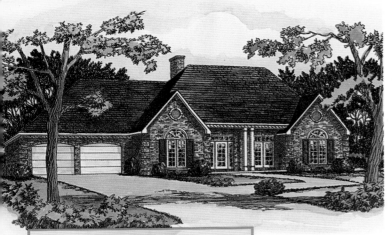

Plan #201023

Images provided by designer/architect.

Dimensions: 67'4" W x 32'10" D
Levels: 1
Square Footage: 1,390
Bedrooms: 3
Bathrooms: 2
Foundation: Crawl space, slab
Materials List Available: Yes
Price Category: B

Plan #201024

Images provided by designer/architect.

Dimensions: 50'10" W x 38'10" D
Levels: 1
Square Footage: 1,324
Bedrooms: 3
Bathrooms: 2
Foundation: Crawl space, slab
Materials List Available: Yes
Price Category: B

Copyright by designer/architect.

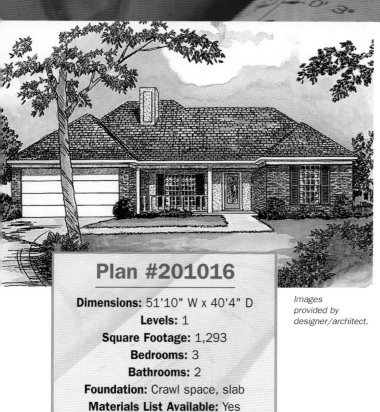

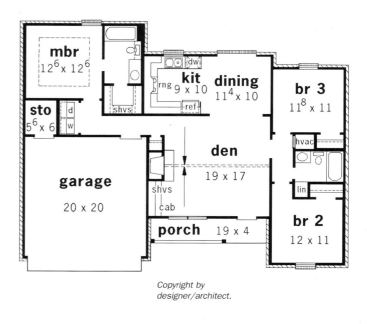

Plan #201016

Dimensions: 51'10" W x 40'4" D

Levels: 1

Square Footage: 1,293

Bedrooms: 3

Bathrooms: 2

Foundation: Crawl space, slab

Materials List Available: Yes

Price Category: B

Images provided by designer/architect.

Copyright by designer/architect.

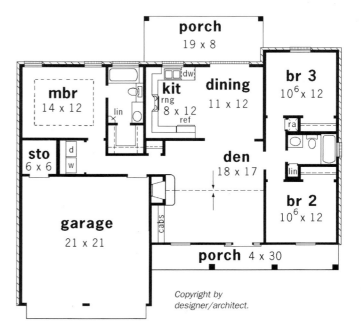

Plan #201018

Dimensions: 51'10" W x 47' D

Levels: 1

Square Footage: 1,294

Bedrooms: 3

Bathrooms: 2

Foundation: Crawl space, slab

Materials List Available: Yes

Price Category: B

Images provided by designer/architect.

Copyright by designer/architect.

Plan #271067

Dimensions: 72'2" W x 46'5" D
Levels: 2
Square Footage: 3,015
Main Level Sq. Ft.: 1,367
Upper Level Sq. Ft.: 1,648
Bedrooms: 3
Bathrooms: 2½
Foundation: Basement, crawl space
Materials List Available: No
Price Category: G

This stunning home borrows from Georgian architecture for a design that will get compliments from passersby.

Features:

- **Living Room:** To the left of the foyer, stately columns introduce this lovely space, which beckons all for a few moments of quiet reflection.

- **Dining Room:** This formal space will nicely host your most elegant occasions with ease.

- **Kitchen:** An L-shaped island is the focal point here, with its handy cooktop and snack bar. A menu desk is a thoughtful touch. The adjacent bayed dinette leads directly to the backyard.

- **Family Room:** A handsome fireplace warms this space and imparts a friendly ambience.

- **Master Suite:** Double doors and a tray ceiling enhance the sleeping chamber, while a whirlpool tub is the highlight in the private bath.

- **Bonus Room:** This versatile area contains a fun phone booth!

Images provided by designer/architect.

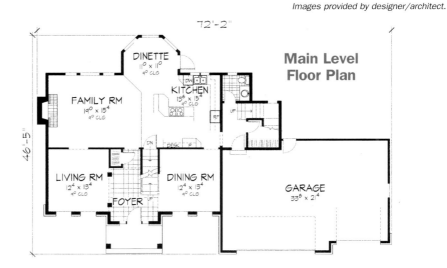

Main Level Floor Plan

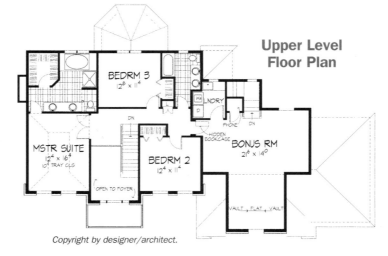

Upper Level Floor Plan

Copyright by designer/architect.

Plan #271068

Dimensions: 72' W x 36' D
Levels: 2
Square Footage: 2,214
Main Level Sq. Ft.: 1,150
Upper Level Sq. Ft.: 1,064
Bedrooms: 4
Bathrooms: 2½
Foundation: Basement
Materials List Available: No
Price Category: E

Images provided by designer/architect.

This traditional home is reminiscent of the Federal styling of a bygone era.

Features:

- **Living Room:** To the right of the foyer, this room is a perfect spot for adults to chat while the kids are playing elsewhere.

- **Dining Room:** Imagine hosting holiday feasts here! This room is quiet, but is also nicely situated near the kitchen for ease of service.

- **Kitchen:** A central work island, a useful menu desk, and a handy pantry equip the family chef for culinary successes. The casual dinette offers sliding glass doors to your prize-winning garden.

- **Family Room:** This space is large enough for a game of charades. The fireplace will be a welcome feature when the family comes inside after playing in the snow.

- **Master Suite:** A tray ceiling makes the sleeping chamber seem special. The private bath flaunts a whirlpool tub to soak away the cares of the day.

Main Level Floor Plan

Copyright by designer/architect.

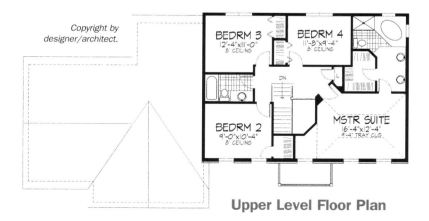

Upper Level Floor Plan

Plan #271070

Dimensions: 70'3" W x 60' D

Levels: 2

Square Footage: 2,144

Main Level Sq. Ft.: 1,156

Upper Level Sq. Ft.: 988

Bedrooms: 4

Bathrooms: 2½

Foundation: Basement, crawl space

Materials List Available: No

Price Category: D

Images provided by designer/architect.

A nice example of a country farmhouse design on the outside, this home is thoroughly modern on the inside.

Features:

• Living Room: To the left of the foyer, this secluded space offers a moment of peace and quiet after a long day at the office.

• Dining Room: An interesting ceiling treatment makes this elegant room even more sophisticated.

• Kitchen: You won't find a more well-appointed space than this! You'll love the central work island, this useful menu desk

and nearby pantry. The adjacent dinette hosts casual meals and offers outdoor access via sliding glass doors.

• Family Room: A handsome fireplace sets the mood in this expansive area.

• Master Suite: A vaulted ceiling presides over the sleeping room, while a walk-in closet organizes your entire wardrobe. The private bath boasts a refreshing shower and a linen closet.

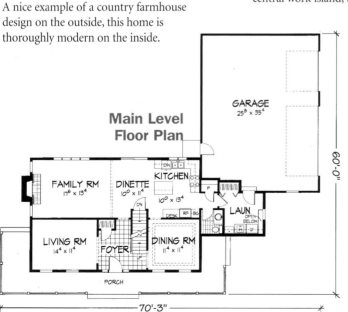

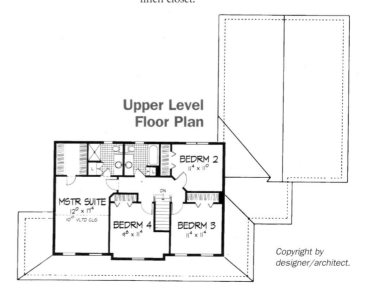

Copyright by designer/architect.

Plan #111006

Dimensions: 56' W x 67' D

Levels: 1

Square Footage: 2,241

Bedrooms: 4

Bathrooms: 2½

Foundation: Slab

Materials List Available: No

Price Category: E

Images provided by designer/architect.

You'll love this plan if you're looking for a home with fantastic curb appeal on the outside and comfortable amenities on the inside.

Features:

- Foyer: This lovely foyer opens to both the living and dining rooms.

- Dining Room: Three columns in this room accentuate both its large dimensions and its slightly formal air.

- Living Room: This room gives an airy feeling, and the fireplace here makes it especially inviting when the weather's cool.

- Kitchen: This G-shaped kitchen is designed to save steps while you're working, and the ample counter area adds even more to its convenience. The breakfast bar is a great gathering area.

- Master Suite: Two walk-in closets provide storage space, and the bath includes separate vanities, a standing shower, and a deluxe corner bathtub.

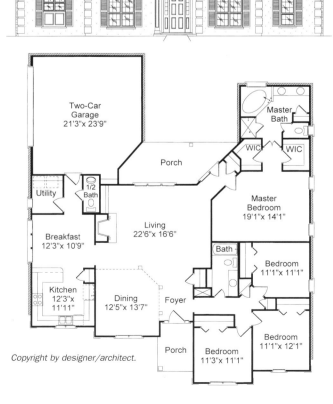

Front Elevation

Copyright by designer/architect.

Images provided by designer/architect.

Copyright by designer/architect.

Plan #321030

Dimensions: 61' W x 51' D
Levels: 1
Square Footage: 2,029
Bedrooms: 4
Bathrooms: 2
Foundation: Basement
Materials List Available: Yes
Price Category: D

SMARTtip

Measuring Angles

A sure-fire way to accurately measure the wall-frame acute angle is to cut a piece of scrap lumber to emulate the angle, and then measure it.

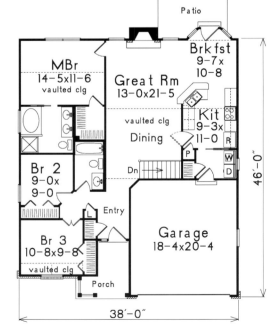

Images provided by designer/architect.

Plan #321033

Dimensions: 38' W x 46' D
Levels: 1
Square Footage: 1,268
Bedrooms: 3
Bathrooms: 2
Foundation: Basement
Materials List Available: Yes
Price Category: B

Copyright by designer/architect.

Plan #111048

Dimensions: 62' W x 65' D

Levels: 2

Square Footage: 2,665

Main Level Sq. Ft.: 1,916

Upper Level Sq. Ft.: 749

Bedrooms: 4

Bathrooms: 3

Foundation: Slab, optional crawl space

Materials List Available: No

Price Category: F

Images provided by designer/architect.

Main Level Floor Plan

Two Car Garage 21'4"x 21'4"
Patio
Porch
Utility 12'2"x 7'6"
Living 20'2"x 20'
WIC
Master Bedroom 18'x 14'2"
Breakfast 14'2"x 9'6"
Master Bath
Kitchen 12'2"x 12'
Dining 11'6"x 15'
Bath
Bedroom 11'6"x 11'4"
Porch

Upper Level Floor Plan

WIC
Bath
WIC
Bedroom 14'8"x 12'6"
Bedroom 14'8"x 12'6"

Copyright by designer/architect.

Plan #111050

Dimensions: 77' W x 51' D

Levels: 2

Square Footage: 2,333

Main Level Sq. Ft.: 1,685

Upper Level Sq. Ft.: 648

Bedrooms: 4

Bathrooms: 3

Foundation: Basement

Materials List Available: No

Price Category: E

Images provided by designer/architect.

Main Level Floor Plan

Patio
Porch
Breakfast 10'8"x 10'
Two-Car Garage 21'8"x 23'4"
Master Bedroom 15'x 13'6"
WIC
Living 19'4"x 17'4"
Kit. 10'8"x 12'
Ma. Bath
Bedroom 11'10"x 11'7"
Dining 11'10"x 13'3"
Utility

Copyright by designer/architect.

Upper Level Floor Plan

Unfin. Bedroom 10'8"x 12'
Bath
Balcony
Bedroom 11'10"x 11'
Open to Below
Bedroom 11'10"x 13'

Plan #271035

Dimensions: 43'4" W x 46' D
Levels: 2
Square Footage: 1,891
Main Level Sq. Ft.: 1,075
Upper Level Sq. Ft.: 816
Bedrooms: 3
Bathrooms: 2½
Foundation: Basement
Materials List Available: Yes
Price Category: D

This compact traditional home reflects a thrifty attitude, while still providing the proper necessities for today's families.

Features:

• Great Room: From the entry, this large, eye-catching great room features a vaulted ceiling.

• Dining Room: Open to the living room, this formal dining space basks in the glow from a bay window.

• Kitchen: The U-shaped kitchen keeps everything within arm's reach. The boxed-out window above the sink is a cheery touch.

• Family Room: Offering room for everyone to stretch their legs, this family gathering space is blessed with a warm fireplace and French-door access to a backyard deck.

• Master Suite: This hideaway is the stuff of dreams, and includes a vaulted ceiling, two closets, and a private bath.

• Secondary Bedrooms: Two more bedrooms complete the upper floor and share a second full bath.

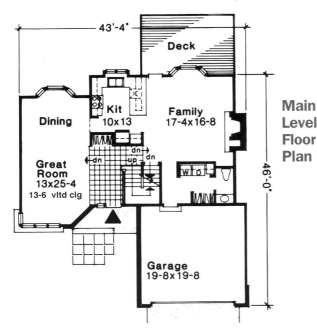

Main Level Floor Plan

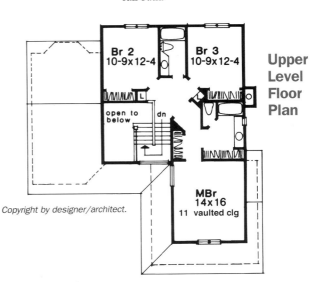

Upper Level Floor Plan

Copyright by designer/architect.

Plan #271038

Dimensions: 60' W x 35'4" D
Levels: 2
Square Footage: 1,820
Main Level Sq. Ft.: 987
Upper Level Sq. Ft.: 833
Bedrooms: 4
Bathrooms: 2½
Foundation: Basement
Materials List Available: No
Price Category: D

This well-designed home easily accommodates four bedrooms while maintaining an open feel throughout.

Features:

- Foyer: This two-story foyer can be reached from the sheltered front porch or through the three-car garage.

- Living Room: This room is spacious enough for any occasion, and lends itself to friendly conversation.

- Dining Room: Columns define this space, while wide windows overlook trees and gardens in the backyard.

- Kitchen: A cooktop island is the highlight here, and a pantry keeps the family chef organized. A cheery breakfast nook opens directly to a breezy deck.

- Family Room: With a bay window and a big fireplace, this room will be popular with guests and residents alike.

- Master Suite: A vaulted ceiling adds a dramatic flair to the bedroom. The private bath hosts a separate tub and shower.

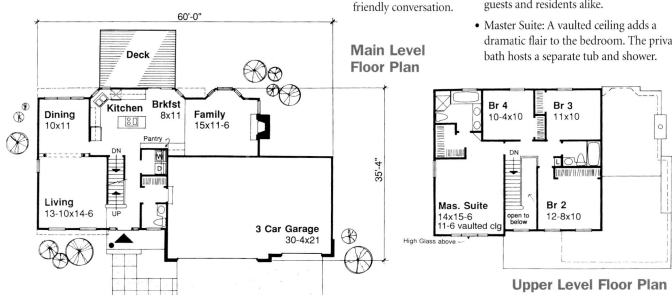

Main Level Floor Plan

60'-0"

Deck

Dining 10x11

Kitchen

Brkfst 8x11

Family 15x11-6

Pantry

DN

UP

Living 13-10x14-6

3 Car Garage 30-4x21

35'-4"

Copyright by designer/architect.

Upper Level Floor Plan

Br 4 10-4x10

Br 3 11x10

DN

Mas. Suite 14x15-6 11-6 vaulted clg

open to below

Br 2 12-8x10

High Glass above

Plan #161002

Dimensions: 64'2" W x 44'2" D
Levels: 1
Square Footage: 1,860
Bedrooms: 3
Bathrooms: 2
Foundation: Basement
Materials List Available: Yes
Price Category: D

Images provided by designer/architect.

The brick, stone, and cedar shake facade provides color and texture to the exterior, while the unique nooks and angles inside this delightful one-level home give it character.

Features:

- Great Room/Dining Room: This spacious great room is furnished with a wood-burning fireplace, a high ceiling, and French doors. Wide entrances to the breakfast room and dining room expand its space to comfortably hold large gatherings.

- Kitchen: The breakfast bar offers additional seating. The covered porch lets you enjoy a view of the landscape and is conveniently located for outdoor meals off this kitchen and breakfast area.

- Master Bedroom: The master bedroom is a private retreat. An alcove creates a comfortable sitting area, and an angled entry leads to the bath with whirlpool and a double-bowl vanity.

Left Side Elevation

Right Side Elevation

Rear Elevation

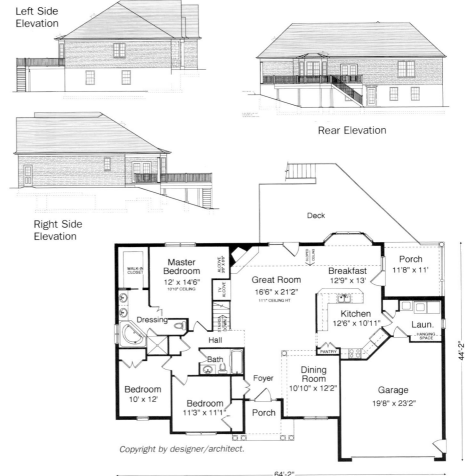

Copyright by designer/architect.

Dining Room

Living Room / Dining Room

Great Room/Breakfast Area

Great Room

SMARTtip

Installing Rods and Poles

The way to install a rod or pole depends on the type it is, the brackets that will hold it, the weight of the window treatment, and the surface to which it is being fastened. Given below are some general guidelines, but for specific installation procedures, refer to the instructions that accompany the rod or pole.

- Use a stepladder to reach high places.

- Use the proper tools.

- Take accurate measurements.

- Work with a helper.

- If attaching a bracket to wood, first drill small pilot holes to avoid splitting the wood.

- Consider using wall anchors, particularly for the heavier window treatments.

- Use a level as needed to help you position the brackets for the pole or rod.

- Take care not to drill or hammer into any pipes or electrical wiring.

Because they're designed to stand out, decorative poles and their finials require more room for installation than conventional drapery rods. Finials add inches to the ends of a window treatment, so make sure you have enough wall room to display your hardware to its full advantage. And because decorative rods are often heavy, be certain your window frames and walls can support the weight.

Plan #271043

Dimensions: 57'8" W x 36'4" D
Levels: 2
Square Footage: 2,396
Main Level Sq. Ft.: 1,238
Upper Level Sq. Ft.: 1,158
Bedrooms: 4
Bathrooms: 2½
Foundation: Basement
Materials List Available: Yes
Price Category: E

Images provided by designer/architect.

This grand home receives guests well, with brilliant windows, classic columns, and gorgeous gables.

Features:

- Living Room: Stately columns introduce this equally elegant room, which comes complete with a handsome fireplace flanked by shelves. A vaulted ceiling soars above it all.

- Dining Room: Opposite, the dining room is defined by its own columns. A butler's pantry joins it to the kitchen.

- Kitchen: This island-equipped kitchen and the breakfast area merge for easy casual dining. You'll find a built-in desk, two pantry closets, and laundry facilities here, too.

- Family Room: Corner windows brighten this fun space, which opens to a backyard deck through a lovely French door.

- Master Suite: The upper-floor master bedroom flaunts a vaulted ceiling and a private bath with dual vanities, a garden tub and a separate shower.

Main Level Floor Plan

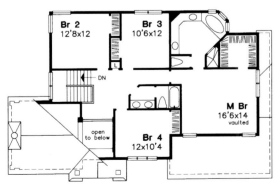

Upper Level Floor Plan

Copyright by designer/architect.

Plan #271044

Dimensions: 61' W x 54'4" D
Levels: 2
Square Footage: 2,341
Main Level Sq. Ft.: 1,750
Upper Level Sq. Ft.: 591
Bedrooms: 4
Bathrooms: 2½
Foundation: Basement
Materials List Available: No
Price Category: E

This traditional home uses hipped rooflines and shingle siding to recall the warmth of English architecture.

Features:

- **Living Room:** A vaulted ceiling crowns this formal room, which immediately welcomes guests from the entry.

- **Dining Room:** Decorative columns introduce this formal dining room, where sumptuous meals are the perfect complement to the surroundings.

- **Kitchen/Breakfast:** This smart pairing ensures a fail-safe spot for casual dining. Note the island cooktop and sliding-glass-door access to the backyard deck.

- **Family Room:** Winter evenings will be less tiresome in this spacious gathering room. A serving bar from the breakfast room, a fireplace, and corner windows make it perfect.

- **Master Bedroom:** This is heaven! A private patio, private bath—and a vaulted ceiling over the sleeping chamber. Lovely!

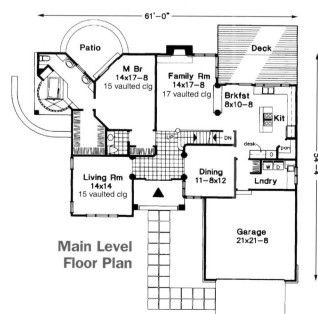

Main Level Floor Plan

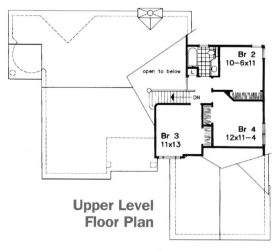

Upper Level Floor Plan

Copyright by designer/architect.

Plan #151034

Dimensions: 58'6" W x 68'4" D
Levels: 1
Square Footage: 2,133
Bedrooms: 3
Bathrooms: 2
Foundation: Crawl space, slab, or basement
Materials List Available: Yes
Price Category: D

You'll love the high ceilings, open floor plan, and contemporary design features in this home.

Features:

- Great Room: A pass-through tiled fireplace between this lovely large room and the adjacent hearth room allows you to notice the mirror effect created by the 10-ft. boxed ceilings in both rooms.

- Dining Room: An 11-ft. ceiling and 8-in. boxed column give formality to this lovely room, where you're certain to entertain.

- Kitchen: If you're a cook, this room may become your favorite spot in the house, thanks to its great design, which includes plenty of work and storage space, and a very practical layout.

- Master Suite: A 10-ft. boxed ceiling gives elegance to this room. A pocket door opens to the private bath, with its huge walk-in closet, glass-blocked whirlpool tub, separate glass shower, and private toilet room.

Images provided by designer/architect.

Plan #151012

Dimensions: 47' W x 94'1" D
Levels: 2
Square Footage: 3,730
Main Level Sq. Ft.: 2,648
Upper Level Sq. Ft.: 1,082
Bedrooms: 3
Bathrooms: 2½
Foundation: Crawl space or slab.
Optional full basement plan available
for extra fee.
Materials List Available: Yes
Price Category: H

Amenities in this charmer include skylights over the foyer and a built-in cedar storage chest.

Features:

- **Living Room:** Enjoy the vaulted ceiling and warming fireplace in this gracious room.

- **Den:** A gas fireplace and built-in media center and bookshelves add up to a relaxing space.

- **Dining Room:** 10-in. columns give formality and built-in cabinets give practicality.

- **Kitchen:** Open to the morning room, the kitchen has an island work area that's built for efficiency.

- **Morning Room:** Enjoy the morning light that streams through the bay window in this room.

- **Rear Covered Porch:** Reach it from the morning room, dining room, or master bedroom.

Main Level Floor Plan

Upper Level Floor Plan

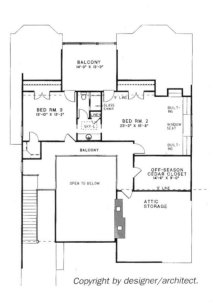

Copyright by designer/architect.

Plan #131025

Dimensions: 62'4" W x 65'10" D
Levels: 1½
Square Footage: 3,204
Main Level Sq. Ft.: 2,196
Upper Level Sq. Ft.: 1,008
Bedrooms: 4
Bathrooms: 4
Foundation: Basement, crawl space, or slab
Materials List Available: Yes
Price Category: H

Images provided by designer/architect.

You'll appreciate the flowing layout that's designed for entertaining but also suits an active family.

Features:

• Ceiling Height: 8 ft.

• Great Room: Decorative columns serve as the entryway to the great room that's made for entertaining. A fireplace makes it warm in winter; built-in shelves give a classic appearance; and the serving counter it shares with the kitchen is both practical and attractive.

• Kitchen: A door into the backyard makes outdoor entertaining easy, and the full bathroom near the door adds convenience.

• Master Suite: Enjoy the sunny sitting area that's a feature of this suite. A tray ceiling adds character to the room, and a huge walk-in closet is easy to organize. The bathroom features a corner spa tub.

• Upper Level Bedrooms: Each of the additional 3 bedrooms is bright and cheery.

Main Level Floor Plan

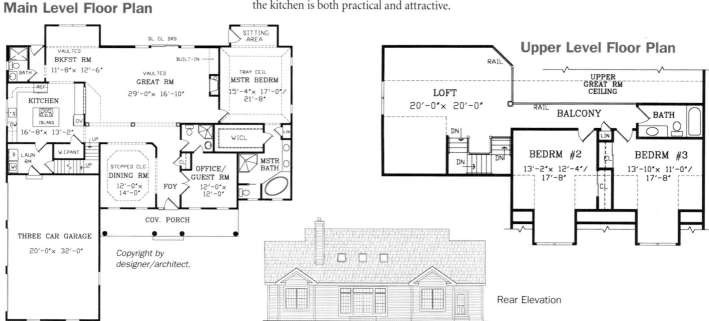

Upper Level Floor Plan

Copyright by designer/architect.

Rear Elevation

Plan #121026

Dimensions: 66'8" W x 76' D
Levels: 2
Square Footage: 3,926
Main Level Sq. Ft.: 2,351
Upper Level Sq. Ft.: 1,575
Bedrooms: 4
Bathrooms: 3 full, 2 half
Foundation: Basement
Materials List Available: Yes
Price Category: H

Images provided by designer/architect.

Plenty of space and architectural detail make this a comfortable and gracious home.

Features:

- Ceiling Height: 8 ft. unless otherwise noted.

- Great Room: A soaring cathedral ceiling makes this great room seem even more spacious than it is, while the fireplace framed by windows lends warmth and comfort.

- Eating Area: There's a dining room for more formal entertaining, but this informal eating area to the left of the great room will get plenty

of daily use. It features a built-in desk for compiling shopping lists and recipes and access to the backyard.

- Kitchen: Next door to the eating area, this kitchen is designed to make food preparation a pleasure. It features a center cooktop, a recycling area, and a corner pantry.

- Lockers: You'll find a bench and lockers at the service entry and additional lockers in the laundry room next door.

Main Level Floor Plan

Upper Level Floor Plan

Copyright by designer/architect.

Plan #161032

Dimensions: 75'8" W x 70'6" D
Levels: 2
Square Footage: 4,517
Main Level Sq. Ft.: 2,562
Finished Lower Level Sq. Ft.: 1,955
Bedrooms: 3
Full Baths: 2
Half Baths: 3
Foundation: Basement
Materials List Available: Yes
Price Category: I

Images provided by designer/architect.

The brick-and-stone exterior, a recessed entry, and a tower containing a large library combine to convey the strength and character of this enchanting house.

Features:

- Hearth Room: Your family or guests will enjoy this large, comfortable hearth room, which has a gas fireplace and access to the rear deck, perfect for friendly gatherings.

- Kitchen: This spacious kitchen features a walk-in pantry and a center island.

- Master Suite: Designed for privacy, this master suite includes a sloped ceiling and opens to the rear deck. It also features a deluxe whirlpool bath, walk-in shower, separate his and her vanities, and a walk-in closet.

- Lower Level: This lower level includes a separate wine room, exercise room, sauna, two bedrooms, and enough space for a huge recreation room.

SMARTtip

Art Underfoot

Make a simple geometric pattern with your flooring materials. Create a focal point in a courtyard or a small area of a patio by fashioning an intricate mosaic with tile, stone, or colored concrete. By combining elements and colors, a simple garden room floor becomes a wonderful work of art. Whether you commission a craftsman or do it yourself, you'll have a permanent art installation right in your own backyard.

Rear View

Main Level
Floor Plan

Deck

Deck

Hearth Room
19'10" x 17'7"

9' ceiling height

Master Bedroom
15'4" x 18'9"

Breakfast
11'7" x 9'6"
irregular

stairs down

Great Room
17'9" x 17'10"
11' ceiling height

Kitchen
15'5" x 13'10"
irregular

Garage
13'8" x 20'

Dressing

Bath

Laun.

walk-in closet

Foyer

Dining Room
12' x 15'

Pantry

Library
13' x 14'7"

Porch

Two Car Garage
23' x 30'6"

Basement Level
Floor Plan

Rec. Room
15' x 17'2"

Bedroom
15' x 12'

Rec. Room
34'5" x 19'6"

stairs up

Bath

walk-in closet

cabinets

Exercise
Room
9'7" x 15'3"

Unexcavated

Bedroom
16'6" x 13'

Bath

Wine Room

Sauna

walk-in closet

Basement

Unexcavated

*Copyright by
designer/architect.*

Rear Elevation

Kitchen

Kitchen

Living Room

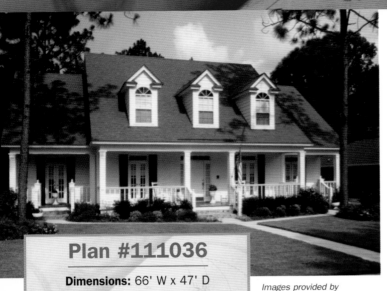

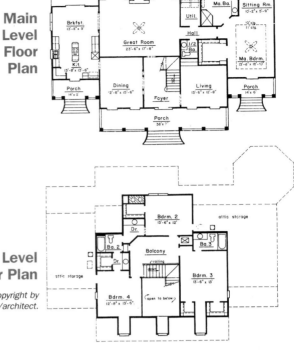

**Main
Level
Floor
Plan**

*Images provided by
designer/architect.*

**Upper Level
Floor Plan**

*Copyright by
designer/architect.*

Plan #111036

Dimensions: 66' W x 47' D

Levels: 2

Square Footage: 3,149

Main Level Sq. Ft.: 2,033

Upper Level Sq. Ft.: 1,116

Bedrooms: 4

Bathrooms: 3½

Foundation: Pier

Materials List Available: No

Price Category: G

**Main Level
Floor Plan**

*Images provided by
designer/architect.*

Upper Level Floor Plan

Copyright by designer/architect.

Plan #111037

Dimensions: 66' W x 84' D

Levels: 2

Square Footage: 3,176

Main Level Sq. Ft.: 2,183

Upper Level Sq. Ft.: 993

Bedrooms: 4

Bathrooms: 3½

Foundation: Slab

Materials List Available: No

Price Category: G

Main Level Floor Plan

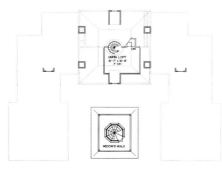

Rear Elevation

Images provided by designer/architect.

Copyright by designer/architect.

Upper Level Floor Plan

Plan #121049

Dimensions: 82' W x 60'8" D

Levels: 2

Square Footage: 3,335

Main Level Sq. Ft.: 2,054

Upper Level Sq. Ft.: 1,281

Bedrooms: 4

Bathrooms: 3½

Foundation: Slab

Materials List Available: Yes

Price Category: G

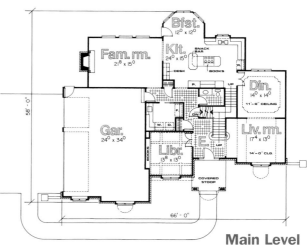

Main Level Floor Plan

Images provided by designer/architect.

Upper Level Floor Plan

Copyright by designer/architect.

Plan #121096

Dimensions: 66' W x 58' D

Levels: 2

Square Footage: 3,611

Main Level Sq. Ft.: 1,857

Upper Level Sq. Ft.: 1,754

Bedrooms: 4

Bathrooms: 2½

Foundation: Basement

Materials List Available: Yes

Price Category: G

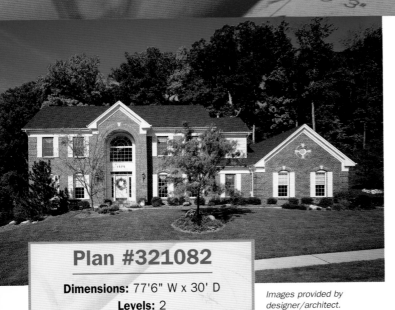

Main Level Floor Plan

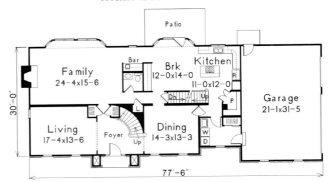

Plan #321082

Dimensions: 77'6" W x 30' D

Levels: 2

Square Footage: 3,144

Main Level Sq. Ft.: 1,724

Upper Level Sq. Ft.: 1,420

Bedrooms: 4

Bathrooms: 4½

Foundation: Basement

Materials List Available: Yes

Price Category: G

Images provided by designer/architect.

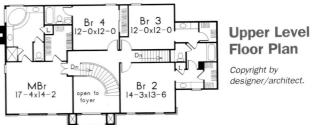

Upper Level Floor Plan

Copyright by designer/architect.

Plan #141020

Dimensions: 58' W x 40'4" D

Levels: 2

Square Footage: 3,140

Main Level Sq. Ft.: 1,553

Upper Level Sq. Ft.: 1,587

Bedrooms: 5

Bathrooms: 4

Foundation: Basement

Materials List Available: No

Price Category: G

Images provided by designer/architect.

Main Level Floor Plan

Upper Level Floor Plan

Copyright by designer/architect.

Upper Level Floor Plan

Main Level Floor Plan

Images provided by designer/architect.

Copyright by designer/architect.

Plan #151121

Dimensions: 66'8" W x 60'4" D
Levels: 2
Square Footage: 3,108
Main Level Sq. Ft.: 2,107
Upper Level Sq. Ft.: 1,001
Bedrooms: 3
Bathrooms: 2½
Foundation: Crawl space, slab (basement option for fee)
Materials List Available: Yes
Price Category: G

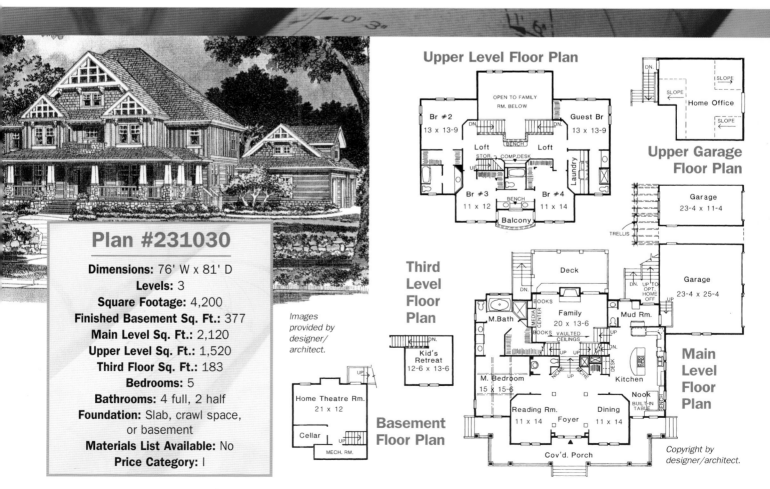

Upper Level Floor Plan

Upper Garage Floor Plan

Third Level Floor Plan

Basement Floor Plan

Main Level Floor Plan

Images provided by designer/architect.

Copyright by designer/architect.

Plan #231030

Dimensions: 76' W x 81' D
Levels: 3
Square Footage: 4,200
Finished Basement Sq. Ft.: 377
Main Level Sq. Ft.: 2,120
Upper Level Sq. Ft.: 1,520
Third Floor Sq. Ft.: 183
Bedrooms: 5
Bathrooms: 4 full, 2 half
Foundation: Slab, crawl space, or basement
Materials List Available: No
Price Category: I

Plan #151031

Dimensions: 60'2" W x 60'2" D

Levels: 2

Square Footage: 3,130

Main Level Sq. Ft.: 1,600

Upper Level Sq. Ft.: 1,530

Bedrooms: 3

Bathrooms: 3½

Foundation: Crawl space, slab

Materials List Available: Yes

Price Category: G

Images provided by designer/architect.

Main Level Floor Plan

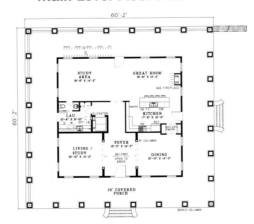

Upper Level Floor Plan

Copyright by designer/architect.

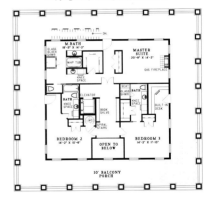

If you love traditional Southern plantation homes, you'll want this house with its wraparound porches that are graced with boxed columns.

Features:

- Great Room: Use the gas fireplace for warmth in this comfortable room, which is open to the kitchen.

- Living Room: 8-in. columns add formality as you enter this living and dining room.

- Kitchen: You'll love the island bar with a sink. An elevator here can take you to the other floors.

- Master Suite: A gas fireplace warms this area, and the bath is luxurious.

- Bedrooms: Each has a private bath and built-in bookshelves for easy organizing.

- Optional Features: Choose a 2,559-sq.-ft. basement and add a kitchen to it, or finish the 1,744-sq.-ft. bonus room and add a spiral staircase and a bath.

Basement Level Floor Plan

Optional Upper Level Floor Plan

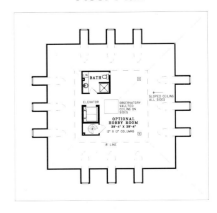

Plan #271031

Dimensions: 88' W x 87'4" D
Levels: 2
Square Footage: 3,062
Main Level Sq. Ft.: 2,389
Upper Level Sq. Ft.: 673
Bedrooms: 4
Bathrooms: 3½
Foundation: Basement
Materials List Available: Yes
Price Category: G

Images provided by designer/architect.

The distinctive look of this elegant, trendsetting estate reflects a refined sense of style and taste.

Features:

- **Parlor/Dining:** Off the vaulted foyer, this cozy sunken parlor boasts a vaulted ceiling and a warm fireplace. Opposite the parlor, this formal dining room is serviced by a stylish wet bar.

- **Kitchen:** This open room features an angled snack bar and serves a skylighted breakfast room.

- **Family Room:** Defined by columns, this skylighted, vaulted family room offers a handsome fireplace with a built-in log bin. Sliding glass doors open to a backyard deck.

- **Master Suite:** This deluxe getaway boasts a vaulted ceiling and unfolds to a skylighted sitting area and a private deck. The garden tub in the master bath basks under its own skylight.

- **Library/Guest Room:** This versatile room enjoys a high ceiling and a walk-in closet.

- **Secondary Bedrooms:** Two reside on the upper floor.

Main Level Floor Plan

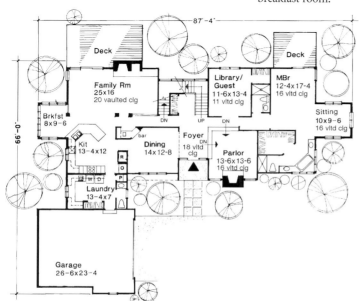

Upper Level Floor Plan

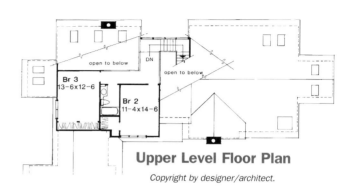

Copyright by designer/architect.

Plan #151020

Dimensions: 96'10" W x 75'10" D
Levels: 2
Square Footage: 4,532
Main Level Sq. Ft.: 3,732
Upper Level Sq. Ft.: 800
Bedrooms: 3
Bathrooms: 3
Foundation: Crawl space or slab; optional full basement plan available for extra fee
Materials List Available: Yes
Price Category: I

From the arched entry to the lanai and exercise and game rooms, this elegant home is a delight.

Features:

- Foyer: This spacious foyer with 12-ft. ceilings sets an open-air feeling for this home.

- Hearth Room: This cozy hearth room shares a 3-sided fireplace with the breakfast room. French doors open to the rear lanai.

- Dining Room: Entertain in this majestic dining room, with its arched entry and 12-ft. ceilings.

- Master Suite: This stunning suite includes a sitting room and access to the lanai. The bath

Images provided by designer/architect.

features two walk-in closets, a step-up whirlpool tub with 8-in. columns, and glass-block shower.

- Upper Level: You'll find an exercise room, a game room, and attic storage space upstairs.

Rear View

Main Level Floor Plan

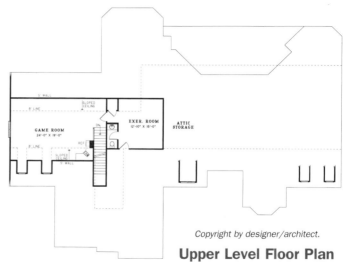

Upper Level Floor Plan

Plan #271029

Dimensions: 53' W x 55'8" D
Levels: 2
Square Footage: 3,039
Main Level Sq. Ft.: 1,612
Upper Level Sq. Ft.: 1,427
Bedrooms: 4
Bathrooms: 2½
Foundation: Basement
Materials List Available: Yes
Price Category: G

Images provided by designer/architect.

This English cottage-style home is packed with fabulous amenities.

Features:

• Living Room: The vaulted entry reveals an elegant stairway and this vaulted formal living room, which boasts oversized windows and a dramatic corner fireplace.

• Dining Room: Decorative columns introduce this adjoining formal dining room, which opens to a screened porch.

• Kitchen: An island cooktop punctuates this large kitchen, which flows into a spacious breakfast room.

• Family Room: The certain hot spot of the home, this generously proportioned room boasts a warming fireplace and access to a jaw-dropping wraparound deck that promises truly awesome views.

• Master Suite: Secluded to a corner of the upper floor, the master bedroom features its own fireplace and private bath. Two more bedrooms and a bonus room finish the floor.

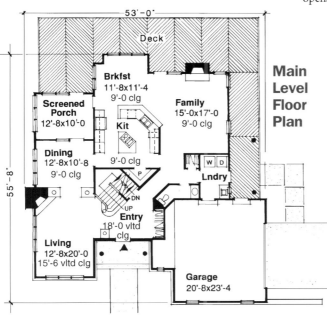

Main Level Floor Plan

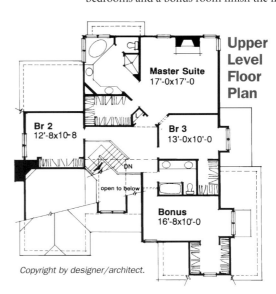

Upper Level Floor Plan

Copyright by designer/architect.

Plan #131031

Dimensions: 69'8" W x 48'4" D
Levels: 2
Square Footage: 4,027
Main Level Sq. Ft.: 2,198
Upper Level Sq. Ft.: 1,829
Bedrooms: 5
Bathrooms: 4½
Foundation: Crawl space, basement
Materials List Available: Yes
Price Category: I

If you love dramatic lines and contemporary design, you'll be thrilled by this lovely home.

Features:

- Foyer: A gorgeous vaulted ceiling sets the stage for a curved staircase flanked by a formal living room and dining room.

- Living Room: The foyer ceiling continues in this room, giving it an unusual presence.

- Family Room: This sunken family room features a fireplace and a wall of windows that look out to the backyard. It's open to the living room, making it an ideal spot for entertaining.

- Kitchen: With a large island, this kitchen flows into the breakfast room.

- Master Suite: The luxurious bedroom has a dramatic tray ceiling and includes two walk-in closets. The dressing room is fitted with a sink, and the spa bath is sumptuous.

Foyer

Breakfast Area

Main Level Floor Plan

Upper Level Floor Plan

Copyright by designer/architect.

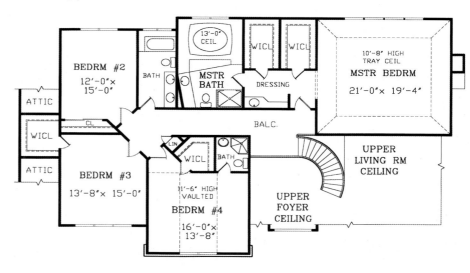

Butler's Pantry

Kitchen

Master Bedroom

Master Bathroom

Copyright by designer/architect.

Images provided by
designer/architect.

**Optional
Basement Level
Floor Plan**

Plan #321034

Dimensions: 75'8" W x 52'6" D

Levels: 1

Square Footage: 3,508

Bedrooms: 4

Bathrooms: 3

Foundation: Daylight basement

Materials List Available: Yes

Price Category: H

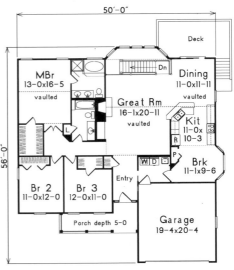

Rear View

Plan #321029

Dimensions: 50' W x 56' D

Levels: 1

Square Footage: 2,334

Bedrooms: 3

Bathrooms: 2

Foundation: Daylight basement

Materials List Available: Yes

Price Category: E

Images provided by
designer/architect.

**Optional
Basement
Level
Floor Plan**

Copyright by designer/architect.

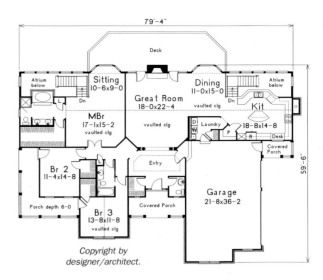

Great Room 18-0x22-4 vaulted clg

Sitting 10-6x9-0

Dining 11-0x15-0 vaulted clg

Atrium below

Atrium below

Deck

Kit 18-8x14-8

MBr 17-1x15-2 vaulted clg

Laundry

Dn

Dn

Covered Porch

Br 2 11-4x14-8

Entry

Covered Porch

Garage 21-8x36-2

Br 3 13-8x11-8 vaulted clg

Porch depth 6-0

Copyright by designer/architect.

Plan #321031

Dimensions: 79'4" W x 59'6" D

Levels: 1

Square Footage: 3,200

Bedrooms: 3

Bathrooms: 2½

Foundation: Daylight basement

Materials List Available: Yes

Price Category: G

Images provided by designer/architect.

Optional Basement Level Floor Plan

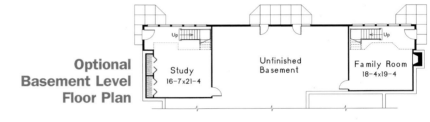

Study 16-7x21-4

Unfinished Basement

Family Room 18-4x19-4

Up

Up

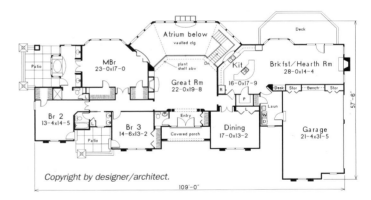

Atrium below vaulted clg

MBr 23-0x17-0

Great Rm 22-0x19-8

Kit 16-0x17-9

Brkfst/Hearth Rm 28-0x14-4

Deck

Patio

plant shelf abv

Dn

Br 2 13-4x14-5

Br 3 14-6x13-2

Entry

Dining 17-0x13-2

Garage 21-4x31-5

Patio

Covered porch

Laun

Patio

Copyright by designer/architect.

109'-0"

Plan #321032

Dimensions: 109' W x 57'6" D

Levels: 1

Square Footage: 4,826

Bedrooms: 4

Bathrooms: 2½

Foundation: Daylight basement

Materials List Available: Yes

Price Category: I

Images provided by designer/architect.

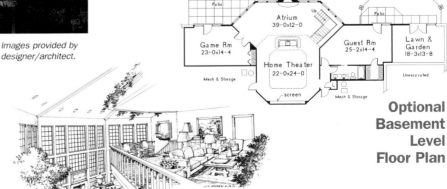

Atrium 39-0x12-0

Game Rm 23-0x14-4

Home Theater 22-0x24-0

Guest Rm 25-2x14-4

Lawn & Garden 18-3x13-8

Patio

Patio

Up

Mech & Storage

Mech & Storage

Unexcavated

screen

Optional Basement Level Floor Plan

Main Level Floor Plan

Plan #181079

Dimensions: 60' W x 47'8" D

Levels: 2

Square Footage: 3,016

Main Level Sq. Ft.: 1,716

Upper Level Sq. Ft.: 1,300

Bedrooms: 6

Bathrooms: 4½

Foundation: Crawl space

Materials List Available: Yes

Price Category: G

Images provided by designer/architect.

Upper Level Floor Plan

Copyright by designer/architect.

Upper Level Floor Plan

Plan #201126

Dimensions: 82'10" W x 54' D

Levels: 2

Square Footage: 3,813

Main Level Sq. Ft.: 2,553

Upper Level Sq. Ft.: 1,260

Bedrooms: 4

Bathrooms: 3½

Foundation: Crawl space, slab

Materials List Available: Yes

Price Category: H

Images provided by designer/architect.

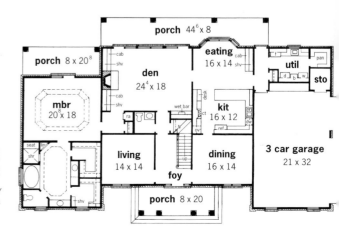

Main Level Floor Plan

Copyright by designer/architect.

Main Level Floor Plan

Deck 27' x 12'

Breakfast 11'3" x 16'6'

Porch 30'x 8'

Master Bedroom 16'4" x 16'6'

Living Room 24'x 17'4"

Util.

Kitchen 11'3"x 19'

WIC

WIC

Bath

Ma. Bath

Porch 11'8"x 6'

Dining Room 13'3"x 13'10"

Guest Bedroom 12'6"x 12'

Porch 11'8"x 6'

Porch 26'x 7'

Images provided by designer/architect.

Plan #111038

Dimensions: 62' W x 67' D

Levels: 2

Square Footage: 3,223

Main Level Sq. Ft.: 2,213

Upper Level Sq. Ft.: 1,010

Bedrooms: 4

Bathrooms: 4

Foundation: Pier

Materials List Available: No

Price Category: G

Upper Level Floor Plan

Bath

Balcony

Exercise Room 12'6" x 12'5"

WIC

WIC

WIC

Bedroom 13'6" x 12'6"

Open to Below

Bedroom 12'6"x 12'6"

Copyright by designer/architect.

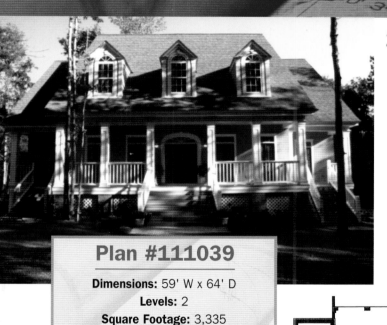

Images provided by designer/architect.

Main Level Floor Plan

Copyright by designer/architect.

Wood Deck 30'10"x 13'

Breakfast 11'4"x 13'

Porch 30'5"x 8'

Master Bedroom 16'4"x 16'4"

Living 21'6"x 17'2"

Util.

Kitchen 11'4" x 18'4"

WIC

WIC

Bath

WIC

Ma. Bath

Dining 13'6" x 13'10"

Foyer

Study 13'8"x 12'

Porch

Porch

Porch 36'x 7'

Plan #111039

Dimensions: 59' W x 64' D

Levels: 2

Square Footage: 3,335

Main Level Sq. Ft.: 2,129

Upper Level Sq. Ft.: 1,206

Bedrooms: 4

Bathrooms: 4

Foundation: Basement

Materials List Available: No

Price Category: G

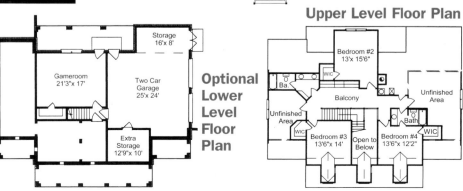

Storage 16'x 8'

Gameroom 21'3" x 17'

Two Car Garage 25'x 24'

Optional Lower Level Floor Plan

Extra Storage 12'9"x 10'

Upper Level Floor Plan

Bedroom #2 13'x 15'6"

Ba.

WIC

Unfinished Area

Balcony

Unfinished Area

WIC

Bath

WIC

Bedroom #3 13'6"x 14'

Open to Below

Bedroom #4 13'6"x 12'2"

Plan #111002

Dimensions: 58' W x 59' D

Levels: 2

Square Footage: 3,266

Main Level Sq. Ft.: 2,036

Upper Level Sq. Ft.: 1,230

Bedrooms: 4

Full Bathrooms: 3½

Foundation: Aboveground basement

Price Category: G

Materials List Available: No

This design has every feature that you'll want in a home for a joyful family life.

Features:

- Ceiling Height: 10 ft.

- Front Porch: Stairs lead up to this wraparound porch, where you can group rockers and a swing.

- Dining Room: This formal room opens from the foyer for the convenience of your guests.

- Study: French doors from the foyer open to this area, which could also serve as an office.

- Living Room: The French doors in this room lead to the screened-in porch at the rear of the house.

- Multimedia Room: On the second floor, this room is convenient to all three secondary bedrooms, so the children will love it.

- Master Suite: Two walk-in closets give a practical touch to this luxurious bedroom, and the two vanities, standing shower, and deluxe bathtub make you feel pampered by the bathroom.

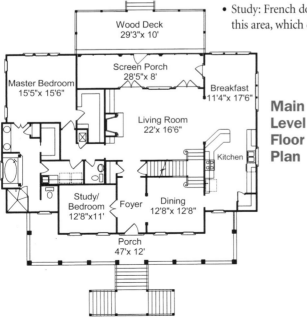

Main Level Floor Plan

- Wood Deck 29'3"x 10'
- Screen Porch 28'5"x 8'
- Master Bedroom 15'5"x 15'6"
- Breakfast 11'4"x 17'6"
- Living Room 22'x 16'6"
- Kitchen
- Study/Bedroom 12'8"x11'
- Foyer
- Dining 12'8"x 12'8"
- Porch 47'x 12'

Upper Level Floor Plan

- Multimedia Room 12'7"x 15'4"
- Bedroom 15'x 11'
- Bedroom 12'7"x 14'2"
- Bedroom 13'8"x 15'8"

Kitchen

Living Room

Woodstove Safety

A couple of issues need special emphasis with regard to stoves. The first is protecting children from contact burns. Several manufacturers make sturdy fireproof safety screens.

The second issue is making sure that logs are the right length to fit into the firebox. Once a log that's too long is popped into a hot stove, removing it safely can be tricky. Seasoned logs catch fire quickly. Nevertheless, should you insert a log that's too long in the stove, remove it immediately and transport it in a fireproof container (such as a metal ashcan) to a safe place outside: a gravel driveway, a sandbox, or a stone or concrete patio. Remember that a scorched log may be slowly burning, even if you can't see smoke. Dousing it with water from a bucket or garden hose will help.

Inadvertently closing a glass door on a slightly oversized log represents a whole set of hazards: broken glass, the need to remove the log, and a fire burning without a protective barrier between it and the combustibles in the room. If there are only embers in the firebox or the fire is low-burning and small, remove the log as described above and close what's left of the door. Open some windows, and let the fire burn down naturally. Then smother the embers with cold ashes from your ash bucket or with sand. If the fire is still crackling and sparking, create a fireproof barrier in front of the opening to prevent sparks from shooting onto combustible materials. (Possibilities for makeshift screens include metal cookie sheets or an all-metal window screen propped against the stove front.) Make sure the embers have burned out.

If there are shooting sparks and flames, get children out and call the fire department. While you wait, try to contain the flames in the firebox. (Throwing water on a fire is a last resort because of the steam and smoke that will result.) Don't cancel the SOS to the fire department even if it looks as if the flames are out.

Images provided by designer/architect.

Plan #211111

Dimensions: 66' W x 74' D
Levels: 2
Square Footage: 3,035
Main Level Sq. Ft.: 2,008
Upper Level Sq. Ft.: 1,027
Bedrooms: 4
Bathrooms: 3½
Foundation: Crawl space
Materials List Available: Yes
Price Category: G

Kids can be kids without disturbing the adults, thanks to the rear stair in this large family house.

Features:

- Ceiling Height: 9 ft. unless otherwise noted.

- Formal Living Room: This large formal living room is connected to the formal dining room and to the family room by a pair of French doors, making this an ideal home for entertaining.

- Wet Bar: This wet bar is neatly placed between the kitchen and the family room, adding to the entertainment amenities.

- Deck: Step out of the family room onto a covered porch that leads to this spacious deck and a breezeway.

- Master Suite: This master suite is isolated for privacy. The master bath is flooded with natural light from sky windows in the sloped ceiling, and it has a dressing vanity with surrounding mirrors.

- Secondary Bedrooms: All secondary bedrooms have bath access and dual closets.

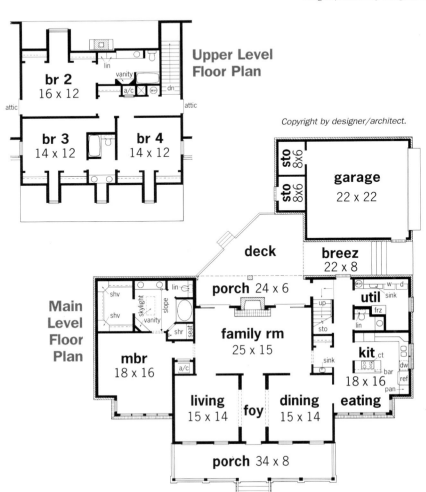

Copyright by designer/architect.

Plan #191017

Dimensions: 78' W x 51' D

Levels: 1

Square Footage: 2,605

Bedrooms: 4

Bathrooms: 3½

Foundation: Crawl space, slab, or basement

Materials List Available: No

Price Category: F

Images provided by designer/architect.

You'll love the elegance of this gorgeous home, which includes every amenity you can imagine.

Features:

- Great Room: An archway from the foyer welcomes you to this expansive room, with its recessed ceiling, gas fireplace, custom cabinets, and French doors leading to the covered rear porch.

- Kitchen: This large room includes a pantry, stove on an island, angled sink, snack bar, and built-in desk close to the hall stairs.

- Laundry Room: You'll find a sink, storage closets, and wall-to-wall cabinets above the washer/dryer and freezer area in this practical spot.

- Master Suite: A wall of windows greets you in the bedroom, and built-in cabinets add storage space. The huge walk-in closet is close to the dressing area. The luxurious bath has a skylight over the dual sinks and is located so that one person can sleep while the other uses it.

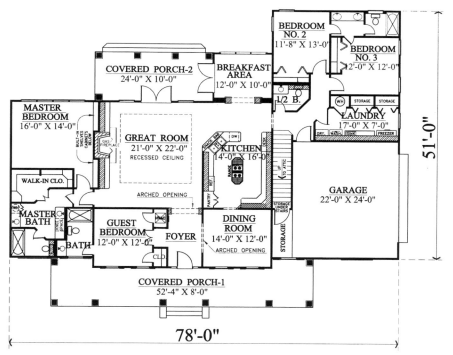

Copyright by designer/architect.

Plan #271037

Dimensions: 66' W x 65' D

Levels: 2

Square Footage: 4,220

Main Level Sq. Ft.: 2,768

Upper Level Sq. Ft.: 1,452

Bedrooms: 4

Bathrooms: 4½

Foundation: Basement

Materials List Available: No

Price Category: I

This design allows family members to carry out their work and leisure activities inside the home. The options for leisure and study are almost countless!

Features:

- "Us" Room: The home's sunken "Us" room is the center of attention, with its vaulted ceiling and two-story fireplace. The room is surrounded by the family living areas.

- Master Suite: Relax in this oasis, which offers twin walk-in closets and a lovely bath.

- Upper Floor: Study areas, an office, and an exercise space are just the beginning!

Dining Room / "Us" Room

Main Level Floor Plan

66—0

Patio

Activity Area
18—4x13—8
13 vaulted clg

Master Suite
17x18—4
13 vaulted clg

glass block

Lndry 6x16

Lndry tub

desk

Garden

Kit

bar

Dining
11—4x12
10 clg

'US' Room
27—4x19—8
23—6 clg

half wall

10—6 clg

Garden

shower tub

65—0

Entry
10 clg

cabinet

Mud

DN

sink

Garage
22—4x21

stor

Porch

Multi-Purpose
17—4x19
13 vaulted clg

Upper Level Floor Plan

glass block

Exercise
11—8x9—4
9—6 clg

DN

cabinet

desk

Kid's Study
11—6
sloped clg

open to below

Office
11—6
sloped clg

desk

skylight above

glass block

Stor.

Br 2
11—4x13
9—6 vltd clg

Br 3
11—4x13
9—6 vltd clg

Plan #271042

Dimensions: 69'8" W x 71'4" D
Levels: 2
Square Footage: 3,469
Main Level Sq. Ft.: 2,132
Upper Level Sq. Ft.: 1,337
Bedrooms: 5
Bathrooms: 3½
Foundation: Basement
Materials List Available: No
Price Category: G

Images provided by designer/architect.

This thoroughly up-to-date home features two deluxe suites.

Features:

- **Dining/Living:** Flanking the soaring entry, these formal rooms are perfect for elegant parties.

- **Swing Suite:** At the rear of the home, this suite can house guests or an elderly parent.

- **Family Room:** Big and welcoming, this space includes a fireplace and a TV nook.

Kitchen

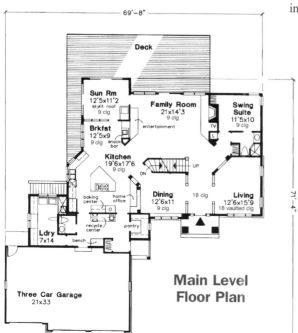

Main Level Floor Plan

Upper Level Floor Plan

Copyright by designer/architect.

- **Master Suite:** The home's second suite offers all of today's best amenities, including a vaulted ceiling and private bath.

Images provided by designer/architect.

Plan #211076

Dimensions: 95' W x 90' D
Levels: 2
Square Footage: 4,242
Main Level Sq. Ft.: 3,439
Upper Level Sq. Ft.: 803
Bedrooms: 4
Bathrooms: 4 full, 3 half
Foundation: Raised slab
Materials List Available: Yes
Price Category: I

Build this country manor home on a large lot with a breathtaking view to complement its beauty.

Features:

• Foyer: You'll love the two-story ceiling here.

• Living Room: A sunken floor, two-story ceiling, large fireplace, and generous balcony above combine to create an unusually beautiful room.

• Kitchen: Use the breakfast bar at any time of the day. The layout guarantees ample working space, and the pantry gives room for extra storage.

• Master Suite: A sunken floor, wood-burning fireplace, and 200-sq.-ft. sitting area work in concert to create a restful space.

• Bedrooms: The guest room is on the main floor, and bedrooms 2 and 3, both with built-in desks in special study areas, are on the upper level.

• Outdoor Grilling Area: Fitted with a bar, this area makes it a pleasure to host a large group.

Kitchen

Kitchen

Main Level Floor Plan

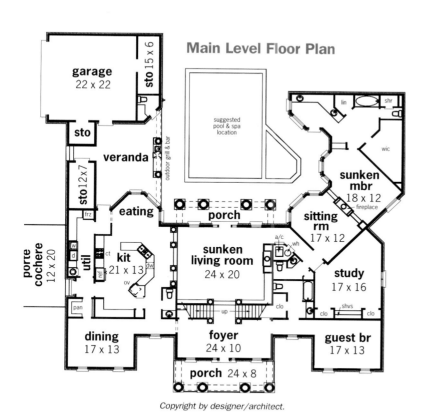

garage 22 x 22

sto 15 x 6

sto

veranda

outdoor grill & bar

sto 12 x 7

eating

frz

porte cochere 12 x 20

w
d

util

ct

kit 21 x 13

ref

ov

dw

pan

suggested pool & spa location

porch

sunken living room 24 x 20

a/c
wh

up

clo

dining 17 x 13

foyer 24 x 10

porch 24 x 8

lin

shr

sunken mbr 18 x 12

fireplace

sitting rm 17 x 12

wic

study 17 x 16

shvs

clo

clo

clo

guest br 17 x 13

Copyright by designer/architect.

Master Bathroom

Upper Level Floor Plan

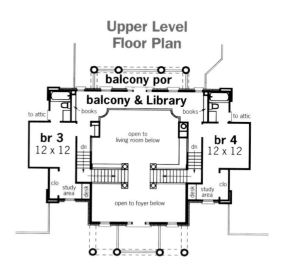

balcony por

balcony & Library

to attic

books

books

to attic

br 3 12 x 12

open to living room below

br 4 12 x 12

clo

dn

dn

clo

study area

desk

desk

study area

clo

open to foyer below

Dining Room

Living Room

Plan #211074

Dimensions: 64' W x 89' D
Levels: 2
Square Footage: 3,486
Main Level Sq. Ft.: 2,575
Upper Level Sq. Ft.: 911
Bedrooms: 4
Bathrooms: 3
Foundation: Crawl space
Materials List Available: Yes
Price Category: G

Images provided by designer/architect.

This plantation-style home may have an old-fashioned charm, but the energy-efficient design and many amenities inside make it thoroughly contemporary.

Features:

- Ceiling Height: 9 ft.
- Porches: This wraparound front porch is fully 10 ft. wide, so you can group rockers, occasional tables, and even a swing here and save the rear porch for grilling and alfresco dining.

- Entry: A two-story ceiling here sets an elegant tone for the rest of the home.
- Living Room: Somewhat isolated, this room is an ideal spot for quiet entertaining. It has built-in bookshelves and a nearby wet bar.
- Kitchen: You'll love the large counter areas and roomy storage space in this lovely kitchen, where both friends and family are sure to congregate.
- Master Suite: It's easy to pamper yourself in this comfortable bedroom and luxurious bath.

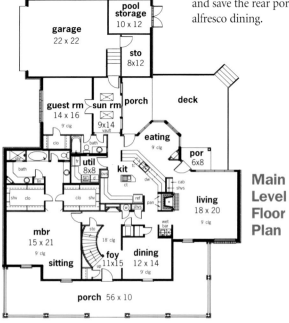

Main Level Floor Plan

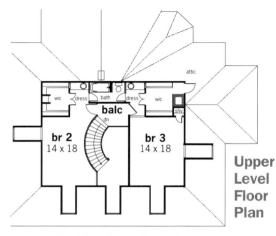

Upper Level Floor Plan

Copyright by designer/architect.

Plan #271096

Dimensions: 66' W x 90' D
Levels: 2
Square footage: 3,190
Main Level Sq. Ft.: 2,152
Upper Level Sq. Ft.: 1,038
Bedrooms: 4
Bathrooms: 3½
Foundation: Crawl space
Materials List Available: No
Price Category: G

Images provided by designer/architect.

This traditional home contains quite possibly everything you're dreaming of, and even more!

Features:

• **F**ormal Rooms: These living and dining rooms flank the entry foyer, making a large space for special occasions.

• **Family Room:** A fireplace is the highlight of this spacious area, where the kids will play with their friends and watch TV.

• **Kitchen:** A central island makes cooking a breeze. The adjoining dinette is a sunny spot for casual meals.

• **Master Suite:** A large sleeping area is followed by a deluxe private bath with a whirlpool tub and a walk-in closet. Step through a French door to the backyard, which is big enough to host a deck with an inviting hot tub!

• **Guest Suite:** One bedroom upstairs has its own private bath, making it perfect for guests.

• A future room above the garage awaits your decision on how to use it.

Main Level Floor Plan

Upper Level Floor Plan

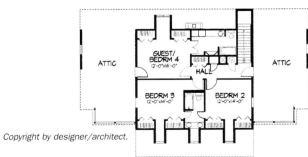

Copyright by designer/architect.

Plan #271098

Dimensions: 68'10" W x 81'5" D

Levels: 2

Square Footage: 3,382

Main Level Sq. Ft.: 2,136

Upper Level Sq. Ft.: 1,246

Bedrooms: 4

Bathrooms: 3½

Foundation: Slab

Materials List Available: No

Price Category: G

Images provided by designer/architect.

Arched windows and a charming front door lend a look of classic elegance to this popular traditional home.

Features:

- Porch: With striking columns, this space is beautiful to behold. But it is also a lovely spot for relaxation on a summer afternoon.

- Living Room: You'll want to use this quiet corner for conversations with friends.

- Family Room: For larger groups, this area is perfect. Gather everyone around the fireplace and play charades.

- Dining Room: Holiday feasts are ably handled here, with the messy kitchen concealed behind double doors.

- Master Suite: You deserve to be pampered by the deluxe private bath, with its soothing whirlpool tub. The big walk-in closet keeps your wardrobe in order.

- Game Room: There are endless uses for this versatile space. Would you like a place to set up your various hobbies?

Upper Level Floor Plan

Copyright by designer/architect.

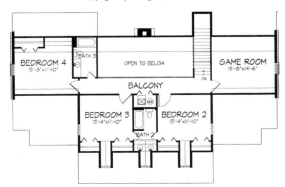

Plan #271095

Dimensions: 70' W x 75' D

Levels: 2

Square Footage: 3,220

Main Level Sq. Ft.: 2,040

Upper Level Sq. Ft.: 1,180

Bedrooms: 3

Bathrooms: 3½

Foundation: Crawl space, slab

Materials List Available: No

Price Category: G

Images provided by designer/architect.

Triple dormers add a touch of charm to this upscale country-style home.

Features:

- **Porch:** A columned porch gives a warm welcome to visiting relatives and friends.

- **Dining Room:** Columns define this formal dining room, which is perfect for all of your entertaining needs.

- **Family Room:** This two-story high family room is warmed by a fireplace and brightened by lots of windows.

- **Kitchen:** With a nice serving bar, a menu desk and a good-sized pantry, this open kitchen will be the envy of any cooking enthusiast.

- **Master Suite:** Double doors introduce this suite, where a spacious sitting room is superseded only by the sumptuous master bath.

- **Secondary Bedrooms:** On the upper level, each bedroom boasts its own private bath.

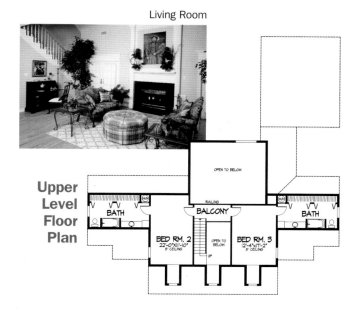

Living Room

Plan #161060

Dimensions: 113'10" W x 60'6" D
Levels: 2
Square Footage: 5,143
Main Level Sq. Ft.: 3,323
Upper Level Sq. Ft.: 1,820
Bedrooms: 4
Bathrooms: 3½
Foundation: Basement,
walkout basement
Materials List Available: Yes
Price Category: I

Images provided by designer/architect.

Luxury, comfort, beauty, spaciousness—
this home has everything you've been wanting,
including space for every possible activity.

Features:

• Courtyard: Enjoy the privacy here before
entering this spacious home.

• Great Room: Open to the foyer, dining area,
and kitchen, this great room has a fireplace
flanked by windows and leads to the open
rear deck.

• Dining Room: Situated between the foyer
and the kitchen, this room is ideal for formal
dining.

• Library: Located just off the foyer, this
library offers a calm retreat from activities in
the great room.

• Utility Area: The mudroom, pantry, half-bath
and laundry room add up to household
convenience.

• Master Suite: You'll love the huge walk-in
closet, extensive window feature, and bath
with a dressing room and two vanities.

Left Side Elevation

Stairs

Rear Elevation

Right Side Elevation

Dining Room

Media Room

Main Level Floor Plan

Master Bedroom
17'8" X 17'

Dressing

Hakk

Walk In Closet
DRAWER BASE

Library
14' X 16'4"

Great Room
17'9" X 29'4"
CEILING HEIGHT 10'4"

Dining

Kitchen
16'9" X 19'6"

CUSTOM CABINETS

Foyer
17'9" X 11'4"

Court Yard

Deck

Laun.

Pantry

Mud Room

Bath

Dining Room
14' X 16'4"

Three Car Garage
23'6" x 37'2"

Upper Level Floor Plan

Copyright by designer/architect.

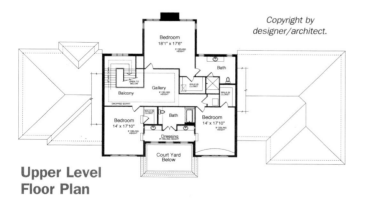

Bedroom
18'1" x 17'6"
9' CEILING HEIGHT

Balcony

Gallery
9' CEILING HEIGHT

Bath

OPEN TO BELOW

DROPPED SOFFIT

Bedroom
14' x 17'10"

Bath

Dressing
9' CEILING HEIGHT

Bedroom
14' x 17'10"
9' CEILING HEIGHT

Court Yard Below

Great Room

Basement Level Floor Plan

Patio

Sitting Room

Exercise Room
13'11" x 17'9"

STAIRS UP

Media Area
17'9" x 32'

Basement

Bath

Wine Storage

Basement

Unexcavated

Unexcavated

Unexcavated

Kitchen

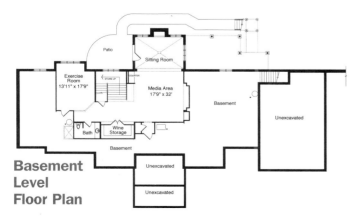

Window Treatments

With window treatments, function is just as important as form, if not more so. You need something that is attractive and easy to use and wears well. Start by addressing the practical issues: will the material provide the desired degree of privacy as well as light? Will the fabrics hold up to the sun? Is the pattern and repeat appropriate to the size of the windows? Is the material the right weight? Is it light enough to drape or hang gracefully, or is it heavy and bulky? Is the cost within your budget? (Window treatments require a lot of fabric.) Is it easily adjustable?

General Considerations

Next move on to what is appropriate for the room and your home.

Aesthetics. Does the look complement the style of your house? The rest of your furnishings? The architecture and shape of your windows? Be sure to consider the time of day you use the room most—daytime or evening—and the room's exposure. For example, south- or west-facing rooms get lots of sunlight, which may need to be controlled if you use the rooms during the day, particularly in the afternoon. North- or east-facing rooms used during the day cannot afford to lose one iota of light. At night, any bare window will look like a gaping black hole in a wall.

A simple café curtain made from a cotton mini print has country-style charm.

Insulation. What condition are your windows in? Can they benefit from the insulation window treatments can provide? Appropriately lined curtains or shades can help keep a room warm or cool. But some window treatments (such as heavy lined panels) can cut off the airflow from a radiator or an air conditioner. If there are windy spots, blinds and louvers ("hard treatments") will clang and clatter whenever the window is open. Look for a soft alternative, such as a fabric shade.

Mechanics. Don't overlook the mechanics of the window treatment you've chosen. Will it work without banging a wall or scraping the window trim? If blinds are door-mounted, you don't want to grab them every time you reach for the doorknob. You may need hold-down brackets for blinds or tiebacks for your curtains. Certain kinds of shades for skylights and other inaccessible windows can be motorized and operated at the push of a button by remote control.

"Does the look complement the style of your house? The rest of your furnishings? The architecture and shape of your windows?"

Lace panels and a vintage-style glass hold back strike a romantic Victorian pose on a window.

Plain white roll-up shades, left, are easy to operate. Use them alone or as an under-treatment with curtains.

Blinds, opposite left, are a versatile choice for controlling light and privacy. They have great contemporary appeal.

Roman shades, opposite right, can be made from your choice of translucent, sun-filtering, or sun-blocking fabric.

Classic curtain panels, below, that are attached to a pole with rings will glide open or closed effortlessly.

Inside or Outside Mount

Sometimes you have an option of installing a window treatment on the inside or outside surface of the window frame. Often the decision is based on whether you are buying stock items, which are available in a limited number of sizes, or custom-made treatments. When deciding where to install your window treatment, and before buying stock items, take accurate measurements of the window, and use the information below as guidelines.

An Outside Mount

- May be necessary if buying a stock item that will not fit the inside width measurement across the window frame.
- May be necessary if the window frame is not deep enough to contain at least the shade or blind mounting brackets, if not the entire depth of the unit.

- Can compensate for unattractive or nonexistent window trim.
- Can make a window that seems too narrow appear wider.

An Inside Mount

- Cannot be used if the blind or shade will not fit within the inside measurements of the window opening.
- Is recommended if the blind or shade will be covered by draw curtains or draperies, which may be impeded by the shade or blind.
- Allows handsome trimwork around the window to remain visible.
- Can enhance the shape of a decorative or architectural window.

You can install a rod or pole anywhere on the wall above the window trim, even just under the ceiling line. This will make small windows look larger.

It's Not Guesswork

Correct measurements will help you determine whether ready-made options will work for you. Without them, you cannot accurately price the elements you need, and you'll waste your time returning items to the store.

Use a metal measuring tape for accuracy, and record the dimensions on a small slip of paper that you can keep on you and have handy when you're shopping.

Inside-Mounted Treatments

Inside the window frame, measure the width across the top, center, and bottom. Use the narrowest measurement, and round down to the nearest ⅛ inch. Measure the height of the window from the top of the opening to the sill.

Outside-Mounted Treatments

Figure out the amount of space that you want to cover with your treatment on each side of the window and above and below the window. Then decide on bracket placement—on the window frame or the wall. Here are some tips.

- Professionals recommend extending outside-mounted shades or blinds 2 inches beyond the sash on each side.
- To determine the appropriate rod length, measure from bracket to bracket. For a decorative pole with finials, add 5 to 8 inches on each side; the actual amount depends on the finial size. Be sure that you have enough room on either side of window before you buy this type of decorative hardware.
- For a fuller curtain look, the width of the panels you use should be at least twice the measurement from bracket to bracket. Some opulent styles call for an amount of fabric that is three times the bracket-to-bracket measurement.
- To determine the appropriate length of curtain and drapery panels, measure from the bracket placement down to the top of the sill, to below the sill, or to the floor, depending on the length you desire. If the panel heading extends above the rod or pole, include that measurement with the overall length.

Plan #161029

Dimensions: 87' W x 82' D

Levels: 2

Square Footage: 4,470

Main Level Sq. Ft.: 3,300

Upper Level Sq. Ft.: 1,170

Bedrooms: 4

Bathrooms: 3 full; 2 half

Foundation: Basement

Materials List Available: Yes

Price Category: I

Images provided by designer/architect.

This gracious home is so impressive — inside and out — that it suits the most discriminating tastes.

Features:

- **Foyer:** A balcony overlooks this gracious area decorated by tall columns.

- **Hearth Room:** Visually open to the kitchen and the breakfast area, this room is ideal for any sort of gathering.

- **Great Room:** Colonial columns also form the entry here, and a magnificent window treatment that includes French doors leads to the terrace.

- **Library:** Built-in shelving adds practicality to this quiet retreat.

- **Kitchen:** Spread out on the oversized island with a cooktop and seating.

- **Additional Bedrooms:** Walk-in closets and private access to a bath define each bedroom.

Main Level Floor Plan

Copyright by designer/architect.

Upper Level Floor Plan

Rear View

Living Room

Living Room/Kitchen

Ideas for Entertaining

Whether an everyday family meal or a big party for 50, make it memorable and fun. With a world of options, it's easier than you think. Be imaginative with food and decoration. Although it is true that great hamburgers and hot dogs will taste good even if served on plain white paper plates, make the meal more fun by following a theme of some sort—color, occasion, or seasonal activity, for example. Be inventive with the basic elements as well as the extraneous touches, such as flowers and lighting. Here are some examples to get you started.

- For an all-American barbecue, set a picnic table with a patchwork quilt having red, white, and blue in it. Use similar colors for the napkins, and perhaps even bandannas. Include a star-studded centerpiece.

- Make a children-size dining set using an old door propped up on crates, and surround it with appropriate-size benches or chairs. Cover the table with brightly colored, easy-to-clean waxed or vinyl-covered fabric.

- If you're planning an elegant dinner party, move your dining room table outside and set it with your best linens, china, silver, and crystal. Add romantic lighting with candles in fabulous candelabras, and set a beautiful but small floral arrangement at each place setting.

- Design a centerpiece showcasing the flowers from your garden. Begin the arrangement with a base of purchased flowers, and fill in with some of your homegrown blooms. That way your flower beds will still be full of blossoms when the guests arrive.

- Base your party theme on the vegetables growing in your yard, and let them be the inspiration for the menu. When your zucchini plants are flowering, wow your family or guests by serving steamed squash blossoms. Or if the vegetables are starting to develop, lightly grill them with other young veggies—they have a much more delicate flavor than mature vegetables do.

- During berry season, host an elegant berry brunch. Serve mixed-berry crepes on your prettiest plates.

Plan #161036

Dimensions: 74'10" W x 65' D

Levels: 2

Square Footage: 3,664

Main Level Sq. Ft.: 2,497

Upper Level Sq. Ft.: 1,167

Bedrooms: 4

Bathrooms: 2½

Foundation: Basement

Materials List Available: No

Price Category: H

The traditional European brick-and-stone facade on the exterior of this comfortable home will thrill you and make your guests feel welcome.

Features:

- **Pub:** The beamed ceiling lends a casual feeling to this pub and informal dining area between the kitchen and the great room.

- **Dining Room:** Columns set off this formal dining room, from which you can see the fireplace in the expansive great room.

- **Library:** Close to the master suite, this room lends itself to quiet reading or work.

- **Master Suite:** The ceiling treatment makes the bedroom luxurious, while the whirlpool tub, double-bowl vanity, and large walk-in closet make the bath a pleasure.

- **Upper Level:** Each of the three bedrooms features a large closet and easy access to a convenient bathroom.

Main Level Floor Plan

Upper Level Floor Plan

Copyright by designer/architect.

Rear Elevation

Left Elevation

Right Elevation

Living Room

Kitchen

Dining Room

Living Room

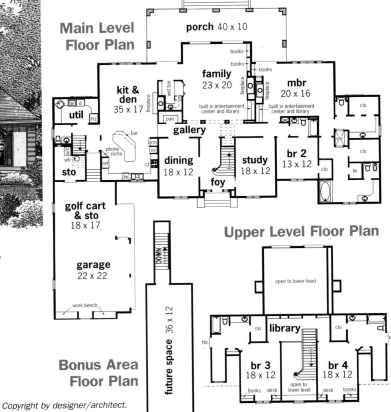

Main Level Floor Plan

porch 40 x 10

books

family 23 x 20

mbr 20 x 16

kit & den 35 x 17

wet bar

fireplace

built in entertainment center and library

built in entertainment center and library

clo

clo

util

wh

gallery

br 2 13 x 12

clo

lin

dining 18 x 12

study 18 x 12

sto

golf cart & sto 18 x 17

foy

up

Upper Level Floor Plan

garage 22 x 22

DOWN

open to lower level

library

work bench

future space 36 x 12

clo

clo

br 3 18 x 12

br 4 18 x 12

Bonus Area Floor Plan

books desk

open to lower level

desk books

Images provided by designer/architect.

Copyright by designer/architect.

Plan #211125

Dimensions: 94' W x 92' D

Levels: 2

Square Footage: 4,440

Main Level Sq. Ft.: 3,465

Upper Level Sq. Ft.: 975

Bedrooms: 4

Bathrooms: 5½

Foundation: Crawl space

Materials List Available: Yes

Price Category: I

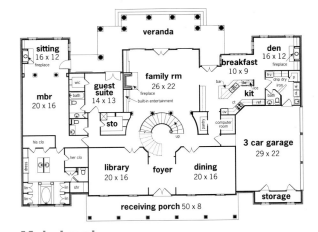

veranda

sitting 16 x 12

den 16 x 12

fireplace

breakfast 10 x 9

family rm 26 x 22

fireplace

wic

bath

guest suite 14 x 13

built-in entertainment

kit

mbr 20 x 16

his clo

sto

3 car garage 29 x 22

her clo

library 20 x 16

foyer

dining 20 x 16

storage

receiving porch 50 x 8

Main Level Floor Plan

open to family room below

bath

wic

open to foyer below

wic

bath

attic

dress rm

desk

down

desk

dress rm

attic

Upper Level Floor Plan

br 3 17 x 16

study

up to attic

br 4 17 x 16

veranda

Images provided by designer/architect.

Copyright by designer/architect.

Plan #211127

Dimensions: 94' W x 71' D

Levels: 2

Square Footage: 5,474

Main Level Sq. Ft.: 4,193

Upper Level Sq. Ft.: 1,281

Bedrooms: 4

Bathrooms: 4 full, 2 half

Foundation: Slab, crawl space

Materials List Available: No

Price Category: I

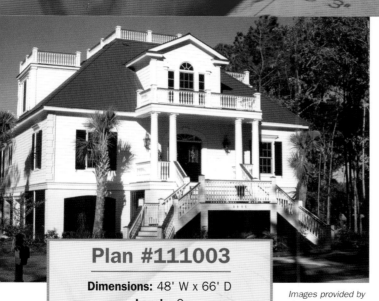

Main Level
Floor Plan

*Copyright by
designer/architect.*

Master
Bedroom
16'10"x 17'8"

Wood Deck
30'10"x 16'

Master
Bath

Porch
17'7"x 12'

Breakfast
12'8"x 13'4"

Walk-In
Closet

Family
17'6"x 20'6"

Kitchen
12'8"x 16'

Utility

1/2
Ba.

Study
12'6"x 13'

Foyer

Dining
12'4"x 14'4"

Porch
18'x 8'

Balcony
17'5"x 10'

Bath

Playroom
13'11"x 12'1"

Dress

Bedroom
12'3"x 11'5"

Bath

Bedroom
12'3"x 11'5"

Upper Level
Floor Plan

Library/
Office
11'5"x 12'1"

Plan #111003

Dimensions: 48' W x 66' D
Levels: 2
Square Footage: 3,319
Main Level Sq. Ft.: 2,331
Upper Level Sq. Ft.: 988
Bedrooms: 3
Bathrooms: 3½
Foundation: Pier
Materials List Available: No
Price Category: G

*Images provided by
designer/architect.*

Main Level
Floor Plan

Garage
22'6"x 24'6"

Covered Porch

Master
Bedroom
17'2"x 16'4"

Living
22'2"x 18'

Gameroom
13'6"x 15'6"

Bedroom
11'2"x 10'6"

Dining
11'6"x 14'

Breakfast
12'6"x 10'

Upper Level Floor Plan

Copyright by designer/architect.

Bedroom
12'x 11'

Bedroom
11'x 16'

Open to
Below

Bedroom
11'x 16'

Plan #111035

Dimensions: 68'6" W x 74'7" D
Levels: 2
Square Footage: 3,064
Main Level Sq. Ft.: 2,143
Upper Level Sq. Ft.: 921
Bedrooms: 4
Bathroom: 3½
Foundation: Slab
Materials List Available: No
Price Category: G

*Images provided by
designer/architect.*

Plan #291013

Dimensions: 72' W x 75' D

Levels: 2

Square Footage: 3,553

Main Level Sq. Ft.: 1,830

Upper Level Sq. Ft.: 1,723

Bedrooms: 4

Bathrooms: 2½

Foundation: Basement

Materials List Available: No

Price Category: H

Images provided by designer/architect.

Copyright by designer/architect.

Main Level Floor Plan

Upper Level Floor Plan

Plan #291014

Dimensions: 104' W x 60' D

Levels: 2

Square Footage: 4,372

Main Level Sq. Ft.: 3,182

Upper Level Sq. Ft.: 1,190

Bedrooms: 3

Bathrooms: 3 full, 2 half

Foundation: Basement

Materials List Available: No

Price Category: I

Images provided by designer/ architect.

Copyright by designer/architect.

Main Level Floor Plan

Upper Level Floor Plan

Plan #211117

Dimensions: 74' W x 78' D

Levels: 2

Square Footage: 3,284

Main Level Sq. Ft.: 2,655

Upper Level Sq. Ft.: 629

Bedrooms: 4

Bathrooms: 4

Foundation: Slab

Materials List Available: Yes

Price Category: G

Images provided by designer/architect.

Main Level Floor Plan

Upper Level Floor Plan

Copyright by designer/architect.

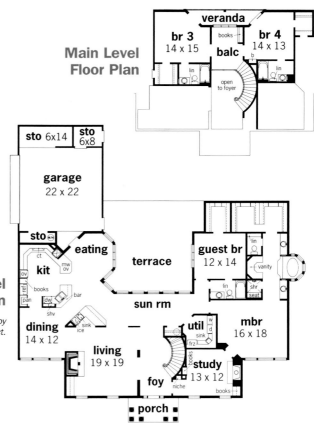

Plan #271032

Dimensions: 78' W x 40' D

Levels: 2

Square Footage: 3,195

Main Level Sq. Ft.: 1,758

Upper Level Sq. Ft.: 1,437

Bedrooms: 4

Bathrooms: 2½

Foundation: Basement

Materials List Available: No

Price Category: E

Images provided by designer/architect.

Main Level Floor Plan

Upper Level Floor Plan

Copyright by designer/architect.

Plan #191001

Dimensions: 62' W x 72' D

Levels: 1

Square Footage: 2,156

Bedrooms: 4

Bathrooms: 3

Foundation: Crawl space, slab, or basement

Materials List Available: No

Price Category: D

This lovely home has the best of old and new — a traditional appearance combined with fabulous comforts and conveniences.

Features:

- **Great Room:** A tray ceiling gives stature to this expansive room, and its many windows let natural light stream into it.

- **Kitchen:** When you're standing at the sink in this gorgeous kitchen, you'll have a good view of the patio. But if you turn around, you'll see the island cooktop, wall oven, walk-in pantry, and snack bar, all of which make this kitchen such a pleasure.

- **Master Suite:** Somewhat isolated for privacy, this area is ideal for an evening or weekend retreat. Relax in the gracious bedroom or luxuriate in the spa-style bath, with its corner whirlpool tub, large shower, two sinks, and access to the walk-in closet, which measures a full 8 ft. x 10 ft.

- **Mudroom:** No matter whether you live where mud season is as reliable as spring thaws or where rain is a seasonal event, you'll love having a spot to confine the muddy mess.

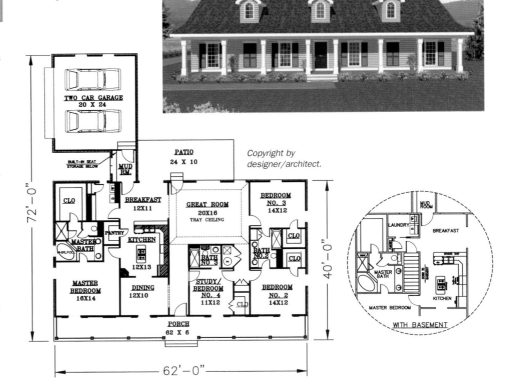

Copyright by designer/architect.

Plan #121061

Dimensions: 56' W x 52' D
Levels: 2
Square Footage: 3,025
Main Level Sq. Ft.: 1,583
Upper Level Sq. Ft.: 1,442
Bedrooms: 4
Bathrooms: 3 ½
Foundation: Basement
Materials List Available: Yes
Price Category: G

This large home with a contemporary feeling is ideal for the family looking for comfort and amenities.

Features:

• Entry: Stacked windows bring sunlight into this two-story entry, with its stylish curved staircase.

• Library: French doors off the entry lead to this room, with its built-in bookcases flanking a large, picturesque window.

• Family Room: Located in the rear of the home, this family room is sunken to set it apart. A spider-beamed ceiling gives it a contemporary feeling, and a bay window, wet bar, and pass-through fireplace add to this impression.

• Kitchen: The island in this kitchen makes working here a pleasure. The corner pantry joins a breakfast area and hearth room to this space.

Main Level Floor Plan

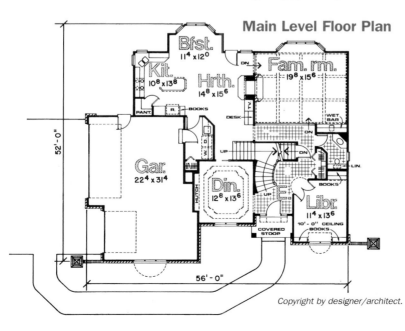

Copyright by designer/architect.

Upper Level Floor Plan

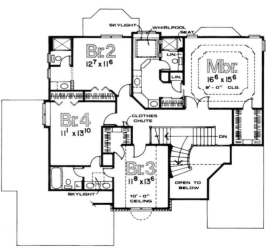

Plan #161035

Dimensions: 75' W x 64'11" D
Levels: 2
Square Footage: 3,688
Main Level Sq. Ft.: 2,702
Upper Level Sq. Ft.: 986
Bedrooms: 4
Bathrooms: 3½
Foundation: Basement
Materials List Available: No
Price Category: H

You'll appreciate the style of the stone, brick, and cedar shake exterior of this contemporary home.

Features:

• **Hearth Room:** Positioned for an easy flow for guests and family, this hearth room features a bank of windows that integrate it with the yard.

• **Breakfast Room:** Move through the sliding doors here to the rear porch on sunny days.

• **Kitchen:** Outfitted for a gourmet cook, this kitchen is also ideal for friends and family who can perch at the island or serve themselves at the bar.

• **Master Suite:** A stepped ceiling, crown moldings, and boxed window make the bedroom easy to decorate, while the two walk-in closets, lavish dressing area, and whirlpool tub in the bath make this area comfortable and luxurious.

Main Level Floor Plan

Upper Level Floor Plan

Copyright by designer/architect.

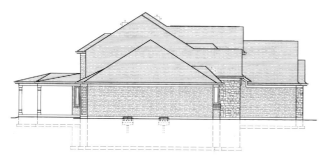

Left Elevation

Right Elevation

Kitchen

SMARTtip

How to Arrange Seating Around Your Fireplace

When the TV is near or on the same wall as the fireplace, you can arrange seating that places you at the best advantage to enjoy both. Position sofas and chairs in front of the fire, and remember that the distance between you and the TV should be at least three times the size of the screen.

Dining Room

Living Room

Master Bathroom

Plan #221025

Dimensions: 69'8" W x 72' D

Levels: 2

Square Footage: 3,009

Main Level Sq. Ft.: 2,039

Upper Level Sq. Ft.: 970

Bedrooms: 4

Bathrooms: 2½

Foundation: Basement

Materials List Available: No

Price Category: G

Images provided by designer/architect.

Designed to resemble a country home in France, this two-story beauty will delight you with its good looks and luxurious amenities.

Features:

- **Great Room:** You'll look into this great room as soon as you enter the two-story foyer. A fireplace flanked by built-in bookcases and large windows looking out to the deck highlight this room.

- **Dining Room:** This formal room is located just off the entry for the convenience of your guests.

- **Kitchen:** A huge central island and large pantry make this kitchen a delight for any cook. The large nook looks onto the deck and opens to the lovely three-season porch.

- **Master Suite:** You'll love this suite, with its charming bay shape, great windows, walk-in closet, luxurious bath, and door to the deck.

- **Upper Level:** Everyone will love the two bedrooms, large bath, and huge game.

Main Level Floor Plan

Upper Level Floor Plan

Copyright by designer/architect.

Plan #161045

Dimensions: 57' W x 49'8" D

Levels: 2

Square Footage: 2,077

Main Level Sq. Ft.: 1,532

Upper Level Sq. Ft.: 545

Bedrooms: 3

Bathrooms: 2½

Foundation: Basement

Materials List Available: Yes

Price Category: D

Images provided by designer/architect.

Multiple gables, arched windows, and the stone accents that adorn the exterior of this lovely two-story home create a dramatic first impression.

Features:

- **Great Room:** With multiple windows to light your way, grand openings, varied ceiling treatments, and angled walls let you flow from room to room. Enjoy the warmth of a gas fireplace in both this great room and the dining area.

- **Master Suite:** Experience the luxurious atmosphere of this master suite, with its coffered ceiling and deluxe bath.

- **Additional Bedrooms:** Angled stairs lead to a balcony with writing desk and to two additional bedrooms.

- **Porch:** Exit two sets of French doors to the rear yard and a covered porch, perfect for relaxing in comfortable weather.

Main Level Floor Plan

Copyright by designer/architect.

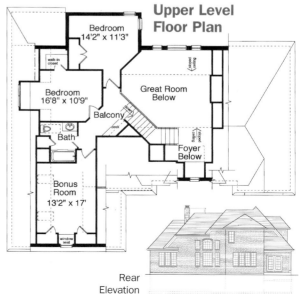

Upper Level Floor Plan

Rear Elevation

Plan #221023

Dimensions: 90'3" W x 65'8" D
Levels: 2
Square Footage: 3,511
Main Level Sq. Ft.: 1,931
Upper Level Sq. Ft.: 1,580
Bedrooms: 4
Bathrooms: 3½
Foundation: Basement
Materials List Available: No
Price Category: H

The curb appeal of this traditional two-story home, with its brick-and-stucco facade, is well matched by the luxuriousness you'll find inside.

Images provided by designer/architect.

Features:

- Ceiling Height: 9 ft.

- Family Room: This large room is open to the kitchen and the dining nook, making it an ideal spot in which to entertain.

- Living Room: The high ceiling in this room contributes to its somewhat formal feeling, and the fireplace and built-in bookcase allow you to decorate for a classic atmosphere.

- Master Suite: The bedroom in this suite has a luxurious feeling, partially because of the double French doors that are flanked by niches for displaying small art pieces or collectables. The bathroom here is unusually large and features a walk-in closet.

- Upper Level: You'll find four bedrooms, three bathrooms, and a large bonus room to use as a study or play room on this floor.

Main Level Floor Plan

FAM. RM.
22'4" × 17'0"

NK.
VAULT CEILING
11'0" × 10'0"

KIT.
18'8" × 13'6"

LIV.
10'-1 1/8" CEILING
14'4" × 18'6"

DEN
10'-1 1/8" CEILING
11'4" × 19'0"

STOR.

3 CAR GAR.
22'0" × 43'4"

BUTLER'S PANTRY

DIN.
13'0" × 15'0"

E.
2 STORY

90'-3"

65'-8"

Upper Level Floor Plan

BR. #3
11'4" × 14'0"

BR. #2
11'6" × 12'4"

MBR.
14'4" × 18'0"

ART NICHE

SHELVES

BONUS RM.
11'4" × 33'8"

BR. #4
CATHEDRAL CEILING
13'0" × 13'0"

OPEN TO E.

Copyright by designer/architect.

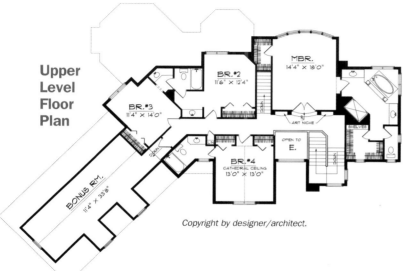

Competing Interests- Fireplace, Media Center, and Windows

What should you do if the only place for the television is next to the fireplace? If the TV is small enough to keep on a cart that you can wheel away when the set is not in use, that's ideal. But with cable hookups, VCRs, DVDs, and large-screen TVs, that might be impractical. A cabinet that lets you store the all of this equipment behind closed doors may be the answer, especially if the storage unit is part of a large built-in paneled wall system that incorporates the fireplace into its overall design.

When large windows or glass doors share the wall with a fireplace, easy-to-adjust window treatments are essential: drapery panels on a traverse rod or suspended from rings on a pole, or shutters, shades, or blinds are options that can help with glare when viewing a TV during the daytime. But by all means, make certain your selection allows the sun shine in during the day when appropriate.

Also be aware that a pleasant window view by day just becomes a large dark hole at night. So in the evening, close the curtains while the fire sets the mood, whether you're entertaining or relaxing alone.

Rear Elevation

Plan #121077

Dimensions: 64' W x 46' D
Levels: 2
Square Footage: 2,480
Main Level Sq. Ft.: 1,369
Upper Level Sq. Ft.: 1,111
Bedrooms: 4
Bathrooms: 2½
Foundation: Basement
Materials List Available: Yes
Price Category: E

Images provided by designer/architect.

You'll love this design if you've been looking for a home that mixes formal and informal living spaces.

Features:

- **Entry**: An angled staircase is the focal point in this lovely two-story entry.
- **Living Room**: To the left of the entry, a boxed ceiling, transom-topped windows, and corner columns highlight this formal living room and the dining room.
- **Den**: On the right side of the entry, French doors open to this cozy den with its boxed window and built-in bookcase.
- **Family Room**: Sunken to set it off, the family room has a beamed ceiling and a fireplace flanked by windows.

Main Level Floor Plan

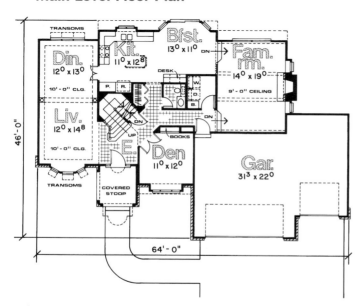

Upper Level Floor Plan

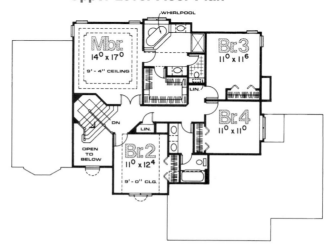

Copyright by designer/architect.

Plan #121081

Dimensions: 76'8" W x 68' D
Levels: 2
Square Footage: 3,623
Main Level Sq. Ft.: 2,603
Upper Level Sq. Ft.: 1,020
Bedrooms: 4
Bathrooms: 4½
Foundation: Basement
Materials List Available: Yes
Price Category: G

Images provided by designer/architect.

You'll love this impressive home if you're looking for perfect spot for entertaining as well as a home for comfortable family living.

Features:

- **Entry:** Walk into this grand two-story entryway through double doors, and be greeted by the sight of a graceful curved staircase.

- **Great Room:** This two-story room features stacked windows, a fireplace flanked by an entertainment center, a bookcase, and a wet bar.

- **Dining Room:** A corner column adds formality to this room, which is just off the entryway for the convenience of your guests.

- **Hearth Room:** Connected to the great room by a lovely set of French doors, this room features another fireplace as well as a convenient pantry.

Main Level Floor Plan

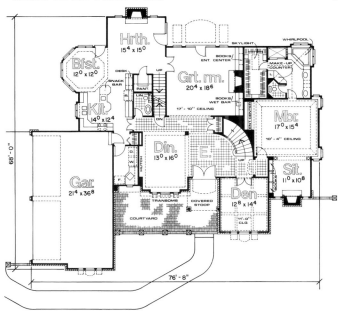

Upper Level Floor Plan

Copyright by designer/architect.

Plan #211077

Dimensions: 94' W x 68' D

Levels: 2

Square Footage: 5,560

Main Level Sq. Ft.: 4,208

Upper Level Sq. Ft.: 1,352

Bedrooms: 4

Bathrooms: 4 full, 2 half

Foundation: Slab, or crawl space

Materials List Available: No

Price Category: I

This palatial home has a two-story veranda and offers room and amenities for a large family.

Features:

- Ceiling Height: 10 ft.

- Library: Teach your children the importance of quiet reflection in this library, which boasts a full wall of built-in bookshelves.

- Master Suite: Escape the pressures of a busy day in this truly royal master suite. Curl up in front of your own fireplace. Or take a long, soothing soak in the private bath, with his and her sinks and closets.

- Kitchen: This room offers many modern comforts and amenities, and free-flowing traffic patterns.

Images provided by designer/architect.

Main Level Floor Plan

Copyright by designer/architect.

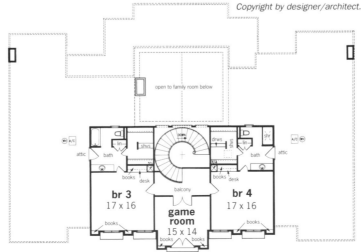

Upper Level Floor Plan

Plan #211075

Dimensions: 80' W x 84' D
Levels: 2
Square Footage: 3,568
Main Level Sq. Ft.: 2,330
Upper Level Sq. Ft.: 1,238
Bedrooms: 4
Bathrooms: 3½
Foundation: Crawl space
Materials List Available: Yes
Price Category: H

Images provided by designer/architect.

The porte-cochere—or covered passage over a driveway—announces the quality and beauty of this spacious country home.

Features:

- Front Porch: Spot groups of potted plants on this 779-sq.-ft. porch, and add a glider and some rocking chairs to take advantage of its comfort.

- Family Room: Let this family room become the heart of the home. With a fireplace to make it cozy and a wet bar for easy serving, it's a natural for entertaining.

- Game Room: Expect a crowd in this room, no matter what the weather.

- Kitchen: A cooktop island and a pantry are just two features of this fully appointed kitchen.

- Master Suite: The bedroom is as luxurious as you'd expect, but the quarter-circle raised tub in the master bath might surprise you. Two walk-in closets and two vanities add a practical touch.

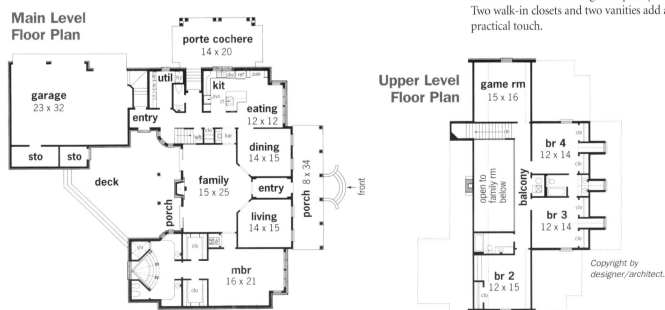

Main Level Floor Plan

Upper Level Floor Plan

Copyright by designer/architect.

Plan #161033

Dimensions: 78'2" W x 74'6" D
Levels: 2
Square Footage: 5,125
Main Level Sq. Ft.: 2,782
Upper Level Sq. Ft.: 1,027
Optional Basement Level Sq. Ft.: 1,316
Bedrooms: 4
Bathrooms: 3½
Foundation: Poured foundation
Materials List Available: Yes
Price Category: I

Images provided by designer/architect.

The dramatic design of this home, combined with its comfort and luxuries, suit those with discriminating tastes.

Features:

- Great Room: Let the fireplace and 14-ft. ceilings in this room set the stage for all sorts of gatherings, from causal to formal.

- Dining Room: Adjacent to the great room and kitchen fit for a gourmet, the dining room allows you to entertain with ease.

- Music Room: Give your music the space it deserves in this specially-designed room.

- Library: Use this room as an office, or reserve it for quiet reading and studying.

- Master Suite: You'll love the separate dressing area and walk-in closet in the bedroom.

- Lower Level: A bar and recreational area give even more space for entertaining.

Rear View

Main Level Floor Plan

Copyright by designer/architect.

Patio
22' x 18'

Dining Room
15'3" x 15'3"
9' ceiling ht.

Kitchen
20' x 15'4"

Master Bedroom
14'6" x 15'4"

Great Room
21'5" x 27'8"
14' ceiling ht.

Library
15'6" x 15'2" irr.

Pantry

9' ceiling ht.

Dressing

Laun.

Hall

Foyer
11' ceiling ht.
9' ceiling ht.

Music Room
14'9" x 12'2"
11' ceiling ht.

walk-in closet

walk-in closet

Porch

Three Car Garage
21' x 28'9"

Upper Level Floor Plan

Bedroom
12'10" x 12'10"

Bedroom
14'4" x 12'

Balcony
10'2" x 6'4"

wood rails

walk-in closet

Mech.

Bath

Bedroom
17' x 12'

walk-in closet

Sitting Area
8'8" x 11'7"

window seat

Optional Basement Level Floor Plan

Media Room
12'7" x 15'

Billiards
19'6" x 22'3"

Hobby Room
14' x 16'5"

Bar
12' x 11'6"

Bath

walk-in closet

Basement

Basement

Unexcavated

Unexcavated

Color Wheel Combinations

The color wheel is the designer's most useful tool for pairing colors. Basically, it presents the spectrum of pigment hues as a circle. The primary colors (yellow, blue, and red) are combined in the remaining hues (orange, green, and purple). The following are the most often used configurations for creating color schemes.

Dining Room

Living Room

Plan #161023

Dimensions: 71'8" W x 38'10" D
Levels: 2
Square Footage: 3,445
Main Level Sq. Ft.: 1,666
Mid Level Sq. Ft.: 743
Upper Level Sq. Ft.: 1,036
Bedrooms: 4
Bathrooms: 3½
Foundation: Poured
Materials List Available: No
Price Category: G

You'll love the versatility that the mixture of formal and informal spaces gives to this home.

Features:

- Dining Room: Let guests move from the formal dining room into the adjoining cozy hearth room.

- Hearth Room: Also situated close to the kitchen and breakfast room, the hearth room is a true center of this home. The fireplace, wood ceiling, and a recessed entertainment center add charm.

- Mid Level Wing: A computer area and 2 bedrooms highlight this separate space.

- Master Suite: A sitting area, fireplace, and dressing room attached to the master bath make this area a dream come true.

- Guest Room: This area includes a private bath and walk-in closet.

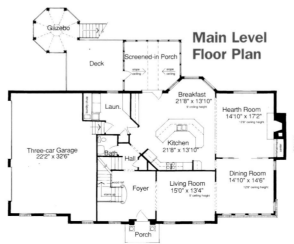

Living Room

Kitchen

Dining Room

Plan #121037

Dimensions: 46' W x 47'10" D
Levels: 2
Square Footage: 2,292
Main Level Sq. Ft.: 1,158
Upper Level Sq. Ft.: 1,134
Bedrooms: 4
Bathrooms: 2½
Foundation: Basement
Materials List Available: Yes
Price Category: E

Images provided by designer/architect.

This convenient and comfortable home is filled with architectural features that set it apart.

Features:

- Ceiling Height: 8 ft. unless otherwise noted.

- Foyer: You'll know you have arrived when you enter this two-story area highlighted by a decorative plant shelf and a balcony.

- Great Room: Just beyond the entry is the great room where the warmth of the two-sided fireplace will attract family and friends to gather. A bay window offers a more intimate place to sit and converse.

- Hearth Room: At the other side of the fireplace, the hearth offers a cozy spot for smaller gatherings or a place to sit alone and enjoy a book by the fire.

- Breakfast Area: With sunlight streaming into its bay window, the breakfast area offers the perfect spot for informal family meals.

- Master Suite: This private retreat is made more convenient by a walk-in closet. It features its own tub and shower.

Main Level Floor Plan

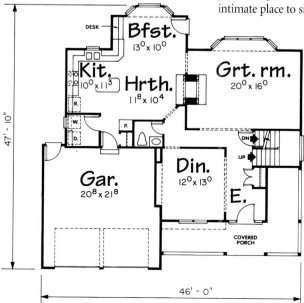

Upper Level Floor Plan

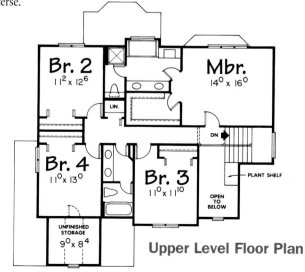

Copyright by designer/architect.

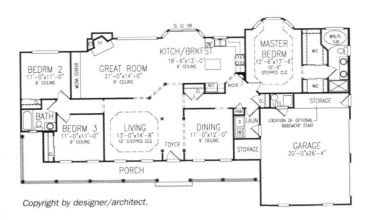

Plan #131016

Dimensions: 75' W x 45' D

Levels: 1

Square Footage: 1,902

Bedrooms: 3

Bathrooms: 2

Foundation: Basement, crawl space, or slab

Materials List Available: Yes

Price Category: E

Copyright by designer/architect.

Images provided by designer/architect.

Great Room

Plan #131017

Dimensions: 69'8" W x 39'4" D

Levels: 1

Square Footage: 1,480

Bedrooms: 3

Bathrooms: 2

Foundation: Basement, crawl space, or slab

Materials List Available: Yes

Price Category: C

Images provided by designer/architect.

Alternate Floor Plan

Part Plan with Optional Basement

Rear Elevation

Copyright by designer/architect.

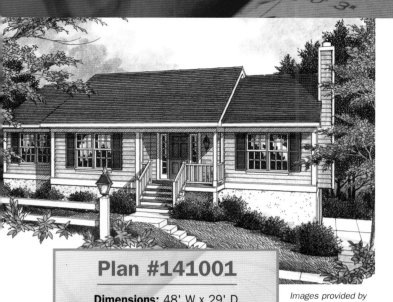

Images provided by designer/architect.

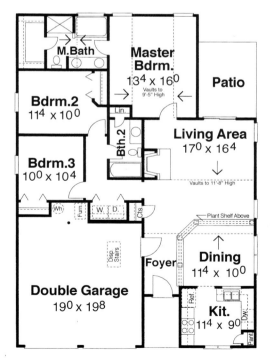

Copyright by designer/architect.

Plan #141001

Dimensions: 48' W x 29' D
Levels: 1
Square Footage: 1,208
Bedrooms: 3
Bathrooms: 2
Foundation: Basement
Materials List Available: Yes
Price Category: B

SMARTtip

Hydro-seeding

An alternative to traditional seeding is hydro-seeding. In this process, a slurry of grass seed, wood fibers, and fertilizer is spray-applied in one step. Hydro-seeding is relatively inexpensive. Compared with seeding by hand, hydro-seeding is also very fast.

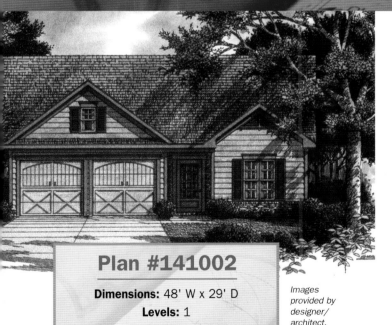

Images provided by designer/architect.

Plan #141002

Dimensions: 48' W x 29' D
Levels: 1
Square Footage: 1,365
Bedrooms: 3
Bathrooms: 2
Foundation: Slab, basement
Materials List Available: No
Price Category: B

Copyright by designer/architect.

Plan #181085

Dimensions: 56'4" W x 44' D
Levels: 2
Square Footage: 2,183
Main Level Sq. Ft.: 1,232
Second Level Sq. Ft.: 951
Bedrooms: 3
Bathrooms: 2½
Foundation: Basement
Materials List Available: Yes
Price Category: D

Images provided by designer/architect.

This country home features an inviting front porch and a layout designed for modern living.

Features:

- Ceiling Height: 8 ft.

- Solarium: Sunlight streams through the windows of this solarium at the front of the house.

- Living Room: Walk through French doors, and you will enter this inviting living room. Family and friends will be drawn to the corner fireplace.

- Formal Dining Room: Usher your guests directly from the living room into this formal dining room. The kitchen is located on the other side of the dining room for convenient service.

- Kitchen: This generously sized kitchen is a delight, it offers a center island, separate eat-in area, and access to the back deck.

- Bonus Room: This room just off the entry hall can become a family room, a bedroom, or an office.

- Master Suite: Curl up by the corner fireplace in this master retreat, with its walk-in closet and lavish bath with separate shower and tub.

Main Level Floor Plan

Upper Level Floor Plan

Copyright by designer/architect.

Plan #141014

Dimensions: 72' W x 38' D
Levels: 2
Square Footage: 2,091
Main Level Sq. Ft.: 1,362
Upper Level Sq. Ft.: 729
Bedrooms: 3
Bathrooms: 2½
Foundation: Basement
Materials List Available: Yes
Price Category: D

The wraparound front porch and front dormers evoke an old-fashioned country home.

Features:

- Ceiling Height: 8 ft. unless otherwise noted.

- Living Room: This spacious area has an open flow to the dining room, so you can graciously usher guests when it is time to eat.

- Dining Room: This elegant dining room has a bay that opens to the sun deck.

- Kitchen: This warm and inviting kitchen looks out to the front porch. Its bayed breakfast area is perfect for informal family meals.

- Master Suite: The bedroom enjoys a view through the front porch and features a master bath with all the amenities.

- Flexible Room: A room above the two-bay garage offers plenty of space that can be used for anything from a home office to a teen suite.

- Study Room: The two second-floor bedrooms share a study that is perfect for homework.

Images provided by designer/architect.

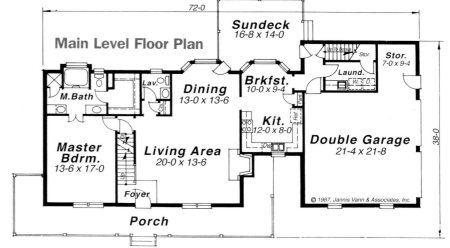

Main Level Floor Plan

Sundeck 16-8 x 14-0
Stor. 7-0 x 9-4
Laund.
M.Bath
Lav.
Dining 13-0 x 13-6
Brkfst. 10-0 x 9-4
Kit. 12-0 x 8-0
Double Garage 21-4 x 21-8
Master Bdrm. 13-6 x 17-0
Living Area 20-0 x 13-6
Foyer
Porch

© 1987, Jannis Vann & Associates, Inc.

Upper Level Floor Plan

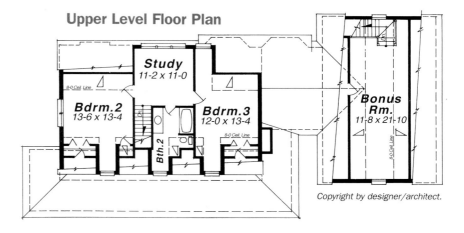

Study 11-2 x 11-0
Bdrm.2 13-6 x 13-4
Bth.2
Bdrm.3 12-0 x 13-4
Bonus Rm. 11-8 x 21-10

Copyright by designer/architect.

**Main Level
Floor Plan**

*Copyright by
designer/architect.*

*Images provided by
designer/architect.*

**Basement
Level Floor
Plan**

**Upper
Level
Floor
Plan**

Plan #111009

Dimensions: 56' W x 49' D

Levels: 2

Square Footage: 2,514

Main Level Sq. Ft.: 1,630

Upper Level Sq. Ft.: 884

Bedrooms: 4

Bathrooms: 3½

Foundation: Basement

Materials List Available: No

Price Category: E

**Main Level
Floor Plan**

*Images provided by
designer/architect.*

Plan #111026

Dimensions: 66' W x 65' D

Levels: 2

Square Footage: 2,406

Main Level Sq. Ft.: 1,796

Upper Level Sq. Ft.: 610

Bedrooms: 4

Bathrooms: 4

Foundation: Crawlspace

Materials List Available: No

Price Category: E

**Upper Level
Floor Plan**

Copyright by designer/architect.

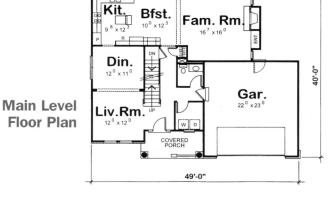

Main Level Floor Plan

Kit.
9⁸ x 12³

Bfst.
10⁰ x 12³

Fam. Rm.
16⁷ x 16⁰

Din.
12⁰ x 11⁰

Liv. Rm.
12⁰ x 12⁰

Gar.
22⁰ x 23⁰

COVERED PORCH

40'-0"

49'-0"

Upper Level Floor Plan

Copyright by designer/architect.

Mbr.
12⁰ x 16⁶

9'-0" CEILING

BOOKS

Br. 4
11⁰ x 10⁶

Br. 2
10⁰ x 11⁷

Br. 3
11⁰ x 11⁰

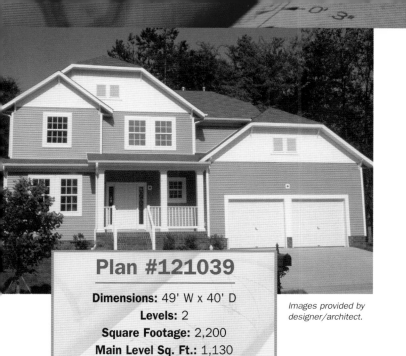

Plan #121039

Dimensions: 49' W x 40' D

Levels: 2

Square Footage: 2,200

Main Level Sq. Ft.: 1,130

Upper Level Sq. Ft.: 1,070

Bedrooms: 4

Bathrooms: 2½

Foundation: Basement

Materials List Available: Yes

Price Category: E

Images provided by designer/architect.

Main Level Floor Plan

Mbr.
15⁰ x 13⁰
10'-0" CEIL.

Fam. Rm.
14⁶ x 15⁴

Bfst.
9⁴ x 11⁰

Kit.
13³ x 11²

Gar.
19⁸ x 20⁴

Den
10⁰ x 10⁶

COVERED PORCH

47'-8"

40'-0"

Upper Level Floor Plan

Copyright by designer/architect.

OPTIONAL EXPANSION

COMP. AREA

Br. 3
10⁰ x 10⁰

Br. 2
10⁰ x 10⁶

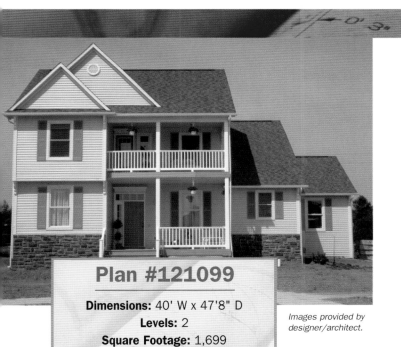

Plan #121099

Dimensions: 40' W x 47'8" D

Levels: 2

Square Footage: 1,699

Main Level Sq. Ft.: 1,268

Upper Level Sq. Ft.: 431

Bedrooms: 3

Bathrooms: 2½

Foundation: Basement

Materials List Available: Yes

Price Category: C

Images provided by designer/architect.

Plan #131041

Dimensions: 42' W x 45' D
Levels: 2
Square Footage: 1,679
Main Level Sq. Ft.: 1,134
Upper Level Sq. Ft.: 545
Bedrooms: 3
Bathrooms: 2½
Foundation: Crawl space, slab, or basement
Materials List Available: Yes
Price Category: D

This rustic-looking two-story cottage includes contemporary amenities for your total comfort.

Features:

- Great Room: With a 9-ft.-4-in.-high ceiling, this large room makes everyone feel at home. A fireplace with raised hearth and built-in niche for a TV will encourage the whole family to gather here on cool evenings, and sliding glass doors leading to

the rear covered porch make it an ideal entertaining area in mild weather.

- Kitchen: When people aren't in the great room, you're likely to find them here, because the convenient serving bar welcomes casual dining, and this room also opens to the p porch.

- Master Suite: Relax at the end of the day in this room, with its 9-ft.-4-in.-high ceiling and walk-in closet, or luxuriate in the private bath with whirlpool tub and dual-sink vanity.

- Optional Basement: This area can include a tuck-under two-car garage if you desire it.

Main Level Floor Plan

Upper Level Floor Plan

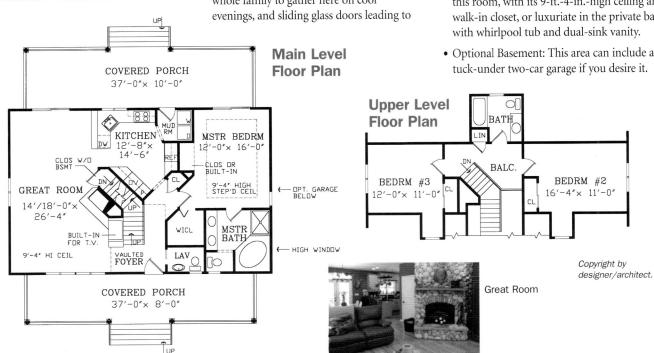

Great Room

Plan #251008

Dimensions: 44'4" W x 73' 2" D
Levels: 2
Square Footage: 1,808
Main Level Sq. Ft.: 1,271
Upper Level Sq. Ft.: 537
Bedrooms: 3
Bathrooms: 2½
Foundation: Basement
Materials List Available: Yes
Price Category: D

Images provided by designer/architect.

An elegant front dormer adds distinction to this country home and brings light into the foyer.

Features:

• Ceiling Height: 9 ft. unless otherwise noted
• Front Porch: A full-length front porch adds to the country charm and provides a relaxing place to sit.

• Foyer: This impressive foyer soars to two stories thanks to the front dormer.

• Dining Room: This dining room has ample space for entertaining. After dinner, guests can step out of the dining room directly onto the rear deck.

• Kitchen: This well-designed kitchen has a double sink. It features a snack bar with plenty of room for impromptu meals.

• Master Bedroom: This distinctive master bedroom features a large-walk-in closet.

• Master Bath: This master bath features walk-in closets in addition to a double vanity and a deluxe tub.

Main Level Floor Plan

Copyright by designer/architect.

Upper Level Floor Plan

Plan #131027

Dimensions: 62'4" W x 53'6" D
Levels: 2
Square Footage: 2,567
Main Level Sq. Ft.: 2,017
Upper Level Sq. Ft.: 550
Bedrooms: 4
Bathrooms: 3
Foundation: Crawl space, slab, or basement
Materials List Available: Yes
Price Category: F

The features of this home are so good that you may have trouble imagining all of them at once.

Images provided by designer/architect.

Features:

- Great Room: Imagine a stepped ceiling, corner fireplace, built-media center, and wall of windows with a glass door to the backyard—in one room.

- Dining Room: A stepped ceiling and server with a sink add to the elegance of this formal room.

- Breakfast Room: Eat at the bar this room shares with the island kitchen, and admire the 12-ft. cathedral ceiling and bayed group of

8- and 9-ft. windows. Or go through the sliding glass door to the covered side porch.

- Master Suite: The bedroom has a tray ceiling and cozy sitting area, and a whirlpool tub, shower, and walk-in closet are in the skylighted bath.

- Optional Study: The private bath in bedroom 2 makes it ideal for a study or home office.

- Bonus Room: Enjoy the extra 300 sq. ft.

Breakfast Nook

Rear View

Great Room

Main Level Floor Plan

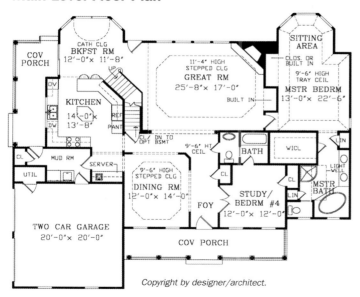

Copyright by designer/architect.

Upper Level Floor Plan

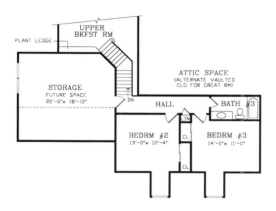

Painting Tips

As with any skill, there is a right and a wrong way to paint. There is a right way to hold a brush, a right way to maneuver a roller, a right way to spray a wall, etc. Follow these basic professional tips:

Brushing vs. Rolling. Some painters insist that only a brush-painted job looks right. However, most painters will "cut in" the edges with a brush, and then finish the main body of a wall or ceiling using a roller. Brushing alone can be time-consuming, and it is typically reserved for architectural woodwork.

Using the Right Brush. Use the largest brush with which you are comfortable. Professional painters seldom pick up anything smaller than a 4-inch brush. Most homeowners will achieve good results using a 4-inch brush for "cutting in" and for large surfaces, and an angled 2½- to 3-inch sash brush for trim around windows and doors. Be sure, also, to use brushes that are appropriate for the type of paint being applied. Oil-based paints require a natural bristle (also called "China bristles"), while water-based paints are applied with a synthetic bristle brush.

Handling a Brush. Many people grip a paintbrush as if they were shaking someone's hand. It is better to grip a brush more like a pencil, with the fingers and thumb wrapped around the metal ferrule. This grip provides the hand and wrist with a wider range of motion and therefore greater speed and precision. If your hand cramps, switch hands or switch temporarily to the handshake grip.

Wiping Rags. Before you begin painting, put a dust rag in your pocket. This is helpful for clearing away cobwebs and dust before painting. It is also handy for wiping off paint drips before they have a chance to dry.

Paint Hooks. When working on a ladder, use a good-quality paint hook to secure the paint bucket to your ladder. Avoid makeshift hooks made with wire or coat hangers. Paint hooks are inexpensive and available at virtually all paint and hardware stores.

Plan #101014

Dimensions: 52' W x 28' D
Levels: 2
Square Footage: 1,598
Main Level Sq. Ft.: 812
Upper Level Sq. Ft.: 786
Bedrooms: 3
Bathrooms: 2½
Foundation: Slab, crawl space
Materials List Available: No
Price Category: C

Images provided by designer/architect.

This lovely Victorian home has a perfect balance of ornamental features and modern amenities.

Features:

- Ceiling Height: 8 ft. unless otherwise noted.
- Foyer: An impressive beveled glass-front door invites you into this roomy foyer.
- Kitchen: This bright and open kitchen offers an abundance of counter space to make cooking a pleasure.

- Breakfast Room: You'll enjoy plenty of informal family meals in this sunny and open spot next to the kitchen.
- Family Room: The whole family will be attracted to this handsome room. A full-width bay window adds to the Victorian charm.
- Master Suite: This dramatic suite features a multi-faceted vaulted ceiling and his and her closets and vanities. A separate shower and 6-ft. garden tub complete the lavish appointments.

Main Level Floor Plan

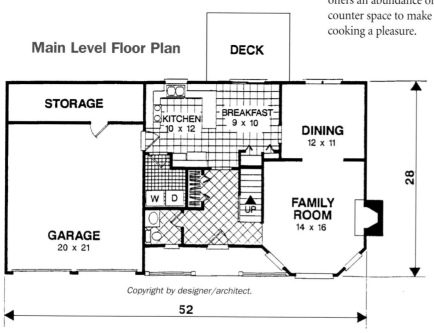

Copyright by designer/architect.

Upper Level Floor Plan

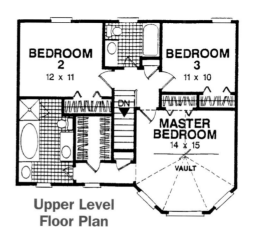

Plan #131046

Dimensions: 68' W x 57'6" D
Levels: 2
Square Footage: 2,245
Main Level Sq. Ft.: 1,720
Upper Level Sq. Ft.: 525
Bedrooms: 3
Bathrooms: 2½
Foundation: Crawl space, slab, or basement
Materials List Available: Yes
Price Category: F

You'll love the mixture of country charm and contemporary amenities in this lovely home.

Features:

- Porch: The covered wraparound porch spells comfort, and the arched windows spell style.

- Great Room: Look up at the 18-ft. vaulted ceiling and the balcony that looks over this room from the upper level, and then notice the wall of windows and the fireplace that's set into a media wall for decorating ease.

- Kitchen: This roomy kitchen is also designed for convenience, thanks to its ample counter space and work island.

- Breakfast Room: The kitchen looks out to this lovely room, with its vaulted ceiling and sliding French doors that open to the rear covered porch.

- Master Bedroom: A 10-ft-ceiling and a dramatic bay window give character to this charming room.

Images provided by designer/architect.

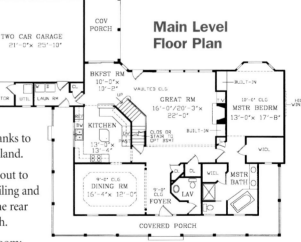

Main Level Floor Plan

Upper Level Floor Plan

Copyright by designer/architect.

Plan #171017

Dimensions: 84' W x 54' D

Levels: 2

Square Footage: 2,558

Main Level Sq. Ft.: 1,577

Upper Level Sq. Ft.: 981

Bedrooms: 4

Bathrooms: 2½

Foundation: Slab, crawl space

Materials List Available: Yes

Price Category: E

Images provided by designer/architect.

Main Level Floor Plan

Upper Level Floor Plan

Copyright by designer/architect.

Plan #281003

Dimensions: 71' W x 35' D

Levels: 2

Square Footage: 2,370

Main Level Sq. Ft.: 1,252

Upper Level Sq. Ft.: 1,118

Bedrooms: 4

Bathrooms: 2½

Foundation: Full basement

Materials List Available: Yes

Price Category: E

Images provided by designer/architect.

Upper Level Floor Plan

Copyright by designer/architect.

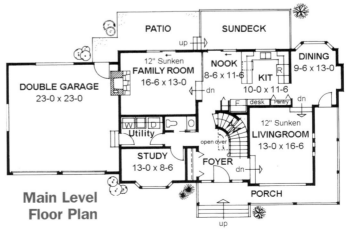

Main Level Floor Plan

Main Level Floor Plan

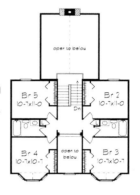

Upper Level Floor Plan

Copyright by designer/architect.

Images provided by designer/architect.

Plan #321081

Dimensions: 70'6" W x 55'6" D
Levels: 2
Square Footage: 2,828
Main Level Sq. Ft.: 2,006
Upper Level Sq. Ft.: 822
Bedrooms: 5
Bathrooms: 3½
Foundation: Basement, crawl space, or slab
Materials List Available: Yes
Price Category: F

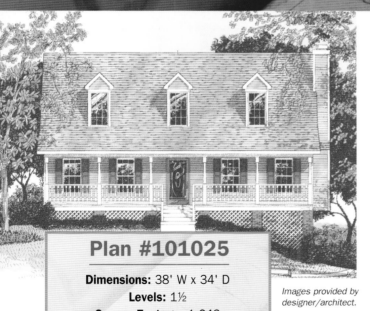

Main Level Floor Plan

Upper Level Floor Plan

Copyright by designer/architect.

Images provided by designer/architect.

Plan #101025

Dimensions: 38' W x 34' D
Levels: 1½
Square Footage: 1,643
Main Level Sq. Ft.: 1,064
Upper Level Sq. Ft.: 579
Bedrooms: 3
Bathrooms: 2½
Foundation: Basement, crawl space
Materials List Available: No
Price Category: C

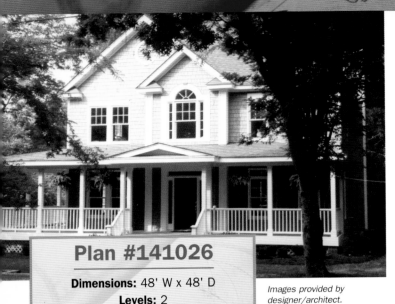

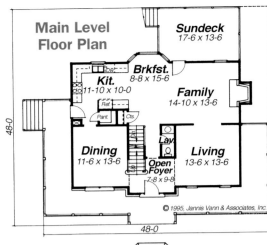

Main Level Floor Plan

Sundeck 17-6 x 13-6

Brkfst. 8-8 x 15-6

Kit. 11-10 x 10-0

Family 14-10 x 13-6

Ref

Pant

Cts

Dining 11-6 x 13-6

Lav

Open Foyer 7-8 x 9-8

Living 13-6 x 13-6

48-0

48-0

© 1995, Jannis Vann & Associates, Inc.

Plan #141026

Dimensions: 48' W x 48' D

Levels: 2

Square Footage: 1,993

Main Level Sq. Ft.: 1,038

Upper Level Sq. Ft.: 955

Bedrooms: 3

Bathrooms: 2½

Foundation: Basement

Materials List Available: Yes

Price Category: D

Images provided by designer/architect.

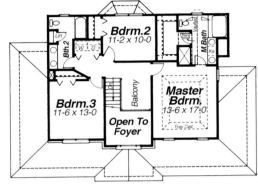

Upper Level Floor Plan

Lin

Bth.2

W D

Bdrm.2 11-2 x 10-0

M.Bath

Bdrm.3 11-6 x 13-0

Balcony

Open To Foyer

Master Bdrm 13-6 x 17-0

Tray Ceil.

Copyright by designer/architect.

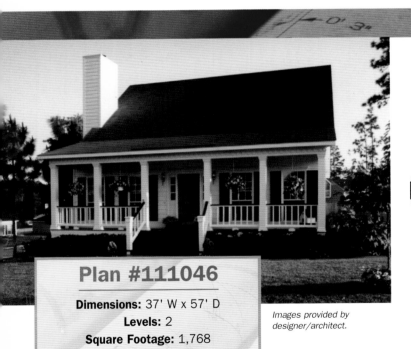

Plan #111046

Dimensions: 37' W x 57' D

Levels: 2

Square Footage: 1,768

Main Level Sq. Ft.: 1,247

Upper Level Sq. Ft.: 521

Bedrooms: 3

Bathrooms: 2½

Foundation: Crawl space

Materials List Available: No

Price Category: C

Images provided by designer/architect.

Wood Deck 12'6"x 8'

Covered Porch 12'2"x 10'

Ext. Storage

Master Bath

WIC

Breakfast 11'10"x 9'6"

Utility

Master Bedroom 12'6"x 15'6"

1/2 Ba.

Kitchen 10'x 11'6"

Living 14'4"x 17'6"

Dining 13'x 12'

Porch 32'x 5'

Main Level Floor Plan

Bedroom 12'6"x 14'

Bedroom 10'6"x 13'2"

Balcony

Upper Level Floor Plan

Copyright by designer/architect.

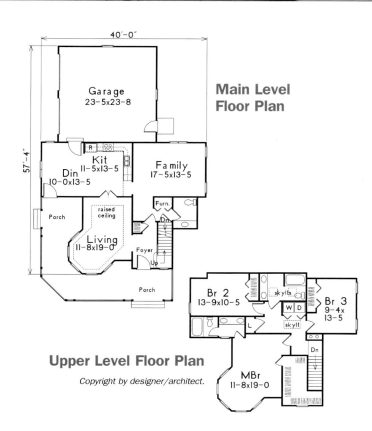

Main Level Floor Plan

Garage
23-5x23-8

Din
10-0x13-5

Kit
11-5x13-5

Family
17-5x13-5

Porch

raised
ceiling

Living
11-8x19-0

Foyer

Porch

40'-0"

57'-4"

Images provided by designer/architect.

Upper Level Floor Plan

Br 2
13-9x10-5

skylts

Br 3
9-4x
13-5

W D

skylt

MBr
11-8x19-0

Copyright by designer/architect.

Plan #321080

Dimensions: 40' W x 57'4" D
Levels: 2
Square Footage: 2,050
Main Level Sq. Ft.: 1,028
Upper Level Sq. Ft.: 1,022
Bedrooms: 3
Bathrooms: 2½
Foundation: Basement, crawl space, or slab
Materials List Available: Yes
Price Category: D

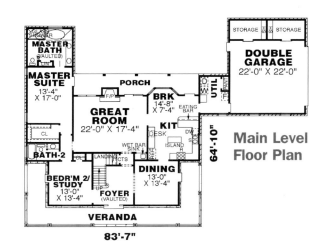

GLASS SHOWER

MASTER BATH (VAULTED)

MASTER SUITE
13'-4" X 17'-0"

PORCH

BRK
14'-8" X 7'-4"

STORAGE   STORAGE

DOUBLE GARAGE
22'-0" X 22'-0"

UTIL

GREAT ROOM
22'-0" X 17'-4"

KIT

BATH-2

WET BAR SINK

EATING BAR

ISLAND

BEDR'M 2/ STUDY
13'-0" X 13'-4"

LANDING

DINING
13'-0" X 13'-4"

FOYER (VAULTED)

VERANDA

83'-7"

64'-10"

Main Level Floor Plan

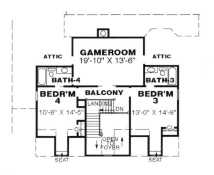

ATTIC

GAMEROOM
19'-10" X 13'-6"

ATTIC

BATH-4

BATH-3

BEDR'M 4
10'-8" X 14'-5"

BALCONY

LANDING   DN

BEDR'M 3
13'-0" X 14'-8"

OPEN TO FOYER

SEAT

SEAT

Upper Level Floor Plan

Copyright by designer/architect.

Plan #241018

Dimensions: 83'7" W x 64'10" D
Levels: 1½
Square Footage: 2,519
Main Level Sq. Ft.: 2,096
Upper Level Sq. Ft.: 423
Bedrooms: 4
Bathrooms: 4
Foundation: Slab
Materials List Available: No
Price Category: E

Images provided by designer/architect.

Plan #121083

Dimensions: 72' W x 45'4" D
Levels: 2
Square Footage: 2,695
Main Level Sq. Ft.: 1,881
Upper Level Sq. Ft.: 814
Bedrooms: 4
Bathrooms: 3½
Foundation: Basement
Materials List Available: Yes
Price Category: F

Images provided by designer/architect.

You'll love this home for its soaring entryway ceiling and well-designed layout.

Features:

- Entry: A balcony from the upper level looks down into this two-story entry, which features a decorative plant shelf.
- Great Room: Comfort is guaranteed in this large room, with its built-in bookcases framing a lovely fireplace and trio of transom-topped windows along one wall.
- Living Room: Save both this formal room and the formal dining room, both of which flank the entry, for guests and special occasions.
- Kitchen: This convenient work space includes a gazebo-shaped breakfast area where friends and family will gather at any time of day.

Main Level Floor Plan

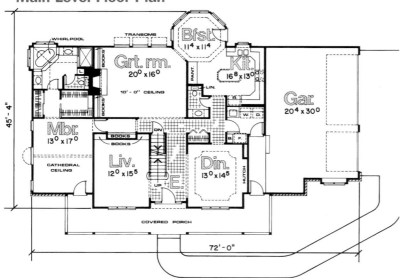

Upper Level Floor Plan

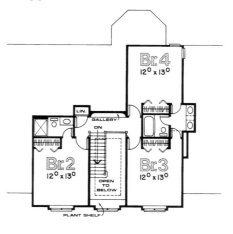

Copyright by designer/architect.

Plan #131001

Dimensions: 72'4" W x 32'4" D
Levels: 1
Square Footage: 1,615
Bedrooms: 3
Bathrooms: 2
Foundation: Basement, crawl space, or slab
Materials List Available: Yes
Price Category: D

Images provided by designer/architect.

Cathedral ceilings and illuminating skylights add drama and beauty to this practical ranch house.

Features:

Ceiling Height: 8 ft.

- Front Porch: Watch the rain in comfort from the covered front porch.

- Foyer: The stone-tiled foyer flows into the living areas.

- Living Room: Oriented towards the front of the house, the living room opens to the dining room and shares a lovely three-sided fireplace with the family room.

- Family Room: Conveniently located to share the fireplace with the living room, this room is bright and cheery thanks to its skylights as well as the sliding glass doors that open onto the rear patio.

- Kitchen: An island makes this sunny room both efficient and attractive.

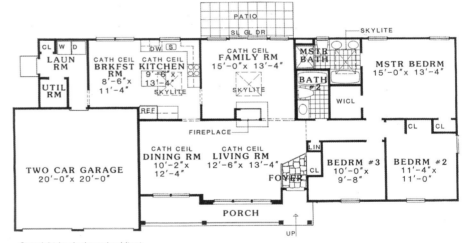

Copyright by designer/architect.

- Breakfast Nook: Located just off the kitchen, this area can serve double-duty as a spot for kitchen visitors to sit.

- Dining Room: The open design between the dining and living rooms adds to the spacious feeling that the cathedral ceiling creates in this area.

- Laundry Room: This area opens from the kitchen for convenience.

- Master Suite: A walk-in closet makes this room practical, but the master bathroom with a skylight, dual-sink vanity, soaking tub, and separate shower makes it luxurious.

- Bedrooms: The two additional bedrooms share a bathroom.

Main Level
Floor Plan

Images provided by designer/architect.

Upper Level
Floor Plan

Copyright by designer/architect.

Plan #181078

Dimensions: 58' W x 42'2" D

Levels: 2

Square Footage: 2,292

Main Level Sq. Ft.: 1,266

Upper Level Sq. Ft.: 1,026

Bedrooms: 4

Bathrooms: 2½

Foundation: Full basement

Materials List Available: Yes

Price Category: E

Main Level
Floor Plan

Images provided by designer/architect.

Upper Level
Floor Plan

Copyright by designer/architect.

Plan #181094

Dimensions: 50' W x 39' D

Levels: 2

Square Footage: 2,099

Main Level Sq. Ft.: 1,060

Upper Level Sq. Ft.: 1,039

Bedrooms: 4

Bathrooms: 2½

Foundation: Full basement

Materials List Available: Yes

Price Category: D

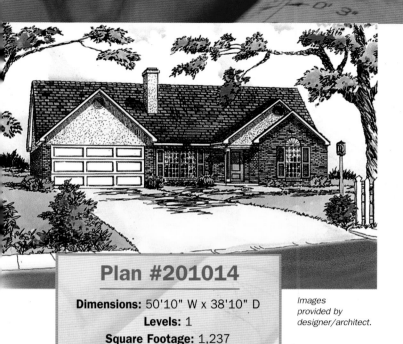

Plan #201014

Dimensions: 50'10" W x 38'10" D
Levels: 1
Square Footage: 1,237
Bedrooms: 3
Bathrooms: 2
Foundation: Crawl space, slab
Materials List Available: Yes
Price Category: B

Images provided by designer/architect.

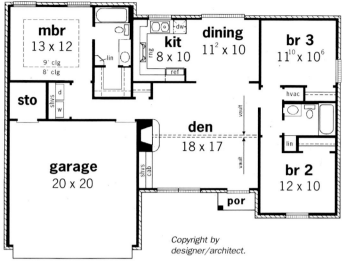

Copyright by designer/architect.

Plan #201017

Dimensions: 64'10" W x 38'10" D
Levels: 1
Square Footage: 1,265
Bedrooms: 3
Bathrooms: 2
Foundation: Crawl space, slab
Materials List Available: Yes
Price Category: B

Images provided by designer/architect.

SMARTtip

Kitchen Underlayment

Check with the manufacturer when selecting an underlayment material. Two that most manufacturers reject:

- Particleboard because it swells greatly when wet. If you have particleboard on the floor now, remove it or cover it with underlayment-grade plywood.

- Hardboard because some tile manufacturers do not consider it a suitable underlayment for their products.

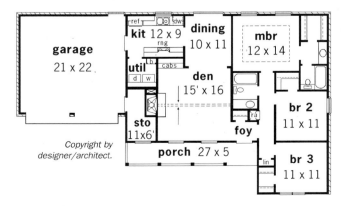

Copyright by designer/architect.

Plan #211069

Dimensions: 58' W x 42' D
Levels: 1½
Square Footage: 1,600
Main Level Sq. Ft.: 1,136
Upper Level Sq. Ft.: 464
Bedrooms: 3
Bathrooms: 2
Foundation: Crawl space
Materials List Available: Yes
Price Category: C

Images provided by designer/architect.

Enjoy the large front porch on this traditionally styled home when it's too sunny for the bugs, and use the screened back porch at dusk and dawn.

Features:

• **Living Room:** Call this the family room if you wish, but no matter what you call it, expect friends and family to gather here, especially when the fireplace gives welcome warmth.

• **Kitchen:** You'll love the practical layout that pleases everyone from gourmet chefs to beginning cooks.

• **Master Suite:** Positioned on the main floor to give it privacy, this suite has two entrances for convenience. You'll find a large walk-in closet here as well as a dressing room that includes a separate vanity and mirror makeup counter.

• **Storage Space:** The 462-sq.-ft. garage is roomy enough to hold two cars and still have space to store tools, out-of-season clothing, or whatever else that needs a dry, protected spot.

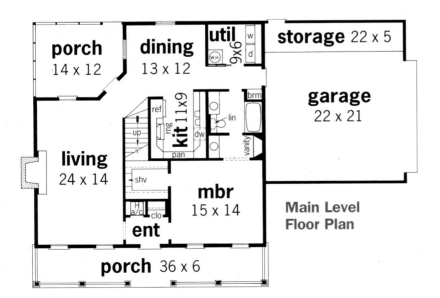

Main Level Floor Plan

Upper Level Floor Plan

Copyright by designer/architect.

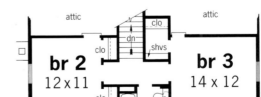

Plan #131004

Dimensions: 59'4" W x 35'8" D
Levels: 1
Square Footage: 1,097
Bedrooms: 3
Bathrooms: 2
Foundation: Basement, crawl space, or slab
Materials List Available: Yes
Price Category: B

You'll love the extra features you'll find in this charming but easy-to-build ranch home.

Features:

• **Porch:** This full-width porch is graced with impressive round columns, decorative railings, and ornamental moldings.

• **Living Room:** Just beyond the front door, the living room entrance has a railing that creates the illusion of a hallway. The 10-ft. tray ceiling makes this room feel spacious.

• **Dining Room:** Flowing from the living room, this room has a 9-ft.-high stepped ceiling and leads to sliding glass doors that open to the large rear patio.

• **Kitchen:** This kitchen is adjacent to the dining room for convenience and has a large island for efficient work patterns.

• **Master Suite:** Enjoy the privacy in this bedroom with its private bathroom.

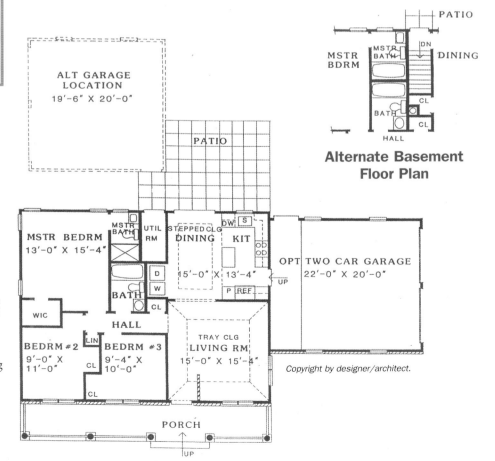

Alternate Basement Floor Plan

Plan #181151

Dimensions: 50' W x 46' D
Levels: 2
Square Footage: 2,283
Main Level Sq. Ft.: 1,274
Second Level Sq. Ft.: 1,009
Bedrooms: 3
Bathrooms: 2½
Foundation: Basement
Materials List Available: Yes
Price Category: E

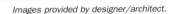

Images provided by designer/architect.

- Kitchen: This efficient and well-designed kitchen has double sinks and offers a separate eating area for those impromptu family meals.

- Master Bedroom: This master retreat has a walk-in closet and its own sumptuous bath.

- Home Office: Whether you work at home or just need a place for the family computer and keeping track of family finances, this home office fills the bill.

Multiple porches, stately columns, and arched multi-paned windows adorn this country home.

Features:

- Ceiling Height: 8 ft. unless otherwise noted.

- Great Room: The second-floor mezzanine overlooks this great room. With its soaring ceiling, this dramatic room is the centerpiece of a spacious and flowing design that is just as suited to entertaining as it is to family life.

- Dining Area: Guests will naturally flow into this dining area when it is time to eat. After dinner they can step directly out onto the porch to enjoy coffee and dessert when the weather is fair.

Main Level Floor Plan

21'-0" X 20'-8"
6,30 X 6,20

17'-0" X 11'-8"
5,10 X 3,50

9'-8" X 8'-8"
2,90 X 2,80

9'-0" X 10'-0"
2,70 X 3,00

10'-0" X 12'-0"
3,00 X 3,60

9'-8" X 9'-4"
2,90 X 2,80

12'-0" X 20'-8"
3,60 X 6,20

46'-0"
13,8 m

50'-0"
15,0 m

Upper Level Floor Plan

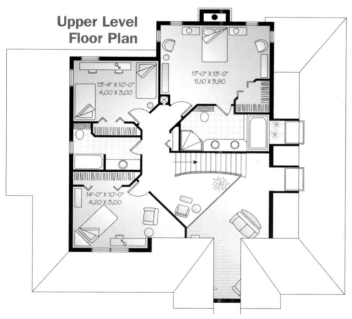

13'-4" X 10'-0"
4,00 X 3,00

17'-0" X 13'-0"
5,10 X 3,90

14'-0" X 10'-0"
4,20 X 3,00

Copyright by designer/architect.

SMARTtip

Coping Chair Rails

If the teeth of your rasp tend to break out thin edges of the cope, try wrapping the rasp with sandpaper to make fine adjustments.

Dining Room

Living Room

Master Bath

Plan #131002

Dimensions: 70'1" W x 60'7" D
Levels: 1
Square Footage: 1,709
Bedrooms: 3
Bathrooms: 2½
Foundation: Basement, crawl space, or slab
Materials List Available: Yes
Price Category: D

Images provided by designer/architect.

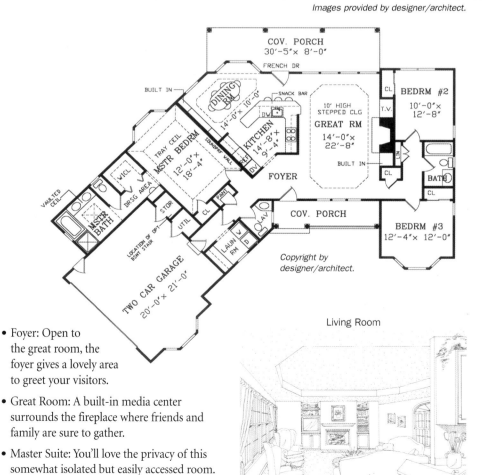

Copyright by designer/architect.

Rear View

Living Room

You'll love the way this angled ranch brings out the best in a corner lot or on a slope.

Features:

• Ceiling Height: 8 ft.

• Front Porch: Hang baskets of plants from the roof of this porch, which is just the right size for a couple of rockers and a side table.

• Dining Room: Well-placed windows flood this room with sunlight during the day and a built-in cabinet gives ample storage space for all your china, linens, and collectables.

• Foyer: Open to the great room, the foyer gives a lovely area to greet your visitors.

• Great Room: A built-in media center surrounds the fireplace where friends and family are sure to gather.

• Master Suite: You'll love the privacy of this somewhat isolated but easily accessed room. Decorate to show off the large bay window and tray ceiling, and enjoy the luxury of a compartmented bathroom.

Plan #271074

Dimensions: 68' W x 86' D
Levels: 1
Square Footage: 2,400
Bedrooms: 4
Bathrooms: 3
Foundation: Crawl space or slab
Materials List Available: No
Price Category: E

Perfect for families with aging relatives or boomerang children, this home includes a completely separate suite at the rear.

Features:

• **Living Room:** A corner fireplace casts a friendly glow over this gathering space.

• **Kitchen:** This efficient space offers a serving bar that extends toward the eating nook and the formal dining room.

• **Master Suite:** A cathedral ceiling presides over this deluxe suite, which boasts a whirlpool tub, dual-sink vanity, and walk-in closet.

• **In-law Suite:** This separate wing has its own vaulted living room, plus a kitchen, a dining room, and a bedroom suite.

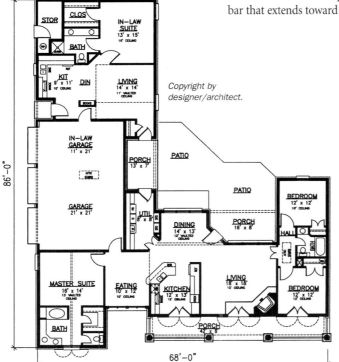

Copyright by designer/architect.

SMARTtip

Adding Professional Flair to Window Treatments

You can give your window treatment designs a professional look by using decorator tricks to customize readymades or dress your own home-sewn designs. These could include contrast linings, tassels, cording, ribbons, or couture trimmings such as buttons, coins, or bows applied to edges. Another trick is to sew a fine wire into the hem of curtains or valances to create a pliable edge that you can shape yourself. Small weights that you can sew into the hem of drapery panels or jabots will make them hang better. For more inspiration look at fashion magazines and visit showrooms.

Plan #131034

Dimensions: 40' W x 32' D
Levels: 2 (Upper unfinished)
Square Footage: 1,040
Bedrooms: 5
Bathrooms: 2½
Foundation: Crawl space, slab, or basement
Materials List Available: Yes
Price Category: C

You'll love the versatility this expandable ranch-style home gives, with its unfinished, second story that you can transform into two bedrooms and a bath if you need the space.

Features:

- **Porch:** Decorate this country-style porch to accentuate the charm of this warm home.

- **Living Room:** This formal room features a wide, dramatic archway that opens to the kitchen and the dining room.

- **Kitchen:** The angled shape of this kitchen gives it character, while the convenient island and well-designed floor plan make cooking and cleaning tasks unusually efficient.

- **Bedrooms:** Use the design option in the blueprints of this home to substitute one of the bedrooms into an expansion of the master bedroom, which features an amenity-laden, private bathroom for total luxury.

Images provided by designer/architect.

Optional Main Level Floor Plan

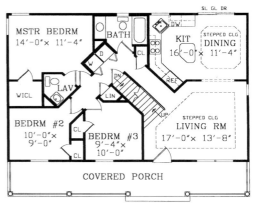

Main Level Floor Plan

Kitchen

Upper Level Floor Plan

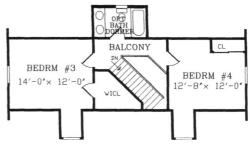

Copyright by designer/architect.

Plan #131043

Dimensions: 65'8" W x 43'10" D
Levels: 2
Square Footage: 1,945
Main Level Sq. Ft.: 1,375
Upper Level Sq. Ft.: 570
Bedrooms: 3
Bathrooms: 2½
Foundation: Crawl space, slab, or basement
Materials List Available: Yes
Price Category: E

This home will delight you with its three dormers and half-round transom windows, which give a nostalgic appearance, and its amenities and conveniences that are certainly contemporary.

Features:

- **Porch:** This covered porch forms the entryway.
- **Great Room:** Enjoy the fireplace in this large, comfortable room, which is open to the dining area. A French door here leads to the covered porch at the rear of the house.
- **Kitchen:** This large, country-style kitchen has a bayed nook, and oversized breakfast bar, and pass-through to the rear porch to simplify serving and make entertaining a pleasure.
- **Master Suite:** A tray ceiling sets an elegant tone for this room, and the bay window adds to it. The large walk-in closet is convenient, and the bath is sumptuous.
- **Bedrooms:** These comfortable rooms have convenient access to a bath.

Main Level Floor Plan

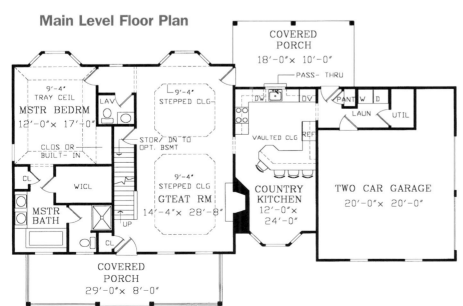

Upper Level Floor Plan

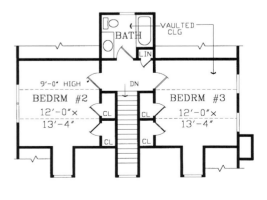

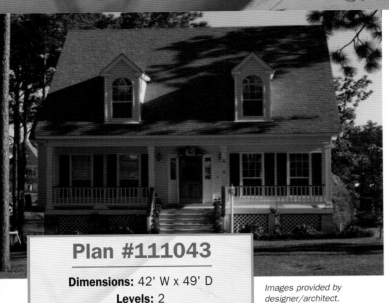

Main Level Floor Plan

Upper Level Floor Plan

Plan #111043

Dimensions: 42' W x 49' D
Levels: 2
Square Footage: 1,737
Main Level Sq. Ft.: 1,238
Upper Level Sq. Ft.: 499
Bedrooms: 3
Bathrooms: 2½
Foundation: Crawl space
Materials List Available: No
Price Category: C

Main Level Floor Plan

Upper Level Floor Plan

Plan #111045

Dimensions: 41' W x 50' D
Levels: 2
Square Footage: 1,880
Main Level Sq. Ft.: 1,244
Upper Level Sq. Ft.: 636
Bedrooms: 3
Bathrooms: 2½
Foundation: Slab
Materials List Available: No
Price Category: D

Plan #211072

Dimensions: 62' W x 86' D

Levels: 2

Square Footage: 3,012

Main Level Sq. Ft.: 2,202

Upper Level Sq. Ft.: 810

Bedrooms: 4

Bathrooms: 3½

Foundation: Crawl space, optional basement

Materials List Available: Yes

Price Category: G

Images provided by designer/architect.

Main Level Floor Plan

sto | sto | sto

garage 22 x 22

porch 18 x 6

util 14 x 9

built-in entertainment ctr and library

family rm 25 x 16

kit 14 x 13

bath 17 x 9

built-in entertainment ctr and library

sitting 14 x 12

mbr 16 x 13

dining 16 x 12

eating 14 x 10

foy

porch 34 x 8

future space 28 x 12

Upper Level Floor Plan

Copyright by designer/architect.

outline of lower level

br 4 11 x 12

balcony

br 2 13 x 13

br 3 13 x 12

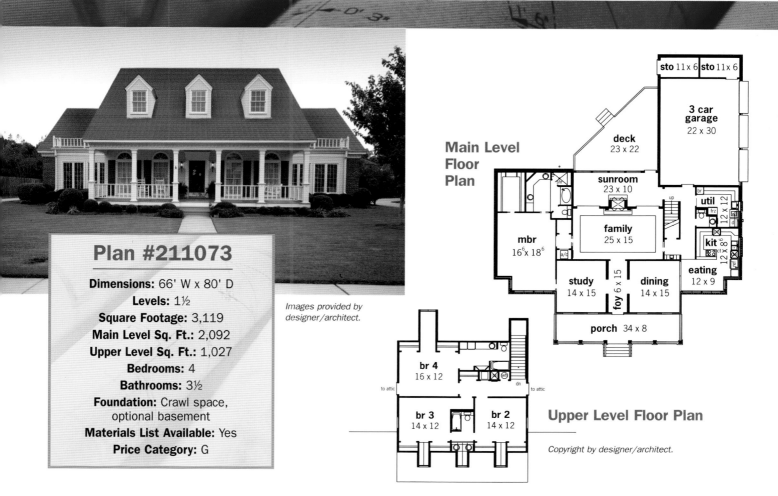

Plan #211073

Dimensions: 66' W x 80' D

Levels: 1½

Square Footage: 3,119

Main Level Sq. Ft.: 2,092

Upper Level Sq. Ft.: 1,027

Bedrooms: 4

Bathrooms: 3½

Foundation: Crawl space, optional basement

Materials List Available: Yes

Price Category: G

Images provided by designer/architect.

Main Level Floor Plan

sto 11 x 6 | sto 11 x 6

3 car garage 22 x 30

deck 23 x 22

sunroom 23 x 10

util 12 x 12

mbr 16⁶ x 18⁶

family 25 x 15

kit 12 x 8⁶

study 14 x 15

foy 6 x 15

dining 14 x 15

eating 12 x 9

porch 34 x 8

br 4 16 x 12

to attic

br 3 14 x 12

br 2 14 x 12

to attic

dn

Upper Level Floor Plan

Copyright by designer/architect.

Plan #121006

Dimensions: 46' W x 58' D

Levels: 1

Square Footage: 1,762

Bedrooms: 3

Bathrooms: 2

Foundation: Basement, crawl space, or slab

Materials List Available: Yes

Price Category: C

The entry has a trio of arched openings that leads you to other areas of this amenity-packed home.

Features:

- Ceiling Height: 8 ft. except as noted.

- Eating Bar: Conveniently located between the kitchen and family room, this is sure to be a favorite spot for informal entertaining and family gatherings.

- Family room: A wall of windows, a fireplace, and a vaulted ceiling stretching to 11 ft. work together to make this a bright and warm room.

- Kitchen: There's no shortage of counter space in this well-planned kitchen that features a center island in addition to the eating bar.

- Master Suite: Luxuriate at the end of the day in this large bedroom with its decorative tray ceiling and walk-in closet. Enjoy the pampering bath with its sunlit corner whirlpool flanked by vanities.

- Garage: Two bays provide room for cars and plenty of storage as well.

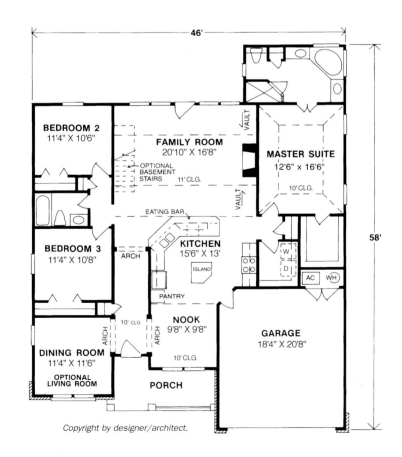

Plan #121010

Dimensions: 50' W x 62' D
Levels: 1
Square Footage: 1,902
Bedrooms: 2
Bathrooms: 2
Foundation: Basement
Materials List Available: Yes
Price Category: D

This home is replete with architectural details that provide a convenient and gracious lifestyle.

Features:

- **Ceiling Height:** 8 ft.

- **Great Room:** The entry enjoys a long view into this room. Family and friends will be drawn to the warmth of its handsome fireplace flanked by windows.

- **Breakfast Area:** You'll pass through cased openings from the great room into the cozy breakfast area that will lure the whole family to linger over informal meals.

- **Kitchen:** Another cased opening leads from the breakfast area into the well-designed kitchen with its convenient island.

- **Master Bedroom:** To the right of the great room special ceiling details highlight the master bedroom where a cased opening and columns lead to a private sitting area.

- **Den/library:** Whether you are listening to music or relaxing with a book, this special room will always enhance your lifestyle.

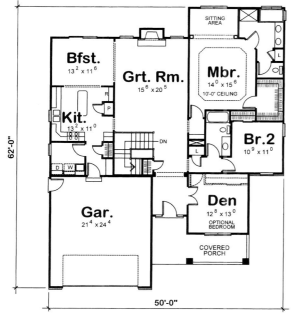

SMARTtip

Accentuating Your Fireplace with Faux Effects

Experiment with faux effects to add an aged look or a specific style to a fireplace mantel and surround. Craft stores sell inexpensive kits with directions for adding the appearance of antiqued or paneled wood or plaster, rusticated stone, marble, terra cotta, and other effects that make any style achievable.

Plan #251001

Dimensions: 61'3" W x 40'6" D
Levels: 1
Square Footage: 1,253
Bedrooms: 3
Bathrooms: 2
Foundation: Crawl space, basement
Materials List Available: Yes
Price Category: B

This charming country home has a classic full front porch for enjoying summertime breezes.

Features:

- Ceiling Height: 8 ft.

- Foyer: Guests will walk through the front porch into this foyer, which opens to the family room.

- Screened Porch: A second porch is screened and is located at the rear of the home off the dining room, so your guests can step out for a bit of fresh air after dinner.

- Family Room: Family and friends will be drawn to this large open space, with its handsome fireplace and sloped ceiling.

- Kitchen: This open and airy kitchen is a pleasure in which to work. It has ample counter space and a pantry.

- Master Bedroom: This master bedroom features a large walk-in closet. It has its own master bath with a single vanity, a tub, and a walk-in shower.

- Garage: This attached garage provides plenty of extra storage space, as well as parking for two cars.

Images provided by designer/architect.

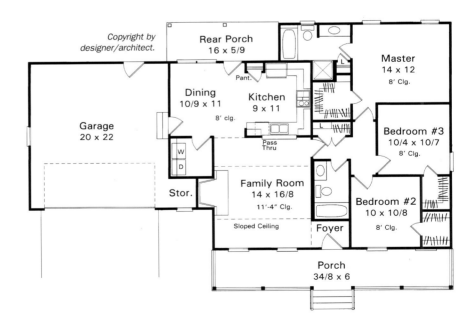

Plan #251002

Dimensions: 55'6" W x 64'3" D
Levels: 1
Square Footage: 1,333
Bedrooms: 3
Bathrooms: 2
Foundation: Crawl space, slab
Materials List Available: Yes
Price Category: B

Although compact, this farmhouse has all the amenities for comfortable modern living.

Features:

• Ceiling Height: 8 ft. unless otherwise noted.

• Foyer: This gracious and welcoming foyer opens to the family room.

• Family Room: This inviting family room is designed to accommodate all kinds of family activities. It features a 9-ft. ceiling and a handsome, warming fireplace.

• Kitchen: Cooking in this kitchen is a real pleasure. It includes a center island, so you'll never run out of counter space for food preparation.

• Master Bedroom: This master bedroom features a large walk-in closet and an elegant 9-ft. recessed ceiling.

• Master Bath: This master bath offers a double vanity, a tub, and a walk-in shower.

• Garage: This attached garage provides plenty of extra storage space, as well as parking for two cars.

SMARTtip

Arts and Crafts Style

The heart of this style rests in its earthy connection. The more you can bring nature into it, the more authentic it will be. An easy way to do this is with plants. A bonus is that plants naturally thrive in the bathroom, where they enjoy the humid environment.

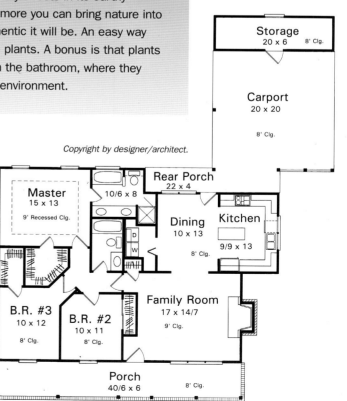

Copyright by designer/architect.

Images provided by designer/architect.

Plan #121012

Dimensions: 40' W x 48'8" D
Levels: 1
Square Footage: 1,195
Bedrooms: 3
Bathrooms: 2
Foundation: Basement
Materials List Available: Yes
Price Category: B

This compact one-level home uses an open plan to make the most of its square footage.

Features:

- Ceiling Height: 8 ft.
- Covered Porch: This delightful area, located off the kitchen, provides a private spot to enjoy some fresh air.
- Open Plan: The family room, dining area and kitchen share a big open space to provide a sense of spaciousness. Moving so easily between these interrelated areas provides the convenience demanded by a busy lifestyle.
- Master Suite: An open plan is convenient, but it is still important for everyone to have their private space. The master suite enjoys its own bath and walk-in closet. The secondary bedrooms share a nearby bath.
- Garage: Here you will find parking for two cars and plenty of extra storage space as well.

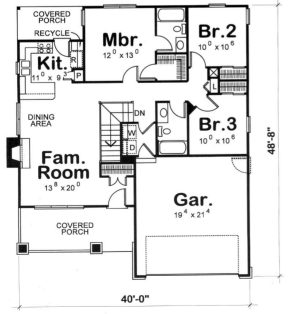

Copyright by designer/architect.

SMARTtip
Painting Doors

To protect the door finish while working, cover the sawhorses with towels or carpet scraps. Be sure to allow sufficient time for the door to dry before flipping it over.

To paint both sides of the door at one time, drive a pair of 16d nails into the top and bottom edges of the door, and then rest the door on the sawhorses, as shown below. After painting one side, simply flip the door over to paint the other side. (Note: This method may not work quite as well with very heavy wood or steel doors.)

Plan #121038

Dimensions: 54' W x 52' D
Levels: 2
Square Footage: 2,332
Main Level Sq. Ft.: 1,597
Upper Level Sq. Ft.: 735
Bedrooms: 4
Bathrooms: 2½
Foundation: Basement
Materials List Available: Yes
Price Category: E

Images provided by designer/architect.

Offering plenty of architectural style, this home is designed with the busy modern lifestyle in mind.

Features:

- Ceiling Height: 8 ft. unless otherwise noted.

- Family Room: The visual spaciousness of this stylish family room is enhanced by a cathedral ceiling and light streaming through stacked windows.

- Kitchen: This is sure to be a popular informal gathering place. The kitchen features a

convenient center island with a snack bar, pantry, and planning desk. The breakfast area is perfect for quick family meals.

- Master Suite: This peaceful retreat is thoughtfully located apart from the rest of the house. It includes a walk-in closet and a private bath.

- Bedrooms: Bedroom 2 has its own walk-in closet and private bath. Bedrooms 3 and 4 share a full bath.

**Main Level
Floor Plan**

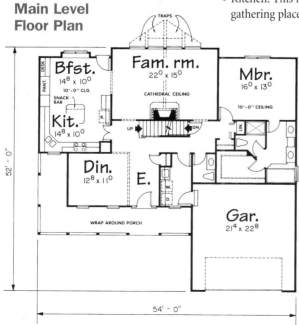

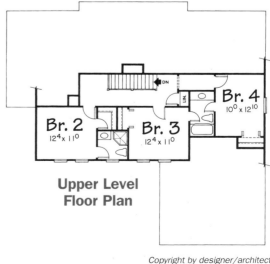

**Upper Level
Floor Plan**

Copyright by designer/architect.

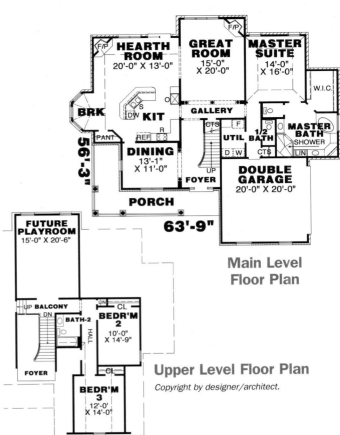

Main Level Floor Plan

Images provided by designer/architect.

HEARTH ROOM 20'-0" X 13'-0"

GREAT ROOM 15'-0" X 20'-0"

MASTER SUITE 14'-0" X 16'-0"

W.I.C.

BRK

KIT

GALLERY

MASTER BATH SHOWER

PANT

DINING 13'-1" X 11'-0"

1/2 BATH

UTIL

FOYER

UP

DOUBLE GARAGE 20'-0" X 20'-0"

PORCH

56'-3"

63'-9"

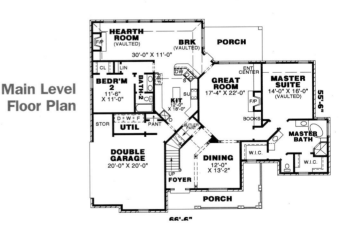

FUTURE PLAYROOM 15'-0" X 20'-6"

UP BALCONY DN

BATH-2

BEDR'M 2 10'-0" X 14'-9"

HALL

FOYER

BEDR'M 3 12'-0" X 14'-0"

Upper Level Floor Plan

Copyright by designer/architect.

Plan #241012

Dimensions: 63'9" W x 56'3" D

Levels: 2

Square Footage: 2,743

Main Level Sq. Ft.: 2,153

Upper Level Sq. Ft.: 590

Bedrooms: 3

Bathrooms: 2½

Foundation: Slab

Materials List Available: No

Price Category: E

Main Level Floor Plan

Images provided by designer/architect.

HEARTH ROOM (VAULTED) 30'-0" X 11'-0"

BRK (VAULTED)

PORCH

BEDR'M 2 11'-6" X 11'-0"

BATH-2

GREAT ROOM 17'-4" X 22'-0"

MASTER SUITE 14'-0" X 16'-0" (VAULTED)

55'-6"

ENT CENTER

STOR

KIT 12'-0" X 18'-0"

UTIL

PANT

BOOKS

F/P

MASTER BATH

DOUBLE GARAGE 20'-0" X 20'-0"

DINING 12'-0" X 13'-2"

W.I.C.

UP

FOYER

PORCH

66'-6"

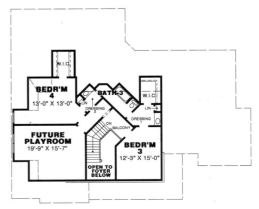

Upper Level Floor Plan

Copyright by designer/architect.

W.I.C.

BEDR'M 4 13'-0" X 13'-0"

BATH-3

W.I.C.

DRESSING

DRESSING

DN BALCONY

FUTURE PLAYROOM 19'-9" X 15'-7"

BEDR'M 3 12'-3" X 15'-0"

OPEN TO FOYER BELOW

Plan #241014

Dimensions: 66'6" W x 55'6" D

Levels: 2

Square Footage: 3,046

Main Level Sq. Ft.: 2,292

Upper Level Sq. Ft.: 754

Bedrooms: 4

Bathrooms: 3

Foundation: Slab

Materials List Available: No

Price Category: G

Plan #251007

Dimensions: 71' W x 42'6" D

Levels: 2

Square Footage: 1,597

Main Level Sq. Ft.: 982

Upper Level Sq. Ft.: 615

Bedrooms: 4

Bathrooms: 2½

Foundation: Basement

Materials List Available: Yes

Price Category: C

Images provided by designer/architect.

Main Level Floor Plan

Upper Level Floor Plan

Copyright by designer/architect.

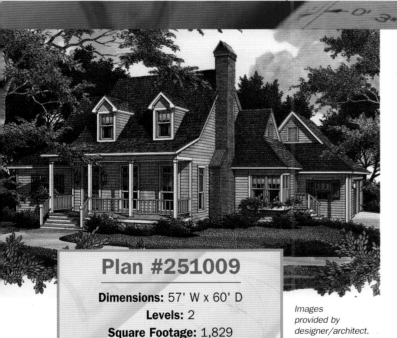

Plan #251009

Dimensions: 57' W x 60' D

Levels: 2

Square Footage: 1,829

Main Level Sq. Ft.: 1,339

Upper Level Sq. Ft.: 490

Bedrooms: 4

Bathrooms: 2½

Foundation: Basement

Materials List Available: No

Price Category: D

Images provided by designer/architect.

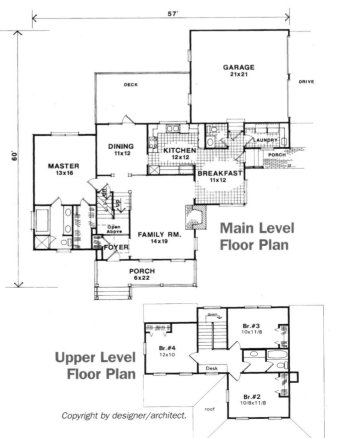

Main Level Floor Plan

Upper Level Floor Plan

Copyright by designer/architect.

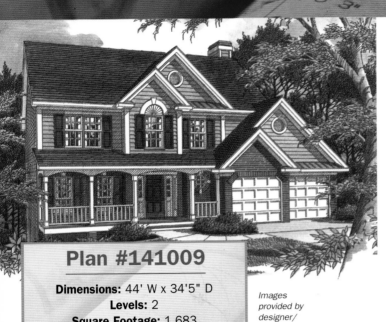

Plan #141009

Dimensions: 44' W x 34'5" D

Levels: 2

Square Footage: 1,683

Main Level Sq. Ft.: 797

Upper Level Sq. Ft.: 886

Bedrooms: 3

Bathrooms: 2½

Foundation: Basement, crawl space or slab

Materials List Available: No

Price Category: C

Images provided by designer/architect.

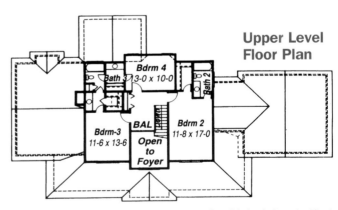

Main Level Floor Plan

Sundeck 16-0 x 12-0

Brkfst. 8-0 x 9-6

Kitchen 9-4 x 11-8

Living Area 18-0 x 11-8

Stor. 5-6 x 12-0

Dining 11-0 x 13-4

Open Foyer 8-4 x 11-10

Double Garage 19-8 x 21-4

Porch

Upper Level Floor Plan

Copyright by designer/architect.

M.Bath

Bdrm. 3 13-0 x 9-6

Master Bdrm. 15-6 x 11-0

Bdrm. 2 13-0 x 9-6

Open Foyer

Plan #141017

Dimensions: 82' W x 49' D

Levels: 2

Square Footage: 2,480

Main Level Sq. Ft.: 1,581

Upper Level Sq. Ft.: 899

Bedrooms: 4

Bathrooms: 3½

Foundation: Basement, crawl space, or slab

Materials List Available: No

Price Category: E

Images provided by designer/architect.

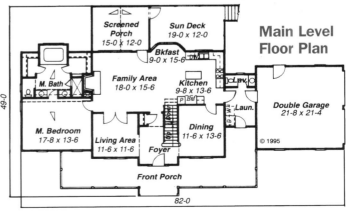

Upper Level Floor Plan

Copyright by designer/architect.

Bdrm 4 13-0 x 10-0

Bath

Bath 2

Bdrm-3 11-6 x 13-6

BAL Open to Foyer

Bdrm 2 11-8 x 17-0

Main Level Floor Plan

Screened Porch 15-0 x 12-0

Sun Deck 19-0 x 12-0

Bkfast 9-0 x 15-6

M. Bath

Family Area 18-0 x 15-6

Kitchen 9-8 x 13-6

Laun.

Double Garage 21-8 x 21-4

M. Bedroom 17-8 x 13-6

Living Area 11-6 x 11-6

Foyer

Dining 11-6 x 13-6

© 1995

Front Porch

82-0

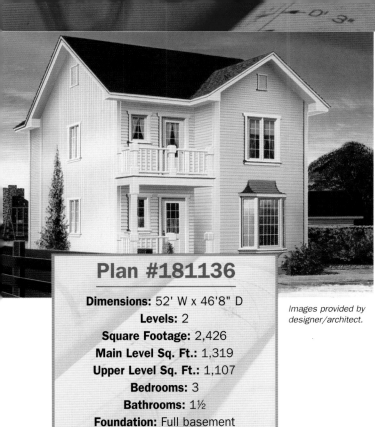

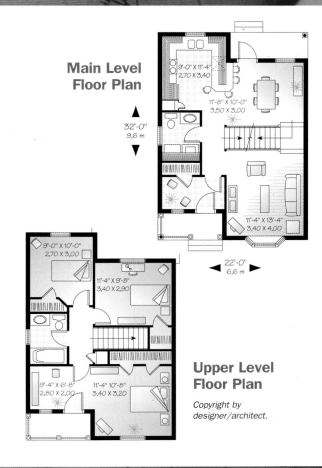

**Main Level
Floor Plan**

9'-0" X 11'-4"
2,70 X 3,40

11'-8" X 10'-0"
3,50 X 3,00

11'-4" X 13'-4"
3,40 X 4,00

32'-0"
9,6 m

22'-0"
6,6 m

Plan #181136

Dimensions: 52' W x 46'8" D

Levels: 2

Square Footage: 2,426

Main Level Sq. Ft.: 1,319

Upper Level Sq. Ft.: 1,107

Bedrooms: 3

Bathrooms: 1½

Foundation: Full basement

Materials List Available: Yes

Price Category: E

*Images provided by
designer/architect.*

9'-0" X 10'-0"
2,70 X 3,00

11'-4" X 9'-8"
3,40 X 2,90

9'-4" X 6'-8"
2,80 X 2,00

11'-4" 10'-8"
3,40 X 3,20

**Upper Level
Floor Plan**

*Copyright by
designer/architect.*

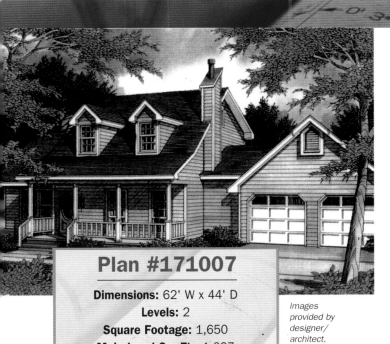

62'

PORCH
22 X 8

CLOSET

BATH

DINING
10 x 12

KITCHEN
11 x 11

MASTER SUITE
13 x 17

GREAT RM
19 x 17

UTILITY

GARAGE
21 x 24

FOYER

PORCH
22 X 6

44'

**Main Level
Floor Plan**

Plan #171007

Dimensions: 62' W x 44' D

Levels: 2

Square Footage: 1,650

Main Level Sq. Ft.: 1,097

Upper Level Sq. Ft.: 553

Bedrooms: 3

Bathrooms: 2

Foundation: Slab, crawl space

Materials List Available: Yes

Price Category: C

*Images
provided by
designer/
architect.*

BEDRM
13 x 10

BATH

BEDRM
14 x 11

STOR

**Upper Level
Floor Plan**

*Copyright by
designer/architect.*

Plan #121040

Dimensions: 50' W x 48' D
Levels: 2
Square Footage: 1,818
Main Level Sq. Ft.: 1,302
Upper Level Sq. Ft.: 516
Bedrooms: 3
Bathrooms: 2½
Foundation: Basement
Materials List Available: Yes
Price Category: D

Offering plenty of architectural style, this home is designed with the busy modern lifestyle in mind.

Features:

• Ceiling Height: 8 ft. unless otherwise noted.

• Great Room: This is sure to be the central gathering place of the home with its volume ceiling, abundance of windows, and its handsome fireplace.

• Kitchen: This convenient and attractive kitchen offers a center island. It includes a snack bar that will get lots of use for impromptu family meals.

• Breakfast Area: Joined to the kitchen by the snack bar, this breakfast area will invite you to linger over morning coffee. It includes a pantry and access to the backyard.

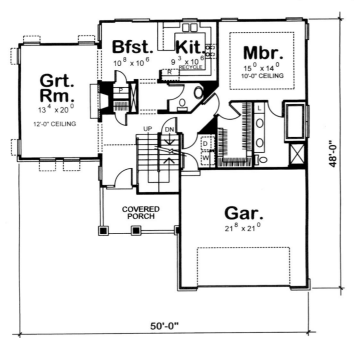

Main Level Floor Plan

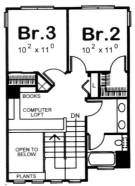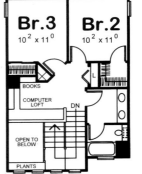

Upper Level Floor Plan

• Master Bedroom: This private retreat offers the convenience of a walk-in closet and the luxury of its own whirlpool bath and shower.

• Computer Loft: Designed with the family computer in mind, this loft overlooks a two-story entry.

Plan #121044

Dimensions: 40' W x 55'8" D

Levels: 2

Square Footage: 1,923

Main Level Sq. Ft.: 1,351

Upper Level Sq. Ft.: 572

Bedrooms: 3

Bathrooms: 3

Foundation: Basement

Materials List Available: Yes

Price Category: D

Images provided by designer/architect.

The layout of this gracious home is designed with the contemporary family in mind.

Features:

- Ceiling Height: 8 ft. unless otherwise noted.

- Foyer: This elegant entry is graced with an open stairway that enhances the sense of spaciousness.

- Kitchen: Located just beyond the entry, this convenient kitchen features a center island that doubles as a snack bar.

- Breakfast Area: A sloped ceiling unites this area with the family room. Here you will find a planning desk for compiling menus and shopping lists.

- Master bedroom: This bedroom has a distinctively contemporary appeal, with its cathedral ceiling and triple window.

- Computer Loft: Designed to house a computer, this loft overlooks the family room.

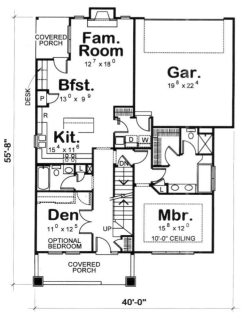

Main Level Floor Plan

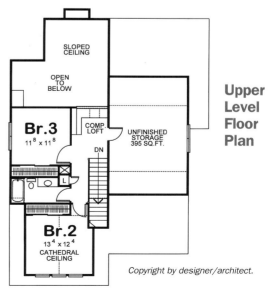

Upper Level Floor Plan

Copyright by designer/architect.

Plan #251004

Dimensions: 50'9" W x 42'1" D
Levels: 1
Square Footage: 1,500
Bedrooms: 3
Bathrooms: 2
Foundation: Crawl space, slab
Materials List Available: Yes
Price Category: C

Combine the old-fashioned appeal of a country farmhouse with all the comforts of modern living.

Features:

• Ceiling Height: 9 ft.

• Foyer: When guests enter this inviting foyer, they will be greeted by a view of the lovely family room.

• Family Room: Usher family and friends into this welcoming family room, where they can warm up in front of the fireplace. The room's 12-ft. ceiling enhances its sense of spaciousness.

• Kitchen: Gather around and keep the cook company at the snack bar in this roomy kitchen. There's still plenty of counter space for food preparation, thanks to the kitchen island.

• Master Bedroom: This elegant master bedroom features a large walk-in closet and a 9-ft. recessed ceiling.

• Master Bath. This master bath includes a double vanity, a tub, and a walk-in shower.

• Garage: This attached garage provides plenty of extra storage space, as well as parking for two cars.

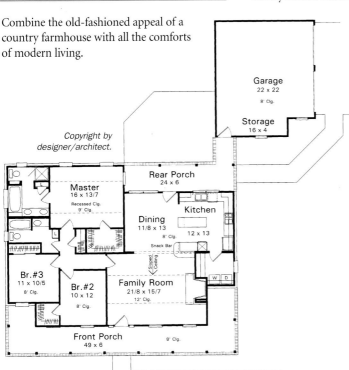

Copyright by designer/architect.

SMARTtip

Shaker Style in Your Bathroom

This warm, likable style fits in perfectly with a country home because of its old-fashioned values. But it blends in well with contemporary interiors, too, because of its clean lines and plain geometric shapes. In fact, adding a few Shaker elements can warm up the sometimes cold look of a thoroughly modern room.

Plan #131035

Dimensions: 65'4" W x 45'10" D
Levels: 1
Square Footage: 1,892
Bedrooms: 3
Bathrooms: 2½
Foundation: Basement, crawl space, of slab
Materials List Available: Yes
Price Category: E

Images provided by designer/architect.

Families who love a mixture of traditional — a big front porch, simple roofline, and bay windows—and contemporary—an open floor plan—will love this charming home.

Features:

- Great Room: Central to this home, the open living and entertaining areas allow the family to gather effortlessly and create the perfect spot for entertaining.

- Dining Room: Volume ceilings both here and in the great room further enhance the spaciousness the open floor plan creates.

- Master Suite: Positioned on the opposite end of the other two bedrooms in the split-bedroom plan, this master suite gives an unusual amount of privacy and quiet in a home of this size.

- Bonus Room: Located over the attached garage, this bonus room gives you a place to finish for a study or a separate game room.

Rear Elevation

Copyright by designer/architect.

Bonus Area

Plan #121047

Dimensions: 67'8" W x 57' D
Levels: 2
Square Footage: 3,072
Main Level Sq. Ft.: 2,116
Upper Level Sq. Ft.: 956
Bedrooms: 4
Bathrooms: 3½
Foundation: Slab
Materials List Available: Yes
Price Category: G

Images provided by designer/architect.

A long porch and a trio of roof dormers give this gracious home a sophisticated country look.

Features:

• Ceiling Height: 8 ft. unless otherwise noted.

• Balcony: This balcony overlooks the entry and the staircase hall.

• Dining Room: Columns and a cased opening lend elegance, making this the perfect venue for stylish dinner parties.

• Family Room: A cathedral ceiling gives this room a light and airy feel. The handsome fireplace framed by windows is sure to become a favorite family gathering place.

• Master Bedroom: This architecturally distinctive bedroom features a bayed sitting area and a tray ceiling.

• Bedrooms: One of the bedrooms enjoys a private bath, making it a perfect guest room. Other bedrooms feature walk-in closets.

Main Level Floor Plan

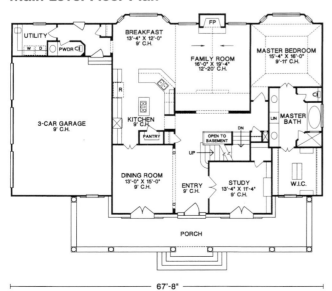

Upper Level Floor Plan

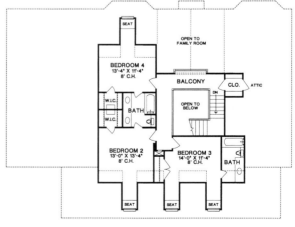

Copyright by designer/architect.

Plan #121016

Dimensions: 56' W x 48' D
Levels: 2
Square Footage: 2,594
Main Level Sq. Ft.: 1,322
Upper Level Sq. Ft.: 1,272
Bedrooms: 4
Bathrooms: 3
Foundation: Basement
Materials List Available: Yes
Price Category: E

A huge wraparound porch gives this home warmth and charm.

Features:

• Ceiling Height: 8 ft. except as noted.

• Family Room: This informal sunken room's beamed ceiling and fireplace flanked by windows makes it the perfect place for family gatherings.

• Formal Dining Room: Guests will enjoy gathering in this large elegant room.

• Master Suite: The second-floor master bedroom features its own luxurious bathroom.

• Compartmented Full Bath: This large bathroom serves the three secondary bedrooms on the second floor.

• Optional Play Area: This special space, included in one of the bedrooms, features a cathedral ceiling.

• Kitchen: A large island is the centerpiece of this modern kitchen's well-designed food-preparation area.

Main Level Floor Plan

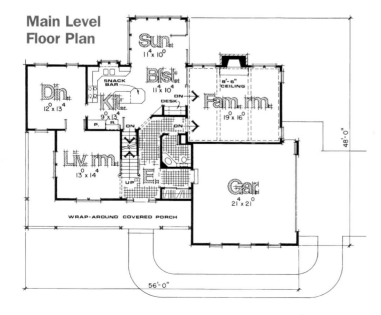

Upper Level Floor Plan

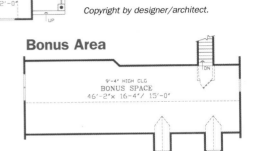

Copyright by designer/architect.

Plan #131047

Dimensions: 69'10" W x 51'8" D

Levels: 1

Square Footage: 1,793

Bedrooms: 3

Bathrooms: 2

Foundation: Basement, crawl space, or slab

Materials List Available: Yes

Price Category: E

Images provided by designer/architect.

Bonus Area

Rear Elevation

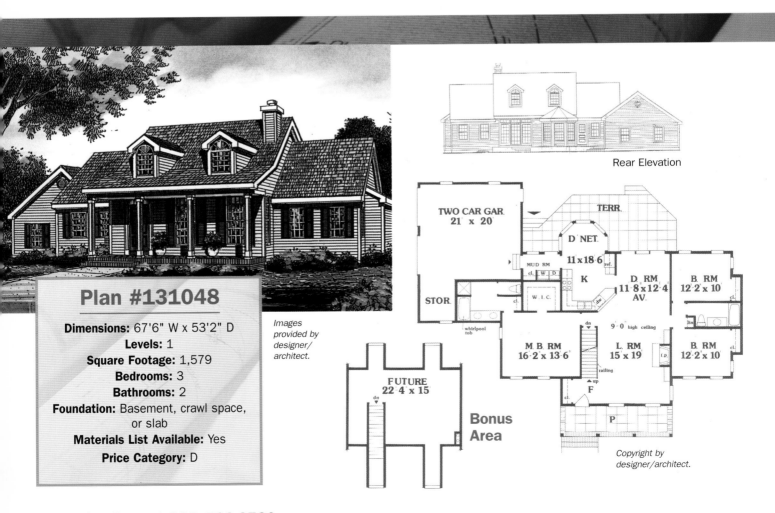

Rear Elevation

Plan #131048

Dimensions: 67'6" W x 53'2" D

Levels: 1

Square Footage: 1,579

Bedrooms: 3

Bathrooms: 2

Foundation: Basement, crawl space, or slab

Materials List Available: Yes

Price Category: D

Images provided by designer/architect.

Bonus Area

Copyright by designer/architect.

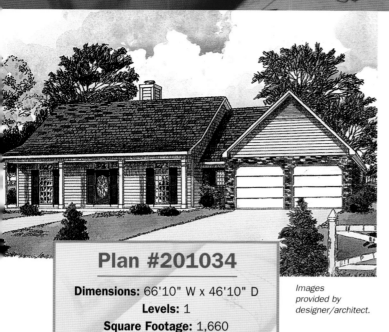

Plan #201034

Dimensions: 66'10" W x 46'10" D
Levels: 1
Square Footage: 1,660
Bedrooms: 3
Bathrooms: 2
Foundation: Crawl space, slab
Materials List Available: Yes
Price Category: C

Images provided by designer/architect.

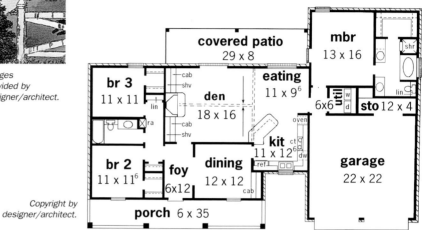

SMARTtip

Wall Frame Widths

Trim Tip: Depending on the room, widths of wall frames usually vary from wall to wall. This is okay as long as you keep variations as small as possible while trying to maintain dimensions close to the ideal 1:0.635 ratio of the Golden Rectangle. Doors and windows will dictate exceptions to the rule.

Plan #201051

Dimensions: 58'10" W x 59'5" D
Levels: 1
Square Footage: 1,899
Bedrooms: 3
Bathrooms: 2
Foundation: Crawl space, slab
Materials List Available: Yes
Price Category: D

Images provided by designer/architect.

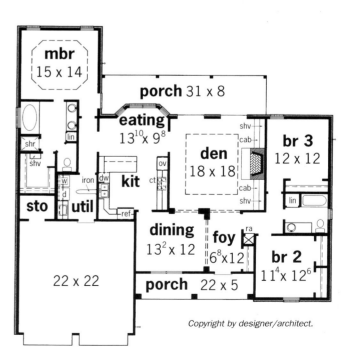

Decks

Many people are reluctant to make design decisions because they don't think of themselves as designers. But if you take the time to think things through carefully, you may be surprised at the ideas you generate. Start with memories of places you have enjoyed. Of course, dreams can rarely be re-created in the real world. But by letting your imagination run loose and tapping into those images, you can develop a font of design concepts that will help you come up with a deck design.

Beginning Your Design

Begin by imagining your ideal deck, and ask family members to do the same. Think about its design, accessories, and any special elements you would like your deck to contain. Keep track of your ideas by drawing a series of rough sketches as you proceed. Expect to fill a wastebasket or two with these. Don't think of them as actual designs so much as focal points for conversations—it's easier to point to a drawing than to walk around the house.

Feel free to steal ideas from other people. (The best architects do not hesitate to do so.) When you see a deck you like, take photos and jot down some notes. Talk to the owners about how their deck works for them. Most people will be flattered that you like their deck and will be more than glad to talk to you about it. You will not only learn about pleasing designs and materials, but you can avoid the mistakes they made.

Screened porches, left, are popular deck amenities.

Eating areas, above, require ample room for tables and chairs.

Multilevel decks, opposite, provide room for separate activity areas.

Uses for Your New Deck

Call a family meeting to discuss your deck plans. Find out everyone's vision of the deck. What would they like it to look like? Where would they like it to be? The backyard is the logical choice, but an enlarged front porch may better suit your needs. Or it may make more sense to design a deck that wraps around two sides of your house. How large a deck do you want? If a large deck would cut into your yard area, making it tough to play croquet, or if it would throw shade on the flower bed, you may want to scale back your plans. But if you rarely use your yard or hate maintaining the lawn, a larger deck will make gardening chores easier. Most importantly at this point, consider the activities that will take place on the deck.

Cooking and Entertaining

Entertainment is high on many people's list. Plan for a cooking area as well as a place for a good-sized table for seating smaller groups or for buffet settings if you have large parties. For nighttime entertaining, think about installing lighting.

Locate the grill area as far as possible from other use areas so that you don't have to worry about kids bumping into a hot barbecue. Leave ample room for cooking "assistants" so that friends can gather around and talk as you turn the steaks.

Make the deck easy to get to. The more entrances, the better. Large doorways and oversized windows tend to entice people outside. If you plan on eating on the deck often, make sure it is close to the kitchen. Ideally, try to plan for a direct connection between the deck and kitchen.

A Place to Relax

Consider what your future deck will be like during all the seasons when you are likely to use it.

Decide how much sun and how much shade you want, and take this into account when siting your deck. If you live in the northern hemisphere, a north-facing space will be in shade most of the day. This can be an advantage if you live in a very hot climate and a disadvantage for most everyone else. An eastern exposure gives the deck morning sun and afternoon shade; this is often the best choice in warm climates. In cold climates, a southwest exposure usually provides full and late afternoon sun.

Shade structures, left, offer protection from late afternoon sun.

Built-in seating, below, makes a deck inviting and contributes to its design.

Separate activity areas, opposite, help define the uses of the new deck.

Lighting. If you tend to eat and entertain after dark, consider your deck's lighting. A motion-sensing floodlight provides security and lights your way as you bring in groceries, but it makes for an unappealing dining ambiance. Subtle, low-voltage fixtures set into steps or posts provide a better solution for dining and entertaining on the deck. Most lighting plans call for a combination of both types of lighting.

In addition to placing low-voltage lights in steps and posts, consider lining a path that leads up to the deck with small lights. When choosing these fixtures, be sure to select fixtures that are attractive during the day as well as at night.

You may also want to consider using lights for decorative effect. For example, you can install low-voltage lights in the garden to highlight plantings that are visible from the deck. In-ground fixtures cast their light upward, creating interesting areas of shadow and light on trees and shrubs. Many fixtures have lenses that let you aim the light beam.

Avoid installing too many lights. With low-voltage layouts, a few well-placed lights is more dramatic than the glare produced by too many lights.

Private Spaces

Decks are often raised off the ground, which might mean you and your family will be on display for all the neighborhood to see. Existing fences may be too low to shield you from view. Sometimes the problem can be solved by stepping the deck down in stages. In most settings, decks work best when built low to the ground. If your entry door occupies a high position, you'll find it best to build a landing and stairs or a series of tiers leading down to a low-built main deck.

Privacy Options. You may have to take direct action to achieve privacy. You don't have to build an unfriendly, solid wall to avoid the feeling you are being watched. If you feel overexposed, a well-placed trellis provides the base for some nice climbing plants to look at and creates a pleasant enclosure. Another solution is to plant border trees and shrubs.

Fences are another option. There are many styles and materials from which to choose. High solid fences provide the most privacy, but an imposing design isn't very friendly, and it can make your yard seem closed in and smaller than it really is. Soften fences by using them as a backdrop for plantings.

Family members need some privacy among themselves as well. By building with different levels, including a conversation pit, or even by just letting the deck ramble a bit, you can create areas that are separate but not walled off. Careful placement of activity areas can also help create private sections. For example, if you are installing a spa or a cooking center—areas that tend to draw a crowd—place private areas on the other side of the deck.

Open or Cozy. Think about whether you want your deck to feel airy and open to the world or cozy and secluded. These effects can be achieved in many ways. A small deck will feel cozier than a large deck. Low benches and railings designed with large open spaces in them give an open feeling. A deck that hugs the house will have a more sequestered feel than one that juts out into the yard.

Plan #131030

Dimensions: 51' W x 41'10" D
Levels: 2
Square Footage: 2,470
Main Level Sq. Ft.: 1,290
Upper Level Sq. Ft.: 1,180
Bedrooms: 4
Bathrooms: 2½
Foundation: Crawl space, slab, basement, or walk-out basement
Materials List Available: Yes
Price Category: F

Images provided by designer/architect.

Master Bedroom

Master Bathroom

Entry

If high ceilings and spacious rooms make you happy, you'll love this gorgeous home.

Features:

• Family Room: An 18-ft. vaulted ceiling that's open to the balcony above, a corner fireplace, and a wall of windows make this room feel special.

• Dining Room: This formal room, which flows into the living room, also opens to the front porch and optional backyard deck.

• Kitchen: A bright breakfast room joins with this kitchen and opens to the backyard deck.

• Master Suite: You'll smile when you see the 11-ft. vaulted ceiling, stunning arched window, and two walk-in closets in the bedroom. A skylight lets natural light into the private bath, with its spa tub, separate shower, and dual-sink vanity.

• Bedrooms: To reach these three charming bedrooms, you'll admire the view into the family room below as you walk along the balcony hall.

Main Level Floor Plan

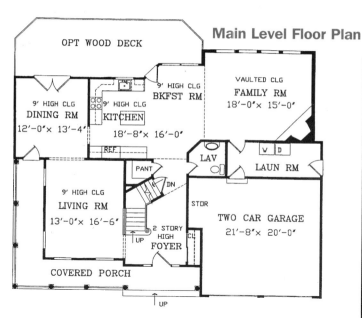

OPT WOOD DECK

9' HIGH CLG
DINING RM
12'-0" x 13'-4"

9' HIGH CLG
KITCHEN

9' HIGH CLG
BKFST RM

VAULTED CLG
FAMILY RM
18'-0" x 15'-0"

18'-8" x 16'-0"

REF

LAV

W D
LAUN RM

PANT

DN

9' HIGH CLG
LIVING RM
13'-0" x 16'-6"

UP

2 STORY
HIGH
FOYER

STOR

CL

TWO CAR GARAGE
21'-8" x 20'-0"

COVERED PORCH

UP

Upper Level Floor Plan

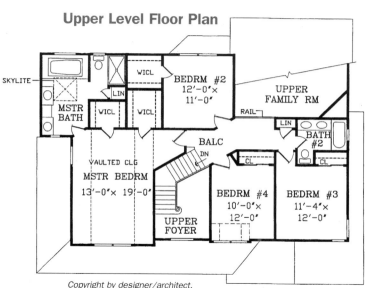

SKYLITE

WICL

LIN

MSTR
BATH

WICL

WICL

BEDRM #2
12'-0" x
11'-0"

UPPER
FAMILY RM

RAIL

LIN

BATH
#2

BALC

DN

CL

CL

VAULTED CLG
MSTR BEDRM
13'-0" x 19'-0"

UPPER
FOYER

BEDRM #4
10'-0" x
12'-0"

BEDRM #3
11'-4" x
12'-0"

Copyright by designer/architect.

Kitchen/Breakfast Area

Dining Room

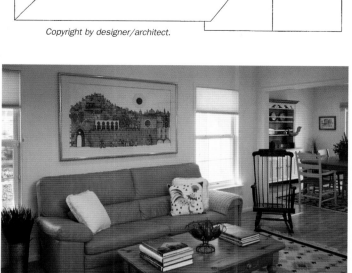

Living Room   Kitchen/Breakfast Area

Plan #121021

Dimensions: 46' W x 48' D
Levels: 2
Square Footage: 2,270
Main Level Sq. Ft.: 1,150
Upper Level Sq. Ft.: 1,120
Bedrooms: 4
Bathrooms: 3
Foundation: Basement
Materials List Available: Yes
Price Category: E

Images provided by designer/architect.

With its wraparound porch, this home evokes the charm of a traditional home.

Features:

• Ceiling Height: 8 ft.

• Foyer: The dramatic two-story entry enjoys views of the formal dining room and great room. A second floor balcony overlooks the entry and a plant shelf.

• Formal Dining Room: This gracious room is perfect for family holiday gatherings and for more formal dinner parties.

• Great Room: All the family will want to gather in this comfortable, informal room which features bay windows, an entertainment center, and a see-through fireplace.

• Breakfast Area: Conveniently located just off the great room, the bayed breakfast area features a built-in desk for household bills and access to the backyard.

• Kitchen: An island is the centerpiece of this kitchen. Its intelligent design makes food preparation a pleasure.

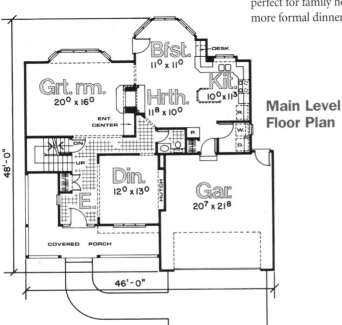

Main Level Floor Plan

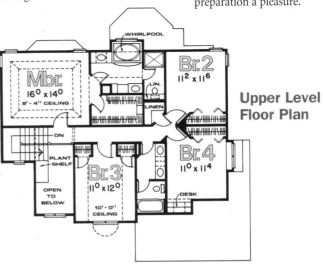

Upper Level Floor Plan

Copyright by designer/architect.

Plan #121035

Dimensions: 45'4" W x 38' D

Levels: 2

Square Footage: 1,471

Main Level Sq. Ft.: 716

Upper Level Sq. Ft.: 755

Bedrooms: 3

Bathrooms: 2½

Foundation: Basement

Materials List Available: Yes

Price Category: B

Images provided by designer/architect.

This convenient and elegant home is designed to expand as the family does.

Features:

- Ceiling Height: 8 ft. unless otherwise noted.
- Family Room: An open staircase to the second level visually expands this room where a built-in entertainment center maximizes the floor space. The whole family will be drawn to the warmth from the handsome fireplace.
- Kitchen: Cooking will be a pleasure in this

bright and efficient kitchen that features an island and a corner pantry. A snack bar offers a convenient spot for informal family meals.

- Dining Area: This lovely bayed area adjoins the kitchen.
- Room to Expand: Upstairs is 258 sq. ft. of unfinished area offering plenty of space for expansion as the family grows.
- Garage: This two-bay garage offers plenty of storage space in addition to parking for cars.

Main Level Floor Plan

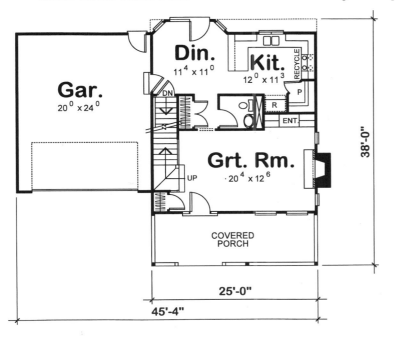

Upper Level Floor Plan

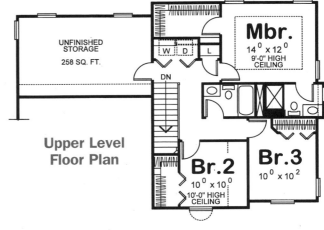

Copyright by designer/architect.

Plan #121045

Dimensions: 40' W x 48' D
Levels: 2
Square Footage: 1,575
Main Level Sq. Ft.: 787
Upper Level Sq. Ft.: 788
Bedrooms: 3
Bathrooms: 2½
Foundation: Basement
Materials List Available: Yes
Price Category: C

This home is carefully laid out to provide the convenience demanded by busy family life.

Features:

- Ceiling Height: 8 ft.
- Family Room: This charming family room, with its fireplace and built-in cabinetry, will become the central gathering place for family and friends.
- Kitchen: This kitchen offers a central island that makes food preparation more convenient and doubles

as a snack bar for a quick bite on the run. The breakfast area features a pantry and planning desk.

- Computer Loft: The second-floor landing includes this loft designed to accommodate the family computer.
- Room to Grow: Also on the second-floor landing you will find a large unfinished area waiting to accommodate the growing family.

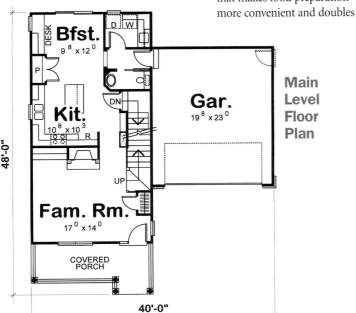

Main Level Floor Plan

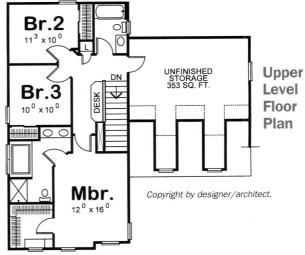

Upper Level Floor Plan

Plan #121014

Dimensions: 52' W x 47'4" D
Levels: 2
Square Footage: 1,869
Main Level Sq. Ft.: 1,421
Upper Level Sq. Ft.: 448
Bedrooms: 3
Bathrooms: 2
Foundation: Basement
Materials List Available: Yes
Price Category: D

This compact home is packed with all the amenities you'll need for a gracious lifestyle.

Features:

- Ceiling Height: 8 ft. except as noted.

- Great Room: A soaring ceiling and six tall transom-topped windows make this a light and airy spot for entertaining.

- Formal Dining Room: This elegant room is ideal for entertaining dinner guests.

- Breakfast Area: This sunny area shares a see-through fireplace with the great room. It's the perfect place to start the day.

- Master Suite: Here are all the features you expect to find in large luxury homes. Wake up to tall, sloped ceilings, and enjoy the corner whirlpool, separate shower, and vanity. A large walk-in closet provides plenty of wardrobe storage.

- Attached Garage: The garage provides two bays of parking plus plenty of storage space.

Main Level Floor Plan

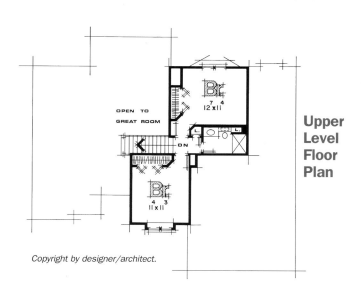

Upper Level Floor Plan

Plan #151029

Dimensions: 59'4" W x 74'2" D

Levels: 1½

Square Footage: 2,777

Main Level Sq. Ft.: 2,082

Upper Level Sq. Ft.: 695

Bedrooms: 4

Bathrooms: 2

Foundation: Crawl space, slab; optional basement plan available for extra fee

Materials List Available: Yes

Price Category: F

Images provided by designer/architect.

This grand home combines historic Southern charm with modern technology and design. A two-car garage and covered front porch allow for optimum convenience.

Features:

- Foyer: This marvelous foyer leads directly to an elegant dining room and comfortable great room.

- Great Room: With high ceilings, a built-in media center, and a fireplace, this will be your

favorite room during the chilly fall months.

- Kitchen: An eat-in-bar with an optional island, computer area, and adjoining breakfast room with a bay window make a perfect layout.

- Master Suite: Relax in comfort with a corner whirlpool tub, a separate glass shower, double vanities, and large walk-in closets.

- Upper Level Bedrooms: 2 and 3 both have window seats.

Main Level Floor Plan

Copyright by designer/architect.

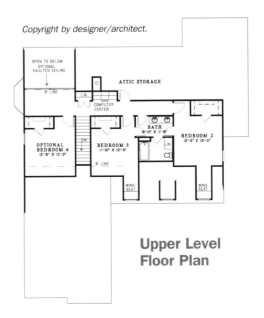

Upper Level Floor Plan

Plan #271049

Dimensions: 74' W x 44' D
Levels: 2
Square Footage: 2,464
Main Level Sq. Ft.: 1,288
Upper Level Sq. Ft.: 1,176
Bedrooms: 4
Bathrooms: 2½
Foundation: Basement, crawl space
Materials List Available: Yes
Price Category: E

Images provided by designer/architect.

This classic farmhouse design features a wraparound porch for enjoying conversation on warm afternoons.

Features:

- Living Room: A central fireplace warms this spacious gathering place, while French doors offer porch access.
- Dining Room: On formal occasions, this room is perfect for hosting elegant meals.
- Country Kitchen: An island workstation and a handy pantry keep the family chef organized and productive.
- Family Room: The home's second fireplace warms this cozy area, which is really an extension of the kitchen. Set up a kitchen table here, and enjoy casual meals near the crackling fire.
- Master Suite: The master bedroom is certainly vast. The walk-in closet is large as well. The private, compartmentalized bath offers a sit-down shower and a separate dressing area.

Main Level Floor Plan

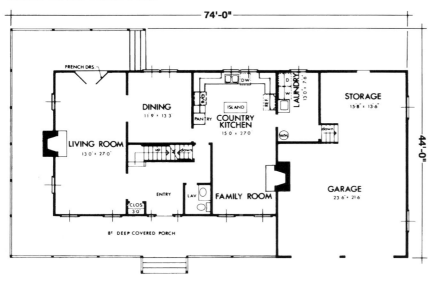

Upper Level Floor Plan

Copyright by designer/architect.

Plan #131021

Dimensions: 60'0" W x 52'4" D
Levels: 2
Square Footage: 3,110
Main Level Sq. Ft.: 1,818
Upper Level Sq. Ft.: 1,292
Bedrooms: 5
Bathrooms: 2½
Foundation: Basement, crawl space, or slab
Materials List Available: Yes
Price Category: H

Images provided by designer/architect.

Amenities abound in this luxurious two-story beauty with a cozy gazebo on one corner of the spectacular wraparound front porch. Comfort, functionality, and spaciousness characterize this home.

Features:

- Ceiling Height: 8 ft.

- Foyer: This two-story high foyer is breathtaking.

- Family Room: Roomy with open views of the kitchen, the family room has a vaulted ceiling and boasts a functional fireplace and a built-in entertainment center.

- Dining Room: Formal yet comfortable, this spacious dining room is perfect for entertaining family and friends.

- Kitchen: Perfectly located with access to a breakfast room and the family room, this

U-shaped kitchen with large center island is charming as well as efficient.

- Master Suite: Enjoy this sizable room with a vaulted ceiling, two large walk-in closets, and a lovely compartmented bath.

Rear Elevation

Main Level Floor Plan

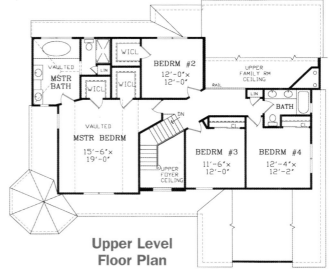

Upper Level Floor Plan

Copyright by designer/architect.

Plan #131024

Dimensions: 36' W by 54'4" D
Levels: 2
Square Footage: 1,635
Main Level Sq. Ft.: 880
Upper Level Sq. Ft.: 755
Bedrooms: 3
Bathrooms: 2 ½
Foundation: Basement, crawl space, or slab
Materials List Available: Yes
Price Category: D

Images provided by designer/architect.

You'll love the combination of early-American detailing on the outside and the contemporary, open layout of the interior.

Features:

• Ceiling Height: 8 ft.

• Front Porch: Use this wraparound front porch as an extra room when the weather's fine.

• Living Room: Separated only by columns, the open arrangement of the living and dining rooms enhances the spacious feeling in this home.

• Family Room/Kitchen: This combination family room/country kitchen includes a large work island and snack bar for convenience.

• Master Suite: A tray ceiling creates a contemporary look in the spacious master bedroom, and three closets make it practical. A compartmented full bath completes the suite.

• Bedrooms: Two additional bedrooms share a second full bath.

• Attic: Finish the attic space that's over the garage for even more living space.

Main Level Floor Plan

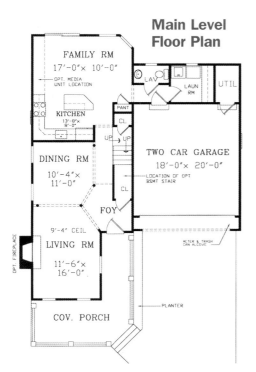

Upper Level Floor Plan

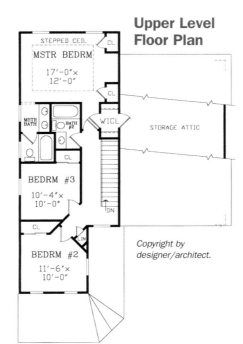

Copyright by designer/architect.

Rear Elevation

Plan #131029

Dimensions: 56'4" W x 46'6" D
Levels: 2
Square Footage: 2,936
Main Level Sq. Ft.: 1,680
Upper Level Sq. Ft.: 1,256
Bedrooms: 4
Bathrooms: 2½
Foundation: Crawl space, slab, or basement
Materials List Available: Yes
Price Category: G

Images provided by designer/architect.

This home is ideal if you love the look of a country-style farmhouse.

Features:

- Foyer: Walk across the large wraparound porch that defines this home to enter this two-story foyer.
- Living Room: French doors from the foyer lead into this living room.

- Family Room: The whole family will love this room, with its vaulted ceiling, fireplace, and sliding glass doors that open to the wooden rear deck.
- Kitchen: A beautiful sit-down center island opens to the family room. There's also a breakfast nook with a lovely bay window.
- Master Suite: Luxury abounds with vaulted ceilings, walk-in closets, private bath with whirlpool tub, separate shower, and dual sinks.
- Loft: A special place with vaulted ceiling and view into the family room below.

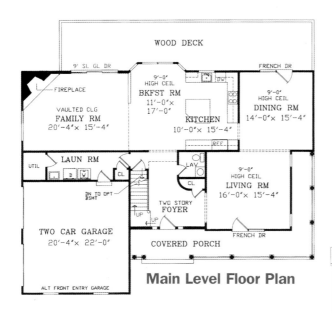

Main Level Floor Plan

Upper Level Floor Plan

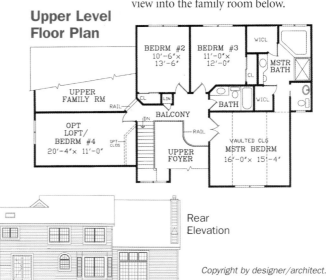

Rear Elevation

Copyright by designer/architect.

Dining Room

Breakfast Area

Kitchen Island

Kitchen

Master Bathroom

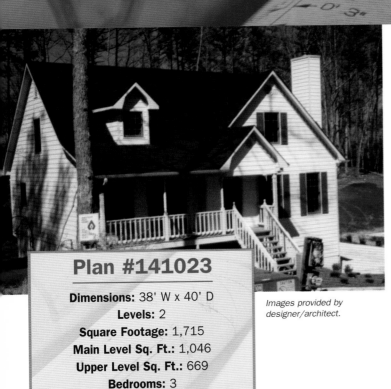

Plan #141023

Dimensions: 38' W x 40' D

Levels: 2

Square Footage: 1,715

Main Level Sq. Ft.: 1,046

Upper Level Sq. Ft.: 669

Bedrooms: 3

Bathrooms: 2½

Foundation: Basement

Materials List Available: Yes

Price Category: C

Images provided by designer/architect.

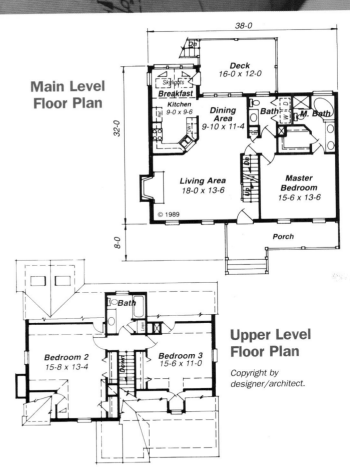

Main Level Floor Plan

38-0

Deck 16-0 x 12-0

Skylights
Breakfast
Kitchen 9-0 x 9-6
Dining Area 9-10 x 11-4
Bath
M. Bath

32-0

Living Area 18-0 x 13-6

Master Bedroom 15-6 x 13-6

© 1989

8-0

Porch

Upper Level Floor Plan

Bath

Bedroom 2 15-8 x 13-4

Bedroom 3 15-6 x 11-0

Copyright by designer/architect.

Plan #141024

Dimensions: 59' W x 46' D

Levels: 2

Square Footage: 1,732

Main Level Sq. Ft.: 1,128

Lower Level Sq. Ft.: 604

Bedrooms: 3

Bathrooms: 2½

Foundation: Basement

Materials List Available: Yes

Price Category: C

Images provided by designer/architect.

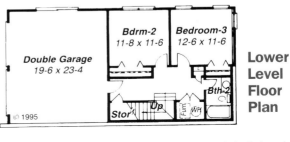

Lower Level Floor Plan

Double Garage 19-6 x 23-4

Bdrm-2 11-8 x 11-6

Bedroom-3 12-6 x 11-6

Bth-2

Stor
Up
Furn.
WH

© 1995

Copyright by designer/architect.

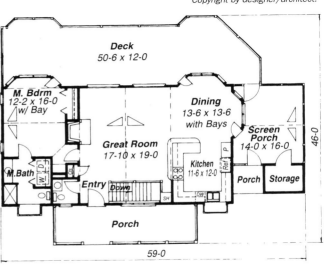

Main Level Floor Plan

Deck 50-6 x 12-0

M. Bdrm 12-2 x 16-0 w/ Bay

Dining 13-6 x 13-6 with Bays

Screen Porch 14-0 x 16-0

Great Room 17-10 x 19-0

Kitchen 11-6 x 12-0

M.Bath

Entry

Porch Storage

Porch

46-0

59-0

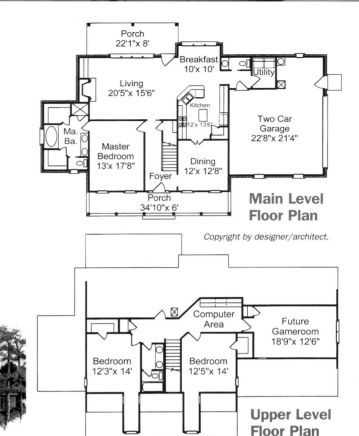

Main Level Floor Plan

Porch 22'1"x 8'

Breakfast 10'x 10'

Utility

Living 20'5"x 15'6"

Kitchen 12'x 13'6"

Two Car Garage 22'8"x 21'4"

Ma. Ba.

Master Bedroom 13'x 17'8"

Dining 12'x 12'8"

Foyer

Porch 34'10"x 6'

Copyright by designer/architect.

Plan #111022

Dimensions: 62' W x 36'4" D

Levels: 2

Square Footage: 3,105

Main Level Sq. Ft.: 1,470

Upper Level Sq. Ft.: 1,635

Bedrooms: 4

Bathrooms: 2½

Foundation: Finished basement

Materials List Available: Yes

Price Category: G

Images provided by designer/architect.

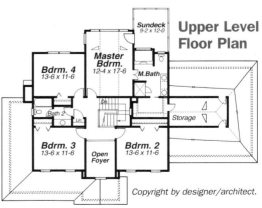

Computer Area

Future Gameroom 18'9"x 12'6"

Bedroom 12'3"x 14'

Bedroom 12'5"x 14'

Upper Level Floor Plan

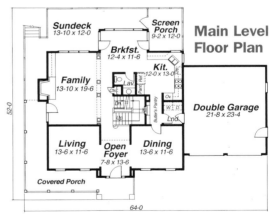

Sundeck 13-10 x 12-0

Screen Porch 9-2 x 12-0

Main Level Floor Plan

Brkfst. 12-4 x 11-6

Kit. 12-0 x 13-0

Family 13-10 x 19-6

Lav.

Double Garage 21-8 x 23-4

52-0

Living 13-6 x 11-6

Open Foyer 7-8 x 13-6

Dining 13-6 x 11-6

Covered Porch

64-0

Plan #141016

Dimensions: 64' W x 52' D

Levels: 2

Square Footage: 2,416

Main Level Sq. Ft.: 1,250

Upper Level Sq. Ft.: 1,166

Bedrooms: 4

Bathrooms: 2½

Foundation: Basement

Materials List Available: Yes

Price Category: E

Images provided by designer/architect.

Sundeck 9-2 x 12-0

Upper Level Floor Plan

Master Bdrm. 12-4 x 17-6

Bdrm. 4 13-6 x 11-6

M.Bath

Bath 2

Storage

Bdrm. 3 13-6 x 11-6

Open Foyer

Bdrm. 2 13-6 x 11-6

Copyright by designer/architect.

Plan #131051

Dimensions: 64'4" W x 53'4" D
Levels: 3
Square Footage: 2,431
Main Level Sq. Ft.: 1,293
Upper Level Sq. Ft.: 1,138
Bedrooms: 4
Bathrooms: 2½
Foundation: Basement, crawl space,
or slab
Materials List Available: Yes
Price Category: F

Gracious and charming with a wraparound front porch and a backyard terrace, this home also has a ready-to-finish third floor all-purpose room and a full bath.

Features:

- Main Level Ceiling Height: 8 ft.

- Family Room: A comfortable space for the entire family to gather, this delightful room can be warmed by a heat-circulating fireplace.

- Dining Room: A cozy dinette boasts a sliding glass door with access to a gorgeous backyard terrace with an optional calm reflecting pool.

- Kitchen: Adjoining the dining area, the kitchen offers plenty of storage and counter space. The laundry room and half-bath are nearby for convenience.

- Garage: The garage is tucked way back to keep it from intruding into the traditional facade.

Main Level Floor Plan

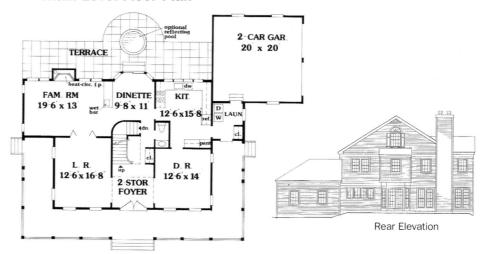

Images provided by designer/architect.

Rear Elevation

Upper Level Floor Plan

3rd Level Floor Plan

Copyright by designer/architect.

Images provided by designer/architect.

Plan #151027

Dimensions: 37' W x 73' D
Levels: 2
Square Footage: 2,332
Main Level Sq. Ft.: 1,713
Upper Level Sq. Ft.: 619
Bedrooms: 3
Bathrooms: 3
Foundation: Crawl space, slab; optional basement plan available for extra fee
Materials List Available: Yes
Price Category: E

A traditional design with a covered front porch and high ceilings in many rooms gives this home all the space and comfort you'll ever need.

Features:

- **Foyer:** A formal foyer with 8-in. wood columns will lead you to an elegant dining area.

- **Great Room:** This wonderful gathering room has 10-ft. boxed ceilings, a built-in media center, and an atrium door leading to a rear grilling porch.

- **Kitchen:** Functional yet cozy, this kitchen opens to the breakfast area with built-in computer desk and is open to the great room as well.

- **Master Suite:** Pamper yourself in this luxurious bedroom with 10-ft. boxed ceilings, large walk-in closets, and a bath area with a whirlpool tub, shower, and double vanity.

- **Second Level:** A game room and two bedrooms with walk-thru baths make this floor special.

Main Level Floor Plan

37'-0"

73'-0"

GARAGE
19'-4" X 20'-0"

GRILLING PORCH
16'-8" X 8'-0"

MEDIA CENTER

GREAT RM.
10" BOXED CEILING
16'-8" X 14'-8"

LIN.

D W
L A U

HANG ROD

M. BATH
8'-6" X 14'-8"

WHP TUB

8" COLUMNS

BREAKFAST ROOM
16'-8" X 10'-0"

COMPUTER DESK

MASTER SUITE
10" BOXED CEILING
14'-7" X 13'-0"

PANTRY

DW.

REF.

UP

KITCHEN

RG.

BATH

GUEST RM. / STUDY
12'-3" X 10'-0"

FOYER
7'-6" X 11'-0"

DINING RM.
13'-3" X 11'-0"

8" COLUMNS

COVERED PORCH
37'-0" X 8'-0"

Upper Level Floor Plan

ATTIC STORAGE

LIN.

BED RM. 2
15'-6" X 10'-6"

GAME RM. / BONUS
12'-10" X 27'-7"

BED RM. 3
15'-6" X 11'-0"

8" LINE

6' WALL

Copyright by designer/architect.

Plan #151028

Dimensions: 36' W X 69' D
Levels: 2
Square Footage: 2,252
Main Level Sq. Ft.: 1,694
Upper Level Sq. Ft.: 558
Bedrooms: 3
Bathrooms: 3
Foundation: Crawl space, slab; optional basement plan available for extra fee
Materials List Available: Yes
Price Category: E

You'll love entertaining in this elegant home with its large covered front porch, grilling porch off the kitchen and breakfast room, and great room with a gas fireplace and media center.

Features:

- **Foyer:** A wonderful open staircase from the foyer leads you to the second floor.

- **Guest Room/Study:** A private bath makes this room truly versatile.

- **Dining Room:** Attached to the great room, this dining room features 8-in. wooden columns that you can highlight for a formal atmosphere.

- **Kitchen:** This cleverly laid-out kitchen with access to the breakfast room is ideal for informal gatherings as well as family meals.

- **Master Suite:** French doors here open to the bath, with its large walk-in closet, double vanities, corner whirlpool tub, and corner shower.

Main Level Floor Plan

36'-0"

- GRILLING PORCH 16'-6" X 7'-8"
- BREAKFAST ROOM 16'-2" X 8'-0"
- KITCHEN 11'-8" X 12'-2"
- REF.
- PANTRY
- KID'S NOOK
- W.LAU.D
- DINING RM. 11'-4" X 10'-6"
- COMPUTER DESK
- 8" COLUMNS
- GARAGE 18'-10" X 20'-0"
- BENCH W/ HANGING & STORAGE BINS
- M. BATH 13'-0" X 13'-2"
- WHP TUB
- LIN
- KNEE SPACE
- GREAT RM. 18'-0" X 18'-4"
- MEDIA CENTER
- MASTER SUITE 13'-0" X 15'-0"
- FOYER
- COVERED PORCH 20'-0" X 8'-0"
- GUEST RM. / STUDY 13'-0" X 11'-0"

69'-0"

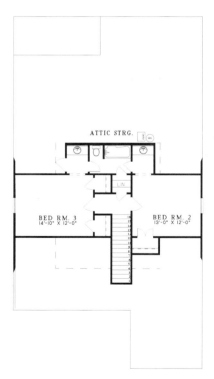

Upper Level Floor Plan

- ATTIC STRG.
- LIN
- BED RM. 3 14'-10" X 12'-0"
- BED RM. 2 13'-0" X 12'-0"

Plan #121036

Dimensions: 42' W x 43' D

Levels: 2

Square Footage: 1,297

Main Level Sq. Ft.: 603

Upper Level Sq. Ft.: 694

Bedrooms: 3

Bathrooms: 2½

Foundation: Basement

Materials List Available: Yes

Price Category: B

This bright and cheery home offers the growing family plenty of room to expand.

Features:

- Ceiling Height: 8 ft. unless otherwise noted.
- Living Room: Family and friends will be drawn to this delightful living room. A double window at the front and windows framing the fireplace bring lots of sunlight that adds to the appeal.
- Dining Room: From the living room, you'll usher guests into this large and inviting dining room.
- Kitchen: A center island is the highlight of this attractive and well-designed kitchen.
- Three-Season Porch: This appealing enclosed porch is accessible from the dining room.
- Master Bedroom: A dramatic angled ceiling highlights a picturesque window in this bedroom.
- Bonus Area: With 354 sq. ft. of unfinished area, you'll never run out of space to expand.

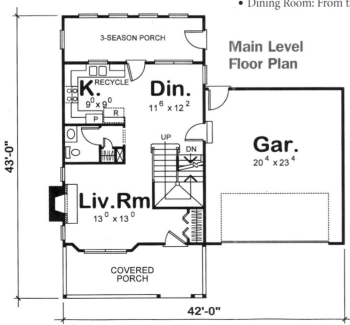

Main Level Floor Plan

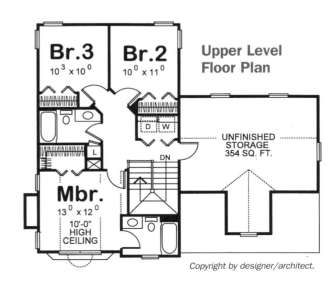

Upper Level Floor Plan

Plan #161031

Dimensions: 99'8" W x 68'8" D

Levels: 2

Square Footage: 5,381

Main Level Sq. Ft.: 3,793

Upper Level Sq. Ft.: 1,588

Bedrooms: 4

Bathrooms: 3½

Foundation: Basement

Materials List Available: Yes

Price Category: I

Images provided by designer/architect.

If you're looking for a compatible mixture of formal and informal areas in a home, look no further!

Features:

- Great Room: Columns at the entry to this room and the formal dining room set a gracious tone that is easy around which to decorate.

- Library: Set up an office or just a cozy reading area in this quiet room.

- Hearth Room: Spacious and inviting, this hearth room is positioned so that friends and family can flow from here to the breakfast area and kitchen.

- Master Suite: The luxury of this area is capped by the access it gives to the rear yard.

- Lower Level: Enjoy the 9-ft.-tall ceilings as you walk out to the rear yard from this area.

Entry

Rear View

Main Level Floor Plan

Copyright by designer/architect.

Deck

Bedroom
16'8" x 12'

Hearth Room

Breakfast
23' x 16' irr.

Bath

Master Bedroom
15'8" x 22"

Bath

Hall

Great Room
16' x 21'6"

Bedroom
16'8" x 12'

Laun.

Kitchen
17'7" x 14'8"

Sloped Ceiling

Sloped Ceiling

Dressing

walk-in closet

Foyer

walk-in closet

Three Car Garage
20' x 33'4"

Dining Room
13'6" x 15'3" irr.

Porch

Library
12'4" x 16'2" irr.

Basement Level Floor Plan

Bedroom
12' x 10'

Rec Room
44'1" x 31'2" Irreg.

Unfinished Basement

Bath

Bar

Dining Room

Rear Elevation

Left Elevation

Right Elevation

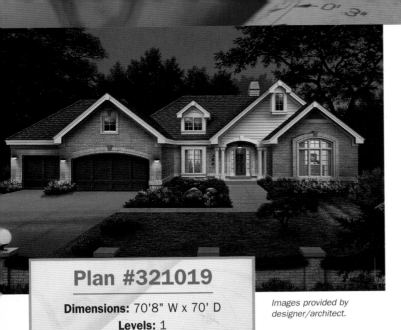

Plan #321019

Dimensions: 70'8" W x 70' D

Levels: 1

Square Footage: 2,452

Bedrooms: 4

Bathrooms: 2½

Foundation: Basement

Materials List Available: Yes

Price Category: E

Images provided by designer/architect.

Copyright by designer/architect.

Plan #231008

Dimensions: 60' W x 62' D

Levels: 1

Square Footage: 1,941

Bedrooms: 3

Bathrooms: 2½

Foundation: Crawl space

Materials List Available: No

Price Category: A

Images provided by designer/architect.

Copyright by designer/architect.

Optional Bonus Area

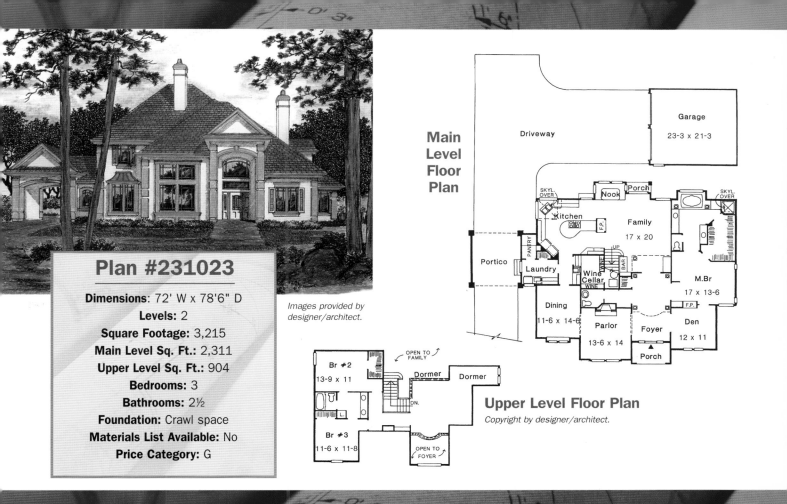

Plan #231023

Dimensions: 72' W x 78'6" D

Levels: 2

Square Footage: 3,215

Main Level Sq. Ft.: 2,311

Upper Level Sq. Ft.: 904

Bedrooms: 3

Bathrooms: 2½

Foundation: Crawl space

Materials List Available: No

Price Category: G

Images provided by designer/architect.

Main Level Floor Plan

Driveway

Garage 23-3 x 21-3

SKYL. OVER — Nook — Porch — SKYL. OVER

Kitchen — F.P. — Family 17 x 20

Portico — PANTRY

Laundry — Wine Cellar WINE — UP — BAR — M.Br 17 x 13-6

Dining 11-6 x 14-6 — Parlor 13-6 x 14 — Foyer — F.P. — Den 12 x 11

Porch

Upper Level Floor Plan

Copyright by designer/architect.

OPEN TO FAMILY

Br #2 13-9 x 11 — Dormer — Dormer

DN.

Br #3 11-6 x 11-8

OPEN TO FOYER

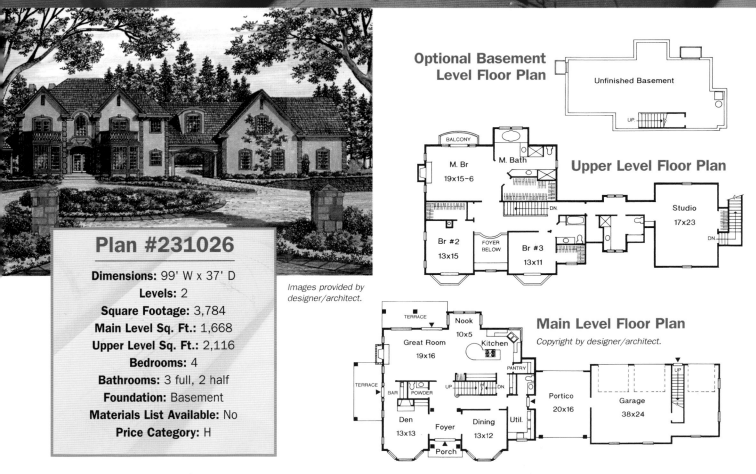

Plan #231026

Dimensions: 99' W x 37' D

Levels: 2

Square Footage: 3,784

Main Level Sq. Ft.: 1,668

Upper Level Sq. Ft.: 2,116

Bedrooms: 4

Bathrooms: 3 full, 2 half

Foundation: Basement

Materials List Available: No

Price Category: H

Images provided by designer/architect.

Optional Basement Level Floor Plan

Unfinished Basement

UP

Upper Level Floor Plan

BALCONY

M. Br 19x15-6 — M. Bath

DN.

Studio 17x23

Br #2 13x15 — FOYER BELOW — Br #3 13x11

DN.

Main Level Floor Plan

Copyright by designer/architect.

TERRACE — Nook 10x5

Great Room 19x16 — Kitchen

TERRACE — PANTRY

BAR — POWDER — UP — DN

Portico 20x16 — Garage 38x24 — UP

Den 13x13 — Foyer — Dining 13x12 — Util.

Porch

Plan #161027

Dimensions: 59'10" W x 37'4" D

Levels: 2

Square Footage: 2,388

Main Level Sq. Ft.: 1,207

Upper Level Sq. Ft.: 1,181

Bedrooms: 4

Bathrooms: 2½

Foundation: Basement

Materials List Available: No

Price Category: E

Double gables, wood trim, an arched window, and sidelights at the entry give elegance to this family-friendly home.

Features:

- Foyer: Friends and family will see the angled stairs, formal dining room, living room, and library from this foyer.

- Family Room: A fireplace makes this room cozy in the evenings on those chilly days, and multiple windows let natural light stream into it.

- Kitchen: You'll love the island and the ample counter space here as well as the butler's pantry. A breakfast nook makes a comfortable place to snack or just curl up and talk to the cook.

- Master Suite: Tucked away on the upper level, this master suite provides both privacy and luxury.

- Additional Bedrooms: These three additional bedrooms make this home ideal for any family.

Images provided by designer/architect.

Main Level Floor Plan

Deck

Breakfast 16'11" x 15'10"

Family Room 20'0" x 13'6"

Kitchen

Two-car Garage 21' x 22'2"

pantry

butler's pantry

Laun.

Bath

Living Room /Library 11'6" x 15'4"

Dining Room 13'2" x 12'0"

Foyer

Porch

37'4"

59'10"

Upper Level Floor Plan

Bedroom 16'8" x 10'8"

walk in closet

Dress.

Bath

Bedroom 12'11" x 10'

Master Bedroom 12' x 17'6"

stairs dn.

Bedroom 12'11" x 11'

Balcony

Copyright by designer/architect.

Plan #121020

Dimensions: 64' W x 46' D

Levels: 2

Square Footage: 2,480

Main Level Sq. Ft.: 1,369

Upper Level Sq. Ft.: 1,111

Bedrooms: 4

Bathrooms: 3

Foundation: Basement

Materials List Available: Yes

Price Category: E

Images provided by designer/architect.

Tapered columns and an angled stairway give this home a classical style.

Features:

- Ceiling Height: 8 ft.
- Living Room: Just off the dramatic two-story entry is this distinctive living room, with its tapered columns, transom-topped windows, and boxed ceiling.
- Formal Dining Room: The tapered columns, transom-topped windows, and boxed ceiling found in the living room continue into this gracious dining space.
- Family Room: Located on the opposite side of the house from the living room and dining room, the family room features a beamed ceiling and fireplace framed by windows.
- Kitchen: An island is the centerpiece of this convenient kitchen.
- Master Suite: Upstairs, a tiered ceiling and corner windows enhance the master bedroom, which is served by a pampering bath.

Main Level Floor Plan

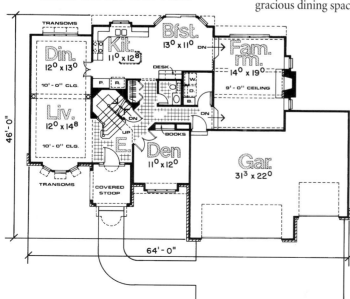

Upper Level Floor Plan

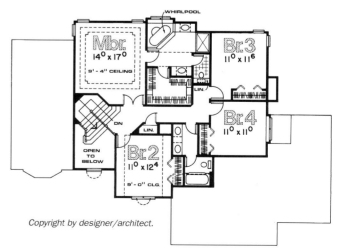

Copyright by designer/architect.

Plan #211009

Dimensions: 72' W x 60' D
Levels: 1
Square Footage: 2,396
Bedrooms: 4
Bathrooms: 2
Foundation: Slab
Materials List Available: Yes
Price Category: E

Beautiful arched windows lend a luxurious feeling to the exterior of this one-story home.

Features:

- Ceiling Height: 9 ft. unless otherwise noted.

- Entry: Guests will be greeted by a dramatic 12-ft. ceiling in this elegant foyer.

- Living Room: The 12-ft. ceiling continues through the foyer into this inviting living room. Everyone will feel welcomed by the crackling fire in the handsome fireplace.

- Covered Porch: When the weather is warm, invite guests to step out of the living room directly into this covered porch.

- Kitchen: This bright and cheery kitchen is designed for the way we live today. It includes a pantry and an angled eating bar that will see plenty of impromptu family meals.

- Energy-Efficient Walls: All the outside walls are framed with 2x6 lumber instead of 2x4. The extra thickness makes room for more insulation to lower your heating and cooling bills.

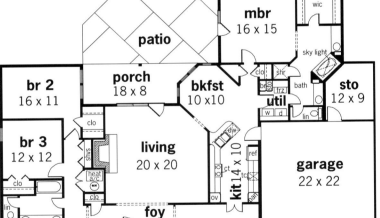

SMARTtip

Ornaments in a Garden

Placement is everything with ornaments in a garden. Some elements are best sitting by themselves. Others are better when they are part of a cohesive whole, perhaps placed in the greenery at a corner or flanking a structure.

Plan #271025

Dimensions: 61'4" W x 56'4" D
Levels: 2
Square Footage: 2,223
Main Level Sq. Ft.: 1,689
Upper Level Sq. Ft.: 534
Bedrooms: 3
Bathrooms: 2½
Foundation: Basement
Materials List Available: Yes
Price Category: E

Images provided by designer/architect.

This traditional home's unique design combines a dynamic, exciting exterior with a fantastic floor plan.

Features:

- Living Room: To the left of the column-lined, barrel-vaulted entry, this inviting space features a curved wall and corner windows.
- Dining Room: A tray ceiling enhances this formal meal room.

- Kitchen: This island-equipped kitchen includes a corner pantry and a built-in desk. Nearby, the sunny breakfast room opens onto a backyard deck via sliding glass doors.
- Family Room: A corner bank of windows provides a glassy backdrop for this room's handsome fireplace. Munchies may be served on the snack bar from the breakfast nook.
- Master Suite: This main-floor retreat is simply stunning, and includes a vaulted ceiling, access to a private courtyard, and of course, a sumptuous bath with every creature comfort.

Main Level Floor Plan

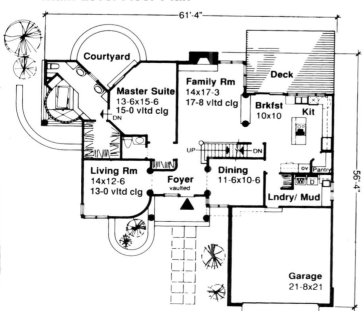

Upper Level Floor Plan

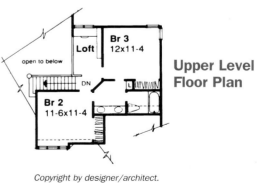

Copyright by designer/architect.

Plan #151001

Dimensions: 70' W x 88' D
Levels: 1
Square Footage: 3,124
Bedrooms: 4
Bathrooms: 3½
Foundation: Crawl space, slab
Materials List Available: Yes
Price Category: G

Images provided by designer/architect.

From the double front doors to sleek arches, columns, and a gallery with arched openings to the bedrooms, you'll love this elegant home.

Features:

- **Grand Room:** With a 13-ft. pan ceiling and column entry, this room opens to the rear covered porch as well as through French doors to the bay-windowed morning room that, in turn, leads to the gathering room.

- **Gathering Room:** A majestic fireplace, built-in entertainment center, and book shelves give comfort and ease.

- **Kitchen:** A double oven, built-in desk, and a work island add up to a design for efficiency.

- **Master Suite:** Enjoy the practicality of walk-in closets, the comfort of a private sitting area, and the convenience of an adjacent study or nursery. The bath features a step-up whirlpool tub and separate shower.

Copyright by designer/architect.

Images provided by designer/architect.

Plan #121009

Dimensions: 50' W x 58' D
Levels: 1
Square Footage: 1,422
Bedrooms: 3
Bathrooms: 2
Foundation: Basement
Materials List Available: Yes
Price Category: B

This amenity-filled home is perfect for the growing family or as a retirement retreat.

Features:

- Ceiling Height: 8 ft. unless otherwise noted.
- Great Room: This inviting space is the perfect place for gatherings of all sizes. It shares 12-ft. ceilings with the dining room and kitchen.

- Dining Room: In addition to the 12-ft. ceiling, arched openings, and built-in book cases make this an elegant place to dine.
- Private Porch: After dinner, step through a door in the dining room to enjoy a summer breeze in this inviting porch.
- Master Suite: The boxed ceiling lends drama to this suite and a walk-in closet adds convenience. Luxury comes from the whirlpool bath.
- Garage: You won't be short of parking and storage space in this two-bay garage. As a bonus there is space for a workbench.

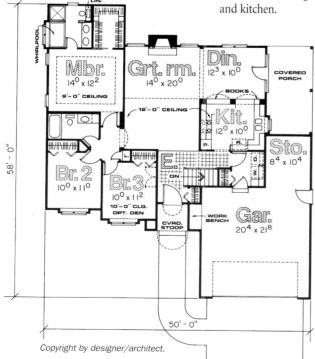

Copyright by designer/architect.

SMARTtip
Window Cornices

You can transform plain rooms by making jogs in cornice molding that will hold shades, blinds, and other window treatments. You can create individual pockets over each window or continue the molding past narrow wall sections between windows to form a more expansive detail. Housings below the cornice can be painted or papered.

Plan #121011

Dimensions: 50' W x 50' D
Levels: 1
Square Footage: 1,724
Bedrooms: 3
Bathrooms: 2
Foundation: Basement
Materials List Available: Yes
Price Category: C

This one-level home is perfect for retirement or for convenient living for the growing family.

Features:

- Ceiling Height: 8 ft.

- Master Suite: For privacy and quiet, the master suite is segregated from the other bedrooms.

- Family Room: Sit by the fire and read as light streams through the windows flanking the fireplace. Or enjoy the built-in entertainment center.

- Breakfast Area: Located just off the family room, the sunny breakfast area will lure you to linger over impromptu family meals. Here you will find a built-in desk for compiling shopping lists and menus.

- Private Porch: Step out of the breakfast area to enjoy a breeze on this porch.

- Kitchen: Efficient and attractive, this kitchen offers an angled pantry and an island that doubles as a snack bar.

SMARTtip

Measuring for Kitchen Countertops

Custom cabinetmakers will sometimes come to your house to measure for a countertop, but home centers and kitchen stores may require that you come to them with the dimensions already in hand. Be sure to double-check measurements carefully. Being off by only ½ in. can be quite upsetting.

To ensure accuracy, sketch out the countertop on a sheet of graph paper. Include all the essential dimensions. To be on the safe side, have someone else double-check your numbers.

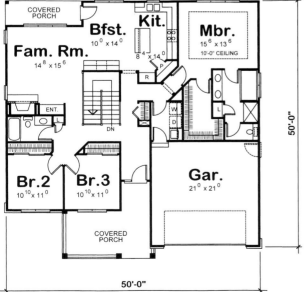

Plan #271086

Dimensions: 56'6" W x 67'6" D
Levels: 2
Square Footage: 1,910
Main Level Sq. Ft.: 1,192
Upper Level Sq. Ft.: 586
Bedrooms: 3
Bathrooms: 2
Foundation: Daylight basement, crawl space
Materials List Available: Yes
Price Category: D

Images provided by designer/architect.

A passive-solar sunroom is the highlight of this popular home and helps to minimize heating costs.

Features:

- Living/Dining Area: This expansive space is brightened by numerous windows and offers panoramic views of the outdoor scenery. A handsome woodstove gives the area a delightful ambiance, especially when the

weather outside is frightful. Your dining table goes in the corner by the sun room.

- Kitchen: This room's efficient design keeps all of the chef's supplies at the ready. A snack bar could be used to help serve guests during parties.

- Bedrooms: With three bedrooms to choose from, all of your family members will be able to find secluded spots of their very own.

- Lower Level: This optional space includes a recreation room with a second woodstove. Let the kids gather here and make as much noise as they want.

Optional Basement Level Floor Plan

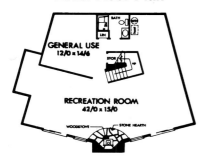

Copyright by designer/architect.

Main Level Floor Plan

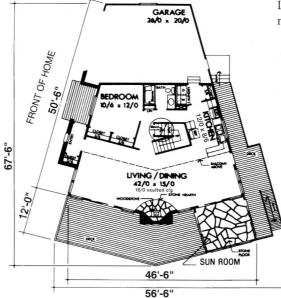

Upper Level Floor Plan

Plan #121017

Dimensions: 54' W x 50' D
Levels: 2
Square Footage: 2,353
Main Level Sq. Ft.: 1,653
Upper Level Sq. Ft.: 700
Bedrooms: 4
Bathrooms: 3
Foundation: Basement
Materials List Available: Yes
Price Category: E

Images provided by designer/architect.

The dramatic two-story entry with bent staircase is the first sign that this is a gracious home.

Features:

- Ceiling Height: 8 ft. except as noted.
- Great Room: A row of transom-topped windows and a tall, beamed ceiling add a sense of spaciousness to this family gathering area.
- Formal Dining Room: The bayed window helps make this an inviting place to entertain.

- See-through Fireplace: This feature spreads warmth and coziness throughout the informal areas of the home.
- Breakfast Area: This sunny area shares a see-through fireplace with the great room. It's the perfect place to start the day.
- Master Suite: Here are all the features you expect to find in large luxury homes. Wake up to tall, sloped ceilings, and enjoy the corner whirlpool, separate shower, and vanity. A large walk-in closet provides plenty of wardrobe storage.

Main Level Floor Plan

Upper Level Floor Plan

Copyright by designer/architect.

Plan #121025

Dimensions: 60' W x 59'4" D

Levels: 2

Square Footage: 2,562

Main Level Sq. Ft.: 1,875

Upper Level Square Footage: 687

Bedrooms: 4

Bathrooms: 2½

Foundation: Basement

Materials List Available: Yes

Price Category: E

Images provided by designer/architect.

Dramatic arches are the reoccurring architectural theme in this distinctive home.

Features:

- Ceiling Height: 8 ft. unless otherwise noted.
- Foyer: This is a grand two-story entrance. Plants will thrive on the plant shelf thanks to light streaming through the arched window.
- Great Room: The foyer flows into the great room through dramatic 15-ft.-high arched openings.

- Kitchen: An island is the centerpiece of this highly functional kitchen that includes a separate breakfast area.
- Office: French doors open into this versatile office that features a 10-ft. ceiling and transom-topped windows.
- Master Suite: The master suite features a volume ceiling, built-in dresser, and two closets. You'll unwind in the beautiful corner whirlpool bath with its elegant window treatment.

Main Level Floor Plan

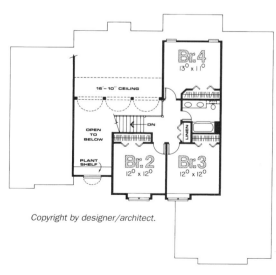

Upper Level Floor Plan

Copyright by designer/architect.

Plan #121029

Dimensions: 58'8" W x 54' D
Levels: 2
Square Footage: 2,576
Main Level Sq. Ft.: 1,735
Upper Level Sq. Ft.: 841
Bedrooms: 4
Bathrooms: 2½
Foundation: Basement
Materials List Available: Yes
Price Category: E

This gracious home is designed with the contemporary lifestyle in mind.

Features:

- Ceiling Height: 8 ft. unless otherwise noted.
- Great Room: This room features a fireplace and entertainment center. It's equally suited for family gatherings and formal entertaining.
- Breakfast Area: The fireplace is two-sided so it shares its warmth with this breakfast area — the perfect spot for informal family meals.
- Master Suite: Halfway up the staircase you'll find double-doors into this truly distinctive suite featuring a barrel-vault ceiling, built-in bookcases, and his and her walk-in closets. Unwind at the end of the day by stretching out in the oval whirlpool tub.
- Computer Loft: This loft overlooks the great room. It is designed as a home office with a built-in desk for your computer.
- Garage: Two bays provide plenty of storage in addition to parking space.

Main Level Floor Plan

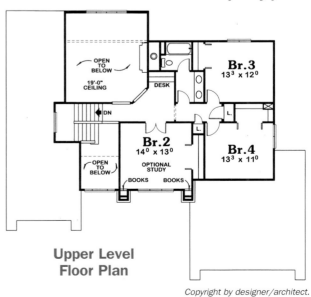

Upper Level Floor Plan

Plan #121031

Dimensions: 52' W x 51'4" D

Levels: 2

Square Footage: 1,772

Main Level Sq. Ft.: 1,314

Upper Level Sq. Ft.: 458

Bedrooms: 3

Bathrooms: 2½

Foundation: Basement

Materials List Available: Yes

Price Category: C

This home features architectural details reminiscence of earlier fine homes.

Features:

- Ceiling Height: 8 ft. unless otherwise noted.
- Foyer: This grand entry soars two-stories high. The U-shaped staircase with window leads to a second-story balcony.
- Great Room: You'll be drawn to the impressive views through the triple-arch windows at the front and rear of this room.
- Kitchen: Designed for maximum efficiency, this kitchen is a pleasure to be in. It features a center island, a full pantry, and a desk for added convenience.
- Breakfast Area: This area adjoins the kitchen. Both rooms are flooded with sunlight streaming from a shared bay window.
- Master Suite: The stylish bedroom includes a walk-in closet. Luxuriate in the whirlpool tub at the end of a long day .

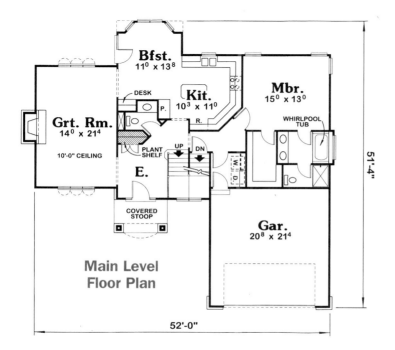

Main Level Floor Plan

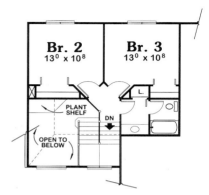

Copyright by designer/architect.

Upper Level Floor Plan

Plan #121024

Dimensions: 60' W x 58' D

Levels: 2

Square Footage: 3,057

Main Level Sq. Ft.: 1,631

Second Level Sq. Ft.: 1,426

Bedrooms: 4

Bathrooms: 2½

Foundation: Basement

Materials List Available: Yes

Price Category: G

This distinctive home offers plenty of space and is designed for gracious and convenient living.

Features:

- Ceiling Height: 8 ft. unless otherwise noted.

- Foyer: A curved staircase in this elegant entry will greet your guests.

- Living Room: This room invites you with a volume ceiling flanked by transom-topped windows that flood the room with sunlight.

- Screened Veranda: On warm summer nights, throw open the French doors in the living room and enjoy a breeze on the huge screened veranda.

- Dining Room: This distinctive room is overlooked by the veranda.

- Family Room: At the back of the home is this comfortable family retreat with its soaring cathedral ceiling and handsome fireplace flanked by bookcases.

- Master Bedroom: This bayed bedroom features a 10-ft. vaulted ceiling.

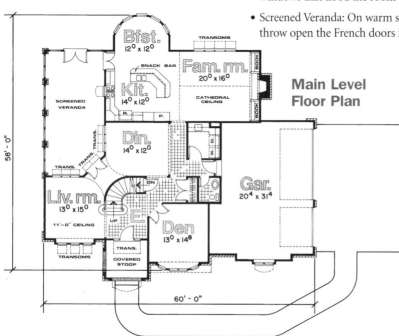

Main Level Floor Plan

Upper Level Floor Plan

Copyright by designer/architect.

Plan #121015

Dimensions: 52' W x 47'4" D
Levels: 2
Square Footage: 1,999
Main Level Sq. Ft.: 1,421
Upper Level Sq. Ft.: 578
Bedrooms: 3
Bathrooms: 3
Foundation: Basement
Materials List Available: Yes
Price Category: D

Images provided by designer/architect.

Hipped roofs and a trio of gables bring distinction to this plan.

Features:

• Ceiling Height: 8 ft.

• Open Floor Plan: The rooms flow into each other and are flanked by an abundance of windows. The result is a light and airy space that seems much larger than it really is.

• Formal Dining Room: Here is the perfect room for elegant entertaining.

• Breakfast Nook: This bright, bayed nook is the perfect place to start the day. It's also great for intimate get-togethers.

• Great Room: The family will enjoy gathering in this spacious area.

• Bedrooms: This large master bedroom, along with three secondary bedrooms and an extra room, provides plenty of room for a growing family.

• Attached Garage: The garage provides two bays of parking plus plenty of storage space.

Main Level Floor Plan

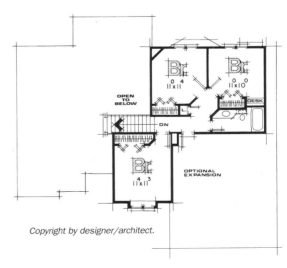

Upper Level Floor Plan

Copyright by designer/architect.

Plan #151026

Dimensions: 34' W x 66'8" D
Levels: 2
Square Footage: 1,574
Main Level Sq. Ft.: 1,131
Upper Level Sq. Ft.: 443
Bedrooms: 3
Bathrooms: 2
Foundation: Crawl space, slab; optional full basement plan available for extra fee
Materials List Available: Yes
Price Category: C

This French Country home gives space for entertaining and offers privacy.

Features:

- **Great Room:** Move through the gracious foyer framed by wooden columns into the great room with its lofty 10-ft. ceilings and gas fireplace.

- **Dining Room:** Set off by 8-in. columns, the dining room opens to the kitchen, both with 9-foot ceilings.

- **Master Suite:** Enjoy relaxing in the bedroom with its 10-ft. boxed ceiling and well-placed windows. Atrium doors open to the backyard, where you can make a secluded garden. A glass-bricked corner whirlpool tub, corner shower, and double vanity make the master bath luxurious.

- **Bedrooms:** Upstairs, two large bedrooms with a walk-through bath provide plenty of room as well as privacy for kids or guests.

Main Level Floor Plan

Copyright by designer/architect.

Upper Level Floor Plan

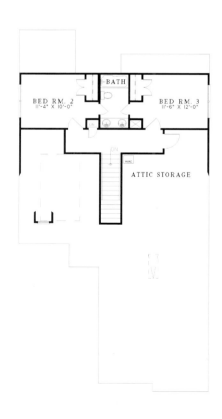

Plan #271011

Dimensions: 36' W x 41' D
Levels: 2
Square Footage: 1,296
Main Level Sq. Ft.: 891
Upper Level Sq. Ft.: 405
Bedrooms: 3
Bathrooms: 2
Foundation: Basement
Materials List Available: Yes
Price Category: B

Images provided by designer/architect.

Perfectly sized for a narrow lot, this charming modern cottage boasts space efficiency and affordability.

Features

• **Living Room:** The inviting raised foyer steps down into this vaulted living room, with its bright windows and eye-catching fireplace.

• **Dining Room:** This vaulted formal eating space includes sliding-glass-door access to a backyard deck.

• **Kitchen:** Everything is here: U-shaped efficiency, handy pantry—even bright windows.

• **Master Suite:** Main-floor location ensures accessibility in later years, plus there's a walk-in closet and full bathroom.

• **Secondary Bedrooms:** On the upper floor, a bedroom and a loft reside near a full bath. The loft can be converted easily to a third bedroom, or use it as a study or play space.

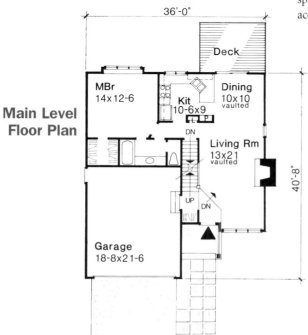

Main Level Floor Plan

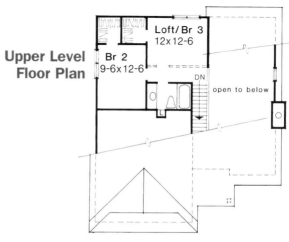

Upper Level Floor Plan

Copyright by designer/architect.

Plan #271013

Dimensions: 43' W x 46' D
Levels: 2
Square Footage: 1,498
Main Level Sq. Ft.: 1,044
Upper Level Sq. Ft.: 454
Bedrooms: 2
Bathrooms: 2½
Foundation: Basement
Materials List Available: Yes
Price Category: B

Images provided by designer/architect.

Smart in looks, function, and cost, this design is filled with flexible spaces.

Features:

- Great Room: Straight ahead from the entry, this broad space serves as one large, flexible living space. It features a cathedral ceiling, a built-in wet bar, a cozy fireplace, and lots of glass overlooking the backyard deck.

- Kitchen/Breakfast: There's space enough here for morning meals. The pass-through to the great room is a bonus.

- Master Bedroom: Main-floor accessibility combines with a window seat, walk-in closet, and private bath to deliver a getaway that is worth the wait.

- Secondary Bedrooms: An upper-floor bedroom and a loft share a full bath. The loft can be framed in to create a study or media room, or simply keep it open and let the kids use it as a playroom.

Main Level Floor Plan

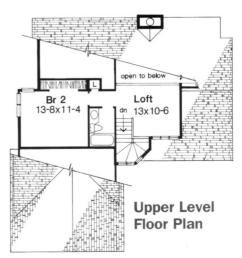

Upper Level Floor Plan

Copyright by designer/architect.

Plan #271015

Dimensions: 48' W x 28' D
Levels: 2
Square Footage: 1,359
Main Level Sq. Ft.: 668
Upper Level Sq. Ft.: 691
Bedrooms: 3
Bathrooms: 2½
Foundation: Basement
Materials List Available: Yes
Price Category: B

Images provided by designer/architect.

Strong vertical lines and pairs of narrow windows give this compact home an airy feel. Its clever floor plan makes good use of every square foot of space.

Features:

• **Living Room:** Beyond the sidelighted front door, the living room enjoys a vaulted ceiling and a flood of light from a striking corner window arrangement.

• **Kitchen/Dining:** A central fireplace separates the living room from this kitchen/dining room, where a French door opens to a rear deck.

• **Master Suite:** Sacrifice no luxuries in this sweet, upper-floor retreat, where a boxed-out window catches morning rays or evening stars. Next to the roomy walk-in closet, the private split bath enjoys a window of its own.

• **Secondary Bedrooms:** A balcony overlooks the living room and leads to one bedroom and the flexible loft.

Main Level Floor Plan

Upper Level Floor Plan

Copyright by designer/architect.

Plan #131033

Dimensions: 84'10" W x 48' D
Levels: 2
Square Footage: 2,813
Main Level Sq. Ft.: 1,890
Upper Level Sq. Ft.: 923
Bedrooms: 5
Bathrooms: 3½
Foundation: Crawlspace, slab, or basement
Materials List Available: Yes
Price Category: G

Contemporary styling, luxurious amenities, and the classics that make a house a home are all available here.

Features:

- **Family Room:** A sloped ceiling with skylight and a railed overlook to make this large space totally up to date.

- **Living Room:** Sunken for comfort and with a cathedral ceiling for style, this room features a fireplace flanked by windows and sliding glass doors.

- **Master Suite:** Unwind in this room, with its cathedral ceiling, with a skylight, walk-in closet, and private access to the den.

- **Upper Level:** A bridge overlooks the living room and foyer and leads through the family room to three bedrooms and a bath.

- **Optional Guest Suite:** 500 sq. ft. above the master suite and den provides total comfort.

Images provided by designer/architect.

Main Level Floor Plan

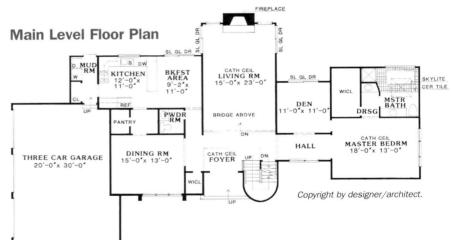

Copyright by designer/architect.

Upper Level Floor Plan

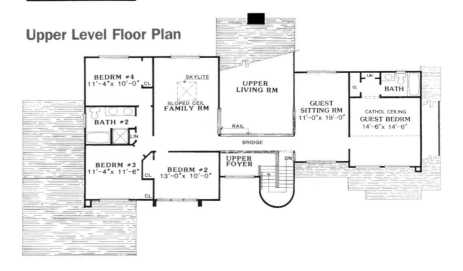

Entry

Living Room / Foyer

Living Room

Rear View

Plan #271016

Dimensions: 45'4" W x 49'6" D

Levels: 2

Square Footage: 2,170

Main Level Sq. Ft.: 1,169

Upper Level Sq. Ft.: 1,001

Bedrooms: 3

Bathrooms: 2½

Foundation: Basement

Materials List Available: Yes

Price Category: D

Images provided by designer/architect.

With plenty of living space, this attractive design is just right for a growing family.

Features:

- **Entry:** This two-story reception area welcomes guests with sincerity and style. A coat closet stands ready to take winter wraps.

- **Great Room:** This sunken and vaulted space hosts gatherings and formal meals of any size, and a handsome fireplace adds warmth and ambiance.

- **Kitchen:** A U-shaped counter keeps the family cook organized. A bayed breakfast nook overlooks a backyard deck.

- **Family Room:** The home's second fireplace adds a cozy touch to this casual area. Relax here with the family after playing in the snow!

- **Master Suite:** A vaulted ceiling presides over the master bedroom. The private bath hosts a separate tub and shower, a dual-sink vanity, and two walk-in closets.

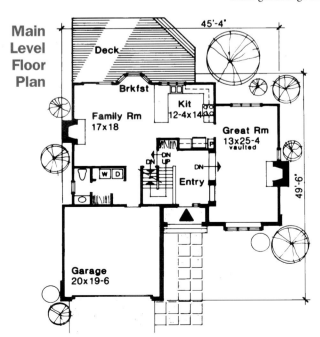

Main Level Floor Plan

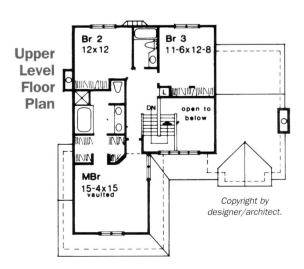

Upper Level Floor Plan

Copyright by designer/architect.

Plan #271018

Dimensions: 67' W x 37' D
Levels: 2
Square Footage: 2,445
Main Level Sq. Ft.: 1,290
Upper Level Sq. Ft.: 1,155
Bedrooms: 4
Bathrooms: 2½
Foundation: Basement
Materials List Available: Yes
Price Category: E

Images provided by designer/architect.

This traditional home re-creates the charm and character of days gone by.

Features:

- **Living Room:** A dramatic skylighted entry preludes this formal, sunken living room, which includes a stunning corner fireplace, a vaulted ceiling, and an adjoining formal dining room.

- **Dining Room:** This quiet space offers a built-in hutch beneath a vaulted ceiling.

- **Kitchen:** A built-in desk and a pantry mark this smartly designed space, which opens to a breakfast room and the family room beyond.

- **Family Room:** Sunken and filled with intrigue, this gathering room features a fireplace flanked by windows, plus French doors that open to a backyard deck.

- **Master Suite:** This luxurious upper-floor retreat boasts a vaulted ceiling, an angled walk-in closet, and a private bath.

Main Level Floor Plan

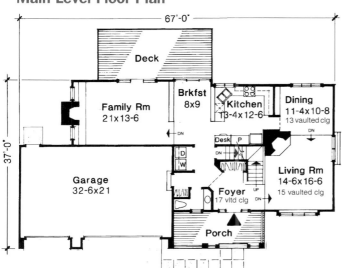

Upper Level Floor Plan

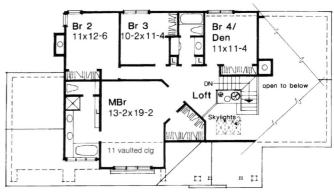

Copyright by designer/architect.

Plan #271019

Dimensions: 40'4" W x 41'8" D

Levels: 2

Square Footage: 1,556

Main Level Sq. Ft.: 834

Upper Level Sq. Ft.: 722

Bedrooms: 3

Bathrooms: 2½

Foundation: Basement

Materials List Available: Yes

Price Category: C

Images provided by designer/architect.

This traditional home features a combination of stone and wood, lending it a distinctive old-world flavor.

Features:

• Kitchen: The centerpiece of the home, this country kitchen features ample work surfaces, a nice-sized eating area with built-in bookshelves, and access to a large backyard deck.

• Dining Room: This formal eating space is highlighted by a dramatic three-sided fireplace that is shared with the adjoining living room.

• Living Room: Enhanced by a dramatic vaulted ceiling, this living room also boasts corner windows that flood the area with natural light.

• Master Suite: Residing on the upper floor along with two other bedrooms, the master bedroom features a vaulted ceiling and a plant shelf that tops the entry to a private bath and walk-in closet.

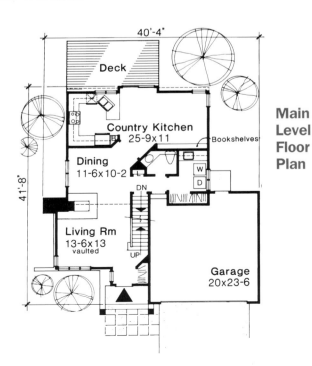

Main Level Floor Plan

Deck

Country Kitchen
25-9x11

Bookshelves

Dining
11-6x10-2

W D

DN

Living Rm
13-6x13
vaulted

UP

Garage
20x23-6

40'-4'

41'-8'

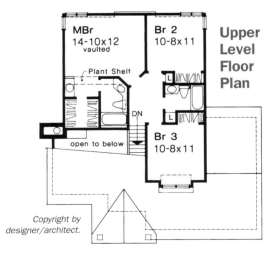

Upper Level Floor Plan

MBr
14-10x12
vaulted

Br 2
10-8x11

Plant Shelf

DN

Br 3
10-8x11

open to below

Copyright by designer/architect.

Plan #271033

Dimensions: 40' W x 42' D
Levels: 2
Square Footage: 1,516
Main Level Sq. Ft.: 817
Upper Level Sq. Ft.: 699
Bedrooms: 3
Bathrooms: 2½
Foundation: Basement
Materials List Available: Yes
Price Category: C

Images provided by designer/architect.

A pronounced roofline and a pleasing mix of brick and lap siding give a sunny disposition to this charming home.

Features:

- **Great Room:** Introduced by the sidelighted entry, this large space offers tall corner windows for natural light and a cheery corner fireplace for warmth.

- **Dining Room:** Joined to the great room only by air, this formal dining room basks in the glow from a broad window.

- **Kitchen:** Plenty of open space allows this kitchen to include ample counter space and incorporate an eating area into it. From here, a door leads to the backyard.

- **Family Room:** Flowing directly from the kitchen, this large family room allows passage to a backyard deck via sliding glass doors.

- **Master Suite:** Secluded to the upper floor, the master bedroom offers a private bath with a walk-in closet beyond.

Main Level Floor Plan

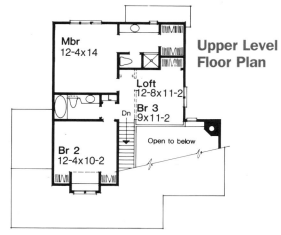

Upper Level Floor Plan

Copyright by designer/architect.

Plan #181039

Dimensions: 38' W x 36' D

Levels: 2

Square Footage: 1,661

Main Level Sq. Ft.: 923

Upper Level Sq. Ft.: 738

Bedrooms: 3

Bathrooms: 1½

Foundation: Full basement

Materials List Available: Yes

Price Category: C

Images provided by designer/architect.

Main Level Floor Plan

Upper Level Floor Plan

Copyright by designer/architect.

Plan #231020

Dimensions: 53' W x 35' D

Levels: 2

Square Footage: 2,166

Main Level Sq. Ft.: 1,538

Upper Level Sq. Ft.: 628

Bedrooms: 3

Bathrooms: 2½

Foundation: Slab, basement

Materials List Available: No

Price Category: D

Images provided by designer/architect.

Main Level Floor Plan

Upper Level Floor Plan

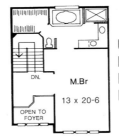

Garage Level Floor Plan

Copyright by designer/architect.

Plan #321036

Dimensions: 78'4" W x 68'6" D
Levels: 1, optional lower
Square Footage: 2,900
**Optional Basement Level
Sq. Ft.:** 1,018
Bedrooms: 4
Bathrooms: 2½
Foundation: Basement
Materials List Available: Yes
Price Category: F

Images provided by designer/architect.

**Optional Basement Level
Floor Plan**

Copyright by designer/architect.

Plan #181061

Dimensions: 56' W x 53'2" D
Levels: 2
Square Footage: 2,111
Main Level Sq. Ft.: 1,545
Upper Level Sq. Ft.: 566
Bedrooms: 3
Bathrooms: 2½
Foundation: Basement, crawl space
Materials List Available: Yes
Price Category: D

Images provided by designer/architect.

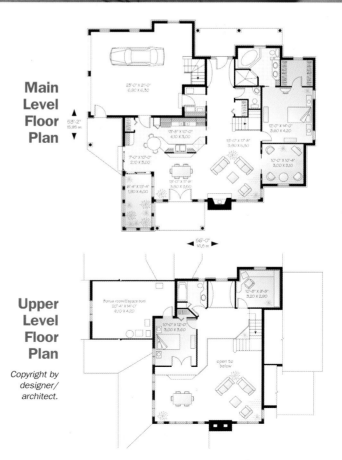

**Main
Level
Floor
Plan**

**Upper
Level
Floor
Plan**

Copyright by designer/ architect.

Plan #271034

Dimensions: 45' W x 43' D
Levels: 2
Square Footage: 1,531
Main Level Sq. Ft.: 1,062
Upper Level Sq. Ft.: 469
Bedrooms: 4
Bathrooms: 2
Foundation: Basement
Materials List Available: Yes
Price Category: C

Images provided by designer/architect.

This versatile home design adapts to today's constantly changing and nontraditional families.

Features:

• Great Room: Both old and young are sure to enjoy this great room's warm and charming fireplace. The vaulted ceiling and high fixed windows add volume and light to the room.

• Family/Kitchen: This joined space is perfect for weekend get-togethers. On warm evenings, step through the sliding glass doors to the backyard deck.

• Den/Bedroom: The flexible den can serve as a nursery or as a guest room for visiting family members of any age.

• Master Bedroom: When the golden years near, you'll appreciate its main-floor locale.

Main Level Floor Plan

Upper Level Floor Plan

Copyright by designer/architect.

Plan #271052

Dimensions: 57' W x 67' D

Levels: 2

Square Footage: 1,779

Main Level Sq. Ft.: 1,309

Upper Level Sq. Ft.: 470

Bedrooms: 3

Bathrooms: 2

Foundation: Daylight basement, crawl space

Materials List Available: Yes

Price Category: C

Images provided by designer/architect.

Designed for relaxation, this home offers a gigantic deck and an irresistible spa room.

Features:

• **Great Room:** A covered porch welcomes guests into the entry hall and this spectacular great room beyond. Outlined by windows and sliding glass doors, this great room offers panoramic views of scenic beauty. Step outside onto the deck to commune with nature one on one.

• **Kitchen:** This U-shaped kitchen flows into a cozy breakfast nook. A formal dining room is just steps away.

• **Master Suite:** This main-floor master suite features direct access to a passive-solar spa room and a sunning area beyond. A walk-in closet and a window seat round out the suite.

• **Secondary Bedrooms:** On the upper floor, a balcony hall overlooks the great room, while leading to these two good-sized bedrooms. A hall bath is located between them.

Basement Level Floor Plan

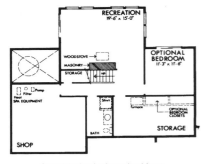

Copyright by designer/architect.

Main Level Floor Plan

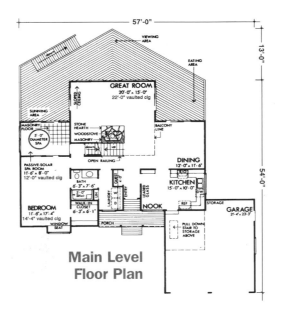

Upper Level Floor Plan

Plan #271005

Dimensions: 48'4" W x 48'4" D
Levels: 1
Square Footage: 1,368
Bedrooms: 3
Bathrooms: 2
Foundation: Basement
Materials List Available: Yes
Price Category: B

Images provided by designer/architect.

This traditional home boasts an open floor plan that is further expanded by soaring vaulted ceilings.

Features:

- **Great Room:** Front and center, this large multipurpose room features a gorgeous corner fireplace, an eye-catching boxed out window, and dedicated space for casual dining—all beneath a vaulted ceiling.

- **Kitchen:** A vaulted ceiling crowns this galley kitchen and its adjoining breakfast nook.

- **Master Suite:** This spacious master bedroom, brightened by a boxed-out window, features a vaulted ceiling in the sleeping chamber and the private bath.

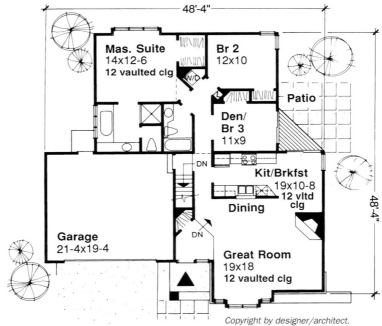

Copyright by designer/architect.

SMARTtip

Design with Computers

Consider using a computer-aided design (CAD) program to plan your deck. Some programs let you see three-dimensional views of your design complete with railings, stairs, planters, hot tubs, and the surrounding landscaping.

Plan #151021

Dimensions: 75'2" W x 89'6" D
Levels: 2
Square Footage: 3,385
Main Level Sq. Ft.: 2,633
Upper Level Sq. Ft.: 752
Bedrooms: 4
Bathrooms: 4
Foundation: Crawl space, or slab
Materials List Available: Yes
Price Category: G

Images provided by designer/architect.

From the fireplace in the master suite to the well-equipped game room, the amenities in this home will surprise and delight you.

Features:

- **Great Room:** A bank of windows on the far wall lets sunlight stream into this large room. The fireplace is located across the room and is flanked by the built-in media center and built-in bookshelves. Gracious brick arches create an entry into the breakfast area and kitchen.

- **Breakfast Room:** Move easily between this room with 10-foot ceiling either into the kitchen or onto the rear covered porch.

- **Game Room:** An icemaker and refrigerator make entertaining a snap in this room.

- **Master Suite:** A 10-ft. boxed ceiling, fireplace, and access to the rear porch give romance, while the built-ins in the closet, whirlpool tub with glass blocks, and glass shower give practicality.

Main Level Floor Plan

Upper Level Floor Plan

Copyright by designer/architect.

Plan #121062

Dimensions: 70' W x 62' D
Levels: 2
Square Footage: 3,448
Main Level Sq. Ft.: 2,375
Upper Level Sq. Ft.: 1,073
Bedrooms: 4
Bathrooms: 3½
Foundation: Basement
Materials List Available: Yes
Price Category: G

Images provided by designer/architect.

You'll love this design if you're looking for a comfortable home with dimensions and details that create a sense of grandeur.

Features:

• Entry: A soaring ceiling, curved staircase, and balcony that overlooks a tall plant shelf combine to create your first impression of grandeur in this home.

• Great Room: A transom-topped bowed window highlights this room, with its 11-ft., beamed ceiling, built-in wet bar, and see-through fireplace.

• Kitchen: Designed for the gourmet cook, this kitchen has every amenity you could desire.

• Breakfast Room: Adjacent to the great room and the kitchen, this gazebo-shaped breakfast area lights both the kitchen and hearth room.

Main Level Floor Plan

Upper Level Floor Plan

Copyright by designer/architect.

Plan #151004

Dimensions: 64'8" W x 62'1" D

Levels: 1

Square Footage: 2,158

Bedrooms: 4

Bathrooms: 2½

Foundation: Basement, slab, crawl space

Materials List Available: Yes

Price Category: D

Images provided by designer/architect.

You'll love the spacious feeling in this comfortable home designed for a family.

Features:

- **Foyer:** A 10-ft. ceiling greets you in this home.

- **Great Room:** A 10-ft. ceiling complements this large room, with its fireplace, built-in cabinets, and easy access to the rear covered porch.

- **Dining Room:** The 9-ft. boxed ceiling in this large room helps to create a beautiful formal feeling.

- **Kitchen:** The island in this kitchen is open to the breakfast room for true convenience.

- **Breakfast Room:** Morning light will stream through the bay window here.

- **Master Suite:** A 9-ft. pan ceiling adds a distinctive note to this room with access to the rear porch. In the bath, you'll find a whirlpool tub, separate shower, double vanities, and two walk-in closets.

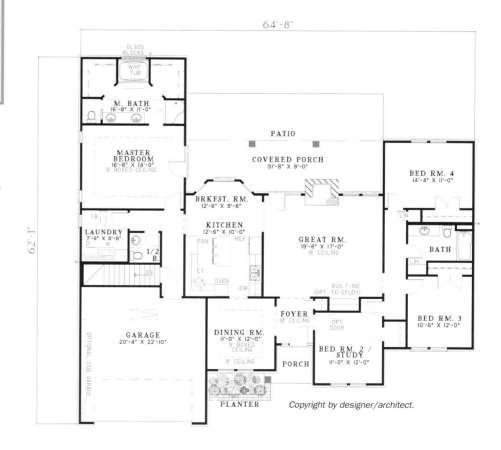

Copyright by designer/architect.

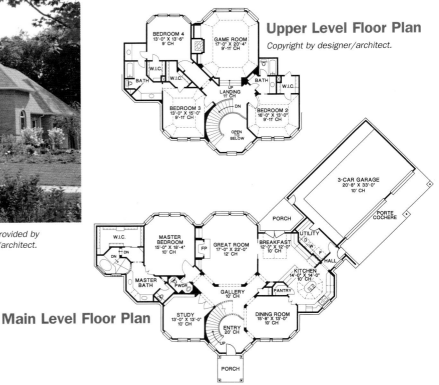

Upper Level Floor Plan

Copyright by designer/architect.

BEDROOM 4
13'-0" X 13'-6"
9' CH

GAME ROOM
17'-0" X 20'-4"
9'-11" CH

W.I.C.

BATH

W.I.C.

LANDING
11' CH

DN

BATH

W.I.C.

BEDROOM 3
13'-0" X 15'-0"
9'-11" CH

BEDROOM 2
16'-0" X 13'-0"
9'-11" CH

OPEN TO BELOW

3-CAR GARAGE
20'-8" X 33'-0"
10' CH

PORTE COCHERE

PORCH

W.I.C.

MASTER BEDROOM
15'-0" X 18'-4"
10' CH

GREAT ROOM
17'-0" X 22'-0"
12' CH

BREAKFAST
12'-0" X 12'-0"
10' CH

UTILITY

FP

DN

MASTER BATH

PWDR

GALLERY
10' CH

PANTRY

KITCHEN
14'-0" X 14'-0"
10' CH

HALL

Main Level Floor Plan

STUDY
13'-0" X 13'-0"
10' CH

ENTRY
20' CH

UP

DINING ROOM
15'-8" X 13'-0"
10' CH

PORCH

Plan #121100

Dimensions: 100'10" W x 80'5" D

Levels: 2

Square Footage: 3,750

Main Level Sq. Ft.: 2,274

Upper Level Sq. Ft.: 1,476

Bedrooms: 4

Bathrooms: 3½

Foundation: Slab

Materials List Available: No

Price Category: G

Images provided by designer/architect.

Main Level Floor Plan

Two Car Garage
21'4" x 21'4"

Patio

Porch

Master Bedroom
14' x 17'

Family
19'4" x 17'

Breakfast

Dining
15' x 11'3"

Living
11'4" x 11'4"

Bedroom
12' x 12'

Porch

Upper Level Floor Plan

Copyright by designer/architect.

Rear View

Bedroom
13' x 16'

Bedroom
11'6" x 12'

Plan #111033

Dimensions: 67' W x 65' D

Levels: 2

Square Footage: 2,824

Main Level Sq. Ft.: 2,120

Upper Level Sq. Ft.: 704

Bedrooms: 4

Bathrooms: 3

Foundation: Slab

Materials List Available: No

Price Category: F

Images provided by designer/architect.

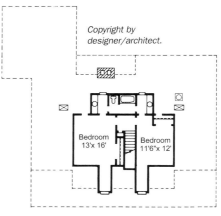

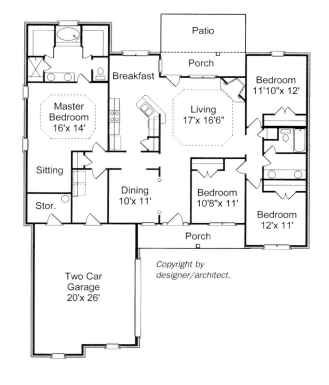

Images provided by designer/architect.

Copyright by designer/architect.

Plan #111015

Dimensions: 64' W x 58' D

Levels: 1

Square Footage: 2,208

Bedrooms: 4

Bathrooms: 2

Foundation: Crawl space

Materials List Available: No

Price Category: E

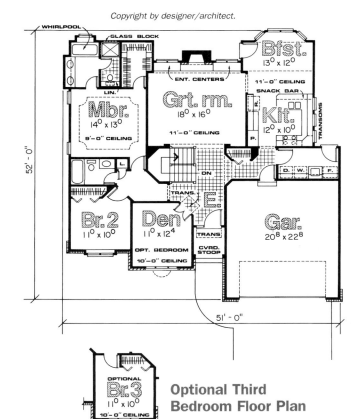

Images provided by designer/architect.

Plan #121055

Dimensions: 51' W x 52' D

Levels: 1

Square Footage: 1,622

Bedrooms: 3

Bathrooms: 2

Foundation: Basement

Materials List Available: Yes

Price Category: C

Plan #161040

Dimensions: 63'4" W x 48' D
Levels: 2
Square Footage: 2,403
Main Level Sq. Ft.: 1,710
Upper Level Sq. Ft.: 695
Bedrooms: 4
Bathrooms: 3½
Foundation: Basement
Materials List Available: Yes
Price Category: E

Designed with attention to detail, this elegant home will please the most discriminating taste.

Images provided by designer/architect.

Features:

- Great Room: The high ceiling in this room accentuates the fireplace and the rear wall of windows. A fashionable balcony overlooks the great room.

- Dining Room: This lovely formal dining room is introduced by columns and accented by a boxed window.

- Kitchen: This wonderful kitchen includes a snack bar, island, and large pantry positioned to serve the breakfast and dining rooms with equal ease.

- Master Suite: This master suite features a dressing room, private sitting area with 11-ft.

ceiling, whirlpool tub, double-bowl vanity, and large walk-in closet.

- Additional Bedrooms: Three additional bedrooms complete this spectacular home.

Rear Elevation

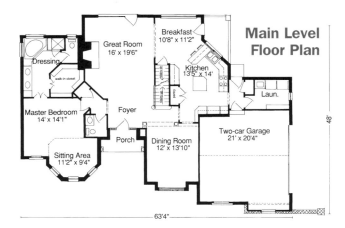

Main Level Floor Plan

Great Room 16' x 19'6"
Breakfast 10'8" x 11'2"
Dressing
Kitchen 13'5" x 14'
walk-in closet
Laun.
Master Bedroom 14' x 14'1"
Foyer
Porch
Dining Room 12' x 13'10"
Two-car Garage 21' x 20'4"
Sitting Area 11'2" x 9'4"
48'
63'4"

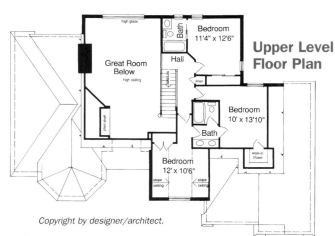

Upper Level Floor Plan

high glass
Bath
Bedroom 11'4" x 12'6"
Great Room Below
high ceiling
Hall
linen
Bedroom 10' x 13'10"
Bath
walk-in closet
Bedroom 12' x 10'6"
slope ceiling   slope ceiling

Copyright by designer/architect.

Plan #101019

Dimensions: 58'4" W x 55'2" D
Levels: 2
Square Footage: 2,954
Main Level Sq. Ft. 2093
Upper Level Sq. Ft. 861
Bedrooms: 4
Bathrooms: 3½
Foundation: Slab, crawl space, or basement
Materials List Available: No
Price Category: F

Images provided by designer/architect.

This luxurious home features a spectacular open floor plan and a brick exterior.

Features:

- Ceiling Height: 9 ft. unless otherwise noted.
- Foyer: This inviting two-story foyer, which vaults to 18 ft., will greet guests with an impressive "welcome."
- Dining Room: To the right of the foyer is this spacious dining room surrounded by decorative columns.

- Family Room: There's plenty of room for all kinds of family activities in this enormous room, with its soaring two-story ceiling.
- Master Suite: This sumptuous retreat boasts a tray ceiling. Optional pocket doors provide direct access to the study. The master bath features his and her vanities and a large walk-in closet.
- Breakfast Area: Perfect for informal family meals, this bayed breakfast area has real flair.
- Secondary Bedrooms: Upstairs are three large bedrooms with 8-ft. ceilings. One has a private bath.

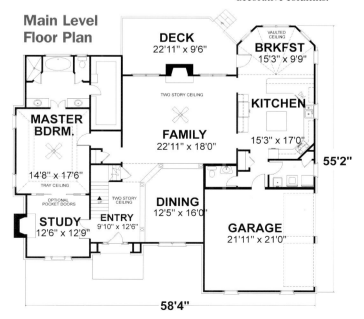

Plan #221022

Dimensions: 79' W x 55' D
Levels: 2
Square Footage: 3,382
Main Level Sq. Ft.: 2,376
Upper Level Sq. Ft.: 1,006
Bedrooms: 4
Bathrooms: 3½
Foundation: Basement
Materials List Available: No
Price Category: G

Images provided by designer/architect.

- **Master Suite:** Located on the main floor for privacy, this area includes a walk-in closet and a deluxe full bathroom.
- **Upper Level:** Look into the great room and entryway as you climb the stairs to the three large bedrooms and a full bath on this floor.

The traditional-looking facade of stone, brick, and siding opens into a home you'll love for its spaciousness, comfort, and great natural lighting.

Features:

- Ceiling Height: 9 ft.

- Great Room: The two-story ceiling here emphasizes the dimensions of this large room, and the huge windows make it bright and cheery.

- Sunroom: Use this area as a den or an indoor conservatory, where you can relax in the midst of health-promoting and beautiful plants.

- Kitchen: This well-planned kitchen features a snacking island and opens into a generous dining nook where everyone will gather.

Main Level Floor Plan

SMARTtip

Clearing the Canvas- Arranging Furniture

If you are having trouble creating a pleasing arrangement of furniture in a room, it can help to remove all of the contents and start from scratch. This is a good idea if you have trouble picturing things on paper or if you aren't going to buy a lot of new furniture and just need a fresh start. If at all possible, strip the room down completely, removing all of the furnishings, including window treatments, rugs, wall art, and accessories. This way you can observe the true architectural nature of the space without distractions that influence your perceptions. For example, minus the trappings of curtains, you can see that two windows may be slightly different sizes or installed too close to a corner. Other things you may notice might be odd corners, uneven walls, radiators or heating registers that are conspicuously located, or any other quirky features that are unique to your home.

Don't be in a rush to start filling up the room again. Live with it empty for a few days so that you can really get a sense of the space. Then slowly begin to bring things back inside, starting with the largest objects. You'll know immediately when you've crossed the line with something that doesn't belong. But you have to be willing to pull back and pare down.

OPEN TO
FAM. RM.

LINEN

BR. #2
13'4" X 12'8"

OPEN TO
E.

BR. #4
11'8" X 12'4"

BR. #3
11'8" X 12'6"

**Upper Level
Floor Plan**

Copyright by designer/architect.

Rear
Elevation

Plan #211002

Dimensions: 68' W x 62' D
Levels: 1
Square Footage: 1,792
Bedrooms: 3
Bathrooms: 2
Foundation: Crawl space
Materials List Available: Yes
Price Category: C

Arched windows on the front of this home give it a European style that you're sure to love.

SMARTtip

Water Features

Water features create the ambiance of a soothing oasis on a deck. A water-filled urn becomes a mirror that reflects the sky— making a small deck look larger. Fish flashing in an ornamental pool add color and act as a focal point for a deck with no view.

A water fountain introduces a pleasant rhythmical sound that helps drown out the background noises of traffic and nearby neighbors.

Features:

- Living Room: The 12-ft. ceiling in this large, open room enhances its spacious feeling. A fireplace adds warmth on chilly days and cool evenings.

- Dining Room: Decorate to accentuate the 12-ft. ceiling and formal feeling of this room.

- Kitchen: Designed for comfort and efficiency, this room also has a 12-ft. ceiling. The cozy breakfast bar is a natural gathering spot for friends and family.

- Master Suite: A split design guarantees privacy here. A sloped cathedral ceiling adds elegance, and a walk-in closet makes it practical. The bath has two vanities, a tub, and a walk-in shower.

- Garage: Park two cars here, and use the balance of this 520 sq. ft. area as a handy storage area.

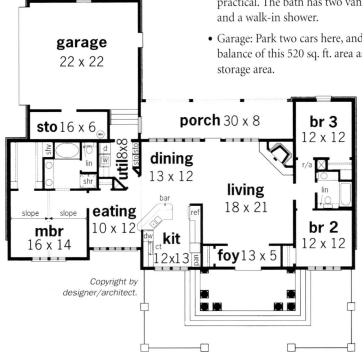

Copyright by designer/architect.

Plan #121063

Dimensions: 84' W x 52' D
Levels: 2
Square Footage: 3,473
Main Level Sq. Ft.: 2,500
Upper Level Sq. Ft.: 973
Bedrooms: 4
Bathrooms: 3½
Foundation: Basement
Materials List Available: Yes
Price Category: G

Enjoy the many amenities in this well-designed and gracious home.

Features:

- **Entry:** A large sparkling window and a tapering split staircase distinguish this lovely entryway.

- **Great Room:** This spacious great room will be the heart of your new home. It has a 14-ft. spider-beamed window that serves to highlight its built-in bookcase, built-in entertainment center, raised hearth fireplace,

wet bar, and lovely arched windows topped with transoms.

- **Kitchen:** Anyone who walks into this kitchen will realize that it's designed for both convenience and efficiency.

- **Master Suite:** The tiered ceiling in the bedroom gives an elegant touch, and the bay window adds to it. The two large walk-in closets and the spacious bath, with columns setting off the whirlpool tub and two vanities, complete this dream of a suite.

Main Level Floor Plan

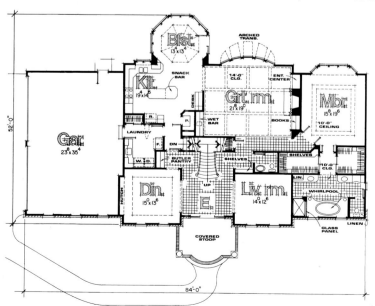

Upper Level Floor Plan

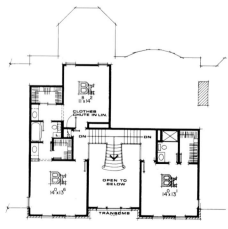

Copyright by designer/architect.

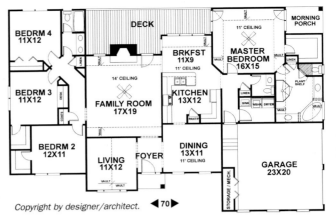

DECK

BEDRM 4
11X12

MORNING
PORCH

BRKFST
11X9

MASTER
BEDROOM
16X15
11' CEILING

BEDRM 3
11X12

FAMILY ROOM
17X19
14' CEILING

KITCHEN
13X12
11' CEILING

BEDRM 2
12X11

LIVING
11X12

FOYER

DINING
13X11
11' CEILING

GARAGE
23X20

STORAGE / MECH.

47

Copyright by designer/architect. ◄ 70 ►

Plan #101010

Dimensions: 70' W x 47' D

Levels: 1

Square Footage: 2,187

Bedrooms: 4

Bathrooms: 2½

Foundation: Slab, crawl space, basement

Materials List Available: Yes

Price Category: D

Images provided by designer/architect.

Copyright by designer/architect.

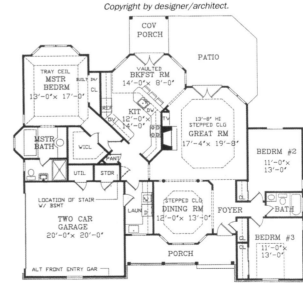

COV
PORCH

PATIO

TRAY CEIL
MSTR
BEDRM
13'-0" x 17'-0"

VAULTED
BKFST RM
14'-0" x 8'-0"

13'-8" HI
STEPPED CLG
GREAT RM
17'-4" x 19'-8"

BEDRM #2
11'-0" x
13'-0"

KIT
12'-0" x
14'-0"

MSTR
BATH

WICL

UTIL

STOR

PANT

LOCATION OF STAIR
W/ BSMT

TWO CAR
GARAGE
20'-0" x 20'-0"

LAUN

STEPPED CLG
DINING RM
12'-0" x 13'-0"

FOYER

BATH

BEDRM #3
11'-0" x
13'-0"

PORCH

ALT FRONT ENTRY GAR

Plan #131015

Dimensions: 57'4" W x 56'10" D

Levels: 1

Square Footage: 1,860

Bedrooms: 3

Bathrooms: 2

Foundation: Basement, crawl space, or slab

Materials List Available: Yes

Price Category: D

Images provided by designer/architect.

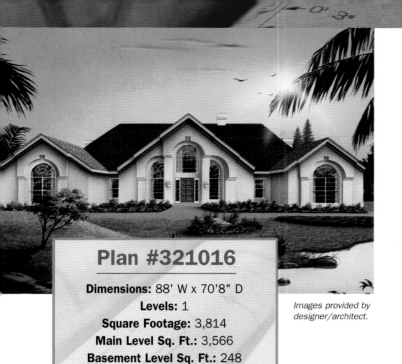

Plan #321016

Dimensions: 88' W x 70'8" D
Levels: 1
Square Footage: 3,814
Main Level Sq. Ft.: 3,566
Basement Level Sq. Ft.: 248
Bedrooms: 3
Bathrooms: 2½
Foundation: Daylight basement
Materials List Available: Yes
Price Category: H

Images provided by designer/architect.

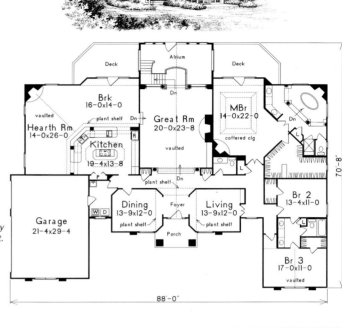

Rear View

Copyright by designer/architect.

Plan #321026

Dimensions: 67' W x 42'4" D
Levels: 1
Square Footage: 1,712
Bedrooms: 3
Bathrooms: 2½
Foundation: Crawl space
Materials List Available: Yes
Price Category: C

Images provided by designer/architect.

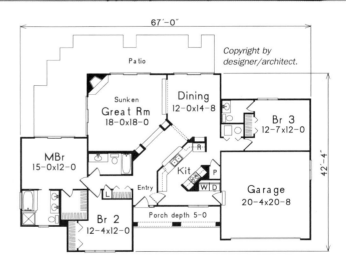

Copyright by designer/architect.

SMARTtip

Deck Design with Computers

Consider using a computer-aided design (CAD) program to plan your deck. Some programs let you see three-dimensional views of your design complete with railings, stairs, planters, hot tubs, and the surrounding landscaping.

Plan #121065

Dimensions: 62' W x 55'4" D
Levels: 2
Square Footage: 3,407
Main Level Sq. Ft.: 1,719
Upper Level Sq. Ft.: 1,688
Bedrooms: 4
Bathrooms: 2½
Foundation: Basement
Materials List Available: Yes
Price Category: G

Images provided by designer/architect.

If you love contemporary design, the unusual shapes of the rooms in this home will delight you.

Features:

- Entry: You'll see a balcony from the upper level that overlooks this entryway, as well as the lovely curved staircase to this floor.
- Great Room: This room is sunken to set it apart. A fireplace, wet bar, spider-beamed ceiling, and row of arched windows give it character.
- Dining Room: Columns define this lovely octagon room, where you'll love to entertain guests or create lavish family dinners.
- Master Suite: A multi-tiered ceiling adds a note of grace, while the fireplace and private library create a real retreat. The gracious bath features a gazebo ceiling and a skylight.

Main Level Floor Plan

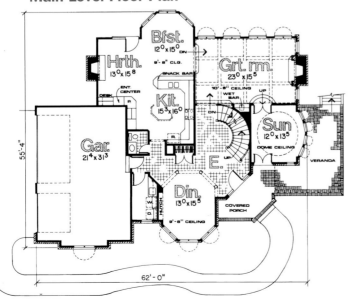

Upper Level Floor Plan

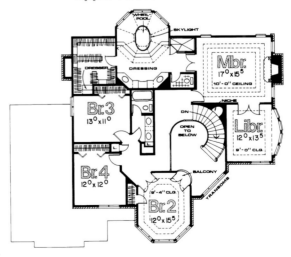

Copyright by designer/architect.

Plan #121067

Dimensions: 56' W x 59'4" D
Levels: 2
Square Footage: 2,708
Main Level Sq. Ft.: 1,860
Upper Level Sq. Ft.: 848
Bedrooms: 4
Bathrooms: 3½
Foundation: Basement
Materials List Available: Yes
Price Category: F

Images provided by designer/architect.

You'll love this home because it is such a perfect setting for a family and still has room for guests.

Features:

- **Family Room:** Expect everyone to gather in this room, near the built-in entertainment centers that flank the lovely fireplace.

- **Living Room:** The other side of the see-through fireplace looks out into this living room, making it an equally welcoming spot in chilly weather.

- **Kitchen:** This room has a large center island, a corner pantry, and a built-in desk. It also features a breakfast area where friends and family will congregate all day long.

- **Master Suite:** Enjoy the oversized walk-in closet and bath with a bayed whirlpool tub, double vanity, and separate shower.

Main Level Floor Plan

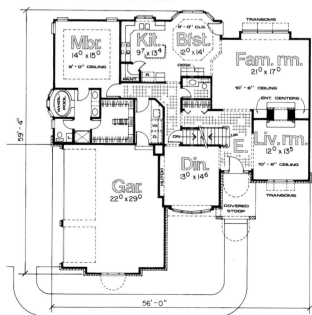

Upper Level Floor Plan

Copyright by designer/architect.

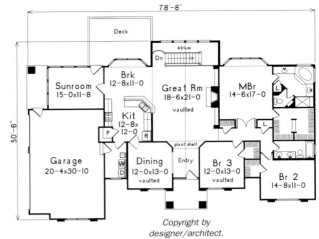

Images provided by
designer/architect.

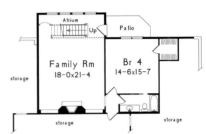

*Copyright by
designer/architect.*

Plan #321037

Dimensions: 78'8" W x 50'6" D

Levels: 1

Square Footage: 2,397

Bedrooms: 3

Bathrooms: 2

Foundation: Basement

Materials List Available: Yes

Price Category: E

**Optional
Basement Level
Floor Plan**

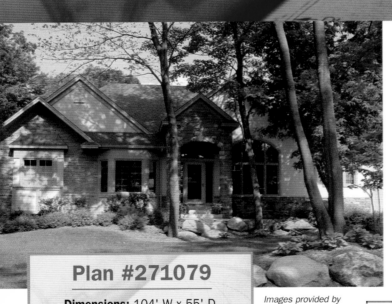

Optional Basement Level Floor Plan

Plan #271079

Dimensions: 104' W x 55' D

Levels: 1

Square Footage: 2,228

Bedrooms: 1-3

Bathrooms: 1½

Foundation: Daylight basement

Materials List Available: No

Price Category: E

Images provided by
designer/architect.

*Copyright by
designer/architect.*

Copyright by designer/architect.

Images provided by designer/architect.

Plan #271059

Dimensions: 67' W x 57' D
Levels: 1
Square Footage: 1,790
Bedrooms: 1-3
Bathrooms: 1½-2½
Foundation: Daylight basement
Materials List Available: No
Price Category: C

Optional Basement Level Floor Plan

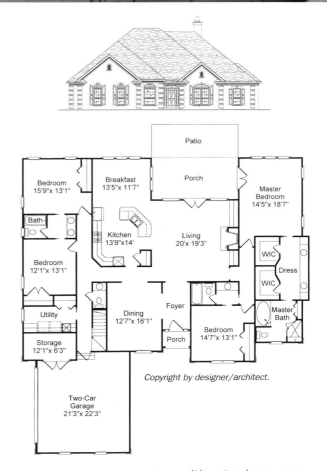

Images provided by designer/architect.

Copyright by designer/architect.

Plan #111018

Dimensions: 67' W x 79' D
Levels: 1
Square Footage: 2,745
Bedrooms: 4
Bathrooms: 3½
Foundation: Basement
Materials List Available: No
Price Category: F

Plan #121069

Dimensions: 58' W x 59'4" D
Levels: 2
Square Footage: 2,914
Main Level Sq. Ft.: 1,583
Upper Level Sq. Ft.: 1,331
Bedrooms: 4
Bathrooms: 3½
Foundation: Basement
Materials List Available: Yes
Price Category: F

Images provided by designer/architect.

You'll love this design if you're looking for a home to complement a site with a lovely rear view.

Features:

- Great Room: A trio of lovely windows looks out to the front entry of this home. The French doors in this room open to the breakfast area for everyone's convenience.

- Kitchen: Designed to suit a gourmet cook, this kitchen includes a roomy pantry and an island with a snack bar.

- Breakfast Area: The boxed window here is perfect for houseplants or a collection of culinary herbs. A door leads to the rear porch, where you'll love to dine in good weather.

- Master Suite: On the upper level, the bedroom features a cathedral ceiling, two walk-in closets, and a window seat. The bath also has a cathedral ceiling and includes dual lavatories, a large dressing area, and a sunlit whirlpool tub.

Main Level Floor Plan

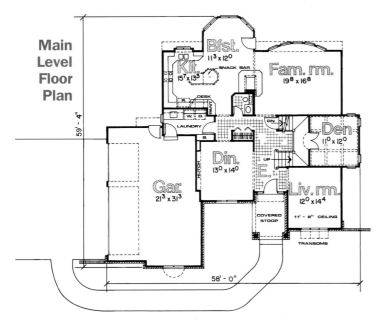

Upper Level Floor Plan

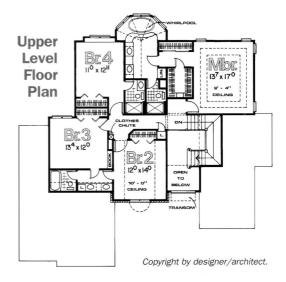

Copyright by designer/architect.

Plan #161028

Dimensions: 84'6" W x 69'4" D

Levels: 1

Square Footage: 3,570

Optional Finished Basement Sq. Ft.: 2,367

Bedrooms: 3

Bathrooms: 3½

Foundation: Basement

Materials List Available: Yes

Price Category: H

Images provided by designer/architect.

From the gabled stone-and-brick exterior to the wide-open view from the foyer, this home will meet your greatest expectations.

Features:

- Great Room/Dining Room: Columns and 13-ft. ceilings add exquisite detailing to the dining room and great room.

- Kitchen: The gourmet-equipped kitchen with an island and a snack bar merges with the cozy breakfast and hearth rooms.

- Master Bedroom: The luxurious master bed room pampers with a separate sitting room with a fireplace and a dressing room boasting a whirlpool tub and two vanities.

- Additional: Two bedrooms upstairs include a private bath and walk-in closet. The optional finished basement solves all your recreational needs: bar, media room, billiards room, exercise room, game room, as well as an office and fourth bedroom.

Rear Elevation

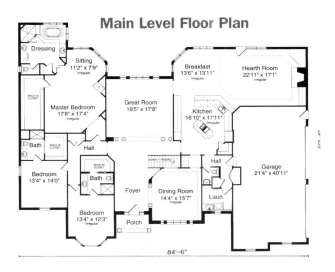

Main Level Floor Plan

Basement Level Floor Plan

Copyright by designer/architect.

Plan #211006

Dimensions: 61' W x 77' D
Levels: 1
Square Footage: 2,177
Bedrooms: 3
Bathrooms: 2
Foundation: Slab, optional basement
Materials List Available: Yes
Price Category: D

This traditional home with a stucco exterior is distinguished by its 9-ft. ceilings throughout and its sleek, contemporary interior.

Features:

- **Living Room:** A series of arched openings that surround this room adds strong visual interest. Settle down by the fireplace on cold winter nights.

- **Dining Room:** Step up to enter this room with a raised floor that sets it apart from other areas.

- **Kitchen:** Ideal for cooking as well as casual socializing, this kitchen has a stovetop island and a breakfast bar.

- **Master Suite:** The sitting area in this suite is so big that you might want to watch TV here or make it a study. In the bath, you'll find a skylight above the angled tub with a mirror surround and well-placed plant ledge.

- **Rear Porch:** This 200-sq.-ft. covered porch gives you plenty of space for entertaining.

SMARTtip

DECK Furniture Style

Mix-and-match tabletops, frames, and legs are stylish. Combine materials such as glass, metal, wood, and mosaic tiles.

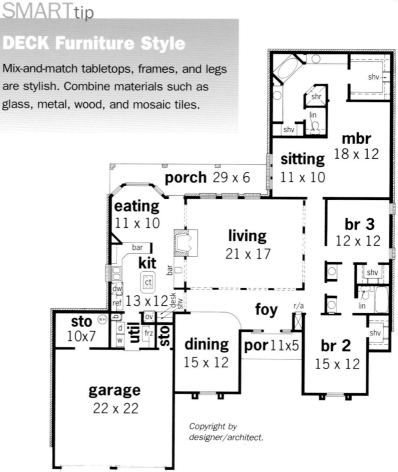

Copyright by designer/architect.

Plan #121073

Dimensions: 70' W x 52' D
Levels: 2
Square Footage: 2,579
Main Level Sq. Ft.: 1,933
Upper Level Sq. Ft.: 646
Bedrooms: 4
Bathrooms: 2½
Foundation: Basement
Materials List Available: Yes
Price Category: E

Images provided by designer/architect.

Luxury will surround you in this home with contemporary styling and up-to-date amenities at every turn.

Features:

• Great Room: This large room shares both a see-through fireplace and a wet bar with the adjacent hearth room. Transom-topped windows add both light and architectural interest to this room.

• Den: Transom-topped windows add visual interest to this private area.

• Kitchen: A center island and corner pantry add convenience to this well-planned kitchen, and a lovely ceiling treatment adds beauty to the bayed breakfast area.

• Master Suite: A built-in bookcase adds to the ambiance of this luxury-filled area, where you're sure to find a retreat at the end of the day.

Main Level Floor Plan

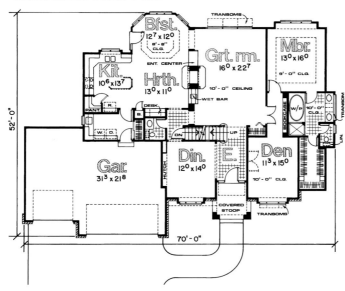

Upper Level Floor Plan

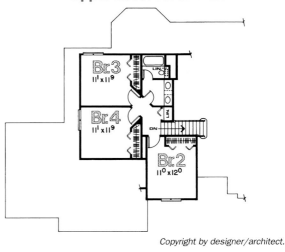

Copyright by designer/architect.

Plan #121074

Dimensions: 68'8" W x 47'8" D

Levels: 2

Square Footage: 2,486

Main Level Sq. Ft.: 1,829

Upper Level Sq. Ft.: 657

Bedrooms: 4

Bathrooms: 2½

Foundation: Basement

Materials List Available: Yes

Price Category: E

Images provided by designer/architect.

Enjoy the natural light that streams through the many lovely windows in this well-designed home.

Features:

• Living Room: This room is sure to be your family's headquarters, thanks to the lovely 15-ft. ceiling, stacked windows, central location, and cozy fireplace.

• Dining Room: A boxed ceiling adds formality to this well-positioned room.

• Kitchen: The island cooktop in this kitchen is so large that it includes a snack bar area. A pantry gives ample storage space, and a built-in desk—where you can set up a computer station or a record-keeping area— adds efficiency.

• Master Suite: For the sake of privacy, this master suite is located on the opposite side of the home from the other living areas. You'll love the roomy bedroom and luxuriate in the private bath with its many amenities.

Main Level Floor Plan

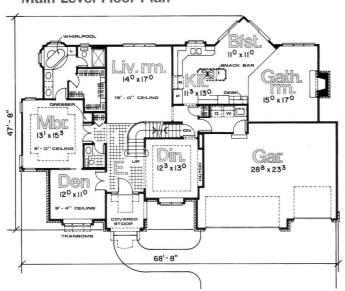

Upper Level Floor Plan

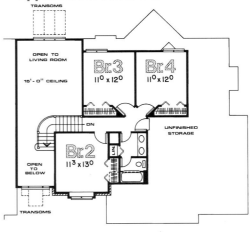

Copyright by designer/architect.

Plan #151010

Dimensions: 38'4" W x 68'6" D
Levels: 1
Square Footage: 1,379
Bedrooms: 3
Bathrooms: 2
Foundation: Crawl, slab
Materials List Available: Yes
Price Category: B

This French Country home has a spacious great room for friends and family to gather, but you can sneak away to the covered rear porch or patio off the master suite for cozy tête-à-têtes.

Features:

- Entry: Take advantage of the marvelous 10-ft. ceilings to hang groups of potted flowering plants.

- Great Room: This spacious room, with an optional 10-ft. boxed ceiling, is the place to curl up by the gas fireplace on a cold winter night.

- Kitchen: The kitchen includes a bar for casual meals, and is open to the breakfast room.

- Rear Porch: Enjoy leisurely meals on the covered rear porch that you can access from both the master suite and the breakfast room.

- Master Suite: The 10-ft. boxed ceiling in the bedroom and the master bath with a whirlpool tub and separate shower make this suite a luxurious place to end a long day.

Plan #121077

Dimensions: 64' W x 46' D
Levels: 2
Square Footage: 2,480
Main Level Sq. Ft.: 1,369
Upper Level Sq. Ft.: 1,111
Bedrooms: 4
Bathrooms: 2½
Foundation: Basement
Materials List Available: Yes
Price Category: E

Images provided by designer/architect.

You'll love this design if you've been looking for a home that mixes formal and informal living spaces.

Features:

- **Entry:** An angled staircase is the focal point in this lovely two-story entry.
- **Living Room:** To the left of the entry, a boxed ceiling, transom-topped windows, and corner columns highlight this formal living room and the dining room.
- **Den:** On the right side of the entry, French doors open to this cozy den with its boxed window and built-in bookcase.
- **Family Room:** Sunken to set it off, the family room has a beamed ceiling and a fireplace flanked by windows.

Main Level Floor Plan

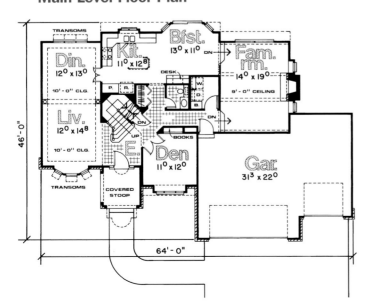

Upper Level Floor Plan

Copyright by designer/architect.

Plan #161030

Dimensions: 96'6" W x 61'5" D
Levels: 2
Square Footage: 4,562
Main Level Sq. Ft.: 3,364
Upper Level Sq. Ft.: 1,198
Bedrooms: 4
Bathrooms: 3½
Foundation: Basement
Materials List Available: Yes
Price Category: I

You'll be charmed by this impressive home, with its stone-and-brick exterior.

Features:

- **Great Room:** The two-story ceiling here adds even more dimension to this expansive space.

- **Hearth Room:** A tray ceiling and molding help to create a cozy feeling in this room, which is located so your guests will naturally gravitate to it.

- **Dining Room:** This formal room features columns at the entry and a butler's pantry for entertaining.

- **Master Suite:** A walk-in closet, platform whirlpool tub, and 2-person shower are only a few of the luxuries in the private bath, and tray ceilings and moldings give extra presence to the bedroom.

- **Upper Level:** A balcony offers a spectacular view of the great room and leads to three large bedrooms, each with a private bath.

Images provided by designer/architect.

Main Level Floor Plan

Upper Level Floor Plan

Copyright by designer/architect.

Plan #121053

Dimensions: 66' W x 68' D
Levels: 1
Square Footage: 2,456
Bedrooms: 3
Bathrooms: 2½
Foundation: Basement
Materials List Available: Yes
Price Category: E

Images provided by designer/architect.

Copyright by designer/architect.

SMARTtip

Installing Plastic Molding

Foam trim is best cut with a backsaw. Power miter saws with fine-toothed blades also work. Larger-toothed blades tend to tear the foam unevenly.

Plan #211041

Dimensions: 49' W x 64' D
Levels: 1
Square Footage: 1,891
Bedrooms: 3
Bathrooms: 2
Foundation: Slab
Materials List Available: Yes
Price Category: D

Images provided by designer/architect.

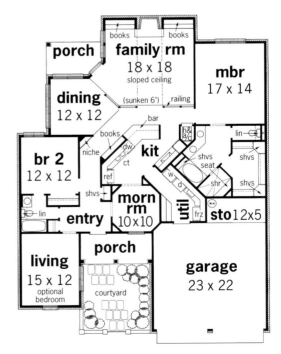

Copyright by designer/architect.

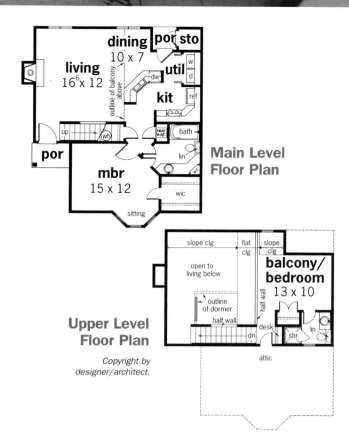

dining
10 x 7

living
16⁶ x 12

por **sto**

util

kit

por

mbr
15 x 12

**Main Level
Floor Plan**

*Images provided by
designer/architect.*

slope clg | flat clg | slope clg

open to
living below

**balcony/
bedroom**
13 x 10

outline
of dormer

half wall

desk

**Upper Level
Floor Plan**

attic

*Copyright by
designer/architect.*

Plan #211078

Dimensions: 28' W x 34' D
Levels: 2
Square Footage: 1,081
Main Level Sq. Ft.: 814
Upper Level Sq. Ft.: 267
Bedrooms: 2
Bathrooms: 2
Foundation: Slab, optional crawl
space, or basement
Materials List Available: Yes
Price Category: B

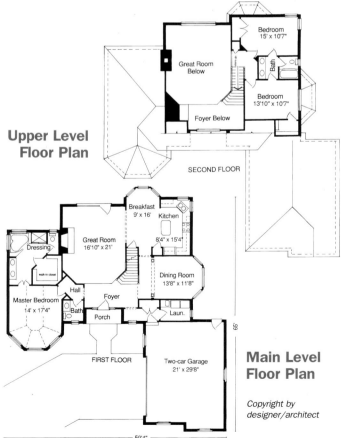

**Upper Level
Floor Plan**

Bedroom
15' x 10'7"

Great Room
Below

Bath

Bedroom
13'10" x 10'7"

Foyer Below

SECOND FLOOR

Breakfast
9' x 16'

Kitchen
8'4" x 15'4"

Great Room
16'10" x 21'

Dressing

Dining Room
13'8" x 11'8"

Master Bedroom
14' x 17'4"

Hall

Bath

Foyer

Laun.

walk-in closet

Porch

FIRST FLOOR

Two-car Garage
21' x 29'8"

**Main Level
Floor Plan**

59'4"

*Copyright by
designer/architect*

Plan #161042

Dimensions: 59'4" W x 65' D
Levels: 2
Square Footage: 2,198
Main Level Sq. Ft.: 1,706
Upper Level Sq. Ft.: 492
Bedrooms: 3
Bathrooms: 2½
Foundation: Basement
Materials List Available: Yes
Price Category: D

*Images
provided by
designer/
architect.*

Planning Your Landscape

Landscapes change over the years. As plants grow, the overall look evolves from sparse to lush. Trees cast cool shade where the sun used to shine. Shrubs and hedges grow tall and dense enough to provide privacy. Perennials and ground covers spread to form colorful patches of foliage and flowers. Meanwhile, paths, arbors, fences, and other structures gain the comfortable patina of age.

Constant change over the years—sometimes rapid and dramatic, sometimes slow and subtle—is one of the joys of landscaping. It is also one of the challenges. Anticipating how fast plants will grow and how big they will eventually get is difficult, even for professional designers, and was a major concern in formulating the designs for this book.

As Your Landscape Grows

To illustrate the kinds of changes to expect in a planting, these pages show one of the designs at three different "ages." Even though a new planting may look sparse at first, it will soon fill in. And because of careful spacing, the planting will look as good in 10 to 15 years as it does after 3 to 5. It will, of course, look different, but that's part of the fun.

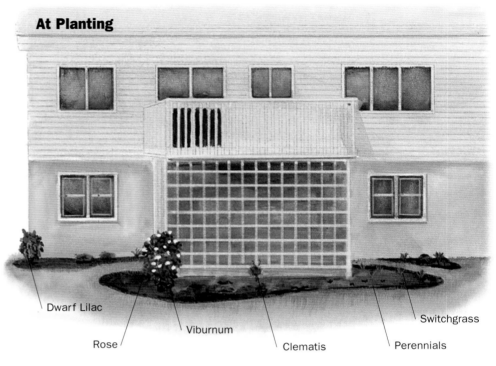

At Planting

Dwarf Lilac

Rose

Viburnum

Clematis

Switchgrass

Perennials

Three to Five Years

Rose

Switchgrass

Dwarf Lilac

Juniper

Viburnum

Juniper

Clematis

Perennials

At Planting—Here's how a raised-deck planting might appear in late spring immediately after planting. The rose and clematis haven't begun to climb the new lattice trellis. The viburnum and lilac, usually sold in 2- to 5-gal. cans, start blooming as young plants and may have flowers when you buy them, but there will be enough space that you may want to plant some short annuals around them for the first few growing seasons. You can put short annuals between the new little junipers, too. The switchgrass and perennials, transplanted from quart- or gallon-size containers, are just low tufts of foliage now, but they grow fast enough to produce a few flowers the first summer.

Three to Five Years—As shown here in midsummer, the rose and clematis now reach most of the way up the supports. Although they aren't mature yet, the lilac, viburnum, and junipers look nice and bushy, and they're big enough that you don't need to fill around them with annuals. So far, the vines and shrubs have needed only minimal pruning. Most grasses and perennials reach full size about three to five years after planting; after that, they need to be divided and replanted in freshly amended soil to keep them healthy and vigorous.

Ten to Fifteen Years—Shown again in summer, the rose and clematis now cover their supports, and the lilac and viburnum are as tall as they'll get. To maintain all of these plants, you'll need to start pruning out some of the older stems every year in early spring. The junipers have spread sideways to form a solid mass; prune them as needed along the edge of the lawn and pathways. When the junipers crowd them out, move the daylilies to another part of your property, or move them to the front of the bed to replace the other perennials, as shown here.

Ten to Fifteen Years

Rose

Clematis

Dwarf Lilac

Juniper

Viburnum

Juniper

Daylily

Switchgrass

A Step Up

Plant a Foundation Garden

Homes on raised foundations usually have foundation plantings. These simple skirtings of greenery hide unattractive concrete-block underpinnings and help overcome the impression that the house is hovering a few feet above the ground. Useful as these plantings are, they are too often just monochromatic expanses of clipped junipers, dull as dishwater. But, as this design shows, a durable, low-maintenance foundation planting can be more varied, more colorful, and more fun.

Because a foundation planting should look good year-round, the design is anchored by a row of cherry laurels, broad-leaved evergreens covered each spring by heavily scented flowers. A small garden of shrubs, perennials, and a graceful arching grass will catch the eye of visitors approaching the front door. Colorful perennials bloom from spring to fall along the edge of the bed. At the far end is a tidy viburnum, whose spicy-scented flowers will encourage springtime strolls around that corner of the house.

'Morning Light' D
Japanese silver grass

'Autumn Joy' sedum E

'Crimson Pygmy' C
Japanese barberry

Lamb's ears I

Plants & Projects

From spring to fall, something is always blooming here, but foliage texture and color play an even greater role than flowers in this design. From the slender, shimmering leaves of Japanese silver grass rising behind mounded barberries, to furry lamb's ears, feathery coreopsis, and fleshy sedum, textures abound, colored in a variety of reds, greens, and silvers. Winter offers glossy green cherry laurels, the tawny leaves and striking seed heads of silver grass, and the rich russets of the sedum. Other than an annual cutback in spring and a little pruning to shape the viburnum, the planting requires little maintenance.

A Korean spice viburnum (use 1 plant)
At the corner of the house, this deciduous shrub produces spicy-scented flowers in spring (preceded by pretty pink buds) and dense green foliage in summer and fall. Shape by annual pruning.

B 'Otto Luyken' cherry laurel (use 4)
The glossy dark leaves and spreading habit of these evergreen shrubs will clothe the foundation year-round. As a bonus, spring produces a profusion of fragrant white flowers in spikes.

C 'Crimson Pygmy' Japanese barberry (use 3)
A compact deciduous shrub with small, teardrop-shaped maroon leaves that turn crimson in fall, when they are joined by bright red berries.

D 'Morning Light' Japanese silver grass (use 1)
A rustling sentinel by the door, this grass is silvery all summer, then turns tawny after frost. Its fluffy seed heads last through the winter.

E 'Autumn Joy' sedum (use 3)
Flat-topped flower clusters emerge in late summer above clumps of fleshy gray-green leaves, turning from white through shades of ever deeper pink to rust-colored seed heads that can stand through the winter.

F 'East Friesland' salvia (use 4)
Shown against the green backdrop, reddish purple flower spikes cover these perennials from May through fall.

G 'Longwood Blue' bluebeard (use 1)
A small deciduous shrub with silvery gray foliage and fringed blue flowers from late summer to frost.

H 'Moonbeam' coreopsis (use 4)
A perennial with fine foliage and tiny pale yellow flowers from July into September.

I Lamb's ears (use 3)
A perennial with fuzzy silver-white leaves. Use the large-leaved, wide-spreading cultivar 'Helene von Stein' (sometimes called 'Big Ears').

J 'Big Blue' lilyturf (use 4)
This grasslike evergreen perennial under the viburnum has dark blue flowers in summer.

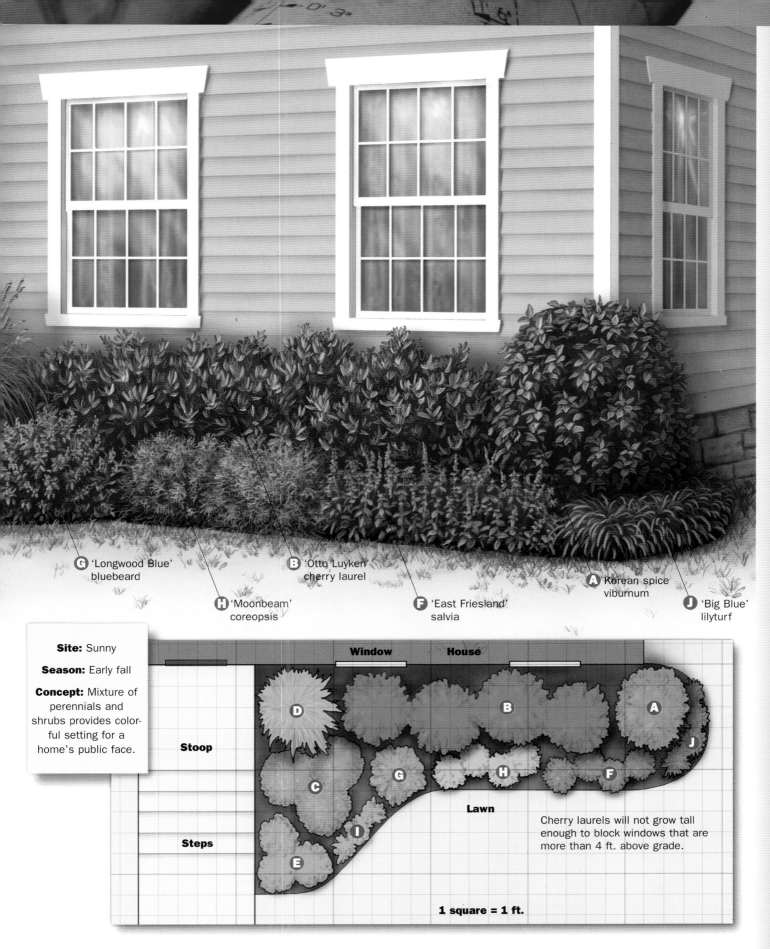

G 'Longwood Blue' bluebeard

B 'Otto Luyken' cherry laurel

A Korean spice viburnum

H 'Moonbeam' coreopsis

F 'East Friesland' salvia

J 'Big Blue' lilyturf

Site: Sunny

Season: Early fall

Concept: Mixture of perennials and shrubs provides colorful setting for a home's public face.

Window   House

Stoop

Steps

D

C

G

E

I

H

B

A

J

F

Lawn

Cherry laurels will not grow tall enough to block windows that are more than 4 ft. above grade.

1 square = 1 ft.

Note: All plants are appropriate for USDA Hardiness Zones 5, 6, and 7.

A Pleasing Postal Planting

Provide a Leafy Setting

For some, the lowly mailbox may seem a surprising candidate for landscaping. But posted like a sentry by the driveway entrance, it is highly visible to visitors and passersby. And it is one of the few places on your property that you visit every day. A pretty planting pleases the passing public and rewards your daily journey.

Foliage provides months of interest in this planting. Large clumps of feather reed grass are eye-catching from early summer through winter, with graceful leaves and plumes of flowers that rustle in the wind. At their feet, the grayish foliage of yarrow, catmint, and beach wormwood contrasts with reddish sedum and the grassy blue leaves of the cottage pinks. When the pinks are in bloom, take one or two of these sweet-scented flowers back to the house with you each day; they'll perfume a whole room. For a quick olfactory fix, rub your fingers on the aromatic catmint leaves.

Plants & Projects

Despite the frequent visits, this is not a spot for a high-maintenance garden. The plants selected here are carefree, able to withstand summer drought and piles of winter snow. A heavy mulch will control weeds not crowded out by the vigorous plants.

A **'Karl Foerster' feather reed grass** (use 3 plants)
This perennial grass is the focal point of the planting. Slender leaves arch but don't flop. Narrow flower plumes rise above the foliage from midsummer on. Seed heads and leaves turn a lovely tan in fall, fare well in winter conditions. .

B **'Coronation Gold' yarrow** (use 5)
A perennial, it forms a clump of lacy but tough green-gray foliage. In midsummer thick flower stalks support clusters of very bright golden yellow flowers.

C **'Dropmore' catmint** (use 7)
A perennial that forms a casual, sometimes floppy mound of arching stems and small gray leaves. Airy clouds of small violet-blue flowers seem to hover over the plant from early summer on.

D **'Silver Brocade' beach wormwood** (use 3)
A low, spreading perennial grown here for its striking silver-gray foliage, which offers a nice contrast in color and texture to the nearby sedum and feather reed grass.

E **'Vera Jameson' sedum** (use 5)
A perennial forming a low mound of distinctive, dusty gray-purple succulent leaves on stout stalks. Domed clusters of small pink flowers hover over the foliage in late summer.

F **'Aqua' cottage pink** (use 5)
A perennial with grassy bluish evergreen foliage and deliciously scented frilly white flowers in late spring.

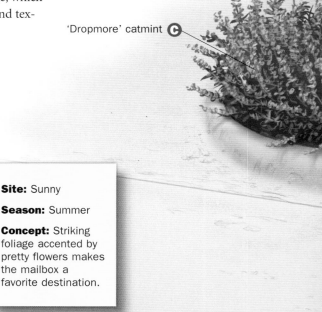

'Aqua' cottage pink **F**

'Dropmore' catmint **C**

1 square = 1 ft.

Lawn

Driveway

Street   Flagstone paver (optional)   Mailbox

Site: Sunny

Season: Summer

Concept: Striking foliage accented by pretty flowers makes the mailbox a favorite destination.

'Karl Foerster' **A**
feather reed grass

'Coronation **B**
Gold'
yarrow

Fill area between post and
curb with flagstone paver
or extend the plantings
from either side.

'Vera Jameson' **E**
sedum

'Silver Brocade' **D**
beach wormwood

Plan #121082

Dimensions: 68'8" W x 60' D
Levels: 2
Square Footage: 2,932
Main Level Sq. Ft.: 2,084
Upper Level Sq. Ft.: 848
Bedrooms: 4
Bathrooms: 3½
Foundation: Basement
Materials List Available: Yes
Price Category: F

Images provided by designer/architect.

Enjoy the spacious covered veranda that gives this house so much added charm.

Features:

• Great Room: A volume ceiling enhances the spacious feeling in this room, making it a natural gathering spot for friends and family. Transom-topped windows look onto the veranda, and French doors open to it.

• Den: French doors from the entry lead to this room, with its unusual ceiling detail, gracious fireplace, and transom-topped windows.

• Hearth Room: Three skylights punctuate the cathedral ceiling in this room, giving it an extra measure of light and warmth.

• Kitchen: This kitchen is a delight, thanks to its generous working and storage space.

Main Level Floor Plan

Upper Level Floor Plan

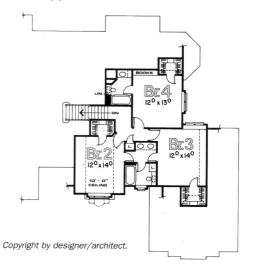

Copyright by designer/architect.

Plan #211004

Dimensions: 64' W x 62' D
Levels: 1
Square Footage: 1,828
Bedrooms: 4
Bathrooms: 2
Foundation: Slab, crawl space, basement
Materials List Available: Yes
Price Category: D

This super-energy-efficient home has the curb appeal of a much larger house.

Features:

- Ceiling Height: 9 ft.

- Kitchen: You will love cooking in this bright, airy, and efficient kitchen. It features an angled layout that allows a great view to the outside through a window wall in the breakfast area.

- Breakfast Area: With morning sunlight streaming through the wall of windows in this area, you won't be able to resist lingering over a cup of coffee.

- Rear Porch: This breezy rear porch is designed to accommodate the pleasure of old-fashioned rockers or swings.

- Master Bedroom: Retreat at the end of a long day to this bedroom, which is isolated for privacy yet conveniently located a few steps from the kitchen and utility area.

- Attic Storage: No need to fuss with creaky pull-down stairs. This attic has a permanent stairwell to provide easy access to its abundant storage.

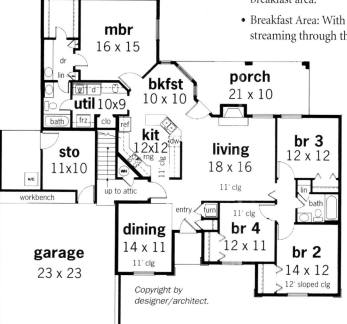

Copyright by designer/architect.

SMARTtip

Resin Furniture

Resin furniture is made of molded plastic. Most resin pieces are quite affordable, but lacquered resin with brass fittings is a high-end item. Resin doesn't corrode and cleans easily, but a scratched finish cannot be repaired. However, lacquered resin can be touched up.

Plan #211005

Dimensions: 68' W x 64' D
Levels: 1
Square Footage: 2,000
Bedrooms: 3
Bathrooms: 2
Foundation: Slab
Materials List Available: Yes
Price Category: D

A brick veneer exterior complements the columned porch to make this a striking home.

Images provided by designer/architect.

Features:

- Ceiling Height: 9 ft. unless otherwise noted.

- Living Room: From the front porch, the foyer unfolds into this expansive living room. Family and friends will be drawn to the warmth of the living room's cozy fireplace.

- Formal Dining Room: This elegant room is designed for dinner parties of any size.

- Kitchen: Located between the formal dining room and the dinette, the kitchen can serve formal meals as easily as quick family repasts.

- Master Suite: There's plenty of room to unwind at the end of a long day in the huge master bedroom. Luxuriate in the private bath, with its spa tub, separate shower, dual sinks, and two walk-in closets.

- Home Office: The home office, accessible from the master bedroom, is the perfect quiet spot to work, study, or pay the bills.

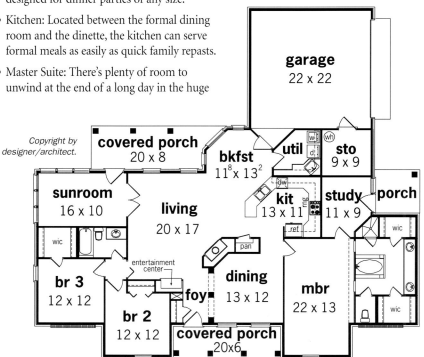

Copyright by designer/architect.

Plan #121089

Dimensions: 54' W x 51'8" D
Levels: 2
Square Footage: 1,976
Main Level Sq. Ft.: 1,413
Upper Level Sq. Ft.: 563
Bedrooms: 4
Bathrooms: 2½
Foundation: Basement
Materials List Available: Yes
Price Category: D

Images provided by designer/architect.

Enjoy the natural light that streams into every room through a variety of window types.

Features:

• **Entry:** This two-story entryway is distinguished by its many windows, which flood the area with light.

• **Great Room:** Tall windows frame the large fireplace in this room. A high, sloped ceiling accentuates its spacious dimensions, and its convenient position makes it a natural

gathering place for friends and family.

• **Kitchen:** An island provides an extra measure of convenience in this well-designed kitchen. The sunny breakfast area with its many windows is defined by the snack bar that it shares with the kitchen area.

• **Master Suite:** Placed in the opposite side of the home for privacy, this master suite features unusual detailing on the ceiling. The bath includes a corner whirlpool tub and double vanity.

Main Level Floor Plan

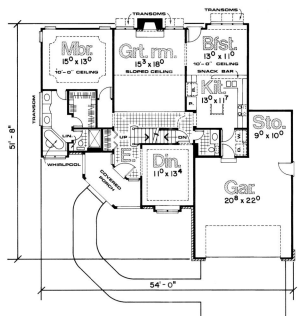

Upper Level Floor Plan

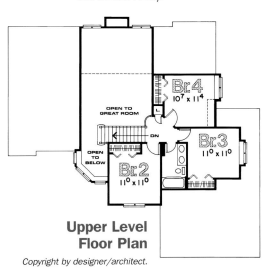

Copyright by designer/architect.

Plan #121092

Dimensions: 65'4" W x 52'8" D
Levels: 1
Square Footage: 1,887
Bedrooms: 3
Bathrooms: 2½
Foundation: Basement
Materials List Available: Yes
Price Category: D

Images provided by designer/architect.

This is the design if you want a home that will be easy to expand as your family grows.

Features:

- Entry: Both the dining room and great room are immediately accessible from this lovely entry.

- Great Room: The transom-topped bowed windows highlight the spacious feeling here.

- Gathering Room: Also with an angled ceiling, this room has a fireplace as well as built-in

entertainment center and bookcases.

- Dining Room: This elegant room features a 13-ft. boxed ceiling and majestic window around which you'll love to decorate.

- Kitchen: Designed for convenience, this kitchen includes a lovely angled ceiling and gazebo-shaped breakfast area.

- Basement: Use the plans for finishing a family room and two bedrooms when the time is right.

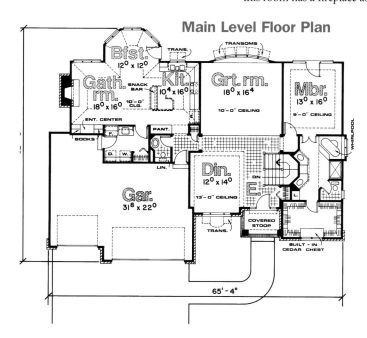

Main Level Floor Plan

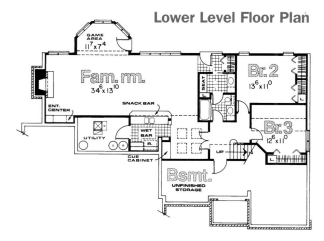

Lower Level Floor Plan

Copyright by designer/architect.

Plan #121008

Dimensions: 62' W x 56' D
Levels: 1
Square Footage: 1,651
Bedrooms: 3
Bathrooms: 2
Foundation: Basement
Materials List Available: Yes
Price Category: C

This elegant home is packed with amenities that belie its compact size.

Features:

• Ceiling Height: 8 ft.

• Dining Room: The foyer opens into a view of the dining room, with its distinctive boxed ceiling.

• Great Room: The whole family will want to gather around the fireplace and enjoy the views and sunlight streaming through the transom-topped window.

• Breakfast Area: Next to the great room and sharing the transom-topped windows, this cozy area invites you to linger over morning coffee.

• Covered Porch: When the weather is nice, take your coffee through the door in the breakfast area and enjoy this large covered porch.

• Master Suite: French doors lead to this comfortable suite featuring a walk-in. Enjoy long, luxurious soaks in the corner whirlpool accented with boxed windows.

Optional Bedroom

Br. 3
10² x 10⁰

Copyright by designer/architect.

SMARTtip
Finishing Your Fireplace with Tile

An excellent finishing material for a fireplace is tile. Luckily, there are reproductions of art tiles today. Most showrooms carry examples of Arts and Crafts, Art Nouveau, California, Delft, and other European tiles. Granite, limestone, and marble tiles are affordable alternatives to custom stone slabs.

Plan #161016

Dimensions: 59'4" W x 58'8" D
Levels: 2
Square Footage: 2,101
Main Level Sq. Ft.: 1,626
Upper Level Sq. Ft.: 475
Bedrooms: 3
Bathrooms: 2½
Foundation: Basement
Materials List Available: Yes
Price Category: D

Images provided by designer/architect.

Features:

- **Great Room:** Made for relaxing and entertaining, the great room is sunken to set it off from the rest of the house. A balcony from the second floor looks down into this spacious area, making it easy to keep track of the kids while they are playing.

- **Kitchen:** Convenience marks this well laid-out kitchen where you'll love to cook for guests and for family.

- **Master Bedroom:** A vaulted ceiling complements the unusual octagonal shape

of the master bedroom. Located on the first floor, this room allows some privacy from the second floor bedrooms. It is also ideal for anyone who no longer wishes to climb stairs to reach a bedroom.

Rear Elevation

You'll love the exciting roofline that sets this elegant home apart from its neighbors as well as the embellished, solid look that declares how well-designed it is—from the inside to the exterior.

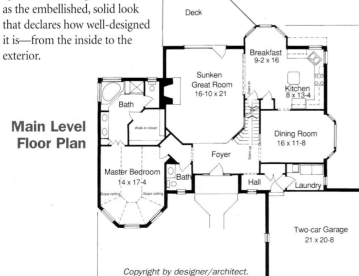

Main Level Floor Plan

Deck

Breakfast 9-2 x 16

Sunken Great Room 16-10 x 21

Kitchen 8 x 13-4

Bath

Walk-in closet

Foyer

Dining Room 16 x 11-8

Master Bedroom 14 x 17-4

Bath

Hall

Laundry

Slope ceiling   Slope ceiling

Two-car Garage 21 x 20-8

58'-8"

59'-4"

Copyright by designer/architect.

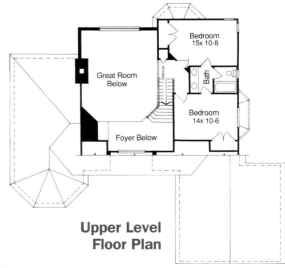

Upper Level Floor Plan

Bedroom 15 x 10-8

Great Room Below

Bath

Bedroom 14 x 10-6

Foyer Below

Plan #351001

Dimensions: 78'8" W x 51' D
Levels: 1
Square Footage: 1,855
Bedrooms: 3
Bathrooms: 2½
Foundation: Basement, crawl space, or slab
Materials List Available: Yes
Price Category: D

From the lovely arched windows on the front to the front and back covered porches, this home is as comfortable as it is beautiful.

Features:

- Great Room: Come into this room with 12-ft. ceilings, and you're sure to admire the corner gas stove and three windows overlooking the porch.

- Dining Room: Set off from the open design, this room is designed to be used formally or not.

- Kitchen: You'll love the practical walk-in pantry, broom closet, and angled snack bar here.

- Breakfast Room: Brightly lit and leading to the covered porch, this room will be a favorite spot.

- Bonus Room: Develop a playroom or study in this area.

- Master Suite: The large bedroom is complemented by the private bath with garden tub, separate shower, double vanity, and spacious walk-in closet.

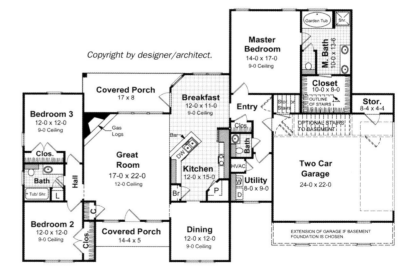

Copyright by designer/architect.

Kitchen/Great Room

Plan #151002

Dimensions: 67' W x 66' D

Levels: 1

Square Footage: 2,444

Bedrooms: 3

Bathrooms: 2

Foundation: Basement, crawl space, or slab

Materials List Available: Yes

Price Category: E

Images provided by designer/architect.

This gracious, traditional home is designed for practicality and convenience.

Features:

- Ceiling Height: 9 ft. except as noted below.

- Great Room: This room is ideal for entertaining, thanks to its lovely fireplace and French doors that open to the covered rear porch. Built-in cabinets give convenient storage space.

- Family Room: With access to the kitchen as well as the rear porch, this room will become your family's "headquarters."

- Study: Enjoy the quiet in this room with its 12-ft. ceiling and doorway to a private patio on the side of the house.

- Dining Room: Take advantage of the 8-in. wood columns and 12-ft. ceilings to create a formal dining area.

- Kitchen: An eat-in bar is a great place to snack, and the handy computer nook allows the kids to do their homework while you cook.

Copyright by designer/architect.

- Breakfast Room: Opening from the kitchen, this area gives added space for the family to gather any time.

- Master Suite: Featuring a 10-ft. boxed ceiling, the master bedroom also has a door way that opens onto the covered rear porch. The master bathroom has a step-up whirlpool tub, separate shower, and twin vanities with a makeup area.

Plan #211011

Dimensions: 84' W x 54' D
Levels: 1
Square Footage: 2,791
Bedrooms: 3 or 4
Bathrooms: 2
Foundation: Slab or crawl space
Materials List Available: Yes
Price Category: F

SMARTtip

Types of Decks

Ground-level decks resemble a low platform and are best for flat locations. They can be the most economical type to build because they don't require stairs.

Raised decks can rise just a few steps up or meet the second story of a house. Lifted high on post supports, they adapt well to uneven or sloped locations.

Multilevel decks feature two or more stories and are connected by stairways or ramps. They can follow the contours of a sloped lot, unifying the deck with the outdoors.

Plenty of room plus an open, flexible floor plan make this a home that will adapt to your needs.

Features:

- Ceiling Height: 8 ft. unless otherwise noted.
- Living Room: This distinctive room features a 12-ft. ceiling and is designed so that it can also serve as a master suite with a sitting room.
- Family Room: The whole family will want to gather in this large, inviting family room.
- Morning Room: The family room blends into this sunny spot, which is perfect for informal family meals.
- Kitchen: This spacious kitchen offers a smart layout. It is also contiguous to the family room.
- Master Suite: You'll look forward to the end of the day when you can enjoy this master suite. It includes a huge, luxurious master bath with two large walk-in closets and two vanity sinks.
- Optional Bedroom: This optional fourth bedroom is located so that it can easily serve as a library, den, office, or music room.

Copyright by designer/architect.

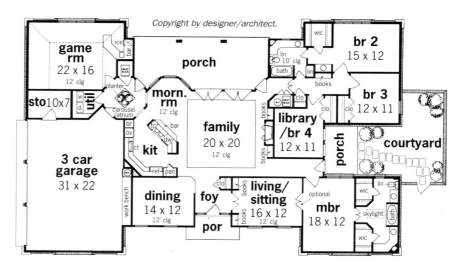

Plan #211001

Dimensions: 52' W x 66' D
Levels: 1
Square Footage: 1,655
Bedrooms: 3
Bathrooms: 2
Foundation: Slab
Materials List Available: Yes
Price Category: C

You'll love this elegant one-story home, both practical and gorgeous, with its many amenities.

Features:

- **Entry:** A covered porch and three glass doors with transoms announce this home.

- **Living Room:** At the center of the house, this living room has a 15-ft. ceiling and a fireplace. A glass door flanked by windows opens to a skylighted porch at the rear of the home.

- **Dining Room:** This elegant octagonal room, which is shaped by columns and cased openings, overlooks both backyard porches.

- **Kitchen:** A 14-ft. sloped ceiling with a skylight adds drama.

- **Master Suite:** Enjoy the seclusion of this area at the rear of the home, as well as its private access to a rear porch. The bath features an oval spa tub, separate shower, dual vanities, and huge walk-in closet.

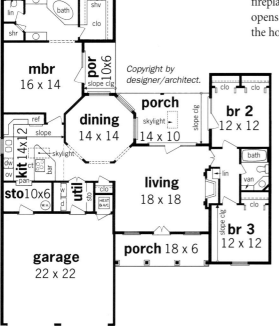

Copyright by designer/architect.

SMARTtip

Plotting a Potting Space

Whether you opt for a simple corner potting bench or a multipurpose shed or greenhouse, organization is key. You'll need a work surface —a counter or table that's a convenient height for standing while at work— plus storage accommodations for hand tools, long-handled tools, watering cans, extra lengths of hose, hose nozzles, flowerpots, bags of fertilizer and potting soil, gardening books, and notebooks. Plastic garbage cans (with lids) are good for soil and seeds. Most of these spaces are small, so use hooks and stacking bins, which keep items neat and at hand's reach. High shelves free up floor space while holding least-used things.

Plan #121022

Dimensions: 76' W x 58'8" D
Levels: 2
Square Footage: 3,556
Main Level Sq. Ft.: 2,555
Upper Level Sq. Ft.: 1,001
Bedrooms: 4
Bathrooms: 4
Foundation: Basement
Materials List Available: Yes
Price Category: H

Images provided by designer/architect.

Dramatic soaring ceilings are the hallmark of the large and luxurious home.

Features:

- Ceiling Height: 8 ft. except as noted.
- Gathering Room: Guests and family will be drawn to this room with its cathedral ceiling and its fireplace flanked by built-ins.
- Den: To the right of the entry, French doors lead to a handsome den with a tall, spider-beamed ceiling.

- Great Room: This room will be flooded with sunlight thanks to stacked windows that take advantage of its 18-ft. ceiling.
- Formal Dining Room: Upon entering the 13-ft. entry, your guests will see this elegant room with its arched windows and decorative ceiling.
- Master Suite: Unwind at day's end in this luxurious suite featuring two walk-in closets, a sky-lit whirlpool and his and her vanities.

Main Level Floor Plan

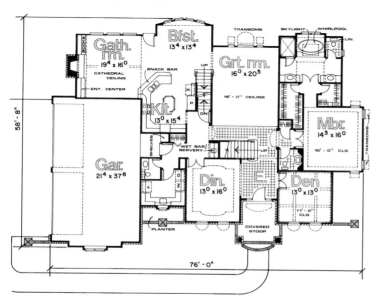

Upper Level Floor Plan

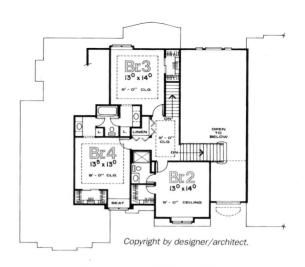

Copyright by designer/architect.

Plan #121019

Dimensions: 70' W x 60' D
Levels: 2
Square Footage: 3,775
Main Level Sq. Ft.: 1,923
Upper Level Sq. Ft.: 1,852
Bedrooms: 4
Bathrooms: 3
Foundation: Basement
Materials List Available: Yes
Price Category: H

Images provided by designer/architect.

The grand exterior presence is carried inside, beginning with the dramatic curved staircase.

Features:

- Ceiling Height: 8 ft.
- Den: French doors lead to the sophisticated den, with its bayed windows and wall of bookcases.
- Living Room: A curved wall and a series of arched windows highlight this large space.
- Formal Dining Room: The living room shares the curved wall and arched windows found in the living room.
- Screened Porch: This huge space features skylights and is accessible by another French door from the dining room.
- Family Room: Family and guests alike will be drawn to this room, with its trio of arched windows and fireplace flanked by bookcases.
- Kitchen: An island adds convenience and distinction to this large, functional kitchen.
- Garage: This spacious three-bay garage provides plenty of space for cars and storage.

Main Level Floor Plan

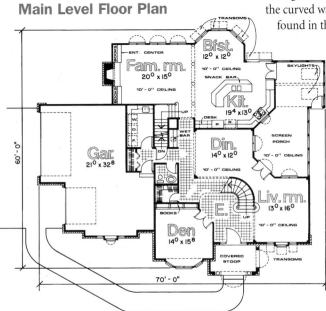

Upper Level Floor Plan

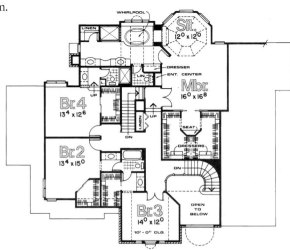

Copyright by designer/architect.

Plan #121046

Dimensions: 65'3" W x 57'2" D

Levels: 2

Square Footage: 2,655

Main Level Sq. Ft.: 1,906

Upper Level Sq. Ft.: 749

Bedrooms: 4

Bathrooms: 2

Foundation: Slab

Materials List Available: Yes

Price Category: F

Images provided by designer/architect.

This home beautifully blends traditional architectural detail with modern amenities.

Features:

- Ceiling Height: 8 ft. unless otherwise noted.
- Foyer: This two-story entry enjoys views of the uniquely shaped study, a second-floor balcony, and the formal dining room.
- Formal Dining Room: With its elegant corner column, this dining room sets the stage for formal entertaining as well as family gatherings.
- Kitchen: This well-appointed kitchen features a center island for efficient food preparation. It has a butler's pantry near the dining room and another pantry in the service entry.
- Breakfast Area: Here's the spot for informal family meals or lingering over coffee.
- Rear Porch: Step out through French doors in the master bedroom and the breakfast area.

Main Level Floor Plan

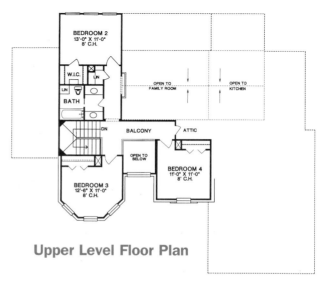

Upper Level Floor Plan

Copyright by designer/architect.

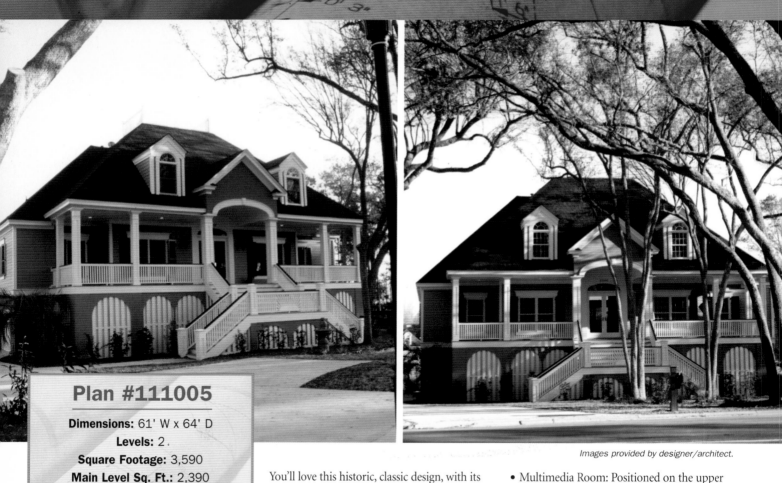

Plan #111005

Dimensions: 61' W x 64' D
Levels: 2
Square Footage: 3,590
Main Level Sq. Ft.: 2,390
Upper Level Sq. Ft.: 1,200
Bedrooms: 5
Bathrooms: 3
Foundation: Above ground basement
Materials List Available: No
Price Category: H

Images provided by designer/architect.

You'll love this historic, classic design, with its slightly Southern and very traditional feeling.

Features:

- Ceiling Height: 9 ft.

- Foyer: This gracious area opens to the formal dining room and, through French doors, to the quiet study.

- Living Room: A two-story ceiling emphasizes the spaciousness of this bright and airy room. A balcony from the upper level looks into the living room below.

- Multimedia Room: Positioned on the upper level for both quiet and the children's convenience, this room will be a gathering point for everyone.

- Kitchen: A working island and snack bar are practical touches. The adjoining breakfast area opens to the rear covered porch.

- Master Suite: French doors lead to the huge wooden deck, and the bath has two vanities, a walk-in closet, a corner tub, and a standing shower.

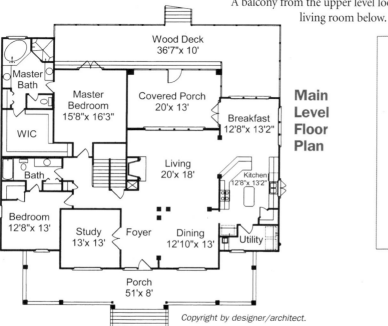

Main Level Floor Plan

Copyright by designer/architect.

Upper Level Floor Plan

Dining Room

Living Room

Living Room

SMARTtip

Window Trims

If conventional trims and braids don't excite you, look for untraditional or unusual elements for decorating your window treatments. Attach single beads, small shells, or crystal drops at regular intervals along the edge. Either glue them in place or, if they have holes, sew them on. A series of stars, leaves, or some other appropriate shape made of stiffened fabric and then glued or stitched on is another idea. Consider old or new buttons, jewelry, or metal chains. If your embroidery skills are good, use them to embellish the window treatment.

Plan #121023

Dimensions: 85'5" W x 74'8" D
Levels: 2
Square Footage: 3,904
Main Level Sq. Ft.: 2,813
Upper Level Sq. Ft.: 1,091
Bedrooms: 4
Bathrooms: 2½
Foundation: Basement
Materials List Available: Yes
Price Category: H

Images provided by designer/architect.

Spacious and gracious, here are all the amenities you expect in a fine home.

Features:

- Ceiling Height: 8 ft. except as noted.

- Foyer: This magnificent entry features a graceful curved staircase with balcony above.

- Sunken Living Room: This sunken room is filled with light from a row of bowed windows. It's the perfect place for social gatherings both large and small.

- Den: French doors open into this truly distinctive den with its 11-ft. ceiling and built-in bookcases.

- Formal Dining Room: Entertain guests with style and grace in this dining room with corner column.

- Master Suite: Another set of French doors leads to this suite that features two walk-in closets, a whirlpool flanked by vanities, and a private sitting room with built-in bookcases.

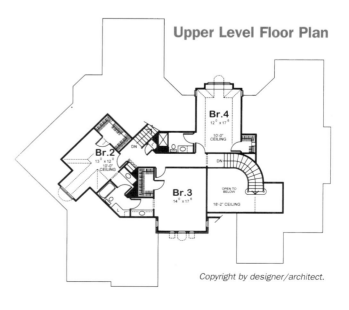

Copyright by designer/architect.

Plan #151024

Dimensions: 60' W x 73'8" D
Levels: 2
Square Footage: 3,623
Main Level Sq. Ft.: 2,391
Upper Level Sq. Ft.: 1,232
Bedrooms: 3
Bathrooms: 3
Foundation: Crawl space, slab; optional full basement plan available for extra fee
Materials List Available: Yes
Price Category: F

Images provided by designer/architect.

The 2-story foyer gives elegance to this traditional home with four fireplaces, 10-ft. ceilings, and multiple pairs of French doors.

Features:

- **Great Room:** With French doors leading to the covered porch, the study, and the master suite, this room is a natural hub for guests and family.

- **Study:** Off the great room, this impressive study features an 11-ft. ceiling and gas fireplace.

- **Master Suite:** Enter from the great room, and enjoy the fireplace, two walk-in closets, the whirlpool tub, and a private patio.

- **Kitchen/Hearth Room:** Always the traditional center of activity, this area includes a computer area, an island, ample storage, a butler's pantry, and a separate laundry/hobby room with a sink.

- **Game Room:** Upstairs, the game room is just the place for hosting large groups.

Main Level Floor Plan

Copyright by designer/architect.

Upper Level Floor Plan

Images provided by designer/architect.

Plan #111031

Dimensions: 56' W x 53' D
Levels: 2
Square Footage: 2,869
Main Level Sq. Ft.: 2,152
Upper Level Sq. Ft.: 717
Bedrooms: 4
Bathrooms: 3
Foundation: Slab
Price Category: F
Materials List Available: No

This home is ideal for any family, thanks to its spaciousness, beauty, and versatility.

Features:

- Ceiling Height: 9 ft.

- Front Porch: The middle of the three French doors with circle tops here opens to the foyer.

- Living Room: Archways from the foyer open to both this room and the equally large dining room.

- Family Room: Also open to the foyer, this room features a two-story sloped ceiling and a balcony from the upper level. You'll love the fireplace, with its raised brick hearth and the

two French doors with circle tops, which open to the rear porch.

- Kitchen: A center island, range with microwave, built-in desk, and dining bar that's open to the breakfast room add up to comfort and efficiency.

- Master Suite: A Palladian window and linen closet grace this suite's bedroom, and the bath has an oversized garden tub, standing shower, two walk-in closets, and double vanity.

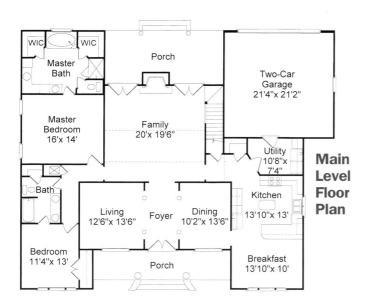

Main Level Floor Plan

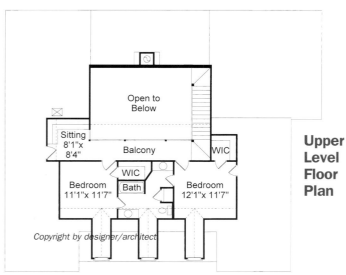

Upper Level Floor Plan

Copyright by designer/architect.

Entry

Kitchen

Living Room

Living Room

SMARTtip

Preparing to Use a Clay Chiminea

Before getting started, there are a couple of general rules about using a clay chiminea. Make sure the chiminea is completely dry before lighting a fire, or else it will crack. Also, line the bottom of the pot with about 4 inches of sand. Finally, always build the fire slowly, and never use kerosene or charcoal lighter fluid.

To cure a new clay chiminea, follow these simple steps:

- Build a small paper fire inside the pot. For kindling, use strips of newspaper rolled into a few balls. Place one newspaper ball on the sand inside the chiminea. Ignite it with a match. Then add another ball, and another, one at a time, until the outside walls of the chiminea are slightly warm. Allow the fire to burn out; then let the pot cool completely before the next step.

- Once the chiminea feels cool, light another small fire, this time using wood. Again, let the fire burn out naturally, and then allow the unit to completely cool.

- Repeat the process of lighting a wood fire three more times, adding more kindling and building a larger fire with each consecutive attempt. Remember to let the chiminea cool completely between fires.

After the fifth fire, the chiminea should be cured and ready to use anytime you want a cozy fire.

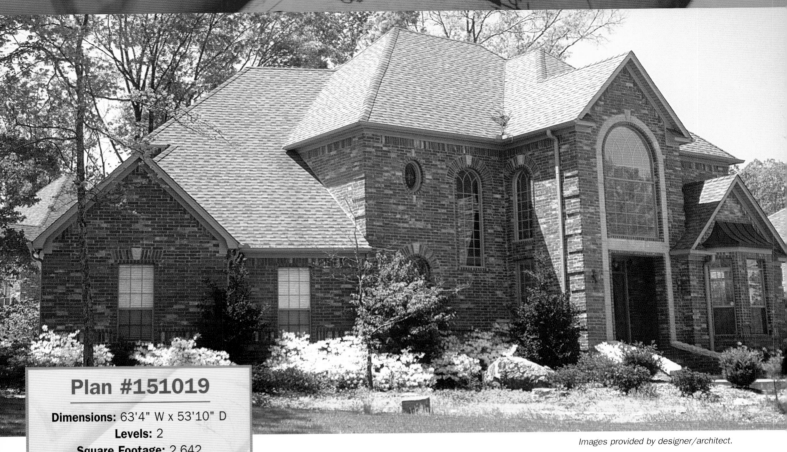

Plan #151019

Dimensions: 63'4" W x 53'10" D
Levels: 2
Square Footage: 2,642
Main Level Sq. Ft.: 1,407
Upper Level Sq. Ft.: 1,235
Bedrooms: 3
Bathrooms: 2
Foundation: Crawl space, slab; optional full basement plan available for extra fee
Materials list available: Yes
Price Category: F

Images provided by designer/architect.

Majestic French doors at the entry and a balcony overlooking the open foyer set the gracious tone that marks every aspect of this fabulous design.

Features:

• **Great Room:** Step down into this large room with its gas fireplace and atrium door to the patio.

• **Study:** Sliding doors and a 9-ft. ceiling give presence to this room.

• **Dining Room:** Entertaining is easy in this conveniently-placed room with sliding glass doors leading to a rear screened porch as well as the patio.

• **Upper Level:** Bedrooms 2 and 3 share access to a bath and the balcony that overlooks the foyer.

• **Master Suite:** A 10-ft. pan ceiling and French doors give elegance to the spacious suite, and you'll enjoy practicality and luxury in the bath, with its two walk-in closets, a corner whirlpool tub, and split vanities.

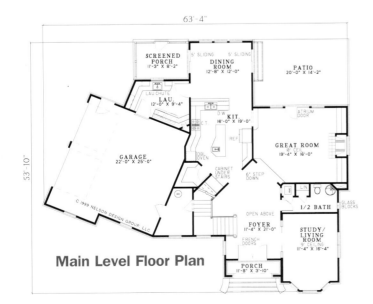

Main Level Floor Plan

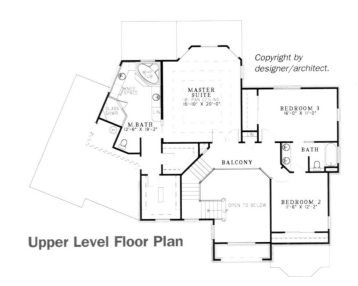

Copyright by designer/architect.

Upper Level Floor Plan

Plan #261012

Dimensions: 58' W x 47' D
Levels: 2
Square Footage: 2,648
Main Level Sq. Ft.: 1,452
Upper Level Sq. Ft.: 1,196
Bedrooms: 4
Bathrooms: 2½
Foundation: Basement
Materials List Available: No
Price Category: F

You'll love the comfort of this spacious, stately home, with its elegant interior design.

Features:

- Dining Room: A stepped ceiling and large window area make this room welcoming.

- Den: This large room is set off from the rest of the house for privacy and quiet.

- Family Room: Highlights in this room include a gas fireplace, large window feature, and pocket doors that can divide it from the living room.

- Kitchen: The center island features a cooktop and an angled snack bar open to the dinette.

- Deck: This large wooden deck opens from the dinette, making it convenient to the kitchen.

- Master Suite: Running the length of the house, this suite includes a walk-in closet and a bath with a whirlpool tub, double vanity, and separate shower.

Rear Elevation

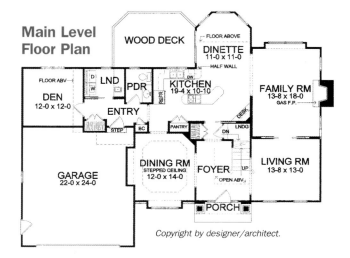

Copyright by designer/architect.

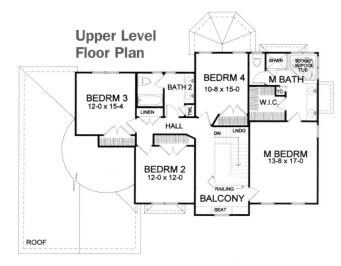

Plan #151011

Dimensions: 59'6" W x 74'4" D
Levels: 2
Square Footage: 3,437
Main Level Sq. Ft.: 2,184
Upper Level Sq. Ft.: 1,253
Bedrooms: 5
Bathrooms: 4
Foundation: Crawl space, slab; optional basement or daylight basement available for an additional fee
Price Category: G

Images provided by designer/architect.

Beauty, comfort, and convenience are yours in this luxurious, split-level home.

Features:

- Ceiling Height: 10 ft. unless otherwise noted.
- Master Suite: The 11-ft. pan ceiling sets the tone for this secluded area, with a lovely bay window that opens onto a rear porch, a pass-through fireplace to the great room, and a sitting room.
- Great Room: The pass-through fireplace makes this spacious room a cozy spot, while the French doors leading to a rear porch make it a perfect spot for entertaining.
- Dining Room: Gracious 8-in. columns set off the entrance to this room.
- Kitchen: An island bar provides an efficient work area that's fitted with a sink.
- Breakfast Room: Open to the kitchen, this room is defined by a bay window and a spiral staircase to the second floor.
- Laundry Room: Large enough to accommodate a folding table, this room can also be fitted with a swinging pet door.
- Play Room: French doors in the children's playroom open onto a balcony where they can continue their games.
- Upper Level Bedrooms: The 9-ft. ceilings on the second story make the rooms feel bright and airy.

Copyright by designer/architect.

Main Level Floor Plan

Upper Level Floor Plan

Plan #151033

Dimensions: 81' W x 93' D
Levels: 2
Square Footage: 5,548
Main Level Sq. Ft.: 3,276
Upper Level Sq. Ft.: 2,272
Bedrooms: 4
Bathrooms: 4
Foundation: Crawl space, slab
Price Category: I

Images provided by designer/architect.

From the exercise room to the home theatre, you'll love the spaciousness and comfort in this beautifully-designed home.

Features:

- Family Room: Everyone can gather around the stone fireplace and built-in media center.

- Hearth Room: Open to the breakfast/kitchen area, this room also has a lovely gas fireplace.

- Computer Areas: Set up work areas in the computer room, as well as the kid's nook.

- Dining Room: Sit by the bay window or go through the swinging door to the adjoining hearth room.

- Master Suite: Somewhat secluded, the bedroom has a vaulted 10-ft. boxed ceiling while the bath features a TV, whirlpool tub, a separate shower, and corner vanities.

- Porch: The rear screened-in porch lets in extra light through skylights on its roof.

Main Level Floor Plan

Upper Level Floor Plan

Plan #121018

Dimensions: 95'9" W x 70'2" D

Levels: 2

Square Footage: 3,950

Main Level Sq. Ft.: 2,839

Upper Level Square Footage: 1,111

Bedrooms: 4

Bathrooms: 2 full, 2 half

Foundation: Basement

Materials List Available: Yes

Price Category: H

Images provided by designer/architect.

A spectacular two-story entry with a floating curved staircase welcomes you home.

Features:

- Ceiling Height: 8 ft. except as noted.
- Den: To the left of the entry, French doors lead to a spacious and stylish den featuring a spider-beamed ceiling.
- Living Room: The volume ceiling, transom windows, and large fireplace evoke a gracious traditional style.

- Gathering Rooms: There is plenty of space for large-group entertaining in the gathering rooms that also feature fireplaces and transom windows.
- Master Suite: Here is the height of luxurious living. The suite features an oversized walk-in closet, tiered ceilings, and a sitting room with fireplace. The pampering bath has a corner whirlpool and shower.
- Garage: An angle minimizes the appearance of the four-car garage.

Main Level Floor Plan

Upper Level Floor Plan

Copyright by designer/architect.

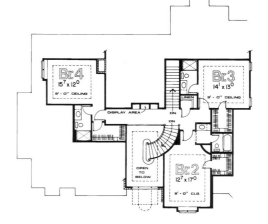

Plan #121004

Dimensions: 55'4" W x 48' D
Levels: 1
Square Footage: 1,666
Bedrooms: 3
Bathrooms: 2
Foundation: Basement
Materials List Available: Yes
Price Category: C

An efficient floor plan and plenty of amenities create a luxurious lifestyle.

Features:

- Ceiling Height: 8 ft. except as noted.

- Entry: Enjoy summer breezes on the porch; then step inside the entry where sidelights and an arched transom create a bright, cheery welcome.

- Great Room: The 10-ft. ceiling and the transom-topped windows flooding the room with light provide a sense of spaciousness. The fireplace adds warmth and style.

- Dining Room: You'll usher your guests into this room located just off the great room.

- Breakfast Area: Also located off the great room, the breakfast area offers another dining option.

- Master Suite: The master bedroom is highlighted by a tray ceiling and a large walk-in closet. Luxuriate in the private bath with its sunlit whirlpool, separate shower, and double vanity.

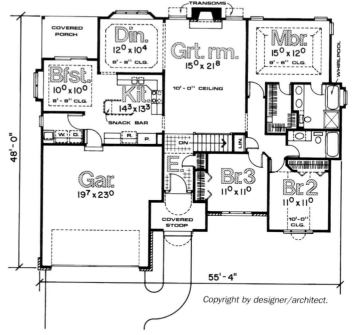

SMARTtip

Carpeting

Install the best underlayment padding available, as well as the highest grade of carpeting you can afford. This will guarantee a feeling of softness beneath your feet and protect your investment for years to come by reducing wear and tear on the carpet.

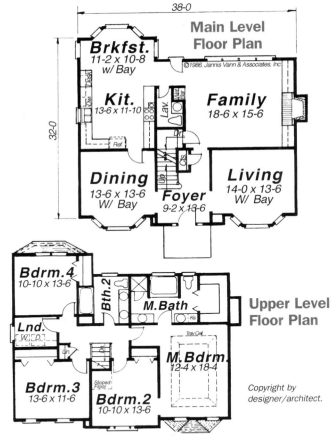

Main Level Floor Plan

38-0

32-0

©1986, Jannis Vann & Associates, Inc.

Brkfst. 11-2 x 10-8 w/ Bay

Kit. 13-6 x 11-10

Lav.

Wet Bar

Family 18-6 x 15-6

Ref.

Dining 13-6 x 13-6 W/ Bay

Up

Dn

Cls.

Foyer 9-2 x 13-6

Living 14-0 x 13-6 W/ Bay

Upper Level Floor Plan

Bdrm.4 10-10 x 13-6

Bth.2

M.Bath

Ks

Lnd. W.C.D.

Tray Ceil.

Bdrm.3 13-6 x 11-6

Sloped Floor

Bdrm.2 10-10 x 13-6

M.Bdrm. 12-4 x 18-4

Copyright by designer/architect.

Plan #141030

Dimensions: 38' W x 32' D

Levels: 2

Square Footage: 2,323

Main Level Sq. Ft.: 1,179

Upper Level Sq. Ft.: 1,144

Bedrooms: 4

Bathrooms: 2½

Foundation: Basement

Materials List Available: Yes

Price Category: E

Images provided by designer/architect.

Upper Level Floor Plan

BDRM. 3 12'-4"x15'-10"

OPEN TO LIVING RM.

BATH 3

TUB RM.

STUDY ALCOVE

BALCONY

CHILDREN'S DEN 11'-6"x15'-6"

BATH 2

OPEN TO FOYER

BDRM. 2 15'-4"x13'-6"

BDRM.4 13'-4"x15'-6"

Copyright by designer/architect.

SUNDECK 20'-0"x12'-0"

PRIVACY DECK 15'-6"x10'-0"

KEEPING RM.

BREAKFAST NOOK

TWO STORY LIVING RM. 20'-0"x15'-6"

SITTING RM.

M.BEDROOM 15'-6"x19'-6"

KITCHEN 12'-4"x14'-0"

M. BATH

OPEN FOYER

LAV.

DINING RM. 15'-4"x13'-6"

LAUND. 9'-6"x10'-6"

LIBRARY 13'-6"x16'-6"

M. CLOSET

GARAGE 21'-4"x20'-8"

Main Level Floor Plan

77'-0"

66'-0"

Plan #141034

Dimensions: 77' W x 66' D

Levels: 2

Square Footage: 3,588

Main Level Sq. Ft.: 2,329

Upper Level Sq. Ft.: 1,259

Bedrooms: 4

Bathrooms: 3 full , 2 half

Foundation: Basement

Materials List Available: Yes

Price Category: H

Images provided by designer/architect.

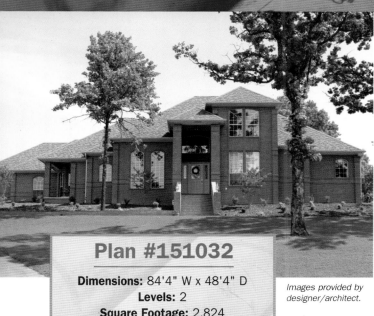

Plan #151032

Dimensions: 84'4" W x 48'4" D
Levels: 2
Square Footage: 2,824
Main Level Sq. Ft.: 2,279
Upper Level Sq. Ft.: 545
Bedrooms: 4
Bathrooms: 3
Foundation: Crawl space, slab (basement option for fee)
Materials List Available: Yes
Price Category: F

Images provided by designer/architect.

Upper Level Floor Plan

Copyright by designer/architect.

Main Level Floor Plan

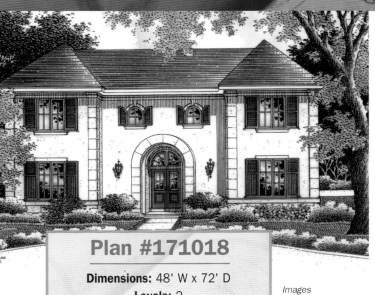

Plan #171018

Dimensions: 48' W x 72' D
Levels: 2
Square Footage: 2,599
Main Level Sq. Ft.: 1,967
Upper Level Sq. Ft.: 632
Bedrooms: 4
Bathrooms: 4
Foundation: Slab, crawl space
Materials List Available: Yes
Price Category: E

Images provided by designer/architect.

Upper Level Floor Plan

Main Level Floor Plan

Plan #121003

Dimensions: 76' W x 55'4" D
Levels: 1
Square Footage: 2,498
Bedrooms: 4
Bathrooms: 3
Foundation: Basement
Materials List Available: Yes
Price Category: E

Repeated arches bring style and distinction to the interior and exterior of this spacious home.

Features:

- Ceiling Height: 8 ft. except as noted.

- Den: A decorative volume ceiling helps make this spacious retreat the perfect place to relax after a long day.

- Formal Living Room: The decorative volume ceiling carries through to the living room that invites large formal gatherings.

- Formal Dining Room: There's plenty of room for all the guests to move into this gracious formal space that also features a decorative volume ceiling.

- Master Suite: Retire to this suite with its glamorous bayed whirlpool, his and her vanities, and a walk-in closet.

- Optional Sitting Room: With the addition of French doors, one of the bedrooms can be converted into a sitting room for the master suite.

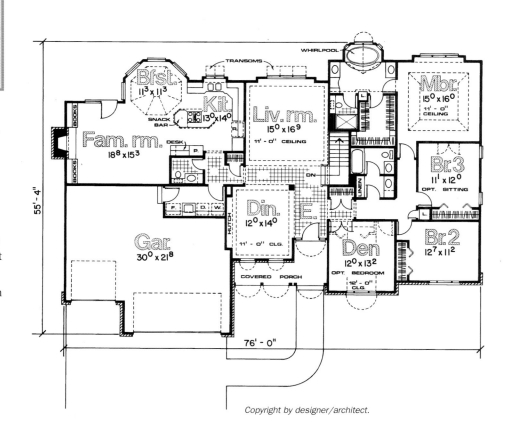

Plan #271063

Dimensions: 61'4" W x 70' D
Levels: 1
Square Footage: 2,572
Bedrooms: 3
Bathrooms: 2
Foundation: Daylight basement
Materials List Available: No
Price Category: D

Images provided by designer/architect.

European detailing gives this home a unique flair and elegant curb appeal.

Features:

- **Entry Rotunda:** This welcoming area opens to a quiet den with a cozy fireplace.

- **Living Room:** This open space leads back to a wall of windows overlooking a backyard deck.

- **Country Kitchen:** A central island and dramatic overhead glass make for a great spot for meal preparation and eating. A four-season porch is nearby.

- **Master Suite:** Double doors and a coffered ceiling enhance this secluded suite. The private bath has everything you can imagine, including a whirlpool tub.

Copyright by designer/architect.

Basement Level Floor Plan

Plan #121007

Dimensions: 74' W x 67'8" D
Levels: 1
Square Footage: 2,512
Bedrooms: 3
Bathrooms: 2½
Foundation: Basement
Materials List Available: Yes
Price Category: E

Images provided by designer/architect.

A series of arches brings grace to this home's interior and exterior.

Features:

- Ceiling Height: 8 ft.

- Formal Dining Room: Tapered columns give this dining room a classical look that lends elegance to any dinner party.

- Great Room: Just beyond the dining room is this light-filled room, with its wall of arched windows and see-through fireplace.

- Hearth Room: On the other side of the fire place you will find this cozy area, with its corner entertainment center.

- Dinette: A gazebo-shaped dinette is the architectural surprise of the house layout.

- Kitchen: This well-conceived working kitchen features a generous center island.

- Garage: With three garage bays you'll never be short of parking space or storage.

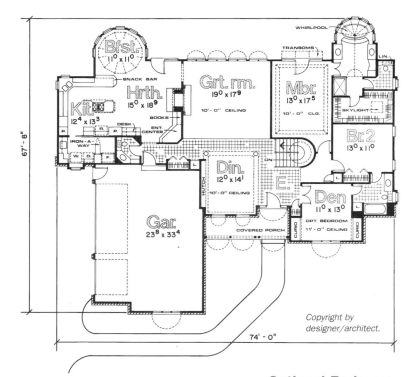

Copyright by designer/architect.

Optional Bedroom

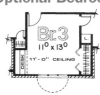

Plan #211010

Dimensions: 81' W x 84' D
Levels: 1
Square Footage: 2,503
Bedrooms: 3
Bathrooms: 2½
Foundation: Slab
Materials List Available: Yes
Price Category: E

Images provided by designer/architect.

A well-designed floor plan makes maximum use of space and creates convenience and comfort.

Features:

- Ceiling Height: 10 ft. unless otherwise noted.

- Living Room: A stepped ceiling gives this living room special architectural interest. There's a full-service wet bar designed to handle parties of any size. When the weather gets warm, step out of the living room into a lovely screened rear porch.

- Master Bedroom: You'll love unwinding at the end of a busy day in this master suite. It's located away from the other bedrooms for more privacy.

- Study: This charming study adjoins the master bedroom. It's the perfect quiet spot to get some work done, surf the internet, or pay the bills.

SMARTtip

Deck Railings

Install caps and post finials to your railings. A rail cap protects the cut ends of the posts from the weather. Finials add another decorative layer to your design, and the styles are endless—ball, chamfered, grooved, and top hat are a few.

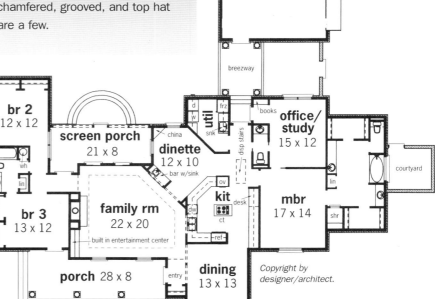

Copyright by designer/architect.

Plan #111051

Dimensions: 72' W x 91' D
Levels: 1
Square Footage: 3,668
Bedrooms: 4
Bathrooms: 2½
Foundation: Crawl space
Materials List Available: No
Price Category: H

You'll find everything you want in this traditional cottage-style home, and it's all on one floor!

Features:

• **Living Room:** Both this room and the dining room are just off the foyer for convenience. A corner fireplace and windows overlooking the backyard give character to the room.

• **Kitchen:** The kitchen island contains a sink and dishwasher as well as a bar. A nearby hall way leads to a half-bath, the utility room, and the two-car garage.

• **Breakfast Area:** Adjacent to the kitchen, the large breakfast area leads to the back porch.

• **Master Suite:** Featuring a walk-in closet and bath with a garden tub, standing shower, and private toilet area, this room opens to the back porch.

• **Additional Bedrooms:** Walk-in closets in two bedrooms and a wide closet with a double door in the third provide good storage space.

Kitchen/Breakfast Area

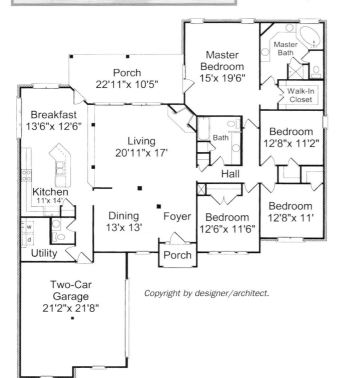

Copyright by designer/architect.

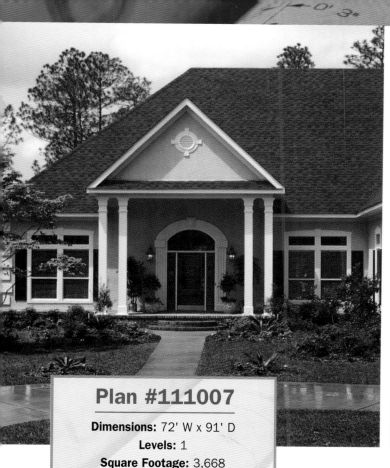

Plan #111007

Dimensions: 72' W x 91' D
Levels: 1
Square Footage: 3,668
Bedrooms: 4
Bathrooms: 3½
Foundation: Crawl space
Materials List Available: No
Price Category: H

This Mediterranean-inspired, traditional manor home offers an enormous amount of space and every amenity you can imagine, but to do it justice, site it on a large lot with wonderful views.

Features:

- **Living Room:** With a fireplace and built-in media center, this room has the potential to become a gathering place for guests as well as family members.

- **Kitchen:** Enjoy this well-designed kitchen which will surely have you whistling as you work.

- **Breakfast Area:** Unusually large for a breakfast room, this space invites a crowd at any time of day. French doors at the back of the room open to the gracious rear porch.

- **Master Suite:** Privacy is guaranteed by the location of this spacious suite. The separate walk-in closets give plenty of storage space, and the master bath features separate vanities as well as a large corner whirlpool tub.

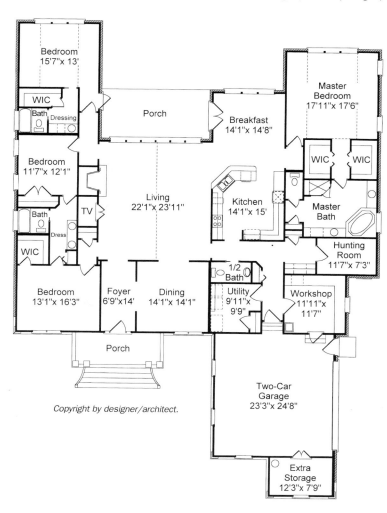

Plan #161001

Dimensions: 67'2" W x 47' D
Levels: 1
Square Footage: 1,782
Bedrooms: 3
Bathrooms: 2
Foundation: Basement
Materials List Available: Yes
Price Category: C

Images provided by designer/architect.

An all-brick exterior displays the solid strength that characterizes this gracious home.

Features:

- Gathering Area: A feeling of spaciousness permeates this gathering area, created by the foyer, great room, and dining room. Multiple windows provide natural light that dances along a sloped ceiling, spilling onto decorative columns and a fireplace.

- Breakfast Area: A continuation of the sloped ceiling leads to this breakfast area, where French doors open to a screened porch.

- Kitchen: An abundance of cabinets and counter space are the hallmarks of this large kitchen, with its easy access to a spacious laundry room and storage area.

- Master Suite: A tray ceiling and spacious walk-in closet in the master bedroom, along with a whirlpool tub and double-bowl vanity in the bathroom, enable you to pamper yourself.

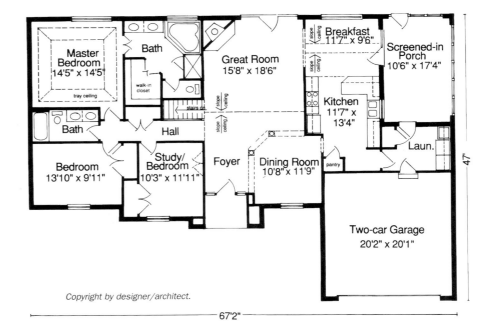

Copyright by designer/architect.

Rear Elevation

Left Side Elevation

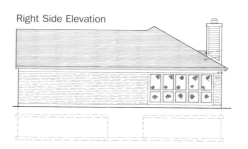

Right Side Elevation

Front View

Great Room / Foyer

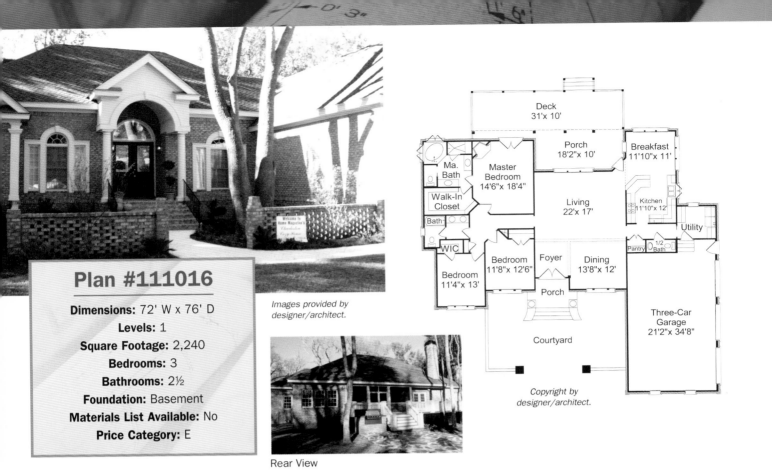

Plan #111016

Dimensions: 72' W x 76' D

Levels: 1

Square Footage: 2,240

Bedrooms: 3

Bathrooms: 2½

Foundation: Basement

Materials List Available: No

Price Category: E

Images provided by designer/architect.

Rear View

Copyright by designer/architect.

Deck 31'x 10'

Porch 18'2"x 10'

Breakfast 11'10"x 11'

Ma. Bath

Master Bedroom 14'6"x 18'4"

Walk-In Closet

Bath

Living 22'x 17'

Kitchen 11'10"x 12'

Utility

WIC

Bedroom 11'8"x 12'6"

Foyer

Dining 13'8"x 12'

Pantry

1/2 Bath

Bedroom 11'4"x 13'

Porch

Three-Car Garage 21'2"x 34'8"

Courtyard

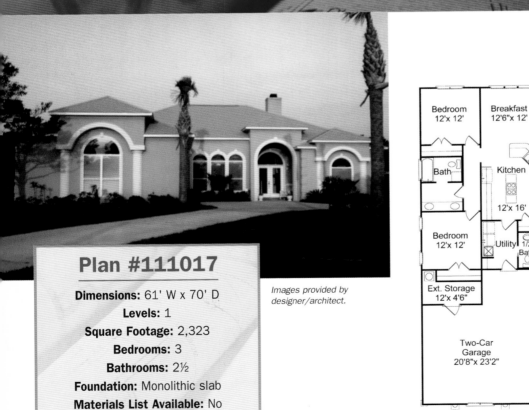

Plan #111017

Dimensions: 61' W x 70' D

Levels: 1

Square Footage: 2,323

Bedrooms: 3

Bathrooms: 2½

Foundation: Monolithic slab

Materials List Available: No

Price Category: E

Images provided by designer/architect.

Copyright by designer/architect.

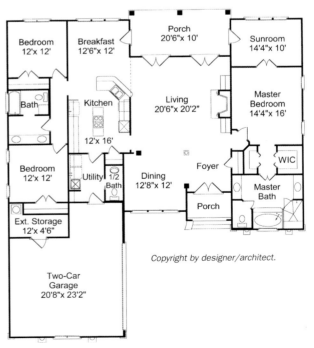

Bedroom 12'x 12'

Breakfast 12'6"x 12'

Porch 20'6"x 10'

Sunroom 14'4"x 10'

Bath

Kitchen 12'x 16'

Living 20'6"x 20'2"

Master Bedroom 14'4"x 16'

Bedroom 12'x 12'

Utility

1/2 Bath

Dining 12'8"x 12'

Foyer

WIC

Ext. Storage 12'x 4'6"

Porch

Master Bath

Two-Car Garage 20'8"x 23'2"

Plan #111029

Dimensions: 65' W x 77' D
Levels: 1½
Square Footage: 2,781
Main Level Sq. Ft.: 2,781
Upper Level Sq. Ft.: 319
Bedrooms: 4
Bathrooms: 3
Foundation: Crawl space
Materials List Available: No
Price Category: F

Images provided by designer/architect.

Upper Level Floor Plan

Copyright by designer/architect.

Main Level Floor Plan

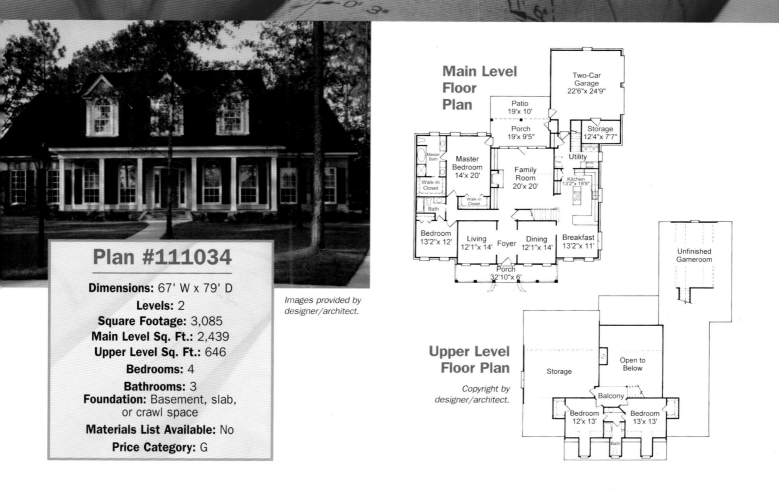

Plan #111034

Dimensions: 67' W x 79' D
Levels: 2
Square Footage: 3,085
Main Level Sq. Ft.: 2,439
Upper Level Sq. Ft.: 646
Bedrooms: 4
Bathrooms: 3
Foundation: Basement, slab, or crawl space
Materials List Available: No
Price Category: G

Images provided by designer/architect.

Main Level Floor Plan

Upper Level Floor Plan

Copyright by designer/architect.

Plan #151007

Dimensions: 54'2" W x 56'2" D

Levels: 1

Square Footage: 1,787

Bedrooms: 3

Bathrooms: 2

Foundation: Basement, crawl space, or slab

Materials List Available: Yes

Price Category: C

This compact, well-designed home is graced with amenities usually reserved for larger houses.

Features:

- Foyer: A 10-ft. ceiling creates unity between the foyer and the dining room just beyond it.

- Dining Room: 8-in. boxed columns welcome you to this dining room, with its 10-ft. ceilings.

- Great Room: The 9-ft. boxed ceiling suits the spacious design. Enjoy the fireplace in the winter and the rear-grilling porch in the summer.

- Breakfast Room: This bright room is a lovely spot for any time of day.

- Master Suite: Double vanities and a large walk-in closet add practicality to this quiet room with a 9-ft. pan ceiling. The master bath includes whirlpool tub with glass block and a separate shower.

- Bedrooms: Bedroom 2 features a bay window, and both rooms are convenient to the bathroom.

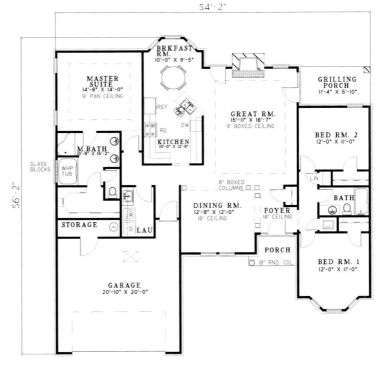

Plan #151008

Dimensions: 42' W x 66'10" D
Square Footage: 1,892
Bedrooms: 3
Bathrooms: 2
Foundation: Crawl space, slab, basement, or daylight basement
Materials List Available: Yes
Price Category: D

Images provided by designer/architect.

This cozy home features a foyer with 8-in. columns and a wide-open welcoming great room and kitchen.

Features:

- **Great Room/Kitchen:** Enjoy the fireplace in the great room while seated at the kitchen island or in the breakfast room. Access to the rear patio and covered porch makes this room a natural spot for family as well as for entertaining.

- **Dining Room:** For a formal evening, entertain in the dining room with its grand entrance through elegant 8-in. columns.

- **Master Suite:** Luxuriate in the privacy of the master suite with its 10-ft. ceiling and private access to the covered porch. The master bath pampers you with a whirlpool tub, separate vanities, a shower, and a walk-in closet.

- **Bedrooms:** A bedroom with walk-in closet and private access to full bath is a cozy retreat, while the other bedroom makes room for one more!

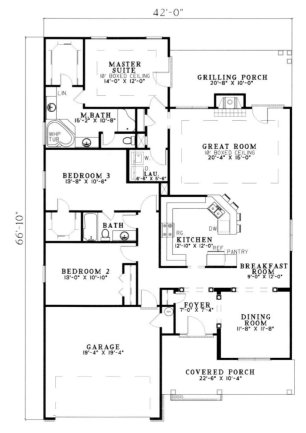

Copyright by designer/architect.

Plan #151003

Dimensions: 51'6" W x 52'4" D
Levels: 1
Square Footage: 1,680
Bedrooms: 3
Bathrooms: 2
Foundation: Basement, slab, or daylight basement.
Materials List Available: Yes
Price Category: C

A lovely front porch, bay windows, and dormers add sparkle to this country-style home.

Features:

- Great Room: Perfect for entertaining, this room features a tray ceiling, wet bar, and a quiet screened porch nearby.

- Dining Room: This bayed dining room facing the front porch is cozy yet roomy enough for family parties during the holidays.

- Kitchen: This eat-in kitchen also faces the front and is ideal for preparing meals for any occasion.

- Master Suite: The tray ceiling here gives an added feeling of space, while the distance from the other bedrooms allows for all the privacy you'll need.

Plan #111041

Dimensions: 34' W x 32' D

Levels: 2

Square Footage: 1,743

Main Level Sq. Ft.: 912

Upper Level Sq. Ft.: 831

Bedrooms: 3

Bathrooms: 3

Foundation: Pier

Materials List Available: No

Price Category: C

You'll love the way this vacation home can accommodate a crowd or make a small family feel cozy and comfortable.

Features:

- **Living Area:** This easy-care living area is perfect for those times when you want to get away from it all—including extra housework.

- **Kitchen:** This kitchen is large enough for friends and family to chat with the cook or help with the dishes after a meal. You'll use the breakfast bar all day long for setting out drinks and snacks.

- **Master Suite:** Relax on the balcony off this master suit, and luxuriate in the bath with double vanities, a whirlpool tub, and a walk-in closet.

- **Study:** Adjacent to the master suite, this room lets you catch up on reading in a quiet spot.

- **Porch:** Let guests spill onto this convenient porch when you're hosting a party, or use it as outdoor space where the children can play.

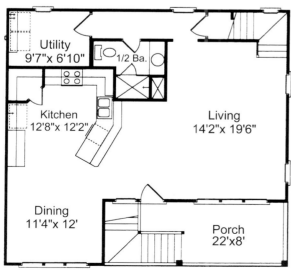

Main Level Floor Plan

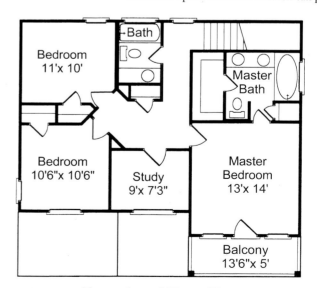

Upper Level Floor Plan

Plan #111010

Dimensions: 34' W x 38' D

Levels: 3

Square Footage: 1,804

Main Level Sq. Ft.: 731

Upper Level Sq. Ft.: 935

Third Level Sq.Ft.: 138

Bedrooms: 3

Bathrooms: 3

Foundation: Piers

Materials List Available: No

Price Category: D

Images provided by designer/architect.

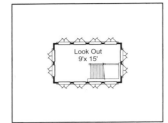

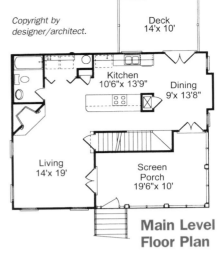

Copyright by designer/architect.

Deck 14'x 10'

Kitchen 10'6"x 13'9"

Dining 9'x 13'8"

Living 14'x 19'

Screen Porch 19'6"x 10'

Main Level Floor Plan

Third Level Floor Plan

Look Out 9'x 15'

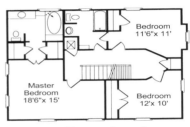

Bedroom 11'6"x 11'

Master Bedroom 18'6"x 15'

Bedroom 12'x 10'

Upper Level Floor Plan

Plan #111021

Dimensions: 34' W x 44'0" D

Levels: 2

Square Footage: 2,221

Main Level Sq. Ft.: 1,307

Upper Level Sq. Ft.: 914

Bedrooms: 4

Bathrooms: 3

Foundation: Pier

Materials List Available: No

Price Category: E

Images provided by designer/architect.

Bedroom 12'x 11'

Bedroom 12'x 11'

Kitchen 12'x 13'

Living 21'x 19'2"

Dining 12'4"x 13'6"

Porch 21'x 8'

Main Level Floor Plan

Upper Level Floor Plan

Copyright by designer/architect.

Study 10'x 10'

Sitting Area 10'9"x 10'

Master Bedroom 12'x 16'

Bedroom 12'4"x 13'

Balcony 21'x 8'

Plan #111040

Dimensions: 37' W x 52' D

Levels: 2

Square Footage: 1,650

Main Level Sq. Ft.: 1,122

Upper Level Sq. Ft.: 528

Bedrooms: 4

Bathrooms: 2

Foundation: Pier

Materials List Available: No

Price Category: C

Images provided by designer/architect.

Main Level Floor Plan

Upper Level Floor Plan

Copyright by designer/architect.

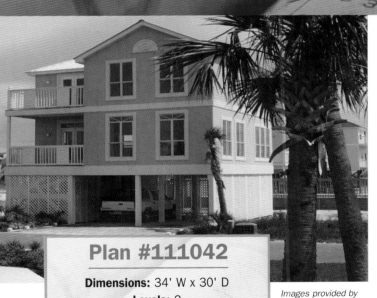

Plan #111042

Dimensions: 34' W x 30' D

Levels: 2

Square Footage: 1,779

Main Level Sq. Ft.: 907

Upper Level Sq. Ft.: 872

Bedrooms: 3

Bathrooms: 2½

Foundation: Pier

Materials List Available: No

Price Category: C

Images provided by designer/architect.

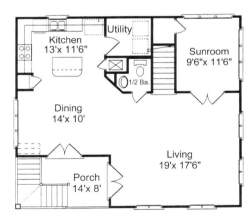

Main Level Floor Plan

Upper Level Floor Plan

Copyright by designer/architect.

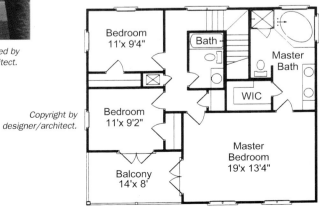

Plan #181120

Dimensions: 32' W x 40' D
Levels: 2
Square Footage: 1,480
Main Level Sq. Ft.: 1,024
Second Level Sq. Ft.: 456
Bedrooms: 2
Bathrooms: 2
Foundation: Basement
Materials List Available: Yes
Price Category: B

Images provided by designer/architect.

Escape to this charming all-season vacation home with lots of view-capturing windows.

Features:

- Ceiling Height: 8 ft. unless otherwise noted.
- Living/Dining Area: The covered back porch opens into this large, inviting combined area. Its high ceiling adds to the sense of spaciousness.
- Family Room: After relaxing in front of the fireplace that warms this family room, family and guests can move outside onto the porch to watch the sun set.
- Kitchen: Light streams through a triple window in this well-designed kitchen. It's conveniently located next to the dining area and features a center island with a breakfast bar and double sinks.
- Master Suite: This first floor suite is located in the front of the house and is enhanced by its large walk-through closet and the adjoining private bath.

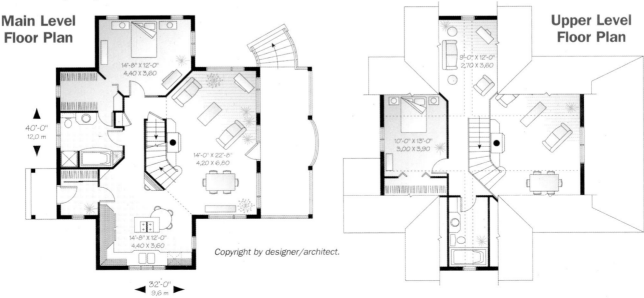

Main Level Floor Plan

Upper Level Floor Plan

Copyright by designer/architect.

Plan #291005

Dimensions: 16' W x 36'10" D

Levels: 2

Square Footage: 896

Main Level Sq. Ft.: 448

Upper Level Sq. Ft.: 448

Bedrooms: 2

Bathrooms: 1½

Foundation: Crawl space

Materials List Available: No

Price Category: A

You'll be as charmed by the interior of this small home as you are by the wood-shingled roof, scroll-saw rake detailing, and board-and-batten siding on the exterior.

Features:

• **Porch:** Relax on this porch, which is the ideal spot for a couple of rockers or a swing.

• **Entryway:** Double doors reveal an open floor plan that makes everyone feel welcome.

• **Living Room:** Create a cozy nook by the windows here.

• **Kitchen:** Designed for convenience, this kitchen has ample counter space as well as enough storage to suit your needs. The stairway to the upper floor and the half-bath divide the kitchen from the living and dining areas.

• **Upper Level:** 9-ft. ceilings give a spacious feeling to the two bedrooms and full bathroom that you'll find on this floor.

Images provided by designer/architect.

Main Level Floor Plan

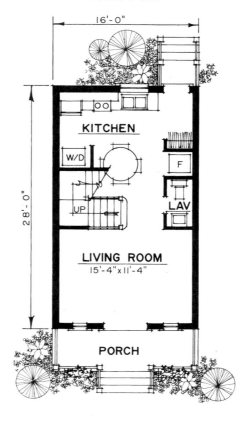

Upper Level Floor Plan

Copyright by designer/architect.

Plan #111049

Dimensions: 60' W x 50' D

Levels: 2

Square Footage: 2,205

Main Level Sq. Ft.: 1,552

Upper Level Sq. Ft.: 653

Bedrooms: 3

Bathrooms: 2

Foundation: Pier

Materials list available: No

Price Code: E

This stately beach home offers many waterfront views.

Images provided by designer/architect.

Features:

- Ceiling Height: 8 ft.

- Entrance: This home features raised stairs, with two wings that lead to the central staircase.

- Front Porch: This area is 110 square feet.

- Living Room: This huge room features a wood-burning fireplace and large windows, and it leads to the rear covered porch and a spacious deck. It is also open to the kitchen and dining area.

- Kitchen: This room has ample counter space

and an island that is open to the dining area.

- Master Suite: This upper level room has a large balcony. This balcony is a perfect place to watch the sun set over the beach. This room also a walk-in closet.

- Master Bath: This room has all the modern amenities, with separate vanities, large corner tub and walk-in shower.

- Lower Level Bedrooms: These rooms each have a walk in closet and share a bathroom.

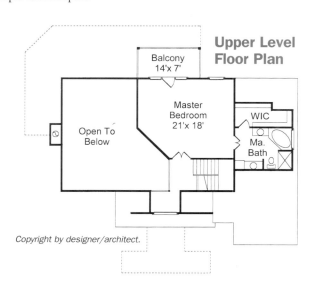

Copyright by designer/architect.

Rear View

Removing Carpet Stains in Kid's Rooms

Kids will be kids, and so accidents will happen. The cardinal rule for removing a stain from carpeting is to always clean up a spot or spill immediately, using white cloths or paper towels. Blot, never rub or scrub, a stain. Work from the outer edge in toward the center of the spot, and then follow up with clean water to remove any residue of the stain. Blot up any moisture remaining from the cleanup by layering white paper towels over the spot and weighing them down with a heavy object.

To remove a water-soluble stain, blot as much of it as possible with white paper towels that have been dampened with cold water. If necessary, mix a solution of ¼ teaspoon of clear, mild, nonbleach laundry detergent with 32 ounces of water, and then spray it lightly onto the spot. Blot it repeatedly with white paper towels. Rinse it with a spray of clean water; then blot it dry.

To treat soils made by urine or vomit, mix equal parts of white vinegar and water, and blot it onto the spot with white paper towels; then clean with detergent solution.

To remove an oil-based stain, blot as much of it as you can; then apply a nonflammable spot remover made specifically for grease, oil, or tar to a clean, white paper towel. Don't apply the remover directly to the carpet, or you may damage the backing. Blot the stain with the treated towel. Wear rubber gloves to protect your hands. Use this method for stains caused by crayons, cosmetics, ink, paint, and shoe polish.

For spots made by cola, chocolate, or blood, apply a solution of 1 tablespoon of ammonia and 1 cup of water to the stain; then go over it with the detergent solution. Do not use ammonia on a wool carpet. Try an acid stain remover—lemon juice or white vinegar diluted with water.

To remove chewing gum or candle wax, try freezing the spot with ice cubes, and then gently scrape off the gum or wax with a blunt object. Follow this with a vacuuming. If this doesn't work, apply a commercial gum remover to the area, following the manufacturer's directions.

Main Level Floor Plan

Copyright by designer/architect.

MBr 17-0x13-10

Deck

Kitchen 11-4x12-0

Great Rm 13-7x18-8 Sunken vaulted

Dining 11-4x12-0

Garage 18-4x21-4

35'-0"

56'-0"

Br 3 12-4x12-5

Br 2 11-0x12-5

open to below

Br 4 11-4x13-3

Upper Level Floor Plan

Plan #321085

Dimensions: 35' W x 56' D

Levels: 2

Square Footage: 1,985

Main Level Sq. Ft.: 1,114

Upper Level Sq. Ft.: 871

Bedrooms: 4

Bathrooms: 3½

Foundation: Basement

Materials List Available: Yes

Price Category: D

Images provided by designer/architect.

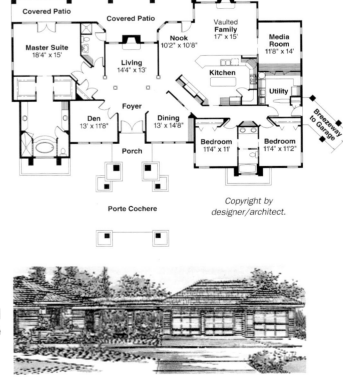

Patio

Covered Patio

Covered Patio

Master Suite 18'4" x 15'

Nook 10'2" x 10'8'

Vaulted Family 17' x 15'

Media Room 11'8" x 14'

Living 14'4" x 13'

Kitchen

Utility

Foyer

Den 13' x 11'8"

Dining 13' x 14'8"

Bedroom 11'4" x 11'

Bedroom 11'4" x 11'2"

Breezeway to Garage

Porch

Porte Cochere

Copyright by designer/architect.

Plan #361001

Dimensions: 81' W x 68'11" D

Levels: 1

Square Footage: 3,055

Bedrooms: 3

Bathrooms: 3

Foundation: Basement, crawl space

Materials List Available: No

Price Category: G

Images provided by designer/architect.

Optional Garage

Plan #181063

Dimensions: 55' W x 41' D

Levels: 2

Square Footage: 2,037

Main Level Sq. Ft.: 1,347

Upper Level Sq. Ft.: 690

Bedrooms: 4

Bathrooms: 2

Foundation: Full basement

Materials List Available: Yes

Price Category: D

Images provided by designer/architect.

Main Level Floor Plan

Upper Level Floor Plan

Copyright by designer/architect.

Plan #321083

Dimensions: 49' W x 42' D

Levels: 2

Square Footage: 2,336

Main Level Sq. Ft.: 1,291

Upper Level Sq. Ft.: 1,045

Bedrooms: 4

Bathrooms: 2½

Foundation: Basement

Materials List Available: Yes

Price Category: E

Images provided by designer/architect.

Main Level Floor Plan

Upper Level Floor Plan

Copyright by designer/architect.

Plan #271087

Dimensions: 43'5½" W x 43'5½" D
Levels: 2
Square Footage: 2,734
Main Level Sq. Ft.: 1,564
Basement Level Sq. Ft.: 1,170
Bedrooms: 4
Bathrooms: 3
Foundation: Daylight basement or crawl space
Materials List Available: No
Price Category: F

Images provided by designer/architect.

This octagonal home offers a choice of exterior finish: wood or stucco.

Features:

- Entry: A seemingly endless deck leads to the main entry, which includes a coat closet.
- Living Room: A fireplace enhances this spacious room, which offers great outdoor views, plus deck access via sliding glass doors.
- Master Suite: At the end of a hallway, the quiet master bedroom boasts a private bath.
- Lower Level: The basement includes a versatile general area, which could be a nice playroom. A handy den, an extra bedroom and a two-car garage round out this level.

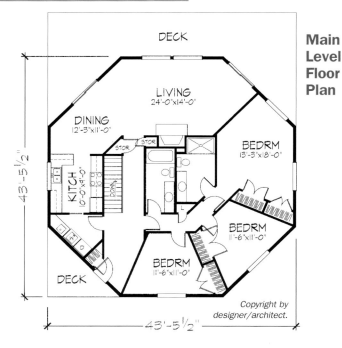

Main Level Floor Plan

Basement Level Floor Plan

Plan #271085

Dimensions: 55' W x 66' D
Levels: 2
Square Footage: 1,541
Main Level Sq. Ft.: 1,028
Upper Level Sq. Ft.: 513
Bedrooms: 3
Bathrooms: 2
Foundation: Basement, crawl space
Materials List Available: Yes
Price Category: C

The soaring, wing-like roof of this plan makes a unique statement and offers fabulous scenic views.

Features:

- Conversation Pit: This central, sunken conversation pit is anchored by a massive stone fireplace and will be a popular gathering place at any time of the day.

- Living Room: This area is augmented by a high ceiling and provides outdoor views through tall windows.

- Dining Room: Enjoy all of your meals in this versatile space. Sliding glass doors allow you to step onto the wraparound deck for dessert and coffee under the stars.

- Kitchen: The U-shaped design of this efficient work space keeps everything you need at your fingertips. A nearby laundry alcove facilitates multitasking.

- Bedrooms: One bedroom has deck access, while another overlooks the living room.

Images provided by designer/architect.

Main Level Floor Plan

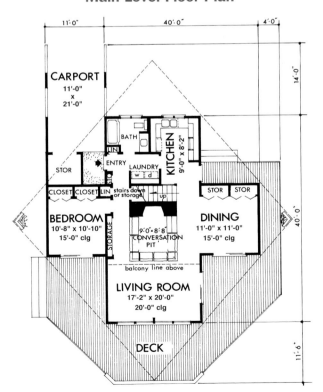

Upper Level Floor Plan

Copyright by designer/architect.

Main Level Floor Plan

UTILITY · HW · PR · UP
D · W · F
PANTRY
KITCHEN 10'-0" x 8'-3"
F.P.
LIVING ROOM 12'-0"x13'-8"
OPEN TO ABOVE
DINING ROOM 10'-2" x 9'-0"
ENTRY · PORCH
24'-0"
25'-4"
1'-4"

Images provided by designer/architect.

Upper Level Floor Plan

LOFT 12'-0"x8'-0" (8'-0" CLG)
DN
OPEN TO ABOVE
RIDGE BEAM
OPEN TO BELOW
TUB/SHWR · BATH
MASTER BEDROOM 12'-0"x11'-0" (12'-0" CEILING)
PLANT SHELF
W.I.C.

Copyright by designer/architect.

Plan #291006

Dimensions: 24' W x 25'4" D

Levels: 2

Square Footage: 965

Main Level Sq. Ft.: 547

Upper Level Sq. Ft.: 418

Bedrooms: 1

Bathrooms: 1½

Foundation: Crawl space

Materials List Available: No

Price Category: A

Upper Level Floor Plan

5'-0" KNEEWALL
CEILING CLIP
LOFT 12'-4"x8'-0"
DN
WOOD RAIL
EXPOSED BEAM
VAULTED CEILING
BATH
MASTER BED 13'-2"x11'-0" CEILING CLIP
W.I.C.
5'-0" KNEEWALL

UTIL · WH · PR · UP
D · W · F
KITCHEN 11'-0"x8'-4"
FP
LIVING ROOM 13'-0"x13'-8"
OPEN TO ABOVE
DINING 15'-0"x9'-0"
ENTRY
PORCH 24'-0"x7'-0"
24'-0"
31'-0"

Main Level Floor Plan

Copyright by designer/architect.

Plan #291007

Dimensions: 24' W x 31' D

Levels: 2

Square Footage: 1,065

Main Level Sq. Ft.: 576

Upper Level Sq. Ft.: 489

Bedrooms: 1

Bathrooms: 1½

Foundation: Crawl space

Materials List Available: No

Price Category: B

Images provided by designer/architect.

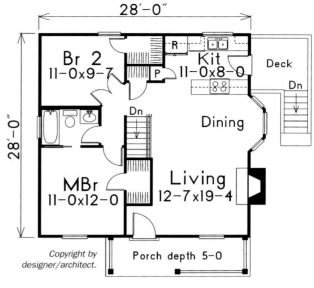

28'-0"

28'-0"

Br 2
11-0x9-7

Kit
11-0x8-0

Deck

Dn

P
R

Dn

Dining

MBr
11-0x12-0

Living
12-7x19-4

Porch depth 5-0

Images provided by designer/architect.

Copyright by designer/architect.

Plan #321025

Dimensions: 28' W x 28' D

Levels: 1

Square Footage: 914

Bedrooms: 2

Bathrooms: 1

Foundation: Daylight basement

Materials List Available: Yes

Price Category: A

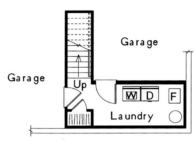

Garage

Garage

Up

W D F

Laundry

Optional Basement Level Floor Plan

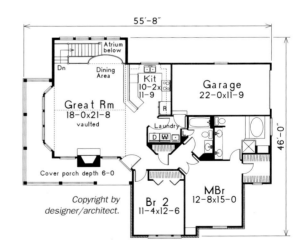

55'-8"

Atrium below

Dn

Dining Area

Kit
10-2x11-9

Garage
22-0x11-9

Great Rm
18-0x21-8
vaulted

R

46'-0"

Laundry
D W

Cover porch depth 6-0

Br 2
11-4x12-6

MBr
12-8x15-0

Copyright by designer/architect.

Plan #321035

Dimensions: 55'8" W x 46' D

Levels: 1

Square Footage: 1,384

Bedrooms: 2

Bathrooms: 2

Foundation: Basement

Materials List Available: Yes

Price Category: B

Images provided by designer/architect.

Rear View

Up

Patio

Family Rm
25-0x21-4

Unexcavated

Unfinished Basement

Optional Basement Level Floor Plan

Plan #181081

Dimensions: 58' W x 33' D

Levels: 2

Square Footage: 2,350

Main Level Sq. Ft.: 1,107

Second Level Sq. Ft.: 1,243

Bedrooms: 3

Bathrooms: 2½

Foundation: Basement

Materials List Available: Yes

Price Category: E

Images provided by designer/architect.

This traditional country home features a wrap-around porch and a second-floor balcony.

Features:

- Ceiling Height: 8 ft. unless otherwise noted.

- Family Room: Double French doors and a fireplace in this inviting front room enhance the beauty and warmth of the home's open floor plan.

- Kitchen: You'll love working in this bright and convenient kitchen. The breakfast bar is the perfect place to gather for informal meals.

- Master Suite: You'll look forward to retiring to this elegant upstairs suite at the end of a busy day. The suite features a private bath with separate shower and tub, as well as dual vanities.

- Secondary Bedrooms: Two family bedrooms share a full bath with a third room that opens onto the balcony.

- Basement: An unfinished full basement provides plenty of storage and the potential to add additional finished living space.

Main Level Floor Plan

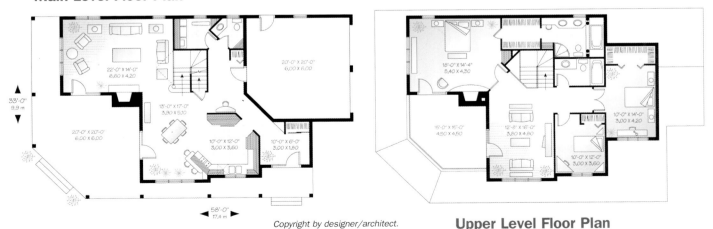

Copyright by designer/architect.

Upper Level Floor Plan

Plan #181109

Dimensions: 26' W x 30' D
Levels: 2
Square Footage: 1295
Main Level Sq. Ft.: 772
Second Level Sq. Ft.: 523
Bedrooms: 2
Bathrooms: 2
Foundation: Basement
Materials List Available: Yes
Price Category: B

This charming home with beautiful windows is the perfect starter or retirement home.

Images provided by designer/architect.

Features:

• Ceiling Height: 8 ft. unless otherwise noted.

• Living Room: This front living room is the centerpiece of a well-designed floor plan that makes excellent use of space. The living room itself has plenty of room for family and friends to gather and relax.

• Kitchen: This bright and efficient kitchen includes an eat-in area that is perfect for informal dining. The eating area flows easily into the living room.

• Guest Bedroom: Guests will stay in comfort thanks to this pleasant downstairs guest room with its own closet and full bath.

• Master Suite: Retire at the end of the day in comfort and privacy in this upstairs master suite, which features a nicely appointed full bathroom and a walk-in closet.

• Mezzanine: This lovely balcony is open to the family room below. It provides space for a reading area or a home office.

Main Level Floor Plan

30'-0"
9,0 m

26'-0"
7,8 m

12'-0" X 11'-4"
3,60 X 3,40

14'-8" X 13'-4"
4,40 X 4,00

10'-0" X 26'-8"
3,00 X 8,00

10'-0" X 16'-8"
3,00 X 5,00

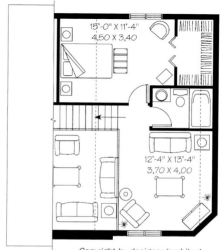

Upper Level Floor Plan

15'-0" X 11'-4"
4,50 X 3,40

12'-4" X 13'-4"
3,70 X 4,00

Copyright by designer/architect.

Plan #181122

Dimensions: 62' W x 36'4" D

Levels: 2

Square Footage: 3,105

Main Level Sq. Ft.: 1,470

Upper Level Sq. Ft.: 1,635

Bedrooms: 4

Bathrooms: 3

Foundation: Finished basement

Materials List Available: Yes

Price Category: G

Images provided by designer/architect.

Main Level Floor Plan

Upper Level Floor Plan

Copyright by designer/architect.

Plan #181125

Dimensions: 39'8" W x 36'8" D

Levels: 3

Square Footage: 2,392

Main Level Sq. Ft.: 967

Upper Level Sq. Ft.: 1,076

Third Level Sq. Ft.: 349

Bedrooms: 4

Bathrooms: 3½

Foundation: Pillars

Materials List Available: Yes

Price Category: E

Images provided by designer/architect.

Main Level Floor Plan

Top Level Floor Plan

Copyright by designer/architect.

Upper Level Floor Plan

Plan #361007

Dimensions: 42' W x 40' D
Levels: 2
Square Footage: 1,306
Main Level Sq. Ft.: 1,047
Upper Level Sq. Ft.: 259
Bedrooms: 3
Bathrooms: 2
Foundation: Crawl space
Materials List Available: No
Price Category: B

Images provided by designer/architect.

Copyright by designer/architect.

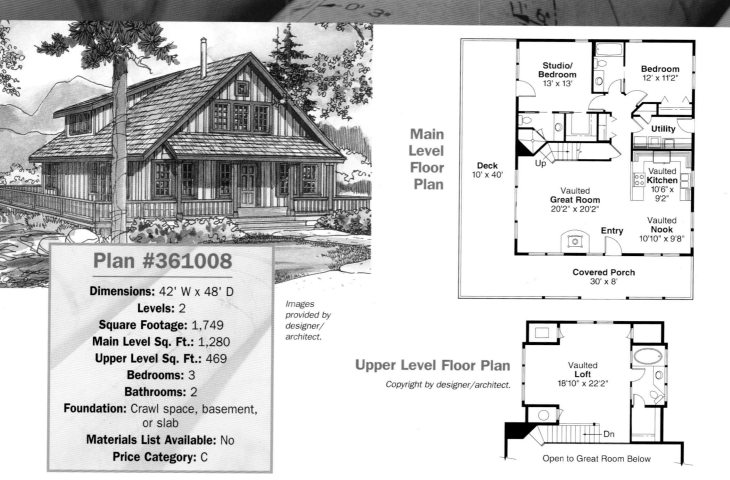

Plan #361008

Dimensions: 42' W x 48' D
Levels: 2
Square Footage: 1,749
Main Level Sq. Ft.: 1,280
Upper Level Sq. Ft.: 469
Bedrooms: 3
Bathrooms: 2
Foundation: Crawl space, basement, or slab
Materials List Available: No
Price Category: C

Images provided by designer/architect.

Copyright by designer/architect.

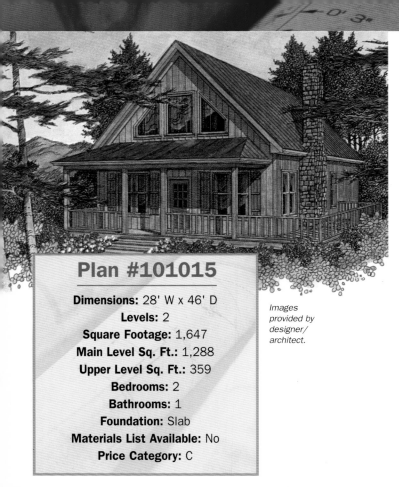

Main Level Floor Plan

BEDROOM 1
11'-10" x 10'-0"

BEDROOM 2
11'-4" x 10'-0"

46'-0"
+ PORCH

LINEN

PANTRY

GREAT ROOM
27'-4" x 29'-5"
20' HIGH CEILING

DECK/PATIO
11'-6" x 18'-8"

VAULT

VAULT

DECK
7'-6" x 36'-0"

PORCH
24'-4" x 7'-6"

◄ 28'-0" ►

LOFT
23'-1" x 15'-6"

VAULT

VAULT

40" KNEE WALL

DN

Upper Level Floor Plan

OPEN BELOW
20' HIGH CEILING

VAULT

VAULT

Images provided by designer/architect.

Copyright by designer/architect.

Plan #101015

Dimensions: 28' W x 46' D
Levels: 2
Square Footage: 1,647
Main Level Sq. Ft.: 1,288
Upper Level Sq. Ft.: 359
Bedrooms: 2
Bathrooms: 1
Foundation: Slab
Materials List Available: No
Price Category: C

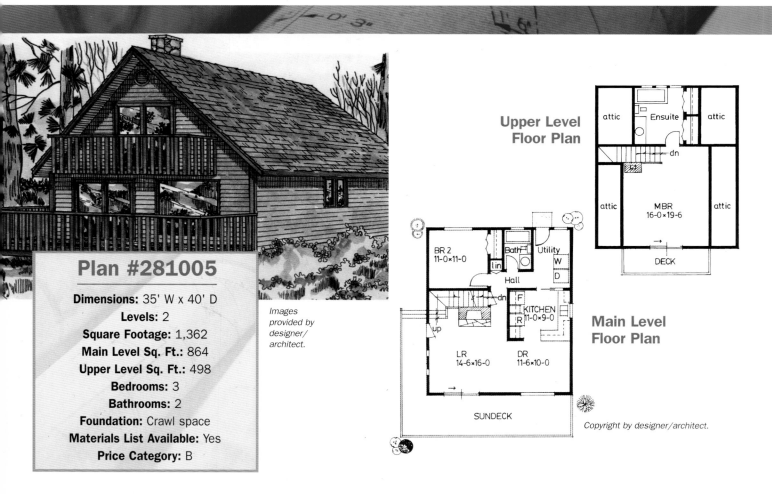

Upper Level Floor Plan

attic

Ensuite

attic

dn

attic

MBR
16-0 x 19-6

attic

DECK

Main Level Floor Plan

BR 2
11-0 x 11-0

Bath

Utility

lin

W
D

Hall

KITCHEN
11-0 x 9-0

F
R

up

dn

LR
14-6 x 16-0

DR
11-6 x 10-0

SUNDECK

Images provided by designer/architect.

Copyright by designer/architect.

Plan #281005

Dimensions: 35' W x 40' D
Levels: 2
Square Footage: 1,362
Main Level Sq. Ft.: 864
Upper Level Sq. Ft.: 498
Bedrooms: 3
Bathrooms: 2
Foundation: Crawl space
Materials List Available: Yes
Price Category: B

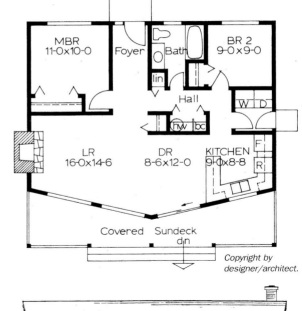

Images provided by
designer/architect.

Copyright by
designer/architect.

Plan #281010

Dimensions: 34' W x 31' D

Levels: 1

Square Footage: 884

Bedrooms: 2

Bathrooms: 1

Foundation: Crawl space

Materials List Available: Yes

Price Category: A

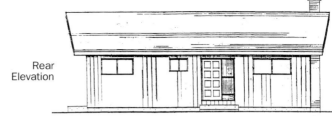

Rear
Elevation

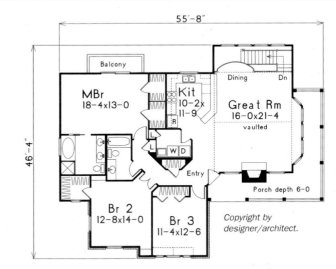

Copyright by
designer/architect.

Plan #321009

Dimensions: 55'8" W x 46'4" D

Levels: 1

Square Footage: 2,295

Bedrooms: 3

Bathrooms: 2

Foundation: Basement

Materials List Available: Yes

Price Category: E

Images provided by
designer/architect.

Rear View

Optional Basement
Level Floor Plan

Plan #111027

Dimensions: 48' W x 57' D

Levels: 2

Square Footage: 2,601

Main Level Sq. Ft.: 1,623

Upper Level Sq. Ft.: 978

Bedrooms: 3

Bathrooms: 2

Foundation: Pier

Materials List Available: No

Price Category: F

Images provided by designer/architect.

Main Level Floor Plan

Dining 12'8"x 12'
Bedroom 13'x 12'
Living 18'6"x 22'
Bedroom 13'x 11'9"
Porch
Deck

Upper Level Floor Plan

Copyright by designer/architect.

Master Bedroom 18'6"x 20'
Study 13'x 15'6"
Balcony

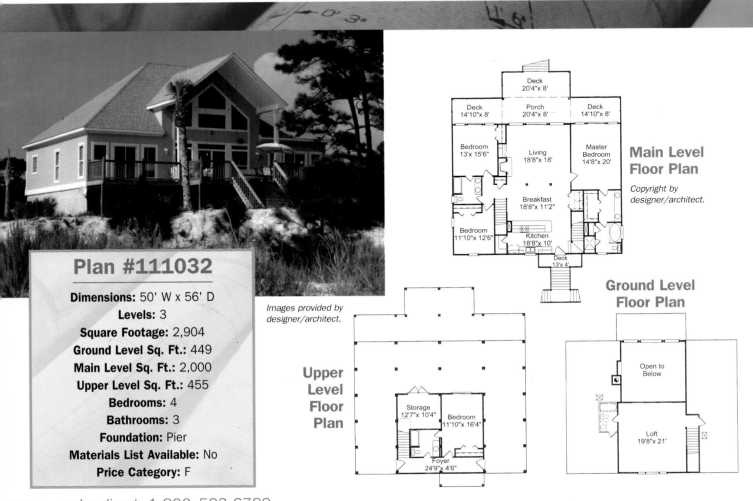

Plan #111032

Dimensions: 50' W x 56' D

Levels: 3

Square Footage: 2,904

Ground Level Sq. Ft.: 449

Main Level Sq. Ft.: 2,000

Upper Level Sq. Ft.: 455

Bedrooms: 4

Bathrooms: 3

Foundation: Pier

Materials List Available: No

Price Category: F

Main Level Floor Plan

Copyright by designer/architect.

Deck 20'4"x 8'
Deck 14'10"x 8'
Porch 20'4"x 8'
Deck 14'10"x 8'
Bedroom 13'x 15'6"
Living 18'8"x 18'
Master Bedroom 14'8"x 20'
Breakfast 18'8"x 11'2"
Bedroom 11'10"x 12'6"
Kitchen 18'8"x 10'
Deck 13'x 4'

Images provided by designer/architect.

Upper Level Floor Plan

Storage 12'7"x 10'4"
Bedroom 11'10"x 16'4"
Foyer 24'9"x 4'6"

Ground Level Floor Plan

Open to Below
Loft 19'8"x 21'

Images provided by designer/architect.

Plan #181133

Dimensions: 38' W x 40' D
Levels: 2
Square Footage: 1,832
Main Level Sq. Ft.: 1,212
Second Level Sq. Ft. 620
Bedrooms: 3
Bathrooms: 2
Foundation: Basement
Materials List Available: Yes
Price Category: D

You'll enjoy sunshine indoors and out with a wraparound deck and windows all around.

Features:

- Ceiling Height: 8 ft.

- Family Room: Family and friends will be drawn to this large sunny room. Curl up with a good book before the beautiful see-through fireplace.

- Screened Porch: This porch shares the see-through fireplace with the family room so you can enjoy an outside fire on cool summer nights.

- Master Suite: This romantic first-floor master suite offers a large walk-in closet and a luxurious private bathroom enhanced by dual vanities.

- Secondary Bedrooms: Upstairs you'll find two generous bedrooms with ample closet space. These bedrooms share a full bathroom.

- Basement: This large walkout basement with large glass door is perfectly suited for future expansion.

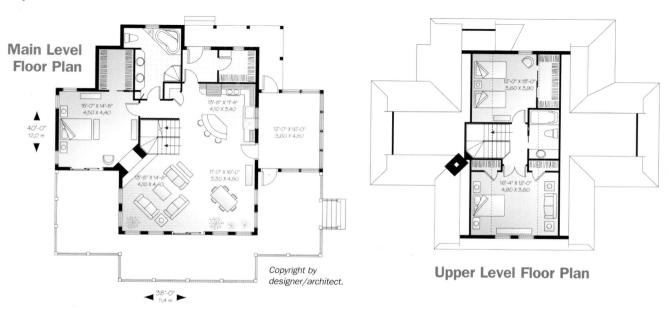

Main Level Floor Plan

Upper Level Floor Plan

Copyright by designer/architect.

Plan #181108

Dimensions: 26' W x 48' D

Levels: 2

Square Footage: 1,484

Main Level Sq. Ft.: 908

Second Level Sq. Ft.: 576

Bedrooms: 3

Bathrooms: 2

Foundation: Basement

Materials List Available: Yes

Price Category: B

This delightful home is well suited to a waterfront property with great views.

Features:

- Ceiling Height: 8 ft.

- Sunroom: This elevated front sunroom fills the house with warmth and is the perfect place in which to watch the sun set over a lake. A lovely deck adjoins the sunroom.

- Family Room: From the sunroom, walk through sliding doors into this inviting room with angled wood-burning fireplace.

- Dining Room: Also accessible from the sunroom, this dining room shares the family room fireplace. The dining room and the family room both get plenty of light from full-length multi-pane windows.

- Kitchen: This kitchen has a breakfast bar at the large center island, double sinks, and a pantry.

- Master Suite: Upstairs you'll find this master getaway with walk-in closet, luxurious full bathroom, and whirlpool tub.

Main Level Floor Plan

Upper Level Floor Plan

Images provided by designer/architect.

Plan #181128

Dimensions: 36' W x 36' D
Levels: 2
Square Footage: 1,634
Main Level Sq. Ft.: 1,087
Second Level Sq. Ft.: 547
Bedrooms: 3
Bathrooms: 2
Foundation: Basement
Materials List Available: Yes
Price Category: C

This stone-accented rustic vacation home offers the perfect antidote to busy daily life.

Features:

- Ceiling Height: 8 ft. unless otherwise noted.
- Family Room: Family and friends will be unable to resist relaxing in this airy two-story family room, with its own handsome fireplace. French doors lead to the front deck.
- Kitchen: This eat-in kitchen features double sinks, ample counter space, and a pantry. It offers plenty of space for the family to gather for informal vacation meals.
- Master Suite: This first-floor master retreat occupies almost the entire length of the home. It includes a walk-in closet and a lavish bath.
- Secondary Bedrooms: On the second floor, two family bedrooms share a full bath.
- Mezzanine: This lovely balcony overlooks the family room.
- Basement: This full unfinished basement offers plenty of space for expansion.

Main Level Floor Plan

36'-0"
10,8 m

36'-0"
10,8 m

14'-0" X 12'-0"
4,20 X 3,60

20'-0" X 14'-0"
6,00 X 4,20

13'-0" X 17'-0"
3,90 X 5,10

Upper Level Floor Plan

10'-0" X 11'-8"
3,00 X 3,50

12'-0" X 11'-8"
3,60 X 3,50

Copyright by designer/architect.

Main Level Floor Plan

Images provided by designer/architect.

Upper Level Floor Plan

Copyright by designer/architect.

Plan #181131

Dimensions: 26'4" W x 37' D

Levels: 2

Square Footage: 1,442

Main Level Sq. Ft.: 922

Upper Level Sq. Ft.: 520

Bedrooms: 3

Bathrooms: 2

Foundation: Full basement

Materials List Available: Yes

Price Category: B

Main Level Floor Plan

Images provided by designer/architect.

Upper Level Floor Plan

Copyright by designer/architect.

Plan #181132

Dimensions: 44' W x 26' D

Levels: 2

Square Footage: 1,437

Main Level Sq. Ft.: 856

Upper Level Sq. Ft.: 581

Bedrooms: 3

Bathrooms: 1½

Foundation: Walk-out basement

Materials List Available: Yes

Price Category: B

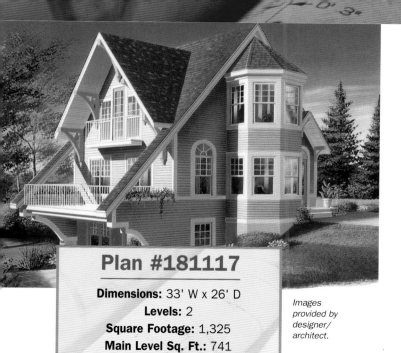

Plan #181117

Dimensions: 33' W x 26' D

Levels: 2

Square Footage: 1,325

Main Level Sq. Ft.: 741

Upper Level Sq. Ft.: 584

Bedrooms: 2

Bathrooms: 1½

Foundation: Walk-out basement

Materials List Available: Yes

Price Category: B

Images provided by designer/architect.

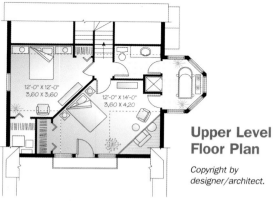

Main Level Floor Plan

Upper Level Floor Plan

Copyright by designer/architect.

Plan #181121

Dimensions: 27'8" W x 48' D

Levels: 2

Square Footage: 1,484

Main Level Sq. Ft.: 908

Upper Level Sq. Ft.: 576

Bedrooms: 3

Bathrooms: 2

Foundation: Walk-out basement

Materials List Available: Yes

Price Category: B

Images provided by designer/architect.

Main Level Floor Plan

Upper Level Floor Plan

Copyright by designer/architect.

Plan #181062

Dimensions: 58' W x 55' D
Levels: 2
Square Footage: 1,953
Main Level Sq. Ft.: 1,301
Second Level Sq. Ft.: 652
Bedrooms: 2
Bathrooms: 2½
Foundation: Half basement, half crawl space
Materials List Available: Yes
Price Category: D

Images provided by designer/architect.

Features:

- Ceiling Height: 8 ft.
- Wall of Doors: The entire back of the house is filled by five sets of multi-pane glass doors.
- Formal Dining Room: This dining room is located adjacent to the kitchen for convenient entertaining.
- Kitchen: This efficient kitchen is a pleasure in which to work, thanks to plenty of counter space, a pantry, double sinks, and access to the laundry room.
- Great Room: This great room is open to the atrium. As a result it is filled with warmth and natural light. You'll love gathering around the handsome fireplace.
- Master Suite: This private first-floor retreat features a walk-in closet and a luxurious full bath with dual vanities.

A magnificent glass enclosed vertical atrium is the focal point of this beautiful country home.

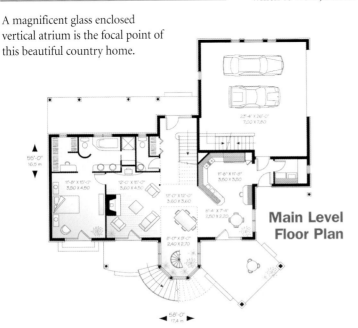

Main Level Floor Plan

Copyright by designer/architect.

Upper Level Floor Plan

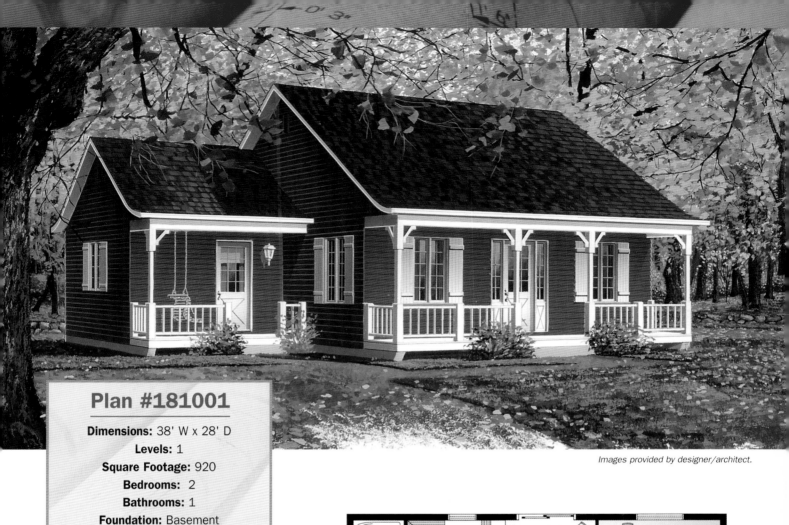

Plan #181001

Dimensions: 38' W x 28' D
Levels: 1
Square Footage: 920
Bedrooms: 2
Bathrooms: 1
Foundation: Basement
Materials List Available: Yes
Price Category: A

Images provided by designer/architect.

This cozy and charming one-story cottage offers many amenities in its well-designed layout.

Features:

- Ceiling Height: 8 ft.

- Porch: Enjoy summer evenings relaxing on the front porch.

- Kitchen: This kitchen has ample work and storage space as well as a breakfast bar and enough room for the family to dine together.

- Family Room: Natural light streaming through the windows makes this an appealing place for family activities.

- Bedrooms: There's a generous master bedroom and one secondary bedroom. Each has its own closet.

- Laundry Room: A fully equipped laundry room is conveniently located adjacent to the kitchen.

- Full Basement: Here is plenty of storage room as well as the opportunity for expanded living space.

28'-0"
8,4 m

19'-0" X 11'-8"
5,70 X 3,50

12'-2" X 11'-8"
3,65 X 3,50

15'-4" X 12'-0"
4,60 X 3,60

9'-0" X 10'-0"
2,70 X 3,00

38'-0"
11,4 m

Copyright by designer/architect.

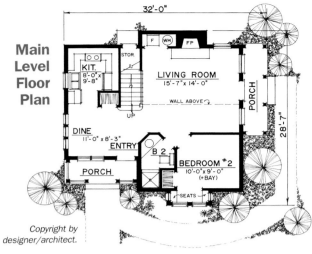

Main Level Floor Plan

32'-0"

KIT.
8'-0" x 9'-8"

STOR.

F | WH | FP

LIVING ROOM
15'-7" x 14'-0"

PORCH

28'-7"

WALL ABOVE

DINE
11'-0" x 8'-3"

ENTRY

B 2

BEDROOM #2
10'-0" x 9'-0"
(+BAY)

PORCH

SEATS

Copyright by designer/architect.

Images provided by designer/architect.

Upper Level Floor Plan

DOWN

D

W

OPEN TO LIVING ROOM

WOOD BEAMS

BATH #1

MASTER BEDROOM
10'-5" x 13'-8"
(11'-8" CEILING)

W.I.C.

BUILT-IN CABINETS

Plan #291008

Dimensions: 32' W x 28'7" D

Levels: 2

Square Footage: 1,183

Main Level Sq. Ft.: 772

Upper Level Sq. Ft.: 411

Bedrooms: 2

Bathrooms: 2

Foundation: Crawl space

Materials List Available: No

Price Category: B

Plan #281006

Dimensions: 34' W x 56' D

Levels: 2

Square Footage: 1,702

Main Level Sq. Ft.: 1,238

Upper Level Sq. Ft.: 464

Bedrooms: 3

Bathrooms: 2

Foundation: Walk-out basement

Materials List Available: Yes

Price Category: C

Images provided by designer/architect.

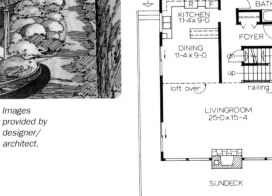

BR 3
11-4 x11-0

BR 2
14-0 x11-6

lin

up

R F

KITCHEN
11-4 x 9-0

DINING
11-4 x 9-0

loft over

BATH

FOYER

dn

up

railing

LIVINGROOM
25-0 x 15-4

SUNDECK

Main Level Floor Plan

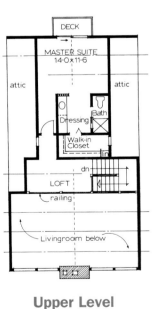

DECK

MASTER SUITE
14-0 x 11-6

attic

attic

Dressing

Bath

Walk-in Closet

dn

LOFT

railing

Livingroom below

Upper Level Floor Plan

Copyright by designer/architect.

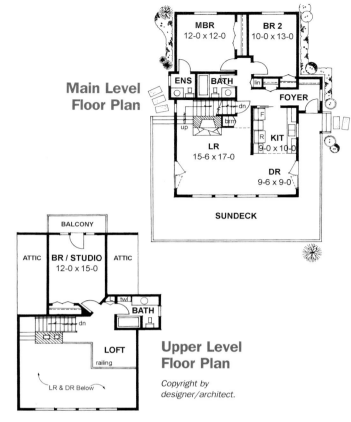

Main Level Floor Plan

MBR 12-0 x 12-0
BR 2 10-0 x 13-0
ENS
BATH
lin
FOYER
dn
up
brm
F
R
KIT 9-0 x 10-0
LR 15-6 x 17-0
DR 9-6 x 9-0
SUNDECK

Images provided by designer/architect.

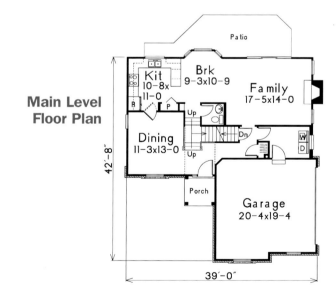

BALCONY
ATTIC
BR / STUDIO 12-0 x 15-0
ATTIC
twl
BATH
dn
LOFT
railing
LR & DR Below

Upper Level Floor Plan

Copyright by designer/architect.

Plan #281004

Dimensions: 36' W x 50' D
Levels: 2
Square Footage: 1,426
Main Level Sq. Ft.: 1,086
Upper Level Sq. Ft.: 340
Bedrooms: 3
Bathrooms: 2½
Foundation: Walk-out basement
Materials List Available: Yes
Price Category: B

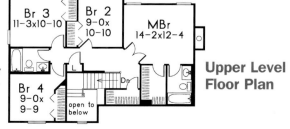

Main Level Floor Plan

Patio
Kit 10-8x 11-0
Brk 9-3x10-9
Family 17-5x14-0
Dining 11-3x13-0
R
P
Up
Dn
Up
W
D
42'-8"
Porch
Garage 20-4x19-4
39'-0"

Images provided by designer/architect.

Br 3 11-3x10-10
Br 2 9-0x 10-10
MBr 14-2x12-4
Br 4 9-0x 9-9
open to below
Dn
L

Copyright by designer/architect.

Upper Level Floor Plan

Plan #321084

Dimensions: 39' W x 42'8" D
Levels: 2
Square Footage: 1,700
Main Level Sq. Ft.: 896
Upper Level Sq. Ft.: 804
Bedrooms: 4
Bathrooms: 2½
Foundation: Basement
Materials List Available: Yes
Price Category: C

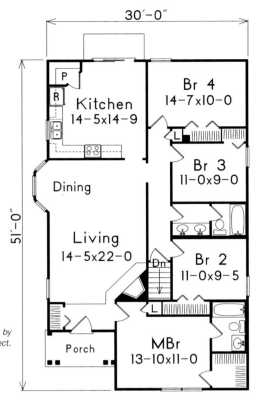

30'-0"

P
R

Kitchen
14-5x14-9

Br 4
14-7x10-0

L

Dining

Br 3
11-0x9-0

51'-0"

Living
14-5x22-0

Dn

Br 2
11-0x9-5

L

Porch

MBr
13-10x11-0

Images provided by designer/architect.

Copyright by designer/architect.

Plan #321038

Dimensions: 30' W x 51' D

Levels: 1

Square Footage: 1,452

Bedrooms: 4

Bathrooms: 2

Foundation: Basement

Materials List Available: Yes

Price Category: B

Plan #321040

Dimensions: 35' W x 40'8" D

Levels: 1

Square Footage: 1,084

Bedrooms: 2

Bathrooms: 2

Foundation: Basement

Materials List Available: Yes

Price Category: B

Images provided by designer/architect.

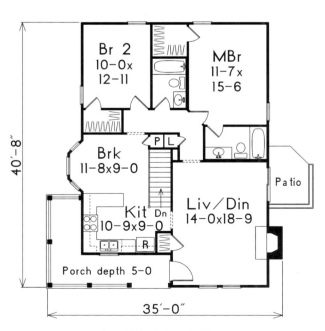

Br 2
10-0x
12-11

MBr
11-7x
15-6

40'-8"

Brk
11-8x9-0

P L

Patio

Kit
10-9x9-0

Dn

Liv/Din
14-0x18-9

R

Porch depth 5-0

35'-0"

Copyright by designer/architect.

Upper Level
Floor Plan

*Copyright by
designer/architect.*

*Images provided by
designer/architect.*

Main Level
Floor Plan

26'-0"
7,8 m

28'-0"
8,4 m

Plan #181112

Dimensions: 28' W x 26' D

Levels: 2

Square Footage: 1,148

Main Level Sq. Ft.: 728

Upper Level Sq. Ft.: 420

Bedrooms: 1

Bathrooms: 1½

Foundation: Full basement

Materials List Available: Yes

Price Category: B

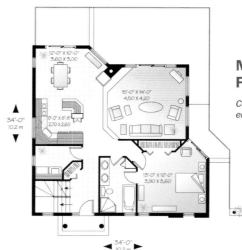

Main Level
Floor Plan

*Copyright by design-
er/architect.*

34'-0"
10,2 m

34'-0"
10,2 m

Upper Level
Floor Plan

*Images
provided by
designer/architect.*

OPEN TO
BELOW

Plan #181116

Dimensions: 34' W x 34' D

Levels: 2

Square Footage: 1,737

Main Level Sq. Ft.: 1,010

Upper Level Sq. Ft.: 727

Bedrooms: 3

Bathrooms: 2

Foundation: Walk-out basement

Materials List Available: Yes

Price Category: C

Plan #111047

Dimensions: 36' W x 54' D
Levels: 2
Square Footage: 1,863
Main Level Sq. Ft.: 1,056
Upper Level Sq. Ft.: 807
Bedrooms: 4
Bathrooms: 3
Foundation: Pier
Materials List Available: No
Price Category: D

Designed for a coastline, this home is equally appropriate as a year-round residence or a vacation retreat.

Features:

- Orientation: The rear-facing design gives you an ocean view and places the most attractive side of the house where beach-goers can see it.

- Entryway: On the waterside, a large deck with a covered portion leads to the main entrance.

- Carport: This house is raised on piers that let you park underneath it and that protect it from water damage during storms.

- Living Room: A fireplace, French doors, and large windows grace this room, which is open to both the kitchen and the dining area.

- Master Suite: Two sets of French doors open to a balcony on the ocean side, and the suite includes two walk-in closets and a fully equipped bath.

Main Level Floor Plan

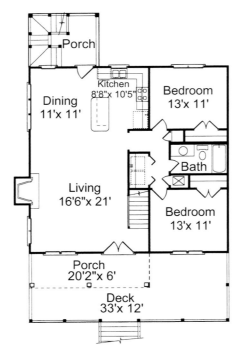

Upper Level Floor Plan

Plan #271053

Dimensions: 70' W x 34' D
Levels: 2
Square Footage: 2,458
Main Level Sq. Ft.: 1,067
Upper Level Sq. Ft.: 346
Bedrooms: 3
Bathrooms: 2½
Foundation: Daylight basement or crawl space
Materials List Available: No
Price Category: E

The octagonal shape and window-filled walls of this home create a powerful interior packed with panoramic views.

Features:

• Great Room: Straight back from the angled entry, this room is brightened by sunlight through windows and sliding glass doors. Beyond the doors, a huge wraparound deck offers plenty of space for tanning or relaxing. A spiral staircase adds visual interest.

• Kitchen: This efficient space includes a convenient pantry.

• Master Suite: On the upper level, this romantic master suite overlooks the great room below. Several windows provide scenic outdoor views. A walk-in closet and a private bath round out this secluded haven.

• Basement: The optional basement includes a recreation room, as well as an extra bedroom and bath.

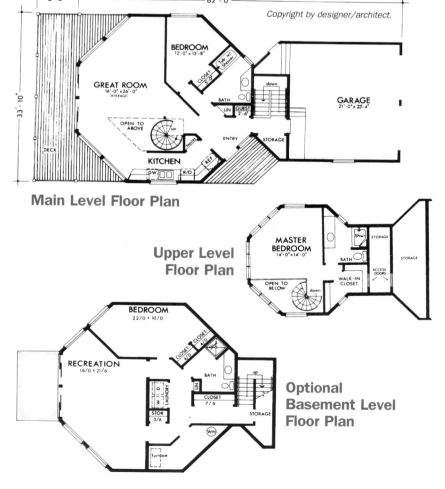

Main Level Floor Plan

Upper Level Floor Plan

Optional Basement Level Floor Plan

Plan #281002

Dimensions: 54' W x 33' D
Levels: 2
Square Footage: 1,859
Main Level Sq. Ft.: 959
Second Level Sq. Ft.: 900
Bedrooms: 3
Bathrooms: 1 full, 2 half
Foundation: Basement
Materials List Available: Yes
Price Category: C

This lovely three-bedroom home has the layout and amenities you need for comfortable living.

Features:

- Ceiling Height: 8 ft. unless otherwise noted.
- Foyer: Guests will walk through the lovely and practical front porch into this attractive foyer, with its vaulted ceiling.

- Living/Dining Room: Family and friends will be drawn to the warmth of the cozy, convenient gas fireplace in this combination living/dining room.

- Master Suite: You'll enjoy retiring at the end of the day to this luxurious master suite. It has a private sitting area with built-in storage for your books and television. Relax in the bath under its skylight.

- Kitchen: At the center of the main floor you will find this kitchen, with its eating nook that takes full advantage of the view and is just the right size for family meals.

- Deck: This large deck is accessible from the master suite, eating nook, and living/dining room.

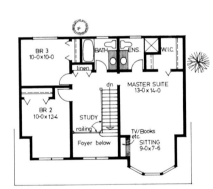

Upper Level Floor Plan

Main Level Floor Plan

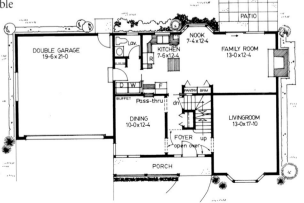

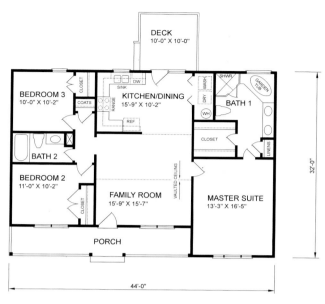

Plan #341019

Dimensions: 44' W x 32' D

Levels: 1

Square Footage: 1,258

Bedrooms: 3

Bathrooms: 2

Foundation: Crawl space, slab, or basement

Materials List Available: Yes

Price Category: B

Images provided by designer/architect.

Copyright by designer/architect.

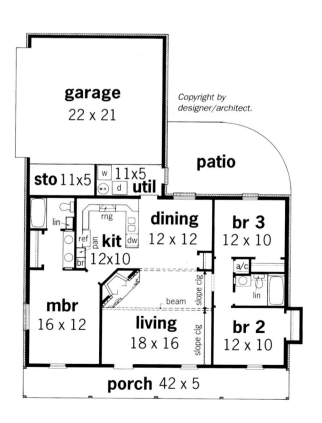

Plan #211016

Dimensions: 44'6" W x 59' D

Levels: 1

Square Footage: 1,191

Bedrooms: 3

Bathrooms: 2

Foundation: Slab

Materials List Available: Yes

Price Category: B

Images provided by designer/architect.

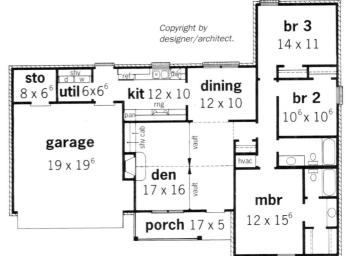

br 3
14 x 11

sto
8 x 6⁶

util 6x6⁶

kit 12 x 10

dining
12 x 10

br 2
10⁶ x 10⁶

ref

rng

pan

shv cab

garage
19 x 19⁶

vault

den
17 x 16

vault

hvac

mbr
12 x 15⁶

porch 17 x 5

Plan #201022

Dimensions: 56'10" W x 45'10" D

Levels: 1

Square Footage: 1,363

Bedrooms: 3

Bathrooms: 2

Foundation: Crawl space, slab

Materials List Available: Yes

Price Category: B

9'-0" X 14'-8"
2,70 x 4,40

11'-0" X 9'-8"
3,30 X 2,90

11'-8" X 13'-0"
3,50 X 3,90

10'-0" X 12'-0"
3,00 X 3,60

34'-0"
10,2 m

12'-0" X 16'-4"
3,60 X 4,90

11'-0" X 11'-0"
3,30 X 3,30

43'-0"
12,9 m

Plan #181152

Dimensions: 43' W x 34' D

Levels: 1

Square Footage: 1,339

Bedrooms: 3

Bathrooms: 1

Foundation: Basement

Materials List Available: Yes

Price Category: B

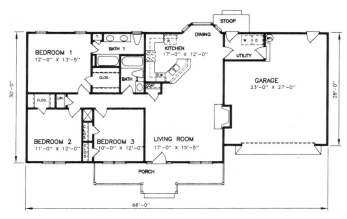

Images provided by designer/architect.

Copyright by designer/architect.

Plan #341005

Dimensions: 66' W x 30' D

Levels: 1

Square Footage: 1,334

Bedrooms: 3

Bathrooms: 2

Foundation: Crawl space, slab, or basement

Materials List Available: Yes

Price Category: B

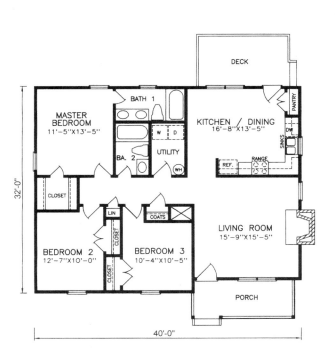

Images provided by designer/architect.

Copyright by designer/architect.

Plan #341028

Dimensions: 40' W x 32' D

Levels: 1

Square Footage: 1,248

Bedrooms: 3

Bathrooms: 2

Foundation: Crawl space, slab, or basement

Materials List Available: Yes

Price Category: B

Plan #191030

Dimensions: 33' W x 36' D

Levels: 1

Square Footage: 864

Bedrooms: 2

Bathrooms: 1

Foundation: Crawl space or slab

Materials List Available: No

Price Category: A

Enjoy the view from the spacious front porch of this cozy cottage, which is ideal for a retirement home, vacation retreat, or starter home.

Features:

- Porch: This 6-ft.-wide porch, which runs the length of the home, gives you plenty of space to set up a couple of rockers next to a potted herb garden.

- Living/Dining Room: This huge living and dining area gives you many options for design. The snack bar that it shares with the kitchen is a practical touch.

- Kitchen: The first thing you'll notice in this well-planned kitchen is how much counter and storage space it offers.

- Laundry Room: Opening to the backyard, this room also features ample storage space.

- Bedrooms: Both rooms have good closet space and easy access to the large, luxurious bath.

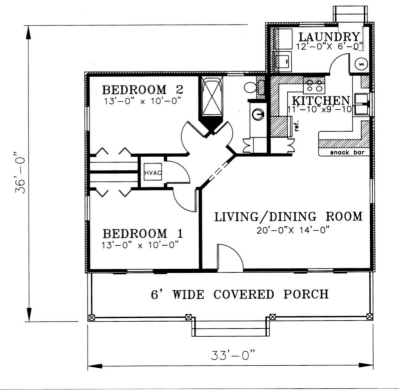

LAUNDRY
12'-0"X 6'-0"

BEDROOM 2
13'-0" x 10'-0"

KITCHEN
11'-10"x9'-10"

ref.

snack bar

HVAC

BEDROOM 1
13'-0" x 10'-0"

LIVING/DINING ROOM
20'-0"X 14'-0"

36'-0"

6' WIDE COVERED PORCH

33'-0"

Plan #211025

Dimensions: 70' W x 44' D
Levels: 1
Square Footage: 1,434
Bedrooms: 3
Bathrooms: 2
Foundations: Crawl space
Materials List Available: Yes
Price Category: B

Images provided by designer/architect.

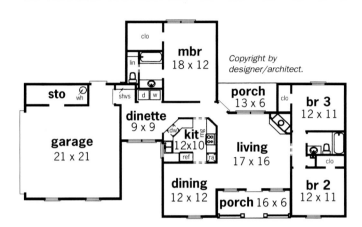

Copyright by designer/architect.

Plan #211021

Dimensions: 61' W x 35' D
Levels: 1
Square Footage: 1,375
Bedrooms: 3
Bathrooms: 2
Foundation: Slab
Materials List Available: Yes
Price Category: B

Images provided by designer/architect.

Copyright by designer/architect.

Plan #211019

Dimensions: 73' W x 37' D

Levels: 1

Square Footage: 1,395

Bedrooms: 3

Bathrooms: 2

Foundation: Slab

Materials List Available: Yes

Price Category: B

Images provided by designer/architect.

Copyright by designer/architect.

Plan #341034

Dimensions: 50' W x 38'2" D

Levels: 1

Square Footage: 1,445

Bedrooms: 3

Bathrooms: 2

Foundation: Crawl space, slab, or basement

Materials List Available: Yes

Price Category: B

Images provided by designer/architect.

Copyright by designer/architect.

Plan #181021

Dimensions: 37' W x 44' D
Levels: 1
Square Footage: 1,124
Bedrooms: 2
Bathrooms: 1
Foundation: Basement
Materials List Available: Yes
Price Category: B

Images provided by designer/architect.

This cozy country cottage is enhanced by lattice trim details over the porch and garage.

Features:

- Ceiling Height: 8 ft.

- Living Room: This living room gets extra architectural interest from a sunken floor. The room, located directly to the left of the entry hall, has plenty of space for entertaining.

- Dining Room: This dining room is located in center of the home. It's adjacent to the kitchen to make it easy to serve meals.

- Kitchen: This bright and efficient kitchen is a real pleasure in which to work. It includes a pantry and double sinks. There's a breakfast bar that will see plenty of informal meals for families on the go.

- Covered Porch: This is the perfect place to which to retire after dinner on a warm summer evening.

- Bedrooms: Each of the two bedrooms has its own closet. They share a full bathroom.

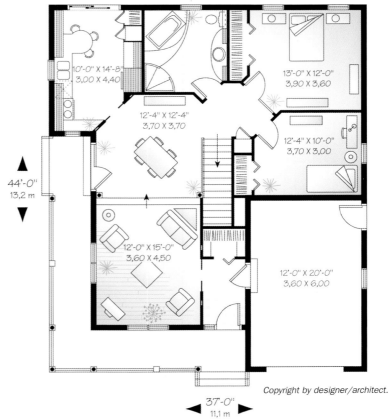

10'-0" X 14'-8"
3,00 X 4,40

13'-0" X 12'-0"
3,90 X 3,60

12'-4" X 12'-4"
3,70 X 3,70

12'-4" X 10'-0"
3,70 X 3,00

44'-0"
13,2 m

12'-0" X 15'-0"
3,60 X 4,50

12'-0" X 20'-0"
3,60 X 6,00

37'-0"
11,1 m

Copyright by designer/architect.

Plan #181015

Dimensions: 58' W x 28'4" D
Levels: 1
Square Footage: 1,776
Bedrooms: 3
Bathrooms: 1
Foundation: Basement
Materials List Available: Yes
Price Category: B

Images provided by designer/architect.

A pillared front porch and beautifully arched windows enhance the stucco exterior.

Features:

- Ceiling Height: 8 ft.

- Kitchen: Cooking will be a pleasure in this bright and spacious kitchen. There is ample counter space for food preparation, in addition to a center island. The kitchen is flooded with light from sliding glass doors that provide access to the outdoors.

- Family Room: Nothing warms you on a cold winter day quite like the radiant heat from the cozy wood-burning fireplace/stove you will find in this family gathering room.

- Front Porch: Step directly out of the living room onto this spacious front porch. Relax in a porch rocker, and enjoy a summer breeze with your favorite book or just rock and watch the sun set.

- Bedrooms: Three family bedrooms share a full bathroom complete with dual vanities and laundry facilities.

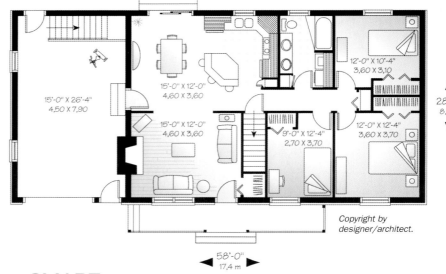

Copyright by designer/architect.

SMARTtip

Electrical Safety in the Kitchen

Sometimes the special needs of the disabled may seem to conflict with those of the very young. A case in point is accessible switch placement, which is lower on a wall. The NKBA recommends locating outlets and switches inside the front of an adult-accessible tilt-down drawer to conceal them from children. Alternatively, an outlet strip can be kept out of a child's reach and at a convenient adult location while lessening the reach to outlets and switches installed in the backsplash.

Plan #151150

Dimensions: 48" W x 54" D

Levels: 1

Square Footage: 1,193

Bedrooms: 3

Bathrooms: 2

Foundation: Crawl space, slab

Materials List Available: Yes

Price Category: B

Images provided by designer/architect.

Copyright by designer/architect.

Plan #151149

Dimensions: 47'5" W x 46'5" D

Levels: 1

Square Footage: 1,157

Bedrooms: 3

Bathrooms: 2

Foundation: Crawl space, slab

Materials List Available: Yes

Price Category: B

Images provided by designer/architect.

Copyright by designer/architect.

Plan #341003

Dimensions: 60' W x 30' D

Levels: 1

Square Footage: 1,200

Bedrooms: 3

Bathrooms: 2

Foundation: Crawl space, slab, or basement

Materials List Available: Yes

Price Category: B

Images provided by designer/architect.

If you're looking for the ideal plan for a first home or an empty-nester, this romantic cottage will meet your needs with style.

Features:

- **Outdoor Living Space:** Use the porch at the front of the house and the deck at the back as extra living area in fine weather.

- **Living Room:** Open to both the dining area and the kitchen, this room also looks out to the deck and backyard.

- **Kitchen:** This well-planned area combines a step-saving layout with conveniently placed counter and storage space.

- **Laundry Closet:** Open the door to this centrally located closet to find a full washer and dryer.

- **Bedrooms:** Choose between the bedrooms with spacious walk-in closets for your room, and depending on need, use the others for children's rooms, a guestroom, or an office.

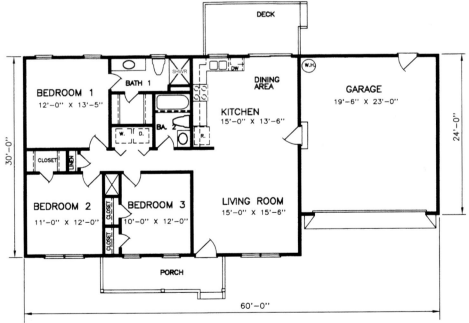

Copyright by designer/architect.

Plan #341004

Dimensions: 56'10" W x 28'6" D

Levels: 1

Square Footage: 1,101

Bedrooms: 3

Bathrooms: 2

Foundation: Crawl space, slab, or basement

Materials List Available: Yes

Price Category: B

Images provided by designer/architect.

You'll love the romantic feeling that the gables and front porch give to this well designed home, with its family-oriented layout.

Features:

- **Living Room:** The open design between this spacious room and the kitchen/dining area makes this home as ideal for family activities as it is for entertaining.

- **Outdoor Living Space:** French doors open to the back deck, where you're sure to host alfresco dinners or easy summer brunches.

- **Kitchen:** Designed for the cook's convenience, this kitchen features ample work area as well as excellent storage space in the nearby pantry.

- **Laundry Area:** Located behind closed doors to shut out the noise, this laundry closet is conveniently placed.

- **Master Suite:** With triple windows, a wide closet, and a private bath, this is a luxurious suite.

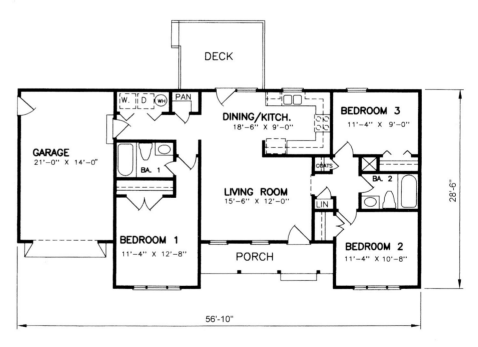

Copyright by designer/architect.

Plan #341009

Dimensions: 44'5" W x 39'4" D

Levels: 1

Square Footage: 1,280

Bedrooms: 3

Bathrooms: 2

Foundation: Crawl space, slab, or basement

Materials List Available: Yes

Price Category: B

Images provided by designer/architect.

If you admire the exterior features of this home — the L-shaped front porch, nested gables, and transom lights — you'll love its interior.

Features:

- Ceiling Height: Ceilings are 9-ft. high to enhance this home's spacious feeling.

- Living Room: A fireplace creates a cozy feeling in this open, spacious room.

- Dining Room: Decorative columns grace the transition between this room and the living room.

- Kitchen: This open kitchen features a serving bar, a large pantry, and access to the back deck.

- Laundry: The washer and dryer are housed in a large utility closet to minimize noise.

- Master Suite: A designer window, vaulted ceiling, and walk-in closet make the bedroom luxurious, and the garden tub and shower make the private bath a true retreat.

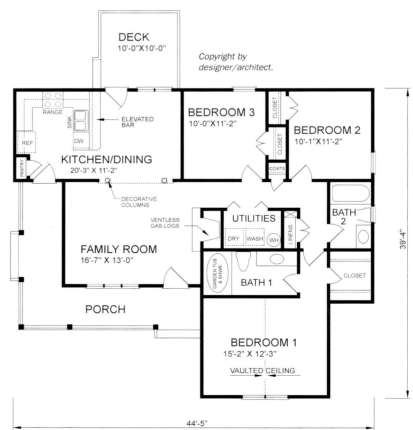

Copyright by designer/architect.

Plan #341013

Dimensions: 44' W x 34' D

Levels: 1

Square Footage: 1,363

Bedrooms: 3

Bathrooms: 2

Foundation: Crawl space, slab, or basement

Materials List Available: Yes

Price Category: B

Images provided by designer/architect.

The luxurious amenities in this compact, well designed home are sure to delight everyone in the family.

Features:

- Ceiling Height: 9-ft. ceilings add to the spacious feeling created by the open design.

- Family Room: A vaulted ceiling and large window area add elegance to this comfortable room, which will be the heart of this home.

- Dining Area: Adjoining the kitchen, this room features a large bayed area as well as French doors that open onto the back deck.

- Kitchen: This step-saving design will make cooking a joy for everyone in the family.

- Utility Room: Near the kitchen, this room includes cabinets and shelves for extra storage space.

- Master Suite: A triple window, tray ceiling, walk-in closet, and luxurious bath make this area a treat.

Copyright by designer/architect.

Images provided by designer/architect.

Bonus Area

Copyright by designer/architect.

Plan #211090

Dimensions: 66' W x 72' D
Levels: 1
Square Footage: 1,932
Bedrooms: 3
Bathrooms: 2
Foundation: Crawl space
Materials List Available: No
Price Category: D

Plan #211036

Dimensions: 80' W x 40' D
Levels: 1
Square Footage: 1,800
Bedrooms: 3
Bathrooms: 2
Foundation: Slab
Materials List Available: Yes
Price Category: D

Images provided by designer/architect.

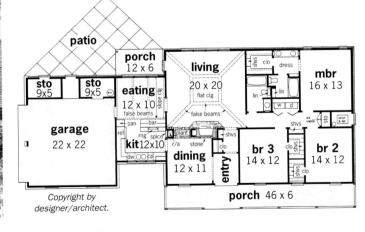

Copyright by designer/architect.

SMARTtip
Dimmer Switches

You can dim lights just slightly to extend lamp life and save energy, and there will be very little perceptible change in light level. For instance, dimming the light to 50 percent will be perceived as though the light were only dimmed to 70 percent. Therefore, there is no dramatic dilation or constriction of the eye due to light level change.

Plan #151022

Dimensions: 79' W x 77'8" D
Levels: 2
Square Footage: 3,059
Main Level Sq. Ft.: 2,650
Upper Level Sq. Ft.: 409
Bedrooms: 4
Bathrooms: 4
Foundation: Basement, crawl space, or slab
Materials List Available: Yes
Price Category: G

The two front porches, a rear covered porch, and a huge rear deck are your first clues to the comfort you'll enjoy in this home.

Features:

- Great Room: This versatile room with a 10-ft. ceiling has a gas fireplace, built-in shelves and entertainment center, a place for an optional staircase, and access to the rear covered porch.

- Dining Room: The 10-ft. ceiling lets you decorate for formal dining but still allows a casual feeling.

- Breakfast Room: This bright space is open to the kitchen, so you can enjoy it at any time of day.

- Hobby Room: Use this space just off the garage for almost any activity.

- Master Suite: Enjoy the 10-ft. boxed ceiling, built-in cabinets, and access to the rear covered porch. The split design gives privacy. The bath has a corner whirlpool tub, separate glass shower, and split vanities.

Upper Level Floor Plan

Copyright by designer/architect.

Main Level Floor Plan

Plan #211038

Dimensions: 72' W x 42' D

Levels: 1

Square Footage: 1,898

Bedrooms: 3

Bathrooms: 2

Foundation: Slab

Materials List Available: Yes

Price Category: D

A railed front porch, a charming cupola, and stylish shutters add classic flair to this home.

Features:

- Ceiling Height: 8 ft. unless otherwise noted.

- Family Room: The welcoming entry flows into this attractive family gathering area. The room features a handsome fireplace and a 14-ft. vaulted ceiling with exposed beams. French doors lead to a backyard patio.

- Formal Dining Room: This elegant room adjoins the living room. You'll usher your guests through a half-wall with decorative spindles.

- Kitchen: Food preparation will be a pleasure working at the wraparound counter.

- Eating Nook: Modern life includes lots of quick, informal meals, and this is the spot to enjoy them. The nook includes a laundry closet, so you can change loads while cooking.

- Master Suite: This private retreat boasts a private bath with a separate dressing area and a roomy walk-in closet.

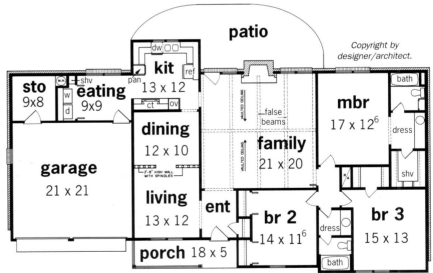

SMARTtip

Efficient Kitchen Appliances

Appliances that carry the **Energy Star** label — a program of the Department of Energy — are significantly more energy efficient than most other appliances. Dishwashers, for example, must be 25 percent more energy efficient than models that meet minimum federal energy requirements. Energy Star refrigerators must be 10 percent more efficient than the newest standards.

Plan #211032

Dimensions: 77' W x 32' D

Levels: 1

Square Footage: 1,751

Bedrooms: 4

Full Baths: 2

Foundation: Slab

Materials List Available: Yes

Price Category: C

Images provided by designer/architect.

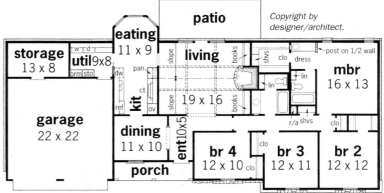

Copyright by designer/architect.

Plan #211042

Dimensions: 66' W x 60' D

Levels: 1

Square Footage: 1,800

Bedrooms: 3

Bathrooms: 2

Foundation: Crawl space

Materials List Available: Yes

Price Category: D

Images provided by designer/architect.

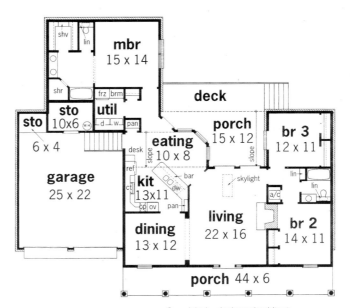

Copyright by designer/architect.

Plan #281016

Dimensions: 46' W x 44' D
Levels: 2
Square Footage: 1,945
Main Level Sq. Ft.: 1,211
Upper Level Sq. Ft.: 734
Bedrooms: 3
Bathrooms: 3
Foundation: Combination basement/slab
Materials List Available: Yes
Price Category: D

The fabulous window shapes on this Tudor-style home give just a hint of the beautiful interior design.

Features:

- **Living Room:** A vaulted ceiling in this raised room adds to its spectacular good looks.

- **Dining Room:** Between the lovely bay window and the convenient door to the covered sundeck, this room is an entertainer's delight.

- **Family Room:** A sunken floor, cozy fireplace, and door to the patio make this room special.

- **Study:** Just off the family room, this quiet spot can be a true retreat away from the crowd.

- **Kitchen:** The family cooks will be delighted by the ample counter and storage space here.

- **Master Suite:** A large walk-in closet, huge picture window, and private bath add luxurious touches to this second-floor retreat.

Images provided by designer/architect.

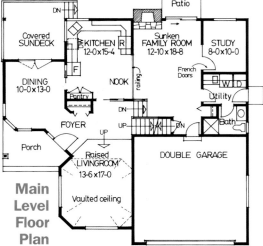

Main Level Floor Plan

Upper Level Floor Plan

Copyright by designer/architect.

Rear Elevation

Left Side Elevation

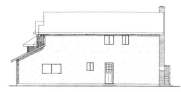

Right Side Elevation

Plan #171008

Dimensions: 72' W x 40' D
Levels: 1
Square Footage: 1,652
Bedrooms: 3
Bathrooms: 2
Foundation: Slab, crawl space
Materials List Available: Yes
Price Category: C

Images provided by designer/architect.

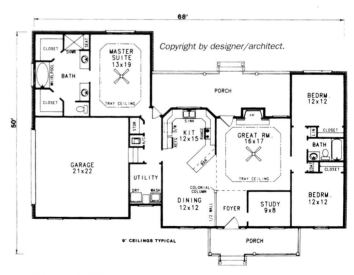

Plan #171009

Dimensions: 68' W x 50' D
Levels: 1
Square Footage: 1,771
Bedrooms: 3
Bathrooms: 2
Foundation: Slab, crawl space
Materials List Available: Yes
Price Category: C

Images provided by designer/architect.

Plan #281018

Dimensions: 50' W x 52'6" D
Levels: 1
Square Footage: 1,565
Bedrooms: 3
Bathrooms: 2
Foundation: Basement
Materials List Available: Yes
Price Category: C

You'll love the arched window that announces the grace of this home to the rest of the world.

Features:

- Living Room: Scissor trusses on the ceiling and a superb window design make this room elegant.

- Dining Room: Open to the living room, this dining room features an expansive window area and contains a convenient, inset china closet.

- Family Room: A gas fireplace in the corner and a doorway to the patio make this room the heart of the house.

- Breakfast Room: The bay window here makes it a lovely spot at any time of day.

- Kitchen: A raised snack bar shared with both the family and breakfast rooms adds a nice touch to this well-planned, attractive kitchen.

- Master Suite: A bay window, walk-in closet, and private bath add up to luxurious comfort in this suite.

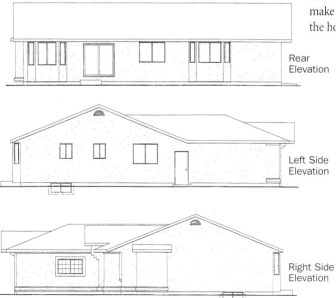

Rear Elevation

Left Side Elevation

Right Side Elevation

Plan #281015

Dimensions: 32' W x 48' D
Levels: 2
Square Footage: 1,660
Main Level Sq. Ft.: 964
Upper Level Sq. Ft.: 696
Bedrooms: 4
Bathrooms: 2½
Foundation: Basement
Materials List Available: Yes
Price Category: C

You'll love the gracious features and amenities in this charming home, which is meant for a narrow lot.

Features:

- **Foyer:** This two-story foyer opens into the spacious living room.

- **Living Room:** The large bay window in this room makes a perfect setting for quiet times alone or entertaining guests.

- **Dining Room:** The open flow between this room and the living room adds to the airy feeling.

- **Family Room:** With a handsome fireplace and a door to the rear patio, this room will be the heart of your home.

- **Kitchen:** The U-shaped layout, pantry, and greenhouse window make this room a joy.

- **Master Suite:** The bay window, large walk-in closet, and private bath make this second-floor room a true retreat.

Images provided by designer/architect.

Main Level Floor Plan

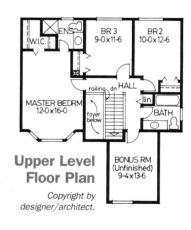

Upper Level Floor Plan

Copyright by designer/architect.

Left Side Elevation

Rear Elevation

Right Side Elevation

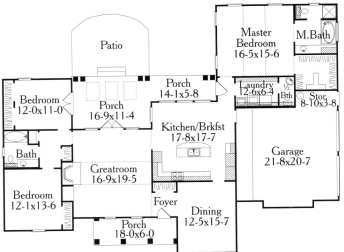

Plan #311017

Dimensions: 72' W x 55'2" D

Levels: 1

Square Footage: 1,974

Bedrooms: 3

Bathrooms: 2½

Foundation: Slab or crawl space or basement

Materials List Available: Yes

Price Category: D

Images provided by designer/architect.

Copyright by designer/architect.

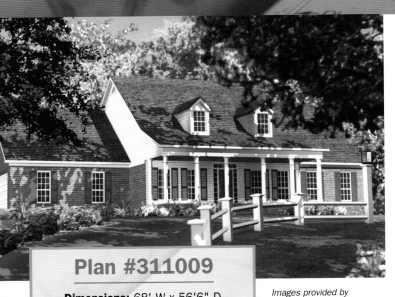

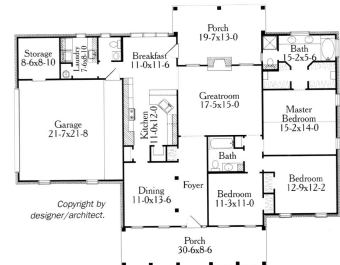

Plan #311009

Dimensions: 68' W x 56'6" D

Levels: 1

Square Footage: 1,894

Bedrooms: 3

Bathrooms: 2½

Foundation: Basement, crawl space, or slab

Materials List Available: Yes

Price Category: D

Images provided by designer/architect.

Copyright by designer/architect.

Basement Stair Option

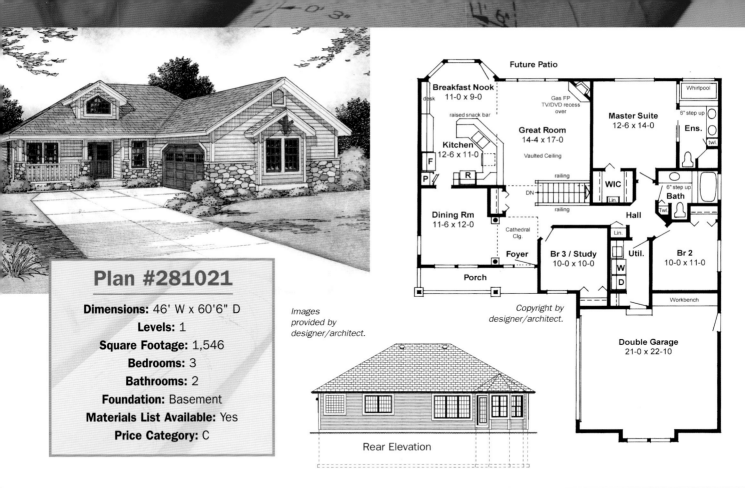

Plan #281021

Dimensions: 46' W x 60'6" D

Levels: 1

Square Footage: 1,546

Bedrooms: 3

Bathrooms: 2

Foundation: Basement

Materials List Available: Yes

Price Category: C

Images provided by designer/architect.

Rear Elevation

Plan #281022

Dimensions: 48' W x 58' D

Levels: 1

Square Footage: 1,506

Bedrooms: 3

Bathrooms: 2

Foundation: Basement

Materials List Available: Yes

Price Category: C

Images provided by designer/architect.

Copyright by designer/architect.

Rear Elevation

Plan #151165

Dimensions: 63' W x 84'4" D

Levels: 1

Square Footage: 1,927

Bedrooms: 3

Bathrooms: 2

Foundation: Crawl space, slab

Materials List Available: Yes

Price Category: D

Optional Bonus Area

Plan #151160

Dimensions: 65'4" W x 86'8" D

Levels: 1

Square Footage: 1,845

Bedrooms: 3

Bathrooms: 2

Foundation: Crawl space, slab

Materials List Available: Yes

Price Category: D

Optional Bonus Area

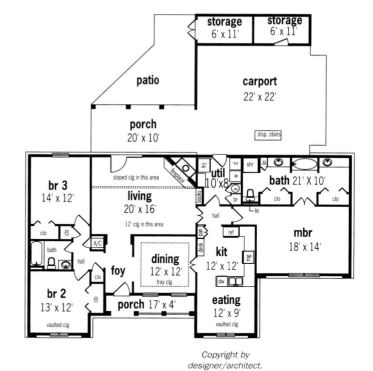

Plan #211129

Dimensions: 62' W x 64' D

Levels: 1

Square Footage: 1,868

Bedrooms: 3

Bathrooms: 2

Foundation: Slab

Materials List Available: No

Price Category: D

Images provided by designer/architect.

Copyright by designer/architect.

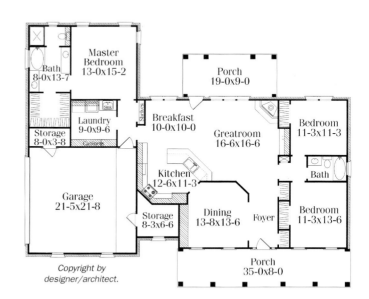

Plan #311012

Dimensions: 65'8" W x 55' D

Levels: 1

Square Footage: 1,836

Bedrooms: 3

Bathrooms: 2

Foundation: Basement, crawl space, or slab

Materials List Available: Yes

Price Category: D

Images provided by designer/architect.

Copyright by designer/architect.

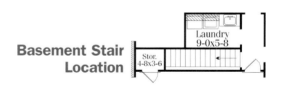

Basement Stair Location

Plan #151161

Dimensions: 63' W x 76' D

Levels: 1

Square Footage: 1,915

Bedrooms: 3

Bathrooms: 2

Foundation: Crawl space, slab

Materials List Available: Yes

Price Category: D

Images provided by designer/architect.

Copyright by designer/architect.

Plan #281020

Dimensions: 60' W x 48' D

Levels: 1

Square Footage: 1,734

Bedrooms: 3

Bathrooms: 2½

Foundation: Basement

Materials List Available: Yes

Price Category: C

Images provided by designer/architect.

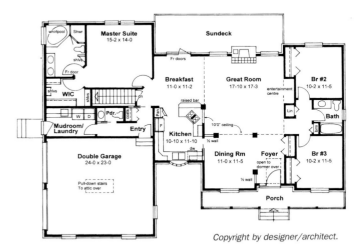

Copyright by designer/architect.

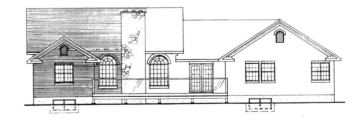

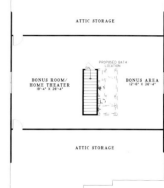

Copyright by designer/architect.

Images provided by designer/architect.

Plan #151145

Dimensions: 42' W x 67'4" D
Levels: 1
Square Footage: 1,774
Bedrooms: 2
Bathrooms: 2
Foundation: Crawl space, slab
Materials List Available: Yes
Price Category: C

Optional Bonus Area

Images provided by designer/architect.

Plan #311018

Dimensions: 70'6" W x 51' D
Levels: 1
Square Footage: 1,867
Bedrooms: 3
Bathrooms: 2
Foundation: Crawl space, slab, or basement
Materials List Available: Yes
Price Category: C

Copyright by designer/architect.

Basement Stair Location

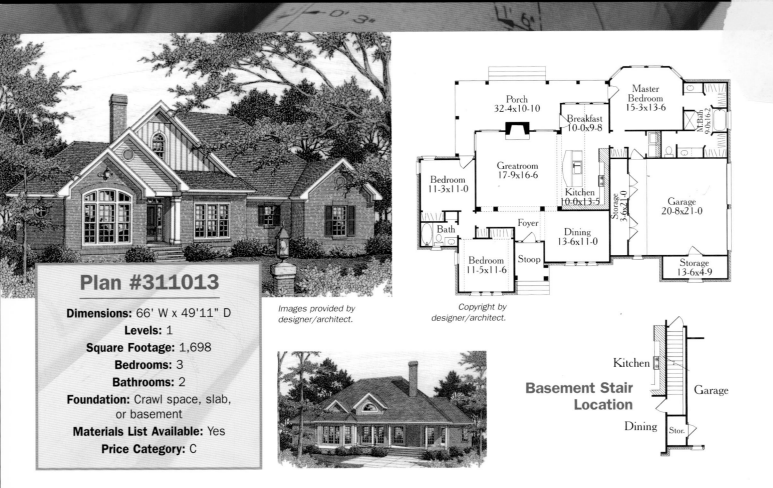

Plan #311013

Dimensions: 66' W x 49'11" D

Levels: 1

Square Footage: 1,698

Bedrooms: 3

Bathrooms: 2

Foundation: Crawl space, slab, or basement

Materials List Available: Yes

Price Category: C

Images provided by designer/architect.

Copyright by designer/architect.

Porch 32-4x10-10

Master Bedroom 15-3x13-6

M.Bath 9-0x16-2

Breakfast 10-0x9-8

Bedroom 11-3x11-0

Greatroom 17-9x16-6

Kitchen 10-0x13-5

Storage 3-6x21-0

Garage 20-8x21-0

Bath

Foyer

Dining 13-6x11-0

Storage 13-6x4-9

Bedroom 11-5x11-6

Stoop

Basement Stair Location

Kitchen

Garage

Dining

Stor.

Plan #311008

Dimensions: 70'1" W x 48' D

Levels: 1

Square Footage: 1,688

Bedrooms: 3

Bathrooms: 2

Foundation: Basement, crawl space, or slab

Materials List Available: Yes

Price Category: C

Images provided by designer/architect.

Copyright by designer/architect.

Porch 31-4x8-0

Master Bedroom 13-6x15-6

Bath

Breakfast 9-10x10-6

Storage 8-6x9-4

Laundry 8-6x9-4

Greatroom 15-4x19-5

Bath

Kitchen 9-6x11-6

Bedroom 13-6x11-6

Bedroom 10-11x11-6

Foyer

Dining 12-0x11-6

Garage 21-6x21-6

Porch 31-4x8-0

Basement Stair Option

Laun. 8-6x5-6

Storage

Images provided by designer/architect.

Plan #151164

Dimensions: 62'4" W x 83'6" D

Levels: 1

Square Footage: 1,848

Bedrooms: 3

Bathrooms: 2

Foundation: Crawl space, slab

Materials List Available: Yes

Price Category: D

Copyright by designer/architect.

Images provided by designer/architect.

Plan #151163

Dimensions: 63' W x 90' D

Levels: 1

Square Footage: 1,832

Bedrooms: 3

Bathrooms: 2

Foundation: Crawl space, slab

Materials List Available: Yes

Price Category: D

Optional Bonus Area

Copyright by designer/architect.

Plan #291002

Dimensions: 63' W x 37' D

Levels: 1

Square Footage: 1,550

Bedrooms: 3

Bathrooms: 2

Foundation: Basement

Materials List Available: No

Price Category: C

Images provided by designer/architect.

This comfortable Southwestern-style ranch house will fit perfectly into any setting.

Features:

- Ceiling Height: 8 ft. unless otherwise noted.

- Front Porch: This scalloped front porch offers plenty of room for enjoying a cool summer breeze.

- Foyer: Upon entering this impressive foyer you'll be greeted by a soaring space encompassing the living room and dining room.

- Living/Dining Area: This combined living room and dining room has a handsome fireplace as its focal point. When dinner is served, guests will flow casually into the dining area.

- Kitchen: Take your cooking up a notch in this terrific kitchen. It features a 42-in.-high counter that will do double-duty as a snack bar for family meals and a wet bar for entertaining.

- Master Suite: This master retreat is separated from the other bedrooms and features an elegant vaulted ceiling. The dressing area has a compartmentalized bath and a walk-in closet.

Rear View

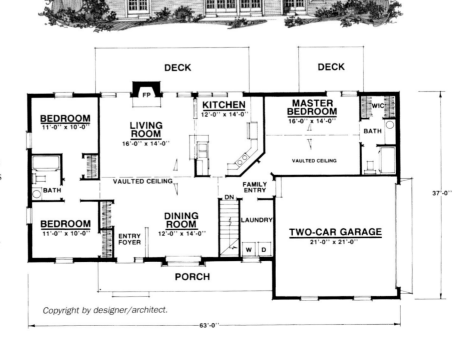

Copyright by designer/architect.

Plan #251005

Dimensions: 48' W x 44' D
Levels: 1
Square Footage: 1,631
Bedrooms: 3
Bathrooms: 2
Foundation: Basement
Materials List Available: Yes
Price Category: C

Images provided by designer/architect.

This elegant home features hip roof lines that will add appeal in any neighborhood.

Features:

- Ceiling Height: 9 ft.

- Front Porch: The porch stretches across the entire front of the home, offering plenty of space to sit and enjoy evening breezes.

- Family Room: This family room features a handsome fireplace and has plenty of room for all kinds of family activities.

- Dining Room: This dining room has plenty of room for dinner parties. After dinner, guests can step through French doors onto the rear deck.

- Kitchen: This kitchen is a pleasure in which to work. It features an angled snack bar with plenty of room for informal family meals.

- Master Bedroom: You'll enjoy retiring at day's end to this master bedroom, with its large walk-in closet.

- Master Bath. This master bath features a double vanity, a deluxe tub, and a walk-in shower.

Copyright by designer/architect.

SMARTtip

Victorian Style

Victorian, today, is a very romantic look. To underscore this, add the scent of lavender or some other dried flower to the room or use potpourri, which you can keep in a bowl on the vanity. Hang a fragrant pomander on a hook, display lavender soaps on a wall shelf, or tuck sachets between towels on a shelf. For an authentic touch, display a Victorian favorite, the spider plant.

Plan #151016

Dimensions: 60'2" W x 39'10" D
Levels: 2
Square Footage: 1,783;
2,107 with bonus
Main Level Sq. Ft.: 1,124
Upper Level Sq. Ft.: 659
Bonus Room Sq. Ft.: 324
Bedrooms: 3
Bathrooms: 2 ½
Foundation: Basement, crawl space,
or slab
Price Category: C

Images provided by designer/architect.

An open design characterizes this spacious home built for family life and entertaining.

Features:

- **Great Room:** Enjoy the fireplace in this spacious, versatile room.

- **Dining Room:** Entertaining is easy, thanks to the open design with the kitchen.

- **Master Suite:** Luxury surrounds you in this suite, with its large walk-in closet, double vanities, and a bathroom with a whirlpool tub and separate shower.

- **Upper Bedrooms:** Window seats make wonderful spots for reading or relaxing, and a nook between the windows of these rooms is a ready-made play area.

- **Bonus Area:** Located over the garage, this space could be converted to a home office, a studio, or a game room for the kids.

- **Attic:** There's plenty of storage space here.

Main Level Floor Plan

Copyright by designer/architect.

Upper Level Floor Plan

Plan #191024

Dimensions: 50' W x 42' D

Levels: 1

Square Footage: 1,700

Bedrooms: 3

Bathrooms: 2

Foundation: Crawl space

Materials List Available: No

Price Category: C

Images provided by designer/architect.

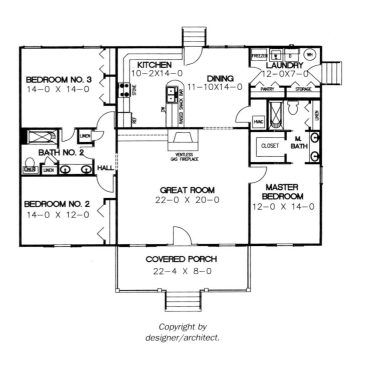

BEDROOM NO. 3 14-0 X 14-0

KITCHEN 10-2X14-0

DINING 11-10X14-0

LAUNDRY 12-0X7-0

FREEZER

PANTRY

STORAGE

STOVE

RAISED SNACK BAR

REF

HVAC

LINEN

BATH NO. 2

CLOSET

M. BATH

LINEN

LINEN

HALL

VENTLESS GAS FIREPLACE

BEDROOM NO. 2 14-0 X 12-0

GREAT ROOM 22-0 X 20-0

MASTER BEDROOM 12-0 X 14-0

COVERED PORCH 22-4 X 8-0

Copyright by designer/architect.

Plan #311010

Dimensions: 56'4" W x 67'4" D

Levels: 1

Square Footage: 1,997

Bedrooms: 4

Bathrooms: 2½

Foundation: Basement, crawl space, or slab

Materials List Available: Yes

Price Category: D

Images provided by designer/architect.

Copyright by designer/architect.

Storage 17-4x5-8

Garage 20-4x21-4

Master Bedroom 12-0x17-1

Bath

Porch 17-4x10-0

1/2 Bath

Laundry 7-4x6-3

Bedroom 11-4x10-0

Bath

Greatroom 17-4x17-4

Pantry

Kitchen/ Breakfast 11-4x20-5

Bedroom 11-4x11-4

Bedroom 11-3x10-1

Foyer

Dining 11-3x13-4

Porch 31-0x8-0

1/2 Bath

Greatroom

Kitchen **Basement Stair Location**

Plan #141038

Dimensions: 40'4" W x 38' D

Levels: 2

Square Footage: 1,668

Main Level Sq. Ft.: 1,057

Upper Level Sq. Ft.: 611

Bedrooms: 3

Bathrooms: 2½

Foundation: Basement with drive-under garage

Materials List Available: No

Price Category: C

Images provided by designer/architect.

If you're looking for the ideal plan for a sloping site, this could be the home of your dreams.

Features:

- **Porch:** Set a couple of rockers on this large porch so you can enjoy the evening views.
- **Living Room:** A handsome fireplace makes a lovely focal point in this large room.
- **Dining Room:** Three large windows over looking the sundeck flood this room with natural light.
- **Kitchen:** The U-shaped, step-saving layout makes this kitchen a cook's dream.
- **Breakfast Room:** With an expansive window area and a door to the sundeck, this room is sure to be a family favorite in any season of the year.
- **Master Suite:** A large walk-in closet and a private bath with tub, shower, and double vanity complement this suite's spacious bedroom.

Main Level Floor Plan

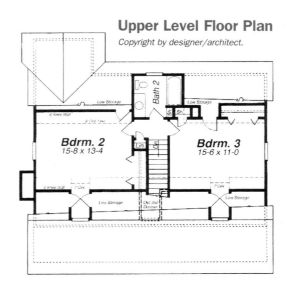

Upper Level Floor Plan
Copyright by designer/architect.

Plan #281026

Dimensions: 40' W x 52' D
Levels: 2
Square Footage: 1,858
Main Level Sq. Ft.: 1,004
Upper Level Sq. Ft.: 854
Bedrooms: 3
Bathrooms: 2½
Foundation: Basement
Materials List Available: Yes
Price Category: D

Images provided by designer/architect.

Main Level Floor Plan

Copyright by designer/architect.

Family Dr 17-0 x 10-2
Gas FP
Great Room 14-0 x 16-6
Two-story high clg.
Kitchen 13-4 x 11-0
up
Laundry
Hall
dn
Foyer
Powder Rm
Flex Room (Dr, Study or Home Office) 11-0 x 14-10
Double Garage 21-0 x 20-6
Porch

Upper Level Floor Plan

Master Suite 16-6 x 14-0
Great Room Below
Ens
WIC
Bath
Study/Computer 14-0 x 9-6
dn
Br 3 9-6 x 10-0
Br 2 10-0 x 9-6

Rear Elevation

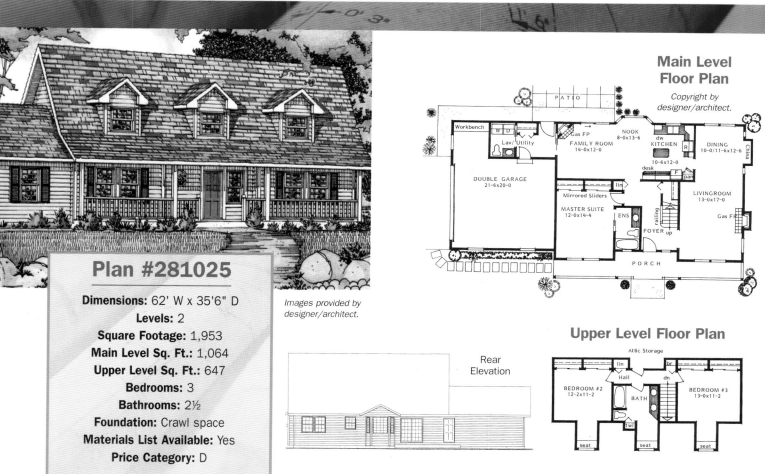

Plan #281025

Dimensions: 62' W x 35'6" D
Levels: 2
Square Footage: 1,953
Main Level Sq. Ft.: 1,064
Upper Level Sq. Ft.: 647
Bedrooms: 3
Bathrooms: 2½
Foundation: Crawl space
Materials List Available: Yes
Price Category: D

Images provided by designer/architect.

Main Level Floor Plan

Copyright by designer/architect.

PATIO
Workbench
W D
Lav/Utility
Gas FP
NOOK 8-0x13-6
KITCHEN 10-6x12-0
DINING 10-0/11-6x12-6
China
FAMILY ROOM 14-0x12-0
desk
DOUBLE GARAGE 21-6x20-0
Mirrored Sliders
lin
MASTER SUITE 12-0x14-4
ENS
railing
LIVINGROOM 13-0x17-0
FOYER
up
Gas FP
PORCH

Rear Elevation

Upper Level Floor Plan

Attic Storage
lin
br
BEDROOM #2 12-2x11-2
Hall
dn
BATH
BEDROOM #3 13-0x11-2
seat
seat
seat

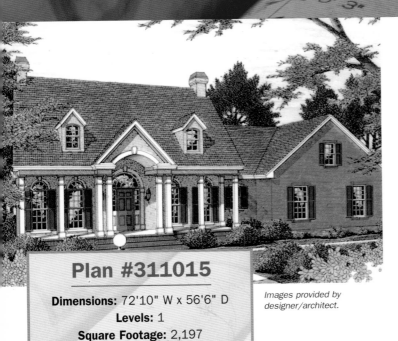

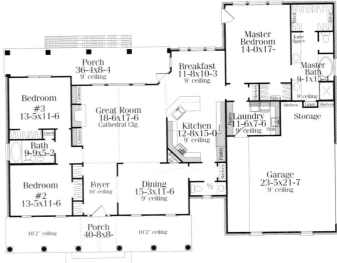

Plan #311015

Dimensions: 72'10" W x 56'6" D

Levels: 1

Square Footage: 2,197

Bedrooms: 3

Bathrooms: 2½

Foundation: Slab, crawl space, or basement

Materials List Available: No

Price Category: D

Images provided by designer/architect.

Copyright by designer/architect.

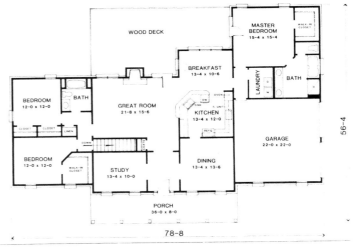

Plan #301004

Dimensions: 78'8" W x 56'4" D

Levels: 1

Square Footage: 2,344

Bedrooms: 3

Bathrooms: 2

Foundation: Crawl space, slab, or basement

Materials List Available: Yes

Price Category: E

Images provided by designer/architect.

Copyright by designer/architect.

Plan #291001

Dimensions: 63' W x 37' D

Levels: 1

Square Footage: 1,550

Bedrooms: 3

Bathrooms: 2

Foundation: Basement

Materials List Available: No

Price Category: C

Images provided by designer/architect.

A handsome porch with Greek Revival details greets visitors to this Early-American style home.

Features:

• Ceiling Height: 8 ft. unless otherwise noted.

• Foyer: Upon entering this foyer you'll be struck by the space provided by the vaulted ceiling in the dining room, living room, and kitchen.

• Dining Room: This dining room is perfectly suited for formal dinner parties as well as less formal family meals.

• Decks: Two rear decks are conveniently accessible from the master bedroom, kitchen, and living room.

• Kitchen: You'll enjoy cooking in this well-designed kitchen, which features an eating area that is perfect for informal family meals.

• Master Bedroom: This master retreat is separated from the other bedrooms for additional privacy. It features an elegant vaulted ceiling and is graced with a dressing area, private bath, and walk-in closet.

Rear View

Copyright by designer/architect.

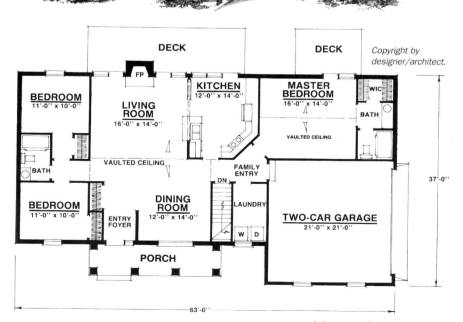

Plan #311007

Dimensions: 71'2" W x 48' D

Levels: 1

Square Footage: 1,688

Bedrooms: 3

Bathrooms: 2

Foundation: Basement, crawl space, or slab

Materials List Available: Yes

Price Category: C

Images provided by designer/architect.

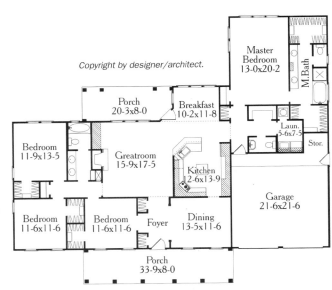

Copyright by designer/architect.

Master Bedroom 13-0x20-2

M.Bath

Porch 20-3x8-0

Breakfast 10-2x11-8

Bedroom 11-9x13-5

Greatroom 15-9x17-5

Kitchen 12-6x13-9

Laun. 5-6x7-5

Stor.

Garage 21-6x21-6

Bedroom 11-6x11-6

Bedroom 11-6x11-6

Foyer

Dining 13-5x11-6

Porch 33-9x8-0

Basement Stair Location

Laun.

Stor.

Plan #311006

Dimensions: 65'1" W x 73'7" D

Levels: 1

Square Footage: 2,465

Bedrooms: 4

Bathrooms: 2½

Foundation: Basement, crawl space, or slab

Materials List Available: Yes

Price Category: E

Images provided by designer/architect.

Storage 21-5x7-6

Sitting Room 12-7x10-0

Garage 21-5x25-4

M.Bath

Master Bedroom 12-7x13-9 9' ceiling

Porch 19-4x12-0

Bedroom 12-0x13-6 9' ceiling

Bath

Greatroom 18-10x17-6 10' ceiling

Pantry

1/2 Bath

Laun. 9-0x8-8

Kitchen 18-0x11-3 9' ceiling

Bedroom 12-0x11-7 9' ceiling

Bedroom 13-7x11-7 10' ceiling

Foyer

Dining 11-7x13-7 10' ceiling

Breakfast 14-0x9-0

Porch 31-5x8-0

Copyright by designer/architect.

Plan #301005

Dimensions: 71' W x 42' D
Levels: 1
Square Footage: 1,930
Bedrooms: 3
Bathrooms: 2
Foundation: Crawl space, slab
Materials List Available: Yes
Price Category: D

This home features an old-fashioned rocking-chair porch that enhances the streetscape.

Features:

• Ceiling Height: 8 ft.

• Dining Room: When the weather is warm, guests can step through French doors from this elegant dining room and enjoy a breeze on the rear screened porch.

• Family Room: This family room is a warm and inviting place to gather, with its handsome fireplace and built-in bookcases.

• Kitchen: This kitchen offers plenty of counter space for preparing your favorite recipes. Its U-shape creates a convenient open traffic pattern.

• Master Suite: You'll look forward to retiring at the end of the day in this truly luxurious master suite. The bedroom has a fireplace and opens through French doors to a private rear deck. The bath features a corner spa tub, a walk-in shower, double vanities, and a linen closet.

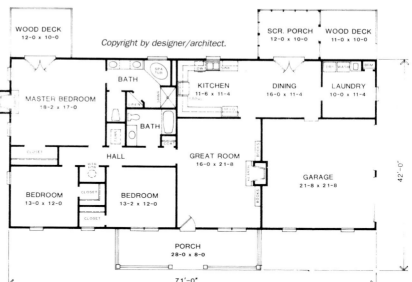

SMARTtip

Light With Shutters

For the maximum the amount of light coming through shutters, use the largest panel possible on the window. Make sure the shutters have the same number of louvers per panel so that all of the windows in the room look unified. However, don't choose a panel that is over 48 inches high, because the shutter becomes unwieldy. Also, any window that is wider than 96 inches requires extra framing to support the shutters.

Plan #211130

Dimensions: 68' W x 70' D

Levels: 1

Square Footage: 2,280

Bedrooms: 3

Bathrooms: 2

Foundation: Slab

Materials List Available: Yes

Price Category: E

Images provided by designer/architect.

Copyright by designer/architect.

Plan #191027

Dimensions: 62' W x 42' D

Levels: 1

Square Footage: 2,354

Bedrooms: 4

Bathrooms: 2½

Foundation: Crawl space

Materials List Available: No

Price Category: E

Images provided by designer/architect.

Copyright by designer/architect.

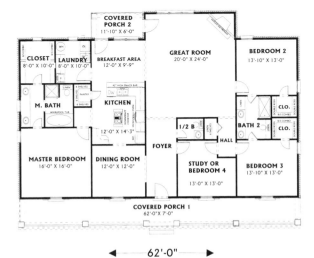

Images provided by designer/architect.

Copyright by designer/architect.

67'-0"
20,1 m

15'-8" X 16'-0"
4,70 X 4,80

12'-0" X 11'-4"
3,60 X 3,30

17'-4" X 16'-4"
5,20 X 4,90

18'-0" X 14'-0"
5,40 X 4,20

12'-0" X 13'-0"
3,60 X 3,90

14'-8" X 16'-4"
4,40 X 4,90

16'-8" X 23'-8"
5,00 X 7,10

50'-0"
15,0 m

Plan #181155

Dimensions: 50' W x 67' D

Levels: 1

Square Footage: 2,118

Bedrooms: 3

Bathrooms: 2½

Foundation: Full basement

Materials List Available: Yes

Price Category: D

Images provided by designer/architect.

Copyright by designer/architect.

Garage
20-4x21-4

M.Bath
17-8x10-6

Porch
22-0x12-0

Stor.
5-0x6-1

1/2 Bath

Laun.
8-4x5-8

Master Bedroom
19-2x13-7

Greatroom
22-0x15-2

Kitchen
12-8x12-0

Bath

Bedroom
10-8x12-0

Bedroom
11-6x11-0

Foyer

Dining
11-6x13-6

Breakfast
12-8x9-10

Porch
30-8x6-0

Bonus Area

Future
14-0x12-0

Future
29-4x16-0

Future
12-8x12-0

Plan #311016

Dimensions: 63'10" W x 64'7" D

Levels: 1

Square Footage: 2,089

Bedrooms: 3

Bathrooms: 2½

Foundation: Slab, crawl space, or basement

Materials List Available: Yes

Price Category: D

Plan #151166

Dimensions: 60'8" W x 79'6" D
Levels: 1½
Square Footage: 2,140
Main Level Sq. Ft.: 1,690
Upper Level Sq. Ft.: 450
Bedrooms: 3
Bathrooms: 2½
Foundation: Crawl space, slab
Materials List Available: Yes
Price Category: D

Images provided by designer/architect.

Main Level Floor Plan

Upper Level Floor Plan

Copyright by designer/architect.

Plan #151167

Dimensions: 58' W x 85'4" D
Levels: 1½
Square Footage: 2,286
Main Level Sq. Ft.: 1,831
Upper Level Sq. Ft.: 455
Bedrooms: 4
Bathrooms: 3
Foundation: Crawl space, slab
Materials List Available: Yes
Price Category: E

Images provided by designer/architect.

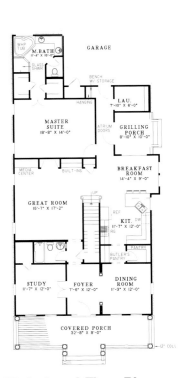

Main Level Floor Plan

Upper Level Floor Plan

Copyright by designer/architect.

Plan #151133

Dimensions: 66'4" W x 58'7" D

Levels: 1

Square Footage: 2,029

Bedrooms: 3

Bathrooms: 2

Foundation: Crawl space, slab, or basement

Materials List Available: Yes

Price Category: D

Images provided by designer/architect.

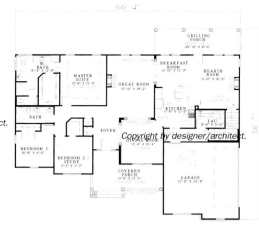

Optional Finished Basement

Copyright by designer/architect.

Plan #191012

Dimensions: 60' W x 76' D

Levels: 1

Square Footage: 2,123

Bedrooms: 3

Bathrooms: 2½

Foundation: Crawl space

Materials List Available: No

Price Category: D

Images provided by designer/architect.

Copyright by designer/architect.

Main Level Floor Plan

Images provided by designer/architect.

Upper Level Floor Plan

Copyright by designer/architect.

Plan #151152

Dimensions: 50' W x 50' D
Levels: 1½
Square Footage: 2,297
Main Level Sq. Ft.: 1,627
Upper Level Sq. Ft.: 670
Bedrooms: 3
Bathrooms: 2½
Foundation: Crawl space, slab
Materials List Available: Yes
Price Category: E

Main Level Floor Plan

Images provided by designer/architect.

Upper Level Floor Plan

Copyright by designer/architect.

Plan #151153

Dimensions: 50' W x 50' D
Levels: 1½
Square Footage: 2,290
Main Level Sq. Ft.: 1,604
Upper Level Sq. Ft.: 686
Bedrooms: 3
Bathrooms: 2½
Foundation: Crawl space, slab
Materials List Available: Yes
Price Category: E

Plan #201084

Dimensions: 66'10" W x 54'5" D
Levels: 1
Square Footage: 2,056
Bedrooms: 3
Bathrooms: 2
Foundation: Crawl space, slab
Materials List Available: Yes
Price Category: D

Images provided by designer/architect.

This classic family home features beautiful country styling with lots of curb appeal.

Features:

- Ceiling Height: 8 ft.
- Open Plan: When guests arrive, they'll enter a foyer that is open to the dining room and den. This open area makes the home seem especially spacious and offers the flexibility for all kinds of entertaining and family activities.
- Kitchen: You'll love preparing meals in this large, well-designed kitchen. There's plenty of counter space, and the breakfast bar is perfect impromptu family meals.
- Master Suite: This spacious and elegant master suite is separated from the other bedroom for maximum privacy.
- Bonus Room: This unfinished bonus room awaits the time to add another bedroom or a home office.
- Garage: This attached garage offers parking for two cars, plus plenty of storage space.

Copyright by designer/architect.

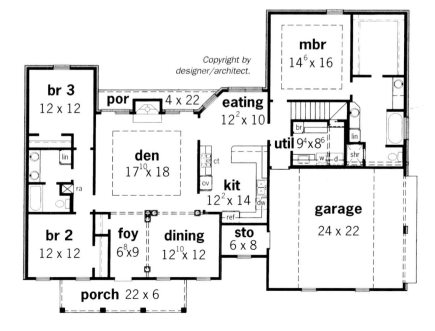

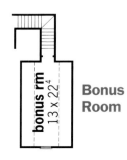

Bonus Room

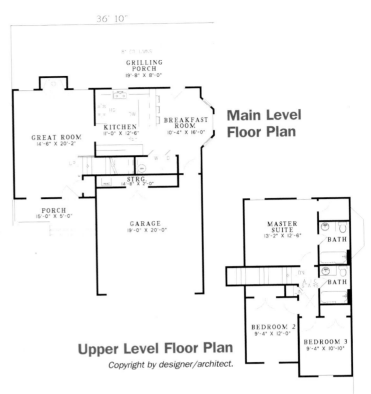

Main Level Floor Plan

GRILLING PORCH 19'-8" X 8'-0"

GREAT ROOM 14'-6" X 20'-2"

KITCHEN 11'-0" X 12'-6"

BREAKFAST ROOM 10'-4" X 16'-0"

STRG. 14'-8" X 2'-0"

PORCH 15'-0" X 5'-0"

GARAGE 19'-0" X 20'-0"

36' 10"

MASTER SUITE 13'-2" X 12'-6"

BATH

BATH

BEDROOM 2 9'-4" X 12'-0"

BEDROOM 3 9'-4" X 10'-10"

Upper Level Floor Plan

Copyright by designer/architect.

Plan #151148

Dimensions: 36'10" W x 47'4" D

Levels: 2

Square Footage: 1,287

Main Level Sq. Ft.: 655

Upper Level Sq. Ft.: 612

Bedrooms: 3

Bathrooms: 2

Foundation: Crawl space, slab

Materials List Available: Yes

Price Category: B

Images provided by designer/architect.

Main Level Floor Plan

62'-0"

COVERED PORCH 16'-10" X 8'-0"

GARAGE 11'-4" X 19'-4"

GRILLING PORCH 8'-0" X 11'-8"

KITCHEN 10'-7" X 10'-8"

NOOK 10'-7" X 6'-8"

OPTIONAL BASEMENT STAIRS

FOYER 6'-4" X 10'-8"

M.BATH

STACKED W/D

MASTER SUITE 13'-10" X 11'-8"

GREAT RM. 16'-2" X 17'-8" OPEN TO ABOVE

STONE FIREPLACE

FRENCH DOORS

DECK

39'-2"

Upper Level Floor Plan

Copyright by designer/architect.

LOFT 16'-2" X 14'-3"

6'8" WALL

BATH 10'-8" X 6'-4"

ATTIC STORAGE

VAULTED CEILING

SLOPED CEILING

BEDROOM 2 14'-2" X 11'-4"

8' LINE

BEAMS

OPEN TO BELOW

5' WALL

Plan #151156

Dimensions: 62' W x 39'2" D

Levels: 2

Square Footage: 1,408

Main Level Sq. Ft.: 917

Upper Level Sq. Ft.: 491

Bedrooms: 2

Bathrooms: 2

Foundation: Crawl space, slab

Materials List Available: Yes

Price Category: B

Images provided by designer/architect.

Plan #191025

Dimensions: 50' W x 68' D

Levels: 1

Square Footage: 2,052

Bedrooms: 3

Bathrooms: 2

Foundation: Crawl space, slab

Materials List Available: No

Price Category: D

Images provided by designer/architect.

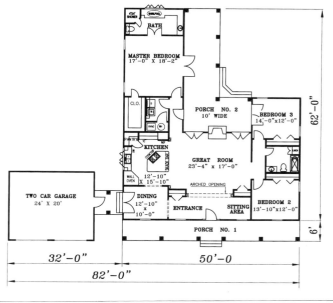

Copyright by designer/architect.

Plan #191026

Dimensions: 50' W x 62' D

Levels: 1

Square Footage: 2,052

Bedrooms: 3

Bathrooms: 2

Foundation: Crawl space, slab

Materials List Available: No

Price Category: D

Images provided by designer/architect.

Copyright by designer/architect.

Plan #171006

Dimensions: 68' W x 50' D
Levels: 1
Square Footage: 2,296
Bedrooms: 3
Bathrooms: 2½
Foundation: Slab, crawl space
Materials List Available: Yes
Price Category: E

This classic country farmhouse features a large, open rocking-chair front porch.

Features:

- Ceiling Height: 9 ft. unless otherwise noted.
- Great Room: This spacious great room is perfect for all types of entertaining.

SMARTtip

Window Shades

While decorative hems add interest to roller shades, they also increase the cost. If you're handy with a glue gun, choose one of the trims available at fabric and craft stores, and consider attaching it yourself. Give your shades fancy pulls for an inexpensive dash of pizzazz.

- Dining Room: This dining room is designed to accommodate formal dinner parties as well as less-formal family occasions. After dinner, step from the dining room onto the covered rear porch.
- Family Room: On cool evenings, enjoy the handsome fireplace in this family room. There's plenty of room for all kinds of family activities.

- Kitchen: This is truly a cook's kitchen with its cooktop range and U-shaped open traffic pattern. The snack bar will see lots of use for quick family meals.
- Master Suite: This master suite is separated from the other bedrooms for additional privacy. The large bedroom has a paddle fan and a roomy walk-in closet. The bathroom features his and her vanities, a deluxe bath, and a walk-in shower.

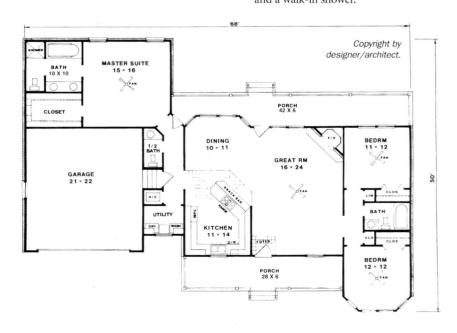

Copyright by designer/architect.

Plan #151155

Dimensions: 50' W x 50' D

Levels: 1½

Square Footage: 2,296

Main Level Sq. Ft.: 1,537

Upper Level Sq. Ft.: 759

Bedrooms: 3

Bathrooms: 2½

Foundation: Crawl space, slab

Materials List Available: Yes

Price Category: E

Images provided by designer/architect.

Main Level Floor Plan

Upper Level Floor Plan

Copyright by designer/architect.

Plan #151162

Dimensions: 59'4" W x 74'6" D

Levels: 1½

Square Footage: 2,231

Main Level Sq. Ft.: 1,698

Upper Level Sq. Ft.: 533

Bedrooms: 3

Bathrooms: 2½

Foundation: Crawl space, slab

Materials List Available: Yes

Price Category: E

Images provided by designer/architect.

Main Level Floor Plan

Upper Level Floor Plan

Copyright by designer/architect.

Plan #211048

Dimensions: 66' W x 60'8" D
Levels: 1
Square Footage: 2,002
Bedrooms: 3
Bathrooms: 2
Foundation: Crawl space, slab
Materials List Available: Yes
Price Category: D

This southern-style home is filled with inviting spaces and will fit into any neighborhood.

Features:

- Ceiling Height: 8 ft.

- Front Porch: Enjoy summer breezes on this porch, which features accented shutters that are both functional and stylish.

- Living Room: From the porch, French doors lead into the side-lit entry and this gracious living room.

- Sundeck: You can bask in the summer sun on this private rear deck, or if you prefer, enjoy a cool breeze under the shade of the rear porch. Each is accessible through its own set of French doors.

- Master Suite: This suite is secluded from the rest of the house for privacy, making it the perfect retreat at the end of a busy day. From the bedroom, open double doors to gain access to the luxurious bath, with a dual-sink vanity and his and her walk-in closets.

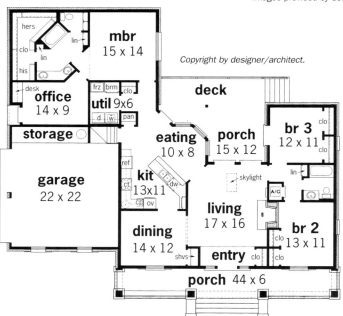

SMARTtip

Eye Appeal

Not everything in a landscaping plan needs to be in the ground. You might want to consider hanging flowering plants on a front porch or placing hardy potted plants on outdoor steps and decks or strategically along a paved walkway. Even a window box, viewed from outside, becomes a part of the landscaping.

Plan #171011

Dimensions: 70' W x 58' D

Levels: 1

Square Footage: 2,069

Bedrooms: 3

Bathrooms: 2½

Foundation: Slab, crawl space

Materials List Available: Yes

Price Category: D

Images provided by designer/architect.

This home combines the charm of a country cottage with all the modern amenities.

Features:

• Ceiling Height: 9 ft. unless otherwise noted.

• Front Porch: Watch the sun set, read a book, or just relax on this spacious front porch.

• Foyer: This gracious foyer has two closets and opens to the formal dining room and the study.

• Dining Room: This big dining room works just as well for family Sunday dinner as it does for entertaining guests on Saturday night.

• Family Room: This inviting family room features an 11-ft. ceiling, a paddle fan, and a corner fireplace.

• Kitchen: This smart kitchen includes lots of counter space, a built-in desk, and a breakfast bar.

• Master Bedroom: This master bedroom is separate from the other bedrooms for added privacy. It includes a paddle fan.

• Master Bath: This master bath has two vanities, walk-in closets, a deluxe tub, and a walk-in shower.

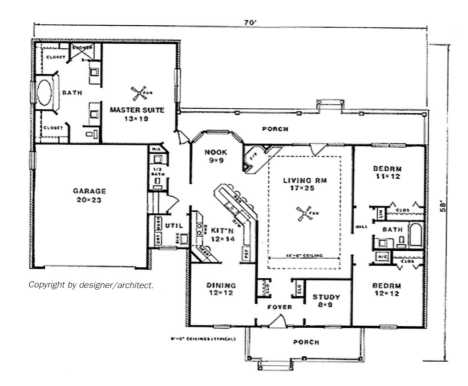

Copyright by designer/architect.

Main Level Floor Plan

Copyright by designer/architect.

PATIO

FAMILY ROOM
15-6x12-8

Gas FP

NOOK
8-0x12-8

KITCHEN
10-0x12-8

BATH

French doors

LIVINGROOM
13-0x16-0

Butler's Pan.

DINING
13-0x12-0

DOUBLE GARAGE
21-6x26-0

Covered Entry

open over up

FOYER

VERANDAH

Upper Level Floor Plan

BR3
11-4x12-0

Bath

whirlpool

ENS.

W.I.C.

Make-up Vanity

BR2
13-0x12-0

railing

MASTER SUITE
13-0x20-4

Foyer below

plant shelf

Images provided by designer/architect.

Rear Elevation

Plan #281024

Dimensions: 63' W x 36' D
Levels: 2
Square Footage: 2,170
Main Level Sq. Ft.: 1,173
Upper Level Sq. Ft.: 997
Bedrooms: 3
Bathrooms: 3
Foundation: Basement
Materials List Available: Yes
Price Category: D

Covered Patio

Copyright by designer/architect.

NOOK
8-6 x 12-6

Family Rm
17-6 x 14-4

9'-0" ceiling

Dining Rm
11-0 x 11-6

Kitchen
14-0 x 13-0

9'-0" ceiling

Livingrm
13-2 x 17-6

Hall

Br #4/Study
10-0 x 10-0

Util.

Open over

Foyer

Porch

Double Garage
22-0 x 23-0

Porch

Main Level Floor Plan

Master Suite
12-8 x 14-0

whirlpool

Ens.

Br #3
10-0 x 10-0

WIC

Shwr

Computer Centre

Br #2
10-0 x 11-0

laundry chute

railing

WIC

Bath

Foyer below

Upper Level Floor Plan

Plan #281017

Dimensions: 50' W x 59' D
Levels: 2
Square Footage: 2,101
Main Level Sq. Ft.: 1,270
Upper Level Sq. Ft.: 831
Bedrooms: 4
Bathrooms: 2½
Foundation: Basement
Materials List Available: Yes
Price Category: D

Images provided by designer/architect.

Rear Elevation

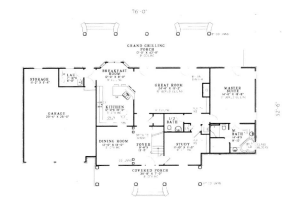

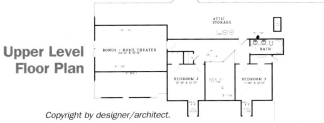

Images provided by designer/architect.

Upper Level Floor Plan

Copyright by designer/architect.

Plan #151147

Dimensions: 76' W x 52'6" D
Levels: 1½
Square Footage: 2,422
Main Level Sq. Ft.: 1,778
Upper Level Sq. Ft.: 644
Bedrooms: 3
Bathrooms: 2½
Foundation: Crawl space, slab
Materials List Available: Yes
Price Category: E

Main Level Floor Plan

Upper Level Floor Plan

Plan #181154

Dimensions: 54' W x 42' D
Levels: 2
Square Footage: 2,406
Main Level Sq. Ft.: 1,296
Upper Level Sq. Ft.: 1,110
Bedrooms: 3
Bathrooms: 2½
Foundation: Full basement
Materials List Available: Yes
Price Category: E

Images provided by designer/architect.

Copyright by designer/architect.

Plan #241001

Dimensions: 65' W x 56'3" D

Levels: 1

Square Footage: 2,350

Bedrooms: 3

Bathrooms: 2½

Foundation: Slab

Materials List Available: No

Price Category: E

Images provided by designer/architect.

Classic, traditional rooflines combine with arched windows to draw immediate attention to this lovely three-bedroom home.

Features:

- Great Room: The foyer introduces you to this impressive great room, with its grand 10-ft. ceiling and handsome fireplace.

- Kitchen: Certain to become the hub of such a family-oriented home, this spacious kitchen, which adjoins the breakfast area and a delightful sunroom, features an abundance of counter space, a pantry, and a convenient eating bar.

- Master Suite: You will enjoy the privacy and comfort of this master suite, which features a whirlpool tub, split vanities, and a separate shower.

- Study: Adjourn to the front of the house, and enjoy the quiet confines of this private study with built-in bookshelves to work, read, or just relax.

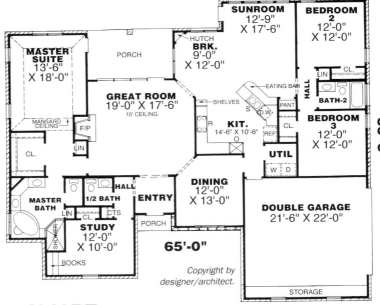

Copyright by designer/architect.

SMARTtip

Kitchen Counters

Make use of counter inserts to help with the cooking chores. For example, ceramic tiles inlaid in a laminate counter create a heat-proof landing zone near the range. A marble or granite insert is tailor-made for pastry chefs. And a butcher-block inlay is a great addition to the food prep area.

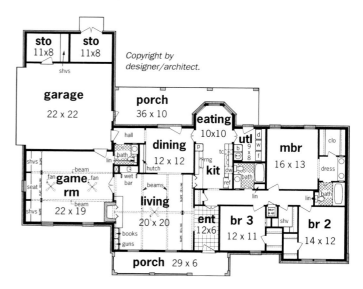

Plan #211054

Dimensions: 80' W x 62' D

Levels: 1

Square Footage: 2,358

Bedrooms: 3

Bathrooms: 2½

Foundation: Slab

Materials List Available: Yes

Price Category: E

Images provided by designer/architect.

SMARTtip

Dressing Up a Simple Fireplace

Painting a wood surround with a faux marble or faux bois (wood) is inexpensive. Adding a simple, prefabricated wooden shelf mantel can add lots of architectural character.

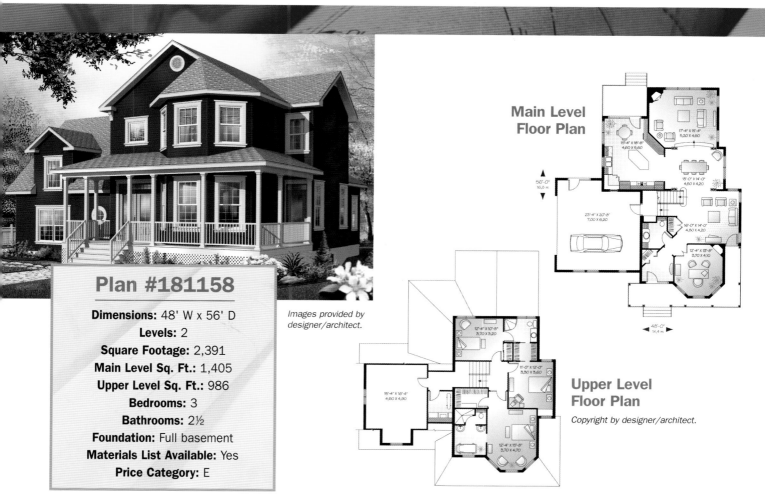

Plan #181158

Dimensions: 48' W x 56' D

Levels: 2

Square Footage: 2,391

Main Level Sq. Ft.: 1,405

Upper Level Sq. Ft.: 986

Bedrooms: 3

Bathrooms: 2½

Foundation: Full basement

Materials List Available: Yes

Price Category: E

Images provided by designer/architect.

Main Level Floor Plan

Upper Level Floor Plan

Copyright by designer/architect.

Plan #321041

Dimensions: 64' W x 34' D
Levels: 2
Square Footage: 2,286
Main Level Sq. Ft.: 1,283
Upper Level Sq. Ft.: 1,003
Bedrooms: 4
Bathrooms: 2½
Foundation: Basement
Materials List Available: Yes
Price Category: E

If you love the way these gorgeous windows look from the outside, you'll be thrilled with the equally gracious interior of this home.

Features:

- **Entryway:** This two-story entryway shows off the fine woodworking on the railing and balustrades.

- **Living Room:** The large front windows form a glamorous background in this spacious room.

- **Family Room:** A handsome fireplace and a sliding glass door to the backyard enhance the open design of this room.

- **Breakfast Room:** Large enough for a crowd, this room makes a perfect dining area.

- **Kitchen:** The angled bar and separate pantry are highlights in this step-saving design.

- **Master Suite:** Enjoy this suite's huge walk-in closet, vaulted ceiling, and private bath, which features a double vanity, tub, and shower stall.

Images provided by designer/architect.

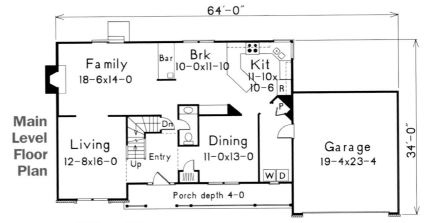

Main Level Floor Plan

Upper Level Floor Plan

Copyright by designer/architect.

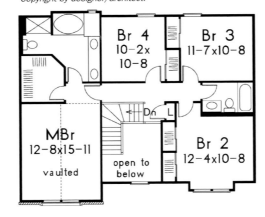

Upper Level Floor Plan

Copyright by designer/architect.

BATH 3
BA 3
CLOS
LINEN
CLOS
BEDROOM 3
15'-11" X 9'-8"
ALCOVE
BEDROOM 4
13'-0" X 12'-2"

Plan #341006

Dimensions: 86'3" W x 35'4" D

Levels: 2

Square Footage: 2,588

Main Level Sq. Ft.: 1,660

Upper Level Sq. Ft.: 928

Bedrooms: 4

Bathrooms: 3

Foundation: Crawl space, slab, or basement

Materials List Available: Yes

Price Category: E

Images provided by designer/architect.

86'-3"

35'-4"

DECK
GARAGE
KITCHEN 13'-3"X9'-2"
DINING 13'-0"X14'-2"
GREAT ROOM 16'-0"X27'-2"
BATH
BATH
DRESSING AREA
CLOSET
BEDROOM 1 13'-0"X16'-10"
COATS
CLOSET
BEDROOM 2 15'-3"X11'-0"
PORCH

Main Level Floor Plan

Plan #341011

Dimensions: 50' W x 58'4" D

Levels: 2

Square Footage: 2,560

Main Level Sq. Ft.: 1,387

Upper Level Sq. Ft.: 1,173

Bedrooms: 4

Bathrooms: 3½

Foundation: Crawl space, slab, or basement

Materials List Available: Yes

Price Category: E

Images provided by designer/architect.

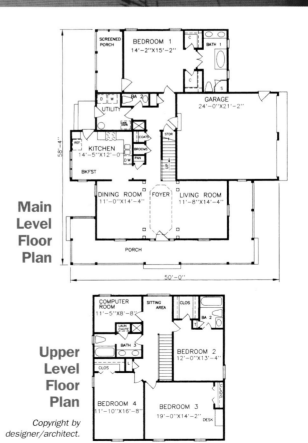

SCREENED PORCH
BEDROOM 1 14'-2"X15'-2"
BATH 1
BA 2
UTILITY
GARAGE 24'-0"X21'-2"
KITCHEN 14'-5"X12'-0"
COATS
BKFST
DINING ROOM 11'-0"X14'-4"
FOYER
LIVING ROOM 11'-8"X14'-4"
PORCH

58'-4"

50'-0"

Main Level Floor Plan

COMPUTER ROOM 11'-5"X8'-8"
SITTING AREA
CLOS
BA 2
LAUN CHUTE
BATH 3
BEDROOM 2 12'-0"X13'-4"
CLOS
BEDROOM 4 11'-10"X16'-8"
BEDROOM 3 19'-0"X14'-2"
DESK

Upper Level Floor Plan

Copyright by designer/architect.

Plan #151015

Dimensions: 72'4" W x 48'4" D
Levels: 2
Square Footage: 2,789
Main Level Sq. Ft.: 1,977
Upper Level Sq. Ft.: 812
Bedrooms: 4
Bathrooms: 3
Foundation: Basement, crawl space, or slab
Price Category: F

Images provided by designer/architect.

The spacious kitchen that opens to the breakfast room and the hearth room make this family home ideal for entertaining.

Features:

• **Great Room:** The fireplace will make a cozy winter focal point in this versatile space.

• **Hearth Room:** Enjoy the built-in entertainment center, built-in shelving, and fireplace here.

• **Dining Room:** A swing door leading to the kitchen is as attractive as it is practical.

• **Study:** A private bath and walk-in closet make this room an ideal spot for guests when needed.

• **Kitchen:** An island work area, a computer desk, and an eat-in bar add convenience and utility.

• **Master Bath:** Two vanities, two walk-in closets, a shower with a seat, and a whirlpool tub highlight this private space.

Main Level Floor Plan

Upper Level Floor Plan

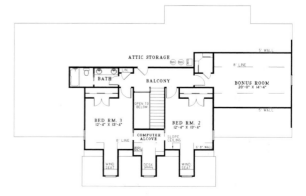

Copyright by designer/architect.

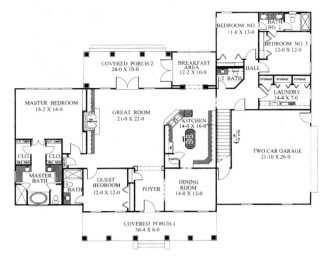

Images provided by
designer/architect.

Plan #191028

Dimensions: 80' W x 63' D

Levels: 1

Square Footage: 2,669

Bedrooms: 4

Bathrooms: 3½

Foundation: Basement, slab

Materials List Available: No

Price Category: F

Copyright by designer/architect.

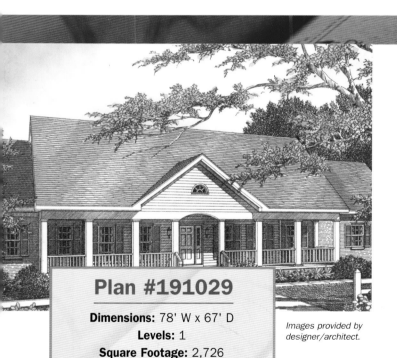

Images provided by
designer/architect.

Plan #191029

Dimensions: 78' W x 67' D

Levels: 1

Square Footage: 2,726

Bedrooms: 4

Bathrooms: 3½

Foundation: Basement, crawl space,
or slab

Materials List Available: No

Price Category: F

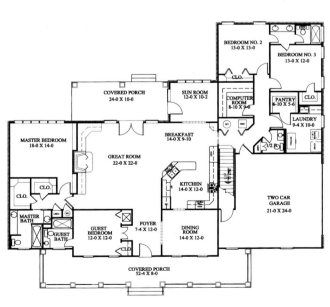

Copyright by designer/architect.

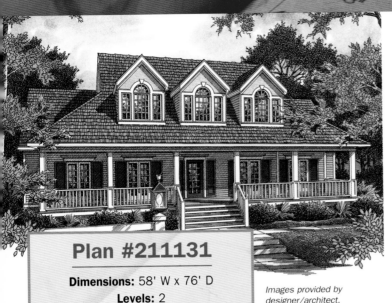

Plan #211131

Dimensions: 58' W x 76' D

Levels: 2

Square Footage: 2,598

Main Level Sq. Ft.: 1,647

Upper Level Sq. Ft.: 951

Bedrooms: 4

Bathrooms: 3½

Foundation: Basement

Materials List Available: No

Price Category: E

Images provided by designer/architect.

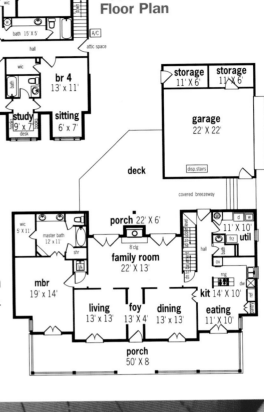

Upper Level Floor Plan

Main Level Floor Plan

Copyright by designer/architect.

Plan #151158

Dimensions: 60'8" W x 82' D

Levels: 2

Square Footage: 2,990

Main Level Sq. Ft.: 1,796

Upper Level Sq. Ft.: 1,194

Bedrooms: 4

Bathrooms: 3½

Foundation: Crawl space, slab

Materials List Available: Yes

Price Category: F

Images provided by designer/architect.

Main Level Floor Plan

Upper Level Floor Plan

Copyright by designer/architect.

Main Level Floor Plan

42'-0"
12.8 m

23'-4" X 12'-8"
7.00 X 3.80

13'-0" X 13'-0"
3.90 X 3.90

20'-4" X 22'-8"
6.10 X 6.80

13'-4" X 18'-0"
4.00 X 5.40

11'-8" X 9'-4"
3.50 X 2.80

54'-0"
16.2 m

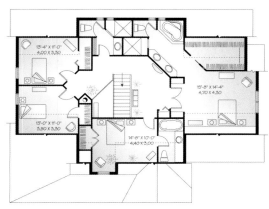

Upper Level Floor Plan

Copyright by designer/architect.

13'-4" X 11'-0"
4.00 X 3.50

15'-8" X 14'-4"
4.70 X 4.30

13'-0" X 11'-0"
3.90 X 3.50

14'-8" X 10'-0"
4.40 X 3.00

Images provided by designer/architect.

Plan #181160

Dimensions: 54' W x 42' D

Levels: 2

Square Footage: 2,768

Main Level Sq. Ft.: 1,296

Upper Level Sq. Ft.: 1,472

Bedrooms: 4

Bathrooms: 3½

Foundation: Basement

Materials List Available: Yes

Price Category: F

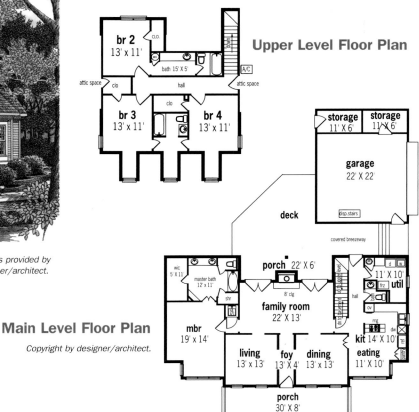

Upper Level Floor Plan

br 2
13' x 11'

bath 15' X 5'

attic space

attic space

hall

br 3
13' x 11'

br 4
13' x 11'

storage
11' X 6'

storage
11' X 6'

garage
22' X 22'

disp.stairs

deck

covered breezeway

wic
5' X 11'

master bath
12' x 11'

porch 22' X 6'

8' clg

11' X 10'

util

family room
22' X 13'

hall

mbr
19' x 14'

living
13' X 13'

foy
13' X 4'

dining
13' X 13'

eating
11' X 10'

kit 14' X 10'

porch
30' X 8'

Main Level Floor Plan

Copyright by designer/architect.

Images provided by designer/architect.

Plan #211132

Dimensions: 58' W x 76' D

Levels: 2

Square Footage: 2,535

Main Level Sq. Ft.: 1,647

Upper Level Sq. Ft.: 888

Bedrooms: 4

Bathrooms: 3½

Foundation: Basement

Materials List Available: No

Price Category: E

Images provided by designer/architect.

Plan #141018

Dimensions: 45' W x 64' D

Levels: 2

Square Footage: 2,588

Main Level Sq. Ft.: 1,320

Upper Level Sq. Ft.: 1,268

Bedrooms: 4

Bathrooms: 2½

Foundation: Basement, crawl space, or slab

Materials List Available: Yes

Price Category: E

This country home features a large wraparound porch, along with many Victorian-style accents.

Features:

• Ceiling height: 9 ft.

• Formal Dining Room: Usher your dinner guests into this large formal dining room.

• Living Room: With a style to match the dining room, this is the perfect place to start an evening's entertainment.

• Family Room: With its handsome warming fireplace, this is the less-formal space where the family will go to unwind.

• Kitchen: Cooking will be a pleasure in this large, sunny kitchen.

• Breakfast Room: Located adjacent to the kitchen, this breakfast room is the perfect spot for informal family meals.

• Master Suite: This luxurious retreat offers a walk-in closet. The master bath has double vanities, a jet tub, and a separate shower.

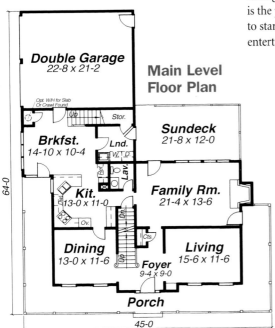

Main Level Floor Plan

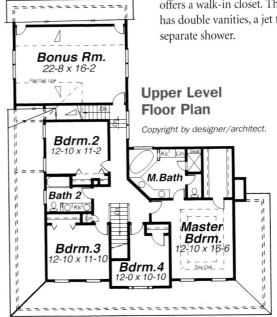

Upper Level Floor Plan

Copyright by designer/architect.

Plan #101020

Dimensions: 55'8" W x 49'2" D
Levels: 2
Square Footage: 2,972
Main Level Sq. Ft.: 1,986
Upper Level Sq. Ft.: 986
Bedrooms: 4
Bathrooms: 3½
Foundation: Basement
Materials List Available: No
Price Category: F

Images provided by designer/architect.

This luxurious country home has an open-design main level that maximizes the use of space.

Features:

- Ceiling Height: 9 ft. unless otherwise noted.

- Foyer: Guests will be greeted by this grand two-story entry, with its graceful angled staircase.

- Dining Room: At nearly 12 ft. x 15 ft., this elegant dining room has plenty of room for large parties.

- Family Room: Everyone will be drawn to

this 17-ft. x 19-ft. room, with its dramatic two-story ceiling and its handsome fireplace.

- Kitchen: This spacious kitchen is open to the family room and features a breakfast bar and built-in table in the cooktop island.

- Master Suite: This elegant retreat includes a bayed 18-ft.-5-in. x 14-ft.-9-in. bedroom and a beautiful corner his and her bath/closet arrangement.

- Secondary Bedrooms: Upstairs you'll find three spacious bathrooms, one with a private bath and two with access to a shared bath.

Main Level Floor Plan

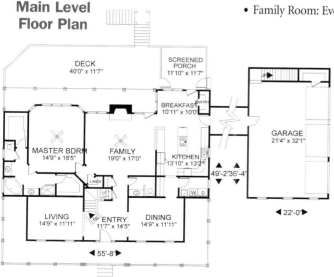

Upper Level Floor Plan

Copyright by designer/architect.

Plan #141036

Dimensions: 57' W x 41' D
Levels: 2
Square Footage: 2,527
Main Level Sq. Ft.: 1,236
Upper Level Sq. Ft.: 1,291
Bedrooms: 4
Bathrooms: 3
Foundation: Basement
Materials List Available: No
Price Category: E

Wood shakes and stone make the exterior of this home distinctive, and a fabulous layout and gorgeous features make the interior spectacular.

Features:

- **Living Room:** This spacious two-story room has a fireplace to make it cozy on chilly nights.

- **Guest Wing:** Guests will love having their own wing just beyond the computer command center.

- **Dining Room:** This room is ideal for entertaining or family dinner times.

- **Kitchen:** This step-saving design features an angled work area and a large pantry.

- **Breakfast Room:** The door to the patio makes this a perfect gathering place at any time of day.

- **Master Suite:** You'll love the stepped ceiling and hinged window seat in the bedroom, the walk-in closet, and the vaulted ceiling, tub, shower, and two vanities in the bath.

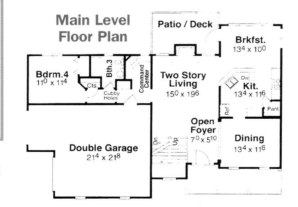

Main Level Floor Plan

Upper Level Floor Plan

Copyright by designer/architect.

Living Room

Kitchen

Master Bedroom

Let Us Help You
Plan Your
Dream Home

Whether you've always dreamed of building your own home or you can't find the right house from among the dozens you've toured, our collection of ultimate home plans can help you achieve the home of your dreams. You could have an architect create a one-of-a-kind home for you, but the design services alone could end up costing up to 15 percent of the cost of construction—a hefty premium for any building project. Isn't it a better idea to select from among the hundreds of unique designs shown in our collection for a fraction of the cost?

What does Creative Homeowner Offer?

In this book, Creative Homeowner provides hundreds of home plans from the country's best architects and designers. Our designs are among the most popular available. Whether your taste runs from traditional to contemporary, Victorian to early American, you are sure to find the best house design for you and your family. Our plans packages include detailed drawings to help you or your builder construct your dream house. **(See page 584.)**

Can I Make Changes to the Plans?

Creative Homeowner offers three ways to help you achieve a truly unique home design. Our customizing service allows for extensive changes to our designs. **(See page 585.)** We also provide reverse images of our plans, or we can give you and your builder the tools for making minor changes on your own. **(See page 586.)**

Can You Help Me Stay on Budget?

Building a house is a large financial investment. To help you stay within your budget, Creative Homeowner can provide you with general construction costs based on your zip code. **(See page 586.)** Also, many of our plans come with the option of buying detailed materials lists to help you price out construction costs.

Is There Anything I Missed?

A typical construction crew consists of a number of skilled professionals. If you plan on doing all or part of the work yourself, or you want to keep tabs on your builder, we offer best-selling building and design books at attractive prices. (See our company Web site at www.creativehomeowner.com.) Our home-building book package covers all phases of home construction, from framing and drywalling to wiring and plumbing.

Our Plans Packages Offer:

All of our home plans are the result of many hours of work by leading architects and professional designers. Most of our home plans include each of the following.

Frontal Sheet

This artist's rendering of the front of the house gives you an idea of how the house will look once it is completed and the property landscaped.

Detailed Floor Plans

These plans show the size and layout of the rooms. They also provide the locations of doors, windows, fireplaces, closets, stairs, and electrical outlets and switches.

Foundation Plan

A foundation plan gives the dimensions of basements, walk-out basements, crawl spaces, pier foundations, and slab construction. Each house design lists the type of foundation included. If the plan you choose does not have the foundation type you require, our customer service department can help you customize the plan to meet your needs.

Roof Plan

In addition to providing the pitch of the roof, these plans also show the locations of dormers, skylights, and other elements.

Exterior Elevations

These drawings show the front, rear, and sides of the house as if you were looking at it head on. Elevations also provide information about architectural features and finish materials.

Interior Elevations and Details

Interior elevations show specific details of such elements as fireplaces, kitchen and bathroom cabinets, built-ins, and other unique features of the design.

Cross Sections

These show the structure as if it were sliced to reveal construction requirements, such as insulation, flooring, and roofing details.

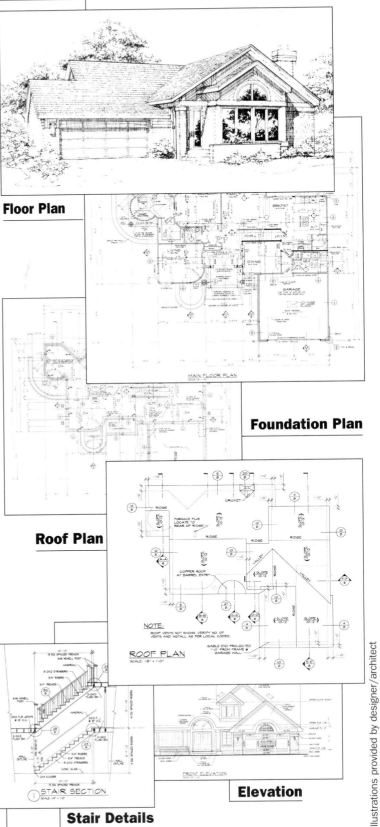

Frontal Sheet

Floor Plan

Foundation Plan

Roof Plan

Cross Sections

Stair Details

Elevation

Illustrations provided by designer/architect

Customize Your Plans in 4 Easy Steps

1 **Select the home plan** that most closely meets your needs. Purchase of a reproducible master is necessary in order to make changes to a plan.

2 **Call 1-800-523-6789 to place your order.** Tell our sales representative you are interested in customizing your plan. To receive your customization cost estimate, we will send you a checklist (via fax or email) for you to complete indicating the changes you would like to make to your plan. There is a $50 nonrefundable consultation fee for this service. If you decide to continue with the custom changes, the $50 fee is credited to the total amount charged.

3 **Fax the completed checklist** to 1-201-760-2431 or email it to us at customize@creativehomeowner.com. Within three business days of receipt of your checklist, a detailed cost estimate will be provided to you.

4 **Once you approve the estimate,** a 75% retainer fee is collected and customization work begins. Preliminary drawings typically take 10 to 15 business days. After approval, we will collect the balance of your customization order cost before shipping the completed plans. You will receive five sets of blueprints or a reproducible master, plus a customized materials list if desired.

Modification Pricing Guide

Categories	Average Cost From...	To
Add or remove living space	Quote required	
Bathroom layout redesign	$120	$280
Kitchen layout redesign	$120	$280
Garage: add or remove	Starting at $400	
Garage: front entry to side load or vice versa	Starting at $300	
Foundation changes	Starting at $220	
Exterior building materials change	Starting at $200	
Exterior openings: add, move, or remove	$65 per opening	
Roof line changes	Starting at $360	
Ceiling height adjustments	Starting at $280	
Fireplace: add or remove	Starting at $90	
Screened porch: add	Starting at $280	
Wall framing change from 2x4 to 2x6	Starting at $200	
Bearing and/or exterior walls changes	Quote required	
Non-bearing wall or room changes	$65 per room	
Metric conversion of home plan	Starting at $400	
Adjust plan for handicapped accessibility	Quote required	
Adapt plans for local building code requirements	Quote required	
Engineering stamping only	Quote required	
Any other engineering services	Quote required	
Interactive illustrations (choices of exterior materials)	Quote required	

Note: *Any home plan can be customized to accommodate your desired changes. The average prices above are provided only as examples of the most commonly requested changes, and are subject to change without notice. Prices for changes will vary according to the number of modifications requested, plan size, style, and method of design used by the original designer. To obtain a detailed cost estimate, please contact us.*

Architectural Seals

Because of differences in building codes, some cities and states now require an architect or engineer licensed in that state to review and "seal" a blueprint, or officially approve it, prior to construction. Delaware, Nevada, New Jersey, and New York require that all plans for houses built in those states be redrawn by an architect licensed in the state in which the home will be built.

Before Customization

After

Decide What Type of Plan Package You Need

How many Plans Should You Order?

Standard 8-Set Package. We've found that our 8-set package is the best value for someone who is ready to start building. Once the process begins, a number of people will require their own set of blueprints. The 8-set package provides plans for you, your builder, the subcontractors, mortgage lender, and the building department.
Minimum 4-Set Package. If you are in the bidding process, you may want to order only four sets for the bidding round and reorder additional sets as needed.
1-Set Study Package. The 1-set package allows you to review your home plan in detail. The plan will be marked as a study print, and it is illegal to build a house from a study print alone. It is a violation of copyright law to reproduce a blueprint without permission.

Buying Additional Sets

If you require additional copies of blueprints for your home construction, you can order additional sets within 60 days of the original order date at a reduced price. The cost is $45.00 for each additional set. For more information, contact customer service.

Reproducible Masters

If you plan to make minor changes to one of our home plans, you can purchase reproducible masters. Printed on vellum paper, an erasable paper that you can reproduce in a copying machine, reproducible masters allow an architect, designer, or builder to alter our plans to give you a customized home design. This package also allows you to print as many copies of the modified plans as you need for construction.

Mirror-Reverse Sets

Plans can be printed in mirror-reverse—we can "flip" plans to create a mirror image of the design. This is useful when the house would fit your site or personal preferences if all the rooms were on the opposite side than shown. As the image is reversed, the lettering and dimensions will also be reversed, meaning they will read backwards. Therefore, when ordering mirror-reverse drawings, you must order at least one set of right-reading plans. A $50.00 fee per order will be charged for mirror-reverse (regardless of the number of mirror-reverse sets ordered).

EZ Quote: Home Cost Estimator

EZ Quote is our response to one of the most frequently asked questions we hear from customers: "How much will the house cost me to build?" EZ Quote: Home Cost Estimator will enable you to obtain a calculated building cost to construct your new home, based on labor rates and building material costs within your zip code area. This summary is useful for those who want to know the total construction costs before purchasing sets of home plans. It will also provide a level of comfort when you begin soliciting bids from builders. The cost is $29.95 for the first EZ Quote and $14.95 for each additional one. Available only in the U.S. and Canada.

CompleteCost Estimator

CompleteCost Estimator is a valuable tool for use in planning and constructing your new home. It combines the detail of a materials list with line-by-line cost estimating. The result is a complete, detailed estimate—similar to a bid—that will act as a checklist for all the items you will need to select or coordinate during our building process. CompleteCost Estimator is only available for certain plans (please see Plan Index) and may only be ordered with the purchase of a set of home plans. The cost is $125 for CompleteCost Estimator.

Materials List

Available for most of our plans, the Materials List provides you an invaluable resource in planning and estimating the cost of your home. Each Materials List outlines the quantity, dimensions, and type of materials needed to build your home (with the exception of mechanical systems). You will get faster, more-accurate bids from your contractors and building suppliers—and avoid paying for unused materials. A Materials List may only be ordered with the purchase of a set of home plans.

Order Toll Free by Phone
1-800-523-6789
By Fax: 201-760-2431

Regular office hours are
8:30AM–7:00PM ET, Mon–Fri

Orders received by 3PM ET, will be processed and shipped within two business days.

Order Online
www.ultimateplans.com

Mail Your Order
Creative Homeowner
Attn: Home Plans
24 Park Way
Upper Saddle River, NJ 07458

Canadian Customers
Order Toll Free 1-800-393-1883

Mail Your Order (Canada)
Creative Homeowner Canada
Attn: Home Plans
113-437 Martin St., Ste. 215
Penticton, BC V2A 5L1

Before You Order

Our Exchange Policy

Blueprints are nonrefundable. However, should you find that the plan you have purchased does not fit your needs, you may exchange that plan for another plan in our collection within 60 days from the date of your original order. The entire content of your original order must be returned before an exchange will be processed. You will be charged a processing fee of 20% of the amount of the original plan set, the cost difference between the new plan set and the original plan set (if applicable), and shipping costs for the new plans. Contact our customer service department for more information. Please note: reproducible masters may only be exchanged if the package is unopened.

Building Codes and Requirements

At the time of creation, our plans meet the building code requirements published by the Building Officials and Code Administrators International, the Southern Building Code Congress International, the International Conference of Building Officials, or the Council of American Building Officials. Because building codes vary from area to area, some drawing modifications and/or the assistance of a professional designer or architect may be necessary to comply with your local codes or to accommodate specific building site conditions. We strongly advise you to consult with your local building official for information regarding codes governing your area.

Blueprint Price Schedule

Price Code	1 Set	4 Sets	8 Sets	Reproducible Masters	Materials List
A	$290	$330	$380	$510	$60
B	$360	$410	$460	$580	$60
C	$420	$460	$510	$610	$60
D	$470	$510	$560	$660	$70
E	$520	$560	$610	$700	$70
F	$570	$610	$670	$750	$70
G	$620	$670	$720	$850	$70
H	$700	$740	$800	$900	$70
I	$810	$850	$900	$940	$80

Shipping & Handling

	1-4 Sets	5-7 Sets	8+ Sets or Reproducibles
US Regular (7–10 business days)	$15	$20	$25
US Priority (3–5 business days)	$25	$30	$35
US Express (1–2 business days)	$40	$45	$50
Canada Reg. (8–12 business days)	$35	$40	$45
Canada Exp. (3–5 business days)	$50	$55	$60
Worldwide Exp. (3–5 business days)	$80	$80	$80

Note: All delivery times are from date the blueprint and package is shipped.

Order Form

Please send me the following:

Plan Number: _____

Price Code: _____ (see Plan Index)

Indicate Foundation Type: (see plan page for availability)
☐ Slab   ☐ Crawl space   ☐ Basement   ☐ Walk-out basement

Basic Blueprint Package   Cost
☐ Reproducible Masters $_____
☐ 8-Set Plan Package $_____
☐ 4-Set Plan Package $_____
☐ 1-Set Study Package $_____

☐ Additional plan sets:
☐ ___ sets at $45.00 per set $_____
☐ Print in mirror-reverse: $50.00 per order $_____
    ___ sets printed in mirror-reverse

Important Extras
☐ Materials List $_____
☐ EZ Quote for Plan #_____ at $29.95 $_____
☐ Additional EZ Quotes for Plan #s_____
    at $14.95 each $_____

Shipping (see chart above) $_____
SUBTOTAL $_____
Sales Tax (NJ residents add 6%) $_____

TOTAL $_____

Order Toll Free: 1-800-523-6789   By Fax: 201-760-2431
Creative Homeowner
24 Park Way
Upper Saddle River, NJ 07458

Name _____
(Please print or type)

Street _____
(Please do not use a P.O. Box)

City _____ State _____

Country _____ Zip _____

Daytime telephone (_____)_____

Fax (_____)_____
(Required for reproducible orders)

E-Mail _____

Payment   ☐ Check/money order *Make checks payable to Creative Homeowner*

☐ VISA   ☐ MasterCard   ☐ American Express Cards   ☐ DISCOVER

Credit card number _____

Expiration date (mm/yy) _____

Signature _____

Please check the appropriate box:
☐ Licensed builder/contractor   ☐ Homeowner   ☐ Renter

SOURCE CODE **CA900**

Copyright Notice

All home plans sold through this publication are protected by copyright. Reproduction of these home plans, either in whole or in part, including any form and/or preparation of derivative works thereof, for any reason without prior written permission is strictly prohibited. The purchase of a set of home plans in no way transfers any copyright or other ownership interest in it to the buyer except for a limited license to use that set of home plans for the construction of one, and only one, dwelling unit. The purchase of additional sets of the home plans at a reduced price from the original set or as a part of a multiple-set package does not convey to the buyer a license to construct more than one dwelling.

Similarly, the purchase of reproducible home plans (sepias, mylars) carries the same copyright protection as mentioned above. It is gener-ally allowed to make up to a maximum of 10 copies for the construction of a single dwelling only. To use any plans more than once, and to avoid any copyright license infringement, it is necessary to contact the plan designer to receive a release and license for any extended use. Whereas a purchaser of reproducible plans is granted a license to make copies, it should be noted that because blueprints are copy-righted, making photocopies from them is illegal.

Copyright and licensing of home plans for construction exist to protect all parties. Copyright respects and supports the intellectual property of the original architect or designer. Copyright law has been rein-forced over the past few years. Willful infringement could cause set-tlements for statutory damages to $150,000.00 plus attorney fees, damages, and loss of profits.

Index

Index

Index

Index